MOTORCYCLE HAND[...]

CHILTON'S™

President	Dean F. Morgantini, S.A.E.
Vice President–Finance	Barry L. Beck
Vice President–Sales	Glenn D. Potere
Executive Editor	Kevin M. G. Maher, A.S.E.
Production Manager	Ben Greisler, S.A.E.
Production Assistant	Melinda Possinger
Project Managers	George B. Heinrich III, A.S.E., S.A.E., Will Kessler, A.S.E., S.A.E., James R. Marotta, A.S.E., S.T.S., Richard Schwartz, A.S.E., Todd W. Stidham, A.S.E.
Schematics Editor	Christopher G. Ritchie
Authors	Ben Greisler, S.A.E., Kevin M. G. Maher, A.S.E.

CHILTON™ Automotive Books
PUBLISHED BY W. G. NICHOLS, INC.

Manufactured in USA
© 1998 W. G. Nichols
1020 Andrew Drive
West Chester, PA 19380
ISBN 0-8019-9099-8
Library of Congress Catalog Card No. 98-71215
2345678901 8765432109

NOV 1999

Contents

Contents

SAFETY NOTICE

Proper service and repair procedures are vital to the safe, reliable operation of all motor vehicles, as well as the personal safety of those performing repairs. This manual outlines procedures for servicing and repairing vehicles using safe, effective methods. The procedures contain many NOTES, CAUTIONS and WARNINGS which should be followed, along with standard procedures, to eliminate the possibility of personal injury or improper service which could damage the vehicle or compromise its safety.

It is important to note that repair procedures and techniques, tools and parts for servicing motor vehicles, as well as the skill and experience of the individual performing the work, vary widely. It is not possible to anticipate all of the conceivable ways or conditions under which vehicles may be serviced, or to provide cautions as to all possible hazards that may result. Standard and accepted safety precautions and equipment should be used during cutting, grinding, chiseling, prying, or any other process that can cause material removal or projectiles.

Some procedures require the use of tools specially designed for a specific purpose. Before substituting another tool or procedure, you must be completely satisfied that neither your personal safety, nor the performance of the vehicle, will be endangered.

Although information in this manual is based on industry sources and is complete as possible at the time of publication, the possibility exists that some vehicle manufacturers made later changes which could not be included here. While striving for total accuracy, NP/Chilton cannot assume responsibility for any errors, changes or omissions that may occur in the compilation of this data.

PART NUMBERS

Part numbers listed in this reference are not recommendations by Chilton for any product brand name. They are references that can be used with interchange manuals and aftermarket supplier catalogs to locate each brand supplier's discrete part number.

SPECIAL TOOLS

Special tools are recommended by the vehicle manufacturer to perform their specific job. Use has been kept to a minimum, but, where absolutely necessary, they are referred to in the text by the part number of the tool manufacturer. These tools can be purchased, under the appropriate part number, from your local dealer or regional distributor, or an equivalent tool can be purchased locally from a tool supplier or parts outlet. Before substituting any tool for the one recommended, read the SAFETY NOTICE at the top of this page.

ABOUT THE AUTHORS

Why This Book?

▶ **See Figures 1, 2, 3, 4 and 5**

Chilton has been around for a long, long time. Many of the people working with the company today used the company's books when they were growing up. How's that to induce a little stage fright?

Chilton has evolved over the years. In it's hay-day, the company published anything and everything, from "How To Fix Your Apple Computer" to the first edition of a once, little known, science fiction novel called Dune.

But, times and people change. Over the years, the people at Chilton, zeroed-in on their one true love. A passion for machines. Chilton's editorial offices are filled to the brim with car lovers and enthusiasts. That's probably no surprise to anyone. But, what some people don't realize, is just how deep the love for things mechanical goes. To many Chilton employees, America's love affair with the automobile is just not enough.

That is not to take anything away from our love for cars. It is not to diminish the time spent, day-in and day-out on every nuance of the automobile. It is just that, over time, many of the people who come to work at Chilton fall further into the grasp of the internal combustion engine and its significance to the world around them.

As-long-as I have been with the editorial staff at Chilton (a dream job when I was hired, and still one today), there have been motorcycle enthusiasts among us. OK, perhaps, in the manner that Chilton has long drilled into me, I understate it. There have always been MOTORCYCLE FREAKS among the staff.

When you think about it, I guess it really just makes sense. There is an undeniable fact that today's automobiles have become sophisticated. Perhaps, at times, they are so sophisticated that we feel these machines no longer need us, the car lovers, to exist. Let's leave behind the obvious calls for psychological counseling. Any car lover will understand what I mean by that.

There was a time when you needed to pay attention to your car. If you didn't, your car would certainly let you know, and at the WRONG TIME. To many, it became a point of pride NOT to let it come to that. If you were a real man, you could keep your car running. And, though today, our society still nurtures some of those feelings, it is just not the same. Having to change spark plugs, ohhhhhh, once every 100,000 miles just doesn't seem like such an accomplishment anymore.

And in the midst of all this, we know that there are still car guys and gals out there. People still take pride in a well running, good looking, home maintained car. The challenge comes more these days as the vehicle ages. It becomes much greater as the car gets older and we get a chance to really strut our stuff keeping it in top running condition. We diagnose problems, make repairs and save ourselves money. All worthwhile goals.

So, WHAT IS IT ABOUT MOTORCYCLES? I mean, many of them are becoming more modern too requiring less attention these days, including advances like Fuel Injection and Anti-Lock Brakes. Well, the key word in that phrase was LESS.

9099ZP16

Fig. 1 Between our love for things mechanical and a large portion of the staff that rides, a new motorcycle book from Chilton was only natural

We said less and NOT, none. That is because motorcycles have an edge to them. It all stems from the fact that THEY FALL DOWN WITHOUT US.

You see, bikes NEED US, and as car guys/gals, or mechanical guys/gals, or machismo laden Americans, we just plain like that. SO WHAT that you no longer have to readjust the points on the side of the road, using a matchbook as a feeler gauge. The truth is that motorcycles help us to face the world around us. We can't just roll up the windows when the rain hits. We can't just turn up the A/C when it is hot. And, we can't just crank up the radio and IGNORE everyone else, because there is a good chance we will get KILLED if we do. We can't simply hide behind the technology of a capable machine.

Why a motorcycle book? Well, it was natural. To keep and maintain a bike is as close to our roots as we can get. And, considering how many of

9099ZP04

Fig. 2 It was good seeing bikes mixed in with the usual parade of cars that come through our shop . . .

9099ZP13

Fig. 3 . . . as a matter of fact, the bikes took over occasionally

9099ZP17

Fig. 4 We received support from all the editors—we considered captioning this photo, "How many Chilton editors does it take to fix a motorcycle?"

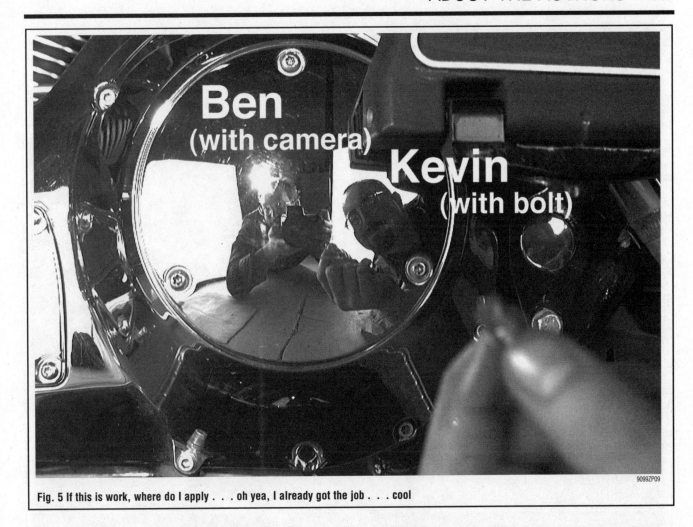

Fig. 5 If this is work, where do I apply . . . oh yea, I already got the job . . . cool

us ride, daily, weekly or seasonally here at Chilton, well, it just made sense.

When Ben and I started lobbying for this book two years ago, we sat back and looked at the cumulative experience of our whole riding staff. We looked at HOW MUCH we had learned from our fellow editors over our past decade each of riding. Each new experience involved a learning curve. "What do you mean no one makes a part to do that! Why Not?" We had asked questions like that of each other and the industry for many years. We had come up with new questions (or so we sometimes thought) and had spent countless hours searching for the answers. At some point, we decided it was time to share those answers, because we figured that if we asked the questions, then other people must be as well.

Ben and I are so GRATEFUL to have been able to work on this project. We took the opportunity to contact members of the motorcycle industry that we had previously not had a good enough excuse to call. What we now realize about most of them is, that we probably didn't need an excuse in the first place. There have been a LOT of people and companies who have contributed to this book. We cannot express our appreciation enough, because we know how little we could have accomplished without them.

What makes matters worse is that we are so painfully aware of our own shortcomings. We know that there are people who are twice our ages, that have spent their entire lives in the industry and probably have more to say than we have managed to get into this entire book. We mean no disrespect to any of them. Our combined experience in the industry and on the road may be meager to some, but somehow we found enough to fill the pages of this book. And our greatest hope with this book is that each person who picks it up will find at least ONE THING new. That each reader will walk away having thought about something a different way.

I for one am torn that this project is finally over. It was shorter than either of us thought it should have been. Two years in the making, and nine months in the slaving. We swear it feels like more. Again, it was probably only because of the great support we received that could have made it possible in that time frame.

We would REALLY like to thank all of the Chilton staff members who leant their expertise, hands and, in some cases, motorcycles to the production of this book. If nothing else, they indulged us as each lunch conversation inevitably turned back to how we were going to cover this or that topic for "the new motorcycle book." Their patience will not soon be forgotten.

We should be planning the annual Chilton Editorial Motorcycle Trip soon. For the past few years it has involved the Blue Ridge Parkway and pure motorcycle destinations like, Deal's Gap. I don't know where we will be heading this year, but it is going to feel extra good with this book behind us. I know that I would like to turn it all off for the trip and just enjoy, but I suspect that I will constantly compare things to what we covered in this book. I'm afraid that I will be sad, realizing other topics that we should have covered, or worse, other points we should have addressed on topics that we did cover. Ben keeps after me with talk of our NEXT edition. I just laugh, nervously, each time he brings it up.

One last thought, for your amusement. Ben and I entered into a proverbial deal with the Devil on this intro. Neither wanted to write an autobiography, so we each agreed to let the OTHER write something about his partner in crime. The key to this was a friendly agreement for each of us to write the piece without seeing what the other was going to write about us, and then NOT EDIT ANYTHING afterwards. I, for one, am torn between having some fun (if only for self-defense reasons) and possibly looking like a complete ass afterwards, if he was to take it too seriously. My decision, tell it like it is (GOD, I hope he has a sense of humor).

BEN, The True Story

♦ **See Figures 6 and 7**

Ben has been around Chilton a little longer than I have, but we discovered motorcycles together. I guess we were infected by the Chilton staff at the same time. He is an Engineer by schooling, trade, hobby and, I sometimes think, by birth.

I can't imagine how he was as a child, but I have often speculated how he may have corrected his own Mother when she used imperfect logic or unsound scientific principles to justify why he should finish all of his vegetables or not sit so close to the TV.

Ben wrote books for a long time, mostly the heavy duty stuff like professional driveability diagnostics (that was almost as hard to type as it was to say). Somewhere between his engineering education, his automotive racing experience (SCCA Pro-Rally) and his general obsession with things mechanical he has accumulated an incredible store of knowledge concerning cars, trucks and motorcycles. He was a Project Manager with the book company for a long time too. What I remember most about those days was his ABSOLUTE insistence about approaching a project the right way in order to maximize the results.

These days, he is Sir Lord of the Dungeon (our respectful name for Chilton's tear-down facility). I guess his experience as a professional photographer, computer geek (can you say Macintosh), Engineer, Chilton Editor and all-around automotive guy, prepared him to run the facility for us. And it is a good thing that he was so prepared, because we seldom let up on him.

It escapes me at this time, who first said "a neat desk is a sign of a sick mind." But, it doesn't matter, whoever said it would probably be sure of Ben's sanity, at least until he worked with Ben.

He is a perfectionist who will probably be in my office complaining about something else he wanted to add to this book, THE DAY AFTER it leaves our offices for the printer. But, maybe that is why I enjoy working with him so much. He is an ever-present check and balance, a sounding board, a fountain of knowledge at the molecular level. If I sound like I am

9099ZP07

Fig. 7 . . . too many late nights and early mornings, and too few showers in between (ugly, but true)

9099ZP06

Fig. 6 The real reason that Ben posed for this picture of he and his bike while wearing a helmet is . . .

fawning, so be it, when it comes to his work, he deserves it. I learned, a long time ago, that if there is a question I need to get answered, but that is too difficult or troublesome for me to bother with, pose it to Ben as a challenge. Do so, and you will almost ALWAYS get an answer (and sometimes even the right one).

It took a long time for us to divide the workload of this book and, somehow, it wound up becoming an even split as far as writing chapters went. For the record, he wrote chapters 5, 6, 7, 8 & 9. Sometimes it was clear whose experience dictated who would write what chapter. BUT, at other times, it was pure irony. I can't get over the fact that he wrote the detailing section, since his car (with over 225 thousand miles on it) has probably NEVER seen a hose (or anything other than rainwater). I will admit this, his current bike (with over 80 thousand miles on it), has been introduced to a hose, and occasionally some wax. He takes better care of his bike. But that is OK, that is probably the whole point of the book in the first place.

He, on the other hand, is probably still laughing at the fact that I wrote the riding gear chapter. Once upon a time, I was the tank-top, no-helmet, riding down the road on a prayer type. I still wear an open face helmet most of the time and occasionally ride without, ahemmmm, proper equipment. BUT, my years of riding have taught me a LOT about what is out there (and why), so I tend to keep most of the safety gear on these days. It is just that Ben won't move his bike across the parking lot without a full set of leathers, so most people would have assumed that he should have written the section on gear . . . well, no one should assume.

For what it is worth, I would like to thank Ben for his help with this project. We work well together. I know what he is going to yell at me about before his face even turns red. Just kidding, mostly. Without a partner who was so steadfast in his goals, I would not have survived this book.

KEVIN, The Ugly Truth

▶ See Figure 8

When Kevin came to work for Chilton, he was a much different man than what he is now. Those were the P.H. days: Pre-Harley. Kevin sat in his cubicle, listening to the Grateful Dead, Jimmy Buffet or something else mellow through a set of headphones. He was slim, studied karate and brewed his own beer. We got to be pretty friendly and he and his future wife, Johanna, threw some pretty groovy parties. He and I were editors, and life was good.

BOOM! (or should I say "potato, potato, potato") Life changed for Kevin. His Suzuki rat bike (just short of having a milk crate strapped to the back) was displaced by a Harley-Davidson 1200 Sportster. He said he had always wanted a Harley and now he had it. Life would never be the same for Kevin (or for us!)

Even when Kev had the Suzuki, motorcycling was a big part of his life. Kev puts on miles beyond what his bikes should be capable of. When Kev bought the 1200 Sporty and had problems with oil dripping out the breathers, the factory essentially told him he was riding too much and too hard! With over 38,000 miles in two years, the Sporty served him well, including a famous trip down the Blue Ridge Parkway, where his Harley didn't have any problems, but every BMW on the trip did! (Although I was much quicker through Deals Gap!)

Kevin got into the Harley lifestyle. He stopped brewing his own beer and quit karate. The gut grew and so did the goatee. Toy runs were the norm and he started to edit the newsletter for his local H.O.G. Chapter. We would have arguments about helmets versus no-helmet, full face versus half shells. He decided that a tattoo was needed to fill out the full picture, so he got one. There was still some hope for him when he presented the results of the needlework on his arm: A cuddly Grateful Dead bear riding a Harley!

9099ZP05

Fig. 8 Working down in the photo studio, we tried our best to keep Kevin away from the chemicals but we just couldn't do it

Realizing that he was riding the wheels off the Sporty, he traded up to a fuel injected Road King. Soon he and Johanna were cruising down Route 66 on a cross-country trip, taking in the sights and making memories for a lifetime. His tattoo Harley bear was further adorned with a Route 66 sign.

Kevin is very passionate about everything he does. It explains his success with Chilton. Due to some good timing and hard work, Kev jumped from an editor position through project manager to now being in charge of the entire editorial department. He is the "big cheese" and officially my boss. Even at that, I try to keep him straight.

When he gets it into his mind to buy something, watch out! We went out one lunch to pick up a case of beer for a party I was having, and Kevin came back with a riding lawn tractor. We were going past a Sears on the way to the beer distributor and Kevin asked if we could take a slight detour. I never did get my beer.

He picked up an old BMW to use as a rain bike and soon was bitten by the Bimmer (Beemer?) bug. As I write this, we are set to head out to a BMW rally in Maryland where he hopes to sell his bike and put the money towards a new one. There is a new R-bike in his future for sure!

Kevin doesn't write as much as he used to now that he is King Guru of Editorial Management. He hasn't had a real reason to work with me in the digital photo studio as an editor. His people work side by side with my photographers and technicians, but he hasn't had to do that. This book changed all that. It was great fun watching him adjust to life down here in the catacombs while we worked on this book. He turned the wrenches on the bike while I set up the shots. I had to constantly remind him of things like, "Hey, don't stand in front of the light," or "If you don't move your hands, I can't see the part you are holding," or finally, "Um, Kev, get your head out of the lens!"

I tease Kevin about being an English major, but it is a good balance to my analytical side. We work well together and it was a natural to write this book as a team. I read his stuff and pointed out technical items that needed correction. He read my stuff and marked up every incorrect **grammer** (NOTE: Kev left this so you would see what he had to put up with) usage and misplaced comma. We argue, we fight, we have a great time. Almost everyone who has seen us together say we are scary as a team. Gee, I don't know what they are talking about!

ACKNOWLEDGMENTS

The authors would like to express the sincerest appreciation to the following companies who supported the production of this book with information, motorcycles, products, cooperation, products and general help:

- American Honda Motors Co., Inc.—Torrance, CA
- American Suzuki Motor Corporation—Brea, CA
- BMW North America—Woodcliff Lake, NJ
- Buell American Motorcycles—Troy, WI
- Cobra Engineering—Anaheim, CA
- Corbin—Hollister, CA
- Deltran Corp. / Battery Tender—Deland, FL
- Ducati North America Inc.
- Gerbing's Heated Clothing, Inc.—Union, WA
- Hannum's Harley-Davidson—Media, PA
- Hannum's Motorsports—West Chester, PA
- Harley-Davidson Motor Company, Inc.—Milwaukee, WI
- Hein Gericke / Intersport Fashions West, Inc.—Tustin, CA
- Kawasaki Motors Corp. USA—Irvine, CA
- Kryptonite Corp.—Canton, MA
- Moto America, Inc. / Moto Guzzi—Angier, NC
- Motorcycle Safety Program of Pennsylvania / Millersville University
- Olympia Sports Company—Hawthorne, NY
- Otto's BMW—West Chester, PA
- Polaris Industries, Inc. / Victory Motorcycles USA—Minneapolis, MN
- Progressive Suspension, Inc.—Hesperia, CA
- RiderWearHouse / Aerostitch—Duluth, MN
- RK BMW/Ducati—Deptford, NJ
- Smaltz's Harley-Davidson—Eagle, PA
- Snell Memorial Foundation—North Highlands, CA
- Summit Industries, Inc. / Lexol—Marietta, GA
- Triumph Motorcycles Limited
- Widder Enterprises—Ojai, CA
- Yamaha Motor Corporation, USA—Cypress, CA

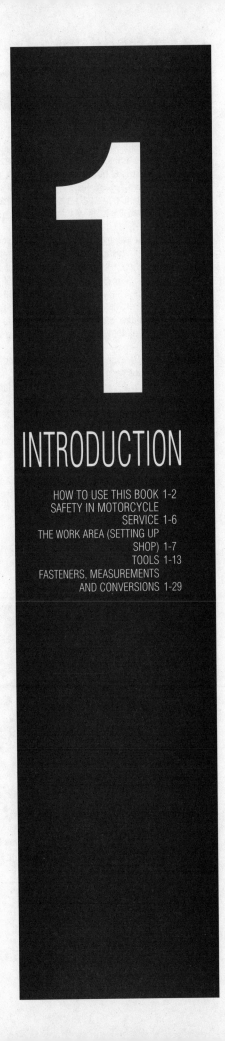

1

INTRODUCTION

HOW TO USE THIS BOOK

◆ **See Figures 1, 2, 3 and 4**

This book is designed to be a handy reference guide to choosing, buying and maintaining your motorcycle, riding gear and accessories. We strongly believe that regardless of how many or how few years of riding or wrenching experience you may have, there is something new waiting here for you. And, probably more importantly, we feel that information contained in this book should be available to all motorcyclists before they throw a leg over a bike or spend money on it.

One of the most fascinating aspects of motorcycling is that it means so many different things to so many people. To some it is the preferred form of transportation, while some only participate as a weekend diversion. Many people view motorcycling as a sport of personal challenge, while to others it is a lifelong passion. For most, it is probably something in between these extremes or some combination. The bottom line, to all of us, it is FUN. In this book, we have attempted to address the most basic needs of all motorcyclists, whether you view your bike as a toy or a tool.

This book IS NOT at complete repair manual and no attempt has been made to supplant the need for one if you desire to fully rebuild or repair a motorcycle. Instead, this manual covers all of the topics that a factory service manual (designed for factory trained technicians) and a manufacturer's owners manual (designed more by lawyers than by motorcyclists these days) will not. This manual will take you through the basics of maintaining a motorcycle, step-by-step to help you understand what the factory trained technicians already know by heart. By using the information in this manual, any motorcyclist should be able to make better informed decisions about what he or she needs to do to maintain and enjoy a motorcycle.

Keeping all of that in mind, we have divided the book into the following topics:
- INTRODUCTION
- BUYING YOUR BIKE
- RIDING GEAR
- ENGINE & DRIVETRAIN MAINTENANCE
- CHASSIS MAINTENANCE
- PREPARING TO RIDE
- ACCESSORIZING THE BIKE
- APPEARANCE AND CARE
- BASIC TROUBLESHOOTING
- WINTER STORAGE

Even if you never plan on touching a wrench (and if so, we hope that you will change your mind), this book will still help you understand what a technician needs to do in order to maintain your bike. And, even if you don't perform the maintenance services, we will provide information from accessorizing to detailing, from pre-ride checks to pre-winter storage preparation.

Fig. 2 . . . and brakes . . .

Fig. 1 This book is designed to help guide you through complete motorcycle care and ownership, from basic maintenance such as fluids . . .

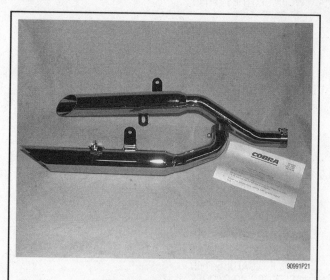

Fig. 3 . . . to choosing and installing accessories . . .

Fig. 4 . . . and even selecting and caring for your riding gear

Fig. 5 Proper care will help prevent mechanical failures, don't trust your life to someone else

I Wish I Was Him

Dweeb!

By following our advice, you are guaranteed to win acceptance from other motorcyclists (REALLY?)

Can You Do It? (and Should You?)

♦ **See Figure 5**

If you are not the type who is prone to taking a wrench to something NEVER FEAR. The procedures in this book cover basic topics at a level virtually anyone will be able to handle. And just the fact that you purchased this book shows your interest in better understanding your motorcycle.

The real truth is that although many people use motorcycles simply as a form of transportation you should never mistake one for an automobile. Although we feel strongly that the driver of an automobile should understand their vehicle, the average mechanical failure (which could be caused by poor maintenance or missed by a lack of periodic inspection) will TYPICALLY have less devastating results on a car or truck (and we realize that we are making a generalization here). The bottom line is that a motorcycle DOES NOT STAND UP ON ITS OWN and a mechanical failure (a tire blowout, an engine seizure or a locked brake, all of which could result from a lack of maintenance) has a much stronger possibility of sending you sliding down some pavement (or dirt) on a motorcycle, than in a car.

So where are we going with this? Simply that not only do we believe that you are capable of maintaining your own motorcycle, but that maintaining it yourself is preferable in most cases. At the very least you should fully understand what proper maintenance entails. You may decide that you would prefer most service be performed by a technician (and that's your call), but every time you throw a leg over a motorcycle, you are placing faith in the technician's work and trusting him or her with your life. Understanding what that technician has done for your motorcycle will allow you to keep an eye on its condition and its adjustments.

Don't believe for a second that we are taking anything away from the professionals who dedicate their lives to being first rate motorcycle technicians. We are just pointing out that it is a VERY HIGH stakes game and the more personal involvement you have in the maintenance of your motorcycle, the better your odds are at coming out a winner.

Nes Pas? (No?).

Where to Begin

Before spending any money on parts or accessories, and before removing any nuts or bolts, read through the entire procedure or topic. This will give you the overall view of what tools and supplies will be required for work or what questions need to be answered before purchasing gear. When it comes to maintenance, there is nothing more frustrating than having to walk to the bus stop on Monday morning (or drive your car on a beautiful, sunny day) because you were short one bolt on Sunday afternoon. So read ahead and plan ahead. Each operation should be approached logically and all procedures thoroughly understood before attempting any work.

Avoiding Trouble

Some procedures in this book may require you to "label and disconnect . . . " a group of lines, hoses or wires. Don't be lulled into thinking you can remember where everything goes — you won't. If you reconnect or install a part incorrectly, the bike may operate poorly, if at all. If you hook up electrical wiring incorrectly, you may instantly learn a very expensive lesson.

A piece of masking tape, for example, on a hose and a piece on its fitting will allow you to assign your own label such as the letter A or a short name. As long as you remember your own code, the lines can be reconnected by matching letters or names. Do remember that tape will dissolve in gasoline or other fluids. If a component is to be washed or cleaned, use another method of identification. A permanent felt-tipped marker can be very handy for marking metal parts. Also, remove any tape or paper labels after assembly.

SAFETY is the most important thing to remember when working on a bike. Be sure to read the information on safety in this book.

Maintenance or Repair?

▶ See Figure 6

Proper maintenance is the key to long and trouble-free motorcycle life, and the work can yield its own rewards. A properly maintained bike performs better than one that is neglected. As a conscientious owner and rider, set aside a Saturday morning, at least once a month, to perform a thorough check of items which could cause problems. Keep your own personal log to jot down which services you performed, how much the parts cost you, the date, and the exact odometer reading at the time. Keep all receipts for parts purchased, so that they may be referred to in case of related problems or to determine operating expenses. As a do-it-yourselfer, these receipts are the only proof you have that the required maintenance was performed. In the event of a warranty problem, these receipts will be invaluable.

The literature provided with your bike when it was originally delivered includes the factory recommended maintenance schedule. If you no longer have this literature, replacement copies are usually available from the dealer, or, you can purchase a repair manual that is written just for your bike. For the most part, we will provide average recommended replacement and inspection guidelines with the information in this book. But, remember that motorcycles and manufacturers do vary. Don't take a chance on missing an odd item or replacement interval that is unique to your year or model. Refer to the manufacturer's recommended maintenance charts, whenever possible.

It's necessary to mention the difference between maintenance and repair. Maintenance includes routine inspections, adjustments, and replacement of parts that show signs of normal wear. Maintenance compensates for wear or deterioration. Repair implies that something has broken or is not working. A need for repair is often caused by lack of maintenance. Example: draining and refilling the brake fluid is maintenance recommended by some manufacturers at specific mileage intervals. Failure to do this can allow internal

corrosion or damage and impair the operation of the brake system, requiring expensive repairs. While no maintenance program can prevent items from breaking or wearing out, a general rule can be stated: MAINTENANCE IS CHEAPER THAN REPAIR.

Two basic mechanic's rules should be mentioned here. First, whenever the left side of the bike is referred to, it is meant to specify the your left while sitting in the riding position. Conversely, the right side of the bike means your right side while seated. Second, most screws and bolts are removed by turning counterclockwise, and tightened by turning clockwise. An easy way to remember: righty, tighty; left loosey. Corny, but effective. And if you are really dense (and we have all been so at one time or another, buy a ratchet that is marked ON and OFF, or mark your own).

Professional Help

▶ See Figure 7

We're not suggesting a psychiatrist. It's just that there are some things when working on a motorcycle that are beyond the capabilities or tools of the average Do-It-Yourselfer (DIYer). This shouldn't include most of the topics of this book, but you will have to be the judge. Some motorcycles require special tools or a selection of special parts, even for basic maintenance.

Talk to other riders of the same model and speak with a trusted dealer or repair shop to find out if some system on your bike is particularly difficult to maintain. For example, although the technique of valve adjustment may be easily understood and even performed by a DIYer, it might require a handy assortment of shims in various sizes and a few hours of disassembly to get to that point. Not having the assortment of shims handy might mean multiple trips back and forth to the parts store, and this might not be worth your time.

You will have to decide for yourself where BASIC maintenance ends and where professional help should begin. BUT, take your time and do your research first (starting with the information in this book) and then make your own decision. If you really don't feel comfortable with attempting a procedure, don't buy the macho crap about a REAL motorcyclist not letting someone else work on his or her bike, obviously PLENTY of people do, or dealer service departments and independent shops wouldn't be busy.

On the other hand, should you take something apart and can't get it back together again, chances are only your ego will be damaged (when the tech-

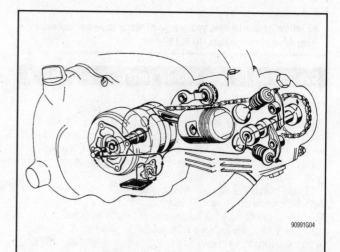

90991P26

Fig. 6 Performing maintenance procedures, like valve lash adjustment, will help prevent costly repairs, like valve replacement

90991G04

Fig. 7 You decide where BASIC maintenance ends, but don't get discouraged too easily, most tasks are within your capabilities

nician comes to pick up the bike and put it back together for you). As long as you approach jobs slowly and carefully, you really have nothing to loose and everything to gain by doing it yourself.

Avoiding the Most Common Mistakes

▶ See Figure 8

Pay attention to the instructions provided. There are 3 common mistakes in mechanical work:

1. Incorrect order of assembly, disassembly or adjustment. When taking something apart or putting it together, performing steps in the wrong order usually just costs you extra time; however, it CAN break something. Read the entire procedure before beginning disassembly. Perform everything in the order in which the instructions say you should, even if you can't immediately see a reason for it. When you're taking apart something that is very intricate, you might want to draw a picture of how it looks when assembled at one point in order to make sure you get everything back in its proper position. When making adjustments, perform them in the proper order; often, one adjustment affects another, and you cannot expect even satisfactory results unless each adjustment is made only when it cannot be changed by any other.

2. Overtorquing (or undertorquing). While it is more common for overtorquing to cause damage, undertorquing may allow a fastener to vibrate loose causing serious damage. Especially when dealing with aluminum parts, pay attention to torque specifications and utilize a torque wrench in assembly. If a torque figure is not available, remember that if you are using the right tool to perform the job, you will probably not have to strain yourself to get a fastener tight enough. The pitch of most threads is so slight that the tension you put on the wrench will be multiplied many times in actual force on what you are tightening.

A good example of how critical torque is can be seen in the case of aluminum side covers on some motorcycles. The polished and chrome aluminum side covers found on many motorcycles today can be damaged by heating and cooling, if a proper clamp load is not evenly distributed around the edge of the component. Failure to use a torque wrench may allow the cover to warp in service causing leaks.

There are many commercial products available for ensuring that fasteners won't come loose, even if they are not torqued just right (a very common brand is Loctite®). If you're worried about getting something together tight enough to hold, but loose enough to avoid mechanical damage during assembly, one of these products might offer substantial insurance. Before choosing a threadlocking compound, read the label on the package and make sure the product is compatible with the materials, fluids, etc. involved.

3. Crossthreading. This occurs when a part such as a bolt is screwed into a nut or casting at the wrong angle and forced. Crossthreading is more likely to occur if access is difficult. It helps to clean and lubricate fasteners, then to start threading with the part to be installed positioned straight in. Always, start a fastener, etc. with your fingers. If you encounter resistance, unscrew the part and start over again at a different angle until it can be inserted and turned several times without much effort. Keep in mind that some parts may have tapered threads, so that gentle turning will automatically bring the part you're threading to the proper angle, but only if you don't force it or resist a change in angle. Don't put a wrench on the part until it has been tightened a couple of turns by hand. If you suddenly encounter resistance, and the part has not seated fully, don't force it. Pull it back out to make sure it's clean and threading properly.

Always take your time and be patient; once you have some experience, working on your bike may well become an enjoyable hobby.

Storing Parts

▶ See Figure 9

Above all, we can't emphasize too strongly the necessity of a neat and orderly disassembly. Even if you are an experienced mechanic, parts can get mislaid, misidentified and just plain lost.

Start with an indelible marker, lots of cans and/or boxes and tags. Each time a part is removed, label it and store it safely. "Parts" includes all fasteners (bolts, nuts, screws, and washers). Bolts and nuts may look the same and not be alike. Similar looking bolts may be different lengths or thread count. Lockwashers may be required in some places and not in others. Everything should go back exactly from where it came.

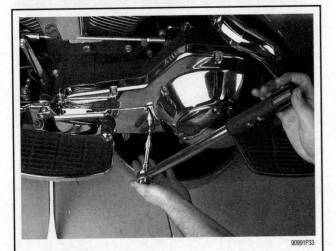

90991P33

Fig. 8 Failure to use a torque wrench on this aluminum cover could lead to a damaged cover and leaks

TCCS3111

Fig. 9 Don't laugh, but that old muffin baking tray can be very helpful in the garage once its life is over in the kitchen

SAFETY IN MOTORCYCLE SERVICE

▶ **See Figure 10**

It is virtually impossible to anticipate all of the hazards involved with motorcycle maintenance and service, but care and common sense will prevent most accidents.

The rules of safety for mechanics range from "don't smoke around gasoline," to "use the proper tool(s) for the job." The trick to avoiding injuries is to develop safe work habits and to take every possible precaution. Whenever you are working on your motorcycle, PAY ATTENTION to what you are doing. The more you pay attention to details and what is going on around you, the less likely you will be to hurt yourself or damage the bike.

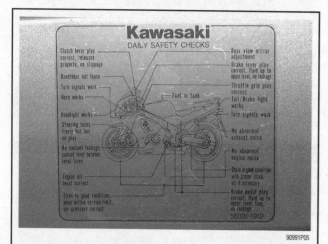

Fig. 10 You perform daily safety checks on your motorcycle (and if you don't, then read Section 6), so pay the same attention in your shop

Do's

▶ **See Figure 11**

• Do keep a fire extinguisher and first aid kit handy.
• Do wear safety glasses or goggles when cutting, drilling, grinding or prying, even if you have 20–20 vision. If you wear glasses for the sake of vision, wear safety goggles over your regular glasses.
• Do shield your eyes whenever you work around the battery. Batteries contain sulfuric acid. In case of contact with the eyes or skin, flush the area with water or a mixture of water and baking soda, then seek immediate medical attention.
• Do use adequate ventilation when working with any chemicals or hazardous materials. Like carbon monoxide, the asbestos dust resulting from some brake lining wear can be hazardous in sufficient quantities.
• Do disconnect the negative battery cable when working on the electrical system. The secondary ignition system contains EXTREMELY HIGH VOLTAGE. In some cases it can even exceed 50,000 volts.
• Do follow manufacturer's directions whenever working with potentially hazardous materials. Most chemicals and fluids are poisonous if taken internally.
• Do properly maintain your tools. Loose hammerheads, mushroomed punches and chisels, frayed or poorly grounded electrical cords, excessively worn screwdrivers, spread wrenches (open end), cracked sockets, slipping ratchets, or faulty droplight sockets can cause accidents.
• Likewise, keep your tools clean; a greasy wrench can slip off a bolt head, ruining the bolt and often harming your knuckles in the process.

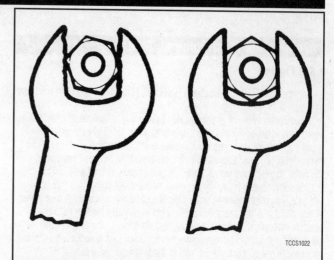

Fig. 11 Using the correct size wrench will help prevent the possibility of rounding off a nut

• Do use the proper size and type of tool for the job at hand. Do select a wrench or socket that fits the nut or bolt. The wrench or socket should sit straight, not cocked.
• Do, when possible, pull on a wrench handle rather than push on it, and adjust your stance to prevent a fall.
• Do be sure that adjustable wrenches are tightly closed on the nut or bolt and pulled so that the force is on the side of the fixed jaw. Better yet, avoid the use of an adjustable if you have a fixed wrench that will fit.
• Do strike squarely with a hammer; avoid glancing blows. But, we REALLY hope you won't be using a hammer much in basic maintenance.

Don'ts

• Don't run the engine in a garage or anywhere else without proper ventilation—EVER! Carbon monoxide is poisonous; it takes a long time to leave the human body and you can build up a deadly supply of it in your system by simply breathing in a little every day. You may not realize you are slowly poisoning yourself. Always use power vents, windows, fans and/or open the garage door.
• Don't work around moving parts while wearing loose clothing. Short sleeves are much safer than long, loose sleeves. Hard-toed shoes with neoprene soles protect your toes and give a better grip on slippery surfaces. Jewelry, watches, large belt buckles, or body adornment of any kind is not safe working around a vehicle. Long hair should be tied back under a hat or cap.
• Don't use pockets for toolboxes. A fall or bump can drive a screwdriver deep into your body. Even a rag hanging from your back pocket can wrap around a spinning shaft or rotor.
• Don't smoke when working around gasoline, cleaning solvent or other flammable material.
• Don't smoke when working around the battery. When the battery is being charged, it gives off explosive hydrogen gas. Aww, just don't smoke, it's bad for you even if it doesn't cause something to blow up.
• Don't use gasoline to wash your hands; there are excellent soaps available. Gasoline contains dangerous additives which can enter the body through a cut or through your pores. Gasoline also removes all the natural oils from the skin so that bone dry hands will suck up oil and grease.
• Don't use screwdrivers for anything other than driving screws! A screwdriver used as an prying tool can snap when you least expect it, causing injuries. At the very least, you'll ruin a good screwdriver.

THE WORK AREA (SETTING UP SHOP)

The size and complexity of your work area will vary with the amount of work you plan to do on your motorcycle. It is easy (and fun) to get carried away when setting up a shop, but the more time you spend in it, the more you will appreciate the preparation work. What we have described here is all that most people would ever need to maintain (repair or possibly even restore) a motorcycle. That doesn't mean you can't maintain your bike if you don't have a garage, it just means that you might not be as comfortable. Face it, trying to check an adjustment in the rain or worse, prepping the bike for winter storage with snow melting down your back just isn't much fun.

So, if you are lucky enough to set up a shop just to work on your bike, here are some things you'll want to consider.

Floor Space

▶ See Figure 12

The average one car garage will give you more than enough work-space, but a decent sized tool shed will also do the trick. A floor plan of 16 X 12 feet (4.8 X 3.6 meters) is more than sufficient for shelving, workbenches, tool shelves or boxes and parts storage areas. 12 X 16 (4.8 X 3.6) works out to 192 square feet (or about 17 square meters). You may think that this sounds like a lot of room, but when you start building shelves, and constructing work benches almost most half of that can be eaten up!

Also, you may wonder why a lot of floor space is needed. There are several reasons, not the least of which is the safety factor. You'll be working around a large, heavy, metal object — your bike. You don't want to be tripping, falling, crashing into things or hurting yourself, because your bike takes up a surprising amount of your work space. Accidents can happen! You can easily trip over a misplaced tool and the LAST thing you want to do is fall on the bike (knocking it over . . . YIKES).

Most garages have concrete floors. Portable bike lifts or work stools roll best on a smooth surface. If your garage floor has cracks with raised sections or blocks with deep grooves, you may have a problem if you plan on using either of these. If the wheels hang up on these cracks or grooves while moving a bike on a stand, you might be in for an unpleasant surprise.

Fig. 12 One of the great advantages to motorcycles is that you can fit a whole bunch in the space an average automobile would occupy

Storage Areas

SHELVES

▶ See Figures 13, 14 and 15

You can't have enough shelf space. Adequate shelf space means that you don't have to stack anything on the floor, where it would be in the way.

Making shelves isn't tough. You can make your own, buy modular or buy prefab units. The best modular units are those made of interlocking shelves and uprights of ABS plastic. They're lightweight and easy to assemble, and their load-bearing capacity is more than sufficient. Also, they are not subject rust or rot as are metal and wood shelves.

Fig. 13 Typical homemade wood shelves, crammed with stuff. These shelves are made from spare ⁵⁄₄ x 6 in. pressure treated decking

Fig. 14 Modular plastic shelves, such as these are inexpensive, weatherproof and easy to assemble

Fig. 15 These shelves were made from the frame of old kitchen cabinets

Fig. 17 A good tool chest has several drawers, each designed to hold a different type tool

Probably the cheapest and best shelves are ones that you make yourself from one inch shelving with 2 X 4 uprights. You can make them as long, wide and high as you want. For at least the uprights, use pressure treated wood. Its resistance to rot is more than worth the additional cost.

TOOL CHESTS

▶ **See Figures 16 and 17**

There are many types and sizes of tool chests. Their greatest advantage is that they can hold a lot of tools, securely, in a relatively small area. If you decide that you need one, make sure that you buy one that's big enough and mobile enough for the work area. Remember, you get what you pay for, so purchase a good brand name, and it should last a lifetime.

There are several things to look for in a tool chest, depending on how much you plan on using it, and just how many tools you plan to stuff in it. Check the overall construction. In general, bolted-together chests are

stronger than riveted or tabbed, because they are sturdier. Drawers that ride on ball bearings are better than compound slide drawers, because they can hold more and are easier to open/close. Heavy-duty, ball bearing casters are better than bushing type wheels, because they will roll better and last longer. Steel wheels are better than plastic, as they are less prone to damage. Compare different boxes, you'll have to make up your own mind exactly what style is best for you.

WORK BENCHES

▶ **See Figure 18**

As with the shelving, work benches can be either store-bought or homemade. The store-bought workbenches can be steel, precut wood, or even plastic kits. They all work (though heavy duty benches are obviously better suited to heavy parts and related work), and most types should be available at your local building supply stores or through tool catalogs.

Homemade benches, as with the shelves have the advantage of being made-to-fit your workshop. A freestanding workbench is best, as opposed to one attached to an outside wall. The freestanding bench can take more abuse since it doesn't transfer the shock or vibration to wall supports.

A good free-standing workbench should be constructed using 4 X 4 pressure treated wood as legs, 2 X 6 planking as header boards and ¾ inch plywood sheathing as a deck. Diagonal supports can be 2 X 4 studs and it's always helpful to construct a full size ¾ inch plywood shelf under the bench. Not only can you use the shelf for storage but also it gives great rigidity to the whole bench structure. Assembling the bench with screws rather than nails takes longer but adds strength and gives you the ability to take the whole thing apart if you ever want to move it.

Lighting

▶ **See Figures 19 and 20**

The importance of adequate lighting can't be over emphasized. Good lighting is not only a convenience but also a safety feature. If you can see what you're working on you're less likely to make mistakes, have a wrench slip or trip over an obstacle. A lot of frustration can be avoided when you can see all the fasteners on which you are working (some of which may be hidden or obscured).

Fig. 16 Different types of mobile, steel tool chests

87933512

Fig. 18 Homemade workbenches

87933023

Fig. 19 At least two of this type of twin tube fluorescent light is essential

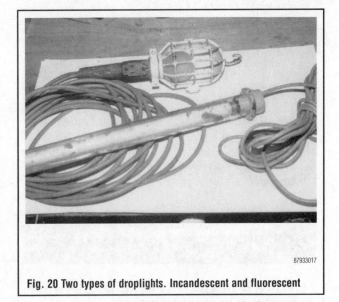

87933017

Fig. 20 Two types of droplights. Incandescent and fluorescent

For overhead lighting, at least 2 twin tube fluorescent shop lights should be in place. Most garages are wired with standard light bulbs attached to the wall studs at intervals. Four or five of these lights, at about a 6 foot height combined with the overhead lighting should suffice. However, no matter where the lights are, your body is going to block some of it so a droplight or clip-on type work light is a great idea.

Ventilation

At one time or another, you'll be working with chemicals that may require adequate ventilation. Now, just about all garages have a big car-sized door and all sheds or workshops have a door. In bad weather the door will have to be closed so at least one window that opens is a necessity. An exhaust fan or regular ventilation fan is a great help, especially in hot weather.

Heaters

If you live in an area where the winters are cold, as do many of us, it's nice to have some sort of heat where we work. If your workshop or garage is attached to the house, you'll probably be okay. If your garage or shop is detached, then a space heater of some sort — electric, propane or kerosene — will be necessary. NEVER run a space heater in the presence of flammable vapors! When running a non-electric space heater, always allow for some means of venting the carbon monoxide!

Electrical Requirements

Obviously, your workshop should be wired according to all local codes. As to what type of service you need, that depends on your electrical load. If you have a lot of power equipment and maybe a refrigerator, TV, stereo or whatever, not only do you have a great shop, but your amperage requirements may exceed the capacity of your wiring. If you are at all in doubt, consult your local electrical contractor.

Safety Equipment

▶ **See Figure 21**

FIRE EXTINGUISHERS

▶ **See Figure 22**

There are many types of safety equipment. The most important of these is the fire extinguisher. You'll be well off with two 5 lbs. extinguishers rated for oil, chemical and wood.

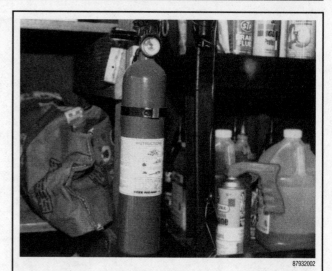
Fig. 22 A good, all-purpose fire extinguisher

FIRST AID KITS

Next you'll need a good first aid kit. Any good kit that can be purchased from the local drug store will be fine. It's a good idea, in addition, to have something easily accessible in the event of a minor injury, such as hydrogen peroxide or other antiseptic that can be poured onto or applied to a wound immediately. Remember, your hands will be dirty. Just as you wouldn't want dirt entering your engine when you open the oil filler plug, you certainly don't want bacteria entering a blood stream that has just been opened!

WORK GLOVES

▶ **See Figure 23**

Unless you think scars on your hands are cool, enjoy pain and like wearing bandages, get a good pair of work gloves. Canvas or leather are the best. And yes, we realize that there are some jobs involving small parts that can't be done while wearing work gloves. These jobs are not the ones usually associated with hand injuries.

A good pair of rubber gloves (such as those usually associated with dish washing) or vinyl gloves is also a great idea. There are some liquids such

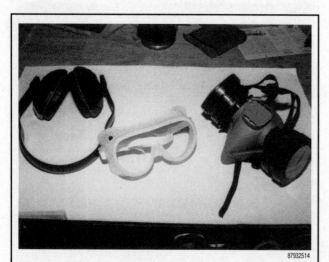
Fig. 21 Three essential pieces of safety equipment. Left to right: ear protectors, safety goggles and respirator

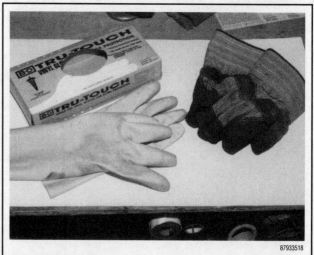
Fig. 23 Three different types of work gloves. The box contains latex gloves

as solvents and penetrants that don't belong on your skin. Avoid burns and rashes. Wear these gloves.

And lastly, an option. If you're tired of being greasy and dirty all the time, go to the drug store and buy a box of disposable latex gloves like medical professionals wear. You can handle greasy parts, perform small tasks, wash parts, etc. all without getting dirty! These gloves take a surprising amount of abuse without tearing and aren't expensive. Note however, that it has been reported that some people are allergic to the latex or the powder used inside some gloves, so pay attention to what you buy.

WORK BOOTS

It's up to you, but I think that a good, comfortable pair of steel-toed work boots is a sensible idea. Primarily because heavy parts or tools get dropped sooner or later. A heavy piece of metal can do significant damage to a sneaker-clad foot.

Good work boots also provide better support, — you're going to be on your feet a lot — are oil-resistant, and they keep your feet warm and dry.

To keep the boots protected, get a spray can of silicone-based water repellent and spray the boots when new, and then periodically thereafter.

EYE PROTECTION

Don't begin any job without a good pair of work goggles or impact resistant glasses! When doing any kind of work, it's all too easy to avoid eye injury through this simple precaution. And don't just buy eye protection and leave it on the shelf. Wear it all the time! Things have a habit of breaking, chipping, splashing, spraying, splintering and flying around. And, for some reason, your eye is always in the way!

If you wear vision correcting glasses as a matter of routine, get a pair made with polycarbonate lenses. These lenses are impact resistant and are available at any optometrist.

EAR PROTECTION

Often overlooked is hearing protection. Power equipment is noisy! Loud noises damage your ears. It's as simple as that!

The simplest and cheapest form of ear protection is a pair of noise-reducing ear plugs. Cheap insurance for your ears. And, they may even come with their own, cute little carrying case.

More substantial, more protection and more money is a good pair of noise reducing earmuffs. They protect from all but the loudest sounds. Hopefully those are sounds that you'll never encounter since they're usually associated with disasters.

WORK CLOTHES

Everyone has "work clothes." Usually this consists of old jeans and a shirt that has seen better days. That's fine. In addition, a denim work apron is a nice accessory. It's rugged, can hold some spare bolts, and you don't feel bad wiping your hands or tools on it. That's what it's for.

If you're so inclined, overalls are a superb work garment. They're rugged and are equipped with numerous pockets, loops and places to put stuff. When bending or reaching, you won't have to worry about your shirt pulling out. Also, they cover your shirt like a work apron.

When working in cold weather, a one-piece, thermal work outfit is invaluable. Most are rated to below zero (Fahrenheit) temperatures and are ruggedly constructed.

Chemicals

There is a whole range of chemicals that you'll find handy for maintenance work. The most common types are, lubricants, penetrants and sealers. Keep these handy, on some convenient shelf. There are also many chemicals that are used for detailing or cleaning, but these are covered elsewhere.

When a particular chemical is not being used, keep it capped, upright and in a safe place. These substances may be flammable, may be irritants or might even be caustic and should always be stored properly, used properly and handled with care. Always read and follow all label directions and be sure to wear hand and eye protection!

LUBRICANTS & PENETRANTS

▶ **See Figures 24 and 25**

In this category, a well-prepared shop should have:
• A full complement of fluids for your bike (engine oil, transmission or drive oil, brake fluid, etc.)
• Anti-seize
• Lithium grease
• Chassis lube
• Assembly lube
• Silicone grease
• Silicone spray
• Penetrating oil

Anti-seize is used to coat certain fasteners prior to installation. This can be especially helpful when two dissimilar metals are in contact (to help prevent corrosion that might lock the fastener in place). This is a good practice

Fig. 24 If your bike requires any unique fluids (like DOT 5 brake fluid), be sure to keep some handy for maintenance checks

Fig. 25 A variety of penetrants and lubricants is a staple of any DIYer's garage

on a lot of different fasteners, BUT, NOT on any fastener which might vibrate loose causing a problem. If anti-seize is used on a fastener, it should be checked periodically for proper tightness.

Lithium grease, chassis lube, silicone grease or a synthetic brake caliper grease can all be used pretty much interchangeably. All can be used for coating rust-prone fasteners and for facilitating the assembly of parts that are a tight fit. Silicone and synthetic greases are the most versatile.

➡**Silicone dielectric grease is a non-conductor that is often used to coat the terminals of wiring connectors before fastening them. It may sound odd to coat metal portions of a terminal with something that won't conduct electricity, but here is it how it works. When the connector is fastened the metal-to-metal contact between the terminals will displace the grease (allowing the circuit to be completed). The grease that is displaced will then coat the non-contacted surface and the cavity around the terminals, SEALING them from atmospheric moisture that could cause corrosion.**

Silicone spray is a good lubricant for hard-to-reach places and parts that shouldn't be gooped up with grease.

Penetrating oil may turn out to be one of your best friends when taking something apart that has corroded fasteners. The most familiar penetrating oils are Liquid Wrench® and WD-40®. These products have hundreds of uses. For your purposes, they are vital!

Before disassembling any part (especially on an exhaust system), check the fasteners. If any appear rusted, soak them thoroughly with the penetrant and let them stand while you do something else. This simple act can save you hours of tedious work trying to extract a broken bolt or stud.

SEALANTS

▶ **See Figure 26**

Sealants are an indispensable part for certain tasks on motorcycles, especially if you are trying to avoid leaks (I think there is a bad Harley-Davidson joke in there somewhere, but we won't take a cheap shot). The purpose of sealants is to establish a leak-proof bond between or around assembled parts. Most sealers are used in conjunction with gaskets, but some are used instead of conventional gasket material.

The most common sealers are the non-hardening types such as Perma-

tex® No.2 or its equivalents. These sealers are applied to the mating surfaces of each part to be joined, then a gasket is put in place and the parts are assembled.

➡**A sometimes overlooked use for sealants like RTV is on the threads of vibration prone fasteners.**

One very helpful type of non-hardening sealer is the "high tack" type. This type is a very sticky material that holds the gasket in place while the parts are being assembled. This stuff is really a good idea when you don't have enough hands or fingers to keep everything where it should be.

The stand-alone sealers are the Room Temperature Vulcanizing (RTV) silicone gasket makers. On some engines, this material is used instead of a gasket. In those instances, a gasket may not be available or, because of the shape of the mating surfaces, a gasket shouldn't be used. This stuff, when used in conjunction with a conventional gasket, produces the surest bonds.

RTV does have its limitations though. When using this material, you will have a time limit. It starts to set-up within 15 minutes or so, so you have to assemble the parts without delay. In addition, when squeezing the material out of the tube, don't drop any glops into the engine. The stuff will form and set and travel around the oil gallery, possibly plugging up a passage. Also, most types are not fuel-proof. Check the tube for all cautions.

CLEANERS

▶ **See Figures 27, 28 and 29**

You'll have two types of cleaners to deal with: parts cleaners and hand cleaners. The parts cleaners are for the bike parts; the hand cleaners are for you.

There are many good, non-flammable, biodegradable parts cleaners on the market. These cleaning agents are safe for you, the parts and the environment. Therefore, there is no reason to use flammable, caustic or toxic substances to clean your parts or tools.

As far as hand cleaners go, the waterless types are the best. They have always been efficient at cleaning, but left behind a pretty smelly odor. Recently though, just about all of them have eliminated the odor and added stuff that actually smells good. Make sure that you pick one that contains

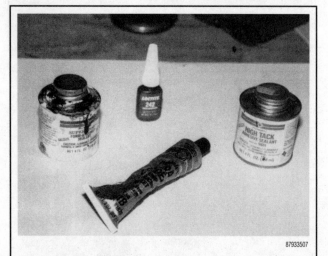

Fig. 26 Sealants are essential. These four types are all that you'll need

Fig. 27 Three types of cleaners. Some are caustic; some are not. Always read and follow label instructions

Fig. 28 This is one type of hand cleaner that not only works well but smells pretty good too

Fig. 29 The best thing to clean up all types of spills is "kitty litter"

lanolin or some other moisture-replenishing additive. Cleaners not only remove grease and oil but also skin oil.

One other note: most women know this already but most men don't. Use a hand lotion when you're all cleaned up. It's okay. Real men DO use hand lotion!

SHOP TOWELS

▶ See Figure 30

One of the most important elements in doing shop work is a good supply of shop towels. Standard household paper towels just don't cut it! Most auto parts stores sell packs of shop towels, usually 50-100 in a pack. They are relatively cheap and can be washed over and over. Some manufacturers now produce a heavy paper towel, just for shop use, and these are often just as good as the cloth types (although they are obviously disposable and might not be considered as environmentally friendly. Not that washing oil soaked rags would be considered "environmentally sound" either . . .). Ideally, you may want to keep both types handy.

One of the best shop towels known to science, is the old-fashioned cloth diaper. They're highly absorbent and rugged, but, in these days of disposable diapers, are hard to find.

Fig. 30 A pack of shop towels

TOOLS

▶ See Figures 31, 32 and 33

Tools; well here is a subject for a whole other book. Again, the first thing you will need to ask yourself, is just HOW involved do you plan to get. Most Asian and European bikes come with a tool kit (perhaps it is a leftover from the days when bikes weren't as reliable as they are today). And, with some, such as the kits supplied with most BMW Airheads, you could reasonably perform all required maintenance using only the kit supplied with the bike. But, that is probably more the exception than the rule and if you are serious about your motorcycle maintenance you will want to gather a quality set of tools to make the job easier, and more enjoyable. BESIDES, TOOLS ARE FUN!!!

Almost every do-it-yourselfer loves to accumulate tools. Though most find a way to perform jobs with only a few common tools, they tend to buy more over time, as money allows. So gathering the tools necessary for bike maintenance does not have to be an expensive, overnight proposition.

When buying tools, the saying "You get what you pay for" is absolutely true! Don't go cheap! Any hand tool that you buy should be drop forged and/or chrome vanadium. These two qualities tell you that the tool is strong enough for the job. With any tool, power or not, go with a name that you've heard of before, or, that is recommended buy your local professional retailer. Let's go over a list of tools that you'll need.

Most of the world uses the metric system. So, if you have anything but a Harley, you can be pretty certain that it was built with metric fasteners and put together using metric measured clearances and adjustments. And, not to spoil anyone's image here, but there are a few metric fasteners on most late-model Harleys too.

So, accumulate your tools accordingly. Any good DIYer should have a decent set of both U.S. and metric measure tools. Don't be confused by terminology. Most advertising refers to "SAE and metric", or "standard and metric." Both are misnomers. The Society of Automotive Engineers (SAE) did not invent the English system of measurement;

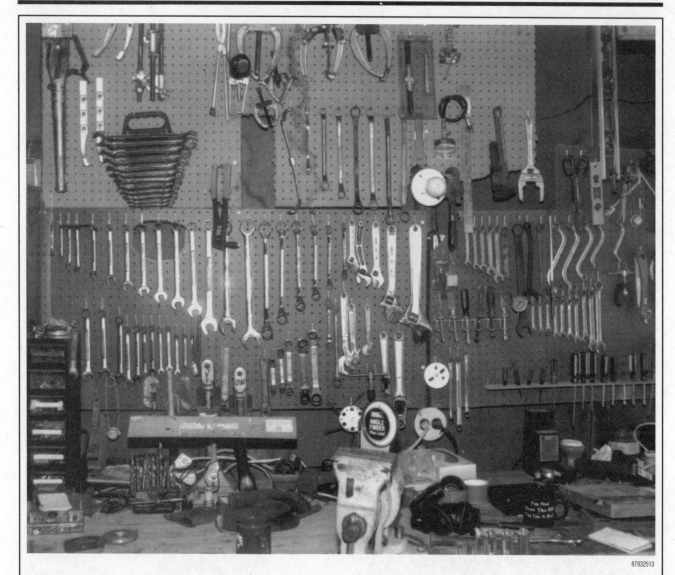

87932513

Fig. 31 The well-stocked garage pegboard. Pegboards can store most tools and other equipment for ease of access. Besides, they're cool looking

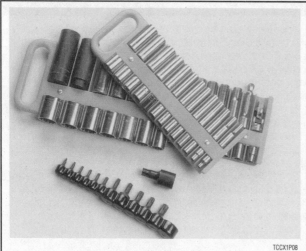

TCCX1P08

Fig. 32 Socket holders, especially the magnetic type, are handy items to keep tools in order

87932007

Fig. 33 A good set of handy storage cabinets for fasteners and small parts makes any job easier

the English did. The SAE likes metrics just fine. Both English (U.S.) and metric measurements are SAE approved. Also, the current "standard" measurement IS metric. So, if it's not metric, it's U.S. measurement.

Hands Tools

SOCKET SETS

♦ **See Figures 34, 35, 36, 37 and 38**

Socket sets are the most basic, necessary hand tools for motorcycle work. For our purposes, socket sets basically come in three drive sizes: ¼ inch, ⅜ inch and ½ inch. Drive size refers to the size of the drive lug on the ratchet, breaker bar or speed handle.

You'll need a good ½ inch set since this size drive lug assures that you won't break a ratchet or socket on large or heavy retainers. Also, torque wrenches with a torque scale high enough for larger fasteners (such as axle nuts) are usually ½ inch drive. The socket set that you'll need should range in sizes from ⁷⁄₁₆ inch through 1 inch for American models, or 6mm through 19mm on Asian and European bikes.

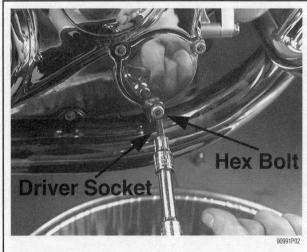

Fig. 36 Internal hex head and Torx® head fasteners are found on various components like engine covers

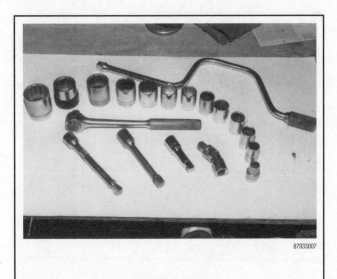

Fig. 34 A good half inch drive socket set

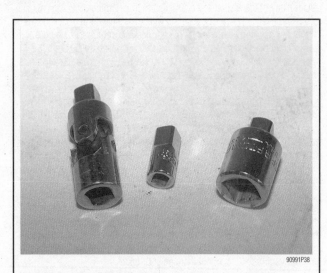

Fig. 37 A swivel (U-joint) adapter, and two types of drive adapters

Fig. 35 Two VERY common drivers for motorcycle service: Left, a Torx® drive socket; right, a hex drive socket

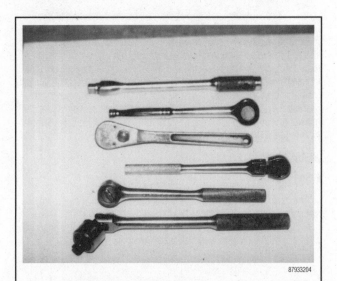

Fig. 38 Ratchets come in all sizes from rigid to swivel-headed

A ⅜ inch set is very handy to have since it allows you to get into tight places that the larger drive ratchets can't. Also, this size set gives you a range of smaller sockets that are still strong enough for heavy duty work.

¼ inch drive sets can be VERY handy in tight places, though they usually duplicate functions of the ⅜ inch set.

As for the sockets themselves, they come in standard and deep lengths as well as standard and thin walled, in either 6 or 12 point.

Standard length sockets are good for just about all jobs, however, some stud-head bolts, hard-to-reach bolts, nuts on long studs, etc., require the deep sockets.

Thin-walled sockets are not too common and aren't usually needed in most work. They are exactly what you think, sockets made with a thinner wall to fit into tighter places. They don't have the wall strength of a standard socket, of course, but their usefulness in a tight spot can make them worth it.

6 and 12 points. This refers to how many sides are in the socket itself. Each has advantages. The 6 point socket is stronger and less prone to slipping which would strip a bolt head or nut. 12 point sockets are more common, usually less expensive and can operate better in tight places where the ratchet handle can't swing far.

Most motorcycle manufacturers use recessed hex-head fasteners to retain many of the engine and chassis parts from engine covers to caliper pins. These fasteners require a socket with a hex shaped driver or a large sturdy hex key. To help prevent torn knuckles, we would recommend that you stick to the sockets on any tight fastener and leave the hex keys for lighter applications. Hex driver sockets are available individually or in sets just like conventional sockets. Any complete tool set should include hex driver sockets.

More and more, manufacturers are using Torx® head fasteners, which were once known as tamper resistant fasteners (because many people did not have tools with the necessary odd driver shape). They are still used on parts of the bike where the manufacturer would prefer only knowledgeable technicians or advanced Do-It-Yourselfers (DIYers) be working. One example would be certain triple-tree fasteners and even the primary cover screws on most late-model Harleys.

There are currently three different types of Torx® fasteners; internal, external and a new tamper resistant. The internal fasteners require a star-shaped driver. The external fasteners require a star-shaped socket. And, the new tamper resistant fasteners use a star-shaped driver with a small hole drilled through the center. The most common are the internal Torx® fasteners, but you might find any of them on your bike.

Torque Wrenches

▶ See Figure 39

In most applications, a torque wrench can be used to assure proper installation of a fastener. Torque wrenches come in various designs and most supply stores will carry a variety to suit your needs. A torque wrench should be used any time you have a specific torque value for a fastener. A torque wrench can also be used if you are following the general guidelines in the charts accompanying the fastener information in this section. Keep in mind that because there is no worldwide standardization of fasteners, the charts are a general guideline and should be used with caution. Again, the general rule of "if you are using the right tool for the job, you should not have to strain to tighten a fastener" applies here.

BEAM TYPE

▶ See Figure 40

The beam type torque wrench is one of the most popular types. It consists of a pointer attached to the head that runs the length of the flexible beam (shaft) to a scale located near the handle. As the wrench is pulled, the beam bends and the pointer indicates the torque using the scale.

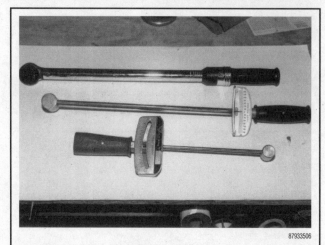

Fig. 39 Three types of torque wrenches. Top to bottom: a ½ inch drive clicker type, a ½ inch drive beam type and a ⅜ inch drive beam type that reads in inch lbs.

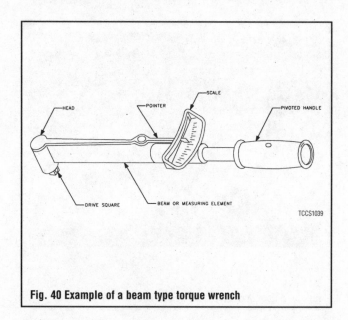

Fig. 40 Example of a beam type torque wrench

CLICK (BREAKAWAY) TYPE

▶ See Figure 41

Another popular torque wrench design is the click type. To use the click type wrench you pre-adjust it to a torque setting. Once the torque is reached, the wrench has a reflex signaling feature that causes a momentary breakaway of the torque wrench body, sending an impulse to the operator's hand.

PIVOT HEAD TYPE

▶ See Figure 42

Some torque wrenches (usually of the click type) may be equipped with a pivot head that can allow it to be used in areas of limited access. BUT, it must be used properly. To hold a pivot head wrench, grasp the handle lightly, and as you pull on the handle, it should be floated on the pivot point. If the handle comes in contact with the yoke extension during the process of pulling, there is a very good chance the torque readings will be

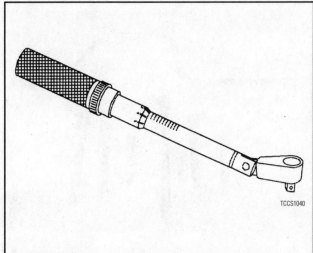

Fig. 41 A click type or breakaway torque wrench—note this one has a pivoting head

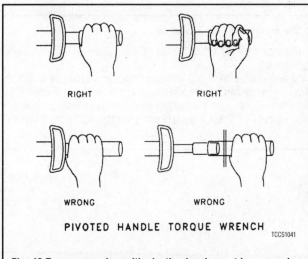

Fig. 42 Torque wrenches with pivoting heads must be grasped and used properly to prevent an incorrect reading

inaccurate because this could alter the wrench loading point. The design of the handle is usually such as to make it inconvenient to deliberately misuse the wrench.

➡ It should be mentioned that the use of any U-joint, wobble or extension would have an effect on the torque readings, no matter what type of wrench you are using. For the most accurate readings, install the socket directly on the wrench driver. If necessary, straight extensions (which hold a socket directly under the wrench driver) will have the least effect on the torque reading. Avoid any extension that alters the length of the wrench from the handle to the head/driving point (such as a crow's foot). U-joint or wobble extensions can greatly affect the readings; avoid their use at all times.

RIGID CASE (DIRECT READING)

▶ See Figure 43

A rigid case or direct reading torque wrench is equipped with a dial indicator to show torque values. One advantage of these wrenches is that they can be held at any position on the wrench without affecting accuracy. These wrenches are often preferred because they tend to be compact, easy to read and have a great degree of accuracy.

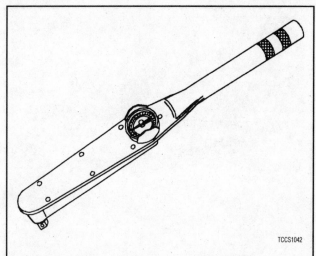

Fig. 43 The rigid case (direct reading) torque wrench uses a dial indicator to show torque

Torque Angle Meters

▶ See Figure 44

Because the frictional characteristics of each fastener or threaded hole will vary, clamp loads which are based strictly on torque will vary as well. In most applications, this variance is not significant enough to cause worry. But, in certain applications, a manufacturer's engineers may determine that more precise clamp loads are necessary (such is the case with many aluminum cylinder heads). In these cases, a torque angle method of installation would be specified. When installing fasteners that are torque angle tightened, a predetermined seating torque and standard torque wrench are usually used first to remove any compliance from the joint. The fastener is then tightened the specified additional portion of a turn measured in degrees. A torque angle gauge (mechanical protractor) is used for these applications. You will probably never have the use for a torque angle meter for most normal maintenance.

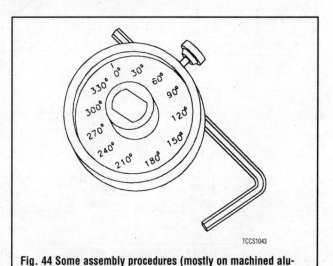

Fig. 44 Some assembly procedures (mostly on machined aluminum parts such as cylinder heads) require the use of a torque angle meter (mechanical protractor)

Breaker Bars

▶ See Figure 45

Breaker bars are long handles with a drive lug. Their main purpose is to provide extra turning force when breaking loose tight bolts or nuts. They

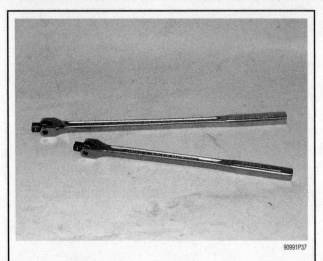

Fig. 45 Breaker bars are great for loosening large or stuck fasteners

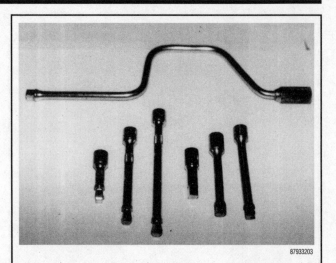

Fig. 46 A speed driver and extensions. The 3 on the left are called "wobbles" since they allow some lateral movement

come in all drive sizes and lengths. Always wear gloves when using a breaker bar

Speed Handles

▶ See Figure 46

Speed handles are tools with a drive lug and angled turning handle that allow you to quickly remove or install a bolt or nut. They don't, however have much torque ability. You might consider one when installing a number of similar fasteners such as an engine cover.

WRENCHES

▶ **See Figures 47, 48, 49 and 50**

Basically, there are 3 kinds of fixed wrenches: open end, box end, and combination.

Open end wrenches have 2-jawed openings at each end of the wrench. These wrenches are able to fit onto just about any nut or bolt. They are extremely versatile but have one major drawback. They can slip on a worn or rounded bolt head or nut, causing bleeding knuckles and a useless fastener.

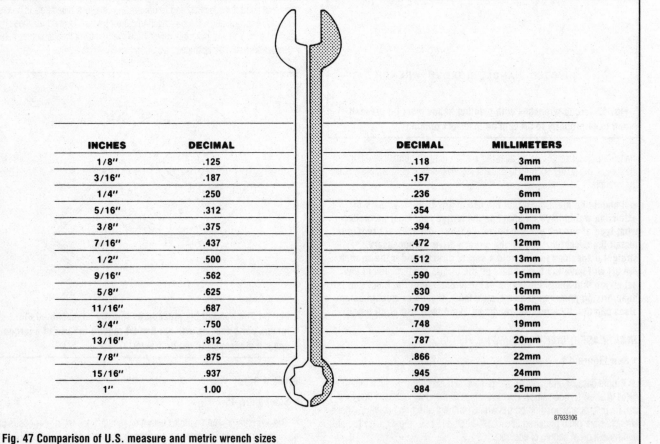

INCHES	DECIMAL	DECIMAL	MILLIMETERS
1/8"	.125	.118	3mm
3/16"	.187	.157	4mm
1/4"	.250	.236	6mm
5/16"	.312	.354	9mm
3/8"	.375	.394	10mm
7/16"	.437	.472	12mm
1/2"	.500	.512	13mm
9/16"	.562	.590	15mm
5/8"	.625	.630	16mm
11/16"	.687	.709	18mm
3/4"	.750	.748	19mm
13/16"	.812	.787	20mm
7/8"	.875	.866	22mm
15/16"	.937	.945	24mm
1"	1.00	.984	25mm

Fig. 47 Comparison of U.S. measure and metric wrench sizes

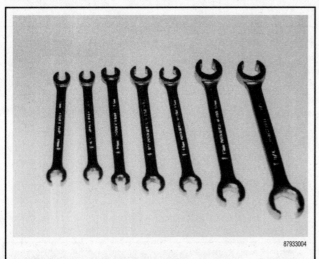

Fig. 48 Flarenut wrenches are critical for brake lines or tubing, to make sure the fittings do not become rounded

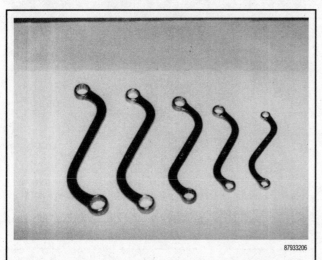

Fig. 49 These S-shaped wrenches are called obstruction wrenches

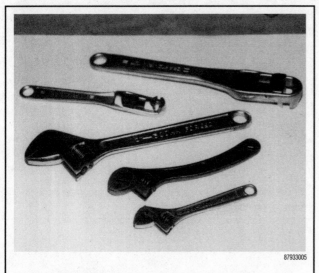

Fig. 50 Several types and sizes of adjustable wrenches

Box-end wrenches have a 360° circular jaw at each end of the wrench. They come in both 6 and 12 point versions just like sockets and each type has the same advantages and disadvantages as sockets.

Combination wrenches have the best of both. They have a 2-jawed open end and a box end. These wrenches are probably the most versatile.

As for sizes, you'll probably need a range similar to that of the sockets, about ¼ inch through 1 inch for American models, or 6mm through 19mm on Asian and European bikes. As for numbers, you'll need 2 of each size, since, in many instances, one wrench holds the nut while the other turns the bolt. On most fasteners, the nut and bolt are the same size.

➡**Although you will typically just need the sizes we specified, there are some exceptions. Occasionally you will find an axle nut or upper fork tube nut which is larger. For these, you will need to buy ONE expensive wrench or a very large adjustable. Or you can always just convince the spouse that we are talking about safety here and buy a whole, expensive, large wrench set.**

One extremely valuable type of wrench is the adjustable wrench. An adjustable wrench has a fixed upper jaw and a moveable lower jaw. The lower jaw is moved by turning a threaded drum. The advantage of an adjustable wrench is its ability to be adjusted to just about any size fastener. The main drawback of an adjustable wrench is the lower jaw's tendency to move slightly under heavy pressure. This can cause the wrench to slip if the wrench is not facing the right way. Pulling on an adjustable wrench in the proper direction will cause the jaws to lock in place. Adjustable wrenches come in a large range of sizes, measured by the wrench length.

PLIERS

♦ **See Figures 51 and 52**

At least 2 pair of standard pliers is an absolute necessity. Pliers are simply mechanical fingers. They are, more than anything, an extension of your hand.

In addition to standard pliers there are the slip-joint, multi-position pliers such as ChannelLock® pliers and locking pliers, such as Vise Grips®.

Slip joint pliers are extremely valuable in grasping oddly sized parts and fasteners. Just make sure that you don't use them instead of a wrench too often since they can easily round off a bolt head or nut.

Locking pliers are usually used for gripping bolts or studs that can't be removed conventionally. You can get locking pliers in square jawed, needle-nosed and pipe-jawed. Pipe jawed have slightly curved jaws for gripping more than just pipes. Locking pliers can rank right up behind duct tape as the handy-man's best friend.

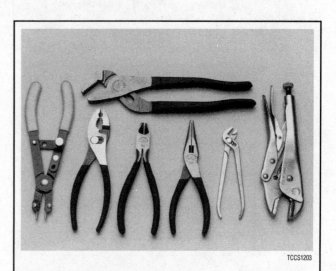

Fig. 51 Pliers and cutters come in many shapes and sizes. You should have an assortment on hand

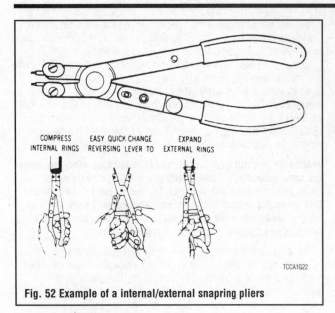

Fig. 52 Example of a internal/external snapring pliers

SCREWDRIVERS

You can't have too many screwdrivers. They come in 2 basic flavors, either standard or Phillips. Standard blades come in various sizes and thicknesses for all types of slotted fasteners. Phillips screwdrivers come in sizes with number designations from 1 on up, with the lower number designating the smaller size. Screwdrivers can be purchased separately or in sets.

HAMMERS

▶ **See Figure 53**

You always need a hammer — for just about any kind of work. For most metal work, you need a ball-peen hammer for using drivers and other like tools, a plastic hammer for hitting things safely, and a soft-faced dead-blow hammer for hitting things safely and hard. Hammers are also VERY useful with impact drivers (if you are not fortunate enough to have an air compressor).

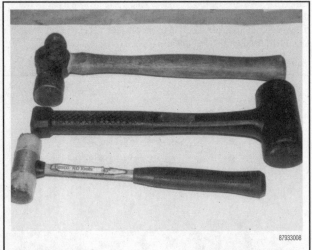

Fig. 53 Three types of hammers. Top to bottom: ball peen, rubber dead-blow, and plastic

OTHER COMMON TOOLS

▶ **See Figures 54 thru 64**

There are a lot of other tools that every workshop will eventually need (though not all for basic maintenance). They include:

- Funnels (for adding fluid)
- Chisels
- Punches
- Files
- Hacksaw
- Bench Vise
- Tap and Die Set
- Flashlight
- Magnetic Bolt Retriever
- Gasket scraper

Fig. 54 A funnel is handy for adding almost every type of fluid (from fork oil to engine oil they help prevent a mess)

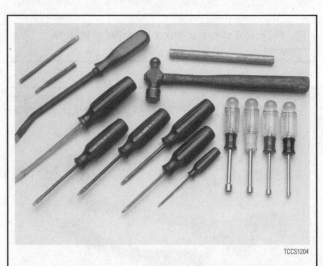

Fig. 55 Various drivers, chisels and prybars are great tools to have in your box

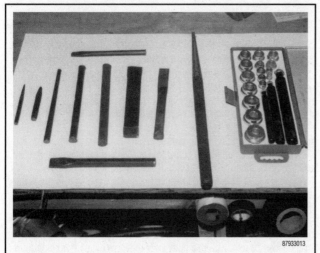

Fig. 56 Punches, chisels and drivers can be purchased separately or in sets

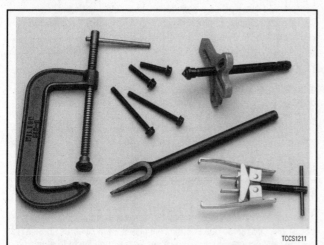

Fig. 57 An assortment of pullers, clamps and separator tools are also needed for many larger repairs (especially engine and suspension work)

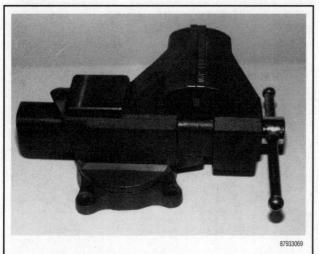

Fig. 58 A good quality, heavy-duty bench vise, like this 5½ in. type, with reversible jaws, is ideal for shop work

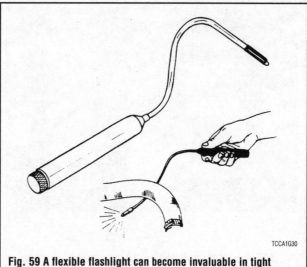

Fig. 59 A flexible flashlight can become invaluable in tight places

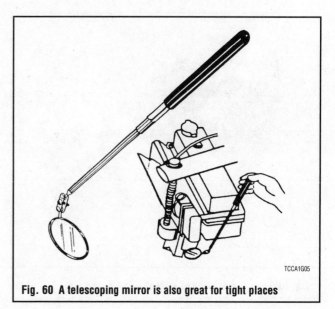

Fig. 60 A telescoping mirror is also great for tight places

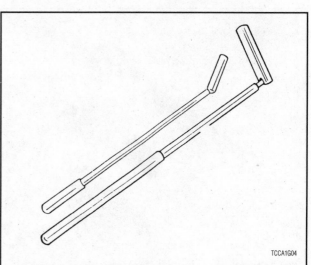

Fig. 61 A magnetic pick-up tool pays for itself the first time you need it

Fig. 62 Two good tap and die sets; US measure (left) and metric

Fig. 63 A set of drill bits and a set of screw extractors

Fig. 64 A really handy tool is the nut splitter. When a frozen nut simply won't budge, use one of these

- Putty Knife
- Screw/Bolt Extractors
- Prybar

Chisel, punches and files are repair tools. Their uses will come up periodically.

Hacksaws have just one use, cutting things off. You may wonder why you'd need one for something as simple as bike maintenance, but you never know. Among other things, guide studs for parts installation can be made from old bolts with their heads cut off.

A large bench vise, of at least 4 inch capacity, is essential. A vise is needed to hold anything being worked on.

A tap and die set might be something you've never needed, but you will eventually. It's a good rule, when everything is apart, to clean-up all threads, on bolts, screws and threaded holes. Also, you'll likely run across a situation in which stripped threads will be encountered. The tap and die set will handle that for you.

Gasket scrapers are just what you'd think, tools made for scraping old gasket material off of parts. You don't absolutely need one. Old gasket material can be remove with a putty knife or single edge razor blade. However, putty knives may not be sharp enough for some really stuck gaskets and razor blades have a knack of breaking just when you don't want them to, inevitably slicing the nearest body part!

Putty knives really do have a use in a motorcycle repair shop. Just because you remove all the bolts from a component sealed with a gasket doesn't mean it's going to come off. Most of the time, the gasket and sealer will hold it tightly. Lightly driving a putty knife at various points between the two parts will break the seal without damage to the parts.

A small — 8-10 inches (20–25 centimeters) long — prybar is extremely useful for removing stuck parts. NEVER, NEVER, use a screwdriver as a prybar! Screwdrivers are not meant for prying. Screwdrivers, used for prying, can break, sending the broken shaft flying!

Screw/bolt extractors are used for removing broken bolts or studs that have broke off flush with the surface of the part.

MOTORCYCLE SPECIALTY TOOLS

▶ **See Figures 65 and 66**

Almost every motorcycle (or motorvehicle) on the road today requires AT LEAST one special tool to perform certain tasks. In most cases, these tools are specially designed to overcome some unique problem or to fit on some oddly sized component.

When manufacturers go through the trouble of making a special tool, it is usually necessary to use it to assure that the job will be done right. A

Fig. 65 Most Japanese and European bike manufacturers include a tool kit with the machine . . .

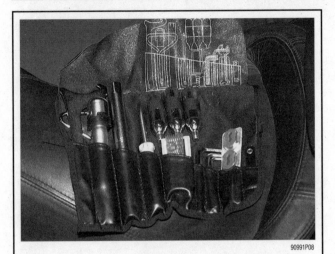

Fig. 66 . . . and these kits often contain most of the tools you would need for basic maintenance

Fig. 67 Pencil style air gauges fit almost all bikes and are easily stored in a tool kit for on-the-road use

Fig. 68 Dial air gauges are GREAT for the shop and are very convenient to use, but they don't always fit into tight motorcycle rims

special tool might be designed to make a job easier, or it might be used to keep you from damaging or breaking a part of the bike.

Don't worry, MOST basic maintenance procedures can either be performed without any special tools OR, because the tools must be used for such basic things, they are commonly available for a reasonable price. It is usually just the low production, highly specialized tools (like a super thin 7-point star-shaped socket capable of 150 ft. lbs. (203 Nm) of torque that is used only on the crankshaft nut of the limited production what-dya-callit cycle) that tend to be outrageously expensive and hard to find. Luckily, you will probably never need such a tool (unless you decide to rebuild or restore a motorcycle, and that is a whole other business).

Special tools can be as inexpensive and simple as an adjustable spanner wrench (which are used on MANY motorcycles to adjust pre-load on the rear shocks) or as complicated as an adjustable axle measurement tool. A few common motorcycle specialty tools are listed here, but check with your dealer or with other riders of your type of bike for help in determining if there are any special tools for YOUR particular model. There is an added advantage is seeking advice from other riders, chances are they may have already found not only what special tool you will need, but how to get it cheaper.

Air (Tire Pressure) Gauge

▶ **See Figures 67 and 68**

Ok, maybe this isn't a MOTORCYCLE ONLY tool, but it is more important to a motorcycle owner than it is to most other people. We all know people who too frequently ignore the air in their car's tires (perhaps someone reading this is even guilty). BUT, on a motorcycle, your tires are your BEST FRIENDS. Treat them well and check the air very often. Keep an accurate tire gauge handy at all times (especially when you travel long distances).

Pressure gauges come in various styles. The pencil type gauge fits just about all bikes and is small enough to keep with you at all times. We prefer dial gauges around the shop. Most are equipped with an air bleed, which makes setting tire pressures a snap. You start by adding some air to a tire. Then, once the gauge is held onto the air valve, you can use the bleed to lower pressure until the desired setting is reached.

Axle Alignment Tool

Although this tool is not absolutely necessary, anyone with a chain or belt final drive will find it VERY useful. There are different versions of this tool available, but all are essentially the same concept, a large sliding scale. Because most belts and chains are adjusted by turning fasteners on BOTH sides of the swingarm, any failure to turn them the exact same distance on

each side will result in the rear tire coming out of alignment with the swingarm (which could lead to dangerously unstable performance).

An axle alignment tool is used to measure the distance from some set point on both sides of the bike, such as the center of the swingarm attachment bolt, to the center of the axle adjusters. By making sure the distance is the same on both sides, you can be certain that the wheel and tire are parallel to the swingarm.

Battery Testers

The best way to test a non-sealed battery is using a hydrometer to check the specific gravity of the acid. Luckily, these are usually very inexpensive and are available at most part stores. Just be careful because the larger ones available at many automotive stores are usually designed for larger, automotive batteries and may require more acid than you will be able to draw from the battery cell. Smaller testers (usually a short, squeeze bulb type) will require less acid and should work on most motorcycle batteries.

Electronic testers are available (and are often necessary to tell if a sealed battery is usable) but these are usually more than most DIYer's are willing to spend. Luckily, many auto part stores have them on hand and are willing to test your battery for you.

Battery Chargers

▶ See Figure 69

If you are not going to ride your bike every day (or at least every week), then you will most likely want to buy a battery charger to keep your battery fresh. There are many types available, from low amperage trickle chargers to electronically controlled battery maintenance tools which monitor the battery voltage to prevent over or undercharging. This last type is especially useful if you must store the bike for any length of time (such as during the severe winter months found in many Northern climates).

Even if you ride your bike every day, you will eventually need a battery charger. Remember that most bike batteries are shipped dry and in a partial charged state. Before a new battery can be put into service it must be filled AND properly charged. Failure to properly charge a battery (which was shipped dry) before it is put into service will prevent it from ever reaching a fully charged state.

Fig. 69 The Battery Tender® is more than just a battery charger, when left connected, it keeps your battery fully charged

Belt Tension Gauge

▶ See Figure 70

Although these are commonly needed for automotive engine applications, most people don't bother using them (opting instead for the old thumb pressure test). But many modern motorcycles (including Harleys and Buells, just to name two) use a belt to drive the rear wheel off the transmission. On such an important and load bearing part you probably want something more accurate than your thumb. There are a few inexpensive belt tension gauges on the market that will accomplish the task without emptying your wallet. If your bike has a drive belt, then chances are your toolbox should have one of these.

Carburetor Synchronization Tool

▶ See Figure 71

If your motorcycle has more than one carburetor, then you'll eventually find a need for a carburetor synchronization tool. Most carb sync tools take the form of vacuum gauges (either mercury tube types or the traditional calibrated dial-type). They are connected to vacuum ports on the individual carburetors or intake manifolds in order to measure the amount of vacuum present at each. By adjusting the carburetor balance screw(s) while watching the sync tool, you can make sure each carburetor runs its cylinder(s) at the same speed as the others.

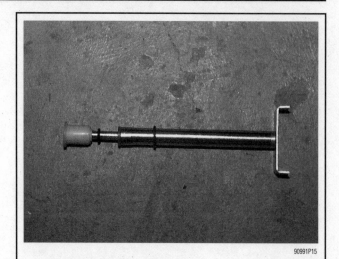

Fig. 70 This inexpensive belt tension gauge is all you need to check the final drive belt on most bikes

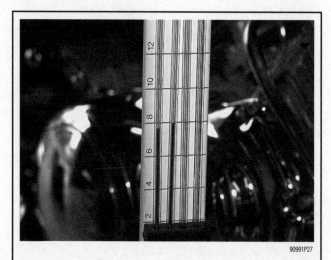

Fig. 71 This carburetor sync tool (the mercury tube-type) can be used on bikes with 2, 3 or 4 carburetors

Chain Breaker/Link Pin Tool

▶ See Figures 72 and 73

If your motorcycle uses a chain final drive, you are probably going to want to buy a chain service tool set. These kits usually consist of a combination, chain breaker, chain link removal and link installation tool. Essentially the tools are usually high strength, threaded presses or c-clamps with the appropriate adapters to enable you to perform the necessary chain service.

➡If your OE and replacement chains use master links, then you can USUALLY get away without this tool, but it still makes master link installation A LOT easier on many models.

Chain Cleaner/Oiler Tool

This is another tool that although it is not absolutely necessary, it can be VERY handy for riders whose bikes use a chain final drive. There are various types available, but many are designed to scrub the chain using a stiff bristled brush, while encasing a few links of the chain at a time to give a mess free spray area for chain oiling.

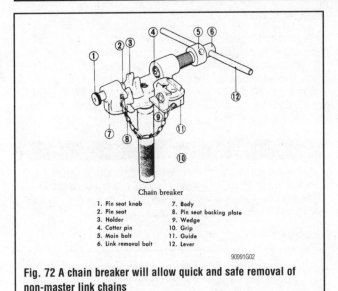

Chain breaker

1. Pin seat knob
2. Pin seat
3. Holder
4. Cotter pin
5. Main bolt
6. Link removal bolt
7. Body
8. Pin seat backing plate
9. Wedge
10. Grip
11. Guide
12. Lever

90991G02

Fig. 72 A chain breaker will allow quick and safe removal of non-master link chains

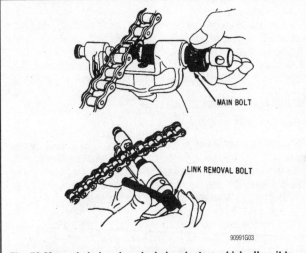

MAIN BOLT

LINK REMOVAL BOLT

90991G03

Fig. 73 Many chain breakers include adapters which allow it to also be used as a link removal or installation tool

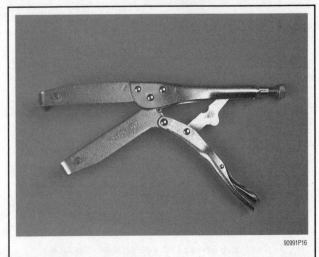

90991P16

Fig. 74 This clutch basket tool is like a pair of locking pliers that met a spanner wrench . . .

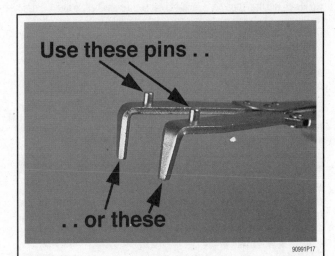

Use these pins . .

. . or these

90991P17

Fig. 75 . . . the pins are inserted into the clutch basket and the tool is held to keep the basket from turning

Clutch Basket Tool

▶ See Figures 74 and 75

Mutli-disc clutch removal (not a basic maintenance item, but they do wear out) will usually require some sort of tool to hold the clutch basket assembly while the fasteners are removed. For many motorcycles (especially most Japanese bikes), the tool is similar to a spanner in that it is a pinned adjustable wrench which keeps the basket from turning. On other bikes, the tool is more like an automotive lockplate tool (the reverse of a puller) that compresses and holds the disks.

Motorcycle Jack/Lift

▶ See Figures 76 and 77

If you have a centerstand, then you may never have a need for one of these, but wouldn't it be nice to stand or sit next comfortably next to your bike during service procedures (or even just during detailing). Of course, if you don't have a centerstand, then simply removing a wheel (to replace a tire, a brake rotor or just to clean and repack the wheel bearings) is impossible without a lift of some type.

Now most people are not going to be able to justify the cost of a pneumatic, full bike, platform lift (like the ones you see in your local shop's

90991P22

Fig. 76 There are many types of motorcycle lifts on the market for home use (this is a very basic one)

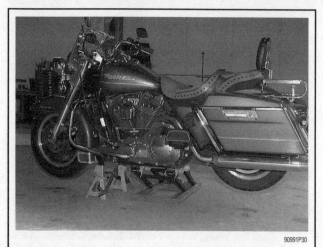

Fig. 77 If your bike doesn't have a centerstand, this lift will allow you to remove wheels (to repack bearings or replace tires)

workbay). But, the good news is that because so many people find the need for these, a lot of companies have come up with RELATIVELY inexpensive bike jacks that will serve the purpose sufficiently.

When purchasing a bike jack, look for one with handy features such as heavy-duty casters (which allow it to be easily rolled around the work area) AND one with some form of protective rubber on the lift points (to help protect the frame or engine of your motorcycle. It is also good for the ends of the lift arms to contain raised stops which will prevent the bike from sliding off the end while you are working on it. The model pictured did not have protective pads (so we added some foam using wire ties . . . not the best solution, but it works).

❊❊ WARNING

Keep in mind that most bike JACKS (as opposed to platform lifts) raise the motorcycle by the frame rail and therefore cannot be used on many models where the exhaust system or even the engine pan extend below the frame rail (unless an adapter is available or can be made to prevent those items from being damaged).

The important thing to keep in mind with a bike jack is to make sure that the bike is well balanced and stable on the lift. If you have other support points, such as a pair of engine guards, then a pair of good old automotive jackstands can be used to provide additional stability to your bike while it is on the jack. And of course, the usual safety precautions must be observed to keep the bike from falling over and damaging the bike or worse, injuring you.

Bike Lift Precautions
• Thoroughly read the bike lift manufacturer's instructions before attempting to raise the bike and be sure to follow them closely when you do.

• Whenever possible secure the bike, either using ratcheting tie-down straps across the frame and around the lift (once the bike is raised and in position), or by stabilizing the bike using automotive jackstands under various frame points (or other large metal parts which are directly bolted to the frame/engine such as a set of engine guards).

• Use extra caution when levering or hammering on a part (not that you want to be hammering your bike much, but a rubber mallet can work wonders now and again) to keep from unbalancing and knocking over the motorcycle.

• Be careful not to bump into the motorcycle when it is on the lift to make sure you don't tip it over (causing massive amounts of damage and grief).

Spanner Wrench

A spanner is different than a normal wrench in that it typically uses 2 or more tabs that are placed within a slot and used to turn the shock sleeve. As mentioned earlier, a spanner wrench is required to adjust the shock pre-load on many motorcycles. There are various types and sizes of spanners available, so make sure the one you are about to buy fits your bike. And, if you have an Asian or European bike, check the tool kit before purchasing one, because they are often (but not always) included.

Measuring Tools

Eventually, you are going to have to measure something whether it is the thickness of a brake pad/rotor or the amount of play in a chain or drive belt. To do this, you will need at least a few precision tools in addition to the special motorcycle tools mentioned earlier.

MICROMETERS & CALIPERS

Micrometers and calipers are devices used to make extremely precise measurements. The simple truth is that you really won't have the need for many of these items just for simple bike maintenance. You will probably want to have at least one precision tool such as an outside caliper to measure rotors or brake pads, but that should be sufficient to most basic maintenance procedures.

Should you decide on becoming more involved in motorcycle mechanics, such as with repair or rebuilding, then these tools will become very important. The success of any rebuild is dependent, to a great extent on the ability to check the size and fit of components as specified by the manufacturer. These measurements are made in thousandths and ten-thousandths of an inch.

Outside Micrometers
▶ See Figure 78

Outside micrometers can be used to check the thickness parts such as the brake rotors. They are also used during many rebuild and repair procedures to measure the diameter of components such as the pistons from a caliper or wheel cylinder. The most common type of micrometer reads in 1/1000 of an inch. Micrometers that use a vernier scale can estimate to 1/10 of an inch.

A micrometer is an instrument made up of a precisely machined spindle which is rotated in a fixed nut, opening and closing the distance between the end of the spindle and a fixed anvil.

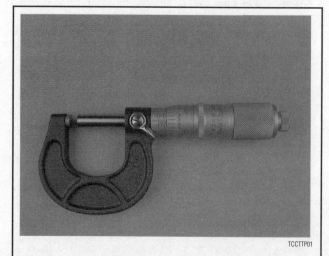

Fig. 78 Outside micrometers can be used to measure bake components including rotors, pads and pistons

To make a measurement, you back off the spindle until you can place the piece to be measured between the spindle and anvil. You then rotate the spindle until the part is contacted by both the spindle and anvil. The measurement is then found by reading the gradations in the handle of the micrometer.

Here's the hard part. we'll try to explain how to read a micrometer. The spindle is threaded. Most micrometers use a thread pitch of 40 threads per inch. One complete revolution of the spindle moves the spindle toward or away from the anvil 0.025 in. (1/40 in.).

The fixed part of the handle (called, the sleeve) is marked with 40 gradations per inch of handle length, so each line is 0.025 in. apart. Okay so far?

Every 4th line is marked with a number. The first long line marked 1 represents 0.100 in., the second is 0.200 in., and so on.

The part of the handle that turns is called the thimble. The beveled end of the thimble is marked with gradations, each of which corresponds to 0.001 in. and, usually, every 5th line is numbered.

Turn the thimble until the 0 lines up with the 0 on the sleeve. Now, rotate the thimble one complete revolution and look at the sleeve. You'll see that one complete thimble revolution moved the thimble 0.025 in. down the sleeve.

To read the micrometer, multiply the number of gradations exposed on the sleeve by 0.025 and add that to the number of thousandths indicated by the thimble line that is lined up with the horizontal line on the sleeve. So, if you've measured a part and there are 6 vertical gradations exposed on the sleeve and the 7th gradation on the thimble is lined up with the horizontal line on the sleeve, the thickness of the part is 0.157 in. (6 x 0.025 = 0.150 . Add to that 0.007 representing the 7 lines on the thimble and you get 0.157). See?

If you didn't understand that, try the instructions that come with the micrometer or ask someone that knows, to show you how to work it. Also, if you didn't understand . . . don't worry. We said you probably won't ever need this for basic maintenance.

Inside Micrometers

Inside micrometers are used to measure the distance between two parallel surfaces. For example, in engine rebuilding work, the inside mike measures cylinder bore wear. Inside mikes are graduated the same way as outside mikes and are read the same way as well.

Remember that an inside mike must be absolutely perpendicular to the work being measured. When you measure with an inside mike, rock the mike gently from side to side and tip it back and forth slightly so that you span the widest part of the bore. Just to be on the safe side, take several readings. It takes a certain amount of experience to work any mike with confidence.

Metric Micrometers

♦ **See Figures 79 and 80**

Metric micrometers are read in the same way as inch micrometers, except that the measurements are in millimeters. Each line on the main scale equals 1 mm. Each fifth line is stamped 5, 10, 15, and so on. Each line on the thimble scale equals 0.01 mm. It will take a little practice, but if you can read an inch mike, you can read a metric mike.

Inside and Outside Calipers

Inside and outside calipers are useful devices to have if you need to measure something quickly and precise measurement is not necessary. Simply take the reading and then hold the calipers on an accurate steel rule.

DIAL INDICATORS

A dial indicator is a gauge that utilizes a dial face and a needle to register measurements. There is a movable contact arm on the dial indicator. When

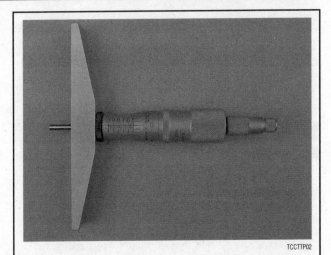

Fig. 79 Depth gauges, like this micrometer, can be used to measure the amount of pad or shoe remaining above a rivet

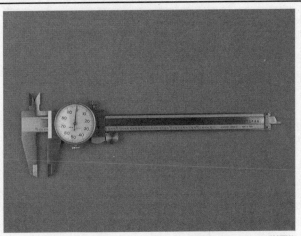

Fig. 80 Outside calipers are fast and easy ways to measure pads or rotors

the arms moves, the needle rotates on the dial. Dial indicators are calibrated to show readings in thousandths of an inch and typically, are used to measure end-play and runout on various parts of a bike and engine. As for maintenance, they may be used to check the end-play on the wheels, and they can also be used to check for warpage (runout) on the brake rotors.

Dial indicators are quite easy to use, although they are relatively expensive. A variety of mounting devices are available so that the indicator can be used in a number of situations. Make certain that the contact arm is always parallel to the movement of the work being measured.

TELESCOPING GAUGES

A telescope gauge is used during rebuilding procedures (NOT usually basic maintenance) to measure the inside of bores. It can take the place of an inside mike for some of these jobs. Simply insert the gauge in the hole to be measured and lock the plungers after they have contacted the walls. Remove the tool and measure across the plungers with an outside micrometer.

DEPTH GAUGES

A depth gauge can be inserted into a bore or other small hole to determine exactly how deep it is. The most common use on maintenance items would be to check the depth of a rivet head (on riveted style brake pads) or to check tire depth. Some outside calipers contain a built-in depth gauge so money can be saved by just buying one tool.

Electric Power Tools

◆ **See Figures 81 and 82**

Power tools are most often associated with woodworking. However, there are a few which are very helpful in bike work.

The most common and most useful power tool is the bench grinder. If you get serious about motorcycle repair, then you will eventually want a grinder with a grinding stone on one side and a wire brush wheel on the other. The brush wheel is indispensable for cleaning parts and the stone can be used to remove rough surfaces and for reshaping, where necessary.

Almost as useful as the bench grinder is the drill. Drills can come in very handy when a stripped or broken fastener is encountered.

Power ratchets and impact wrenches can come in very handy. Power ratchets can save a lot of time and muscle when removing and installing long bolts or nuts on long studs, especially where there is little room to swing a manual ratchet. Impact wrenches can be invaluable especially with frozen bolts, screws with partially damaged heads or on spinning shafts, when it is difficult or impossible to hold the shaft. Let's be real for a second, will you ACTUALLY NEED them for motorcycle maintenance, probably not. But, when you finally do need them one day, BOY WILL YOU BE GLAD YOU HAD EM'.

➡One last thought before you buy any electric tools. If you plan on buying an air compressor (and there are many reasons why you should at least think about it), then you might save money on tools by purchasing air tools instead of electric. Shop around and compare prices to your needs, then make your decision.

Air Tools and Compressors

◆ **See Figures 83 and 84**

Air-powered tools are usually not necessary for simple maintenance procedures. They are, however, useful for speeding up many jobs and for gen-

Fig. 81 Three types of common power tools. Left to right: a hand-held grinder, drill and impact wrench

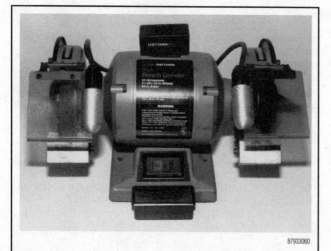

Fig. 82 The bench grinder can be used to clean just about every part removed from the vehicle

Fig. 83 This compressor operates off ordinary house current and provides all the air pressure you'll need

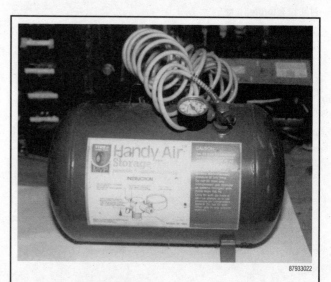

Fig. 84 An air storage tank

eral clean-up of parts. If you don't have air tools, and you want them, be prepared for an initial outlay of a money.

The first thing you need is a compressor. Compressors are available in electrically driven and gas engine driven models. As long as you have electricity, you don't need a gas engine driven type.

The common shop-type air compressor is a pump mounted on a tank. The pump compresses air and forces it into the tank where it is stored until you need it. The compressor automatically turns the pump on when the air pressure in the tank falls below a certain preset level.

There are all kinds of air powered tools, including ratchets, impact wrenches, saws, drills, sprayers, nailers, scrapers, riveters, grinders and sanders. In general, air powered tools are usually cheaper than their electric counterparts (but be careful, there are some cheap electric tools available that might not last as long as comparably priced air tools).

When deciding what size compressor unit you need, you'll be driven by two factors: the Pounds per Square Inch (PSI) capacity of the unit and the deliver rate in Cubic Feet per Minute (CFM). For example, most air powered ratchets require 90 psi at 4 to 5 cfm to operate at peak efficiency. Grinders and saws may require up to 7 cfm at 90 psi. So, before buying the compressor unit, decide what types of tools you'll want so that you don't short-change yourself on the compressor purchase.

If you decide that a compressor and air tools isn't for you, you can have the benefit of air pressure rather cheaply. Purchase an air storage tank, available in sizes up to 20 gallons at most retail stores that sell auto products. These storage tanks can safely store air pressure up to 125 psi and come with a high pressure nozzle for cleaning things and an air chuck for filling tires. The tank can be filled using the common tire-type air compressor, or even at the corner gas station (with their tire pressure hose).

FASTENERS, MEASUREMENTS AND CONVERSIONS

Bolts, Nuts and Other Threaded Retainers

▶ See Figures 85, 86, 87 and 88

Although there are a great variety of fasteners found in the modern motorcycle, the most commonly used retainer is the threaded fastener (nuts, bolts, screws, studs, etc). Most threaded retainers may be reused, provided that they are not damaged in use or during the repair. Some retainers (such as stretch bolts or torque prevailing nuts) are designed to deform when tightened or in use and should not be reinstalled.

➡**Motorcycles more than most vehicles on the road today use recessed socket head fasteners which require hex key or Torx® drivers.**

Whenever possible, we will note any special retainers which should be replaced during a procedure. But you should always inspect the condition of a retainer when it is removed and you should replace any that show signs of damage. Check all threads for rust or corrosion which can increase the torque necessary to achieve the desired clamp load for which that fastener was originally selected. Additionally, be sure that the driver surface of the fastener has not been compromised by rounding or other damage. In some cases a driver surface may become only partially rounded, allowing the driver to catch in only one direction. In many of these occurrences, a fastener may be installed and tightened, but the driver would not be able to grip and loosen the fastener again. (This could lead to frustration down the line should that component ever need to be disassembled again).

If you must replace a fastener, whether due to design or damage, you must ALWAYS be sure to use the proper replacement. In all cases, a retainer of the same design, material and strength should be used. Markings on the heads of most bolts will help determine the proper strength of the fastener. The same material, thread and pitch must be selected to assure proper installation and safe operation of the vehicle afterwards.

Thread gauges are available to help measure a bolt or stud's thread. Most part or hardware stores keep gauges available to help you select the

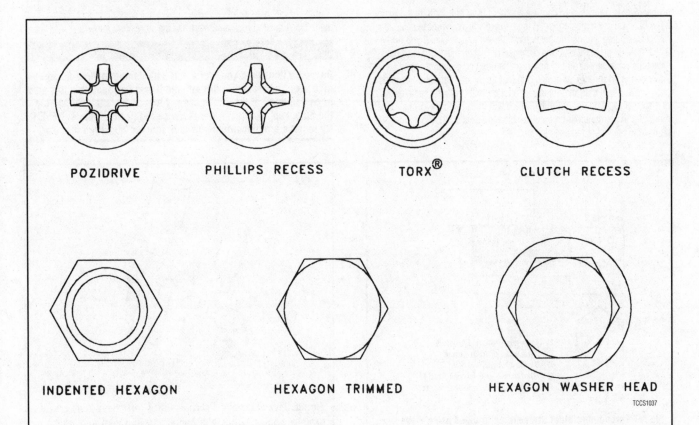

POZIDRIVE PHILLIPS RECESS TORX® CLUTCH RECESS

INDENTED HEXAGON HEXAGON TRIMMED HEXAGON WASHER HEAD

TCCS1037

Fig. 85 Here are a few of the most common screw/bolt driver styles

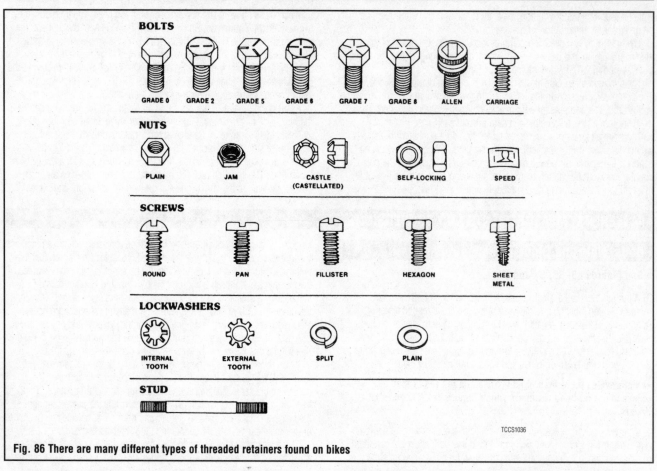

Fig. 86 There are many different types of threaded retainers found on bikes

proper size. In a pinch, you can use another nut or bolt for a thread gauge. If the bolt you are replacing is not too badly damaged, you can select a match by finding another bolt which will thread in its place. If you find a nut which threads properly onto the damaged bolt, then use that nut to help select the replacement bolt. If however, the bolt you are replacing is so badly damaged (broken or drilled out) that its threads cannot be used as a gauge, you might start by looking for another bolt (from the same assembly or a similar location on your bike) which will thread into the damaged bolt's mounting. If so, the other bolt can be used to select a nut; the nut can then be used to select the replacement bolt.

In all cases, be absolutely sure you have selected the proper replacement. Don't be shy, you can always ask the store clerk for help.

✳✳ WARNING

Be aware that when you find a bolt with damaged threads, you may also find the nut or drilled hole it was threaded into has also been damaged. If this is the case, you may have to drill and tap the hole, replace the nut or otherwise repair the threads. NEVER try to force a replacement bolt to fit into the damaged threads.

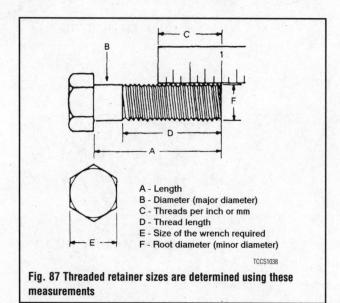

A - Length
B - Diameter (major diameter)
C - Threads per inch or mm
D - Thread length
E - Size of the wrench required
F - Root diameter (minor diameter)

TCCS1038

Fig. 87 Threaded retainer sizes are determined using these measurements

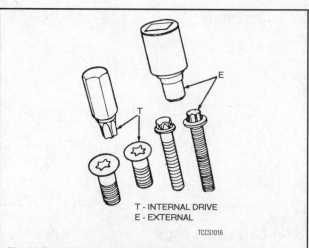

T - INTERNAL DRIVE
E - EXTERNAL

TCCS1016

Fig. 88 Special fasteners such as these Torx® head bolts are used by manufacturers to discourage people from working on vehicles without the proper tools (and knowledge)

Torque

▶ **See Figures 89 and 90**

Torque is defined as the measurement of resistance to turning or rotating. It tends to twist a body about an axis of rotation. A common example of this would be tightening a threaded retainer such as a nut, bolt or screw. Measuring torque is one of the most common ways to help assure that a threaded retainer has been properly fastened.

When tightening a threaded fastener, torque is applied in three distinct areas, the head, the bearing surface and the clamp load. About 50 percent of the measured torque is used in overcoming bearing friction. This is the friction between the bearing surface of the bolt head, screw head or nut face and the base material or washer (the surface on which the fastener is rotating). Approximately 40 percent of the applied torque is used in overcoming thread friction. This leaves only about 10 percent of the applied torque to develop a useful clamp load (the force which holds a joint together). This means that friction can account for as much as 90 percent of the applied torque on a fastener.

	Mark		Class		Mark	Class
Hexagon head bolt	 Bolt head No.	4— 5— 6— 7— 8— 9— 10— 11—	4T 5T 6T 7T 8T 9T 10T 11T	Stud bolt	No mark	4T
		 No mark	4T			
Hexagon flange bolt w/ washer hexagon bolt		 No mark	4T		Grooved	6T
Hexagon head bolt		 Two protruding lines	5T			
Hexagon flange bolt w/ washer hexagon bolt		 Two protruding lines	6T	Welded bolt		4T
Hexagon head bolt		 Three protruding lines	7T			
Hexagon head bolt		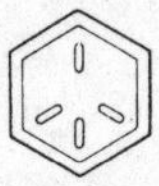 Four protruding lines	8T			

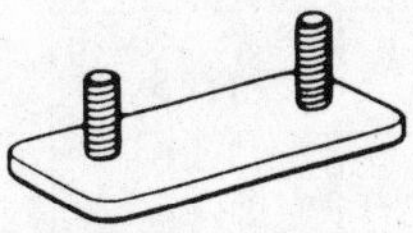

TCCS1240

Fig. 89 Determining bolt strength of metric fasteners—NOTE: this is a typical bolt marking system, but there is no worldwide standard

Class	Diameter mm	Pitch mm	Specified torque					
			Hexagon head bolt			Hexagon flange bolt		
			N·m	kgf·cm	ft·lbf	N·m	kgf·cm	ft·lbf
4T	6	1	5	55	48 in.·lbf	6	60	52 in.·lbf
	8	1.25	12.5	130	9	14	145	10
	10	1.25	26	260	19	29	290	21
	12	1.25	47	480	35	53	540	39
	14	1.5	74	760	55	84	850	61
	16	1.5	115	1,150	83	—	—	—
5T	6	1	6.5	65	56 in.·lbf	7.5	75	65 in.·lbf
	8	1.25	15.5	160	12	17.5	175	13
	10	1.25	32	330	24	36	360	26
	12	1.25	59	600	43	65	670	48
	14	1.5	91	930	67	100	1,050	76
	16	1.5	140	1,400	101	—	—	—
6T	6	1	8	80	69 in.·lbf	9	90	78 in.·lbf
	8	1.25	19	195	14	21	210	15
	10	1.25	39	400	29	44	440	32
	12	1.25	71	730	53	80	810	59
	14	1.5	110	1,100	80	125	1,250	90
	16	1.5	170	1,750	127	—	—	—
7T	6	1	10.5	110	8	12	120	9
	8	1.25	25	260	19	28	290	21
	10	1.25	52	530	38	58	590	43
	12	1.25	95	970	70	105	1,050	76
	14	1.5	145	1,500	108	165	1,700	123
	16	1.5	230	2,300	166	—	—	—
8T	8	1.25	29	300	22	33	330	24
	10	1.25	61	620	45	68	690	50
	12	1.25	110	1,100	80	120	1,250	90
9T	8	1.25	34	340	25	37	380	27
	10	1.25	70	710	51	78	790	57
	12	1.25	125	1,300	94	140	1,450	105
10T	8	1.25	38	390	28	42	430	31
	10	1.25	78	800	58	88	890	64
	12	1.25	140	1,450	105	155	1,600	116
11T	8	1.25	42	430	31	47	480	35
	10	1.25	87	890	64	97	990	72
	12	1.25	155	1,600	116	175	1,800	130

Fig. 90 Typical bolt torques for metric fasteners—WARNING: use only as a guide

TCCS1241

Standard and Metric Measurements

♦ **See Figure 91**

Specifications are often used to help you determine the condition of various components on your bike, or to assist you in their installation. Some of the most common measurements include length (in. or cm/mm), torque (ft. lbs., inch lbs. or Nm) and pressure (psi, in. Hg, kPa or mm Hg).

In some cases, that value may not be conveniently measured with what is available in your toolbox. Luckily, many of the measuring devices which are available today will have two scales so Standard or Metric measurements may easily be taken. If any of the various measuring tools which are available to you do not contain the same scale as listed in the bike's specifications, use the accompanying conversion factors to determine the proper value.

The conversion factor chart is used by taking the given specification and multiplying it by the necessary conversion factor. For instance, looking at the first line, if you have a measurement in inches such as "free-play should be 2 in." but your ruler reads only in millimeters, multiply 2 in. by the conversion factor of 25.4 to get the metric equivalent of 50.8mm. Likewise, if the specification was given only in a Metric measurement, for example in Newton Meters (Nm), then look at the center column first. If the measurement is 100 Nm, multiply it by the conversion factor of 0.738 to get 73.8 ft. lbs.

CONVERSION FACTORS

LENGTH–DISTANCE

Inches (in.)	x 25.4	= Millimeters (mm)	x .0394	= Inches
Feet (ft.)	x .305	= Meters (m)	x 3.281	= Feet
Miles	x 1.609	= Kilometers (km)	x .0621	= Miles

VOLUME

Cubic Inches (in3)	x 16.387	= Cubic Centimeters	x .061	= in3
IMP Pints (IMP pt.)	x .568	= Liters (L)	x 1.76	= IMP pt.
IMP Quarts (IMP qt.)	x 1.137	= Liters (L)	x .88	= IMP qt.
IMP Gallons (IMP gal.)	x 4.546	= Liters (L)	x .22	= IMP gal.
IMP Quarts (IMP qt.)	x 1.201	= US Quarts (US qt.)	x .833	= IMP qt.
IMP Gallons (IMP gal.)	x 1.201	= US Gallons (US gal.)	x .833	= IMP gal.
Fl. Ounces	x 29.573	= Milliliters	x .034	= Ounces
US Pints (US pt.)	x .473	= Liters (L)	x 2.113	= Pints
US Quarts (US qt.)	x .946	= Liters (L)	x 1.057	= Quarts
US Gallons (US gal.)	x 3.785	= Liters (L)	x .264	= Gallons

MASS–WEIGHT

Ounces (oz.)	x 28.35	= Grams (g)	x .035	= Ounces
Pounds (lb.)	x .454	= Kilograms (kg)	x 2.205	= Pounds

PRESSURE

Pounds Per Sq. In. (psi)	x 6.895	= Kilopascals (kPa)	x .145	= psi
Inches of Mercury (Hg)	x .4912	= psi	x 2.036	= Hg
Inches of Mercury (Hg)	x 3.377	= Kilopascals (kPa)	x .2961	= Hg
Inches of Water (H_2O)	x .07355	= Inches of Mercury	x 13.783	= H_2O
Inches of Water (H_2O)	x .03613	= psi	x 27.684	= H_2O
Inches of Water (H_2O)	x .248	= Kilopascals (kPa)	x 4.026	= H_2O

TORQUE

Pounds–Force Inches (in–lb)	x .113	= Newton Meters (N·m)	x 8.85	= in–lb
Pounds–Force Feet (ft–lb)	x 1.356	= Newton Meters (N·m)	x .738	= ft–lb

VELOCITY

Miles Per Hour (MPH)	x 1.609	= Kilometers Per Hour (KPH)	x .621	= MPH

POWER

Horsepower (Hp)	x .745	= Kilowatts	x 1.34	= Horsepower

FUEL CONSUMPTION*

Miles Per Gallon IMP (MPG)	x .354	= Kilometers Per Liter (Km/L)
Kilometers Per Liter (Km/L)	x 2.352	= IMP MPG
Miles Per Gallon US (MPG)	x .425	= Kilometers Per Liter (Km/L)
Kilometers Per Liter (Km/L)	x 2.352	= US MPG

*It is common to covert from miles per gallon (mpg) to liters/100 kilometers (1/100 km), where mpg (IMP) x 1/100 km = 282 and mpg (US) x 1/100 km = 235.

TEMPERATURE

Degree Fahrenheit (°F)	= (°C x 1.8) + 32
Degree Celsius (°C)	= (°F – 32) x .56

TCCS1044

Fig. 91 Standard and metric conversion factors chart

Service Record

Date/Mileage	Service	Next Due

90991G01

Service Record

Date/Mileage	Service	Next Due

Service Record

Date/Mileage	Service	Next Due

Service Record

Date/Mileage	Service	Next Due

90991G01

Service Record

Date/Mileage	Service	Next Due

Service Record

Date/Mileage	Service	Next Due

90991G01

Service Record

Date/Mileage	Service	Next Due

Service Record

Date/Mileage	Service	Next Due

90991G01

Service Record

Date/Mileage	Service	Next Due

90991G01

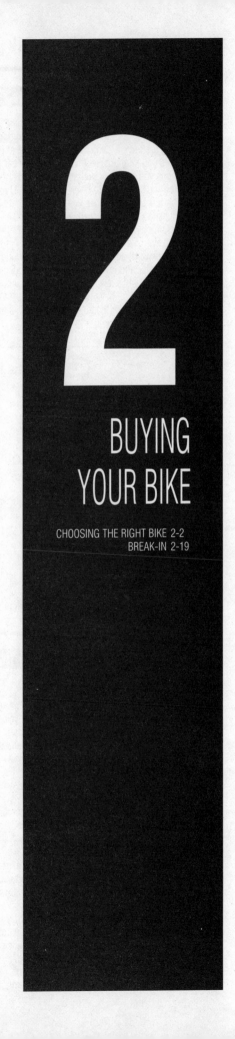

2

BUYING
YOUR BIKE

CHOOSING THE RIGHT BIKE

Volumes of material have been written on the best way to go about purchasing a house or a car. But much less is available to someone who is shopping for a motorcycle, which is probably one of the next most expensive purchases you might make. If you shop for a car or truck, there are many questions you must ask yourself, such as "How will I use this vehicle" and "How much money do I have to spend?" These are valid questions, which must be asked when you are looking at bikes. There is one additional question which is usually not asked of cars, but which MUST be answered before purchasing a motorcycle; "Will it fit me?" The driver's seat of almost every car or truck on the road today is equipped with a fore-aft (forward-backward) adjustment at minimum, though most will tilt and some will even raise and lower or inflate-deflate cushions and supports. On the other hand, only a few motorcycles come with adjustable seats, and if the bike doesn't fit, you have to live with it or customize (which is an option most people take in the long run, even if it is just to make a good bike fit even better).

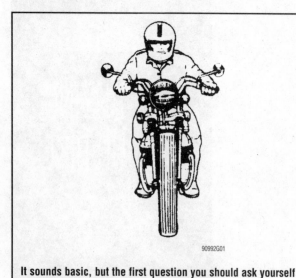

It sounds basic, but the first question you should ask yourself before buying a bike is will it fit your needs

Purpose/Style

▶ See Figures 1, 2, 3, 4 and 5

The first question you have to decide before buying a motorcycle is simple "what do you intend to use it for?" Motorcycles can be anything from weekend toys, to daily transportation or cross-country exploring machines. The non-riding public often doesn't realize the tremendous variety of motorcycles which are available. Frankly, many don't care, viewing motorcycles and their riders with stereotypes as different as outlaw ruffians or bicycle-like nuisances. We even know of a rider who consulted his fiancee for help in picking the color of the first NEW motorcycle he was ever going to buy. Her startled reply was "I thought that all bikes were black?" (It just so happened that his previous bike was, and her mental picture of other motorcycles was based only on her limited real-life experience).

The truth is that motorcycles not only come in a variety of colors, they also come in a great variety of styles. The intended use of the bike will greatly narrow the type of motorcycle which you will want. Do you intend to ride only off-road or only on the street? Perhaps you are looking for a motorcycle to commute 60 miles round-trip everyday or you are looking for a bike just to take out on weekends. A bike which is intended for use on long cross-country tours is usually significantly different from one which is primarily designed for the track or for the weekend brunch ride. And if you can only buy one, you are going to have to make up your mind which is more appropriate by deciding how you plan on using the bike.

Once you have answered the question of how you intend to use the bike, then you should think about what features are important to you. Make a list and order them in priority. Some of the most common features include:

- High performance engine
- High performance chassis
- Long-distance comfort
- Protection from the elements
- Choice of additional accessories

Some of these items can be mutually exclusive at their extremes. To produce motorcycle with cutting edge performance you usually have to sacrifice a certain amount of long-distance comfort or protection from the elements. And likewise, to make a bike which is comfortable for all-day riding in sunshine or downpours, you will likely have to give up some of its top end or cornering performance. But, remember that we are talking about extremes here. Many of today's motorcycles are so well engineered, that VERY few riders have the ability to push them to their performance limits. AND, there is little doubt that no-one should try to push the envelope of the street because most bikes perform so well, that to approach the bike's limits on speed or cornering would likely put you in dangerous situations (and you would probably be breaking the law).

Fig. 1 If you are looking for a sporting bike, you will probably sacrifice some long-distance comfort . . .

Fig. 2 . . . in return for a high performance engine and chassis

Fig. 3 On the other hand, many people prefer the looks and comfort of a cruiser to cutting edge performance

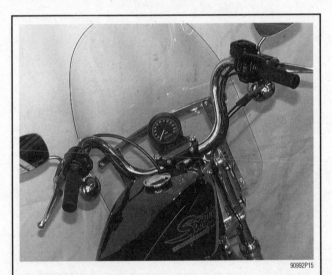

Fig. 4 Accessories, from windshields . . .

Fig. 5 . . . to saddlebags, can change the character of the bike that you choose

Although you want to decide what features are important (because that will help determine the style bike in which you are interested), the truth is that if you leave the extremes out of it, you can probably consider more than one style because their purposes often overlap.

Motorcycles can be roughly grouped in seven categories (Standard, Cruiser, Sport, Sport Touring, Touring, Dual Sport and Dirt), but there is a lot of crossover between categories. Be careful, as an adamant owner of a bike might very much feel his/her bike is a part of one category when you feel it is in another (and this could lead to a protracted and heated debate). Simply put, most motorcycles are designed with one or more intended uses in mind. It is not important to decide whether a bike's use defines its style or if its style defines its use. Just recognize that some bikes are designed to do a particular job better than others and one or more types may best suit your needs.

STANDARD

▶ See Figures 6 thru 12

Public outcries for simplified, all-purpose bikes have spawned the rebirth of the UJM (Universal Japanese Motorcycle) styled standard bike. A standard is usually a street bike, that is capable of performing all or most tasks with confidence but it probably does not excel to greatly at any one. Typically speaking a standard will have little or no bodywork (why waste the money just for looks or for that extra edge of aerodynamics) and could be powered by any simple and effective engine (large or small displacement, 1, 2, 3 or 4-cylinder, inline or V).

Of the features mentioned earlier, a standard, by definition, does not usually excel at any one. But, it may be very capable of all, especially with a few choice accessories.

The nice thing about a standard is its versatility and availability. Because they tend to be basic in design, the price is often kept within reach of the motorcycling public. Most standards do take on some of the particular strengths or characteristics for which their manufacturer's entire line is noted. But, the manufacturers do not waste money on making them the best performing, fastest, "trickest" or hottest looking bikes on the road. Instead, they concentrate on keeping the design simple, relatively easy to maintain and affordable. The versatility and price of these motorcycles makes them highly desirable to many new riders (many of whom have not decided what type of bike they really want yet). And, a little customizing in the form of performance accessories or a windshield and luggage, could easily turn a standard into a very capable sport or touring machine. Arguably, every manufacturer has one or more standard motorcycle in their line up (or has had one at one time).

A possible sub-category to standards would be the power or muscle standard. This group consists of unfaired or naked bikes with predomi-

Fig. 6 A standard is usually a bike-of-all trades, but master of none

90992G50

Fig. 7 Suzuki has long been a champion for the standard motorcycle with models like the GS500E

90992G12

Fig. 10 . . . and Suzuki has built a fine example with their big-bore Bandit 1200S . . .

90992PU1

Fig. 8 Where would you put a bike like the URAL. With a sidecar maybe you would list it under touring, but it is probably just a good, old, standard bike

90992PM2

Fig. 11 . . . while other manufacturer's have followed suit with bikes like the Triumph Speed Triple

90992PM1

Fig. 9 The Yamaha V-Max has defined a sub-group of standards, the power or muscle standard . . .

90992PM3

Fig. 12 Ducati's standard with plenty of muscle is called the M900, otherwise known as the Ducati Monster

nantly standard upright riding positions. What makes them different from a straight standard is that they share many components or at least characteristics with their sport bike siblings. They have VERY powerful engines and capable brakes. What keeps us from calling them sport bikes are the riding positions, lack of wind cutting bodywork and usually a less high performance or cutting edge chassis (the combination of which would usually prevent you from maximizing their potential in track use). In recent history this group was categorized by bikes like the V-Max. But it is also accompanied by a variety of other motorcycles today including the Triumph Speed Triple, Suzuki Bandit 1200 and Ducati M900 Monster.

CRUISER

▶ **See Figures 13 thru 26**

Just like the popular cars of the 50's and 60's, there is something deeply American about a cruiser motorcycle (no matter where it is built). This segment of the market has enjoyed tremendous growth with the successful marketing of these images (most notably with the Harley-Davidson Motor Company who defines the cruiser to many riders). A cruiser motorcycle tends to be a highly stylized statement which screams "look at me" (not that there's anything wrong with that). The style of a cruiser has evolved around a long, low chassis (also making it popular with novice riders because of the low center of gravity and for people who are uhmmm . . . inseamly challenged, and who might find taller bikes more difficult to peddle-around).

Though engines will vary, the stereotypical cruiser contains a big-bore V-twin which is tuned for high torque and little effort. Examples of cruisers can be found from all of the major Japanese manufacturers (Honda, Kawasaki, Suzuki and Yamaha), as-well as from the British (Triumph), Italians (Moto Guzzi) and even the master German bike maker (BMW). Other engines such as inline or V-fours can be found in some of the more adventurous examples which depart from the norm of this segment. The occasional single and, most recently, even an opposed six cylinder has found its way into a cruiser frame. We cannot ignore the British influence on the

Fig. 13 A cruiser is first and foremost a statement of style, and the new BMW would look right at home on the streets of Hollister

Fig. 15 . . . their FXDs or Dynas (and before that their FXRs or Lowriders) . . .

Fig. 14 Few will argue that Harley-Davidson has long defined the cruiser motorcycle with models like their Sportsters . . .

Fig. 16 . . . and, in a most nostalgic way, their Softails

Fig. 17 Though nearly every manufacturer makes a cruiser today—Yamaha Viragos were among the first Japanese bikes to enter the cruiser market

Fig. 18 Cruisers usually have an upright or a slouched back riding position—Kawasaki produces the Vulcan family shown here

Fig. 19 Though many early Japanese cruiser attempts came off slightly like caricatures of Harleys—this Honda Shadow is close, but not quite there yet . . .

cruiser market with the old Triumph twins and happily with the retro-styled Thunderbird and Adventurer triples which came to us with the rebirth of Triumph in the 90's.

Cruiser owners are a varied bunch who are likely to use their bikes very much like a standard. Some will outfit them with windshields and luggage (read: SADDLEBAGS) and use them for long distance riding or touring. Some will only ride them on the weekends (read: BRUNCH at the local place-to-be-seen). In any case, the cruiser usually offers its owner some compromise of modern performance for a blend of retro-style and modern reliability.

90992PC5

Fig. 20 . . . later model cruisers began to hit the looks right on the mark—this is the Honda Shadow American Classic Edition (ACE) Tourer

90992PC7

Fig. 23 Though some have hailed the new BMW as Europe's first cruiser, remember the Moto Guzzi California and new V11 EV were Eurocruisers first

9099VS45

Fig. 21 Suzuki's Intruders have always looked a little quirky (to some) and definitely more Japanese than American . . .

90992PC3

Fig. 24 More recent entries into the cruiser market blur the formerly V-twin dominated cruiser scene—the Triumph Adventurer and Thunderbirds are among these bikes . . .

90992VL5

Fig. 22 . . . but their Intruder 1500LC may have finally changed that

90992PC6

Fig. 25 . . . as well as the bold Honda Valkyrie (a powerful cruiser with tour bike roots)

Fig. 26 But not to be outdone by 3, 4 or 6 cylinder engines, the Polaris Victory is another look at how V-twin cruisers can also be capable, higher performance machines

SPORT BIKE

▶ See Figures 27 thru 41

On the other end of the technical realm from the cruiser market stands the sport bikes. Driven by the bigger, better, faster, "tricker" drive of competition to truly be the baddest on the block. Most of the sport bikes on the market are from the Japanese big-four manufacturers and take the form of high revving, inline four cylinder engined, light alloy-framed machines. But we say MOST, not all, and we cannot exclude the prominent V-twins by Ducati, Buell, Moto Guzzi and various twins or inline 4s from BMW. Nor can we forget the exciting Triumph triples or the most curious MZ singles.

The common thread of sport bikes is that they are based primarily on achieving performance. This usually includes a sophisticated and power-

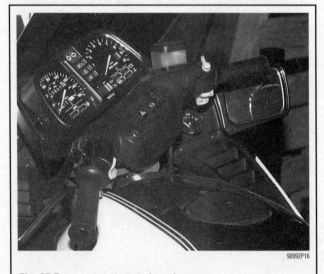

Fig. 27 From compact controls and gauges . . .

Fig. 28 . . . to high performance components, a sport bike is built for curves

90992PS1

Fig. 29 The sport bike market place has long been dominated by Japanese motorcycles—Kawasaki's Ninjas are synonymous with sport bikes in many rider's and even non-rider's minds

90992PS2

Fig. 30 Honda has also had a long reputation with varied sport bikes from twins to water cooled-fours, including the CBR 600 F2s and F3s . . .

90992PS6

Fig. 31 . . . and the "race ready" CBR900RR, a super squid bike if we've ever seen one

90992PS7

Fig. 32 More recently, entries like the Honda Superhawk bring new V-twin sportbikes to battle Ducati

90992PS3

Fig. 33 Yamaha cannot be left out with its YZFs and FZRs . . .

90992GX6

Fig. 34 . . . and neither can Suzuki with their Katanas . . .

90992G6X

Fig. 35 . . . or their famous GSX-R series

90992PS5

Fig. 38 Harley's purchase of the Buell American Motorcycle Company has allowed Buell to compete using models like the S1 Lightning and White Lightning

90992TL1

Fig. 36 More recently, Suzuki upped the ante with liquid-cooled V-twin sport bikes in the form of the TLs

90992PS9

Fig. 39 As usual, the Europeans have their own take on the way things should be, like with sport and sport touring bikes—this example is the Moto Guzzi V10 Centauro

90992PS4

Fig. 37 Triumph has added a European flair to the sport bike market with models like the T595

90992DU1

Fig. 40 Other European exotics include the family of bikes from Ducati, like the 900SS CR

90992BK1

Fig. 41 Another European entry into the serious sport market is the BMW K1200 RS

90992BK2

Fig. 43 Some would say that if BMW didn't invent the sport tourer with the airheads, it perfected them with the oilheads like the R1100 RS

ful engine, highly responsive and adjustable suspension, lightweight chassis, powerful multiple-piston disc brakes and sticky tires, along with colorful and aerodynamic bodywork. At one end of the spectrum, the most capable bikes begin to become so purposely dedicated to performance, that they lack the finesse and comfort necessary for everyday or long-distance riding. At the other end, the segment blurs with sport tourers.

SPORT TOURER

▶ **See Figures 42 thru 48**

For those who are interested in aggressive riding through the canyons, but who are equally worried about comfort on the long stretches of black top, the sport tourer may offer the best of both worlds. A sport touring bike is usually a very capable and technological machine, but without the edge of a pure sport bike. Manufacturers pay attention to the fact that a sport touring rider wants an increased measure of comfort (less radical riding position) and convenience (easier to attach and use luggage), while retaining much of a sport bike's performance.

Some of the most notable examples of this segment include models of both K and R bikes from BMW, the Honda ST1100, The Kawasaki Voy-

90992BK3

Fig. 44 And though many joke about the LT standing for Light Truck on this bike, many of the BMW K models have excellent sport touring records

90992P10

Fig. 42 Many sport tourer motorcycles are equipped with advanced technology from fuel injection to Anti-Lock Brakes

90992ST1

Fig. 45 Honda has some bragging rights of its own with the ST1100

Fig. 46 The Kawasaki Concours is one of the unsung heroes of the sport touring world

Fig. 47 Newer entries, like the S3T Thunderbolt Tourer from Buell deserve a mention for keeping most of the sport bike performance with the comfort necessary for long days in the saddle

Fig. 48 Triumph is not to be left out with models like the Trophy

ager, the Yamaha GTS1000, and even the Buell Thunderbolt. Most sport touring machines come with, or are available with, integral hard-case luggage systems. Again, the panniers long available for BMW arguably define this luggage. Engines can be 2, 3, or 4 cylinders. The common grain being that the engines are all strong performers, but are tame enough to be enjoyed in most circumstances. Many sport tourers are also the recipients of technology such as electronic engine management in the form of fuel injection or advanced brake systems like Anti-Lock Brakes or linked braking systems.

TOUR BIKE

▶ **See Figures 49 thru 54**

For some riders, the ability to gobble up tremendous amounts of blacktop is more important than canyon carving. For these, tour bikes offer the ability and comfort needed for long time and long distance riding. The Honda Gold Wings and Harley-Davidson Ultras typify this segment whose examples usually include ample hard luggage (saddlebags, trunks, glove boxes), a large protective fairing, and large displacement, torquey, but smooth running (and/or rubber-mounted) motors.

Fig. 49 The main purpose of a tour bike is COMFORT, so many are adorned with accessories, from cruise control systems to highway pegs

Fig. 50 But NO motorcycle can really be called a tour bike without the pre-requisite hard luggage

Fig. 51 When people talk about touring bikes, they often say things such as "like a Honda Goldwing" because the name has become synonymous with touring rigs

Fig. 52 But, don't forget the lesser known player from Kawasaki, the Voyager

Fig. 53 A stylish tour bike that is part cruiser too is Harley's Road King (a particular favorite of one author)

Fig. 54 Somewhere between a tour bike and a sport tourer is the BMW R1100 RT, perhaps it just depends on your mood

Again, the lines between categories are blurred by other examples of this market. An argument can be made that the BMW R1100 RT is a either touring or a sport touring bike. The Harley-Davidson FLHS (Electric Glide Sport) and its offspring the highly retro-styled FLHR (Road King) are both built on the Ultra chassis and share the saddlebags, but use a less protective windshield instead of a fairing and do not come with the armchair back-seat or trunk used on the other Harley-Davidson tour bikes. These Harleys are sometimes classified as cruisers instead of tourers, but what's in a name?

DUAL SPORT

▶ **See Figures 55 thru 61**

To some, the ability to explore should not end when the pavement does. But, the majority of their riding will likely be on the street. To these riders is dedicated a small, but specialized, segment of dual sport machines built for both purposes. The typical dual sport is light, but tall allowing for extra suspension travel which is often needed off-road. Extra protection, such as an engine skid plate or hand guards, is often provided, recognizing the increased chance of the bike contacting the ground or other objects off-road.

Fig. 55 How do you tell a dual sport from a dirt bike? Why, by the lights and turn signals for one—examples include the XTs and TWs from Yamaha . . .

90992DS2

Fig. 56 . . . as well as the Kawasaki KE and KLRs—note the long suspension travel and front fender positioned to catch mud

90992DS3

Fig. 59 But the big daddy of dual sports has long been the BMW GS, like this R100 GS PD (Paris Dakar edition) which included a 9.2 gallon fuel tank for exploration

90992DS5

Fig. 57 Honda has its own family of dual sport bikes which includes the XR650L shown here

90992BK4

Fig. 60 The GS legend lives on with BMW oilheads like the R1100 GS, though many people agree the larger and heavier bike is a little less suited to long wilderness crossings

90992DR7

Fig. 58 One large player in this category is the Suzuki DR family, like the DR650SE pictured

90992DS4

Fig. 61 Once again, Triumph was not to be left out (dual sports being a long standing tradition with Europeans anyway), and they brought us the Tiger

Most Japanese manufacturers offer an example of these bikes, but the Europeans have made them an art form with the BMW GS series (the Paris Dakar model includes a voluminous 9.2 gallon gas tank), the KTM and the Ducati Elefant. Arguably, some of the larger and later versions of these bikes, such as the new R1100 GS are less capable off-road cycles because of the increasing size and technology (read: harder to haul out of that ditch than their smaller and older cousins and harder to fix in the middle of the desert). But, they are still very capable machines which can go where you would NEVER want to take your cruiser or sport bike.

DIRT BIKE

▶ **See Figures 62, 63, 64 and 65**

Our final segment is the place where many street riders start and some riders never leave. Dirt bikes are usually small, lightweight, high-revving, small displacement engined bikes which are built tough to take the pounding of off-road antics. The Japanese manufacturers all have extensive lines with bikes sized from teenager-to-adult. Europeans are not to be left out with manufacturer's such as Aprilla, KTM and Husqvarna.

Another reason dirt bikes are built small and light is to ease their handling. Dirt bikes are made to be dropped (as any dirt rider knows—you do that often) and are easily loaded into the backs of trailers or pick-ups for transportation. Perhaps one of the biggest differences between a dirt bike and dual sport is how they are looked at by the government. The dirt bike is usually not legal for use on public roads since it doesn't contain

turn signals, tail lights or other traffic safety devices (which it is really better off not having since they are just more things to break when you drop it).

Fig. 62 Dirt bikes are usually minimalist machines with knobby tires and long suspensions—this example is from the Yamaha YZ family

Fig. 63 Kawasaki also has an extensive lineup, including the KXs, a KX80 is pictured here

Fig. 64 Suzuki has more than a few models to choose from including, JR, RMs and DS80

Fig. 65 And, did you actually expect us to leave out Honda with their XRs?

Does Size Matter?

Once you have decided on the style of bike that fits both your taste and your intended use, the next question is "what size (engine, chassis, seat height) do I want"? To some extent, the style will help decide this since dirt bikes are ALWAYS smaller than tour bikes, but there are a lot of differences, even within a given style.

Contrary to the common American notion that "bigger is always better," the very design of a motorcycle dictates that this is not always true. A heavy and long wheel-based motorcycle is usually not your best choice for the track or canyon curves, while many small, aggressively steering-raked bikes are just not built for highway comfort. You might love the style and function of your R100 GS, but if you have short legs and cannot touch the ground when it is on the center stand, perhaps another dual sport with a little less suspension travel would better suit your needs. Or if you are completely stuck on the GS, suspension and seat modifications may be possible to help the bike fit you better.

Add to this the fact that a rider must be able to maneuver the bike from backing it into a parking spot, or less often but more importantly, picking it up if he/she should happen to have a mishap and size suddenly becomes a major issue. We have heard of one particular petite and elderly (but clever) lady whose ride of choice is a land-yacht-like touring bike. She realized that she could not pick it up without assistance, but wanted to keep riding it

nonetheless. So, she devised a way to use a car scissors jack to pick it up to a point where she could climb aboard, finish the job and deploy the stand. Luckily, the cavernous saddlebags and trunk that this bike is equipped with have plenty of room to store the jack.

But, most of us would prefer a bike that fits us better. A motorcycle should make enough power to safely carry the rider along with a passenger and/or cargo (depending on its use). A rider should be able to sit comfortably on the bike with AT LEAST one foot firmly on the ground. Many of us prefer to be able to plant both feet on the ground (as that will greatly reduce the possibility of a stopped drop if one foot hits gravel or oil). And, as we already touched upon, you should be able to pick up the motorcycle in case you do drop it.

POWER VS CCs

Most people equate the displacement (size) of an engine to the amount of power it makes, but displacement isn't a particularly good indicator if you are comparing different types of engines (air-cooled twins vs liquid cooled, inline 4-cylinders, for example). The old myth that larger means more power (and is therefore better) just isn't always true. Sure, many large displacement engines produce tremendous amounts of power, but many of today's large displacement motorcycle engines are not made for high performance riding. In fact, there are numerous motorcycles available today whose motors are smaller in displacement, but whose output is greater in than some larger motors used in different bikes. So don't think just because your friend has a 1340cc or a 900cc bike that a smaller engine (say 600cc) wouldn't be just fine or even more appropriate for your desires.

What IS important when you are considering the size motor you are looking for in a bike is the motor's design. Is it the appropriate type of motor for the type of bike it is installed in, and for the type of riding you want to do? In general, 3, 4 or even 6-cylinder engines are smoother, higher-revving and produce greater horsepower than their slower-turning, rougher-running and usually more torquey 1 or 2-cylinder cousins. Obviously, there are exceptions to this rule. There are lower-revving torquey 4-cylinder motors available and there are more than a few high-revving, relatively smooth V-twins (what was that sound, did someone just step on a duck?). Again, the engine's design will determine its use and most manufacturers put a lot of thought into matching the engine with the style/purpose of the bike to which it is being installed. When you are deciding on what bike to buy and with what displacement motor, just make sure it is sufficient for your purposes, and that you are comfortable with the way it makes its power. If you like a high-revving engine which requires/allows for a lot of shifting and aggressive riding, than you are looking for a totally different engine than if you were interested in a low-revving, torque producing cruiser.

Just be careful and don't fall into the trap of thinking that because one bike has more displacement than another, that it obviously must be more powerful and faster. One example of this is found in the proliferation of large displacement V-twin cruisers which seem to have been popping-up everywhere for the past few years. A STOCK, Harley-Davidson Evolution Big Twin (1340cc or 80 Cubic Inch) motor averages a claimed 70-72 horsepower at 5000 rpm (54-57 horsepower at 4500 rpm for California motors). These numbers are likely measured at the engine crankshaft, as recent dyno-evaluations have put rear-wheel horsepower on 50 state fuel-injected models in the neighborhood of mid-50s at the rear wheel. The difference is frictional loss that occurs between the crankshaft and the rear wheel (primary drive chain, clutch, transmission and secondary drive belt).

Now a STOCK Harley-Davidson Big Twin is mounted in a motorcycle which weighs anything from 600-800 pounds wet (no, not when it's raining, we mean with all of the fluids in it). These figures show that a stock Evolution motor makes a decent horsepower-to-weight ratio when compared with most cars, but this is far from the ratios available in performance motorcycles. The one thing a Harley Evo motor has going for it is the tremendous amounts of torque it produces, a claimed 80-85 ft. lbs. at 4000 rpm (same amount of torque, but at a lower 2500 rpm for the more constricted/lower horsepower stock California models). The slow turning, low revving Harley-Davidson V-twin is ideal for effortless cruising. It makes tremendous amounts of torque to push the motorcycle and rider along at almost any legal speed. The power is also available for most high gear roll-ons, making the Harley a very pleasant cruising/touring machine.

BUT, now compare the large displacement Evo Big Twin with a much smaller bore production Japanese 4-cylinder, such as the Honda CBR600F3. This motor displaces less than HALF of the 1340cc Harley Big Twin, but it produces a greater power peak of about 90 horsepower at 11,000–12,000 rpm. If you add to this the fact that the motor is installed in a bike which weighs approximately 460 pounds wet (again anywhere from 25-45 percent less than the Harley) you see the tremendous power to weight ratio advantage that a CBR600F3 would have over the larger and greater displacement Harley. But there is a good reason for this, the CBR is not built to be a touring machine, it is a sport-bike. It is a smaller, less comfortable motorcycle which is capable of tremendous speed and handling for track and canyon-carving. And the smaller engine does not produce that much power without a cost. The smooth running 4-cylinder must turn at rpms more than double that of the Harley Big Twin to produce its peak horsepower. Engines of this design give greater rewards in the way of performance, but require more rider control (more shifting and greater attention where the motor makes its best power) than a large bore V-twin. It simply wouldn't be the appropriate engine for a large tour or cruiser bike.

WEIGHT

As you have probably just learned, all is not as it appears when it comes to engine displacement and power. Motorcycle size and weight is somewhat more predictable, but there are a few considerations which would alter the seemingly obvious. The concern here would lie with your physical size and capabilities, along with your intended use of the bike. Unless you plan on ALWAYS riding with a friend (capable of giving you a hand) your bike should not be so large that you would not be a able to right the bike without assistance if it was to fall over. There are a lot of reasons why the bike might hit the ground, and not all of them or your fault. Unfortunately you could return to a parking spot only to find that some careless pedestrian had wanted to look cool sitting on your bike, but had no idea what a side stand was for. The bottom line is simple, motorcycles, by their design, are inherently unstable when stopped. To put it bluntly, without a side or center stand, motorcycles DO NOT STAND UP ON THEIR OWN.

A good rule of thumb is that smaller bikes are lighter and vice versa, but the whole engine displacement thing should have taught you a lesson that nothing in motorcycling is quite that simple. Because of a few simple principles of physics (the details of which are not important here), one must consider where the bike's center of gravity is before deciding how easy it is to pick it up after a drop. A bike with a tall center of gravity (such as some dual-sport and sport bikes) might be smaller than a larger (but lower) standard or cruiser, but might still be harder to pick up in the event of a drop. Physics can be our friend here, in that using the handlebar as a lever can help a person to right a motorcycle which is significantly greater in weight than his or her lifting capabilities.

Unfortunately, most motorcycle dealers and even more motorcycle owners who are looking to sell a bike would probably frown at a request that they lay it over on its side so you can decide if you can pick it up safely. But, because of the inherent tendency of motorcycles to want to fall over, most dealers and some owners will be able to give you some idea how hard it is to pick up a given model.

A better indication if the weight of a bike you are interested in fits YOU, is simply to stand the motorcycle up. Climb aboard (WITH THE OWNER'S PERMISSION PLEASE) and stand it upward from the sidestand or rock it from the center stand and see how comfortable you are with the bike at a standstill. Lean the bike slightly to either side (again be careful here, as an unfamiliar bike might have a lean-point where it suddenly feels very heavy). Your next test is to walk the bike back and forth on a level surface. If all of these seem comfortable to you, there is a good indication that the bike is not too heavy. Of course, common sense must be used here. If you are a particularly petite person, then you might be able to comfortably manipulate even the heavier tour or cruiser motorcycles in the aforementioned manner, but you may NEVER be able to right it after a drop (without a handy scissors jack). That doesn't mean you can't control those heavy bikes while riding, it just means you might need help someday if it falls over. It is a decision that you'll have to make for yourself.

SEAT HEIGHT

▶ **See Figures 66 and 67**

Perhaps one of the most important size requirements (and probably the last one most people think about) is seat height. As we mentioned earlier, a motorcycle must fit YOU and the distance from the seat to the ground is one of the most important factors since it has everything to do with whether or not you can comfortably support the motorcycle at a stop. You obviously must be able to put one foot on the ground when seated on a motorcycle, otherwise you are definitely sitting on the wrong bike and you WILL fall over at the first stop light. But, just being able to touch the ground on the toes of one foot at a time is probably not enough control when it comes to wheeling the bike into a parking spot. And, if you put that one foot down in some loose gravel or oil and it begins to slide, you would do well to have the ability to place the other foot down and throw your weight to the other side of the bike (away from the sliding foot). Ideally, you should be able to place both feet flat on the ground at the same time. Though, being able to touch both feet, one flat and the other pointed slightly is not a bad compromise. The sad fact is, that if your friends call you Stumpy The Moose (because you are inseamly challenged), then you probably can't ride just any motorcycle out there, at least without making some modifications to the bike.

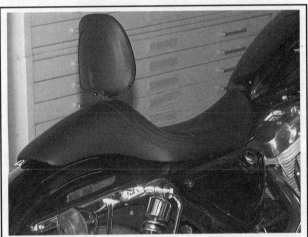

90992P17

Fig. 66 If the seat height is a problem, don't worry since there are many aftermarket manufacturers who can help (like the Corbin seat pictured here) . . .

90992P14

Fig. 67 . . . but make sure the new saddle will also allow you to safely operate the hand and foot controls

Don't be fooled by numbers in a magazine or brochure, the seat height is not the only thing that determines whether your foot will touch down or not. Some highly stylized cruisers, with very low seat heights, loose some of their advantage to very wide seats. This causes you to straddle the bike more, loosing some of your leg's length to the distance they must first spread before beginning the long journey to the tarmac. Again, your best test here is to actually sit on the intended bike and see how it fits.

And if you find that perfect bike, but your feet don't quite touch the ground comfortably, don't despair. Seats are probably one of the most often replaced non-wear parts on the bike. Most manufacturers produce seats of different designs and materials that will offer not only a change in look, but a change in function. Most late-model BMW cycles feature seats that are adjustable by changing how it is mounted into the seat bracket (which is equipped with multiple tiers). And there are many aftermarket suppliers and even custom saddlemakers which offer alternatives. One of the most popular reasons for installing an aftermarket seat, whether it is on a cruiser or a sport bike, is to improve the seat's function. More details on customizing your motorcycle to best fit your needs and taste are found later in this book.

Seat height can also have an affects how your body is positioned in relation to the controls of the bike. When trying a bike out for size, make sure that the hand and foot controls are all within a comfortable reach. If you are thinking of changing a saddle to gain an advantage when it comes to putting your feet down, remember that could come at a cost to usability of the controls.

Riding Clubs

CLUBS, A SOURCE OF INFORMATION

▶ **See Figures 68 and 69**

Back in the day, riding clubs were basically social clubs (not all that dissimilar to your local Elks or Moose lodge) of people who simply shared a hobby of motorcycling. Then, as motorcycles fell out of favor with society and the safetycrats, clubs became associated more with gangs than with family Sundays.

One of the things we have learned in our years of riding is that bikers are a lot like the rest of the world, they come in all different shapes and sizes. And like most people, they enjoy socializing and gathering with others of like minds. That is one of the reasons why there are so MANY different clubs for riders today.

These clubs are fantastic sources of information about new and used bikes. People who love, own and ride a particular brand of motorcycle or

Fig. 68 Many clubs have their own magazines or newsletters which inform you about rallies and other activities . . .

Fig. 69 . . . but clubs are also an opportunity to make a FEW new friends that share your love for bikes

model can be fountains of knowledge about selecting that type of bike, accessorizing it and even performing maintenance on it.

When looking for a motorcycle, it is a great idea to contact riders who belong to these clubs and do some fact finding. And after you purchase the motorcycle, it gets even better. If you have a problem finding a part, accessory or anything else for your bike, these riders may have already solved that problem.

Clubs take many forms, some are factory sponsored and some are independent. There are a large number of national or international clubs out there and an uncountable number of local organizations.

Factory Sponsored Clubs

These clubs are the results of loyal owners and smart marketers. Manufacturer sponsored clubs like, The Harley Owners Group (H.O.G.), the Honda Rider's Club of America (HRCA) or Kawasaki's Good Times Owners Club (GTOC) are all examples of companies who realize that by supporting riders who like their products, they will continue to nurture their customer base. These clubs offer a wide variety of benefits from members only rallies to roadside assistance or towing reimbursements.

Many national factory sponsored organizations also charter local chapters which provide weekend riding companions and all that good information we were talking about earlier.

Independent Clubs

There are a few large (national or international) non-factory sponsored clubs, like the BMW Motorcycle Owner's Association (MOA) and the BMW Rider's Association (RA), just to name two of them. And there are just too many local clubs to think about listing. Although independent clubs cannot usually offer demo rides or discounts on OEM merchandise, they do offer the benefits of networking with other riders. They will usually hold group rides, rallies and other events.

Some, like the BMW MOA, even help you with roadside emergencies. The BMW MOA does this through a club "anonymous" book which is published yearly. The book lists the phone numbers of members (without names) by state and town. Should a member run into trouble, all he/she has to do is make a phone call and a local club member is usually willing to lend a hand.

BREAK-IN

The biggest problem with breaking in a new motorcycle or engine is that, well, everyone has their own opinion. And everyone claims to back it up. Maybe some people even have some data to back it up. This is another one of those items that you are really going to have to decide for yourself. But, there are a few important things to consider.

Warranty

The first, and most important thing to consider when deciding how to break-in a bike is the manufacturer's warranty. The bottom line is that the manufacturer has spent a lot of money on engineering and it was probably those engineers who recommended the break-in conditions for their motorcycle. Also, a manufacturer has a lot in stake in the way of reputation, so they would never steer you wrong, WOULD THEY?

We would also have to assume that a manufacturer is also driven by factors including costs. They would typically recommend something that will not affect their bottom line (meaning will not cost them anything). But most manufacturer's only offer a base warranty of 12 months. Consider the fact that the vast majority of motorcycle riders do NOT place mileage on their machines that would be anywhere close to the 10,000–15,000 mile (16,000–24,000 km) per year average of the automobile driver. That would mean that by the time a machine has 10,000 miles on it, it is usually out of warranty. Many reputable engine builders would tell you that an engine really isn't broken-in until is has at least 10k miles (16k km) on the clock.

So what are you to do??? You don't really think that we are going to recommend you ignore your manufacturer's recommendations for break-in, DO YOU? Of course not, you might void the warranty. If you plan on utilizing that warranty, it is extremely important that you follow the recommendations, ESPECIALLY when it comes fluid changes (which are never a bad idea whether you believe the bike needs it or not).

The same would be true for an engine rebuild. If the rebuilder provides as warranty, then you should follow their instructions. At least most rebuilders have a much more personal stake in the performance of your PARTICULAR motorcycle than a major manufacturer.

Popular Theories

▶ **See Figure 70**

When asked about engine break-in, most people (including manufacturers) will probably fall in one of two camps. Most will caution you to "baby" the machine. Don't go too fast. Don't turn too sharp. Don't jam on the brakes. Don't race the engine. The minority camp is to "beat the living daylight out of it" or break it in the way you plan to use it.

Our experience is that most people fall somewhere in between. The people who want to beat the bike in, tend to ease up and come in somewhere this side of actual abuse. The people who want to baby it usually break down and get on the throttle a little.

We tend to fall in the "realistic use" category. Remember that both extremes can have detrimental affects. Two quick stories apply here. We once saw a very authoritative article from a European bike magazine that performed an experiment. They took multiple models of the same sport bike and broke them into 2 groups. One group had the living daylight run out of them, while the other followed the manufacturer's recommended babying period almost to a "t". Well, after some significant miles they put them all to the dyno, and guess what. The hard used bikes dyno'd a few percent higher in horsepower than the babied machines. Of course, we never saw a LONG term test and we don't know how reliable the machines were 20 or 50 thousand miles later.

We have also witnessed a case where a new rider babied his oil-head BMW, according to the manufacturer's recommendations. By the time the bike had almost 10,000 miles on it, it was using a generous amount of oil. After multiple attempts to remedy the problem, the dealer finally wound up pulling the jugs and examining the cylinders. It turned out that the rings had never fully seated and they were replaced (UNDER WARRANTY).

Fig. 70 Manufacturers tend to feel strongly about break-in, just look at the sticker on this new bike's speedometer

So what is a guy (or gal) to do? We feel you should follow the manufacturer's instructions, within reason. Don't beat the bike, but don't over baby it either. Most manufacturer's say that you should VARY the engine speed and this is probably the single most important point. Also, make sure the engine is fully warmed before taking any liberties with the throttle. Even after break-in, goosing the throttle on a cold engine is just plain a BAD idea.

Typical Recommendations

For the first 50–100 miles (80–160 km):
- Keep the engine speed below $FR1/2 of total rpm before redline
- NO hard starts
- NO hard stops
- NO hard turns

For at least the first 500 miles (805 km):
- Keep the engine speed well below redline for MOST riding, but vary the speed. Do not hold at any one speed on the highway for more than a few minutes. Raise the speed by 5–10 mph (8–16 kmph) for a minute or two, then lower it for a minute or two. Obviously, this will mean avoiding congested traffic, which might not allow you the freedom (or safety) to keep changing your speed.
- AVOID hard starts
- Allow the engine to warm-up fully every-time you ride
- Continue to avoid hard stops or turns, but increase your intensity as the mileage accumulates.
- NO WHEELIES
- NO STOPIES

Then at whatever interval the manufacturer recommends, begin regular service and maintenance with a complete fluid change, inspection and adjustment routine. Be aware than many manufacturers will recommend that a complete break-in inspection be performed at a short interval of 300–500 miles (480–805 km) after delivery. This is because that is the amount of time and distance necessary for all of the new parts to wear in and seat, meaning that adjustments should be performed to make certain everything is operating properly.

Break-In of Other Components

There are 2 commonly overlooked components on a modern motorcycle which require a break-in period, EVERY TIME they are replaced. These components are the tires and the brakes.

TIRES

▶ **See Figure 71**

Every time you have a tire replaced, take extra care for the first 15–20 miles (24–32 km). Remember that most motorcycle tires are treated with a protective coating of mold release compound at the factory. The coating helps to protect the tire while it is in the warehouse or dealer's shop, but unfortunately it also makes the tire VERY SLIPPERY. Slow starts and stops will help allow you to safely remove that first layer of rubber, and with it, the protective coating. ALSO, remember that you should slowly work up to the more aggressive lean angles. Keep in mind that if you rode straight on a highway after mounting a new tire, it might be clean of the treatment at the center, but still have a significant amount of the edge, even 20 miles (32 km) after it was mounted.

Fig. 71 Take it easy on a new set of tires until the rubber is completely scrubbed-in

BRAKES

▶ **See Figure 72**

New brake pads (or shoes) need an adjustment period where they are scrubbed in to provide optimal service. Any time your brakes are replaced, you should avoid HARD stops for the next 100–200 miles (160–320 km). Obviously if you need them in an emergency, USE THEM. Just remember that before they are fully worn-in, it is possible that they might not stop you as well, so ride accordingly, using extra caution.

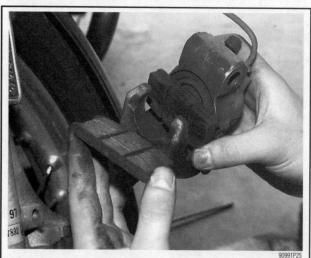

Fig. 72 New brake pads require some time to seat in order to provide optimal service

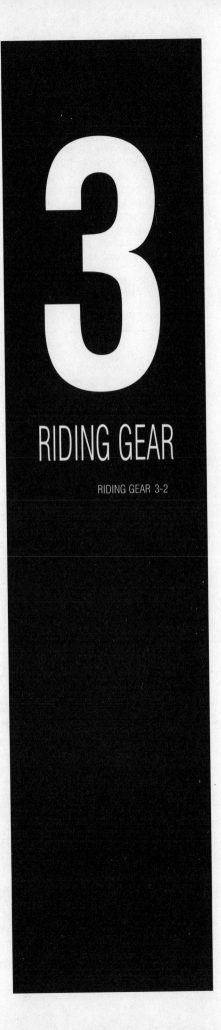

3

RIDING GEAR

RIDING GEAR 3-2

RIDING GEAR

This section is designed to help you choose the proper riding gear for your motorcycling and life style. The goal here is familiarize you with what options are available when it comes to buying protective gear and with what features you should look for in that gear. We have chosen examples of gear from some of the industries known leaders (and in some cases from lesser known but just as high quality manufacturers), and we would like to thank the manufacturers again for their help with the production of this section. That is not to say the brands pictured here are your only options. However it is to say that they are VERY GOOD examples of the high quality motorcycling gear that is available, and as such are excellent standards for comparison with the gear you look at when deciding on a purchase.

What You Are Wearing When . . .

KNOWING YOUR LOCAL LAWS

◗ See Figure 1

It is currently an inescapable fact that there are MANY different laws regarding motorcycling in the United States and in many countries around the world. These laws include regulations on how the bike must be equipped and how you must protect yourself. Before you buy a bike or plan a trip, it would be wise to educate yourself about the laws where you are planning to ride. Remember, what you may choose to do legally in one state of the U.S. may not be legal just across the state line.

Because laws have been known to change with some frequency, we are not going to attempt to give a summary here. Luckily, there are groups who monitor laws about motorcycling for you and publish summaries often. In the U.S., the best source for information on the varying regulations would be from the American Motorcyclist Association (AMA). They publish a list of laws on what is at least a yearly basis. This list will inform you of the different laws regarding Helmets and Eye Protection (for both the rider and passenger), as well as motorcycle safety equipment such as Grab Rails, Headlights and Footpegs.

When you talk about protective gear for motorcycling, people have a lot of varied opinions (which is especially funny considering how many people who have opinions know little or nothing about motorcycles). One thing we want to say about gear is that we don't really want to get into politics. But with that said, laws were designed to protect people from each other instead of themselves and frankly that's not true when they tell you how you must dress to ride a motorcycle. If that is acceptable, then perhaps the government will someday regulate the amount of coffee or alcohol someone is allowed to drink in a given day, or perhaps laws should be passed to decide how much saturated fat or cholesterol you can eat this week. Sounds pretty ridiculous, but wouldn't those examples be things that were just in your best interest?

➡**If you are concerned about the laws in your area, then join a motorcyclists rights group like the AMA or the ABATE (usually known these days as the Alliance of Bikers Aimed Toward Education) and let your voice be heard.**

KEEPING THE RUBBER SIDE DOWN

◗ See Figure 2

When it comes to motorcycling, there is one inescapable fact regarding protective gear (and other forms of clothing), **"What you are wearing when you get ON your bike is what you will be wearing when you get OFF YOUR BIKE!"** There's just no way around it, this is going to be true regardless of whether you PLANNED on getting off your bike at a particular time or not.

Now, the fact that the authors have pointed to what we feel is a flaw in the logic behind laws requiring certain protective gear for adults should not be considered an endorsement for riding without the proper gear. We feel VERY STRONGLY that you should make your own, educated decision on what you are going to wear. And, we feel very strongly that deciding to wear protective gear is a good choice to make.

If you hang around motorcyclists for even a little while, you are going to notice that they treat each other a little differently than most non-riders. When two bikers part, they often say things like "Keep the shiny side up" or "Ride Safe." You rarely see automobile drivers say goodbye by wishing the other well like "drive safe." So why this duality? It's simple, cars don't tend to fall over when you do something wrong (or if you are cut-off by another car). Bikes on the other hand, DON'T STAND UP ON THEIR OWN.

Putting local laws and regulations aside, you are going to have to decide what types of protective gear you plan on wearing. The type of gear you choose should depend as much on your feelings of risk assessment as it will on what type of riding you plan (street riding, off-road riding, commuting, racing . . .). Some people would NEVER consider getting on a motorcycle without full protective gear from helmet to boot, while others think nothing of throwing a leg over their bike wearing nothing more than a t-shirt and jeans. And year after year, a whole lot of people ride without protective clothing and nothing bad happens. So why the big deal?

Well, it is a lot like playing the lottery. If you don't play that number the day it comes up, then you lose. If you don't wear your protective gear the day you

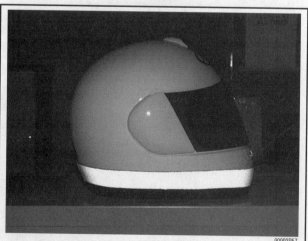

90993P57

Fig. 1 Not only are there laws requiring you to wear a helmet, but some states have laws requiring you to add reflective materials to it

90993P35

Fig. 2 What you are wearing when you get ON your bike is what you will be wearing when you get OFF YOUR BIKE

have a mishap, then you lose. The difference being that when you lose the lottery you probably won't need two ER attendants to hold you down while a nurse scrubs gravel out of your open wounds using a stiff-bristle brush. (It would also probably be interesting to hear the statistics on winning the lottery versus the possibility of having an accident of some sort on a motorcycle, but I suspect the motorcycle accident has better odds of happening.)

BUYING THE RIGHT GEAR

▶ **See Figures 3, 4, 5 and 6**

Choose Something You Like

Probably the single MOST important factor in buying the right gear is to pick items that you like. If you buy a high quality item that is comfortable and versatile, then you are far more likely to WEAR IT. If you hate the look or the fit (or if you think that you look like a complete dork in a piece of gear), then you are probably going to want to leave it at home. And as we already said, the gear doesn't do you ANY GOOD if you are not wearing it when you need it.

One thing that people who are new to motorcycling sometimes don't realize is that a large part of styling with motorcycling gear has been based around functionality. Some people look a bright colored helmets or leathers and snicker ("hey look at that squid"). But high visibility is a function of motorcycle gear that can help to save your life. High visibility gear helps other motorists to NOT only see you, but to recognize you as a motorcyclist and may help to prevent them from running into you. With that said, there are a lot of people who like basic black motorcycle gear. This isn't necessarily a problem, but if you are dressed from head to toe in black, you are not going to stand out in dim light conditions (from dusk to rain) and you should consider this when selecting a style of gear that you are going to buy.

If you don't like bright colors, there are options available for you. A person dressed in black, but who is wearing a white helmet will stand out more than someone who is wearing nothing but black. And, there are even better options today. More and more manufacturers are realizing that you

Fig. 4 . . . or at least looks good to you

can add visibility without taking away from style buy using a few patches of Scotchlite® (a super-reflective material that can be more visible in daylight, but that really catches headlights at night or in dim lighting). Reflective material does not have to look like a highway worker's orange vest, it can be shaped like a bar and shield (if that is your taste), it can be used to spell out a name, it can simply be accent panels in a jacket or pair of boots. If your not familiar with today's high-tech reflective materials you might be surprised how effective they can be and that they can actually enhance the styling of the gear on which they are used.

➡ **A word about bright orange conspicuity vests. Uhhhhhhhhhhh, get over em. They might catch a driver's eye, but what image will it stir first in the driver's mind, hey, here is some guy working on a guardrail or performing a roadway cleanup. We are not convinced that they say "look out, here is a motorcyclist." Remember that a motorist is expecting to quickly overtake and pass a highway worker, not drive along side them or share a roadway. And frankly, they do look pretty silly. Just remember that you have other options.**

Choose Gear To Match Your Riding

The second consideration when buying gear is to ask yourself "how do you ride?" If your motorcycle NEVER leaves the garage unless it is warm and

Fig. 3 Choose high quality gear, that is comfortable to wear and that looks good . . .

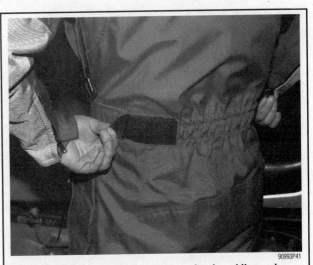

Fig. 5 Your gear should fit both your needs when riding and should properly fit your body

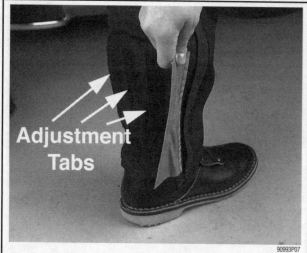

Adjustment Tabs

90993P07

Fig. 6 Each piece of your gear should fit with the other pieces, like these pants can adjust to fit snug over your boots

sunny, then you probably don't need gear that is very warm or completely waterproof. But, if you plan on commuting to your job every day (or even just taking an occasional trip on the bike), then chances are good that you will have to deal with at least some rain and varying temperatures. The gear you choose for more varied or extreme riding conditions is going to have to do a whole lot more than gear purchased only for sunny, warm afternoons.

But, this is not to say that gear can't be versatile enough to use for both. And if your wallet doesn't allow for separate warm, cool and cold riding gear, then you would be wise to select items which can be used in different conditions. Besides, even if you plan on NEVER leaving the garage unless the weather is perfect, there is one thing you can count on, the weather can always change. Even in the desert, it gets cool as the sun sets. Yes, it does actually rain in Southern California (sometimes). And if your riding takes you up in altitude, there can be snow on the top of some mountain roads even when it is warm and sunny down by the sea.

Choose Quality Gear

The last and probably most difficult part of choosing the right gear is making sure that what you have selected is high quality. There are a couple of ways to do this, but they all come down to gathering information about the product. You can never have too much information about something before you buy it.

LOOK AT NAME BRANDS

Now we are not going to say that a certain piece of riding gear is high quality just because a company puts its name brand on it. But, a company that has been around for a long time and that has a good reputation must be doing something right. And you probably want to buy something from a company that has a reputation SPECIFICALLY in the motorcycle industry, not just that has a good reputation for clothing. A boot maker that makes a lot of outdoor gear might make excellent products, but if they don't have the experience in what makes a motorcycle boot different from their other products, they might not make a boot that is any good for motorcycling.

Talk to other motorcyclists and see what brands they have come to trust. If everyone has something good to say about a company, they have probably done something to deserve the praise. Read magazine articles and reviews of gear before deciding to buy something. If you can't find a review on that particular item, look for similar items by the same company and look at how the reviewers feel about that company's products. Often, if someone writes a review for a product that is out of line (good or bad) with what they have come to expect from a manufacturer, they will often tell you that in the review. ". . . although much of the gear we have tested from this company has left us less than dazzled, their new blab blab blab helmet was a real departure from the past and seems to represent a great value . . ."

LOOK AT ATTENTION TO DETAIL

A company that has taken great care on the finish of their product has probably put that quality throughout the gear. A helmet with a poor paint finish or a jacket with seams that are tearing is usually not made of the best materials or workmanship and you would be wise to steer clear of it.

On the other side of the coin, a jacket that has many different features such as a removable lining, vents for cooling, handy pockets with large zipper pulls, etc. obviously has had a lot of thought put into its design and will likely be well made using durable materials.

LOOK AT THE PRICE

We are not going to say that an inexpensive item is no good. Nor are we going to tell you that by spending a whole wad of cash that you are guaranteed to get a high quality item. But it is hard to get away from the old fact that you tend to get what you pay for. Most high quality motorcycle gear will carry a price tag that is higher than their lower quality equivalents (or even higher than their high quality, but non-motorcycle equivalents).

Remember that many companies (even those with very good reputations) have high and low line items. If you are working on a budget, one of their low line items might offer you a chance to get a relatively high quality piece of gear, but that is probably missing some of the more convenient or versatile features of their more expensive counterparts.

A few other things to consider here. One, that good quality gear is normally going to last a long time (especially if it is cared for properly) so that a few dollars invested now may last a LONG TIME. Two, that because gear can be very durable you may be able to find it cheaper used (if you don't mind used clothing). People change and might grow out of a decent piece of gear (especially items like leathers or other snug fitting clothing).

✳✳ WARNING

One warning here. Some types of gear are designed as crash protection use impact absorbent materials (usually some form of foam or hard plastic). These materials lose some of their effectiveness as they age and they are usually designed to do their job only ONCE. If a piece of gear that relies upon this material is exceptionally old or appears to have been dropped or to have been down (meaning it has kissed the ground in use) before, then steer clear of it. Especially when it comes to helmets, a good drop from the seat of the bike or from your kitchen counter may significantly reduce its ability to absorb an impact in the future.

Money is a tough issue when it comes to safety. We really can't tell you what to do here, but remember that gear is designed to PROTECT the user. It's your **butt**, it's your **head**, it's your **fingers** . . . well you probably get the picture here. There are a lot of things we would consider saving money on, but don't save money if it is going to cost you protection.

Choose Something That Fits Properly

Fit is important in motorcycle gear for 2 reasons. The first is simply comfort. If a helmet is too tight, if a jacket restricts movement, if a pair of gloves is so big that they don't allow for proper control of the motorcycle you will be unhappy at best or unsafe at worst. The second reason comes back to safety, which is that basis for protective gear in the first place. A helmet that is too loose may come of during an accident. A jacket that is too big might ride up and expose skin during a slide.

Another thing you should keep in mind with motorcycle gear is that it is designed to fit a certain way and this may not agree with what you have been taught is proper fitting for fashion or other applications. The sleeves of a motorcycle jacket for instance tend to be a little longer than most other jackets. The reason is that you don't want them to ride up too far past the wrist when your arms are bent in a proper riding position. Make sure you consider the unique way the motorcycle gear is used before you decide for sure if an item fits or not.

Unique Problems Of A Woman Motorcyclist

▶ **See Figures 7, 8, 9 and 10**

We've spoken with a lot of women motorcyclists who asked us to say a few words to their fellow sisters of the road (or sisters of the road to be) regarding a problem which is unique to the fairer sex. The truth is that, like many sports, for too long motorcycling has been completely dominated by men. Because we spend the majority of the money in this sport, most companies (who are looking to make money) have spent their efforts on products for men. The problem then comes when women are looking for serious motorcycle gear, which is cut for their unique shapes.

Unfortunately our experience has shown that a lot of the motorcycle gear for women has been designed more for fashion than for function and we caution our women readers when buying products which are highly stylized, to be sure of their functionality. A tight leather, lace-up vest may look REALLY good on most women, but I doubt it is going to do much in a high speed slide. There are more and more garments available which come in unisex styling or which come in both men's and women's versions. This is often a good indication that the garment is really designed for riding and not just looking good, but check it out for yourself. Look at a jacket's cut and stitching as well as the thickness of its leather. Boots with high heels

Fig. 9 It took some searching, but eventually Johanna found a decent pair of women's motorcycle boots with adjustable straps and an oil-resistant sole

Fig. 7 I know it is unfair, but many women have trouble finding riding gear that fits properly

Fig. 10 Some manufacturers, like Olympia® gloves, make products which are specifically designed for women riders

Fig. 8 Don't settle for anything other than quality gear, with the proper cut

are not very practical (though I'm sad to say that is all I see for women in some motorcycle catalogs). Women's hands tend to be shaped differently, and they require gloves cut to match (or the fit won't quite be right).

Luckily some companies really are starting to respond. Olympia® gloves, for example, makes many of their styles in both men's and women's cuts. Also, they have come up with a few types of gloves which are JUST for women and are not just fashion statements. We have also been fortunate enough to see shops which are starting to cater towards women motorcyclists. We hope it is a trend that continues. But for now, don't settle for something that doesn't quite fit right or for something that is more style than function. You need and deserve high quality, protective gear just as much as the rest of us.

Helmets

Laws regarding mandatory helmet use have had a tremendous effect on how many people feel about helmets. Unfortunately, they tend to divide us into two camps. The people who wouldn't be caught dead WITHOUT their helmets (no pun intended) and those who wouldn't be caught dead WITH their helmets (OK, it wasn't that funny the first time either).

The real shame of the matter is that there is so much emotion wrapped up in this issue that it is REALLY DIFFICULT to find the facts. Everyone, whether they are for or against helmets claims to have statistics proving something, "helmets reduce the severity of injury during . . . ." "Education is responsible for a drop in motorcycle deaths, helmet use has nothing to do with . . ." and so on.

Most people with the means to buy a motorcycle are big boys and girls, and are simply going to have to wade through the "FACTS" for themselves. But one thing seems to make sense, "if you are wearing a helmet during a motorcycle accident and you hit your head on something (a rock, curb, bumper, fire hydrant, etc.) the chances are strong that the helmet will do SOMETHING to reduce the trauma of that impact on your head."

➡**Remember that there are laws regarding helmet use all around the world. Another piece of common sense might suggest that if you are going to have to wear a helmet, you might as well choose one that might do you some good if it is ever required to do its job.**

WHAT IS A HELMET?

▸ **See Figures 11 and 12**

A motorcycle helmet is a device that is designed to give some additional protection to your head (and brain!) in the event of a motorcycle accident. It is NOT a panacea for all motorcycle mishaps, but a simple tool that, if used effectively, may REDUCE (not eliminate) the risk to your head during an accident.

Generally speaking, a motorcycle helmet consists of a rigid head covering and a retention system of flexible straps. The rigid covering portion of the helmet has 2 parts, the stiff outer shell and the crushable liner. The job of the outer shell is to protect by spreading a concentrated impact on its surface across a larger area of the liner (and eventually the user's head). The liner does it's job by absorbing impact energy as it compresses. In this way less of the impact energy is conducted directly to your skull.

The helmet retention system is vitally important because the helmet isn't going to do as much good if it comes off or out of place during the acci-

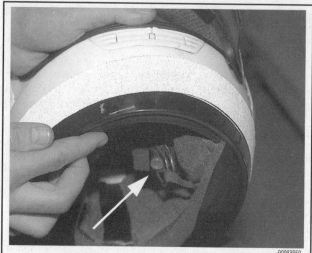

Fig. 12 The helmet chin strap is VERY important, since the helmet won't do any good if it comes off in an accident

dent. So the job of the retention system is exactly as it sounds, to keep the helmet in place during a fall or an accident.

HOW TO SELECT A HELMET

So how do you select a helmet? Remember the 4 basics mentioned at the beginning of this section:
1. Choose something you like.
2. Choose something that fits your riding.
3. Choose something that is high quality.

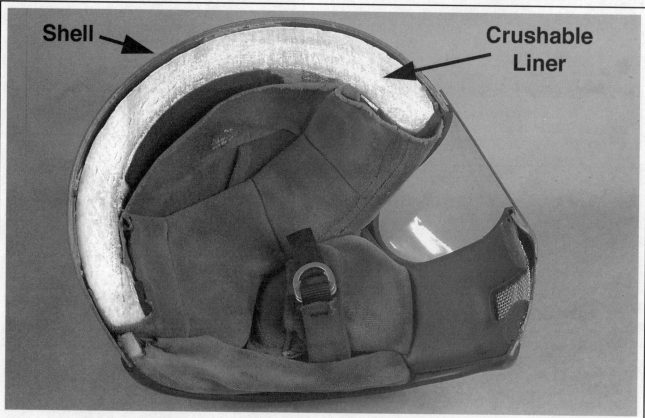

Fig. 11 This helmet has been cut away to reveal the crushable liner found under the hard shell

4. Choose something that fits properly.

But, in order for a helmet to do its job properly there is one additional VERY IMPORTANT requirement:

5. Choose something that has never been damaged or mistreated (READ THIS: Don't buy it used).

Choose a Helmet You Like

♦ See Figure 13

Ok, this one's easy. Choose something that is styled to your tastes. If you think of yourself as boy racer, then you are probably going to be happier with a helmet that contains replica graphics of your favorite motorcycle racer. But if you are pretty sure that James Dean's soul has taken up residence in your body, then you will be much more likely to buy something in basic black.

If you are really worried about style, then you may also want to take into consideration what type (and color) of jacket or bike you will be buying also. A neutral color helmet will go with a lot more bikes than a repli-racer model. Heaven knows you wouldn't want to CLASH on the road???

But like we keep saying, it is just important that you feel comfortable with how your helmet looks, because you are FAR more likely to wear it if you like it.

When you are choosing a style and color of helmet, remember to answer the motorcyclists need for visibility. Bright colors help to provide extra visibility during the day. And, when riding in hot weather a bright color is going to reflect more of the sun's rays then a dark colored helmet to keep your head a little cooler. But when it comes to night riding or foul weather, even the brightest colored helmet won't due. So no matter what color you choose, remember that there are options such as reflective stickers which will help people to see you. Even if you decide on a black helmet, a few well placed stickers will help with low light conditions. One excellent innovation in this area is the helmet Halo® a highly reflective band that looks a lot like a sweat band for your helmet. You wear it around the base of a full face helmet, or even around the brim of an open face helmet to provide reflective surfaces at 360° around your helmet. When riding at night, the Halo® is like adding an additional running light to your motorcycle and can be visible in headlights at distances up to hundreds of yards.

Choose a Helmet To Match Your Riding (Types of Helmets)

♦ See Figure 14

Different riders have different needs. For example, let's face it, dirt riders fall down A LOT, it's just the nature of the sport. And when they do fall down, there is a decent chance that the surface is going to be pretty rough, with things like rocks, plants, mounds of dirt of other protrusions. You will

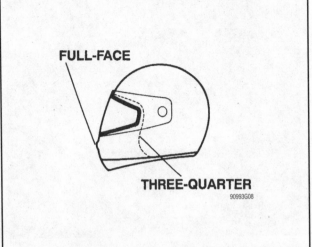

Fig. 14 The most popular style of helmets with people who care about safety are the full face and ¾ styles

notice that most helmets that are specifically designed for off-road use are designed differently than most street helmets. An off-road style helmet, for example, tends to have an exaggerated chin bar which is designed to help keep your face away from the irregular protrusions it might encounter as you are tossed from the bike in dirt riding. That is not to say you can't wear on type for the other use, but it is to say that each type is probably most effective in its own element.

So like any time you are buying motorcycle gear, the first question you will have to decide is "what will I use it for?" and then you can decide what type of helmet will best suit your needs.

There are essentially 3 types of helmets commonly available to motorcyclists, their names give you some idea of the area and degrees of protection they offer your head (and in some cases face):

- Full face
- Open face (or ¾ helmet)
- Halfshell (or half helmet)

FULL FACE HELMETS

♦ See Figures 15, 16, 17 and 18

A full face helmet offers you the most protection in the form of headgear. It is usually defined as a helmet which covers your entire head and that ALSO contains a chin bar. The purpose of the chin bar is to support your

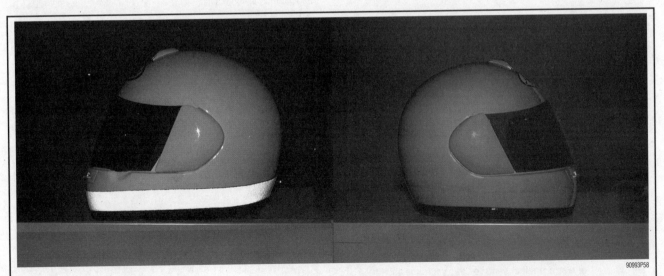

Fig. 13 This white Arai helmet helps keep your head cool and visible during the day, PLUS the Halo® reflective band works GREAT at night

Fig. 15 Full face helmets offer a variety of features from clear and tinted face shields . . .

90993P61

Fig. 16 . . . to cold weather wind deflectors . . .

90993P49

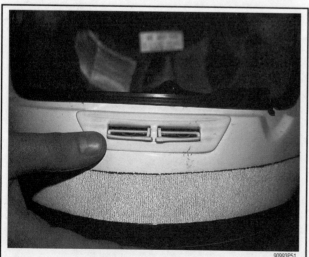

Fig. 17 . . . or warm weather vents to keep your face shield clear and . . .

90993P51

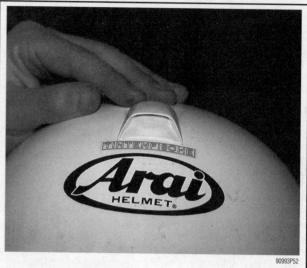

Fig. 18 . . . your head cool

90993P52

face off the ground in the event of a mishap. It should be obvious that in an accident there is a chance your face will slide along the pavement, so a chin bar could save some of those precious features you are so proud of (your nose, your chin . . .). Full face helmets that are designed for street riding usually come with a face shield, so they also serve to provide eye protection. One of the wonderful advantages of a full face helmet is its ability to protect your whole head (face included) from not only accidents, but from the elements. These helmets provide the maximum protection from wind noise, from cold weather riding, riding in heavy downpours and even (if the helmet is well ventilated) decent protection from the sun's rays during warm weather riding.

All of this protection does not come without a cost (like some forms of protection the full face helmet sometimes brings the complaint, "it just doesn't feel the same when I wear one." But that isn't necessarily a good excuse to not wear some protection.) The costs of all this safety include, restricted air flow (including a reduced feeling of actually being in the wind), a reduction in the sounds you hear (including some of the wonderful bangs, clanks and rattles associated with certain v-twin motorcycle engines from various continents), and to some a feeling of being closed in, with that chin bar in the bottom most portion of their peripheral vision, preventing them from easily looking down at themselves or the bike at a stop light.

Now most modern full face helmets have made significant improvements in minimizing the downside of all that protection. One feature that MUST be included in a full face helmet (unless you only plan to ride in sub-freezing temperatures) is adequate ventilation. A good helmet is going to contain a few air inlets and outlets to help keep a flow of forced air through the lining and help cool your head by evaporating sweat.

From these descriptions it should be obvious that a full face helmet is probably the gear of choice for riders who are concerned with maximum protection. This should include any riders with a higher risk of going down (off-road, on-track or aggressive sport riders), or any rider feels the need for the best protection they can get. Unless you are completely helmet-a-phobic from believing all of the anti-helmet propaganda, every serious motorcyclist should own a full face helmet (even if it is just for severe weather riding). Anyone who rides a motorcycle that is not equipped with a windshield of fairing should consider a full face helmet, to help keep from eating bugs and rocks.

OPEN FACE (¾) HELMETS

♦ See Figure 19

An open face or ¾ helmet is a compromise. It provides a large area of protection for your head, but because it does not have a chin bar, it does not provide the same protection for your face that a full face helmet can. Open face helmets therefore also do not provide as much protection from wind

Fig. 19 This ¾ open face helmet offers more protection than a halfshell with a more open feeling than a full face

noise or the elements. So with that said you might ask, "why do people wear them?" It is simple, an open face helmet provides much of the head impact protection of a full face helmet while providing something the full face cannot, visceral pleasure. The open face helmet allows you to enjoy the wind in your face (a great source of enjoyment to many motorcyclists.)

People choose to wear open face helmets for a variety of reasons, all of them having something to do with the lack of a face shield and/or a chin bar. Besides the wind in the face, they provide an enhanced line of vision for non-riding applications (this is not to say that a full face helmet restricts your field of vision for riding, but that the chin bar can make looking at maps, looking down at something on the bike, looking into your pockets or even your jacket zipper a bit awkward). This enhanced line of vision is probably most significant in simply adding to the experience of being outside, on a motorcycle. Some people feel that full face helmets make you feel like you are in a cage (and therefore might as well just be driving a car).

Open face helmets allow you to more easily converse with other riders at stop lights, because they do not muffle your voice. Since they provide less protection from noise, they allow you to hear different sounds that would be muffled by a full face, especially the sweet exhaust note from a v-twin (which might explain the propensity for riders of certain bike types to wear them). Again, this is not to say that full face helmets provide a dangerous restriction of sound. In fact most experts agree that the noise protection of a full face helmet filters out many of the inconsequential road and engine noises allowing you to hear things like horns and sirens better.

Because open face helmets do not provide as much facial protection from the elements, many sport riders and riders of unfaired bikes will stay away from them (the obvious exception being cruiser riders, many of whom cling to a machismo image of not being bothered by the occasional bug or stone in the face). Many riders of bikes with full fairings or windshields choose to wear this style of helmet. Possibly because motorcycles already provide significant protection from wind, bugs, stones, etc. and the addition of a full face helmet under those conditions may prove to be too much (with the drastically reduced air flow that full fairings provide, a full face helmet's ventilation system may be useless).

Like full face helmets, a better made open face is going to have features that make it more useful. These features often include things like vents and snap on face shields or sun visors to make them more adaptable to varied weather conditions.

HALFSHELL (½) HELMETS

Look, at the risk of raising the hairs on the backs of the necks on many of our friends we're going to come right out and say it. This style helmet is primarily produced because there are helmet laws. The person most likely to wear this helmet is also most likely to not wear one if they are given the choice. And considering how much less protection they give you in an

accident than a full face helmet, that may not be much different. We are not saying that they provide no protection at all, just that they are less likely to stay in place during an accident and that because they cover (as the name suggests) only about ½ of your head, they provide significantly less protection than the other styles of helmets.

With that said, the halfshell style helmet does provide a few advantages, similar in nature to the ¾ open face. Because they normally leave part of the ear exposed, they allow you to really enjoy all of the sounds around you during a ride. They provide for easy communication between rider and passenger or even with other riders. They definitely allow for the best feeling of freedom on the motorcycle, while still wearing some head protection. And, most importantly, if they are DOT legal, they allow you to legally operate a motorcycle in areas of the U.S. where a mandatory helmet law is in effect without being required to wear more restrictive head gear like a ¾ open face or full face helmet.

After reading our descriptions of helmets, you might be curious what our choices are when it comes to this important issue of personal protection. Well Ben is a semi-professional race driver (SCCA) and an avid motorcyclist who enjoys sport and sport touring riding. He doesn't get on a motorcycle without full leathers (or an Aerostitch® Roadcrafter suit) and a FULL FACE helmet. But Kevin is more into the just being out there, in the wind and the elements. He rides in various states of protective gear, though he tries to at least keep a jacket on MOST of the time (an Aerostitch® Darien these days). He also owns both a ¾ open face (for most riding conditions) and a full face helmet for severe weather and for more sport oriented riding (read that every chance he gets to hop on a Buell).

Choose a Quality Helmet

▶ **See Figures 20, 21 and 22**

As we stated at the beginning of the section, determining they quality of motorcycle gear is not always a black and white issue. Especially when it comes to helmets, since when deciding if it is high quality has a lot to do with the materials used in construction and the helmet's design. A good starting point is to avoid anything that is $9.99 and is displayed under a sign saying "For novelty purposes only."

In the U.S., the Department of Transportation (DOT) helps us choose a quality helmet by setting standards of impact protection that helmets must meet in order to be legal for use in areas where a mandatory helmet law is in effect. Helmets which meet these standards are equipped with a DOT sticker showing that they meet the requirements and are legal for use. Unfortunately, DOT does not test helmets and publish lists of which ones meet the standards. Instead it is up to the each individual helmet's manufacturer to "certify" that their helmets are in compliance (not very reassuring if you are a suspicious type).

Fig. 20 High quality helmets will display both the DOT and SNELL symbols showing that they have passed both types of certification

There is a non-profit group that tests helmets and certifies them (and whose standards differ from DOT, because they look at different factors). The Snell Memorial Foundation, Inc. was incorporated under California law as a non-profit organization in 1957 and exists solely for the purpose of engaging in scientific and educational activities in order to promote safety, well-being and comfort to people engaged in any type of travel or vehicular transportation. The foundation, formed by friends of William "Pete" Snell, a race car driver who died of massive head injuries received during a racing accident, conducts tests on helmets for various factors. What is comforting about the Snell standard is that the manufacturers participate completely voluntarily by submitting samples for testing (and the foundation will perform random sample testing from stocks intended for retail sales).

The Snell tests are designed to examine a particular helmet's properties which are most critical in providing protection:

- **Impact management** or how well the helmet protects against collisions with large objects.
- **Positional stability** or how well a helmet remains in place on a head when it is properly secured.
- **Retention system strength** or the ability of the helmet chin straps to hold the helmet during an entire accident.
- **Level of protection** or the area of the head that is protected by the helmet.

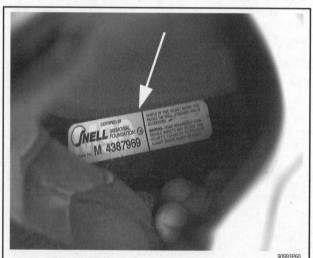

Fig. 21 Check under the helmet lining for certification labels and build dates . . .

Snell tests vary depending on which properties they are checking. One test includes dropping helmets (with a headform installed in the helmet) in a specified manner onto any of three unyielding anvils and then measuring the amount of shock delivered to the headform. Another test involves dropping a metal cone of specified weight, from a specified height onto the helmet and making sure that there is no penetration. Other tests include applying a solvent mix to check resistance to chemical attack from solvents or petrochemicals, testing the permanently attached chin bars of full face helmets, testing the face shields with lead pellets, checking the diameter of ventilation holes, and even checking the peripheral vision allowed by the opening.

This is a lot of testing, and the results are probably a market full of helmets which are significantly safer than if there were no such testing or certifications. But, unfortunately we cannot say that these tests will ASSURE you of a quality helmet every time or that even if you get a quality helmet, that it will protect you from all unforeseen accidents. Remember that we are talking about plastic and Styrofoam here. If you slam your helmeted head into a sharp enough object or even a dull (but immovable) object at a great enough velocity you are not going to have to worry about helmets ever again (unless you believe in reincarnation). Remember that helmets are great tools, but they have their limits. And, although quality control by most modern motorcycle helmet manufacturers is exemplary, there does exist the possibility of a bad helmet slipping through.

Also remember that a helmet may be damaged on display or just from aging. The protective capabilities of a helmet diminish over time and many experts recommend a limited shelf life for helmets. At time of publication, the Snell foundation recommends that all motorcycle helmets be replaced after a maximum of 5 years (or less if the helmet manufacturer has tighter standards).

So how do you try to assure yourself of a quality helmet. Buy a helmet that has BOTH DOT and SNELL stickers showing compliance with both standards. Check the manufacturer helmet labels which should include a production date to be sure it is not excessively old (remember though that you probably won't find a helmet that was produced last week or last month, but keep that 5 year life span in mind). Examine the helmet thoroughly for signs of having been dropped or of other abuse. Look at the helmet shell for evidence of cracks. Check the lining for unusual or irregular depressions showing where it may have been compacted from misuse.

Choose a Helmet That Fits Properly

▶ **See Figures 23 and 24**

A helmet does not do any good if it comes off during an accident. Therefore, the proper fit of a helmet is just as important as the quality of its construction. A helmet should fit snug, but not tight, since a tight helmet will likely place uncomfortable pressure on your head and may give you a headache. But a helmet should not bee too loose, because if it is, it would be much more likely to come off or out of place during an accident.

Any helmet should be snug enough to prevent you from inserting a finger between your forehead and the helmet lining (we are not talking about prying your finger into place, just lightly inserting it). Similarly the padding of a full face helmet should press lightly against your cheeks, but here you are much more likely to be able to insert a finger or two. With the helmet in place, try to rotate it without turning your head. If the helmet turns significantly on your head (especially if it turns enough to interfere with your vision), it is too loose and you should try the next smaller size. Without tightening the chin straps, shake your head briskly from left-to-right a few times. The helmet should follow your head and not come out of place.

➡ **Remember that the crash protective portion of the helmet lining is made of a compactable material and will give slightly during use, which may make a slightly tight helmet just right or a borderline helmet slightly too loose. Take your time when trying on and selecting the right helmet.**

Try out the chin strap retention system. When it has been snugged (in such a way that you can still breath or swallow), make sure it is still comfortable. An awkward retention system is going to discourage you from using it properly and then we are right back to the why bother wearing a helmet thing again because if it is not snugged properly, it may come off during an accident.

Fig. 22 . . . this helmet has a build date stamped on its chin strap—Remember it should be replaced after 5 years

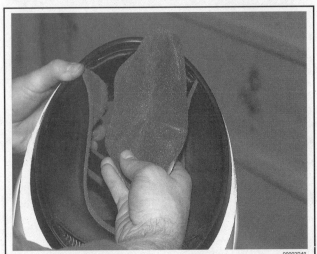

90993P48

Fig. 23 Some of the better helmets on the market, like this Arai, have removable cheek pads so you can adjust the fit . . .

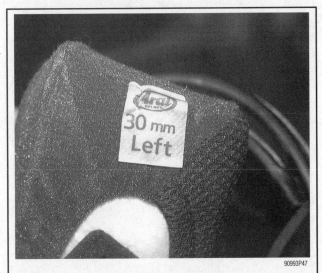

90993P47

Fig. 24 . . . the cheek pads come in various sizes

The Snell foundation recommends a simple method for checking helmet fit and making sure that you have properly secured it on your head EACH TIME you put it on:

"Position the helmet on your head so that it sits low on your forehead; if you can't see the edge of the brim at the extreme upper range of your vision, the helmet is probably out of place. Adjust the chinstraps so that, when in use, it will hold the helmet firmly in place. This positioning and adjusting should be repeated to obtain the very best result possible. The procedure initially may be time consuming. TAKE THE TIME."

"Try to remove the helmet without undoing the retention system closures. If the helmet comes off or shifts over your eyes, readjust and try again. If no adjustment seems to work, this helmet is not for you; try another."

One more thing to consider when it comes to proper helmet fit. If you wear eyeglasses, even part of the time, be sure to try on a helmet with the eyeglasses that you plan to wear with it. Some helmets are better suited than others for glasses and if you have the wrong combination of eyeware and helmet it may place uncomfortable pressure on your temples causing a headache or on the bridge of your nose.

➡I've been sitting here, typing at my computer for about a half an hour and feel like a complete IDIOT, because my wife just walked in and wants to know why I'm wearing my full face helmet and typing. I didn't bother trying to explain that I was just working on the proper fit section and was double-checking a couple of the facts . . . she knows me well enough by now not to pursue it. But it occurs to me that the helmet was still perfectly comfortable the entire time and that the music from the stereo still sounded great . . . thanks Jerry (and the rest of the Dead). But sadly, I just checked the sticker on the production date and it was June of 92 and I am already overdue for another helmet. Hmmmm, what to buy this time?

Don't Buy A Used Helmet

Now we are probably going to take some heat over this one too, but we don't care how honest the guy looks. "I never wore it, I just bought it and it didn't fit and I've never dropped it . . . ever . . . really." Look it is your HEAD, but why take the risk. Remember that a helmet's ability to protect your head is, generally speaking, a one-time thing and it diminishes over time or any time the helmet is mistreated. Repeated bumps into doorways and an occasional drop from the back seat of the bike at a gas station may be enough to significantly reduce its ability to absorb an impact when you really need it.

If you do decide to buy a used helmet. Examine it like you would a new one. ANY evidence of damage should make you extremely suspicious and cautious.

If you have the luxury of examining a used helmet before purchasing it (or if the price was sooooo low that you decided to risk the money), then return the helmet to the original manufacturer for examination before use. This is true of a helmet you have owned for a while and dropped as well. It is too easy to say, "ohhhhh that drop didn't hurt it" when you really don't know.

HOW TO CARE FOR YOUR HELMET

Don't Drop/Bang It

Well, if you read the part on NOT buying a used helmet, you are already aware of the most important form of care for your helmet. "DON'T DROP IT." Don't bang it into things, don't let it bounce around in the trunk of your car. Don't pile things on it in the garage . . . etc.

Don't Leave It Baking In The Sun

But there are other things you should be aware of when it comes to helmet care. Don't let it sit and bake in the sun every day. This is going to have an effect on the shell and the lining. Occasionally leaving it on the seat of your bike may do no real harm, but doing it every day, all day (such as when your are in work) is going to have a cumulative effect and weaken its ability to protect you.

Don't Place It On Mirrors or Sissybars

Sitting a helmet over something, so that it is supported by the impact lining, and not on the edges of the hard shell will compact the foam causing a hard spot which will not crush during an accident. This spot will not only NOT do its job in an accident, but it can directly transmit the shock from the shell to your skull, which is EXACTLY what it was supposed to prevent. Don't leave you helmet sitting on the bikes mirrors or jammed down over your backrest.

Don't Expose It To Solvents

Have you ever poured gasoline in a Styrofoam cup and watched the cup disappear? Well, the impact resistant material under your helmet's shell is remarkable similar to that cup. Read the ingredients of any cleaner or chemical that you plan to use on your helmet and steer clear of those that may damage the shell or lining.

Do Clean And Examine It Regularly

Do yourself a favor and clean the lining with a little water and mild soap (your friends will thank you.). Also, give the hard shell the same treatment.

Remove bugs and dirt so that you will easily notice any damage that may occur through use. A potentially dangerous crack could be hidden by bug goo and road spray. If you are really vain (and aren't we all sometimes) polish it with some high quality wax once in a while, it will make it easier to keep clean.

➡**Be sure to check with the helmet manufacturer before using any chemicals or detergents on your helmet. Be certain that whatever you use will not harm the shell or protective lining.**

Jackets

MOTORCYCLE JACKET FEATURES

♦ **See Figure 25**

When most people think of a jacket, they think of something to protect you from the elements, and that is certainly true of a motorcycle jacket. But riding a motorcycle places certain demands on your gear that would not be applicable to most other activities. And unfortunately, many people either don't realize or don't believe the need for a motorcycle jacket to do something more. A real biker jacket will to protect you in the case of crash or a slide (read that as a motorcycle jacket may be needed to keep your skin on your bones).

A motorcycle jacket will first and foremost offer some protection against abrasion and, if it is truly designed to help minimize the possibility of injury, it will also offer some impact protection. As with helmets, you are going to have to do your own risk assessment here and make a decision with how much of a risk you feel comfortable. Many people don't think twice about riding in a T-shirt or a denim jacket, but unless you have a very minor get-off, neither of these is going to provide significant protection to your upper body.

The best motorcycle jackets will have a combination of these features:
• Abrasion protection
• Impact protection
• A cut to fit your body when riding (and various adjustments or retention systems to keep them in place in the case of a mishap)
• Ventilation to help keep you cool in hot weather
• A lining to help keep you warm in cold weather
• Pockets to store things (with zippers or snaps to keep from losing them)
• Bright colors and/or reflective material to help keep you visible
• Waterproof or water-resistant layer to help keep you dry in damp or wet weather

Fig. 25 A jacket that is designed for motorcycling (and not just to LOOK like a biker jacket) will have a variety of useful features

Abrasion Protection

♦ **See Figure 26**

A jacket that is specifically designed for motorcycle riding will be made of a durable material (leather, Cordura®, etc.) that has been shown to provide a measure of wear-through protection in case of a slide. This is not to say that ANY leather or Cordura® jacket is suitable. There are different weights of leather (a light fashion weight leather jacket won't do as well as a competition weight jacket made of heavier and thicker leather). Also, the seams of a motorcycle jacket are normally reinforced to help keep them from coming apart and preventing the material from doing its job of protecting you.

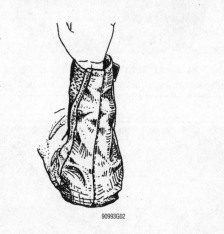

Fig. 26 Jackets should be reinforced along seams and elbows (or other impact areas) to keep the jacket from coming apart in a slide

Impact Protection

♦ **See Figures 27, 28, 29 and 30**

This important part of a motorcycle jacket is often overlooked. Even the fall from a stationary motorcycle can transmit a serious shock to elbows or shoulders. And a good motorcycle jacket should come with some form of padding in these areas to absorb some of the shock for you. A popular fea-

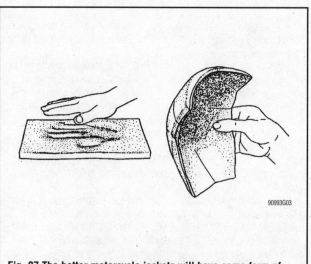

Fig. 27 The better motorcycle jackets will have some form of hard plastic and/or crushable foam impact protectors

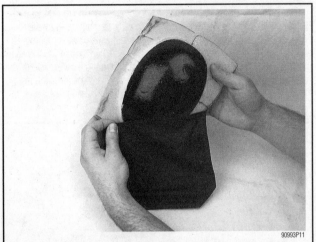

Fig. 28 Impact protectors are usually removable so the jacket can be worn with or without them (and so they can be replaced if necessary)

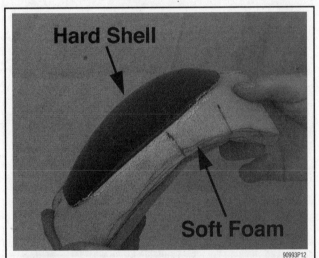

Fig. 29 This protector has a hard plastic shell and crushable foam padding

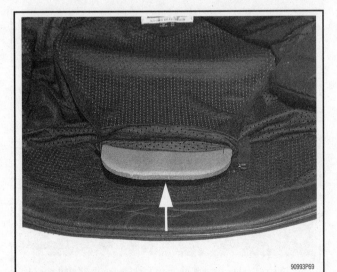

Fig. 30 Many jackets offer a removable back protector too

ture of many high quality jackets is the inclusion of removable plastic and/or foam body armor that works in a similar way to the crushable lining of a helmet. In the event of an impact, the foam condenses to absorb the shock instead of directly transmitting it to your bones.

A Cut To Fit Your Body When Riding

▶ See Figure 31

Take your favorite dress or casual jacket, put it on and sit on your motorcycle. Chances are you will notice a few things that make this jacket comfortable the rest of the time, may not make it suitable for riding. For one thing, when you lean forward, even slightly, and grasp the handle bars, the sleeves will probably pull back exposing your arms, and the hem may pull upward, exposing your back. Depending on the material and the collar, it may flap or even whip you in the wind. And there probably aren't any other retention points, such as cinching system at the waist to seal cold air out and keep it in place in the case of a slide.

Well, these are all the things that a good motorcycle jacket will address. The sleeves of most will be a little long when you are standing around before a ride, but when you climb in the saddle they should fit just right. Sleeves should have a hook and loop tab for adjustment and/or a zipper so it can be sealed to keep the air out on cold days (or nights). Waists should have some sort of belt or adjustment to seal air, and for road racer style jackets, a zipper to attach it to your riding pants (to really keep it in place during a get-off).

Fig. 31 Overlength sleeves with hook and loop and/or zipper adjustments will stay in place when you stretch your arms out in a riding position

Ventilation

▶ See Figures 32 and 33

Any motorcycle jacket (even a black one) will keep you out of direct sunlight on a hot day, and if there is sufficient airflow to allow your sweat to evaporate, it can keep you cool as well. The most popular way to do this is

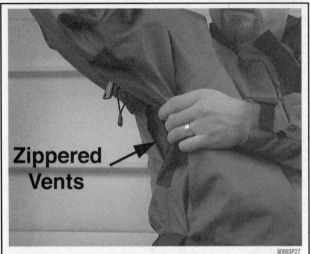

Fig. 32 A good jacket will use some combination of vents to keep you cool in hot weather

Fig. 33 On this leather jacket the thermal layer can be removed in the summer to expose a perforated lining designed to allow airflow

We really can't emphasize the need for zippers or snaps to seal your items in your pockets. Did you ever wonder why so many bikers have those chain drive wallets. Before I had a decent jacket I used to wear one too. Or at least I did after that day the two cute girls in the convertible Saab chased me down, flashing their lights at me (a situation that I otherwise would have enjoyed . . . "hey these chicks dig me I thought . . . looking cool on my Harley . . . they obviously want me"). I was right, they did want me or

Fig. 34 Serious riders want a jacket with a lining that can be removed (making the jacket suitable for all weather)—Some, like the Aerostitch Darien® include a lining which can be worn separately, as a windbreaker

with a series of zippered vents and a mesh or removable liner which will allow air to circulate. Air can enter from unzipped sleeves, or through intake vents (under the arms or on either side of the lapel) and can exit one or more vents across the back.

Linings

▶ See Figures 34 and 35

A lining of insulating material is necessary to keep you warm on cold days or nights. A removable lining is even better since it means the jacket can probably also be used in hot weather. And if you are really going for the gusto, make it a removable lining that can be worn as a jacket by itself once the bike is parked for the night.

Pockets

▶ See Figure 36

Travelling on a motorcycle you learn to pack light. But there are a lot of little things which you like to keep handy from wallets or garage door openers to lip balm, an oil rag or a map. A jacket with a lot of pockets is going to become a convenient traveling companion. Of course, the pockets should have zippers or snaps to close them and prevent these precious items from falling out.

Fig. 35 The double zippers on each lapel make the lining quickly removable as the sun of the day removes the morning chill

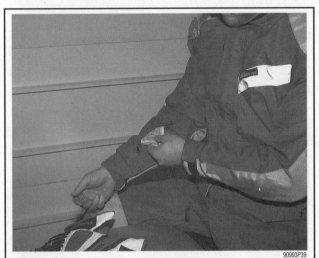

Fig. 36 From toll money to lip balm, an oil rag or a map, multiple pockets make a jacket convenient

more correctly, they wanted to give me back my wallet that had fallen from my jean pocket at the last intersection . . . "uhhhhhhhh, ooooooops, hey thanks ladies, can I buy you a drink?"

❉❉ CAUTION

Be careful what you decide to put in your pockets. Hard and sharp objects are probably not good ideas in the case of a get-off. Remember that a key, a pair of eyeglasses or that little screwdriver you like to keep handy could be driven into your body in a crash. If you wouldn't like to fall on a particular object, DON'T WEAR IT in one of your jacket pockets.

Bright Colors And/Or Reflective Material

▶ See Figure 37

I hope you are not getting sick of hearing this yet. But one more time (for now). Bright colors will keep you cooler in the hot weather and will help keep you seen. If you don't like that, then at least consider something with some reflective material. There are some great options here that will keep you from looking like a complete squid or dork so think about it.

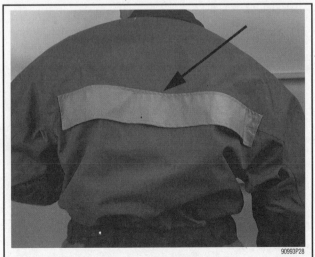

Fig. 37 The reflective panel on the back of this jacket will help assure drivers can see you at night or in foul weather

Waterproof Or Water-Resistant

▶ See Figures 38 and 39

If you tour or commute daily on a motorcycle, you will eventually ride through some rain. Whether it is a damp morning fog or an all day downpour, a jacket that will help keep you warm and dry is a nice plus. You don't NEED a jacket that will do that (because you can carry a rainsuit to wear over the jacket.) But after years of daily and cross country riding, I'm telling you that a jacket which is waterproof too is a REALLY NICE PERK.

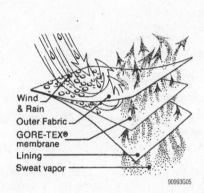

Fig. 38 Fabrics combined with breathable, waterproof materials like Gore-Tex® allow you to stay cool when it is warm and dry when it is wet

Fig. 39 With the storm flaps and zippers all snugged, this jacket will keep you dry even in heavy downpours

Any decent leather jacket will protect you from light rain or mist, especially if you keep it well treated. But, there are options today with materials like Gore-tex® which allow a very high degree of resistance to rain and even all day downpours that are really convenient. For one thing, if your jacket is already waterproof, you will never have to face the decision, "should I start looking for a place to pull over and put my rainsuit on, it is starting to look pretty bad?" And, you never have to take up precious cargo room with a rainsuit if you don't want to.

HOW TO SELECT A JACKET

So how do you select a jacket? Remember the 4 basics mentioned at the beginning of this section:
1. Choose something you like.
2. Choose something that fits your riding.
3. Choose something that is high quality.
4. Choose something that fits properly.

Choose Something You Like

▶ **See Figures 40 and 41**

First thing's first, you've got to like the look of the jacket you pick so we are not going to tell you to buy a bright purple jacket just to be seen if you think you look really dumb in it. Go to dealerships and try on some jackets to get a feel for what you want.

BUT, here are some things to keep in mind. If you do a lot of hot weather riding, a black jacket may not be your best choice. Remember that a lighter color will help to reflect the sun's rays and will keep you cooler in direct sunlight. We've already said a couple of times that a brighter color helps to keep you visible in traffic and in low light conditions, so it helps there too.

➡**Many riders wear a black jacket for the look, and just take it off when the weather is hot. Put the whole safety argument aside for a minute. Keep in mind that in very hot weather and direct sunlight, taking the jacket off will not keep you as cool as you would be under the right jacket. The direct sun will heat your skin, rather than allowing a jacket to reflect some of that heat. The direct sunlight will further warm your skin which will prevent you from fully realizing the benefit of sweat evaporation (and there is that whole sunburn thing to worry about as well). Look at Arabs in the desert, they cover themselves completely with loose fitting, light colored robes. This reflects the sun's rays (and therefore some of its heat) allowing their sweat to evaporate and take body heat with it.**

But if you are dead set with holding that biker image and black it just has to be, you have got a couple of options to help keep you cool and visible.

Fig. 40 Many manufacturers produce multiple jacket styles— Like these from Hein Gericke®, it doesn't matter whether it is a traditional, biker jacket . . .

Fig. 41 . . . or a more modern, competition style jacket, you have to like the way it looks if you are going to wear it

For one thing, make sure your jacket has a ventilation system consisting of zippers (to let air in and out at various points, such as under the arms and across the back) and a mesh lining to encourage airflow. You might also consider breathable materials such as Cordura® nylon and Gore-tex®. And lastly, we come back to the old reflective material thing. Many jackets are made with patches, stripes or lettering of Scotchlite® or an equivalent reflective material that will help greatly to keep you visible at night.

➡**If you find a jacket that you love, but that does not contain any reflective material don't sweat it, you can add that later. One way is to locate a search and rescue equipment supply company (your local fire or park ranger station may be able to help with this) and look for reflective patches or even lettering. I've got an old black leather vest that's just loaded with patches, pins and other memorabilia. I used to wear this over my favorite leather jacket a lot (I especially liked the extra pockets) but I wanted more visibility. My solution; I ordered reflective iron-on letters from a search and rescue equipment catalog (because the reflective "search dog" patch they offered just wouldn't cut it) and spelled my nickname across the back. Not only did it help to keep me seen at night, but I found the added benefit of making it easier to meet people at rallies and in bars (after the bike was asleep for the night, of course).**

Choose Gear To Match Your Riding

▶ **See Figures 42 and 43**

Road racers are probably going to place more emphasis on crash protection (abrasion and impact resistance) than they would on number of pockets. Someone who does a lot of touring or commutes every day is going to want a jacket that protects them from the elements (keeps them warm, cool or dry).

Obviously, if you live in the desert your needs are going to be a little different than if you live in Maine right? But that still doesn't mean the desert dweller NEVER has to worry about cold weather. And I've ridden through Maine in the summer, it can get downright hot in August. You'll have to take an assessment of what your needs and desires are in a jacket, but remember that the more versatile the jacket is, the more likely you are to keep it on all of the time.

Look at the various features we listed earlier and decide which ones are most important to you. Look for a jacket that fills all your needs.

LEATHER OR NOT?

▶ **See Figure 44**

Bikers wear leather, right? Sure, most do. The smell and feel of a good leather jacket has just become a part of motorcycling to many. That is

Fig. 42 Some people call 1-piece garments like the Aerostitch Roadcrafter® a commuter suit, because you can wear normal work clothing underneath, while staying warm, dry and safe

Fig. 44 From Boy Racers to Brando wannabes, the choice for many is still leather—This jacket from Hein Gericke® is an excellent choice for quality and safety

Fig. 43 If your jacket didn't come with a lining, you can remedy that with this fleece jacket, sold by the Riderwearhouse. It can be worn under your riding jacket or separately, as a windbreaker

because leather was the best material they could find years ago to provide protection from elements and from crashes. But football players used to wear leather helmets too (and if you haven't noticed they changed for a reason).

Leather still provides EXCELLENT abrasion protection. There are some very high quality leathers available for motorcycle riders today and you may want to own a set. But, depending on your style of riding, you should at least consider alternatives that offer comparable protection, with some advantages you won't find in most leathers. Non-leather motorcycle jackets are made from a variety of materials such as ballistic nylons, like Cordura® or Coslan® and some jackets even use Kevlar reinforcements at crash points.

This newer breed of non-leather motorcycle jackets usually use a breathable and a waterproof or water-resistant material. There are a few major advantages here. The lighter, breathable materials can be more comfortable to wear and will help to keep you cool on hot days. And, unlike many sealed, nylon or plastic rainsuits, a breathable water-resistant jacket allows your sweat to escape keeping you significantly more comfortable on rainy summer days. These jackets are often easier to clean than leathers (no more saddle soap and leather treatment) as they can often be thrown in the washing machine.

There are a lot of quality options available in non-leather motorcycle jackets. We've shown a few of your options here in the form of the company that arguably invented today's modern non-leather rider jacket. The Aerostitch® line from the Riderwearhouse is the standard that many companies measure against. The Darien jacket, pictured here contains EVERY SINGLE feature we mentioned earlier. From a plethora of pockets to near complete water-resistance (we've worn Darien jackets for all day downpours without a single drop penetrating the outer shell). We've also worn them in temperatures ranging from over 100°F (38®C) to below 32°F (0°C) and they were comfortable the whole time. The Roadcrafter one-piece suit provides similar features and comfort to the Darien, but has the added advantage of protecting your whole body, quickly and easily. The suit is designed with one zipper from head to toe, so that you can quickly step into or out of it (and you can wear just about any street clothing underneath which makes it ideal for commuting). Unfortunately, the full length zipper on the 1-piece suit can also be an Achilles heel. If the seams are not properly sealed or if your riding position allows water to puddle near the base of the zipper, it can seep during ALL DAY downpours.

Now, I'm not saying that I've thrown away my old leather jacket, I'm just saying that since I discovered my Darien my old jacket spends A LOT OF TIME hanging in the closet. If you notice, there aren't any racers out there wearing jackets which aren't leather. A high quality, competition weight leather jacket may still provide more protection than most of the non-leather alternatives for extreme high speed get-offs. If I ever get that Buell and some serious track time, I may opt to wear leathers on the track. But when it comes to just about everything else, well that old leather jacket should last me a very long time, since it doesn't get worn out hanging in the closet (I just have to remember to pull it out and treat it once in a while to keep the old leather from cracking too badly).

Choose Quality Gear

▶ See Figure 45

You might find a high quality leather jacket at a flea-market or at the mall, but NOT LIKELY. Remember that fashion weight leather is not going to protect you as well as heavy, competition weight leather (and you are not often going to find competition weight leather anywhere but a motorcycle shop or supplier).

If the gear is produces or sold by a company that makes its living from motorcyclists (such as Hein Gericke® and Aerostitch®), and has many of the features that we've described, then the chances are it is high quality. Again, there are no guarantees here, so you should do some sleuthing before you decide to buy. Look at motorcycle brand name merchandise. Look at the quality and construction (especially the seams). Even a heavyweight leather jacket won't do you much good if the seams are not reinforced to keep it from coming apart in a slide.

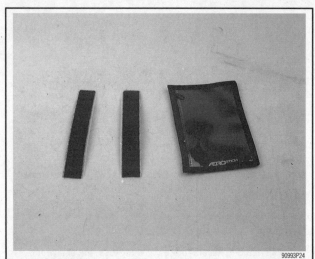

Fig. 45 Features like a removable map pouch are sure signs that this jacket was designed by riders, for riders

Choose Something That Fits Properly

◆ See Figure 46

When you try a jacket on, the best thing to do is to climb on your bike (or bikes if you are so lucky) and see how it fits your riding position. Might the zippers scratch the tank? Do the sleeves pull back or does the waist ride up excessively? If your bike is not handy, try lifting your hands over your head, the sleeves should not expose too much of your wrists. Make sure that the jacket does not bind in the shoulders, but that it is also snug enough to stay in place in the even of the mishap (again, adjustment tabs or belts are handy for this).

If there is a lining, ask yourself if it will be sufficient for all of your riding needs. And if it won't, make sure there is some room under the jacket for one or more additional layers (might we suggest polar fleece and/or electric garments for cold weather). Just make sure the jacket isn't TOO BIG either, since it may balloon and be impossible to seal the wind out.

Fig. 46 Adjustments like these hook and loop waist bands allow you to seal out cold air

HOW TO CARE FOR YOUR JACKET

How you will need to care for your jacket will vary depending on the materials from which it is made. The first thing to do is read the labels or even (in the case of Aerostitch®) the jacket owners manual. The manufacturer will probably give you the best information for the particular materials used in your jacket (especially if it is a non-leather jacket).

Leather Jackets

◆ See Figure 47

In general, leather should be cleaned and treated periodically to help make sure it remains in good condition. Leather is a natural substance which contains oils which help keep the fibers elastic. If it is allowed to completely dry out, the leather will crack and fibers will split. If allowed to continue, this will eventually ruin the leather completely. Leather contains pores that allow the fibers to breath. Dirt, dust and road mung will clog these pores and should be cleaned before treating the leather. There are various products available to clean leather from bottled cleaners to good old saddle-soap. Be sure to read and follow the instructions on the package of the cleaner or the treatment.

➡ **It is natural for some cracks to appear in leather as it ages and this, of itself, does not mean that the leather is damaged or ruined. But, it might mean that you need to pay a little more attention to cleaning and treating it periodically.**

Because water will wash many of the oils out of your leather, you should treat the jacket after anytime it has been exposed to rain or heavy, damp mist.

✳✳ WARNING

Many leather treatments will affect the color of different leather types (especially suede). Be sure to read the instructions closely before using it on your jacket. Whenever possible, test the treatment on a small, inconspicuous area (such as the inside of the lapel or the bottom, inside hem line of the jacket.

Fig. 47 Probably one of the best leather cleaners and leather treatments we've ever used is Lexol®

Non-Leather Jackets

As we stated earlier, because the materials may vary greatly, you really have to follow the jacket manufacturer's instructions for this. In the case of Aerostitch® wear they actually provide a complete owners manual with the jacket because of all the features and the different ways to care for the jacket.

Many non-leather jackets can be cleaned using the gentle cycle of your washing machine. And many can have their water-resistant layer reinforced by a periodic application of a water-repellent spray. Like leather though, it is usually a good idea to keep these fabrics free of road dirt and grime.

Pants/Chaps

When talking about pants as protective gear we are starting to cover topics that are ignored by many motorcyclists. But once again it doesn't matter what many people do, that doesn't change the fact that "what you are wearing when you get on your motorcycle is what you will be wearing when you get off." What you wear in the form of pants will provide crash protection to your entire lower body in the event of a mishap, so once again, you should perform a risk assessment to decide where is your comfort level.

Many, many motorcyclists wear no protective gear from the waist down, other than a pair of jeans. You will sometimes even see some bikers wearing shorts. When it comes to shorts it is easy to see what will happen to your skin in the event of even a small slide or fall. What some people forget is that a motorcycle positions you right over an operating engine and its exhaust system inevitably runs by a portion of your leg(s). If naked skin contacts this exhaust system, for even a second, there is a very good chance that you will suffer a serious and painful burn. At least a pair of jeans helps to prevent this, because you usually feel the heat before it gets too severe.

Now, jeans will provide a VERY limited degree of protection in the case of a get-off, but they will likely wear through in a distance to be measured in feet NOT yards (or meters). It is probably more for their protection from heat and their comfort that many riders wear them in the first place. Otherwise, riders must just be less worried about loosing some skin on their legs or, more likely, that most riders just don't think about it. Face it, jeans are comfortable, relatively rugged and you don't look too strange walking into a hotel or restaurant wearing them. At the same time, casual observation shows that many of these riders also have chosen some other form of protection that they wear (even if it is more for protection from the damp or cold) from time to time.

Chaps

▶ See Figure 48

Probably the most popular form of leg protection for motorcyclists is a pair of chaps. These leftovers from the cowboys of American frontier have become part of the image of the American Biker. A pair of chaps is usually, but not always, made of leather, with zippers running down the sides of both legs and one or more snaps at the ends of the legs. The zippers make them easy to put on over your jeans and a pair of boots, then a belt of some sort fastens them around your waist and you are ready to ride.

Chaps will provide very good protection to your legs in the event of a slide. And they provide advantages over some other forms of leg protection, in that they allow free and clear access to pockets in your jeans (and if you are a guy, the front zipper to your jeans which can be very hand on those pit stops).

Fig. 48 For many, chaps offer the blend of style, convenience and protection for which they are looking

But, the free access that chaps provide come at a cost. The cost is just below your waist at the front and the back . . . where the chaps provide NO protection to the rain, the cold or an unfortunate slide. The occasional rain or cold can be dealt with in others ways, but only your decision regarding risk assessment can answer how comfortable you are with the slide. It is one thing to have gravel scrubbed from your butt, but a completely other thing if that slide occurs face down.

Now even with that said, of the two of us, Kevin owns and wears a pair of chaps quite often. They match his style of riding quite well for many applications. But, like Ben, he also owns a pair of complete riding pants, because of the greater protection offered from crashes and the elements.

Pants

▶ See Figure 49

Now riding pants are very similar to what most of us put on, one leg at a time, just about every day. They tend to come in two major forms, the over-pant (designed to be worn over some other pair of shorts or pants) or the plain riding pant (designed to be worn over your choice of underwear or not, if you go commando).

The difference between over-pants and plain riding pants tends to be the lining and the cut. Over-pants are usually cut a little larger (to give room for that pair of jeans underneath) and they are usually not that concerned with the inside material of the pant (i.e. scratchy fabrics, zippers or seams that might irritate your skin). Regular riding pants however tend to be cut to fit truer to your skin (not allowing for additional pairs of pants underneath) and because they will be riding directly against your skin (or underwear), they are almost always finished on the inside with linings.

Riding pants tend to have something else that is a rare find in a pair of chaps, that is body armor. That same armor described for riding jackets is usually found for knee and sometimes even hip protection in riding pants. So if your riding style helped you decide on a jacket that included impact protection, then you will probably be more interested in a pair of riding pants than in a pair of chaps. Unless of course you are lucky enough to have both.

Fig. 49 Those who are most serious about protection will opt for full leather pants, like these from Hein Gericke®

HOW TO SELECT PANTS OR CHAPS

So how do you select a pair of chaps or riding pants? Remember the 4 basics mentioned at the beginning of this section:

1. Choose something you like.
2. Choose something that fits your riding.
3. Choose something that is high quality.
4. Choose something that fits properly.

Choose Something You Like

◆ See Figure 50

Now if you've read what we wrote about helmets and jackets you'll know that style is important because we want you to actually wear the gear that you buy. But, you will probably also remember that we keep harping on visibility. Well, this time we are not going to harp on it, just mention it. When it comes to pants or chaps, the truth is that on many bikes they don't add a whole lot of visibility because they are hidden by portions of the seat, bodywork or even luggage. We are not going to say that they don't help you to be seen under certain circumstances or on certain types of bikes, just that overall, it is off less concern (especially if you have a bright helmet and a jacket with some reflective material . . . you are already 90 percent there in terms of maximizing your visibility).

When it comes to pants or chaps, the more real advantage of a brighter color is that if you do a lot of hot weather riding, once again the brighter colors will help to keep you cool. Of course, if your decision is to buy chaps, good luck finding something that isn't black (or maybe brown).

Choose Gear To Match Your Riding

◆ See Figures 51, 52, 53, 54 and 55

Once again, we are going to ask you to examine the type of riding which you do, or which you plan to do. If you are planning on riding a sport bike,

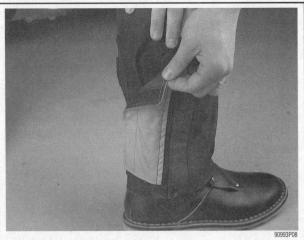

Fig. 50 Although these pants from come in your basic biker black, the adjustment tabs on the legs are covered with reflective material

Fig. 52 One piece suits like the Aerostitch Roadcrafter® are designed to fit quickly and easily over your normal clothing

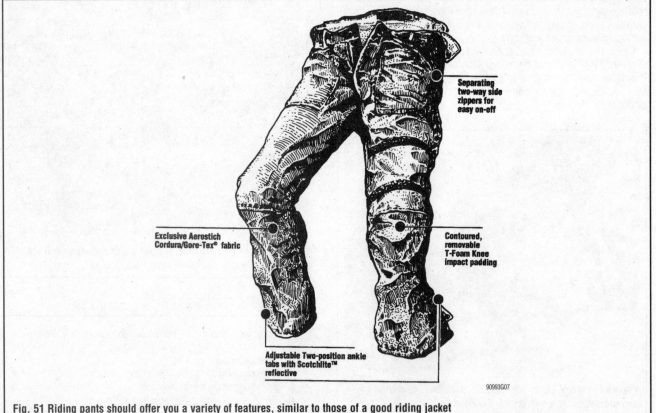

Separating two-way side zippers for easy on-off

Contoured, removable T-Foam Knee impact padding

Exclusive Aerostich Cordura/Gore-Tex® fabric

Adjustable Two-position ankle tabs with Scotchlite™ reflective

Fig. 51 Riding pants should offer you a variety of features, similar to those of a good riding jacket

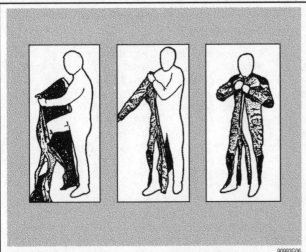

Fig. 53 The Roadcrafter® is designed to quickly step and zipper into it

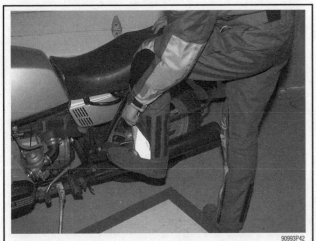

Fig. 54 Pants and one piece suits should be adjustable to fit snug over your boots—the Roadcrafter® uses a reflective panel with hook and loop material for adjustment

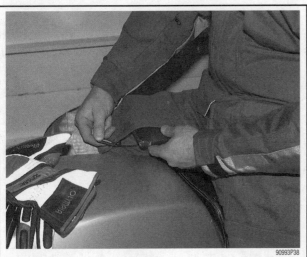

Fig. 55 Just like with jackets, your riding pants should have plenty of pockets for convenience

learning to corner aggressively, go canyon carving, etc. then you are probably going to place more emphasis on crash protection (abrasion and impact resistance) than you would on other features such as number of pockets or even water-resistance. But, if your plans include touring or commuting (which is going to include all sorts of weather) then pants that protect from the elements start to sound really smart.

Many of the features we described for motorcycle jackets are applicable to pants. Look at the various features we listed earlier and decide which ones are most important to you, then look for pants or chaps which fill your needs. Another feature which is more applicable to pants than jackets is whether or not the pants will scratch your bike's bodywork. Remember that a proper riding position includes grabbing the tank with your knees for proper control of the motorcycle and if your chaps have a pair of zippers on the inside and no leather storm flap to protect your tank, or if the riding pants use a rough material on the legs or just the knees (for abrasion resistance), then you will likely scratch the motorcycle's paint over time. Of course, on the other hand, there are tank guards available for many sport bikes to help protect against this very problem. So if you find a pair of pants that really suit your needs, but which have the potential to scratch your baby's paint, you may not be sunk.

Unlike the linings you find in motorcycle jackets, which are usually designed to keep you warm, the linings in motorcycle pants are usually designed more to help you put them on. Since you may slide the pants on with jeans and/or boots on already, a lining usually helps to keep the pants from binding making them more difficult to get into and out of. You don't usually step into chaps, but a lining helps to keep them from binding on your knees when you sit on the bike or if you change positions at all while riding. For cold weather riding, thermal linings are also available for some pants, but for most, you should just get some thermal underwear or fleece ski pant linings.

LEATHER OR NOT?

▶ See Figures 56, 57 and 58

Just like the jackets we described earlier, most bikers wear leather. The smell and feel of leather is simply a part of motorcycling to many. The image is hard to resist, weather it is a black, leather clad biker on a ultra cool cruiser, or a neon leather wearing squid on the hottest sportbike, it just looks and feels right. Competition weight leathers with impact protection still probably provide your best defense from ultra-high speed slides.

Look at your needs and look at what is available in chaps or riding pants. There are some very high quality leathers available for motorcycle riders and you may want pick up a set. But, like jackets, your style of riding might lead you to consider alternatives that offer comparable protection, with advantages you won't find in most leathers. Non-leather motorcycle

Fig. 56 A good set of riding pants, like these leathers from Hein Gericke®, provides the maximum protection in the event of a mishap from abrasion and impact (when equipped with armor)

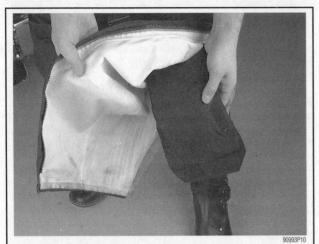

Fig. 57 But materials are available that offer other features as well—The Darien® pants pictured use removable foam armor and are waterproof as well

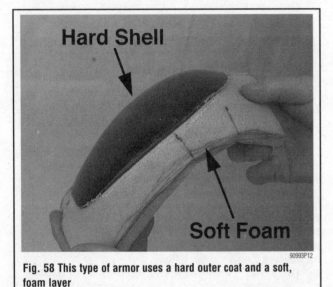

Hard Shell

Soft Foam

Fig. 58 This type of armor uses a hard outer coat and a soft, foam layer

pants are made from a variety of materials like ballistic Cordura® or Coslan® nylons.

Non-leather motorcycle pants usually use a breathable and a waterproof or water-resistant material. There are a few major advantages here. The lighter, breathable materials can be more comfortable to wear and will help to keep you cool on hot days. And, unlike many sealed, nylon or plastic rainsuits, a breathable water-resistant riding pant allows your sweat to escape keeping you significantly more comfortable on rainy summer days. Like their jacket counterparts, these pants are often easier to clean than leathers (no more saddle soap and leather treatment) as they can often be thrown in the washing machine.

Again, we've pictured options here from the company that arguably invented today's modern non-leather rider jacket, but take a look your local shop and in catalogs for other options. The Aerostich® line from the Rider-wearhouse is the standard that many companies measure against. The Darien pants, pictured here contain features including, water-resistant Gore-Tex®, impact protection at the knees (with optional hip protectors available), handy pockets, zippers to access your jeans, zippered legs to help get them over boots, and even reflective materials at the ankle. The Roadcrafter one-piece suit we showed under jackets, also comes in a two-piece version providing the same features, with the versatility to wear either part separately from the other.

Choose Quality Gear

▶ See Figures 59, 60 and 61

The same things we've said about jackets apply to riding pants or chaps. You might find a high quality pair of chaps at a flea-market or at the mall, but NOT LIKELY. Fashion weight leather is not going to protect you as well as heavy, competition weight leather with impact pads (and you are usually not going to find that anywhere but a motorcycle shop or supplier).

When judging the quality of the gear, look for features like zippers which are positioned on the outer portions of the legs, and/or with storm flaps to protect your paint. Check to make sure that a leather garment has a lining which will keep it from binding on your legs, making it more comfortable when riding. Belt buckles can be fashion statements to some, but on riding gear, the more ornate they are, the more likely they would become very uncomfortable during a crash (large, jagged edges should be avoided).

As usual, give preference to gear which is sold by a company that makes its living from motorcyclists. Remember that just buying a name brand does not give you any guarantees, so do your sleuthing. Look for any magazine articles which rate the clothing or the manufacturer. Look at the quality and construction (especially the seams). Even a heavyweight leather riding pant won't do you much good if the seams are not reinforced to keep it from coming apart in a slide.

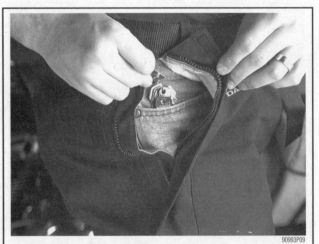

Fig. 59 High quality gear tends to be well thought out, with features like zippers for adjustment and for access to your street clothes

Fig. 60 Another good sign of quality is the inclusion of body armor or protective materials—Some one piece suits use a back protector like the jackets

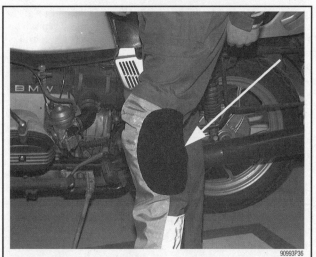

Fig. 61 This suit has optional hook and loop fasteners for knee sliders

Choose Something That Fits Properly

▶ See Figures 62, 63 and 64

Chaps and over-pants are going to fit differently from plain riding pants. When choosing any of them, keep in mind your riding position. If you can, sit on your bike while trying the pants on. They should be long enough so that they still cover your boots when sitting in the riding position (though some people tuck the close cut riding pants into their boots). But, they should not be so long as to trip you when walking.

➥Many leather over-pants and most pairs of chaps can be easily trimmed to the proper length. Even high-quality pairs which have linings usually end the lining a few inches from the bottom, for just this reason. In most instances the extra leather can be neatly cut with a pair of scissors, and no hemming is required. If you find that a hem must be added, your best bet for sewing leather is a saddle and harness maker for horses (these people have the super-heavyweight needles and experience with leather sewing to do the job right).

Now waists can be sensitive issues to some. Look at your weight (and therefore waist) history before buying a tight-fitting pair of riding pants. If you fluctuate in size (and as we get older, most do) then over-pants or chaps may offer you the advantage of allowing extra room for expansion

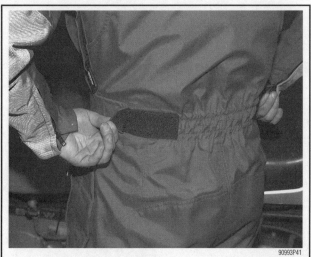

Fig. 62 Pants, chaps or one piece suits should include sufficient adjustments to fit comfortably

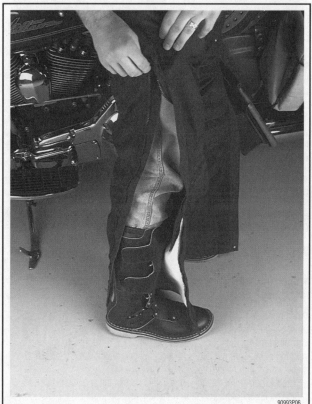

Fig. 63 Almost all will include a full or ¾ length zipper to easily fit over other clothing . . .

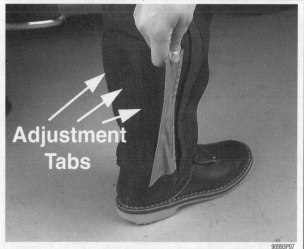

Adjustment Tabs

Fig. 64 . . . and some will include adjustments at the base of the leg so you can tuck them in or snug them over your boots

(and additional layers for cold protection). Some non-leather pants may even come with adjustable waists using snaps or hook and loop expansion panels (these are very handy for allowing a nice fit, or expanding to fit a fleece liner for cold weather).

HOW TO CARE FOR YOUR PANTS OR CHAPS

How you will need to care for your pants or chaps will vary depending on the materials from which it is made. The first thing to do is read the labels or even (in the case of Aerostitch®) the garment owners manual.

The manufacturer will probably give you the best information for the particular materials used in your gear (especially if it is a non-leather riding pant).

The same general advice that we gave for jackets tends to apply to chaps or pants of the same material. One difference, if you ride in foul weather, is the need to clean pants a little more often. The lower legs of your chaps or pants are usually subjected to a lot more road spray than your jacket. After riding through a heavy downpour or even a light rain, it is not unlikely to find that you are COMPLETELY FILTHY from the knees down. Don't try to wipe the dirt off with the garment dry, or you will scratch and tear at the material. Use a damp cloth, or clean it (with saddle-soap for leathers, or as directed for non-leathers).

➡ **It is important to clean grit out of leather garments or it can damage the fibers.**

Boots

WHY SPECIAL MOTORCYCLE BOOTS?

♦ **See Figure 65**

What you wear on your feet when riding is another topic that is sometimes not given its due by motorcyclists. But, think about it for a second, most people have lots of specialized footwear for different purposes, one pair of shoes for the office, another for hiking, a different pair for sports, running or working out. So, why wouldn't you have a special pair of shoes or boots for motorcycling?

A good pair of motorcycle boots will address the specific needs of a motorcyclist, including comfort, functionality and protection. Although you can easily ride a motorcycle in a pair of loafers, the fact is that they won't serve the purpose as well as a pair of boots designed for riding. And, unlike more controversial equipment like helmets, you are more than likely going to wear something on your feet anyway, so why not wear something that offers you some additional benefits.

As usual with motorcycling, an important function of your boots is to provide some protection against injury. It is particularly important that the boots provide support to help protect the ankle. This will help prevent injuries to your feet and joints if your foot is caught by the pegs, shifter or brake pedal in a low speed fall over or slide. Boots should also offer some measure of abrasion protection.

But unlike gear whose sole purpose is crash protection, you will use the most important feature of your boots EVERY time you ride. Probably the single MOST important feature of a good motorcycle boot is an oil resistant sole that will offer you the best traction on varied road conditions.

➡ **Remember that when riding you will often stop the bike (at stop signs, traffic lights or toll booths) and as a motorcyclist you will do something that none of the other drivers on the road do. You will put one or both of your feet on the roadway (sometimes right in a puddle of oil, grease or antifreeze) and you are going to hope that your feet grip enough to support you and your bike.**

Past the key features of a good sole and some measure of crash protection, motorcycle boots can offer a list of additional features similar to that of other motorcycle equipment. Boots can offer you waterproofing (or water resistant materials), walking and riding comfort, and once again, another surface to place some reflective material (though this last one is a stretch, especially if you already have some on the jacket and/or helmet).

HOW TO SELECT A PAIR OF BOOTS

So how do you select a pair of riding boots? Remember the 4 basics mentioned at the beginning of this section:
1. Choose something you like.
2. Choose something that fits your riding.
3. Choose something that is high quality.
4. Choose something that fits properly.

Choose Something You Like

♦ **See Figure 66**

As usual, the easiest of the qualifications for deciding on a good motorcycle boot is to chose something that you like. Remember that if you don't like the way it looks, you probably won't wear it. Of course, the problem can sometimes be finding something that you like the styling of, but that has the functionality of a riding boot. Like so many other types of motorcycle gear, people too often sacrifice functionality for style (while others sacrifice style for functionality).

Before you go making compromises on style or functionality, look for both in one package. One of the best functioning motorcycle boots we've ever used were the old BMW Gore-Tex® boots. I've got a pair with more than 4 years and probably 60,000 miles of riding on them (they still fit great and are still waterproof), but many people didn't like the styling. The old BMW boots were known as Moon Boots, because of their awful resemblance to the boots worn by U.S. Astronauts on Apollo Moon missions. Personally, I don't care about the look, but enough other people did so they were restyled (modernized with more form fitting lines . . . I like the old ones better, but I'm in the minority).

If you really can't find a boot that genuinely matches both the styling and functionality you want, then you can start thinking about compromises.

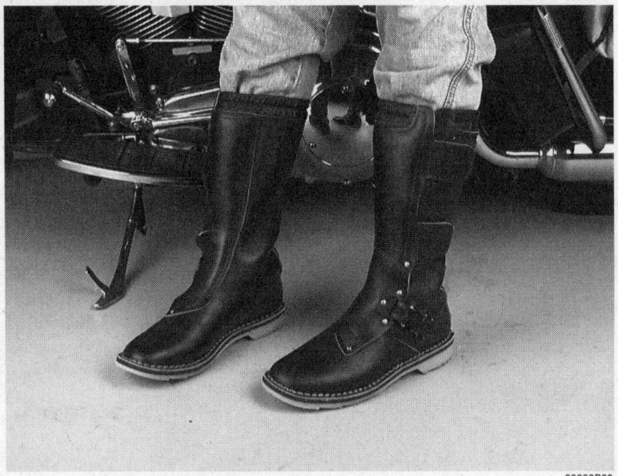

Fig. 65 A good pair of motorcycle boots will be as comfortable as they are durable and functional, these are the Combat Touring boots from the Riderwearhouse

Fig. 66 Reflective material, if you are going to ride at night, there is really no good reason not to have some on everything

Think about your personality when making the decision. Some people are simply more concerned about style while some are more concerned about function. I've found that although I care about style (one of my bikes is a Harley Road King), I also care about function (it is Fuel-Injected, has hard, water-proof bags and a removable windshield). When it comes to boots, if you care enough about the function, an odd styled but very useful boot may look different to you over time (unless it is hot pink, at which point you might never grow to like it . . . of course, there is always leather dye)

Choose Gear To Match Your Riding

Once again, if your only plans are to cruise to the local coffee shop on sunny days, then your needs are significantly different from a dual-sport adventure tourer who plans to make trips through the Mexican Desert. Perhaps these are some extreme examples, but they illustrate the point that is always true in motorcycle gear. Make sure the equipment matches your needs. If all of your riding will be off-road, then an oil-resistant sole is almost pointless, but make sure the sole has a good tread pattern to support you in the dirt.

Waterproofing is not all that common a feature in motorcycling boots (though there are models with Gore-Tex® linings). Most boot manufacturer's seem to feel that the Gore-Tex® is overkill, since people have always applied waterproofing oils and treatments to leather boots with great success. Most people that is, except me. For some reason, I can never seem to properly treat a boot to completely seal out water. Or maybe, I'm just expecting too much (I mean, I am not trying to use the boots as waders to go fly fishing or anything, but I do some serious riding in the rain while touring and commuting, so waterproofing is REALLY important to me).

If you have had success waterproofing work or hiking boots in the past, then you will probably be fine with any high quality leather riding boot and some leather treatment. If you are a complete putz with this subject (like me), then I would suggest a Gore-Tex® lined boot, because the well made ones (like the BMW boots) work REALLY WELL in all day downpours. My boots have NEVER leaked.

Another thing to consider when choosing a boot to match your riding is, does it fit your bike. Some sporty bikes do not give you as much room to get your toes under the shifter and a particularly large boot (including many steel-toed workboots) can make upshifting very difficult. If you can't easily get your foot in and out of position under the shifter, then move on to another boot. You really don't want your foot getting caught under there at each intersection (it can make for embarrassing and potentially dangerous low speed falls at best, or it can help contribute to more serious injuries in the case of an accident.)

There is another question to ask yourself, "are the boots going to match the climate in which I plan to ride?" Will they provide enough insulation on cold morning or winter days or will they provide enough ventilation (to keep from harvesting new and disgusting foot smells) on hot summer days. A good boot will match all of your requirements, but remember that a really warm boot in the winter, may be a bit too warm on really hot summer days.

Choose Quality Gear

▶ See Figure 67

Like with so many things, good motorcycling gear is usually specially designed for motorcycles. Your first place to look for a decent pair of boots is going to be a motorcycle gear supplier. Look at name brands from companies that make MOTORCYCLE gear. It doesn't matter how good a work, hiking or cowboy boot a company produces, if it doesn't understand your specific needs, then the boot will not do as good a job as one which was well thought out for motorcycle use.

Street riders really must pay attention to that all important oil resistant sole. Buy something which will help you hold the bike up at intersections. We know of one particular gentleman who REALLY loved his cowboy boots. He couldn't find anything else that was more comfortable for riding, they didn't interfere with the shifter, they were well treated and waterproofed. His only problem was that they didn't have any grip on slippery pavement (they weren't all that great on dry pavement either). His solution, to have special soles added to them to make the appropriate for riding. This could always

Fig. 67 For street bike riders, the MOST important feature of a motorcycle boot is an oil-resistant sole

be an option if you have found a boot that is perfect in every other way, but it is probably easier to buy one that has already got a decent sole.

Remember to buy boots made of high quality materials with decent workmanship which will provide support and protection in the event of a mishap. And we know that a lot of motorcyclists wear them, but metal adornments, such as buckles or rings (although they can look billy-bad-ass if you are into that sort of thing) are more likely to injure you than protect you in a get-off. Ladies, we probably don't have to tell you that if you are serious about motorcycling, avoid the high and thin heeled fashion boot that, although they will look good on you, will probably get caught on the motorcycle at some point and could help cause an accident. Hey guys and gals, go ahead and buy those good looking biker boots if you want, just wear them when posing, NOT when riding (for your sake).

Choose Something That Fits Properly

▶ See Figure 68

Anyone who has broken-in a new pair of boots at some point in their life knows the pain which can be caused by an ill fitting boot. Luckily, when most boots break-in, the materials stretch and the padding settles so the pain goes away. BUT, if the boot is improperly sized, remember that the pain will probably stay with you as long as you wear the boots.

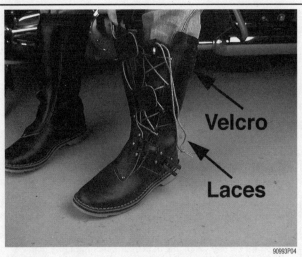

Fig. 68 A boot with lace or tab adjustments will likely be more comfortable than a plain slip-on

A boot which is too small at the time of purchase may not stretch enough to alleviate the pressure (and subsequent pain) in the months of wear that follows. A boot which is too large will move around the foot when walking and will likely cause blisters. Ideally, you want a boot which is SNUG (not tight) when you try it on the first time. If you wear special socks (thick, sweat-wicking sport socks or thin dress socks to wear with the shoes you keep under your desk), then you should be wearing those socks when you try on the boot.

Any motorcyclist will eventually spend some time walking in their boots (at rallies, on vacation, on day-rides to a cool park, or God-forbid . . . walking to the nearest gas station when you pushed it too far on reserve). So it is imperative that you buy a pair of boots which will be comfortable for more than just sitting on a motorcycle.

The best motorcycle boots will offer zippers, laces or hook and loop adjustments to assure proper fit. Remember that a slip-on boot must be loose enough to pull it on and off, and it usually cannot provide the comfort, protection or snug fit that is obtained by adjusting a boot after it is on your foot.

HOW TO CARE FOR YOUR BOOTS

▶ **See Figure 69**

Almost all motorcycle boots are leather, and as such, the same rules of care apply to your boots as to any other leather garment. Keep them clean and keep them fed with natural oils. Saddle soap if the most traditional method of removing dirt, grime and other road mung from your leather boots.

Whenever the boots are exposed to water, from bad weather or from a cleaning, you should immediately coat them with a high quality leather treatment. The water will remove the natural oils which are so important to the leather's well being, allowing the boots to dry-out and crack. Although some cracks in the surface of the leather will happen no matter what, deep cracking will weaken the material and eventually lead to splits (and ruining a good pair of boots).

➡**It is important to clean grit off of leather boots or it can damage the fibers.**

Proper care and treatment is probably more important for your boots than for any other leather garment you own. This is true because of the unusually hard life to which boots are subjected. The heat of the engine (which they often rest against) or exhaust (with which they come into occasional contact), the spray of the road, the bending and twisting under your body weight, all add up to a lot of wear and tear. With proper cleaning and treatment however, you can hold onto a good pair of boots for some time.

90998P11

Fig. 69 Be sure to clean and treat your boots regularly using a quality product made for leather like Lexol®

HOW TO SELECT A PAIR OF GLOVES

Everyone owns a pair of gloves, right? And all gloves have one thing in common, whether they are ski gloves, work gloves, driving gloves, etc. they are all designed to protect your hands. Motorcycle gloves are no different, they are designed to protect your hands from everything you might encounter while riding a motorcycle. And like most types of motorcycle gear, they should be specially designed to live up to all of the varied tasks a motorcyclist will put to them.

A good pair of motorcycle gloves will first and foremost provide some kind of abrasion protection in the event of a slide or crash. But your gloves will likely do a lot more than that. They will protect your hands from the heat of the engine when you fumble under the gas tank for the reserve petcock, or when you reach in between the cylinders on the side of the road to check that hose which looked loose. Your gloves will likely be called upon to help lessen the stinging of rocks or insects which your hands come into contact with while holding the grips going down the highway. They will be asked to keep your hands warm on cool nights (or cold winter days) and dry on rainy afternoons.

In many ways, a good pair of gloves will become another one of your best friends on the road.

So how do you select a pair of riding gloves? Remember the 4 basics mentioned at the beginning of this section:
1. Choose something you like.
2. Choose something that fits your riding.
3. Choose something that is high quality.
4. Choose something that fits properly.

Choose Something You Like

If you've read the rest of this section then you already should have the hang of this category, but just in case you've missed the other gear we've been describing we'll summarize it again. Don't buy gloves which you think LOOK STUPID, you won't wear them. Seems like common sense right? Well, sometime we need to state the obvious.

But there is more to style than just liking the gloves. Remember that highly fashionable gloves with long braids or tassels may look good, but they may also get in the way. Just try riding down the road with one of those tassels caught on something, keeping your left hand from returning safely to the clutch lever, YIKES.

The rule is still simple, buy what you like, just make sure it will work meaning look at the other topics (make sure the glove also fits your needs, is high quality and just plain FITS).

➡**If much of your riding will be taking place in HOT weather, then a light colored glove (white or brightly colored leather) will often keep your hands a little more comfortable than black leather. Perforated gloves and gloves without full fingers can also provide better comfort for hot weather, but remember they come with the price of less protection should they be called upon for the primary purpose of abrasion protection.**

Choose Gear To Match Your Riding

▶ **See Figure 70**

The neat thing about gloves is that compared to other motorcycle gear, they are inexpensive (meaning you may be able to justify owning more than one pair) and they are relatively compact (meaning you should even be able to carry more than one pair with you on trips). We all like to save money and it is really convenient to own just one all purpose pair, so you will probably want to look for that first. But remember that most all purpose garments make compromises and when it comes to gloves you have a real option here to get 2 or 3 specialized pairs each of which does one particular thing VERY WELL.

Fig. 70 Good news, gloves are NOT as expensive as some types of motorcycle gear and you can probably justify owning a variety

SPORT

♦ See Figure 71

If you are planning on some canyon carving or track time, they you would be foolish not to own a good pair of racing weight leather gloves. Heavy leather provides some of the BEST abrasion protection you can buy. Sport riding gloves are often combined with other materials (Kevlar being one of the most popular these days) to provide an additional measure of protection. Though there is some question as to HOW MUCH Kevlar is actually used in a given glove, the very fact that any was used is usually a decent indication that the glove was designed for a sport minded rider.

Any decent sport glove will have reinforced fingers and palms for additional protection. Some palms will be reinforced with additional patches of leather, while others use metal studs (which will in theory slide across pavement will little resistance and little chance of wearing through).

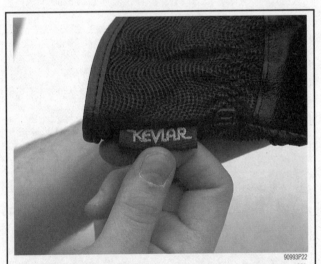

Fig. 71 Materials like Kevlar and competition weight leather will offer abrasion protection

WINTER

♦ See Figures 72 and 73

The first and foremost job of a winter glove is to keep your hands warm. The best winter gloves will have a good layer of insulating material underneath a windproof shell. The shell on many winter gloves is NOT leather, but the better ones will have some sort of leather or ballistic material for the fingers and for the palms (again providing abrasion protection for mishaps).

Many winter gloves will also contain a waterproofing layer (such as Gore-Tex®) which is handy when the cold weather turns wet as well. A medium weight insulated winter glove may be useful for cold summer, spring and fall riding when the weather turns wet. Remember that moisture in the dead of winter usually means snow and you should probably leave the motorcycle at home for this anyway.

✳✳ WARNING

Be careful about oversized or overstuffed winter gloves. If you can't safely operate the controls of the motorcycle, then who cares how warm the glove is, it is useless for riding.

Fig. 72 Decent winter gloves will provide insulation to keep your hands warm, protection to keep them dry and the ability to still move your fingers and control the bike

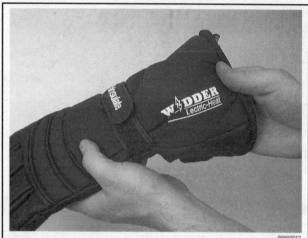

Fig. 73 Gloves with thick insulation are good, but when too thick can interfere with controls, that is when electric gloves offer a significant advantage

Fig. 75 . . . as are fingerless gloves, but REMEMBER that they do provide a LOT less protection to your hands

SUMMER

♦ See Figures 74 and 75

The challenge of a good summer glove is to provide protection to your hand while keeping your hands from sweating to the point of discomfort. There are various methods of achieving this including, bright colors (to reflect heat), lighter leather, breathable materials, perforated materials and fingerless gloves.

❋❋ WARNING

Light leathers, perforated materials and fingerless gloves will provide LESS protection than their heavier, full cut alternatives. This is a good time to think about comfort vs. risk assessment. You'll have to be an adult here and make a decision that you

can live with. If you decide on lighter, cooler materials, at least double check that there is a reinforced palm to provide some abrasion protection.

Some lighter materials may also offer waterproofing, especially the non-leather breathable materials (ballistic nylon and Gore-Tex®). A light weight, but waterproof glove can become invaluable on a long trip, should the weather take a turn for the worse. There are few things more miserable than to be prepared with good waterproof rainwear (jackets, pants and boots), and then to have your cold hands, squishing water out from the fingers of your gloves every time to reach for your bike's hand levers.

GEL

♦ See Figure 76

Motorcycle glove manufacturer's have taken a lesson from mountain bikers and many now offer a variety of gloves with a gel padding in the palm. This can be especially nice on bikes which vibrate heavily through the han-

Fig. 74 Lighter leather gloves, with perforation to improve breathing are good choices for warmer weather . . .

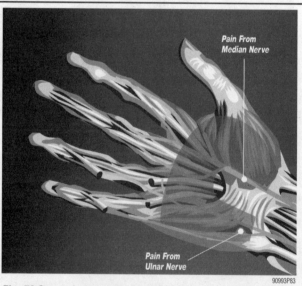

Pain From Median Nerve

Pain From Ulnar Nerve

Fig. 76 Some glove manufacturers, like Olympia®, have learned a lesson from mountain bikers and are making gloves with gel inserts to cushion the nerves in your hands and reduce pain or numbing

dlebars. With these types of gloves comfort can be increased on both high-revving buzzy sportbikes which can transmit a high-frequency, numbing vibration to your hands, and some heavy-throbbing, solid-mounted cruisers which can transmit a low-frequency, but equally numbing vibration.

Choose Quality Gear

◗ See Figures 77 and 78

FUNCTION

Can you ride with a pair of cloth work gloves? Sure, but don't expect them to stay together in a slide. Like most motorcycle gear, the majority of the best stuff was specially designed for motorcycling. You are going to find the best quality gear from shops or catalogs that cater to serious riders.

Look for products from companies that specialize in motorcycle riding apparel. Heavy race weight leather or other high quality ballistic materials are good signs that a company is serious about its gear. Fingers which are constructed of multiple sections, allowing the hand to curl around the grip

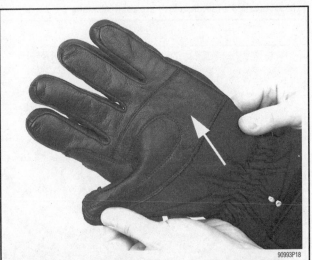
Fig. 77 Probably the single most important sign of a quality motorcycle glove is a thick, abrasion resistant palm

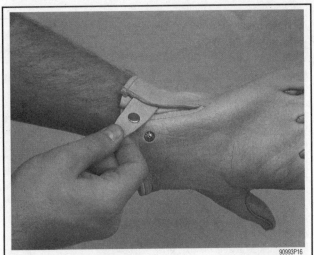
Fig. 78 Snaps, zippers or hook and look adjustments help to seal the glove to your jacket, helping to keep your whole body warm

without stretching the material will allow for the best fit. Reinforced areas on the palm and the fingers are also good hints that the glove is designed for function and not just fashion.

FASHION

In different parts of the U.S. and around the world, it is known by different names. In Los Angeles, CA it is has been called "Hollywood Posing." In Phoenix, AZ it is sometimes referred to as "Scottsdale Syndrome." In rural Pennsylvania it is sometimes called "New Hope Disease" (referring to an arty little town on the Delaware river which was once a popular place for bikers to be seen). No matter where you live, there is probably a term for people who are more concerned with look than reality.

There are many bikers who believe that a motorcycle glove should first and foremost be BLACK and MUST have fringe or chrome buckles or braids. These gloves are usually found in biker "lifestyle" shops or flea markets and NOT in shops for serious motorcyclists. They are usually fashion and nut function. Although these might be decent gloves for looking good, they are not usually the best choice for riding.

➡**We are not saying that black motorcycle gloves are no good (because of fashion, MOST motorcycle gloves, even many of the very good ones are black). We are also not saying that a stereotypical "biker" styled glove won't be high quality, just that in our experience, most are designed more with fashion in mind than function. They often lack the additional stitching, padding, race weight leather and other important protective qualities of a good motorcycle glove. But again, it is a risk assessment issue on which you will have to make your own mind up.**

Choose Something That Fits Properly

◗ See Figure 79

Have you ever tried to pull a zipper or work a throttle in a glove that doesn't fit! If you have too much fabric in the fingers, then you will not be able to grip anything. With gloves that are too big your hands will be stumbling over the levers, grips and controls of your motorcycle. On the other side of the coin, a glove that is too small will pull back on your fingers, fighting your grip. A small glove will make it hard and uncomfortable to maintain your grip of the bike's controls, especially the throttle.

Another thing to consider is whether or not the glove is a gauntlet. A gauntlet-styled glove can be worn over the ends of your jacket sleeves (effectively blocking all air flow). A glove which fits over the sleeves like

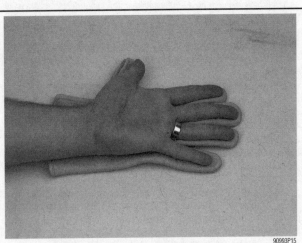
Fig. 79 A glove should be JUST barely larger than your hand, if it is too tight or too loose it will probably make it difficult to work the bike's controls

that is great in the winter because it helps seal out the cold air, but it can be not so great in the summer, if you are looking for a cooling air flow.

HOW TO CARE FOR YOUR GLOVES

▶ **See Figure 80**

Most gloves are leather, or at least contain a leather shell. As usual, the routine to keep leather healthy involves periodic cleaning and treatment to replenish its natural oils. There are some gloves which use ballistic materials and these should be cared for according to their manufacturer's instructions.

Fig. 80 To help keep your gloves in best condition, replenish the natural oils in the leather using a treatment like Lexol®

Eye Wear (Protection)

HOW TO SELECT EYE WEAR

▶ **See Figures 81 and 82**

If you have decided on a full face helmet, then your decisions are easy, be sure to buy a couple of face shields which were designed for your helmet. There, you are done, next topic. But wait one second, before you go. Remember that even if you only plan on riding during the day, things happen and you could find yourself out after dark. So, be sure to have at least one tinted and one clear shield. And, if you are planning on riding in cold weather, you might want something that is fog-free. And then there are those high visibility tint shields. Ohhhhhh forget it, you better read this whole section just to be sure.

And, as for those of us who like to wear open face helmets, we have some important decisions to make. Let's face it, without your eyesight, motorcycling would be VERY DIFFICULT. Think about it before you hop on your bike wearing nothing but a pair of prescription glasses or a stylish pair of Ray-Bans®.

The first and foremost thing that your eye wear MUST do is protect your eyes. This is not just from wind (and dust or dirt), but all the other nasties that you run into on the road. Ever pull into a gas station and decide you really have to clean your windshield? Ever get a crack in your windshield from a pebble kicked up by the car in front of you? Now let's imagine your car didn't have a windshield, YEP, you got it, was I that obvious? That would be the same as riding a motorcycle, and it would have been my face that stopped the rock, I get it.

Fig. 81 Yes Johanna, your shades are stylish, and if they are impact resistant too, then they are good for riding . . .

Fig. 82 . . . but if they are not, then you are better off wearing them under a face shield

✳ CAUTION

Using improper eye wear might lead to a NASTY accident. All it takes is for one stinging piece of dust to distract you long enough to miss that truck which just pulled out and . . . Also, be aware that many areas have laws regarding eye wear, check with your local authorities for standards to be sure that you are not breaking the law.

It's time for a quick, self-effacing story here. Last summer, on a BEAUTIFUL, warm day, I had the windshield off the King and was really enjoying the wind in my face. I was riding through a cool, wooded area just looking around when I glanced to my left only to be struck, under my stylish sunglasses in the right eye. Surprise turned to near panic when I heard the object buzzing under the glasses and then panic turned to OUCH!!!!!!!!!!! as it stung me just next to the edge of my right eye. Luckily I kept the bike on the road as I reached under the glasses, grasped the little SOB (who I was now cursing quite vividly) and threw him away from my face. At the next stop I bought a drink to get some ice to place on the now swollen eye.

Could have been worse I told myself. Owww, I should have worn the riding glasses and not the John Lennon shades. Oooooooooooops.

So how do you select suitable eye wear? Remember the 4 basics mentioned at the beginning of this section:

1. Choose something you like.
2. Choose something that fits your riding.
3. Choose something that is high quality.
4. Choose something that fits properly.

Choose Something You Like

Do we really have to cover this again. OK, in case you used the index and skipped the earlier topics in this section. Don't buy eye wear that you think looks DUMB, you are more likely to just bag it and take unnecessary chances if you hate your gear.

Also remember, that although those little, round, mirrored spectacles may have cost you a couple-of-hundred, they may offer ABSOLUTELY ZIP in the way of impact protection and it is YOUR eyesight.

Choose Gear To Match Your Riding

No matter what type of helmet you have, you should remember that although you may plan to ride only during the day, light conditions will vary. You could get caught in a storm, you might ride through a cool canyon or dark forest. Even on bright sunny days, you may find that tinted eye wear suddenly has become more of a danger than a benefit, so make sure you always keep some clear eye wear handy too.

Also, remember that your needs will vary based on the type of bike you are riding. If you've got a full dresser and/or a big windshield, then your chances of getting plowed with bugs or rocks are significantly less than if your head is hanging over the instruments of a naked bike.

✳✳ CAUTION

A word of warning on some tinted eye wear. Be careful to familiarize yourself with the tint before using it on the bike. Some types of tint will hide sand or gravel on particular road surfaces. This could lead to some unexpected traction difficulties if you didn't know that loose dirt was in a turn because the tinted eye wear hid it from you.

FULL FACE HELMETS

◗ See Figure 83

If you've got a clear shield and a decent pair of sunglasses (which are comfortable under your helmet) then you probably have everything you need to ride with a full face helmet. But, you will probably find a tinted shield (regular or high visibility) is a real nice addition for serious riding. It is never a bad idea to have an extra face shield when you are talking a long trip.

Also, some shields are available in anti-fog versions which are VERY handy for winter riding, cold mornings and even rain storms. Remember that if you have to open the face shield to let in air (to defog the shield) you are letting in other things as well (the cold, the rain, or the other nasties that you were wearing a full face helmet to keep out in the first place).

➡ **There are some products available to reduce or eliminate fogging of your face shield. Probably the best known is the Fog City Fog Shield® which is easily and permanently applied to a helmet face shield. The Fog Shield provides a thin, clear barrier which prevents fogging under most conditions, allowing you to keep the face shield closed (sealing out whatever nasty you are avoiding).**

OPEN FACE (¾ & ½) HELMETS

◗ See Figures 84 and 85

If you wear an open face helmet (even if you have a fairing or a windshield), you will have to take care to avoid injury to the eyes. One popular method with bikers (especially ones on naked cruisers, with no windshield

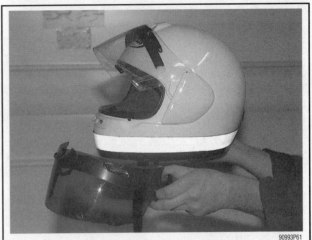

Fig. 83 One advantage of full face helmets is that the manufacturers also produce high quality, impact resistant shields (in clear and tinted versions)

Fig. 84 Safety glasses or goggles that will protect from flying debris and keep your eyes from watering are best with open face helmets

Fig. 85 Probably the best eye protection for open face helmets is a face shield which can be attached to the snaps on most of these helmets

or other protection), is to wear a pair of goggles. A good pair of goggles with impact resistant lenses will effectively seal your eyes from most dirt, debris and bugs, providing you decent protection.

But, some people don't want to ride down the road looking like a welder gone mad. There are many types of sport glasses that are available which provide significant protection and look halfway decent too. Some of the better sports glasses are available with prescription lenses or with frames that hold prescription lenses behind the outer protective lens. The best types will have easily replaceable outer lenses (so that you can replace a damaged lens and/or you can switch the tinted lens for a clear lens when the sun goes down).

Many open face helmets have snaps across the brow to install a face shield. Though most people who wear open face helmets don't use these all of the time (they sort of defeat the purpose of having an open face helmet in the first place), they can be VERY handy for foul weather. Keeping one in your saddlebag can be a God-send should some unexpected rain start to pound down on you. It can be surprising how much rain can sting at speed.

Choose Quality Gear

This one is easy. Look, if you buy it on the boardwalk or from the with the table on the street corner, then it probably isn't going to be impact resistant. Got it? Make sure the face shield, goggles or glasses are intended for sport use like motorcycling and that the lenses are made of an impact resistant or shatterproof material. The only thing worse than having an eye doctor or ER surgeon dig a pebble out of your eye would be to have the same person dig a piece of plastic or glass out instead.

Choose Something That Fits Properly

If you've got a full face helmet, then buy the right shield for it. Don't try to make a different model shield fit, it probably won't. If the shield can close fully and seal the opening in the helmet when closed, then you are probably set.

If you are wearing an open face helmet, then you've got to worry a little more about fit. Goggles are usually adjustable and have straps so they can be snugged to your face. But glasses usually rely on their arms and your ears. A loose fitting pair of glasses can be blown right of your face when you look over your shoulder to see if the lane is clear. Good sport glasses will usually have a retaining strap or stronger arms to help prevent this, but test new glasses out in a safe place before risking them on the highway.

No matter what type of helmet you wear, if you use contact lenses, you are going to want to minimize the airflow over your eyes. The greater the windflow, the greater the rate of evaporation and the quicker your lenses will dry out.

HOW TO CARE FOR YOUR EYE WEAR

The first rule is ALWAYS clean your eye wear with a soft, damp cloth. You may be able to get away with glass cleaner and paper towels on some surfaces and not on others, but a soft damp cloth will never harm your eye wear. If you want to use glass cleaner, first check with the eye wear manufacturer (or any instruction they provided with the eye wear). Second, try it on a corner (which is not important for vision).

Products like Rain-X® can be FANTASTIC on the face shield of some helmets, but some shields are completely destroyed by it. SO, never use a product on your eye wear without first testing it on an inconspicuous area. When it comes to face shields, try it on a small patch of area that is not used to look through (such as where it attaches to the helmet).

Rainsuits

HOW TO SELECT A RAINSUIT

▶ **See Figure 86**

We've said it throughout this book already. We don't care HOW well you plan, in motorcycling there are just too many things that are beyond your control. If you are going to ride seriously, leaving the ten mile radius around your house (and you don't live in the desert), then you are eventu-

Fig. 86 Three different approaches to rainwear, Left: an Aerostitch® suit, Middle: a nylon rainsuit and Right: army surplus plastic overalls

ally going to need some protection from wet weather. There are fewer more miserable experiences than riding in cold, wet jeans (yuck!).

Now some people will just pack the poncho they use when fishing, or that they picked up at the corner drug-store. The problem is that those ponchos weren't designed for high speed winds and they can do a lot of flapping in the breeze. This flapping will tear the poncho apart and may damage the finish on your bike's paint at best, or could get caught in a drive belt/chain or rear tire at worst.

Also, remember that there are riding jackets and pants available (especially most of the non-leather ballistic material clothing) which offer significant water resistance or waterproofing which might make the need for a rainsuit a moot point. You might want to decide on your jacket and riding pants before buying a rainsuit (if you think you might be leaning towards the non-leather wear).

So how do you select gear to protect you from the rain? Remember the 4 basics mentioned at the beginning of this section:
1. Choose something you like.
2. Choose something that fits your riding.
3. Choose something that is high quality.
4. Choose something that fits properly.

Choose Something You Like

▶ **See Figure 87**

Nobody wants to look like the Pillsbury Do-Boy® (I hope) or Joe Wharfman the Dockworker (I think?) when riding their motorcycle, so unless you have some deep seated desire to look like a pastry chef or a fisherman, then you probably want to avoid rainsuits that make you look that way.

Unfortunately, this desire to not look like a total dweeb has led to a lot of people wearing black rainsuits. HELLO, CHECK PLEASE, IS THERE ANYONE HOME OUT THERE. Let's think about this for a second. It is cold, wet and miserable. The idiots in traffic all around you are having trouble seeing through their streaked windshields because they keep forgetting to replace the old wiper blades. Luckily a few of them have actually had the foresight to turn their headlights on, when one runs right over your bike while changing lanes. They couldn't "SEE" you because were wearing BLACK IN THE RAIN. DUHHHHHHHH!

Ok, now that I've gotten that out of the way. The good news is that more and more of the black rainsuits are at least coming with reflective Scotchlite® panels and stripes, which could help the visibility matter greatly. Also, there are more rainsuits available these days in a color other than black. Once again, we're not suggesting that everyone needs to be a human parrot here, but one or two brighter colors (even a light gray) is an improvement over BLACK in the rain. Just remember that a little contrast works to your advantage.

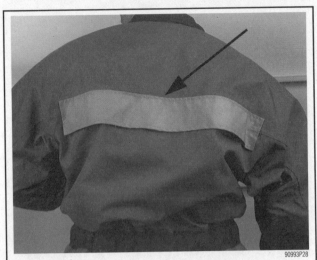

Fig. 87 Reflective materials can help SAVE YOUR LIFE, don't waste money on a rainwear that doesn't have any

So as usual, buy what you like (cause it won't do any good if you're not wearing it), but learn to like something with a little bit of visibility.

Choose Gear To Match Your Riding

▶ See Figure 88

If you have a waterproof jacket, then maybe all you'll need is a pair of rainpants to keep in your saddle or tank bag. Even if you have waterproof riding pants, if you don't plan on wearing them all of the time, an inexpensive rainpants can be rolled-up and carried on the bike for that one occasion when you need them.

If a lot of your riding takes place in cold, nasty, foul weather, then you may wish to opt for an insulated rainsuit. But, if your riding may lead to hot, sticky rain showers, then something breathable is going to offer better comfort (just keep in mind that on a hot, sticky summer night, with rain and humidity in the 100% area, then nothing is going to be particularly comfortable, breathable or not).

You'll have to decide between 1-piece and 2-piece suits. We've often heard that 1-piece suits are supposed to be more storm worthy. Something about there not being much of a chance for water getting in between the jacket and pants. But our experience has proven otherwise with a few different suits. Depending on your riding position, a 1-piece suit may allow water to puddle

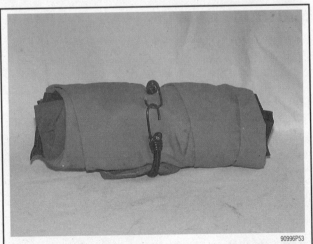

Fig. 88 If you plan on long-distance touring a rainsuit that rolls into a nice tight bundle will not waste much of your precious cargo room

in a bunched crotch area and seep through zippers and seams. Also, the increased difficulty which sometimes comes with pulling these monsters over damp leathers may stress and tear at seam. Add to this a major downside that they are either ON or OFF. If your own a 1-peice suit, you can never wear only the jacket or pants, (like putting the pants on when rain is threatening and only pulling over to add the jacket if the rain gets heavy enough).

A 2-piece suit is nice because of the versatility. You can wear only the pants or jacket (whether you are riding or not, the jacket can be used as a windbreaker or rain coat). If it rained last night, you can put only the pants on to deal with the road spray until it dries out. You can also find more creative ways to pack a 2-piece since each piece folds or rolls into a smaller package than the 1-piece rainsuit. Your only concern with a 2-piece suit should be whether or not it leaks at the waist and, as long as the hem on the jacket is long enough, this should not be an issue. As a matter of fact, if the hem is below your crotch, it may prevent water from pooling and leaking through zippers, a definite advantage over 1-piece suits.

Choose Quality Gear

If the material feels really cheap and the price supports your suspicion, then walk away from it. Chances are, light and cheap rainsuits won't survive their first real day of riding in the rain. Even if a cheap suit makes it through one or two storms, it will probably tear when you are scrambling to put it on at the side of the road with the rain already coming down and the real downpour about to start (usually when you are in the middle of no where, with hours to go before you sleep . . .).

Good signs that a rainsuit will last are those same details we talked about with jackets and pants. Look for a rainsuit with a lining (it doesn't have to be insulated, just a lining which makes is easier to slide the material over damp leather). Storm flaps which help seal zippers (the better storm flaps are usually equipped with hook and loop fasteners to hold them closed over the zippers) are signs that a rainsuit is really designed to keep you dry. Good suits will have plenty of other handy features such as a variety of pockets, bright colors and or reflective materials and, if you are buying a REALLY good suit, heat resistant panels in the legs (to help prevent it from becoming a melted puddle on your engine).

Choose Something That Fits Properly

The key to a decent rainsuit is that it must be big enough to fit over your riding gear (leather jacket and chaps or pants), yet still be small enough to prevent excessive flapping or tearing. If a large rainsuit balloons up too badly, it will give more places for water to find its way in. If it is too oversized you may find yourself tripping over it walking out to the bike, or even worse, slipping on it at an intersection.

HOW TO CARE FOR YOUR RAINSUIT

Whenever you wear a rainsuit the first thing you want to do when you get home is to hang it up in the shower or the garage and let it dry. Even if most of it seems dry already, don't just roll it up and stuff it in a bag, you will be surprised just how bad it can smell when you unroll it at a later date and find it was still damp when you put it away.

If you are completely filthy from road crud, take a moment to rinse the suit off with a hose or even in the shower. If you like, you don't have to take it off to rinse it (remember it is designed to keep you dry). Try to avoid wiping the dirt off it once it is dry because you risk scratching or tearing it.

If the suit is made from Gore-Tex® or some other breathable material, follow the manufacturer's instructions regarding cleaning. Suits like this will vary from the type which can be placed in the washing machine to ones which must be carefully hand rinsed.

Electric Garments/Cold Weather Gear

▶ See Figures 89 and 90

If you put your bike away during winters because you live in a part of the country where the weather gets cold and uninviting, then there may be a way to lengthen your riding season. As a matter of fact, barring snow and ice, we've found that even here in cold Pennsylvania, we can get away without storing our bikes for the winter, largely thanks to owning the right gear.

There are a few things which can make cold weather riding anything from bearable to plain old fun. The first is to make sure your bike is properly equipped (good tires, properly adjusted suspension, and MOST IMPORTANTLY, some form of windshield of fairing). There really is no substitute to just keeping your body out of the cold wind. You and your clothing won't have to work as hard at keeping you warm if you just cut the wind with the proper motorcycle windshield.

The next key to cold weather riding is proper riding gear. A good full face helmet, a high quality jacket, pants and boots which also cut the wind and insulate you will make a tremendous difference. But even when all of this is combined, you may still find a 30 or 40 mile commute or 100 mile weekend ride is tough with snow melting on the sides of the road. The answer then becomes electric garments.

The first time I tried Widder's Lectric Gloves® I nearly exploded from happiness, finally I could make my commute without losing feeling in my hands. I have actually been using a pair of their gloves for years, with great success. I'm telling you that these gloves made a SIGNIFICANT difference in my outlook during countless December toy runs and early January rides. But they also became steady companions for Fall and Spring rides (especially those early morning and late evening commutes). WOW!!!!! I never thought cold weather riding could be so comfortable.

To take matters further, Widder® supplied us with some additional equipment for testing when working on this book. Add the vest to the equation and you are set for just about any weather (at least any weather that the motorcycle will start in). The Widder® vest provides the all important warming of your central core which actually makes the rest of your gear feel like it is doing a better job from your jacket to your boots. One very cool (uhhh, make that warm) feature of the vest we tested was a heated collar that brought heat right up to the base of your neck, just below the helmet.

One product which Widder® did not offer was a fully sleeved electric jacket liner, so we were provided one by Gerbing®, which provided similar results (with the added benefit of warming your arms as well). This sleeved liner proved to be a real advantage on bikes with small windshields or which had no windshield at all (leaving your arms right out in the breeze).

Fig. 89 Nothing matches the warmth or comfort of an electric vest and a pair of electric gloves on a cold day—this combination from Widder® shows the gloves, wiring harness with thermostat and vest with heated collar

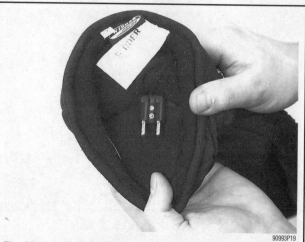

Fig. 90 Most electric gloves are attached to your bike's battery using easy to connect plugs like these banana plugs found on Widder® gear

✳✳ CAUTION

One **VERY IMPORTANT POINT** to make here is that electric components can fail (whether it is the accessory jack, the wiring or the garment itself). Although we have had **NO** problems with the test gear, the fact is that they **COULD** stop working with little notice, so **DO NOT** attempt a long distance ride without enough layers or other gear to keep you warm, **JUST IN CASE.** You'd probably survive a trip home from work if the harness shorted out one day or the fuse blew. But, wouldn't it suck to freeze to death on a Montana plain because you accidentally cut the wiring harness on the muffler clamp while checking the rear chain.

HOW TO SELECT COLD WEATHER GEAR

So how do you select an electric garment? Remember the 4 basics mentioned at the beginning of this section:
1. Choose something you like.
2. Choose something that fits your riding.
3. Choose something that is high quality.
4. Choose something that fits properly.

Choose Something You Like

▶ See Figure 91

Let's face it, most electric garments are worn under your other riding gear so style is not particularly important here. Unless of course someone is dumb enough to make an electric vest in only one color (hot pink), in which case you probably would think twice about buying it anyway.

Of course electric gloves and chaps are a little different since they will probably be seen. Then again, most types that we have seen were not radically styled and would look decent with most riding gear. And it is really hard to escape the fact that even if someone does decide to poke fun at you for how your gear looks, chances are they are freezing their obnoxious asses off in poser gear anyway, while you are riding along toasty. Ohhhhh, what was that? You want to stop for coffee. Nahh let's keep going, I could easily do another hundred miles. Besides, coffee's just gonna make me want to stop too often anyway.

Choose Gear To Match Your Riding

There are two things to keep in mind when selecting electric riding apparel, match your needs AND your motorcycle's alternator output.

Fig. 91 As opposed to the heated vest (which seems to be the most popular electric garment) some manufacturers, like Gerbings® produce heated jacket linings which offer the advantage of heated sleeves

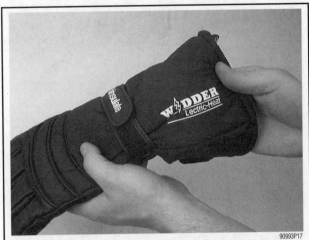

Fig. 93 An electric vest or jacket may be enough, but if not, consider a pair of gloves to keep your hands warm too, especially on unfaired bikes

ASSESS YOUR NEEDS

▶ See Figures 92 and 93

When it comes to your needs, we suggest a conservative approach. Start by riding with your best non-electric gear and see what gets cold. Make sure that you have blocked the wind as effectively as you can. On some motorcycles you can add plastic or vinyl covers over the crash bars to reduce wind flow over your feet. A helmet lining or balaclava will help a lot, and make sure you seal the helmet to your jacket (the BEST method we have found for this is the Aerostitch® wind triangle).

Then, once you have decided that electric garments are the way to go, start with a vest or jacket lining. The act of warming your core will help to keep the rest of your body warmer as blood carries that heat out towards your extremities. If the vest alone does not do the trick, you might want to consider gloves and/or a chaps. We have found that the vest should be sufficient for most situations, but only if you have high quality gear in the form of pants, boots and gloves (as we described in earlier sections). If your hands are not behind some form of windshield or fairing, these are the next likely to get cold (even with a good regular pair of winter gloves) and many companies, like Widder® offer electric gloves to be used with their vest. This combination can make you feel right at home even in sub-freezing temperatures.

Fig. 92 Although not a piece of electric gear, wind triangles, like this one from Aerostitch® can seal your helmet to your jacket, keeping you warm

ASSESS YOUR BIKE'S ABILITY

Your bike has one, important limiting factor when it comes to electric apparel, its alternator output. The simple fact is that if you add enough accessories, you will eventually start consuming more electricity than your bike can produce (you may notice the result if your headlight starts to fade once you have turned on all of your toys). The good news is that virtually all modern bikes have alternators with sufficient capacity to run one or two pieces of electric clothing. It is just that if you ride a dresser with 12 racks of additional running lights all around, a radio, your normal lights, etc, you may exceed your alternator's capacity and slowly drain the battery to the point where the bike will stop running. Our advice is simple, turn off a few of those extra running lights if the headlight starts to dim (otherwise you should be fine).

➡Some models of older bikes are notorious for underpowered charging systems. Many of the BMW airhead boxers (right into their last decade or so of production) may have difficulty keeping up with the demand of electric clothing, once the engine RPM drops below a certain point. On models like this you've got two options; Many bikes with noted charging problems have higher output alternator kits available. And, you can always keeps the revs up (and watch the headlight, if it goes from dim to bright at a certain point, you know where the revs should be).

Choose Quality Gear

▶ See Figures 94 and 95

There aren't that many makers of electric riding apparel. But with that said, even fewer of them have a reputation. Ask around, and look at any articles or reviews you can get your hands on. The two companies who supplied samples for our testing both have EXCELLENT reputations. We have even had some dealing with one of their customer service groups (a few years ago, before we were even working on this book, Widder® was kind enough to repair a glove at no charge which was out of their warranty period, but had developed an open in the heater grid . . . impressive).

Like with most gear, if the company has a name it has earned in the motorcycle industry, that is a good indication of the quality merchandise they sell.

Choose Something That Fits Properly

When it comes to proper fit, most electric garments should fit like their non-heated counterparts. Gloves should not be too big or too small. Chaps or pants should fit comfortably over your jeans. The difference is with vests or with jacket linings. Most manufacturer's recommend that the garment be

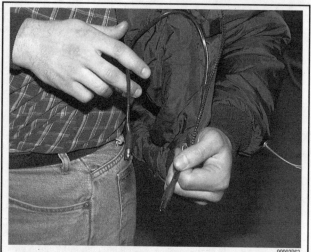

Fig. 94 One of the best thought out features we have seen with electric garments is a wiring harness built into the jacket

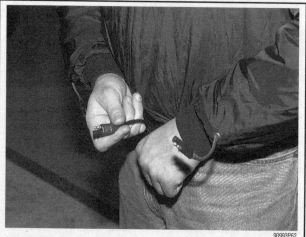

Fig. 95 The wiring for the gloves on this Gerbings® jacket is in the sleeves which keeps you from having to feed the wires through the jacket every time you put it on

comfortable but snug (to prevent cold air from finding its way between you and the garment). You probably want to leave additional room between the garment and the jacket for other insulation layers, especially if you want to be prepared for the worst, should you unexpectedly be unable to use the electric heater one day.

HOW TO CARE FOR YOUR COLD WEATHER GEAR

Because electric apparel has a few features most of your other riding gear lacks (like wires and heating elements) it is important that you follow the manufacturer's instructions closely. Most garments however can be washed. You should periodically inspect the wiring for breaks in the insulation and take care with when connecting or disconnecting it. Never pull directly on a wire, ALWAYS grasp and pull the wiring connector. A little dielectric grease on the connectors won't do any harm and may help make the connections easier to fasten and unfasten.

Any electric gloves which contain leather shells should be treated, just like normal leather. Clean it carefully and treat it with Lexol® or another appropriate leather treatment to restore the material's natural oils.

INSTALLING AN ACCESSORY OUTLET

◆ See Figures 96 thru 102

If you are riding a late-model BMW, then the factory was kind enough to take care of this for you in most cases. But, on most other bikes, you are on your own for installation. One neat feature about installing an accessory jack is that it instantly gives you an easy way to check your battery (using a voltmeter) or to attach a Battery Tender® or other battery maintaining device when you are not riding.

Before installing the outlet, figure out where it should go in relation to the apparel. Start by putting on all of your riding gear and climbing into the saddle. Look at where the wiring harness hangs and where it would be most convenient to locate the outlet. It is really nice to be able to plug and unplug the jack from the seated position, but this is not possible on all models and on some you will have to plug in before climbing on board.

Once you have a good idea where you would like the outlet to go, you will have to access your battery for installation. On many models this will include removing sidecovers, fairings and/or seats. Check your owners manual, as it usually gives you some idea how to get at the battery.

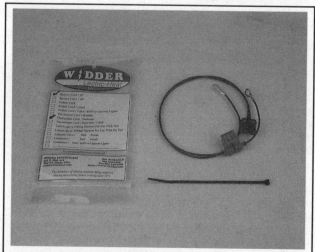

Fig. 96 Most electric garments will come with an adapter that is wired to the battery and becomes your accessory outlet

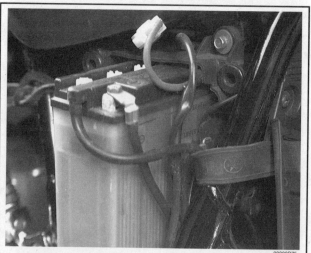

Fig. 97 To install the outlet, start by accessing the battery and disconnecting the wiring

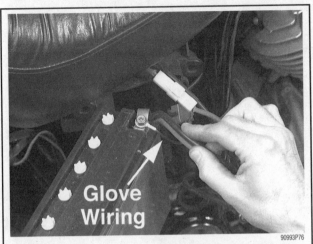

Fig. 98 Place the wiring on the battery cable retaining bolt, but make sure it does not get between the cable and battery (put it on the backside of the cable, closer to the bolt)

1. Make sure the ignition switch is OFF and remove the key.

2. Locate your bike's battery and remove any components necessary to access it. On most Harleys this means removing the seat and/or the battery sidecover. On many Japanese and European bikes this will mean removing the seat and one or more sidecovers. Many bikes with bodywork will have to shed all or part of the fairing for access.

3. Once the battery is accessible, loosen the negative battery cable by turning the retaining bolt counterclockwise. Usually this can be done with a screwdriver, wrench or a socket. The wrench or socket is really the best method to make sure you don't strip the terminal bolt, but it really depends on the amount of access you have.

4. Once the negative cable is disconnected it is always a good idea to wrap some electrical tape around it or put a small plastic baggie over the end to prevent it from touching the battery again and completing a circuit.

5. Loosen the bolt and remove the positive battery cable from the battery. Be careful never to short the battery by allowing the wrench or other tool to bridge the gap between the terminals.

6. Place the accessory outlet wiring over the battery terminal bolts, then insert the bolts back through the cables and into the battery. Start with the positive cable. If there is an inline fuse in the accessory outlet wiring, be sure to connect it to the positive battery cable.

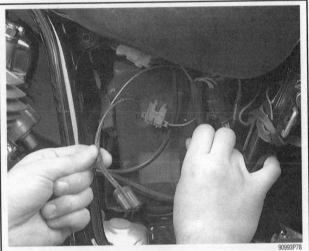

Fig. 99 Route the wiring so that it will not be damaged by rubbing on other components in use

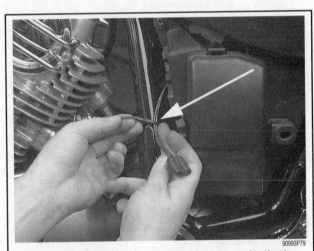

Fig. 101 Once you have finished, use one or more wire ties to hold the outlet securely in place—on this bike we attached it to a frame downtube under a sidecover . . .

Fig. 100 If the battery is removed to install the outlet, be VERY CAREFUL not to pinch the wires as it is reinstalled

Fig. 102 . . . but on this bike, the harness is run under the seat and pokes out from underneath the gas tank (making it easy to access from the saddle)

7. Secure the positive battery cable to the motorcycle battery, then secure the negative cable.

8. Use a voltmeter to check for battery voltage across the terminals of the accessory jack. Then use the voltmeter to check voltage directly across the 2 battery terminals. The voltage should be identical or VERY, VERY close. If not, there is likely a problem with one of the two connections and you should double-check them before proceeding. If there is a significant difference in the voltages, your accessory jack may not work.

9. Once you are sure the connections are good, route the accessory outlet wiring the way you have planned to position the jack. Be sure to keep the wiring away from any moving parts (running it along frame rails and along other chassis wiring is a good idea). If you have a fuel injected motorcycle you want to keep it away from any engine control wiring to prevent possible interference with the engine control computer.

10. Use a few wiring ties to make sure the accessory outlet wiring and jack remain in position.

11. Double-check battery voltage across the jack terminals one last time, then install the seat, sidecovers and/or fairing as necessary. When installing the remaining motorcycle pieces, pay close attention that none of the pieces will interfere with or damage the wiring once they are in position.

12. Ride Warm.

4

ENGINE & DRIVE TRAIN MAINTENANCE

ENGINE MAINTENANCE

▶ See Figures 1 and 2

In this world of throw away appliances and "drive it till it breaks" attitudes, it is easy to see why people often ignore maintenance on things from household oil burners to cars and trucks. BUT, as we stated in the beginning of this manual, motorcycles are different from cars. The majority of mechanical problems with a car or truck will not wind up with the vehicle falling over and the driver hurtling down the road at highway speeds. Motorcycles, on the other hand, tend to go down rather suddenly and spectacularly when a component fails under stress, and the result can be painful.

If you are serious about safety, then you should take a serious interest in the maintenance of your bike. Learn from the examples of those involved with other machines that are unpleasant to be around when mechanical failures occur. Aircraft mechanics and racing pit crews are two examples of people who take their jobs VERY, VERY seriously. They use checklists and keep log books to be certain that no maintenance procedures are overlooked and that no critical part is used beyond its normal working life. To these people, maintenance is PREVENTATIVE not corrective.

Don't wait until a part stops working to give your motorcycle attention. Periodic maintenance to the engine, drivetrain and chassis will help to

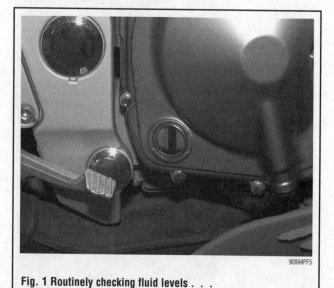

Fig. 1 Routinely checking fluid levels . . .

Fig. 2 . . . and adjustments is the most important thing you can do to maintain your motorcycle

make for a safer riding experience. It doesn't matter if you are racing, touring or just commuting, knowing that your bike is in top shape and that it will get the job done safely will allow you to concentrate on the better things in life, like curvy country roads and long stretches of two-lane.

Before reading any further, be sure that you have a copy of the owners manual for your bike. Although we will provide a lot of information regarding what is common to motorcycle maintenance, you should check the owners manual first. Remember that every bike is different and any manufacturer may have a unique maintenance requirement, that although it is not the norm for the industry, might be very important on your particular model.

For example, Ducati motorcycles use a valve system which is otherwise unique to most vehicles on the road today. Their desmodromic valves are not closed by valve springs, but by the camshaft and a second set of rocker arms. The advantage of this system is that the camshaft does not have to fight the high pressure springs used in most other engines, so it robs less power from the crankshaft. But, the disadvantage is a valve adjustment technique and interval which is unique to THEIR motorcycles.

The topics in this chapter cover most of the powertrain maintenance procedures common to motorcycles on the road today. But not all bikes will contain all systems. For instance, if you have an air cooled engine, then you do not have Glycol coolant to check or replace periodically (your engine uses air and oil for cooling purposes, NOT Glycol coolant). Another example is that motorcycles use various means of final drive, either a chain, a belt or a driveshaft, and your bike will only have one of these. Identify the topics which apply to your motorcycle by comparing the maintenance chart of your owners manual to the list of items in this (and the next) sections' table of contents.

Make sure that you have a complete checklist of maintenance items for your model, then follow the techniques provided to help assure a long and healthy life for you and your bike.

A Word About Warranties

If you have a new motorcycle with a manufacturer's warranty, then it is critically important that you follow ALL OF THE MANUFACTURER'S recommendations regarding care and maintenance. It is also very important that you document everything that you do (or that a mechanic does, if you choose). Keep a log book with receipts, time and dates of services and notes of anything in particular that was noticed during your service. For instance:

June 12th, I performed a 13,000 mile service. Changed all fluids (receipt attached). I noticed that the drive belt was just out of spec (3/4 in. deflection, overnight cold). So I adjusted it, it's dead center of spec now (7/16 in.). I'll make a note to keep a close eye on that . . .

If you perform your own maintenance on a bike that is under warranty, this will be the only proof that the required procedures were performed (just in case something goes wrong that the manufacturer is reluctant about fixing for free).

MANUFACTURER'S FLUIDS

▶ See Figure 3

This is a tough one. Ask anyone involved with bike maintenance and they will probably have an opinion on whose fluids are best for your bike. Some will say to use only specially made motorcycle oils while others will swear that normal automotive fluids are fine. Each will probably have a story to back up their position like, "I once knew a guy who used synthetic car oil in his bike and BAMMM! It blew up! Just like that, I mean he poured it in an' both he and the bike, well they was vaporized in an instant, like one of them thar ray-guns on TV."

Ok, maybe we are exaggerating a little here. Well, we are going to give you some recommendations in the maintenance sections. We may even suggest that there are alternatives to the special products sold by motorcycle manufacturer's (in some cases). BUT, again, remember that if your precious baby is under warranty, you have another source of motivation to buy your oil from the dealer.

Fig. 3 You are never WRONG using a manufacturer's fluid, it is just not always necessary

Manufacturers will have less to complain about if they want to dispute a warranty claim and you can prove that you have used NOTHING but their recommended fluids in your bike. ALSO, the more often you go in and buy oil from your local dealer (the same guy/gal who would be responsible for convincing the manufacturer's rep to go ahead and pay for a warranty repair), the more likely it is that they are going to know you. And they are going to remember you as one of their valued customers, who is always in their shop every couple of months buying oil, a filter, some gaskets and a new T-shirt (hey you didn't think they made ALL their money from bikes and oil did you?).

Once the bike is out of warranty, well, then you have a lot more freedom to make your OWN decision on what fluids to use and where to buy them.

Fuel

SELECTING THE PROPER FUEL

▶ **See Figure 4**

Gasoline is a mixture of hydrocarbons (composed of hydrogen and carbon), produced by refining crude oil. When gasoline burns, these compounds separate into hydrogen and carbon atoms and unite with oxygen atoms. The results obtained from burning gasoline are dependent upon its most important characteristics: octane rating, volatility and density.

Gasoline mixtures and additives will vary slightly from brand-to-brand, but it could also vary from station-to-station too (if a particular station has a problem with moisture or contamination in one or more of its tanks). When deciding on a gasoline, start with the manufacturer's recommended octane rating and try tank fulls from various local stations. Run a few tank fulls of each and settle on the one which gives you the best gas mileage and anti-knock protection. If you get similar results from various brands and stations, then you can likely count of those results from most fill-ups. If one particular gas station or brand seems to give your bike trouble, avoid it. You know, like "Doctor, Doctor it hurts when I do this . . . so don't do that.

➡**DON'T WASTE YOUR MONEY overbuying gasoline with super-high octane. If your manufacturer doesn't require it, and your bike runs fine on a lower octane, then go ahead and use the lower octane. For the most part, the quality of the gasoline and the use of additives will be reasonably comparable from one octane to another with a single brand of gas. Always filling-up with Super-Elite-Mega-Premium 115 octane will probably have ABSOLUTELY no appreciable benefits over the same brand's regular gasoline, unless your engine is seriously high compression (read as extreme aftermarket engine work) or seriously clogged with carbon.**

Octane Rating

Simply put, the octane rating of a gasoline is its ability to resist knock, a detonation or uncontrolled combustion in the cylinder which sounds like a sharp metallic noise. Knock can occur for a variety of reasons, one of which is the incorrect octane rating for the engine in your motorcycle. To understand why knock occurs, you must understand why knock doesn't occur. So let's take a look at the normal combustion process.

Under normal operating conditions, the firing of the spark plug initiates the burning of the fuel/air mixture in the combustion chamber. Once the plug fires, a wall of flame starts outward from the plug in all directions at once. This flame front moves evenly and rapidly throughout the entire combustion chamber until the entire fuel/air mixture is burned. This even, rapid progress of the burning fuel/air mixture is highly dependent on the octane rating of the gasoline. If the octane rating is too low, the last part of the compressed fuel/air mixture may ignite before the flame front reaches it, in effect creating two areas of combustion within the cylinder. The problem occurs because, while the original combustion is proceeding at a carefully controlled rate, this new combustion is simply a sudden sharp explosion. This abrupt increase in pressure is what creates the knocking sound in the combustion chamber. As far as the piston is concerned, the damage it inflicts is exactly like striking the piston top with a heavy hammer. Knock is

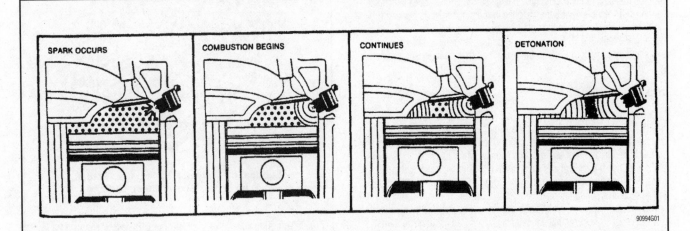

Fig. 4 Using the proper octane fuel will help prevent detonation (a damaging condition which occurs when the anti-knock quality of the fuel used does not meet the engine requirements allowing part of the mixture to combust before the spark plug ignites the rest)

very damaging to the engine, since it causes extraordinary wear to bearings, piston crowns, and other vital engine parts. Engines can actually be destroyed through excessive engine knock.

Engine knock can be controlled by using a gas with the proper octane rating. Octane measurements made under laboratory conditions have led to "Research" and "Motor" octane ratings. In general, the research octane number tends to be about 6 to 10 points higher than the motor octane rating (for what is essentially the same gasoline). Since the early seventies, most octane ratings on gas pumps in the U.S. have been the average of the research and motor octane numbers. For instance, if the gasoline had a research octane rating of 100, and a motor octane rating of 90, the octane rating found on the pump would be 95.

Your owners manual will probably indicate the type and octane of gasoline recommended for use in your bike. however, octane requirements can vary according to the vehicle and the conditions under which it is operating. If you encounter sustained engine knock, wait until your tank is nearly empty, then try a gasoline with a higher octane rating. Don't overbuy—it's a waste of money to buy gasoline of a higher octane than your engine requires in order to satisfy its antiknock need.

As a new motorcycle is driven, combustion deposits build up and the octane requirement increases until an equilibrium level, (usually higher than the new-bike requirement) is reached. Other factors which can increase the octane an engine requires are higher air or engine temperatures, lower altitudes, lower humidity, a more advanced ignition spark timing, a leaner carburetor setting, sudden acceleration, and frequent stop-and-go driving which increases the build-up of combustion chamber deposits.

Volatility

The volatility of any liquid is its ability to vaporize. A highly volatile gasoline will help a cold engine start easily and run smoothly while it is warming up. However, the use of a highly volatile gasoline in warm weather tends to cause vapor lock, a condition not uncommon for older, carbureted automobiles, but almost never seen in motorcycles. The condition occurs when gasoline actually vaporizes before it arrives at the carburetor jet where atomization is supposed to take place. This premature vaporization used to occur in the fuel lines or in a section of the carburetor on automobiles. When use of too highly-volatile fuel leads to vapor lock, the engine becomes starved for fuel and will either lose power or stall. Although refiners used to vary the percentage of volatile components in their gasoline according to season and locality, in order to help prevent this, vapor lock was more likely to occur in the early spring, when some stations may not have received supplies of lower-volatility gasoline.

Luckily, the design of most carbureted motorcycles make vapor lock unlikely. Whereas carbureted automobiles used long fuel lines to travel from the fuel tank to the engine (and a large carburetor fuel bowl which sat right on TOP of the engine), the gasoline in most motorcycles has a short trip to take from the tank to the float bowl (which is smaller than car's) and to the intake manifold. The gasoline spends less time in the lines and float bowls and they are both likely to be cooler than their counterparts on an automobile.

Density

Density is another property of gasoline which can affect your fuel economy. It indicates how much chemical energy the gasoline contains. Density is generally measured in BTU's per gallon (the BTU, or British Thermal Unit, is a standard unit of energy), and usually varies less than 2% among most gasolines but can vary as much as 4–8%. This indicates that gas mileage could vary by as much as 4–8%, depending on the density of the gasoline you happen to choose.

Oxygenated gasoline has become popular (or necessary) in many areas in order to help reduce emissions. Oxygenated gasoline contains less combustible material than a non-oxygenated counterpart. The result is fewer hydrocarbons per gallon. Oxygenated fuels do not harm you motorcycle, they do however rob it of some power and some gas mileage.

Additives

Practically as important as octane rating and volatility are the additives that refiners put into their gasolines. The fuel injector cleaners found in nearly every major brand of gasoline today include detergent additives which help clean the tiny passages in the carburetor or fuel injector systems. This helps to ensure consistent fuel/air mixtures necessary for smooth running and good gas mileage. Winter additives include fuel line de-icers to reduce carburetor icing. Other additives are used to help control combustion chamber deposits, gum formation, rust, and wear.

Engine Oil & Filter

▶ See Figure 5

SELECTING THE PROPER OIL

▶ See Figures 6 and 7

Probably because engine oil is the single most important part of routine engine maintenance (for just about internal combustion engines in the world today), there are probably more myths, misunderstandings and urban legends regarding engine oil, than any other mechanical "thing." What we would like to do here is help demystify engine oil and help you make the best decision for what type of oil to purchase for your motorcycle.

When it comes to engine oil, there are 3 ways you can help improve your motorcycle's mileage and insure that it delivers good economy for a longer time: 1) understand the functions of oil in your engine, 2) choose the proper oil for various operating conditions, and 3) change the oil and filter at the proper intervals.

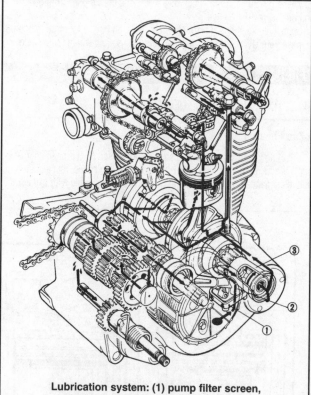

Lubrication system: (1) pump filter screen, (2) oil pump, (3) centrifugal oil filter

90994G02

Fig. 5 This diagram follows an engine oils path through a typical unitized (engine and transmission in one case) motorcycle engine—The point is, look how many vital parts your oil is used to keep lubricated and healthy

The Functions of Engine Oil

What does oil do in your engine? If you answered "lubricate," you're only partially right. While oil is primarily a lubricant, it also performs a number of other functions which are vital to the life and performance of your engine. In addition to being a lubricant, oil also dissipates heat and makes parts run cooler; it helps reduce engine noise; it combats rust and corrosion of metal surfaces; it acts as a seal for pistons, rings, and cylinder walls; it combines with the oil filter to remove foreign substances from the engine.

Types Of Engine Oil

Every bottle of engine oil for sale in the U.S. should have a label describing what standards it meets. Engine oil service classifications are designated by the American Petroleum Institute (API), based on the chemical composition of a given type of oil and testing of samples. The ratings include "S" (normal gasoline engine use) and "C" (commercial and fleet) applications. Over the years, the S rating has been supplemented with various letters, each one representing the latest and greatest rating available at the time of its introduction. During recent years these ratings have included SF, SG, SH and most recently (at the time of this book's publication), SJ. Each successive rating usually meets all of the standards of the previous alpha designation, but also meets some new criteria, meets higher standards and/or contains newer or different additives. Since oil is so important to the life of your motorcycle engine, you should obviously NEVER use an oil of questionable quality. Oils that are labeled with modern API ratings, including the "energy conserving" donut symbol, have been proven to meet the API quality standards.

OIL VISCOSITY

In addition to meeting the classification of the American Petroleum Institute, your oil should be of a viscosity suitable for the outside temperature in which you'll be riding. Oil must be thin enough to get between the close-tolerance moving parts it must lubricate. Once there, it must be thick enough to separate them with a slippery oil film. If the oil is too thin, it won't separate the parts; if it's too thick, it can't squeeze between them in the first place—either way, excess friction and wear takes place. To complicate matters, cold-morning starts require a thin oil to reduce engine resistance, while high speed driving requires a thick oil which can lubricate vital engine parts at temperatures.

According to the Society of Automotive Engineers' (SAE's) viscosity classification system, an oil with a high viscosity number (such as SAE 40 or SAE 50) will be thicker than one with a lower number (SAE 10W). The "W" in 10W indicates that the oil is desirable for use in winter driving. Through the use of special additives, multiple-viscosity oils are available to combine easy starting at cold temperatures with engine protection at turnpike speeds. For example, a 10W40 oil is said to have the viscosity of a 10W oil when the engine is cold and that of a 40 oil when the engine is warm. The use of such an oil will decrease engine resistance and improve your miles per gallon during short trips in which the oil doesn't have a chance to warm up.

Some of the more popular multiple-viscosity oils are 5W30, 10W30, 10W40, 20W-40, 20W-50, and 10W-50. In general, lower weight oils, like 5W-20 or 5W-30 are used for temperatures below 0°F, while medium weight oils like 10W-30 or 10W-40 are used whenever the lowest temperature expected is 0°F., and heavier weight oils like 20W-40 or 20W-50 are recommended whenever the lowest temperature expected is 32°F. However, be certain to consult your owners manual to determine the proper viscosity range for your motorcycle and the outside temperature range in which it operates. Air cooled motorcycles tend to recommend heavier oils for summer or desert operation (which may bring extreme operating temperatures into play), while water cooled motorcycles can usually remain with multi-weight oils because of their more consistent cooling systems.

ADDITIVES

A high-quality engine oil will include a number of chemical compounds known as additives. These are blended in at the refinery and normally fall into the following categories:

Pour Point Depressants help cold starting by making the oil flow more easily at low temperatures. Otherwise, the oil would tend to be a waxy substance just when you need it the most.

Oxidation and Bearing Corrosion Inhibitors help to prevent the formation of gummy deposits which can take place when engine oil oxidizes under high temperatures. In addition, these inhibitors place a protective coating on sensitive bearing metals, which would otherwise be attacked by the chemicals formed by oil oxidation.

Rust and Corrosion Inhibitors protect against water and acids formed by the combustion process. Water is physically separated from the metal parts vulnerable to rust, and corrosive acids are neutralized by alkaline chemicals. The neutralization of combustion acids is an important key to long engine life.

Detergents and Dispersants use teamwork. Detergents clean up the products of normal combustion and oxidation while dispersants keep them suspended until they can be removed by means of the filter or an oil change.

Foam Inhibitors prevent the tiny air bubbles which can be caused by fast-moving engine parts whipping air into the oil. Foam can also occur when the oil level falls too low and the oil pump begins sucking up air instead of oil (like when the kids finish a milkshake). Without foam inhibitors, these tiny air bubbles could cause a loss of lubricating efficiency

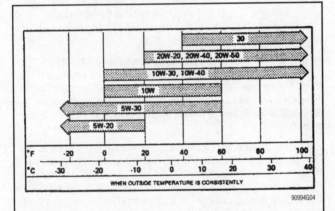

Fig. 6 Oil should be selected based on ambient temperatures for the upcoming months—Note this is an example of typical recommendations, refer to your owners manual to see what your manufacturer recommends

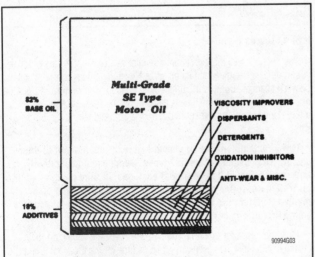

Fig. 7 A typical quart of oil contains more than just the base fluid, it is also comprised of additives

and cause hydraulic valve lifters to collapse while reducing engine performance and economy significantly.

Viscosity Index Improvers reduce the rate at which an oil thins out when the temperature climbs. These additives are what makes multiple-viscosity oils possible. Without them, a single-weight oil which permitted easy starting on a cold morning might thin out and cause you to lose your engine on a hot afternoon. If you use a multiple-viscosity oil, it's this additive that helps your gas mileage during those short trips in cold weather.

Friction Modifiers and Extreme Pressure additives are valuable in so-called boundary lubrication, where there is metal-to-metal contact due to the absence or breaking down of the oil film between moving parts. Friction modifiers, or anti-wear agents, deposit protective surface films which reduce the friction and heat of metal-to-metal contact. Extreme pressure additives work by reacting chemically with metal surfaces involved in high pressure contact.

Automotive Oils

Bring this subject up the next time you are bench racing. We dare ya. OK, our lawyers want us to take back that dare, right now.

✳✳ CAUTION

After a hard day's ride, DO NOT agitate a motorcyclist with whom you have been drinking by bringing up the automotive vs. special motorcycle oil debate. This can be seriously hazardous to your physical and mental well being. DO NOT ATTEMPT THIS at home or in a bar. We are serious. Oh and, if you can't walk home, take a cab.

Ask 10 different bikers and you are almost sure to get as many different opinions on whether or not you can use automotive oils in your motorcycle. Just picking up our enormous stack of bike magazines led us to literally dozens of articles mentioning the subject.

Many of the articles punted, saying that you should always follow the manufacturer's recommendations for your motorcycle. That's a safe position, hard to be wrong with that approach.

Some of the articles mentioned reasons why motorcycle specific oils might be better. On bikes where the engine and transmission share the oil, "automotive oils may not stand up to the punishing conditions of transmission gears and wet clutches." Well, that might be true in some cases?

A few just extolled the virtues of regular oil changes and avoided the issue by recommending that you use a "high quality" oil. Ohhhhhh, go out on a limb won't ya?

Exactly one came out and recommended automotive oils (at least that we found). Motorcycle Consumer News or MCN, is one of our favorite bike magazines because they do not accept advertising and aren't afraid to say if a product stinks. Well, back in 1996, they asked their readers to report on what oils they used, and to relate any problems which might have occurred (or lack thereof). MCN found that out of the 674 responses they'd received by press time, exactly 9 people had reported any problem with clutch slippage or engine damage (the two most popular arguments against automotive oils in a bike). And of those 9 people, 5 who claimed that engine or clutch slipping problems occurred because of synthetic oils, cured the problem by switching to another oil. And the best of it was that 4 of the 5 switched to an automotive synthetic and cured their problems! What MCN concluded was that, at the time, automotive oils were perfectly fine for most motorcycle applications.

Of course time marches on. And, the API has come up with its latest and greatest automotive oil specifications now. A whole new army of "experts" have taken this opportunity to once again denounce automotive oils as not containing enough "special" additives to be used in a motorcycle. Unfortunately, without further surveys, we cannot say for sure that the latest API oil will have the same success in motorcycle engines as MCN found. But then again, most name-brand automotive oils are designed to protect a great variety of internal combustion engines from hard working, slower turning pushrod truck motors to high rpm OHC sports cars.

What do we suggest. Talk to other motorcyclists (preferably those who ride the same model) and see what they use. Choose a name brand oil which meets the requirements set by your bike's manufacturer. Of course, probably more important than anything else, use the correct viscosity for the ambient temperature range and change your oil/filter often.

Synthetic Oil

Synthetic oils are another of those topics which can raise the blood pressure of many motorcyclists who are just "certain" that they have the answer to the world's problems. When synthetics were first marketed, like with so many innovations, people reacted as if this mysterious oil was evil and would surely lead to the downfall of the person who used it (and the engine in which it was used), if not to the complete downfall of our entire civilization.

BUT, take a look around you. Synthetic oils are the first choice of many people who are HARD on their engines. Many racing teams, both in the motorcycle and automotive world, rely upon synthetic oils to protect their high dollar, high rpm and high visibility investments. So what is the big deal?

Conventional oils are based on hydrocarbons, but because they are refined, the sizes and shapes of these molecules are highly irregular. Synthetic oils are assembled from different compounds into specifically sized and shaped hydrocarbons. They are completely compatible with conventional oils, but they benefit from having more predictable reactions to severe conditions. In high heat conditions (such as that which can be found in many motorcycle engines and transmissions), synthetics will resist breaking down better than conventional oils.

➡**Triumph now sells semi-synthetic and fully synthetic oils under their own label. At the time of publication, their full synthetic oil is Mobil 1®. The new Triumph motorcycles use many components and design features that are similar to many Japanese water cooled, multi-cylinder engines, including sharing engine oil with the transmission.**

Also, keep in mind that over the years many companies have tested synthetic oils and it was not always for engineering reasons that one was not marketed. Harley-Davidson Motor CO, for instance, has tested synthetic oils. Their engineers have admitted that no oil related problems were tied to the use of synthetics in their test motors, It seems that Harley stayed away from selling a synthetic motor oil because they thought customers would not like the extra expense (my how times have changed). And remember that today Harley sells synthetic and semi-synthetic gear oils for use in their transmissions and primary drive units.

Synthetic oils are often more expensive than conventional oils, but if the extra protection they offer is worth it to you (sorta like an insurance policy without the hassle of an agent), then you may want to give them a try.

CHECKING YOUR OIL

▶ **See Figures 8 and 9**

You should make this procedure a regular part of your life. Get to know your motorcycle engine, and its appetite. Hopefully it does not eat much oil between changes. But it is important that you monitor how much it does eat. Any change in appetite means a change in mechanical condition (either it has started to use or lose more oil) and you should take steps to find out why.

➡**Two-stroke motors are supposed to use oil, that is part of their design. They usually come in 2 types. Some use a separate oil tank, which should be checked at each gas fill. And some mix the oil with the gasoline during fill-up. Be sure to check your owners manual to determine the proper amount of oil and how to add it to your particular model.**

Most manufacturer's recommend that you check the engine oil HOT. This means that the bike has been run for some time (at least long enough to bring the oil up to normal operating temperature). BUT, this does NOT mean that you have just finished an hour long blast at supersonic speeds

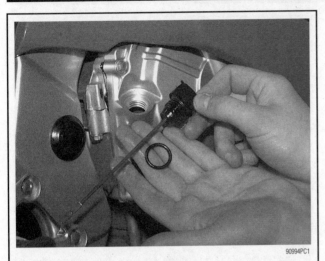

Fig. 8 There are basically 2 ways to check engine oil on most bikes— a dipstick . . .

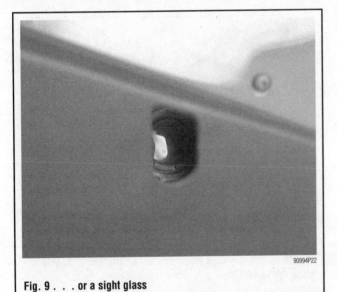

Fig. 9 . . . or a sight glass

across the desert (that is TOO HOT). It also means that the engine has been shut off for a few minutes, giving the oil time to seep back down into the crankcase (unless of course your bike has a separate oil tank because then you want to check it before any seeps back down into the crankcase).

The bike should be parked on a level surface to make sure that you get a correct reading. If your bike has a centerstand (it means that it is probably NOT a Harley, Buell or Ducati, but you knew that already), then the bike should usually be placed on the centerstand for ease of checking. BUT, make sure that it is sitting level (meaning not leaning on just the front of rear tire and not leaning to one side) when you check the oil. You may have to block one wheel up or weight the front tire to bring it down slightly when checking the level. On some bikes with centerstands the manufacturer recommends holding the bike upright and not using the centerstand, and this must be done unless you can level the bike on the stand. Since it is awkward to hold the bike upright and see most sight glasses, it would pay to find another way (such as using the centerstand, and blocking or holding the bike level).

On awkward models, use a friend to find another way to check the fluid. Once you have properly filled the bike (with a friend holding it upright), place it on the centerstand and see how the level changes. Weight the bike on one side or the other, or block a wheel up and see if you can duplicate the correct level reading. Once you have found how to do that, you are set.

If the bike doesn't have a centerstand, then manufacturers are usually nice enough to design the bike so that it can be checked on the sidestand (of course BMW and Harley are included in theose who have occasionally avoided this wisdom). If you have an owners manual, double check to see if your bike has one of these exceptions.

There are basically 2 methods of checking engine oil on most motorcycles, a dipstick or a sight glass.

With A Dipstick

◗ See Figures 10 thru 19

The oil level is usually checked with the motorcycle on its centerstand or sidestand, as applicable. But, always make sure the bike is level.

➡**Most Harley-Davidson Sportsters and Softails are exceptions to the logical sidestand rule. They must be checked with the motorcycle standing straight up and level. This can be a major pain unless you always have someone handy to hold the bike upright when you want to check the oil. You've got a couple of options. (1) Keep a pair of jackstands handy in the garage (these can be used under the engine guards on most models to hold the bike upright). (2) Learn to balance the bike really well with one hand while you pull the dipstick out with the other. OR (3) When you know the oil level is correct (from checking with the bike fully upright), put it on the sidestand and check where the level is now. Make a mark on your dipstick (can you say rotary tool?) and use that mark to check the bike in the future. BUT, be sure to double check and make sure your mark is accurate. Luckily, the oil tanks used by most Harley-Davidsons have a "generous" range to begin with. It shouldn't be hard to fall within the range every time.**

1. With the engine warmed to normal operating temperature, park the bike on a level surface (placing it on its centerstand or sidestand, as applicable).

➡**On bikes which utilize a dry sump (that store their oil in a separate oil tank or bag instead of the crankcase), you must run the engine before checking the oil. This is because some of the oil will usually seep through the oil lines and into the crankcase when the motor sits overnight. Failure to run the engine first (allowing the oil pump return most of the oil to the tank) may result in a false low reading.**

2. Remove the dipstick from the bike. Most Japanese and German bikes use a threaded dipstick, gently turn the tab counterclockwise until it is free, then remove it by pulling straight upward. The dipsticks on most modern Harleys use a large rubber grommet which is simply an interference fit with

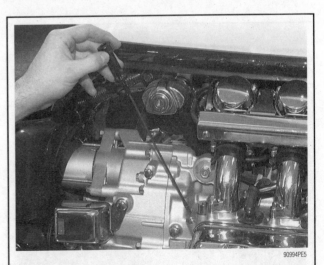

Fig. 10 Though you will find a lot of dipsticks in the engine case like this . . .

Fig. 11 . . . their locations can also vary, from an oil pan behind the motor . . .

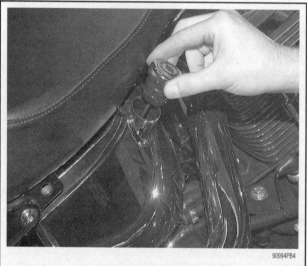

Fig. 12 . . . to an oil tank cradled in the frame . . .

Fig. 13 . . . or even an oil tank that is hidden under the seat

Fig. 14 On models with threaded dipsticks, don't rethread the stick in order to check the level, just insert it and let it sit on top of the threads . . .

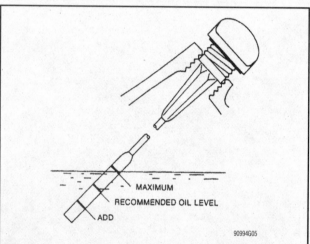

Fig. 15 . . . a threaded dipstick is almost always calibrated to show the correct level only when it is sitting on top of the threads

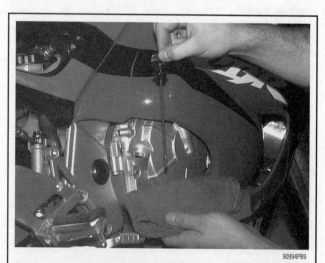

Fig. 16 In all cases, make sure you hold the dipstick vertically to prevent getting a false high reading

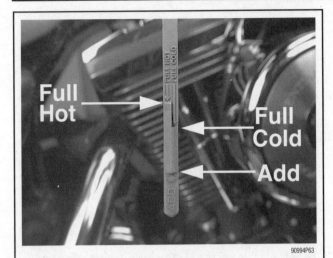

Fig. 17 Read the level on the dipstick—this has two ranges, one for a HOT engine and the other for a COLD engine

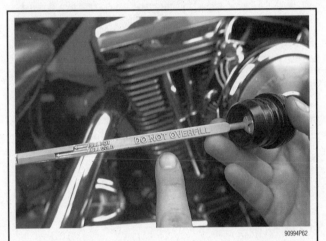

Fig. 18 Some dipsticks have special instructions such as recommended oil grades or, in this case, how important it is NOT TO OVERFILL

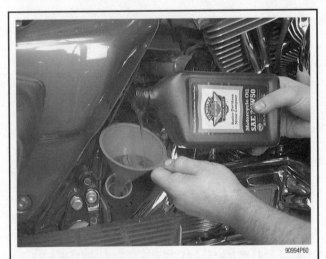

Fig. 19 On bikes with dipsticks, oil is usually added through the same hole in which the dipstick is inserted

the oil bag/tank. These are removed by gently grasping and pulling upward (rocking slightly from side-to-side, if necessary).

➡**If you are still looking for that Buell dipstick, it is usually in the top of an oil tank, located under the seat. So much for checking it at every gas stop.**

3. Wipe the dipstick clean using a rag or paper towel (making sure that no debris or lint is left on the dipstick when it is inserted back into the oil).

4. Insert the dipstick back into the crankcase or oil tank. On most threaded dipsticks the level is marked so that the dipstick is inserted into the hole, BUT is not threaded in place. Instead, leave the dipstick sitting on the top of the threads. The grommet retained Harley dipsticks are designed to be fully seated in order to properly check the level.

5. Remove the dipstick and hold it vertically with the level mark(s) toward the bottom of the dipstick. We know this is contrary to what you have seen every television gas station attendant do. Just trust us here, if you try to hold it horizontally there is a good chance that the oil will flow up the dipstick and give a false high reading (or worse, a false acceptable reading when the level is really low). If however, you follow our advice and hold it vertically the oil will NOT flow up the dipstick and you will never be left with too little oil in your bike.

6. If necessary, add oil (of the proper type and viscosity) to keep the level between the markings.

➡**Most Harley models use a rather large range marked on the dipsticks. Be careful NOT to overfill a Harley. On many models, overfilling will lead to oil carryover to the breathers (and will drip out the air cleaner all over your nice chrome). In most cases you will be fine in the upper ⅓–¼ of the range.**

With A Sight Glass

▸ **See Figures 20, 21, 22, 23 and 24**

Virtually ALL bikes that are equipped with a sight glass are designed to check the oil while the bike is held upright, completely level. This can usually be accomplished using the centerstand (though you may have to weight the front fork to keep the bike level). If you must hold the bike upright, without the aid of a centerstand, then checking the level without the help of a friend can be QUITE A HASSLE.

➡**Checking the fluid level without a centerstand can be a pain. For example, the R1200C from BMW is equipped with a sight glass and NO centerstand, but you are supposed to check the level with the bike upright. If you own one, get used to having someone check it for you, because it is too easy to drop this bike while you are holding it upright, kneeling and bending over to look at the sight glass.**

Fig. 20 If your bike has a sight glass, it is usually found on the lower side of the engine case . . .

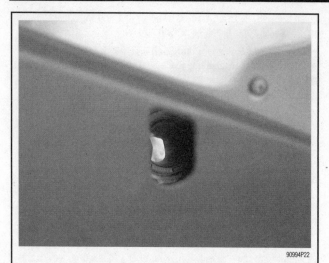

Fig. 21 . . . though bodywork will sometimes make it more difficult to check

Fig. 22 On bikes which use a sight glass, an oil fill cap should be found elsewhere on the engine case

Fig. 23 If bodywork interferes with the fill cap . . .

Fig. 24 . . . then you should use a funnel to prevent making a mess—this manufacturer provided the funnel in the bike's toolkit

1. With the engine warmed to normal operating temperature, park the bike on a level surface (placing it on its centerstand, if possible). Just make sure the bike is perfectly level.

2. Locate the sight glass (usually on the lower, left side of the engine) and check for any markings. Some crankcases are marked with LOW and FULL lines just to the side of the sight glass. Sometimes the sight glass itself is marked with lines or with a dot in the center.

➡️**You are usually in good shape as long as some oil is visible through the glass. BUT, be careful since the glass can be VERY sensitive to lean. If the bike is leaned, even slightly in the wrong direction, the level will appear incorrect (that includes side-to-side and front-to-back).**

3. If necessary, add oil (of the proper type and viscosity) to keep the level between the markings. Add oil slowly since even a small amount of oil will normally make a difference in the sight glass reading.

BUYING AN OIL FILTER

▶ See Figure 25

A quick word about oil filters. Occasionally you hear Joe the ragman talking about how he can save a few bucks by using this spin-on oil filter

Fig. 25 Don't be fooled. Just because spin-on filters LOOK the same as an automotive filter, that doesn't mean they work the same

from a Honda Civic or something on his bike. DON'T DO THAT!!!! Always buy the filter which is designed for and sold for your particular model. You can't tell anything from the outward physical appearance of an oil filter (except by reading the part number) and just because a filter fits does not mean it will do the job properly.

Remember that the oiling systems of each vehicle on the road today varies somewhat. If an oil filter becomes clogged (offering too much resistance to the oil pump to force oil through the filtering media), your engine will be saved by a pressure bypass valve. This valve is spring-loaded and rated ONLY to open at a certain pressure which could be significantly higher (or lower) than your engine's pump pressure if the wrong filter is used.

If a filter with too low a bypass rating is used, then part way through the filter's life that bypass valve may open, preventing it from actually filtering the oil during normal service. But, much worse, if the rating is much higher than your pump, if the filter should clog the valve may NOT open. This would result in starving your bearings of oil and may cause significant engine damage before it is noticed.

A good example is the Harley-Davidson Evolution engine which typically operates under low oil pressure. The roller bearing engine only needs about 15 psi (though it could be as high as 40 psi cold). Many automotive oil filters have a bypass pressure which exceeds the Harley-Davidson peak operating pressure and could starve your Blockhead of oil should the filter clog.

SO, buy an oil filter from a company that manufacturers filters specifically for motorcycles.

CHANGING YOUR OIL AND FILTER

Here we are, with the MOST BASIC, yet MOST IMPORTANT maintenance procedure that you can do for your motorcycle engine. Manufacturers usually differ in their recommendations of how often this should be performed. But your friends here at Chilton are going to simplify it for you.

Change your oil every 3000 miles or 3 months, whichever comes first, period!

Now that recommendation is probably a little more conservative than most manufacturers today (who tend to give ranges from 5000-7500 miles and 6 months). But we are talking about the long term health of your baby. Look at it this way, it depends on how much you paid for it. If you bought the bike new, then the price of the oil is relatively small compared to your overall investment. If you bought a rat and are going to treat it like a rat, you can probably get away with taking the manufacturer's word for the interval and ignore our sage advice.

Notice how we gave a **time** limit along with the mileage. This is one of those "too many people ignore" points we like to make. Mileage is not the only enemy of your oil, so is time. Oil will wear out over time as acids present from combustion attack it. Besides, those acids are one of the items that you want to get OUT of the crankcase (with the used oil) since they will attack the precious metals inside your engine (bearings, etc.).

You see it goes something like this. Oil oxidizes during exposure to air, and this naturally affects its efficiency. Acids get into the oil when the engine is started cold. While the cylinder walls are not yet at normal operating temperature, the acids formed by the combustion process may condense on them and then get into the oil. Unless the lubricant is changed these acids will slowly destroy the oil's lubricating properties.

Most manufacturers give an oil change interval which is based on ideal usage. If the bike is NOT used under any of the following conditions, you may be able to follow their recommendations:

- Extended periods of high-speed operation
- Extended periods of operation at high ambient temperatures
- Operation in extremely dusty environments (read ALL DIRT RIDING and all street riding in the desert).
- Extended periods of stop-and-go driving (traffic, stop signs and lights).
- Infrequent operation (especially during the winter months).
- Extended short hops (such as commuting a short distance or running to the store, or ahhemm, coffee bar hopping)

➥We say Coffee bar hopping because we know none of our readers are dumb enough to go "bar" hopping on a motorcycle. We want you guys/gals to stay alive, buy more vehicles and buy more books. OK?

Usually, one or more of the above conditions applies to all of our riding. Therefore, we stand by our original advice concerning the frequency with which you should change your oil.

No matter what you ride, the first step of a good oil change is to suit up and go for a ride (like you needed an excuse anyway!). The oil should be at normal operating temperature so that it flows better, removing more particulate matter, acids and moisture from the crankcase or oil tank as it is drained.

✳✳ CAUTION

The motorcycle oil will be (1) HOT and (2) toxic. I know a lot of us have poured oil all over ourselves for many years, but the medical profession is seriously frowning on that know. Used engine oil contains a lot of toxins, some of which will be readily absorbed into the skin. Do yourself a favor and buy some disposable plastic gloves, they will definitely protect against the toxins and they will reduce the chance of burning yourself.

BMW

▶ **See Figures 26 thru 43**

As you may already know, BMW's come in basically 2 flavors (ohh, unless you count the F650, then it is 3). Boxers and Bricks and the new one-lungers. Well, the good news is that they all put their oil change pants on the same way, one leg at a time, or so. Most BMWs use a crankcase sump motor, so the oil is drained using a plug in the bottom of the engine. The engine oil is exactly that on these models, it is JUST for the engine. Depending on the model, either a spin-on oil filter (oil-heads and bricks) or a cartridge filter (airheads) are used.

If you are servicing an airhead, be sure to ask your dealer for the complete oil change KIT and not just a filter. The kit comes with everything that you will conceivably need (and as luck will usually have it you will definitely need the whole kit if you only buy the filter). The kit includes new gaskets, seals and sometimes a new crush washer (depends how much your parts guy likes you). Also, check before purchasing the kit, some airheads have been fitted with aftermarket spin-on filters.

If you are changing the oil on an oilhead, you are going to need a cap-type oil filter wrench. If you don't believe us, go kneel under your bike and look at the spin-on filter, I don't think your strap-type wrench is going to do the trick, agree?

Check to see if you are one of the unfortunate few who will have to remove part of the fairing in order to drain your engine oil. To do this, crouch next the bike, then locate your drain plug and oil filter. The drain plug is almost always located on the bottom of the oil pan, but the oil filter

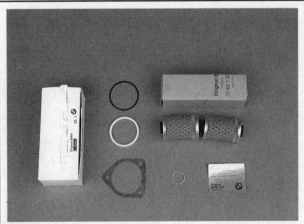

90994PN5

Fig. 26 Owners of airheads should buy the complete filter kit since it will contain the necessary gaskets, seals and O-rings, as well as the filter

Fig. 27 With the motor at operating temperature, loosen and remove the drain plug usually found at the lower rear . . .

Fig. 28 . . . or on the bottom of the motor—BMW normally uses a hex driver type plug on the engine case

Fig. 29 Once the plug has been loosened with a driver, turn the plug out by hand and quickly remove it to keep from getting burned by the hot oil . . .

Fig. 30 . . . then allow the oil to completely drain from the crankcase

location varies. On airheads it is a usually cartridge mounted under a triangular cover on the lower right front of the engine, but some may be equipped with remote spin-on filters. On oilheads it is normally mounted straight upward in an oil pan recess, directly under the motorcycle. On K-bikes it is normally on the lower portion of the engine. You get the idea.

If you are one of these unfortunate few you may wish to remove parts of the bodywork before warming the oil (to save time when you are ready to drain the engine). Luckily BMW seems to have cared when they designed MOST of their bikes and you can usually get away without removing the fairing. Of course, there are a few bikes on which you CAN get away with it, but it is a lot easier on these to take the plastic off.

1. If necessary, remove part of the bodywork to assure easy access to the engine once it is warmed.

❋❋ WARNING

Make sure that removing bodywork will not interfere with operation of the motorcycle. If it would you may want to warm the oil with the bike at idle or just wait to remove the bodywork until after you are done taking the bike for a ride. Convenience is nice, but safety is more important.

2. Warm the engine to normal operating temperature, then park the bike.

3. Position a drain pan (of greater capacity than the bike's crankcase) under the drain plug.

4. Loosen or completely remove the dipstick and/or oil filler cap (as applicable) as this will allow the oil to drain more quickly.

5. Loosen the drain plug using a wrench or a ratchet and socket. Once the plug is loosened, turn it out by hand, keeping inward pressure on the plug to keep oil from escaping past the threads until you are ready to fully withdraw it. When the plug is free, quickly pull the plug, and your hand, out of the way of the hot oil.

6. Allow the engine oil to drain completely. In the meantime, clean the drain plug and, if applicable, get a new crush washer out from your handy stash (purchased at the dealer or with the oil change kit).

7. Install and tighten the drain plug. Be sure to snug the drain plug, but DO NOT overtighten and strip it or your day will get very unhappy, very quickly.

8. On airheads proceed as follows:

a. If equipped with factory crash bars (engine guards) check to see if there is sufficient access to the triangular cover on the lower right side of the engine (the filter housing). If necessary loosen and reposition the right side crash bar for better access.

b. Move the drain pan under the triangular filter housing cover on the lower, right, front side of the engine.

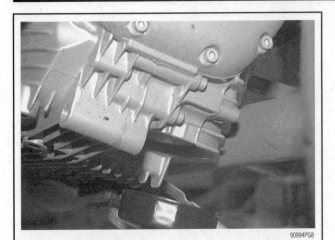

Fig. 31 Most late-model bikes (excluding airheads) are equipped with automotive style spin-on filters, use a cap-type filter wrench to remove them

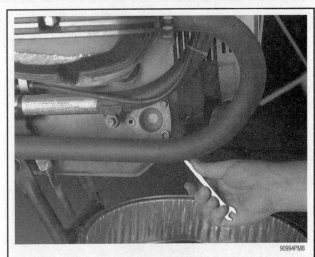

Fig. 34 The type of exhaust and amount of bodywork on your bike will decide how easy it is to remove the cover

Fig. 32 Always apply a light amount of oil to a spin-on oil filter's seal before installation

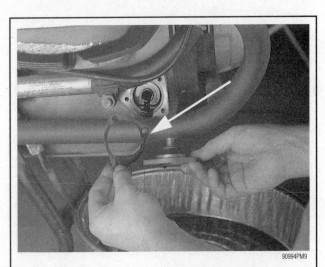

Fig. 35 Once the cover is off be sure to remove the old gasket . . .

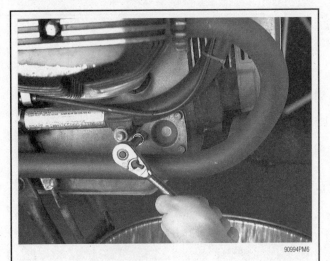

Fig. 33 On some models (like most airheads), the cartridge type filter is installed beneath a filter housing cover

Fig. 36 . . . seal and O-ring (noting the order they were removed for installation purposes)

Fig. 37 Finally, remove and dispose of the old filter cartridge . . .

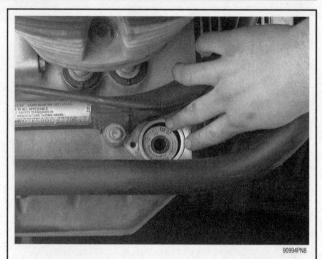

Fig. 40 Install the new filter making sure its grommet seats on the tube in the case . . .

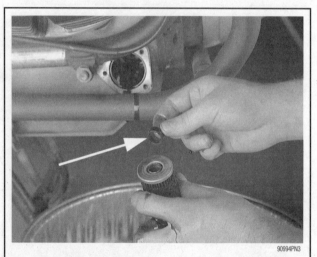

Fig. 38 . . . but remember to be sure the rubber grommet came out with the filter . . .

Fig. 41 . . . then install the cover using the new gasket . . .

Fig. 39 . . . if not you will need a long pair of needle nose pliers to get it out of the case

Fig. 42 . . . seal and O-ring

Fig. 43 Your last step is to properly refill and check the engine oil

➡Although it is not absolutely necessary, we like to prime spin-on oil filters by filling them ½ way with clean, fresh engine oil before installation. On most bikes this will shorten the amount of time necessary for the oil pump to build pressure through the lubricating system on the first start-up since it has less area to fill in the filter.

10. Properly refill the engine using the proper amount of oil. If you do not have the engine oil capacity specification, add the first bottle of oil, then add the rest slowly, checking the level often to prevent overfilling.

11. Start the bike, watching the oil pressure light. It should go out within a second or so of starting the bike. If it does not, STOP the bike immediately and double check the oil level, then restart the bike watching the light again.

12. Once the bike has been warmed, double check the oil level and make sure there is no seepage from the filter or drain plug.

13. Secure any bodywork which was removed or loosened for access.

Harley-Davidson and Buell

▶ **See Figures 44 thru 62**

Harley-Davidson motors are a bit unique to most modern motorcycles, and most of their owners are happy about that. This uniqueness continues with their dry sump oiling system. Instead of storing the oil in the bottom of

c. Loosen and remove the 3 bolts (noting their positions as they may be of different lengths) retaining the filter housing cover.

✷✷ CAUTION

Be careful working around the exhaust pipe, it should still be quite hot from running the engine.

d. Carefully pull the cover from the engine, noting the position of the gasket, seal and O-ring as the cover is removed.

➡On certain RS or RT models with fairings you should be able to replace the filter with the fairing installed, provided that you use the hinged filter cartridge.

e. Remove the filter cartridge from the housing, making sure that the round seal on the engine side of the filter is removed with the filter element. If not, get a small flashlight and look into the housing, you should see the thick, round seal still stuck on the nipple at the back of the housing. Use a pair of long, needle-nose pliers or a strong pair of mechanical fingers to fish the seal out.

f. Carefully install the new filter cartridge, making sure the inner seal is in place on the filter and that it properly seats on the nipple at the back of the housing.

g. Install the filter cover using the new O-ring, seal and gasket from the filter kit.

➡If you didn't get the complete kit, you can take the risk here and reuse the old seals. BUT, if you do, keep a close eye on the filter cover for the next couple of hundred miles (just to make sure it isn't seeping). If you see leakage, then the only thing to do is swallow your pride, then go buy the gaskets and seals.

h. If you have a factory installed oil cooler you may need to take special steps to drain it. Check your owner's manual. BMW supplied a special bolt in the tool kits which came with these bikes. The bolt must be exactly 0.906 in. (23mm) long and it is installed during the oil change to open the thermostatic valve.

9. On models except the airheads, use a filter wrench to loosen and remove the oil filter. On K-models where the filter is installed above an exhaust pipe or fairing, you should use a few paper towels or rags to catch the excess oil which will drain from the filter as it is removed. Lubricate the seal on the lip of the new spin-on filter and install it by hand (unless you are working on an oilhead which obviously doesn't give you the room to turn it by hand). Once the filter is lightly seated, tighten it an additional ½–¾ turn to assure it is fully seated.

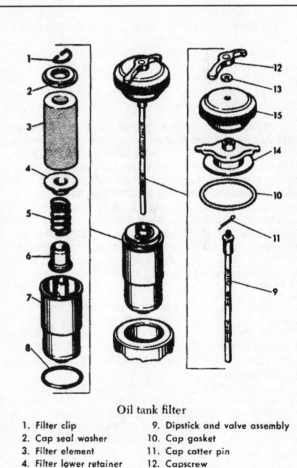

Oil tank filter

1. Filter clip	9. Dipstick and valve assembly
2. Cap seal washer	10. Cap gasket
3. Filter element	11. Cap cotter pin
4. Filter lower retainer	12. Capscrew
5. Cup spring	13. Cap washer
6. Cup seal	14. Capnut
7. Cup	15. Cap top
8. O-ring	

Fig. 44 Some older model Harley's (pre-Evo) utilized an oil tank filter

the crankcase, Harley motors pump their oil in from and out to an separate oil storage tank (often known as an oil bag). Harley motors are not the only motors to use dry sumps (especially going back in history), but today, they certainly represent the majority of dry sumps on the market.

This means very little to the uninitiated, except that if they look for a drain plug right below the motor they will normally come away quite confused. As a matter of fact on some models, such as the Sportster, they are not going to find a drain plug at all, they are going to find a drain hose instead.

All models (current models) are equipped with spin-on oil filters, located at the front of the motor. Some older, pre-Evo models used an oil tank filter. Because of Harleys traditional styling, few have left the factory with body-work that would interfere with access to the oil filter or the plug. Of course, some aftermarket kits, including a few air dams may get in the way a little. But it is a very rare bike that would require bodywork removal in order to perform this basic maintenance.

Take a minute to locate the drain plug on your bike. Typically the drain plug (or hose) will vary based on model:

• **Sportster (XL) models**—A drain hose comes from the back of the oil tank to a nipple located either under the battery tray (early models) or on the back of frame, underneath the swingarm (just in front of the rear wheel).

• **Softails and Buells**—A metal drain plug is normally secured inside a drain hose held in a strap on the lower side of the frame. On Softails you will usually find this hose on the right side.

• **FXR (Lowrider) models**—A drain hose from the oil tank is normally found under the left side cover.

• **Dynas**—Are equipped with an oil pan under the transmission (or between the motor and transmission) and a drain plug is mounted to the lower portion of the pan.

• **FLT models (Touring Chassis bikes)**—Are also usually equipped with an oil pan and a drain plug.

➡**On late-model touring bikes the oil pan is usually a funky one-piece deal located directly under the transmission AND oil tank housing. Here is the trick, the pan is sub-divided in the middle so that it serves as both the engine and transmission oil pans. BUT, be careful because the drain plug is on the OTHER side of the transmission (towards the front of the bike) and is even marked incorrectly in some owners manuals. It is easy to mix the two drain plugs up, since the one closest to the engine oil fill drain the TRANSMISSION and vice versa. So, the first time you drain the oil, pay CLOSE attention to what empties. Remember that the transmission fluid should be cleaner and fresher than used engine oil (unless it is really old) and it has that earthy, gear oil smell.**

1. Warm the engine to normal operating temperature, then park the bike.

2. Position a drain pan (of greater capacity than the bike's oil tank) under the drain plug or hose, as applicable.

3. Loosen or completely remove the dipstick, as this will allow the oil to drain more quickly.

4. If equipped with a drain plug, loosen it using a wrench or a ratchet and socket (on most models the drain plug has a ¾ in. hex). Once the plug is loosened, turn it out by hand, keeping inward pressure on the plug to keep oil from escaping past the threads until you are ready to fully withdraw it. When the plug is free, quickly pull the plug, and your hand, out of the way of the hot oil.

➡**On Softail models, it will be significantly easier to loosen the drain hose clamp if you first free the hose and plug from the strap that holds them to the frame. Once freed, you can pull the hose downward below the frame for better access (and have it pointing at the drain pan for when the plug is removed).**

5. If equipped with a drain hose, use a screwdriver or ratchet and socket to loosen the clamp on the end of the drain hose. On Softails, remove the plug, on Sportsters, pull the hose free of the battery tray or frame tab. Hold the hose downward slightly to direct the oil into the drain pan.

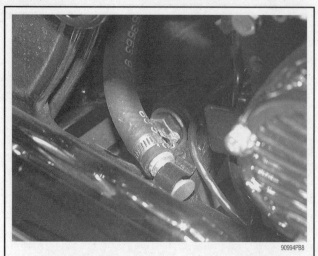

Fig. 45 Like this Softail, most Harley motors are equipped with an oil drain hose that is blocked-off with a metal drain plug . . .

Fig. 46 . . . and is attached to a frame rail like on this Buell— other bikes which use a drain hose include Sportsters and Lowriders

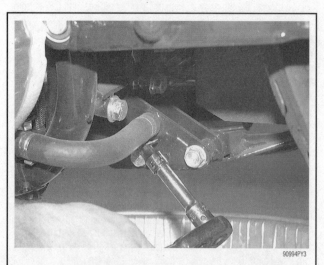

Fig. 47 To change the engine oil on models with a drain hose you should loosen the hose clamp . . .

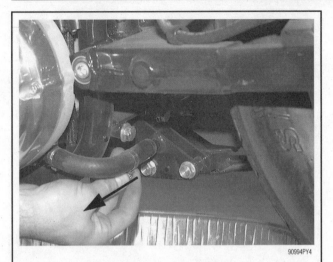

Fig. 48 . . . and slide the clamp back so the hose and plug can be separated

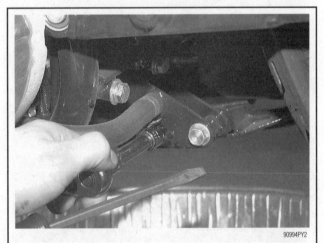

Fig. 49 You can loosen most clamps using a socket or a screwdriver, though some may be spring-tensioned meaning you will need a pair of pliers

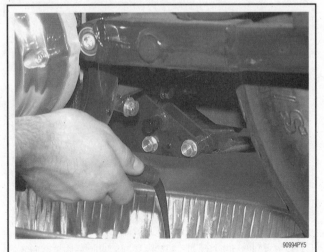

Fig. 50 With the plug removed from the hose, allow the engine oil to completely drain from the oil tank

Fig. 51 On Dyna and Touring models which use an oil pan, loosen and remove the drain plug . . .

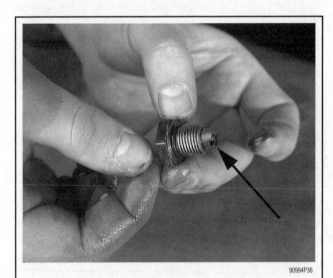

Fig. 52 . . . then check the magnetic plug for debris . . .

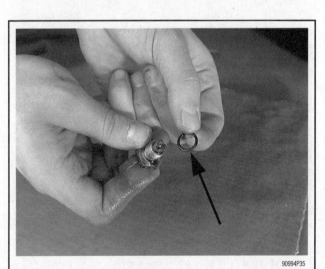

Fig. 53 . . . and replace the O-ring if it is not in good condition (but they can normally be reused a good number of times)

✳✳ **CAUTION**

On late-model Sportsters equipped with the frame mounted drain hose tab, be careful not to bend the drain hose too far. Follow the hose back, just behind the primary case and you will see that it is secured to a hard plastic T-fitting. If you twist at this fitting too hard you risk stressing and cracking it (which would be messy at best and dangerous at worst if you consider where the oil would be leaking . . . on the rear tire).

6. Allow the engine oil to drain completely. In the meantime, clean the drain plug (on models with a plug installed into the pan, the plug is usually magnetic and should be thoroughly cleaned to remove the tiny metal fragments that it was nice enough to remove from suspension in your oil).

7. Install and tighten the drain plug or the hose clamps, as applicable. On drain plugs that are installed into the oil pan, be sure to snug the drain plug, but DO NOT overtighten and strip it or your day will get very unhappy, very quickly. On drain hose models, don't overtighten the clamp (which would cut the hose), but DO BE CERTAIN that it is secure because should it come loose while riding, your rear tire will be the first to know (with you as a close second).

8. Move the drain pan to the front of the motor (under the oil filter).

9. Get a piece of cardboard and bend it in the middle to form a shallow **V**. This will be inserted under the oil filter so that the oil which will run out as it is loosened will run down the cardboard and into the drain pan, instead of all over the front of your engine. Ohhh, and if you have a fuel injected bike, forget that because you have an engine control sensor protruding from the front of the crankcase (and it is RIGHT in your way). If you can't use the cardboard, then place a plastic bag or some rags under the filter to catch the excess oil.

10. Use an oil filter strap or cap wrench to loosen the filter about one turn, then remove the wrench. Again, on fuel injected models, sorry, but many of the strap type wrenches get STUCK on the filter until it is removed (that sensor wiring again, it gives you JUST enough room to put the strap wrench on, but not enough to take it off once the filter has been loosened).

11. Once most of the oil has drained from the filter, unthread and remove it completely (remember there will still be some oil in it so turn it upright as soon as it is clear of the oil filter adapter.

12. Take your new filter and prime it by filling it about ½ way with fresh oil. This will help to make sure that your oil system comes up to pressure more quickly. You can add a decent amount of oil, as some of it will seep through the filter element and fill metal case of the filter. BUT, don't overfill it or you will pour clean oil on the front of the engine as it is installed.

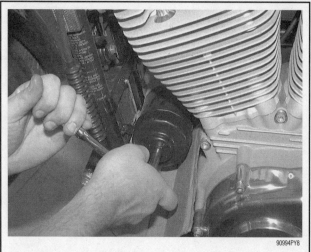

Fig. 55 Use a filter wrench to loosen the oil filter until it can be turned by hand . . .

Fig. 56 . . . then allow the filter to drain using the drip rail to keep the engine oil off your engine case

Fig. 54 Unless you have a fuel injected bike, make a drain rail out of a piece of cardboard by folding it in a V, then insert it under the oil filter

Fig. 57 On fuel injected bikes there is an engine control sensor which makes this impossible AND it usually requires that you use a strap-type filter wrench

Fig. 58 A few well placed rags and a plastic bag can help you to prevent a mess on fuel injected models

Fig. 59 Wipe the oil filter sealing surface using a clean rag

Fig. 60 Prime the new oil filter by filling it about ½ way with clean engine oil . . .

Fig. 61 . . . then lubricate the filter's seal lip using some of the oil

Fig. 62 Install the new filter by hand, giving it ½–¾ turn after it contacts the sealing surface

13. Take a clean, lint free rag or a paper towel and wipe the sealing area of the oil filter adapter.

14. Dip a finger in the clean engine oil and apply a light coating of oil to the rubber oil filter seal.

15. Install the filter, threading it to the adapter quickly and smoothly (to prevent oil from running onto your motor). Once the filter makes contact and is lightly seated, tighten it an additional ½–¾ turn to assure it is fully seated.

16. Clean the hydraulic tappet screen. For details, refer to the information later in this section.

17. Properly refill the engine using the proper amount of oil. If you do not have the engine oil capacity specification, add the first bottle of oil, then add the rest slowly, checking the level often to prevent overfilling.

18. Start the bike, watching the oil pressure light. It should go out within a second or so of starting the bike. If it does not, STOP the bike immediately and double check the oil level, then restart the bike watching the light again.

19. Once the bike has been warmed, double check the oil level (it should have gone down when the engine passages and oil filter were filled, so top it off as necessary) and make sure there is no seepage from the filter and drain plug or hose.

HYDRAULIC TAPPET OIL SCREEN

▶ See Figures 63 thru 68

Each time the engine oil is changed, the hydraulic tappet filter screen should be removed, cleaned, inspected and reinstalled. This is not a big deal, except that the plug can be VERY difficult to remove when the bike is new or if it has been overtightened. On most stock models, the plug is a slotted head which requires a No 1. Screwdriver, anything smaller may begin to strip the screw head. My local dealership tells me that they had Snap-On® make a tool for them so they could use a ratchet to loosen this plug. In our shop we used a Craftsman drag-Link socket and it did the job. But, on my personal bike, I quickly replaced the plug with a hex-head plug available from Harley. Unfortunately, the angle of the engine case prevents a socket from fully gripping the hex-head and I still have to be careful not to strip it.

Once the plug is loosened, unthread and remove it for access to the filter screen and spring. Carefully grab the top of the screen with a pair of needle nose pliers and remove it (the spring will come out with it. Clean the screen using some solvent (a can of evaporative brake cleaner works well) and blow it dry with compressed air. DO NOT allow any solvent to remain on the screen when it is installed back into the motor. Install the spring and

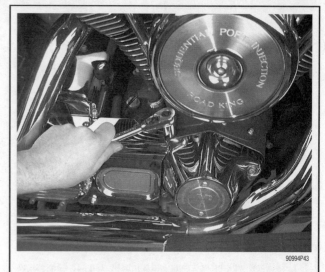
Fig. 65 . . . then you will be able to use a standard socket

Fig. 63 On bikes with the stock tappet screen plug, use a No. 1 screwdriver or a drag link socket to loosen and remove the plug

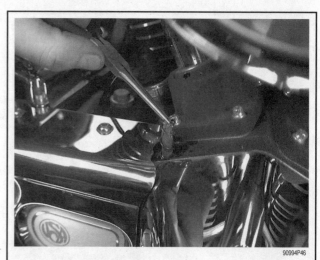
Fig. 66 With the plug removed, you can withdraw the filter screen and spring assembly

Fig. 64 Installation of a hex-head plug will make removal a little easier . . .

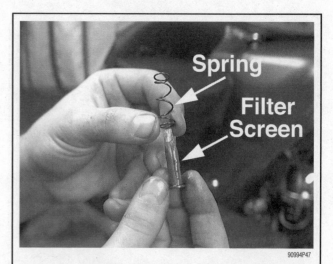
Fig. 67 The spring is mounted on top of the filter screen, and by pushing against the plug, holds the screen in place

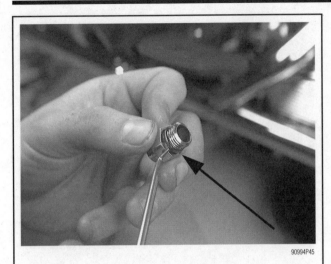

Fig. 68 Before installing the plug, check the O-ring for cuts or damage and replace, if necessary

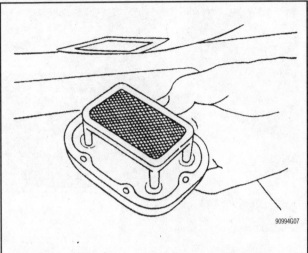

Fig. 69 Some older models may be equipped with reusable filter screens that should be removed and cleaned periodically

screen assembly, then carefully thread the plug. DO NOT overtighten the plug or you will be sorry next oil change when you have trouble getting it out.

Japanese and European Bikes (Except BMW)

FOUR-STROKE ENGINES

▶ See Figures 69 thru 91

Many Japanese and a few European motorcycles with four-stroke engines use the engine oil to lubricate the transmission as well. Most of these motorcycles therefore have one drain plug located centrally under the engine/transmission case. This makes for convenient fluid changes (but it makes the fluid changes all THAT much more important, since acids from old, oxidized and contaminated oils will also be attacking your transmission if left in the bike too long).

Oil filters on almost all modern motorcycles are either of the automotive looking spin-on type (mounted to an oil filter adapter somewhere on the engine), or are of the disposable filter cartridge type (located in a housing mounted to the engine case or oil pan).

➡ Some old models may be equipped with reusable filter screens which are removed, cleaned with a safe solvent, inspected for damage and reinstalled. If you have one of these it might be worth it to buy one or two extras now (if they are still available) so that you will have a spare if the one currently installed becomes unserviceable.

The more bodywork you have on your bike, the more of a chance that you may have to remove some of it to change the oil. BUT, don't let appearances fool you. If you get an opportunity look at a VFR 750 or a CBR 600 while it is parked next to a Katana or a Ninja. The bodywork on all of these bikes hides the spin-on filter, yet the service manuals for the Hondas usually suggest that the change can be done without removing the bodywork. You will have to decide for yourself.

While the motor is overnight cold, check to see if you are one of the unfortunate ones who will have to remove part of the fairing in order to drain your engine oil. To do this, crouch next the bike, then locate your drain plug and oil filter. The drain plug is usually located on the bottom of the engine case, but the oil filter location varies. Most spin-on style filters are mounted to the front of the engine blocks on modern bikes. But we say most, because some are mounted on the side of the engine case and a few are on the lower rear of the engine. Cartridge type filters are usually

installed under a removable cover on the side of the engine case or the bottom of the oil pan.

Here's the good news, MOST bikes are set up so that you can pull the drain plug without touching the fairing, even if you should remove the bodywork to get to the filter. This means that you can go for a ride to warm the oil, come back, pull the drain plug and let the oil drain while you remove the bodywork (allowing the motor to cool). There is an added advantage that the exhaust pipes (which often seem to be mounted near the oil filters on three and four cylinder bikes) should cool down by the time your hands need to be close to them.

If you really don't want to take the bodywork off, check to see if access is possible with it installed. Again, with the bike overnight cold to prevent burns, get your hands and the necessary tools and see if they will all fit. If there is room in the bodywork for the oil to drain from the filter, then the manufacturer intended for you to do it without removing the fairing. But even if there is no drain area for the filter (which is usually the case), you can usually put a few rags or a small oil bottle (with the side cut out) in position under the filter to catch the oil which will escape as it is loosened.

Fig. 70 Loosen the drain plug using a ratchet, extension and appropriate socket . . .

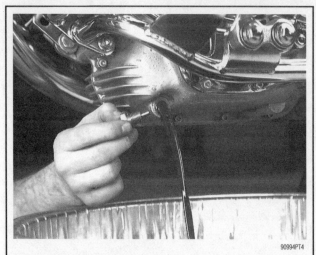

Fig. 71 . . . then remove the plug by hand and allow the engine oil to drain—be careful not to burn yourself on the hot oil

Fig. 74 If you are lucky, your oil filter is a spin-on that is out in the open like this . . .

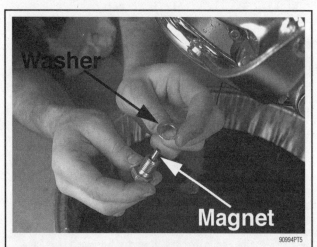

Fig. 72 Inspect the drain plug sealing washer or O-ring (as applicable) and, if it is magnetic, clean the residue from the end of the plug

Fig. 75 . . . or like this, access is easy, just slide a drain pan underneath and use a filter wrench to loosen it

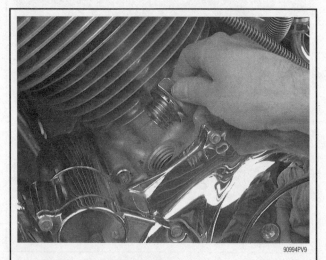

Fig. 73 The oil will usually drain faster if the filler cap is removed

Fig. 76 But if you have a lot of lower bodywork, you will have to decide if any must be removed to access the oil filter

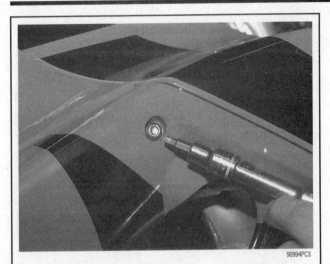

Fig. 77 If so, there are several methods of fastening bodywork, most use some form of capscrew like this hex head . . .

Fig. 78 . . . or this combination Phillips/flathead screw, along with tabs or rubber grommets

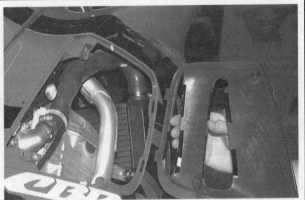

Fig. 79 You may have to remove a side panel before removing a lower fairing, depending on the year and model of your bike, just take your time and you can figure out what piece mounts to what other piece

1. Warm the engine to normal operating temperature, then park the bike.

2. Position a drain pan (of greater capacity than the bike's crankcase) under the drain plug.

3. Loosen or completely remove the dipstick and/or oil filler cap (as applicable) as this will allow the oil to drain more quickly.

4. On some dual-sport and dirt models you may have to remove the engine skid plate for access to the drain plug.

5. Loosen the drain plug using a wrench or a ratchet and socket. Once the plug is loosened, turn it out by hand, keeping inward pressure on the plug to keep oil from escaping past the threads until you are ready to fully withdraw it. When the plug is free, quickly pull the plug, and your hand, out of the way of the hot oil.

6. Allow the engine oil to drain completely. In the meantime, clean the drain plug and, if equipped, get a new crush washer out from your handy stash (what, no stash . . . you may be able to reuse it this time, but by a few extras next time you are at the shop). You really don't want oil leaking from a motorcycle (besides having the potential to ruin your engine, it could get on your REAR TIRE, get it?)

7. While the engine oil is draining remove any bodywork that is necessary to access the filter.

8. Install and tighten the drain plug. Be sure to snug the drain plug, but DO NOT overtighten and strip it or your day will get very unhappy, very quickly.

➡On dry sump motors (especially any dirt or dual sport models) double check your owners manual to make sure there are no other drain plug locations for your particular model. For example for years the Suzuki DR250 and 350 models used an oil storage tank which was part of the frame. In order to completely drain the oil the plug must be removed from the lower portion of the frame tube, as well.

9. Move the drain pan below the filter or filter housing, as applicable.

10. If equipped with a spin-on type oil filter, use a filter wrench (cap or strap-type, whichever you have and will fit) to loosen and remove the oil filter. On models where the filter is installed above an exhaust pipe or fairing, you should use a few paper towels or rags to catch the excess oil which will drain from the filter as it is removed. Lubricate the seal on the lip of the new spin-on filter and install it by hand. Once the filter is lightly seated, tighten it an additional ½–¾ turn to assure it is fully seated.

➡Although it is not absolutely necessary, we like to prime spin-on oil filters by filling them ½ way with clean, fresh engine oil before installation. On most bikes this will shorten the amount of time necessary for the oil pump to build pressure through the lubricating system on the first start-up since it has less area to fill in the filter.

11. On models which use cartridge type filters, locate the cover housing and loosen the retaining bolt(s). Carefully remove the cover, taking care to note any gaskets, seals or O-rings for installation purposes. Although most cartridge filters are interference fit (end-to-end) with the housing, and some are attached to the cover, a few may be retained by circlips. If present, remove the retaining clip before attempting to withdraw the filter element. Install the new element, then install the housing cover, making sure to properly position any seals, gaskets or O-rings. Secure the cover housing bolt(s).

12. Properly refill the engine using the proper amount of oil. If you do not have the engine oil capacity specification, add the first bottle of oil, then add the rest slowly, checking the level often to prevent overfilling.

13. Start the bike, watching the oil pressure light. It should go out within a second or so of starting the bike. If it does not, STOP the bike immediately and double check the oil level, then restart the bike watching the light again.

14. Once the bike has been warmed, double check the oil level and make sure there is no seepage from the filter or drain plug.

15. Secure any bodywork which was removed or loosened for access.

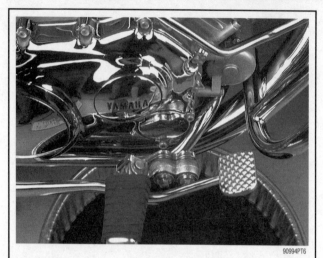

Fig. 80 If however, your bike uses a cartridge type oil filter, you will have to remove an engine cover for access to it . . .

Fig. 81 . . . on this model that means you will have to remove the rear brake pedal . . .

Fig. 82 . . . and the right foot peg mount in order to gain the necessary clearance to remove the cover

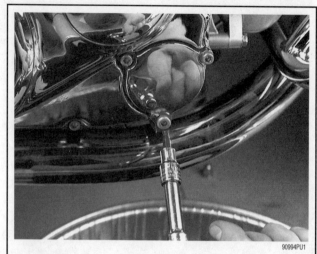

Fig. 83 Once access is gained, loosen and remove the cover retainers . . .

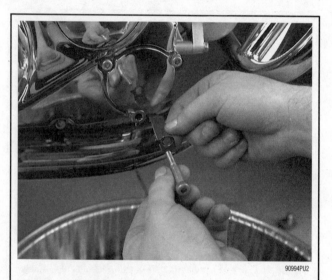

Fig. 84 . . . keeping track of any brackets . . .

Fig. 85 . . . or uneven length bolts for installation purposes

Fig. 86 Remove the filter housing cover, along with any gaskets or O-rings

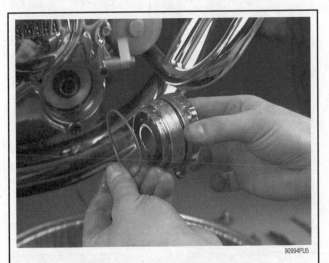

Fig. 87 Check any O-rings for wear, cuts or damage and replace, as necessary

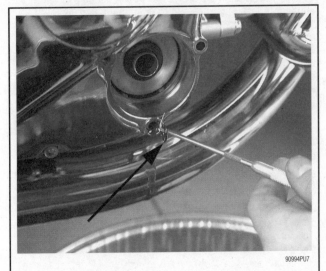

Fig. 88 On some models, the bolt holes may also have O-rings

Fig. 89 Remove and discard the old filter . . .

Fig. 90 . . . but check the new filter against it first, it should be the same size and composition as the old one

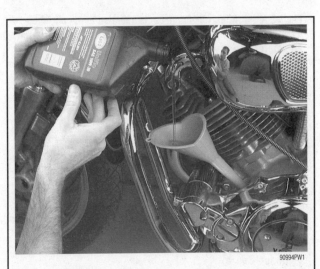

Fig. 91 Once the new filter is installed under the housing cover, properly refill the engine oil

TWO-STROKE ENGINES

The very design of a two-stroke engine means that it usually does not use a high-pressure lubrication system like four-stroke motors. Oil is added to the gasoline mixture in order lubricate the ball or roller bearings of the motor. Some use a separate oil tank, which should be checked at each gas fill. And some mix the oil with the gasoline during fill-up. Be sure to check your owners manual to determine the proper amount of oil and how to add it to your particular model.

For this reason, periodic oil and filter changes are normally not necessary or possible on these motors.

Air Filter

▶ **See Figure 92**

The air filter is used to remove fine particles of dirt or debris present in the air and which are drawn into the air induction system. By removing these particles before the inducted air is fed to the carburetor(s) or throttle body(ies), the engine is protected from unnecessary wear and damage.

A clogged air filter will decrease the efficiency and life of the engine. On carbureted and some open-loop fuel injected motorcycles, a clogged air filter will richen the air/fuel mixture. If the element becomes damaged or torn, it could allow fine particles to enter the engine allowing for rapid wear of delicate parts such as the piston rings, cylinder walls and bearings. Dirt could also clog the tiny passages found in carburetors.

Never run the motorcycle without the air cleaner installed. And be sure to check and clean or replace the air filter regularly.

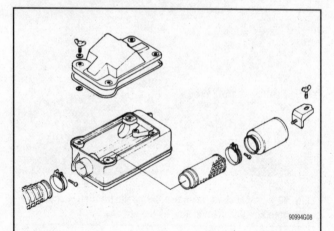

90994G08

Fig. 92 An air filter, of some type, is mounted in the air intake track of all motorcycles in order to remove particles of dirt from air before it is introduced into the engine

INSPECTION & CLEANING

Most manufacturer's recommend checking and/or replacing the air cleaner element every 5000–10,000 miles, depending on the model and filter type. Keep in mind that operation in excessively dusty conditions (off road, dirt riding and desert street riding), requires more frequent inspections. But, especially if access to the air cleaner is easy, we would recommend that you check for excessive dirt, debris or damage at every oil change. Remember that a clogged air cleaner will cost you money (in gas) and fun (in performance). A damaged air cleaner could cost you a lot more in engine damage.

There are basically 4 types of air cleaners found on motorcycles today:
- **Paper**
- **Cotton Gauze**
- **Foam**
- **Metal Mesh**

Paper Elements

▶ **See Figure 93**

Paper filter elements are usually treated in the same manner as automotive air filters. They are simply installed and checked from time to time. Once their recommended life span (in terms of mileage) has expired or once they appear damaged or excessively dirty, they should just be replaced. Be careful when visually inspecting a paper element since it could be very clogged and not appear too dirty to the eye. The best method of checking most paper elements is to see if a light (from a drop light or flash light) will pass through. Hold the element up and place a light in the center of it, then check if you can see the light through the wall of the element. If the element blocks too much of the light it should be replaced.

If a paper element is not excessively dirty, you can service it by gently tapping it on a work surface to dislodge any loose particles, brushing some of the dirt deposits off the outside.

90994P02

Fig. 93 Automotive style paper element air filters are among the most popular style of air filter used in motorcycles today

✻✻ WARNING

Contrary to what you may have heard in the past, you should not use compressed air to blow the element clean. Compressed air, even low level of only a few psi (kPa) can damage or tear the element, allowing particles to pass through the gaps.

➡**Although MOST paper elements are run dry and cannot be cleaned (other than the way we just outlined), there are some exceptions. Harley-Davidson Evolution models are normally equipped from the factory with a paper compound element which Harley recommends washing in warm water, drying and returning to service. Also, some aftermarket companies have offered a paper-like element which is oiled before use, but this last type is rare.**

Cotton Gauze

▶ **See Figure 94**

Used mostly as an aftermarket replacement, this type of filter is noted for excellent filtration ability combined with long life and ease of service. K&N® makes the most widely used and popular versions of these filters, normally consisting of a cotton gauze filter media housed between a metal mesh support.

This type of element MUST be oiled to work properly. It can be removed, inspected, cleaned and re-oiled periodically. Under normal service this type

Fig. 94 This is an example of a K&N filter, the cotton gauze element is behind a metal mesh and is, in this case, secured between 2 metal housings

of element can give very long intervals between cleaning and oiling, but as usual, that varies with the environment in which the engine is run.

➡ Consult the filter manufacturer's recommendations for cleaning or re-oiling techniques and intervals.

In general, these elements can be cleaned with warm soap and water or with a appropriate filter element cleaner. Once the element has dried thoroughly, apply element oil to resaturate the media. Various spray applicator oils are available for this purpose and the appropriate type for your type element should be used.

This type of element may also be available from the manufacturer as an upgrade. For instance, Harley-Davidson sells K&N® gauze filters under their own Screaming Eagle® brand name.

Foam Elements

♦ See Figure 95

Foam air filter elements were quite popular on many motorcycles at one time. They are still in use today and are often used as aftermarket replacements for paper type elements on some types of motorcycles. Foam elements are normally oiled before installation, the oil and foam work together

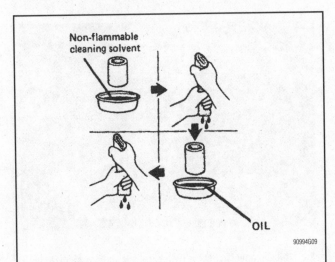

Fig. 95 Most foam air filter elements are designed to be cleaned, oiled and reused

to provide filtering. The foam and oil can capture small bits of foreign matter, while the combination is less restrictive to air than some other styles of filter.

Foam elements also have the advantage of being cleaned using a mild solvent and reused. The combination of high air flow, good filtering ability and long part life has made these filters very popular with high performance applications (or even just mild performance modifications to otherwise almost stock motorcycles).

To service an oiled foam element, you should wash it thoroughly in a mild solvent, letting the filter soak up the solvent like a sponge. Then, squeeze the element dry. Repeat this until the solvent being squeezed from the element ceases to carry off dirt.

✳✳ WARNING

Be sure that you SQUEEZE the solvent from the element and do not wring it out. Twisting the element in a wringing fashion will risk tearing and will likely damage the close-knit pores of the element.

Once the element has been cleaned, soak it the proper type of oil, as recommended by the filter manufacturer. Some use standard engine oils, some use gear oils and others use special filter oil (available in a spray applicator from various companies). Once you are done oiling the element, squeeze off the excess and return it to service.

Like any other air cleaner, even the reusable foam element will have a limited life span. Be sure to check it carefully for damage, deterioration or tears and replace it when it has become unserviceable.

Metal Mesh

We mention this type as more of a history lesson, since you probably won't find one unless you are riding an antique. But, at one point this style of element was very popular. It was constructed as a series of steel screens, one over another. The filtering was accomplished by immersing the filter screens in motor oil. After the excess oil had drained off, a film remained which would trap impurities in the air passing through the filter. Or, at least it would in theory.

One advantage of this style filter was that it could be cleaned by washing in solvent, blown-dry and re-oiled easily and often. One disadvantage was that to maintain effectiveness, this really should be done much more often than most people would. In the past, many owners of bikes which were equipped with this style filter found aftermarket replacements of the foam filter type. Probably a good move for better filtration and less work.

REPLACEMENT

No matter what type of air cleaner element your motorcycle uses one thing is certain. It is mounted in a semi-enclosed housing that has an air inlet track (from outside the bike) and an air outlet track (which goes to the carburetor or throttle body). Accessing the filter element will vary greatly from model to model.

BMW

♦ See Figures 96, 97, 98 and 99

Most BMWs have air cleaners which have been designed for ease of maintenance. Early airheads use a cover on the top, rear, left side of the engine case which was retained by one long bolt. Later airheads and some K-models use a plastic housing which sandwiches the element between upper and lower halves. When installed, the sides of the element are visible, with just the 4 retaining clips (which secure the upper and lower halves around the filter). Later model bikes, including the oilheads, use automotive style plastic housings with lids that are secured by retaining clips and which are usually located under the seat or fairing, depending on the model.

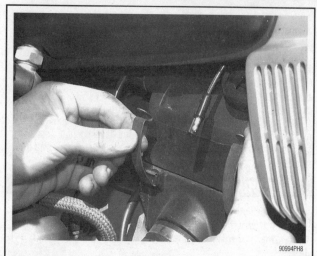

Fig. 96 On most late-model BMWs, the air cleaner element is secured using a few retaining clips . . .

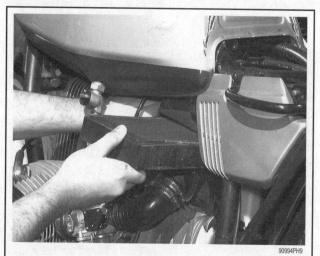

Fig. 97 . . . once the clips are released, the air cleaner is easily removed

Fig. 98 This model was equipped with a K&N® filter element which can be cleaned, oiled and reused (see the information on Cotton Gauze elements earlier in this section)

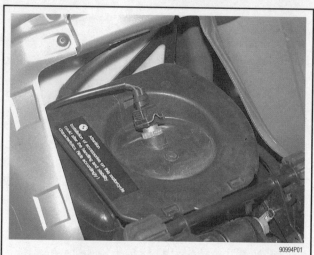

Fig. 99 Late-model bikes, like this oilhead use an automotive style paper element mounted in a plastic housing like this

To access the air cleaners simply undo the retaining bolt (early airheads) or clips and remove the old element. While the element is out, use a damp rag to clean the inside of the housing of any dirt of debris. Then install the new element and secure using the retaining clips.

Harley-Davidson and Buell

▶ See Figures 100, 101, 102, 103 and 104

Most Harley and Buell models use an air cleaner housing which is secured to the carburetor or throttle body (as applicable). The air cleaners are readily identifiable as chromed stamped steel covers, which are either round or oval in shape on the Harleys. Early Buells used a carbon-fiber version of the oval Harley air cleaner cover, but later factory models went to some abysmally shaped plastic housings (which afforded the proper tuning AND still made EPA noise standards).

Element inspection or replacement is a simple matter of unbolting the housing and removing the element. On most late-model Harley EVO big-twins, a single screw holds the cover to the element, while 2 other screws underneath hold the element to the carburetor or throttle body. On Sportsters (and on older, iron head or Shovelhead big-twins), the oval air cleaner is usually bolted to the backing plate by 2 screws and the element sandwiched between them.

Fig. 100 On most Harley Big-Twins, the air cleaner element is bolted to a backing plate and the chrome cover is held on the element by a single, hex-headed bolt

Fig. 101 Because only ONE bolt (or two on Sportsters and some older Iron Heads) is retaining the cover, be sure to use a thread-locking compound like Loctite® on the bolt threads

I knew I should have used Loctite. . . It just fell off!

As a motorcycle rider you will learn that Loctite® can be your BEST friend

Fig. 102 This Fuel Injected twin is equipped with a Screaming Eagle® low restriction air cleaner element that mounts a little differently from stock units . . .

Fig. 103 . . . the element is held onto 3 studs by self-locking nuts (equipped with nylon inserts).

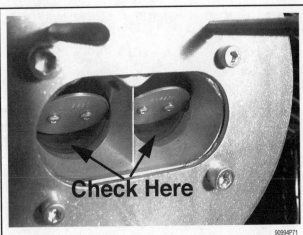

Check Here

Fig. 104 On Fuel Injected units, be sure to periodically check behind the throttle plates for oil residue which could disturb hot idle operation

✳✳ WARNING

Be careful when installing the air cleaner element and cover to these assemblies. Many of the backing plates are made of plastic and are easily stripped (requiring a special order part and some downtime). ALSO, remember that there are only 1 or 2 screws holding the air cleaner cover in place. Most are coated with a thread sealant from the factory. When the sealant starts to wear off, be sure to coat it with fresh sealant, like Loctite® 242 (medium strength, Blue). The thread sealant will help keep the screw(s) from vibrating loose during operation.

While the element is removed, take the opportunity to clean the backing plate and cover using a clean rag. Late-model Harleys tend to carry a little oil over to the air cleaner through the breathers now and again, especially if they sit between use. Don't worry if you see a little oil, just wipe it up. Excessive amounts of oil may be a cause for additional attention (unless you've got an early 90's Sportster and you run at highway speeds a lot). Early 90's Sportsters almost always carried a little extra oil into the air cleaner when run fast. On those models you've got two choices, install a late-model oil pump which has been revised to help solve this or switch to a foam oiled air cleaner and let your breathers do a little extra oiling for you (except of course, in most cases, the oil will be on the wrong side of the filter and may be drawn into the intake before it even gets to the element. Do not mistake this second option as a viable option to cleaning and reoiling a filter, it is more humorous than useful.)

Owners of fuel injected Harleys should take an extra moment when inspecting the air cleaner. If you have some oil carryover, from the breathers, open the throttle body butterflies using the throttle grip and inspect the inside of the bore. Unlike the carbureted models which can rely on the accelerator pump to spray gasoline on this surface now and again, the fuel injected bikes don't have gas introduced until the other end of the intake runner. The result is that oil carryover which would wash away from the throttle bore on a carbureted bike can cake and disrupt idle air on a fuel injected model. If you find some oil caking behind the throttle plates, use a clean rag and some solvent to remove it, and you will prevent hot idle problems down the road.

Japanese and European Bikes (Except BMW)

◆ **See Figures 105 thru 110**

Although some of these bikes have been equipped with an air cleaner hanging out to the side (where it is nice and easy to get at), many are not.

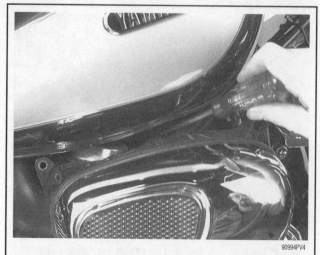

Fig. 107 On this model the housing must be removed to access the filter, but it is a simple matter of removing the screws . . .

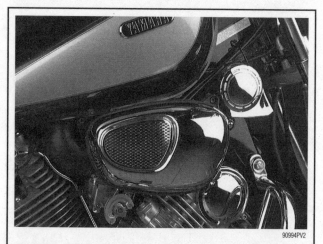

Fig. 105 Most later-model bikes use automotive style filters located in housings either cradled in the frame, or in this case . . .

Fig. 108 . . . and loosening the air intake hose clamp, then gently pulling the housing from the side of the engine

Fig. 106 . . . fastened to the side of the engine using a few retaining screws

Fig. 109 Once the halves of the housing are separated you have access to the filter

Fig. 110 Remove the element for inspection or replacement, as necessary

Fig. 111 Water cooled motorcycles utilize a radiator as a heat exchanger just like most automobiles

Chances are that your air cleaner element is in a plastic housing that is located, under one of the side panels, under the seat, or (heaven forbid) under the gas tank. Obviously, check the easy ones first (before removing the gas tank).

The housing covers are either bolted together, or they are secured by multiple retaining clips (much in the same fashion of today's automobiles). Once the cover is removed, lift the filter element out of the housing for inspection or replacement. Take the opportunity to use a damp rag to clean the inside of the housing of any dirt of debris. Then install the element and secure using the retainers.

Coolant

➡ **Harley guys, you can skip this section. Yep, keep moving, this is for people whose bikes are cooled by something other than air and oil.**

GENERAL INFORMATION

▶ **See Figures 111 and 112**

Motorcycle engines are cooled by 2 basic methods, air and oil or water. Air and oil cooled motors use air passing over cooling fins on the engine cases and, sometimes, air passing over the fins of an oil cooler to remove the heat generated by combustion. Air cooling works well, within limits. But, for the best emission control and most predictable engine performance thermostatically controlled water cooling is usually preferred.

On a water cooled bike, coolant travels through passages in the engine, through a thermostat and out to a radiator, where heat is transferred to the air passing over the radiator fins. Then the coolant, now at a lower temperature, returns to the engine to remove more heat. The term "water cooled" is slightly misleading because the liquid coolant should never be more than 50 percent water. The balance of the solution should usually be a high-quality ethylene-glycol (or propylene-glycol) antifreeze. The term "antifreeze" brings me to another point.

The coolant also serves another purpose. If the bike is placed in winter storage and is exposed to sub-freezing temperatures, the coolant is also an "antifreeze." It serves to protect the bike. Should plain water, or old coolant that has lost some of its ability to resist freezing, be left in the system, then your engine could freeze, cracking the cases. This would lead to some seriously bad realizations come spring.

Water cooling an engine may add performance and reliability, but it also adds complexity. It is another system that must be properly maintained in order to keep the engine working. One of the most common misunderstandings about cooling systems is that the coolant can be ignored. You

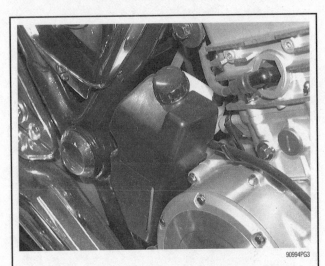

Fig. 112 And, also like automobiles, then usually use an overflow tank for easy level checking and minor fluid top-off

know, I can see some in the tank, so it must be fine. Well, WRONG! Coolant MUST BE CHANGED REGULARLY. It is not sufficient to just have the system full. As coolant ages, it loses its ability to resist boiling and conduct heat. But, more importantly, it also loses its anti-corrosion properties, and this will allow the build-up of scale and residue in the cooling system. This build-up will reduce the cooling system's ability to do its job and could eventually render the system useless. To prevent this oxidation of the aluminum cooling passages you should replace your engine coolant AT LEAST once every 2 years.

Now, there are some long-life coolants available on the market today. If they meet your manufacturer's requirements, then by all means go ahead and use them. BUT, be careful. Normally we would encourage the use of automotive products in motorcycles, but our favorite magazine, Motorcycle Consumer News (MCN) alerted us to a possible problem with coolant and it may be a better idea to use your manufacturer's fluids in this case.

It seems that certain products, including many Honda motorcycles, have experienced unusual problems with water pump seal failures based on the coolant used in the system. It seems to have something to do with the silicates present in many automotive coolants, but that are specifically absent in Honda's brand. There is a school of though that believes these silicates are tearing the seals, leading to early demise of water pumps on that manufacturer's bikes. This is one of those items that you are going to have to decide for yourself. But, motorcycle cooling systems don't use a whole lot of coolant and there probably isn't going to be a really big savings by once every 2 years using an automotive coolant. So, if you are not sure of the compatibility of a coolant with your motorcycle, you may want to trust the manufacturer on this one.

CHECKING YOUR COOLANT

▶ See Figures 113, 114, 115 and 116

You should check the coolant level in your motorcycle as frequently as you check the level of your oil. It can be just as important to the life of your engine. If the level begins to drop suddenly (and you don't see any leaks), then IMMEDIATELY check your oil to see if it is being diluted by the coolant. If so, you must perform a major repair quickly, before the engine is ruined by the diluted oil.

But, most of the time you will probably notice that the coolant level remains the same. Then it is just a matter of keeping an eye on it and replacing it every 2 years.

Most water cooled motorcycles use a coolant reservoir so the level can be checked without removing the radiator or pressure cap. The reservoirs are typically marked with LOW and FULL or COLD and HOT markings.

Usually, manufacturer's suggest that the coolant level should be checked with the bike on the centerstand and with the engine at normal operating temperature. BUT, there are always some exceptions, so check your owners manual to be sure.

If you experience a coolant related problem. Boiling over and pouring out the overflow tube, for example. Check the specific gravity of the coolant using a hydrometer. These should be readily available at most automotive stores. The hydrometer can help you determine if the mixture of coolant to water is incorrect. Of course, if you are unsure just how OLD the coolant in your bike is, then you should replace it immediately and see if the problem goes away.

➡You should always use distilled water in the cooling system since the minerals and chemicals that are usually present in tap or drinking water may contribute to internal system corrosion. And that is exactly what you are trying to avoid by changing the coolant in the first place.

Whenever you check your coolant, take a few minutes to inspect the condition of your coolant hoses as well. With the engine cool, run your hands along the hoses looking for damp or soft spots which indicate a weakening hose that could be getting ready to burst. Check the clamps at the ends to

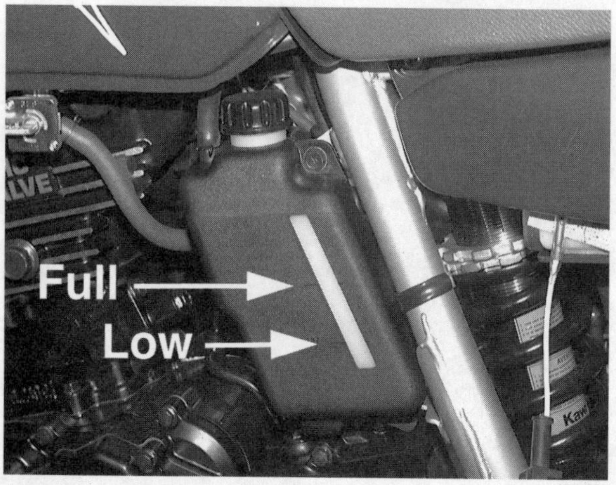

Fig. 113 Most bikes use a coolant reservoir or overflow tank that is marked to indicate proper coolant levels

Fig. 115 If no other method is given to check the coolant, then you must remove the radiator cap—BUT ONLY REMOVE THE CAP when the engine is cold

Fig. 114 But because the overflow tank may not be easily accessible on some bikes there may be other methods, like a level tube

Fig. 116 When you are checking the coolant level, take a moment to inspect the hoses for wear, damage or leaks

be sure the hoses are secure on the fittings. Clamps should be snug, but not over-tight (which might cause the ends of the hose to crack and split). Replace any hose that seems suspect, you wouldn't want it to burst on the road and leave your stranded.

FLUSHING AND FILLING THE SYSTEM

▶ **See Figures 117, 118, 119, 120 and 121**

We'll say it again. AT LEAST, once every 2 years be sure to completely drain, flush and refill your cooling system with a high-quality antifreeze/coolant.

Draining The Cooling System

1. Place the bike on the centerstand, with the engine COLD.
2. If necessary for access, remove the fairing or sidecovers.
3. Position a catch pan and drain the engine cooling system:

   a. Remove the system pressure cap to de-pressurize the system. It usually looks just like a radiator cap, but on motorcycles it isn't always mounted on the radiator.

   b. Most bikes have a water pump drain screw and sealing washer. If equipped, remove the screw and allow the system to drain.

   c. If you cannot find a water pump drain screw, loosen the hose clamp and disconnect the lower radiator hose from the radiator. This will allow the engine and radiator to both drain.

   d. Disconnect the radiator overflow hose from the reservoir tank and siphon the fluid from the tank. If necessary, the tank can be completely removed, rinsed and re-installed.

4. Once the cooling system is empty you have 3 choices. (1) Flush the system by removing the thermostat and using a garden hose. (2) Flush the system using warm water and by running the engine to open the thermostat. (3) Just refill the system. It's your choice, but we've listed them in descending order from best to least best.

Flushing By Removing The Thermostat

1. Locate and remove the thermostat. On some models it is conveniently located directly under the system pressure cap, but on others you will have to unbolt and remove the housing.

2. If you did not remove the lower radiator hose in order to drain the system, disconnect it from the radiator now.

3. Close the rest of the system by reinstalling the pressure cap.

4. With the thermostat removed, but the system sealed everywhere but at the hose your removed, hold a garden hose up to the radiator hose and

Fig. 118 . . . on this CBR the side panel had to be removed . . .

Fig. 119 . . . in order to access and remove the thermostat

allow water to be forced through the system and to exit the bottom of the radiator. Clean water will flow through the engine, through the upper radiator hose and finally through the radiator.

5. Flush the system until the water coming out of the radiator is completely clean.

6. Install the thermostat and the lower radiator hose and refill the cooling system.

Flushing By Running The Engine

1. Install the lower radiator hose and/or the water pump drain screw, as applicable.

2. Fill the cooling system with water through the pressure cap. Then start and run the bike until it reaches normal operating temperature and the thermostat opens. You can tell when this occurs because the upper radiator hose and the radiator will get hot.

3. Shut the engine **OFF** and drain the cooling system. BE CAREFUL as the water will be VERY HOT.

4. Repeat these steps until the water which is drained comes out completely clean.

5. Install the lower radiator hose and/or the water pump drain screw and refill the cooling system.

Fig. 117 When flushing and filling the cooling system you may have to remove body work on some models . . .

Refilling The System

1. Pre-mix the distilled water and coolant in a container by filling it halfway with one and then topping it off with the other. This way you will be certain to maintain the proper 50/50 ration of coolant to water.

2. Carefully pour the solution in the pressure cap opening in the system.

3. Keep filling the system until the level is at the bottom of the filler neck.

4. Fill the reservoir tank to the UPPER, FULL or HOT mark, as applicable.

5. Crank the engine to see if you will be able to run it without closing the system. If you can (without the coolant spraying all over the place) this is the best way to bleed air and make sure the system is full. If so start and run the engine, adding coolant as the level drops until the level remains steadily at the base of the filler neck.

6. If you cannot run the engine with the cap off, close the system and start the engine. As the system approaches operating temperature the thermostat should open. CAREFULLY remove the pressure cap (using a rag to shield you in case you warmed the engine too much). Then add coolant until the level is at the base of the filler neck. Close the system and repeat until the level does not drop when the system is run.

7. Be sure to clean up any antifreeze or coolant that you have spilled and place the remaining solutions in a CHILD PROOF container (then put it where a child can't get at it).

8. Take the bike out for a run and double check the coolant level in the reservoir after it has been at operating temperature for some time.

Fuel Filter

INSPECTION

▶ **See Figures 122, 123 and 124**

The fuel filter is designed to do for your carburetor or fuel injectors what the air filter does for your engine. The only difference is that, as long as the inside of your fuel tank is kept relatively clean and as long as you don't get a particularly bad tank of gas, the filter should be a long-life, trouble free component. If however, the screen becomes clogged, the flow of gasoline will be impeded. This could cause lean fuel mixtures, hesitation and stumbling.

On carbureted vehicles usually have a fuel filter attached to the fuel petcock. Once upon a time it took the form of a sediment bowl and filter screen, usually threaded into the base of the petcock, and occasionally in the carburetor float bowl. But, these days, it is far more likely that a filter screen is mounted to the top of the petcock assembly and is inserted into the gas tank. It is a good idea on carbureted vehicles to remove the petcock, then clean and inspect the fuel filter screen at least once per year.

Some carbureted vehicles are also equipped with one or more inline fuel filters. These are usually similar to the old carbureted automotive style filters, consisting of a filter element in a plastic housing with nipples on either end to attach the fuel lines. On most carbureted bikes you may wish to install one of these filters inline, just below the petcock. These filters are readily available at most automotive supply stores. If you do this, you can usually leave the intank screen alone until you notice a reduction in the fuel flow (meaning that the screen is clogged). One of the additional advantages of adding an inline filter is that most of them are clear plastic and you can actually see if fuel is filling the filter housing. This is helpful in determining if your intank screen is clogged or if the vacuum diaphragm in your petcock (almost all modern bikes use this) is operating correctly.

Fig. 120 On most models you will refill the cooling system through the radiator cap . . .

Fig. 121 . . . and then top off the coolant reservoir

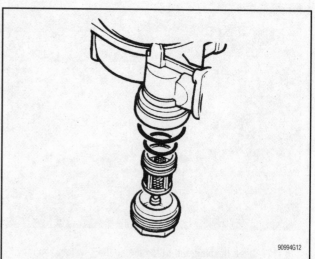

Fig. 122 Once upon a time, carburetors where equipped with a float bowl filter . . .

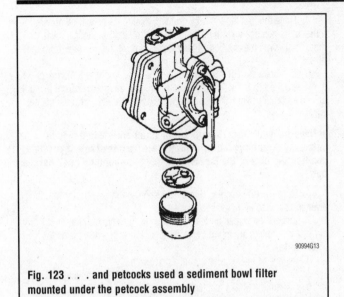

Fig. 123 . . . . and petcocks used a sediment bowl filter mounted under the petcock assembly

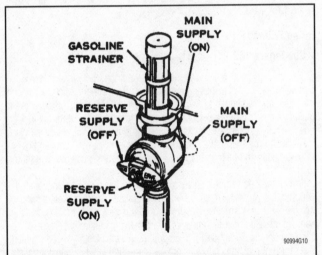

Fig. 124 But, today, the filter is usually mounted on the petcock and inserted into the tank instead

Because of their design, fuel injected vehicles use a pressurized fuel system where an electric pump (usually mounted inside the fuel tank) delivers high pressure fuel to the tiny, intricate valves of the fuel injectors. It is extremely important that no debris is allowed to enter the fuel lines, as it can cause havoc with your fuel injectors. For this reason, most fuel injected bikes are equipped with a high quality canister fuel filter (similar to those found in fuel injected automobiles). The canister is often found inside the fuel tank, as it should NOT require periodic maintenance. But, the filter can be mounted inline between the tank and the throttle body. If a fuel delivery problem occurs, then the filter should be checked and replaced as one of the possible troubleshooting steps.

REPLACEMENT

❊❊ CAUTION

For those of you who have led a sheltered life. YOU ARE DEALING WITH A HIGHLY FLAMMABLE SUBSTANCE HERE! Do not allow any open flames, sparks or other sources of combustion anywhere near the work area. Make sure you are working in a well ventilated area. Protect your skin from gasoline by wearing vinyl gloves. AND DON'T SMOKE!!!

Petcock Filter Screens

Just about every fuel petcock is equipped with some form of fuel filter screen. It makes sense since the petcock is the first valve that could become clogged by debris from the fuel tank. Your filter screen probably takes one of two forms. A sediment bowl type was very popular until the mid 1970's. The intank mounted type is the most popular form today, and if you are riding a modern, carbureted motorcycle, it is VERY likely that your bike uses one.

SEDIMENT BOWL TYPE

▶ See Figure 125

If you have a motorcycle produced in the 1970's or earlier, check the fuel petcock to see if there is a bowl or fitting at the bottom. If so, shut the petcock **OFF**, then unscrew and remove the sediment bowl. Remove the o-ring seal and filter screen. Wash the filter screen using a mild solvent, then reinstall. Make sure the o-ring is in position and snug the fitting. Turn the fuel **ON** and make sure there are no leaks.

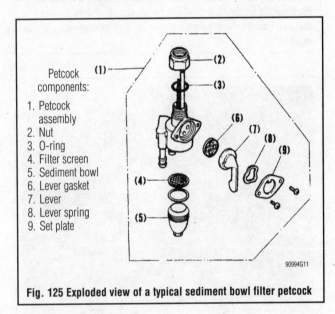

Petcock components:
1. Petcock assembly
2. Nut
3. O-ring
4. Filter screen
5. Sediment bowl
6. Lever gasket
7. Lever
8. Lever spring
9. Set plate

Fig. 125 Exploded view of a typical sediment bowl filter petcock

INTANK MOUNTED TYPE

▶ See Figures 126, 127 and 128

1. Disconnect the fuel line from the carburetor or from the petcock (whichever is easier). If you must remove the line from the petcock itself, obtain a short length of fuel line (with the same inner diameter as the petcock nipple) to use as a drain hose, then attach it to the petcock. Keep this extra line in your tool kit because it could become VERY helpful on the road if you or a buddy runs out of gas.

2. Turn the gas to **RESERVE** or, if equipped, to **PRIME** and allow the fuel to drain.

➡**If you have a vacuum actuated petcock, turning the valve to the PRIME setting (when equipped) will usually allow the tank to drain without applying vacuum to the valve diaphragm. If your bike doesn't have a prime setting, or if prime does not allow it to fully drain, then you will need a hand-held pump to apply vacuum to the diaphragm. These pumps are relatively inexpensive and are available at most automotive supply stores and are handy for other things such as brake bleeding (so they are a good investment).**

3. If necessary, remove the vacuum line from the back of the petcock and connect a small, hand-held vacuum pump. Gently apply a small amount of vacuum, no more than 10 in Hg. at first and see if the fuel flows. If no fuel is flowing, check that the petcock valve is in the **RESERVE** position and, if necessary, apply a little more vacuum. Don't apply too much vacuum or you will destroy the valve diaphragm.

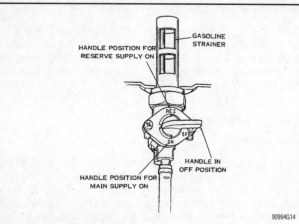

Fig. 126 On most modern carbureted motorcycles, a fuel filter (strainer) is mounted to the top of the petcock, inside the fuel tank, so you will have to remove the petcock to inspect, clean or replace it

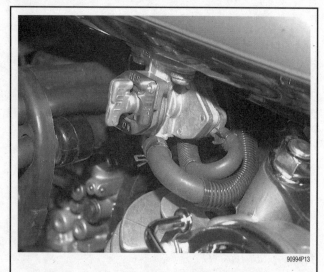

Fig. 127 Most petcocks are either bolted to the fuel tank . . .

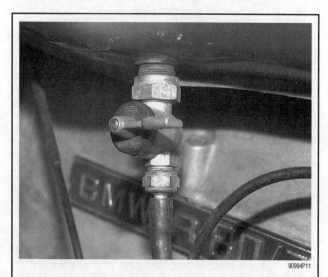

Fig. 128 . . . or they are threaded into it

4. Once the fuel tank is fully drained, decide if you will be able to remove the petcock with the tank installed. You can on most models, but there is always an exception. If necessary, remove the fuel tank from the bike.

5. Petcocks are either threaded into the bottom of the fuel tank or they are bolted to it. Either loosen and unthread the petcock from the tank or is a suitable driver to remove the bolts and carefully withdraw the petcock.

➡Have a few disposable rags and a small drain pan handy to catch any remaining fuel with may drain from the tank. If possible, position the bike or the fuel tank so any remaining fuel will not run out.

6. Clean the filter screen with a mild solvent and blow it dry with low level compressed air (if available).

7. Inspect the screen for tears, damage or uncleanable clogging. If any of these conditions are found, replace the screen with a new element.
To install:

8. Install the filter screen and petcock assembly.

9. Reconnect the vacuum line and/or fuel line(s), as applicable.

10. Carefully refill the fuel tank.

11. Turn the petcock **ON** and check for leaks.

12. If you have a vacuum actuated petcock, start and idle the motor, then recheck for leaks.

Inline Filters

▶ See Figure 129

On most carbureted vehicles, replacement of the inline filter is a very simple matter or disconnecting the fuel lines from either end and removing the filter. Just remember to shut the fuel petcock **OFF** first. To help prevent making a mess, turn the petcock **OFF**, then idle the motor until the fuel line is empty (it is easy to tell with a see-through filter, but otherwise you may have to run it until the carburetor float bowl or bowls is/are empty.) With the lines and filter empty, you will spill less or no gas removing the filter.

In fuel injected vehicles, this should not be a basic maintenance item. If you find that you must replace a filter, do yourself a favor and get a shop manual for the bike or have a technician do this one. Most fuel injected engines operate under high pressure (and many maintain that pressure once the engine is shut **OFF**). You should follow the factory recommended fuel pressure relief procedure before disconnecting any fuel lines of a fuel injected machine. Also, on bikes where the canister mounted inside the tank, you may have other important steps to follow to be sure the tank is opened and sealed safely.

Fig. 129 Even if not included from the manufacturer, an inline filter can easily be added to most carbureted motorcycles

ENGINE TUNE-UP

Once upon a time, riders would have to perform lengthy and sometimes complicated rituals every few thousand miles in order to keep their machines running properly. Bikes of yesterday used components that wore out quickly like ignition points which would have to be replaced and valves which would require adjustment often. In those days of yore, machines could get temperamental if valve, ignition and carburetor adjustments were not performed regularly (and properly).

A tune-up is a sequence of component replacement and adjustment which is designed to restore engine performance which is lost to normal use and wear. Just like the preventive maintenance described earlier, a tune-up should be performed based on time, mileage and your particular pattern of usage. A bike used in competition will require a tune-up before each race, while a weekend warrior's mount might only need one every few months.

To properly perform a tune-up, you must follow a set order of events. For instance, valve adjustment and ignition timing should always precede carburetor adjustment, since they can both affect engine rpm (which is one of the items you would adjust while working on the carburetors). A typical tune-up could consist of the following items (as applicable to any one motorcycle):

- A compression test
- Spark plug inspection and replacement

The traditional tune-up involves tools for basic spark plug service . . .

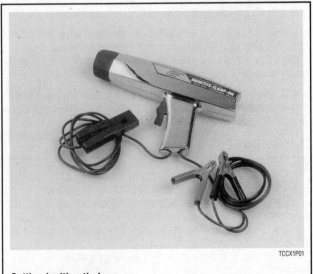

Setting ignition timing . . .

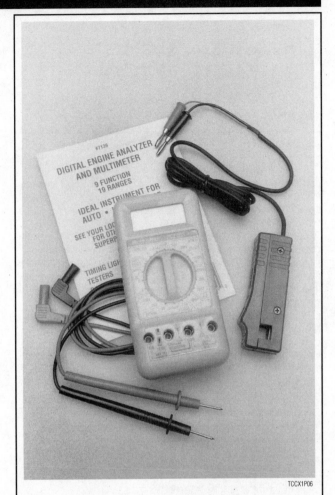

. . . and checking/setting engine RPM—this multimeter can be used as an inductive tachometer

- Valve adjustment
- Ignition timing inspection
- Carburetor synchronization, idle speed and mixture adjustments
- Road test

But, you should note that the tune-up of yesterday is completely gone from the automotive world and it is slowly, but surely, disappearing from the world of motorcycles. Advances in engine management technology (including fuel injection and electronic ignitions), anti-tamper devices used with emission controlled vehicles (like sealed covers over air/fuel mixture screws), and low maintenance mechanical components (such as hydraulic lifters) leaves today's rider with not too much to tweak.

The one thing that you CAN count on is that you will have to periodically check and replace your spark plugs. As a matter of fact, on a few bikes, that is the sum total of your tune-up, since valve, timing and carburetor adjustments may not be possible or necessary. On other bikes spark plug replacement is just the beginning. Once again, grab your owners manual and check for the following items, then perform each of them in the proper sequence (which will usually be in the order we have presented them, although valve adjustment and ignition timing are sometimes reversed).

➡ The steps of a tune-up ASSUME that all engine maintenance from fluid to filter changes has been properly performed. If you are performing carburetor or timing adjustments, BE CERTAIN that there are no air or fuel filter problems before proceeding.

Engine Compression

A compression check is a great way to keep an eye on engine condition. But, if you have a new bike, then you probably won't NEED to do this. Of course, performing a compression check on a new bike (one that has been broken-in already) is a great way to set the baseline for years to come. You will know what the compression was when new and how to compare that with wear on future readings.

CHECKING COMPRESSION

♦ **See Figure 130**

An engine compression test is performed by cranking the motor (using the starter) while a pressure gauge is threaded into (or held into) the spark plug port. The gauge will measure the amount of pressure (read as psi or kPa depending on your gauge) which the piston, rings and valves are capable of building.

Compression readings are a fast and effective way to determine engine condition. Although specifications vary greatly from motor-to-motor, the important thing to watch for in a compression test are changes. Does this test read significantly lower than the previous check for this cylinder (last tune-up). Is one cylinder significantly lower than the other(s). Typically speaking, compression readings should be above 100 psi and no cylinder should be more than 15% lower than the highest reading you have taken.

To obtain a proper reading you should be sure that the engine has been warmed to normal operating temperature (so all components are properly seated). This may be awkward on some bikes where you will have to run the engine up to temperature, then quickly (but carefully) remove the fuel tank for access to the spark plugs.

If possible, a threaded compression gauge should be used. Threaded gauges are more accurate, since they all but eliminate the possibility of compression leaking out the spark plug threads, which is a common cause for low readings when using a non-threaded, hold-in-place gauge. Threaded gauges are also easier to use, since they leave both your hands free to do other things, like hitting the starter button.

1. Warm the engine to normal operating temperature.

2. If you have a fuel petcock, shut it off to empty the float bowl or bowls (this will prevent gasoline from spraying in the cylinders during the compression test. Allow the engine to stall.

3. If your bike does not have a fuel petcock (or does not have one with a full OFF position), shut the engine **OFF**.

4. Disable the ignition system.

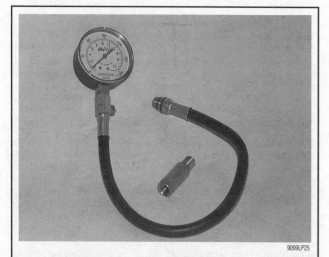

Fig. 130 A compression gauge is a relatively inexpensive tool that can help you determine engine condition

➡Disabling the ignition system can be done in a variety of ways. Check a service manual to find the preferred method for your bike. It may involve disconnecting the ignition coil primary wiring, removing a relay or fuse, or it may be as simple as using the engine kill switch on the handlebar (since some models will allow the starter to work, but will disable the ignition system when the switch is thrown).

5. Carefully clean the area around the spark plug bores, then remove the spark plugs and place them in order (so that you can inspect them more closely after the test and you can remember which cylinders from which they came).

➡Unless you have a single cylinder bike (that uses only 1 spark plug, as some use 2), don't risk forgetting which spark plug lead goes where, LABEL EACH WIRE BEFORE YOU REMOVE IT FROM THE PLUG.

6. Install the gauge to the cylinder being checked. When using a threaded gauge, be sure the proper sized adapter is attached, then thread it carefully into the bore.

7. Hold the throttle wide open using the throttle grip and crank the motor a few times. If you have a dirt bike without an electric starter, you will have to give the starter pedal a good, strong kick to be sure that you get the highest reading of which that cylinder is capable.

➡Remember that it is assumed that all maintenance has been performed, meaning that the throttle cable is properly adjusted. If you are in doubt, visually check that the carburetor or throttle body butterfly is fully open before cranking the motor.

8. Note the compression reading, release the pressure and repeat for that cylinder 1–2 more times to be certain that you have the highest possible reading.

9. Although not all manufacturer's provide specifications, most four-stroke engines should have compression readings somewhere above 100 psi. Figures in the 150–160 psi range are not uncommon on high performance machines. Two-stroke motors tend to have lower readings, closer to 110 psi.

10. On multi-cylinder machines repeat the check for each of the cylinders. Compare the highest readings for each cylinder. Ideally all readings should be within 10% of each other, but a variance of 15% between the lowest and the highest is usually considered the outer limit.

11. If one or more cylinders of a four-stroke motor read lower than specification, or lower than the recommended percentage of the highest cylinder's reading, you should repeat the test. But, this time, add a tablespoon of fresh, clean engine oil to the cylinder (through the spark plug hole) before taking the readings. If the compression readings come up with the oil added, then it is likely that the piston rings and cylinder walls for that cylinder are worn. If the compression remains low your problem is likely in the head (valve train or gasket).

➡Remember that improperly adjusted valves can lower compression readings, so if the valves for that cylinder are checked and shown to be out of adjustment, you should repeat the test to see if compression will then come up to specification.

12. On two-stroke engines, watch over a series of tune-ups. If the compression increases dramatically, the piston crown and chamber are probably becoming carboned-up and should be decarbonized.

LEAK-DOWN TESTS

An even better (and easier) way to check cylinder condition is with the use of a leak-down tester. The only problem to the home mechanic is expense. A leak-down tester is an expensive and specialized tool which is used along with an air compressor. Instead of using the engine to build compression, a leak-down tester pressurizes a cylinder with compressed air and then monitors how much leaks out.

To use a leak-down tester you start by warming the motor and then removing the spark plugs (just like a compression check). But, then you find TDC of the compression stroke the cylinder which is about to be tested (meaning you turn the engine until both valves are shut and the piston is at the top of its travel). At this point the tester pressurizes the cylinder and you watch the gauge to see if it is leaking.

If leaks are found, listen at the tailpipe, oil fill (if crankcase mounted) and the carburetor or throttle body. Hissing sounds coming from these places will tell you what components are worn. Sounds coming from the tailpipe only mean damaged exhaust valve(s). Sounds heard at the carburetor or throttle body point to intake valve problems. Sounds coming from the crankcase (such as through an oil fill) indicate a problem with the pistons, rings and cylinder walls. If you have a water cooled bike, bubbles in the radiator are an indication of head gasket problems.

If you become serious about playing with and/or rebuilding motors (cars and bikes), then a leak-down tester may be worth the investment. If not, check your local tool rental shops, they may have one available for a reasonable fee.

Spark Plugs

GENERAL INFORMATION

▶ **See Figure 131**

Unlike automobiles, whose plug life has increased dramatically over the years with the use of high voltage, electronic ignition systems (as opposed to points which were used in days gone by), most motorcycles still seem to be hard on their spark plugs. A set of spark plugs usually requires replacement after about 5,000–10,000 miles (8,000–16,000 km), depending on your style of riding, type of motor and your ignition system. During normal use, the plug gap increases and the sharp edge of the center electrode tends to dull. As the gap increases and the electrode's edge rounds off, the plug's voltage requirement increases. It requires a greater voltage to jump the wider gap and about two to three times as much voltage to fire the plug at high speeds than at idle. The improved air/fuel ratio control of modern carburetors and fuel injection combined with the higher voltage output of modern electronic ignition systems will often allow an engine to run significantly longer on a set of standard spark plugs, but keep in mind that efficiency will drop as the gap widens. As the plugs wear gas mileage and performance will drop over time. You will know if the plugs have been ignored for too long, as the engine may very well start to sputter or miss under load (it can feel a lot like forgetting to turn the petcock on or that drop in rpm you feel right before a bike starts to hit reserve).

A typical spark plug consists of a metal shell surrounding a ceramic insulator. A metal electrode extends downward through the center of the insulator and protrudes a small distance. Located at the end of the plug and attached to the side of the outer metal shell is the side electrode. The side electrode bends in at a 90° angle so that its tip is just past and parallel to the tip of the center electrode. The distance between these two electrodes (measured in thousandths of an inch or hundredths of a millimeter) is called the spark plug gap.

The spark plug does not produce a spark but instead provides a gap across which the current can arc. The coil produces anywhere from 20,000 to 50,000 volts (depending on the type and application) which travels through the wires to the spark plugs. The current passes along the center electrode and jumps the gap to the side electrode, and in doing so, ignites the air/fuel mixture in the combustion chamber.

SPARK PLUG HEAT RANGE

▶ **See Figure 132**

Spark plug heat range is the ability of the plug to dissipate heat. The longer the insulator (or the farther it extends into the engine), the hotter the plug will operate; the shorter the insulator (the closer the electrode is to the block's cooling passages) the cooler it will operate. A plug that absorbs little heat and remains too cool will quickly accumulate deposits of oil and carbon since it is not hot enough to burn them off. This leads to plug fouling and consequently to misfiring. A plug that absorbs too much heat will have no

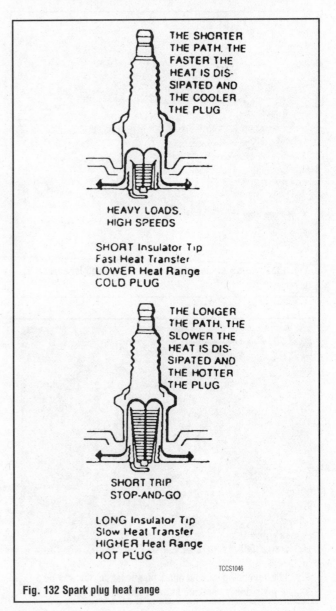

THE SHORTER THE PATH, THE FASTER THE HEAT IS DISSIPATED AND THE COOLER THE PLUG

HEAVY LOADS. HIGH SPEEDS

SHORT Insulator Tip
Fast Heat Transfer
LOWER Heat Range
COLD PLUG

THE LONGER THE PATH, THE SLOWER THE HEAT IS DISSIPATED AND THE HOTTER THE PLUG

SHORT TRIP STOP-AND-GO

LONG Insulator Tip
Slow Heat Transfer
HIGHER Heat Range
HOT PLUG

TCCS1046

Fig. 132 Spark plug heat range

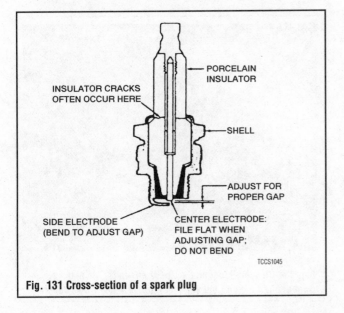

PORCELAIN INSULATOR

INSULATOR CRACKS OFTEN OCCUR HERE

SHELL

ADJUST FOR PROPER GAP

SIDE ELECTRODE (BEND TO ADJUST GAP)

CENTER ELECTRODE: FILE FLAT WHEN ADJUSTING GAP; DO NOT BEND

TCCS1045

Fig. 131 Cross-section of a spark plug

deposits but, due to the excessive heat, the electrodes will burn away quickly and might possibly lead to preignition or other ignition problems. Preignition takes place when plug tips get so hot that they glow sufficiently to ignite the air/fuel mixture before the actual spark occurs. This early ignition will usually cause a pinging during low speeds and heavy loads.

The general rule of thumb for choosing the correct heat range when picking a spark plug is: if most of your riding is long distance, high speed travel, use a colder plug; if most of your riding is stop and go, around town, use a hotter plug. Original equipment plugs are generally a good compromise between the 2 styles and most people never have the need to change their plugs from the factory-recommended heat range.

REMOVAL & INSTALLATION

▶ **See Figures 133 thru 144**

When you're removing spark plugs on a multi-cylinder bike, work on one at a time. Don't start by removing the plug wires all at once, because, unless you number them, they may become mixed up. Take a minute before you begin and number the wires with tape.

1. Disconnect the negative battery cable, and if the bike has been run recently, allow the engine to cool.

Fig. 135 . . . or a more difficult one forcing you to work in confined space

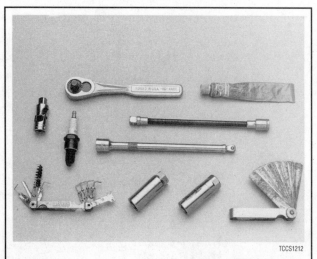

Fig. 133 A variety of tools and gauges are needed for spark plug service

Fig. 136 On many multi-cylinder, inline engines, you may have to remove components, like bodywork or the fuel tank for access

Fig. 134 Depending on your spark plug location, this can be a simple job requiring nothing but wire and plug removal . . .

Fig. 137 On some models, like BMW oilheads, the plugs are right out in the open, but you must first remove a wire cover

2. If necessary for access, remove the gas tank and/or any body work which is in the way of the spark plugs.

➡If you are trying to take a compression reading than you obviously don't want the engine too cool off. BUT, be careful because removing spark plugs from a HOT ALUMINUM cylinder head can cause damage to the threads. If plug removal is difficult, forget the test for now (save your HEAD!!!) and allow the cylinder to cool. Once the cylinder has cooled sufficiently, remove the spark plugs, clean the threads on the plug and give them a good coating of anti-seize paste. Then install the plugs, warm-up the engine and start again. The anti-seize paste should allow you to safely remove the plugs from a hot head (but BE CAREFUL and DON'T FORCE THEM).

3. Carefully twist the spark plug wire boot to loosen it, then pull upward and remove the boot from the plug. Be sure to pull on the boot and not on the wire, otherwise the connector located inside the boot may become separated.

4. Using compressed air, blow any water or debris from the spark plug well to assure that no harmful contaminants are allowed to enter the combustion chamber when the spark plug is removed. If compressed air is not available, use a rag or a brush to clean the area.

➡Some computer or office supply stores sell cans of compressed air which are used to clean electronic components. If you don't have a compressor or a portable air tank, then one of these can serve the purpose for blowing dirt out of spark plug ports.

5. Using a spark plug socket that is equipped with a rubber insert to properly hold the plug, turn the spark plug counterclockwise to loosen and remove the spark plug from the bore.

➡Remove the spark plugs when the engine is cold, if possible, to prevent damage to the threads. If removal of the plugs is difficult, apply a few drops of penetrating oil or silicone spray to the area around the base of the plug, then give it a few minutes to work.

❊❊ WARNING

Be sure not to use a flexible extension on the socket. Use of a flexible extension may allow a shear force to be applied to the plug. A shear force could break the plug off in the cylinder head, leading to costly and frustrating repairs.

To install:
6. Inspect the spark plug boot for tears or damage. If a damaged boot is found, the spark plug boot or boot and wire must be replaced.

Fig. 139 BMW is nice enough to provide you with the special tools necessary to remove their plugs . . .

Fig. 140 . . . like the spark plug wire removal tool . . .

Fig. 138 Once you have accessed the plugs, disconnect the wiring BY PULLING ON THE BOOT, NOT THE WIRE

Fig. 141 . . . and a thin walled socket . . .

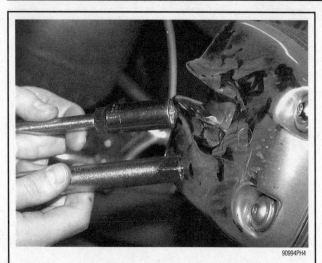

Fig. 142 . . . which can fit where a traditional spark plug socket would have trouble

Fig. 143 Once the plug is gapped, place a thin coating of anti-seize on the threads to keep the plug from getting stuck in the head . . .

Fig. 144 . . . then ALWAYS install the plug by hand, NEVER try to thread it using a ratchet and socket or you might crossthread the plug

7. Using a wire feeler gauge, check and adjust the spark plug gap. When using a gauge, the proper size should pass between the electrodes with a slight drag. The next larger size should not be able to pass while the next smaller size should pass freely.

8. Place a thin coating of anti-seize on the plug threads to make sure they will be easy to remove next time. Don't overdue it with the paste, a small dab is more than enough.

9. Carefully thread the plug into the bore by hand. If resistance is felt before the plug is almost completely threaded, back the plug out and begin threading again. In small, hard to reach areas, an old spark plug wire and boot could be used as a threading tool. The boot will hold the plug while you twist the end of the wire and the wire is supple enough to twist before it would allow the plug to crossthread.

✳ WARNING

Do not use the spark plug socket to thread the plugs. Always carefully thread the plug by hand or using an old plug wire to prevent the possibility of crossthreading and damaging the cylinder head bore.

10. Carefully tighten the spark plug. If the plug you are installing is equipped with a crush washer, seat the plug, then tighten about ¼ turn to crush the washer. If you are installing a tapered seat plug, tighten the plug to specifications provided by the bike or plug manufacturer.

11. Apply a small amount of silicone dielectric compound to the end of the spark plug lead or inside the spark plug boot to prevent sticking, then install the boot to the spark plug and push until it clicks into place. The click may be felt or heard, then gently pull back on the boot to assure proper contact.

12. Unless further checks or adjustments need to be made, install the gas tank or any body work which was removed.

13. Connect the negative battery cable.

SPARK PLUG INSPECTION

▶ See Figures 145 and 146

Whenever the spark plugs are removed from the engine they should be examined for deposits and wear. Your used spark plugs can lend important clues to engine mechanical and operating conditions.

The best method for checking spark plugs is to look at them immediately after they have been under typical operating conditions, under load, but WITHOUT allowing the bike to return to idle operation (which could significantly alter what you might find). The best way to check engine condition using the spark plugs is to use the following proce-dure:

1. Take the bike for a ride and allow it to come up to normal operating temperature.

2. On a secluded roadway (with a safe place to pull WELL OFF THE ROAD, preferably in a rest area or side street), ride the bike for a short distance at full throttle. You don't need to be on a highway to do this, you can be in any gear).

3. With the throttle still wide open, simultaneously hit the engine **KILL** switch while you pull in the clutch cable or shift into Neutral.

4. Coast the bike to a safe spot and brake to a full stop, then place the bike on its stand.

5. Remove one spark plug at a time and examine the deposits to help determine the condition of each cylinder. Compare the plugs to the illustrations and descriptions we have provided.

6. If the plug insulator has turned white or is burned, the plug is too hot and should be replaced with the next colder one available for your bike.

7. If the plugs you are using are too cold, then you will notice sooty or oily deposits. These deposits could be black or only a dark brown. If found, you should try the next hotter plug. If a hotter plug does not remedy the situation, then suspect an overly rich fuel system, or that your engine is burning oil. A compression or leak-down test would be the next step.

8. If the plugs have a damp or oil film over the firing end, a black tip, and a carbon layer over the entire face of the plug, it has been oil fouled. Although you can clean and reuse the plug, it should be replaced. You

A normally worn spark plug should have light tan or gray deposits on the firing tip.

A carbon fouled plug, identified by soft, sooty, black deposits, may indicate an improperly tuned vehicle. Check the air cleaner, ignition components and engine control system.

This spark plug has been **left in the engine too long,** as evidenced by the extreme gap- Plugs with such an extreme gap can cause misfiring and stumbling accompanied by a noticeable lack of power.

An oil fouled spark plug indicates an engine with worn poston rings and/or bad valve seals allowing excessive oil to enter the chamber.

A physically damaged spark plug may be evidence of severe detonation in that cylinder. Watch that cylinder carefully between services, as a continued detonation will not only damage the plug, but could also damage the engine.

A bridged or almost bridged spark plug, identified by a build-up between the electrodes caused by excessive carbon or oil build-up on the plug.

TCCA1P40

Fig. 145 The condition of used spark plugs can give you a good idea what is happening with your engine

GAP BRIDGED

IDENTIFIED BY DEPOSIT BUILD—UP CLOSING GAP BETWEEN ELECTRODES.

CAUSED BY OIL OR CARBON FOULING. REPLACE PLUG, OR, IF DEPOSITS ARE NOT EXCESSIVE THE PLUG CAN BE CLEANED.

OIL FOULED

IDENTIFIED BY WET BLACK DEPOSITS ON THE INSULATOR SHELL BORE ELECTRODES.

CAUSED BY EXCESSIVE OIL ENTERING COMBUSTION CHAMBER THROUGH WORN RINGS AND PISTONS, EXCESSIVE CLEARANCE BETWEEN VALVE GUIDES AND STEMS, OR WORN OR LOOSE BEARINGS. CORRECT OIL PROBLEM. REPLACE THE PLUG.

CARBON FOULED

IDENTIFIED BY BLACK, DRY FLUFFY CARBON DEPOSITS ON INSULATOR TIPS, EXPOSED SHELL SURFACES AND ELECTRODES.

CAUSED BY TOO COLD A PLUG, WEAK IGNITION, DIRTY AIR CLEANER, DEFECTIVE FUEL PUMP, TOO RICH A FUEL MIXTURE, IMPROPERLY OPERATING HEAT RISER OR EXCESSIVE IDLING. CAN BE CLEANED.

NORMAL

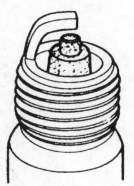

IDENTIFIED BY LIGHT TAN OR GRAY DEPOSITS ON THE FIRING TIP.

PRE-IGNITION

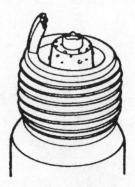

IDENTIFIED BY MELTED ELECTRODES AND POSSIBLY BLISTERED INSULATOR. METALIC DEPOSITS ON INSULATOR INDICATE ENGINE DAMAGE.

CAUSED BY WRONG TYPE OF FUEL, INCORRECT IGNITION TIMING OR ADVANCE, TOO HOT A PLUG, BURNT VALVES OR ENGINE OVERHEATING. REPLACE THE PLUG.

OVERHEATING

IDENTIFIED BY A WHITE OR LIGHT GRAY INSULATOR WITH SMALL BLACK OR GRAY BROWN SPOTS AND WITH BLUISH-BURNT APPEARANCE OF ELECTRODES.

CAUSED BY ENGINE OVER-HEATING, WRONG TYPE OF FUEL, LOOSE SPARK PLUGS, TOO HOT A PLUG, LOW FUEL PUMP PRESSURE OR INCORRECT IGNITION TIMING. REPLACE THE PLUG.

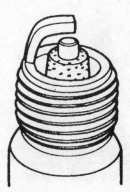

FUSED SPOT DEPOSIT

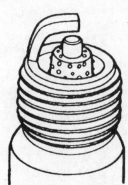

IDENTIFIED BY MELTED OR SPOTTY DEPOSITS RESEMBLING BUBBLES OR BLISTERS.

CAUSED BY SUDDEN ACCELERATION. CAN BE CLEANED IF NOT EXCESSIVE, OTHERWISE REPLACE PLUG.

TCCS2002

Fig. 146 Inspect the spark plug to determine engine running conditions

should also perform a compression or leak-down test to determine the cause of oil fouling.

9. If the plugs exhibit light tan or gray deposits, along with no excessive gap or electrode wear, the engine is running properly and you are using the correct spark plugs.

GAPPING

▶ See Figures 147, 148, 149 and 150

If the spark plugs are not going to be replaced, clean the plugs thoroughly. Remember that any kind of deposit will decrease the efficiency of the plug. Plugs can be cleaned on a spark plug cleaning machine, which can sometimes be found in service stations, or you can do an acceptable job of cleaning with a stiff brush. If the plugs are cleaned, the electrodes must be filed flat. Use an ignition points file, not an emery board or the like, which will leave deposits. The electrodes must be filed perfectly flat with sharp edges; rounded edges reduce the spark plug voltage by as much as 50%.

Check spark plug gap before installation. The ground electrode (the L-shaped one connected to the body of the plug) must be parallel to the center electrode and the specified size wire gauge must pass between the electrodes with a slight drag.

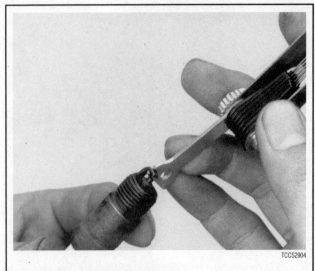

Fig. 149 Adjusting the spark plug gap

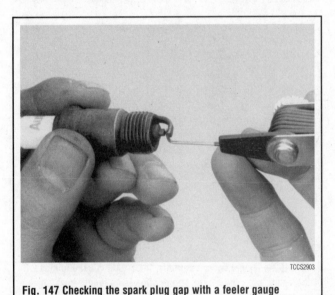

Fig. 147 Checking the spark plug gap with a feeler gauge

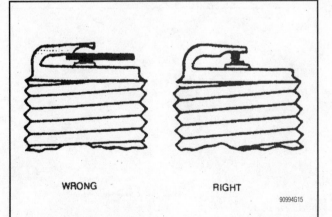

WRONG   RIGHT

90994G15

Fig. 148 This illustration shows why you must use a wire-type gauge to check the gap on a used spark plug, a flat-type feeler gauge can give an incorrect reading

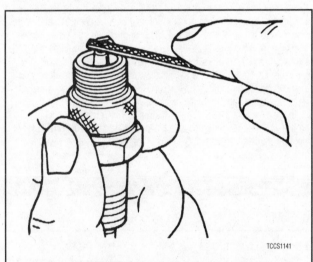

Fig. 150 If the standard plug is in good condition, the electrode may be filed flat—WARNING: do not file platinum plugs

➡ NEVER adjust the gap on a used platinum type spark plug.

Always check the gap on new plugs as they are not always set correctly at the factory. Do not use a flat feeler gauge when measuring the gap on a used plug, because the reading may be inaccurate. A round-wire type gapping tool is the best way to check the gap. The correct gauge should pass through the electrode gap with a slight drag. If you're in doubt, try one size smaller and one larger. The smaller gauge should go through easily, while the larger one shouldn't go through at all. Wire gapping tools usually have a bending tool attached. Use that to adjust the side electrode until the proper distance is obtained. Absolutely never attempt to bend the center electrode. Also, be careful not to bend the side electrode too far or too often as it may weaken and break off within the engine, requiring removal of the cylinder head to retrieve it.

CHECKING AND REPLACING SPARK PLUG WIRES

▶ See Figure 151

At every tune-up, visually check the spark plug cables for burns cuts, or breaks in the insulation. Check the boots and the nipples on the coil. Replace any damaged wiring.

As wires ages internal strands will break, the connectors on either end may corrode or become physically damaged, and the insulation will break down,

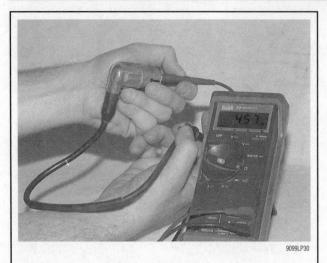

Fig. 151 An ohmmeter can be used to check spark plug wire resistance

allowing for further corrosion and for arcing of the spark during use. All of these items add up to a loss of power for your bike, harder starts, and sometimes to a total loss of spark in the RAIN or under damp, misty conditions.

Every 2 years the resistance of the spark plug wires should be checked with an ohmmeter. If wires are shown to have excessive resistance, they should be replaced. Typically speaking, wire resistance for an electronic ignition system should be below 10,000 ohms. Check a shop manual to see if resistance specifications are available for your model.

To check resistance, disconnect the wire at both ends. Connect the probes of a multi-meter (such as a digital volt ohmmeter or DVOM) set to the 10K or 20K ohm scale to the ends of the spark plug wire. Read the resistance on the meter.

Valve Lash

GENERAL INFORMATION

♦ **See Figures 152, 153 and 154**

Cylinder heads use valves to admit the fuel/air mixture into the combustion chamber, to seal the combustion chamber for compression, and to allow the spent exhaust gases to escape. All of these functions are timed using the valve train (camshaft, lifters/shims and sometimes rocker arms and/or pushrods) to occur at the proper times.

In order for the valves to operate properly, they must be adjusted to assure that the full benefit of the camshaft lobe lift is realized, but they also must be able to close fully once the lobe of the camshaft has gone by. Valves are adjusted by increasing or decreasing their LASH, which is the amount of free-play in the valve train when the valve is closed (meaning the camshaft lobe is NOT actuating the shim, pushrod or rocker arm). Valve lash therefore, is basically a gap that exists between components (the valve stem and a rocker arm or a camshaft lobe and a shim depending on the engine design) when the valve is fully closed.

Since valves open and close with every turn of the crankshaft, their movement becomes a blur at engine speeds, which can create a pounding on the entire valve train. As this use wears the components valve lash will tend to change (increase or decrease depending on the model). On some engines, the valve seats and heads will wear slowly, causing the valve to come further into the cylinder head (moving the stem closer to the shim or rocker arm and decreasing valve lash). On other models, the stem, shim or other valve train components will wear, causing the gap to increase.

But whether the valve lash is increasing or decreasing slowly through use doesn't really matter, either one will eventually lead to the valve being out of adjustment, and this will adversely affect engine performance.

Increased valve lash will not allow a valve to fully open since some of the camshaft lobe lift will be wasted on taking up the excess lash. If an intake valve does not open sufficiently, the full fuel/air charge will not make it into the cylinder and power will be lost during combustion. If an exhaust valve does not open enough, some the exhaust gases will be left in the cylinder, displacing some of the fuel/air mixture which will try to enter the cylinder on the next stroke. Again, the result will be a reduction in engine power.

Decreased valve lash will have a less noticeable effect on engine power, but could have a more devastating effect on your engine. As valve lash is decreased beyond specification, the valve train components may not allow the valve to fully come into contact with the seat. This will prevent the valve from cooling through heat transfer with the valve seat. The term "burnt valve" which you have likely heard someone mention before means that a valve was ruined by heat. A burnt valve will not properly seal the combustion chamber (a will not do its job), but it can also come flying apart, destroying your piston and cylinder wall. As valve lash decreases, the engine could lose power if valves are held partially open by the valve train (not allowing for proper compression).

You can see from these examples why you would want to keep an eye on your valve lash.

Intake and exhaust valves usually have different specifications, because of the differences in their sizes and jobs. The exhaust valve is usually set a little looser than the intake, because of the harsh environment it lives in (superheated gases pass over it into the exhaust system when it is open). Intake

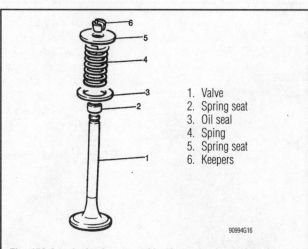

1. Valve
2. Spring seat
3. Oil seal
4. Sping
5. Spring seat
6. Keepers

Fig. 152 A typical valve assembly, the spring is used to close the valve, once the rocker arm or shim is no longer pushing downward

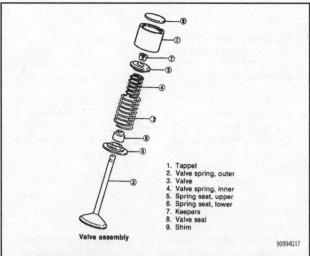

Valve assembly

1. Tappet
2. Valve spring, outer
3. Valve
4. Valve spring, inner
5. Spring seat, upper
6. Spring seat, lower
7. Keepers
8. Valve seal
9. Shim

Fig. 153 Another popular valve and spring assembly, this model uses two valve springs

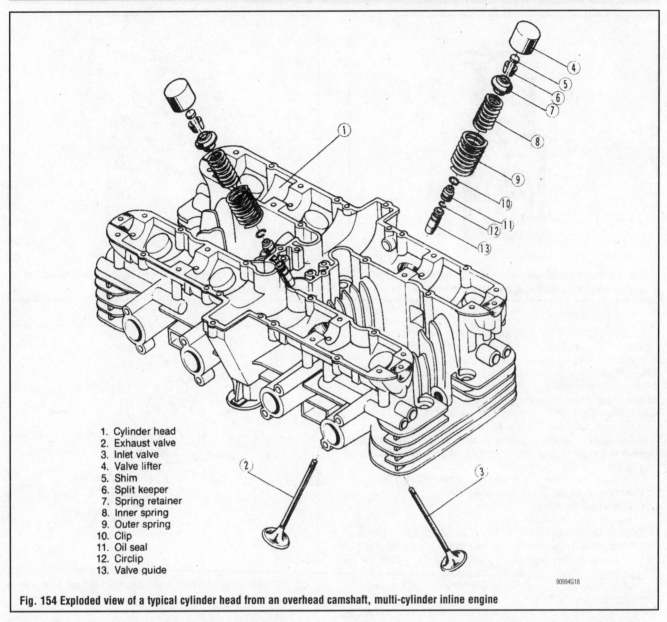

1. Cylinder head
2. Exhaust valve
3. Inlet valve
4. Valve lifter
5. Shim
6. Split keeper
7. Spring retainer
8. Inner spring
9. Outer spring
10. Clip
11. Oil seal
12. Circlip
13. Valve guide

Fig. 154 Exploded view of a typical cylinder head from an overhead camshaft, multi-cylinder inline engine

valves have it easy (for a valve) as they are in contact with the cylinder head when they are exposed to combustion gases and temperatures (when they are open, relatively cool air/fuel mixture passes over their surface).

To identify an exhaust or intake valve, look at its position in relation to the rest of the cylinder head. In most cases, the intake valve will be closest to and in alignment with the intake manifold, while the exhaust valve is closest to and adjacent to the exhaust pipe. I think we can skip further explanation as to why this is true, their purposes being relatively obvious.

ADJUSTMENT

▶ See Figure 155

✳✳ CAUTION

Great care must be taken when adjusting the valves. While some small error is permitted on the loose side (which will result in noisy valves and a slight reduction in performance), setting the clearances too tight will often burn the valves after few miles

With the higher quality metals and components used in modern motorcycle engines, the need for periodic valve adjustments has often been reduced. This is not to say that it has been eliminated in most cases, but that the maintenance intervals have been increased. What was once a ritual which was as common as the oil change is now more likely a once a year task. It also has been eliminated on some models, thanks to hydraulic lifters.

Be sure to consult your owners manual for recommendations on mileage intervals and model valve lash specifications. The specifications can also sometimes be found on emission labels which are mounted to the bikes themselves. Although the specific lash adjustment procedures will vary from model-to-model (and you should consult a shop manual before attempting this), there are a few basic designs and points to keep in mind when trying it for the first time.

To begin with, since valve lash is an measurement of the amount of free-play in the valve train, you must be CERTAIN that you always measure it with the valve fully closed. That means that the actuator (shim, pushrod or lifter) for that particular valve MUST be in contact with the BASE circle of the camshaft lobe (NOT THE RAISED PORTION). This means that you should turn the crankshaft (which can be done with a kickstarter pedal or with the rear wheel if the bike is placed in gear and the spark plugs are removed to relieve compression) until that cylinder is at Top Dead Center (TDC) of its compression stroke. This is when the cylinder would be ready to fire and the valves would have to be closed.

Fig. 155 Proper adjustment assures that all valves for a given cylinder will be closed during the compression stroke

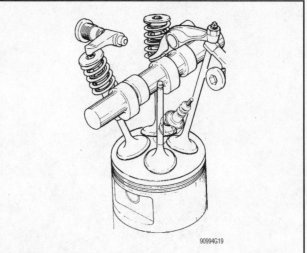

Fig. 156 Rocker arms with screw-type adjusters are the easiest valves to adjust

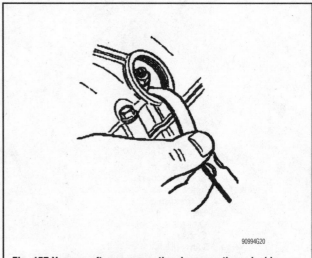

Fig. 157 You can often measure the clearance through side-covers which were designed for periodic service

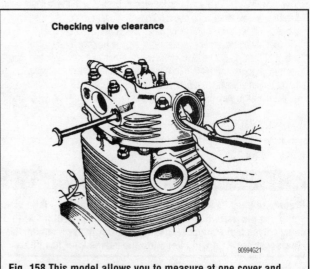

Checking valve clearance

Fig. 158 This model allows you to measure at one cover and adjust at another

In almost all cases, valves must be adjusted on a cold engine. This is important since metal components will expand with heat. Specifications for the same valve will be larger when the valve is cold than when it is hot. If a valve is adjusted to a cold specification when it is hot, that adjustment will be far too tight at operating temperatures, which could lead to a burnt valve. Most importantly here, follow the specifications, they should ALWAYS be presented with the information on whether it is a hot or cold spec.

ALSO, most manufacturers will have you retorque the cylinder head before adjusting the valve lash. Check your owners or shop manual for the proper torque sequence, specification and to be certain that this is necessary for your model before proceeding.

Motorcycles typically use one of three systems to adjust valve lash:
- **Rocker Arms and Screw-type adjusters**
- **Shims and buckets**
- **Hydraulic valve lifters**

Ducati motorcycles are UNIQUE TO THE INDUSTRY and use their own specific adjustment procedures. Their desmodromic valves are not closed by valve springs, but by a camshaft and a second set of rocker arms. The advantage of this system is that the camshaft does not have to fight the high pressure springs used in most other engines, so it robs less power from the crankshaft. But, the disadvantage is a valve adjustment technique and interval which is unique to THEIR motorcycles. If you own a Duck, do yourself a favor and get a good shop manual before attempting this.

Rocker Arms and Screw-Type Adjusters

▶ See Figures 156 thru 169

Probably the most popular form of lash adjustment is a simple screw fitting on the end of a rocker arm. These are especially popular with riders because they usually do not require any special tools to make the adjustments (with the exception of a feeler gauge). You can find these adjusters on many different models from Japan and Europe. They are common on pushrod engines (that don't use hydraulic lifters) and on some overhead cam motors as well.

On most machines with rocker arms and screw-type adjusters, valve lash is adjusted as follows:

1. Place the bike on its centerstand or use a bike lift to block it upright for easier access.

2. Remove the gas tank or any bodywork which interferes with access to the valve cover(s). For a change, you BMW Boxer guys can laugh at everyone else now, since those strange looking motors you have place the valve covers RIGHT where you want them for this.

3. Remove the spark plugs (unless you still haven't installed them from the compression or spark plug condition check) to make the engine easier to turn.

Fig. 159 Check your bike for access covers that allow measurement . . .

Fig. 160 . . . and adjustment, then remove them for access to the valves

Fig. 161 On some models however, the entire valve cover must be removed by loosening any nuts . . .

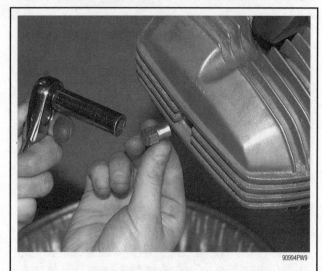

Fig. 162 . . . or bolts that retain the cover . . .

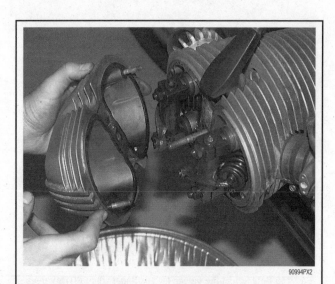

Fig. 163 . . . then pulling the cover free of the cylinder head

Fig. 164 If required on your bike, be sure to retorque the cylinder head to specification

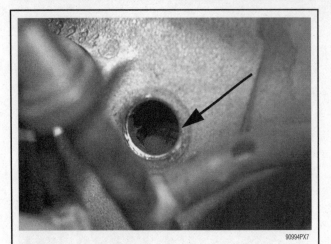

Fig. 165 On this bike, we used the timing mark to make sure the cylinder was at TDC, but without the mark it would still be easy to tell

Fig. 168 . . . then if adjustment is necessary, loosen the lock-nut . . .

Fig. 166 Only adjust the valves for a cylinder when BOTH valves are closed (the valve springs will not be compressed at all)

Fig. 169 . . . and rotate the adjusting nut until the proper clearance is obtained

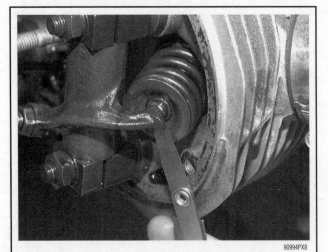

Fig. 167 Check the valve clearance using the proper sized feeler gauge between the valve stem and the rocker . . .

4. Remove the valve adjustment access covers or the valve cover(s), as necessary for access to the rocker arms.

5. Set the cylinder on TDC of the compression stroke, making sure that both valves are fully closed. Unless the valve lash is way out of spec on the tight side, the rocker arms should be a little loose with the cylinder at TDC. If necessary, place the bike in gear and turn the rear wheel in order to turn the cylinders (this shouldn't be too hard with the spark plugs removed, but BE CAREFUL if you are using a bike lift, don't knock it over).

6. If your model requires it, retorque the cylinder head to specification using the proper torque sequence.

7. The proper sized feeler gauge for each valve's specification (remember that the intake and exhaust valves are usually set at different specs) should slide between the tip of the valve stem and the rocker arm with only a slight drag.

8. If the lash must be adjusted, loosen the locknut and rotate the adjuster until the proper clearance is obtained. Hold the adjuster in position while tightening the locknut, then recheck the valve clearance to be certain that the adjuster did not turn.

➡Some machines, like the old 350 Hondas, have the rocker arms mounted on eccentric shafts, and these shafts are rotated to provide more or less clearance.

9. Repeat the adjustment for each valve, making sure each time that the cylinder is at TDC of the compression stroke.

10. Install the valve cover(s), using a new gasket when necessary.

11. Install the spark plugs.

12. Install any bodywork or other components which were removed for access to the valve cover.

13. If raised on a bike lift or blocked up, lower the bike.

Shim and Bucket Adjusters

▶ See Figures 170 thru 175

Some bikes, especially many of the high performance, multi-cylinder bikes from Japan, are equipped with overhead cams and usually NO rocker arms. These motors use shims between the cam lobes and the valve stems to adjust the clearance, and in these instances you will need a micrometer and a selection of shims of the proper thickness in order to adjust the lash.

➡**There are 2 basic designs: shim under bucket and shim over bucket. On the shim under bucket designs, the camshaft must be removed in order to access the shims. On most of the shim over bucket designs, the valve spring can be depressed slightly (sometimes using a special tool to lever on the bucket or valve stem only), allowing for shim removed WITHOUT removing the camshaft.**

The advantage of these setups include smaller, simplified valve trains with less components to rob the crankshaft of power. The disadvantage is that the camshafts are going to have to be removed in order to adjust the valve lash. Again, you are going to want a good shop manual too make sure that you don't miss something important, like the proper camshaft bearing removal or installation sequence and bolt torques (if you have the shim under bucket design or a shim over bucket on which the shaft must be removed for some reason).

Basically, shim and bucket adjustment involves accessing the cams, measuring the valves and installing new shims (where necessary):

1. Make sure the engine is completely COLD. If you did a compression check earlier and you are done gapping new spark plugs. Take a break, grab some lunch, find something to wax, but make sure the engine is COLD.

2. Place the bike on its centerstand or use a bike lift to block it upright for easier access.

3. Remove the gas tank or any bodywork which interferes with access to the valve cover(s).

4. Remove the spark plugs (unless you still haven't installed them from the compression or spark plug condition check) to make the engine easier to turn.

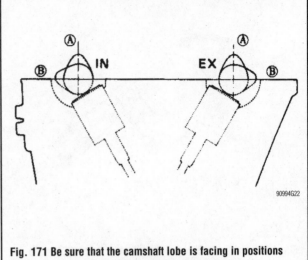

Fig. 171 Be sure that the camshaft lobe is facing in positions "A" or "B" in order to get an accurate reading

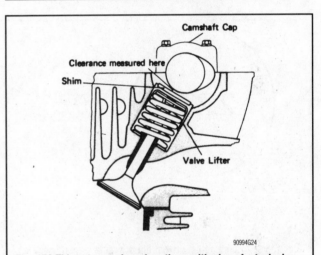

Fig. 172 This cutaway view show the positioning of a typical valve, camshaft and shim adjuster (shim OVER bucket design shown)

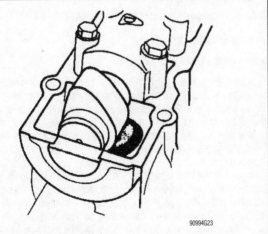

Fig. 170 In order to measure valve clearance on shim and bucket adjustment engines, the camshaft lobe must be facing AWAY from the shim and bucket

Fig. 173 With the lobe facing the proper direction, use a set of feeler gauges to determine the valve clearance

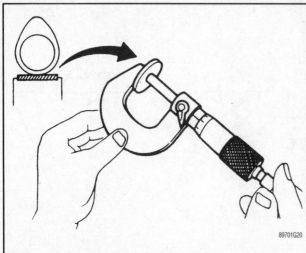

Fig. 174 If clearance is out of specification, you will have to remove the shim and measure it . . .

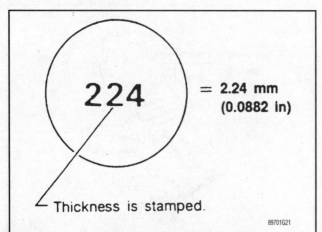

Fig. 175 . . . then select an appropriate replacement based on that size (plus or minus the difference to obtain proper clearance)—Note that many shims have their sizes stamped right on the face

5. Remove the valve cover(s) for access to the valve train.

6. You are going to have to turn the engine over manually in order to set each cylinder at TDC of the compression stroke. Most bikes have an engine cover which can be removed for access to the crankshaft snout. With the cover removed you can turn the crankshaft directly. If you cannot find a cover (or would rather not remove it), you can place the bike in gear and use the rear wheel to turn the shaft (as long as the wheel is off the ground, but be CAREFUL if you are using a bike lift to raise the wheel).

7. Use a feeler gauge set to check the clearance between the base of each camshaft lobe and its shim (over bucket) or between the lobe and the bucket (shim under bucket). Note the clearances for the intake and exhaust valves for each cylinder, then rotate the engine until the next cylinder is on TDC of compression.

➡It is a REALLY GOOD idea to draw a picture of the engine and all of the valves, then note the clearances on the picture. This will help prevent self-doubt later when you go, did I call that the intake for number one, or did I mean it was the exhaust . . . ?

8. Once you have measured the lash on all valves it is time to remove the camshaft (if necessary to access the shims on your engine). Follow your shop manual closely for this but it typically involves:

a. Rotate the engine to TDC of the number one cylinder with all appropriate timing marks aligned.

b. Use a small marker or bottle of White Out® to make alignment marks between the camshaft sprockets and the camshaft drive chain (or belt, if applicable). This will assure that you preserve proper valve timing when installing the cams.

c. Tie the camshaft timing belt or chain in position (this can often be done using safety wire between the frame and the chain/belt).

d. Place a clean rag over the opening in the timing cover and anywhere else you don't want an errant bolt or small part to fall during your work.

e. Loosen each of the camshaft bearing cap bolts using the proper sequence.

➡BE SURE to properly tag and arrange ALL components which are removed from the valve train including the camshaft bearing caps, bolts and bearings. These should all be installed in the same positions from which they were removed. An old baking tray or egg carton works well for this.

f. Remove the bearing caps, then carefully remove the camshafts and sprockets.

➡On some models the camshaft sprockets may need to be removed before each camshaft is removed.

9. Remove and measure each of the valve shims which must be replaced to achieve proper lash. Based on the measurement, calculate what size replacement shims you will need and get going to the local bike shop. If the measurement for a cylinder was too tight, then you will need a shim which is that much smaller for that cylinder. If the measurement was too loose, then you will need a shim which is that much thicker.

➡On shim over bucket engines where the camshaft is not removed, use an appropriate tool to gently pry downward on the the bucket or the valve stem to provide clearance necessary to remove the shim. In some cases special tools for this are available from the manufacturer. In other cases, tools are available from aftermarket sources, or some automotive tools may do the trick. If in doubt, check with your dealer for advice on how to safely slide the shims from under the camshaft.

10. Position the new shims

11. If removed, install the camshafts, making sure that all of the timing marks have remained in proper alignment. Tighten the bearing caps to specification using the proper torque sequence.

12. Install the valve cover(s) and any engine covers which were removed.

13. Install the spark plugs.

14. Install any bodywork or other components which were removed for access to the valve cover.

15. If raised on a bike lift or blocked up, lower the bike.

Hydraulic Valve Lifters

◆ **See Figures 176 and 177**

You've got hydraulic valve lifters? Well then, boy this is your lucky day. Hydraulic valve lifters are designed to automatically compensate for changing valve lash. They work by using a multi-piece, spring loaded lifter body to maintain zero lash in the valve train (allowing valves to open and close fully regardless of normal wear and tear to the valve train). For this reason, bikes with hydraulic valve lifters normally do NOT require any periodic valve adjustments.

It is argued that this design can rob the engine of some power (by loosing a little camshaft lift to hydraulic lifter lash, depending on the design and condition of the lifter). So you will probably see that hydraulic lifters tend to be more popular on models those primary purpose does NOT involve cutting edge engine performance. Hydraulic lifters provide excellent, long-term ease of maintenance at a reasonable cost to overall engine performance and are quite likely to be found on many touring and cruiser models for this reason.

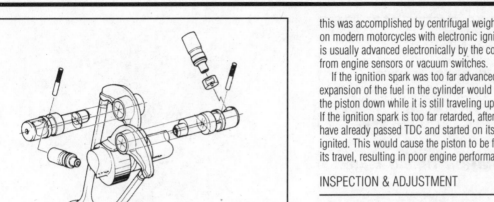

Fig. 176 Cross-sectional view of a Honda hydraulic lifter valve train used on some Nighthawk and Shadow models

1. Tappet guide screw (4)
2. Pushrod hydraulic unit (2)
3. Pushrod cover cork washer (2)
4. Tappet guide
5. Tappet and roller assembly (2)
6. Tappet guide gasket

Fig. 177 Exploded view of a typical hydraulic roller lifter mounting for a V-Twin

Ignition Timing

GENERAL INFORMATION

Ignition timing is the measurement, in degrees of crankshaft rotation, of the point at which the spark plugs fire in each of the cylinders. It is measured in degrees before or after Top Dead Center (TDC) of the compression stroke.

Because it takes a fraction of a second for the spark plug to ignite the mixture in the cylinder, the spark plug must fire a little before the piston reaches TDC. Otherwise, the mixture will not be completely ignited as the piston passes TDC and the full power of the explosion will not be used by the engine.

The timing measurement is given in degrees of crankshaft rotation before the piston reaches TDC (BTDC). If the setting for the ignition timing is 5° BTDC, the spark plug must fire 5° before each piston reaches TDC. This only holds true, however, when the engine is at idle speed.

As the engine speed increases, the pistons go faster. The spark plugs have to ignite the fuel even sooner if it is to be completely ignited when the piston reaches TDC. To do this, ignition systems have various means of advancing the spark timing as the engine speed increases. On older bikes,

this was accomplished by centrifugal weights on a breaker point rotor. But on modern motorcycles with electronic ignition systems, the ignition timing is usually advanced electronically by the control module based on input from engine sensors or vacuum switches.

If the ignition spark was too far advanced (BTDC), the ignition and expansion of the fuel in the cylinder would occur too soon and tend to force the piston down while it is still traveling up. This would cause engine ping. If the ignition spark is too far retarded, after TDC (ATDC), the piston will have already passed TDC and started on its way down when the fuel is ignited. This would cause the piston to be forced down for only a portion of its travel, resulting in poor engine performance and lack of power.

INSPECTION & ADJUSTMENT

▶ **See Figures 178 and 179**

Before transistorized ignitions took over in the late 70's and very early 80's riders would have to check, adjust and replace their breaker points very frequently. Failure to do so would lead to hard starts and eventual, no starts as the point gap widened or the points eventually became worn or burned beyond service. If you are riding a bike with points, then God bless you. But, if it is not a show-able antique, you are crazy. There are many retrofit kits available to convert a points machine over to electronic ignition. Don't listen to those people who are afraid of electronic ignition (because "if it breaks I can't just fix it on the side of the road"), it works better and breaks down much less often than mechanical breaker points. As a matter of fact, it is a good thing that those die-hards who insist on keeping points CAN fix them on the side of the road, because eventually THEY ARE GOING TO HAVE TO.

Every modern motorcycle is equipped with an electronic ignition, usually known as transistorized ignition, breakerless discharge or capacitor discharge ignitions. On these systems, the mechanical breaker points have been replaced with an ignition module and a signal rotor of some sort. Where the mechanical breaker points were once used to physically break the primary ignition circuit, causing the ignition coil to discharge and fire the secondary circuit, an ignition module now performs that function. The module knows WHEN to perform that function based on a signal received from a signal rotor (usually a magnetized pick-up coil of some sort, which sends signals to the ignition module). The pick-up coil normally sends signals to the module based on changes to a magnetic field caused by notches machined into a part of the crankshaft, or a part turned by the crankshaft. The advantages of electronic ignition include long life (because no mechanical contacts are used to break the primary circuit which could wear like points), along with a significantly higher voltage capacity. The higher voltage is an advantage when it comes to firing plugs with larger gaps or under adverse conditions like oil soaked plugs on a bad cylinder.

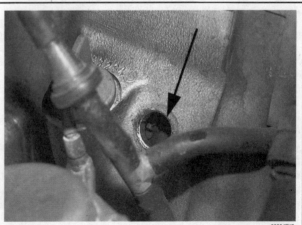

Fig. 178 If the ignition timing is adjustable on your bike, there will be one or more timing marks accessible under a cover or plug

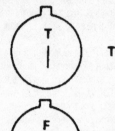

TOP DEAD CENTER

IGNITION TIMING MARK

90994G27

Fig. 179 Marks may be letters, numbers, lines or just dots depending on the model—A given model may have more than one mark, showing TDC for each of the cylinders, or like in this case, showing TDC for No. 1 and a mark to show when proper advance is set

The newer your bike, the lesser the chance that the ignition timing can or should be adjusted. Although many modern bikes still have the capacity to adjust their ignition timing, it is no longer recommended as a periodic procedure. Timing marks are usually provided ONLY to be used as a check to make sure all ignition components are installed correctly and functioning properly. Check your owners manual for recommendations regarding checking ignition timing.

If your bike is equipped with timing marks they will usually consist of notches, dots, or letters that are either machined directly on a part of the crankshaft, or a part which the crankshaft turns such as the alternator rotor. There is usually a cover or plug which can be easily removed to view the timing mark. For instance, most Harley V-Twins are equipped with a timing plug at the base of the cylinders. Most BMW airhead boxers were equipped with a plug on the left side of the engine case. Many Japanese motorcycles have either a crankcase plug or small engine cover which can be removed to find the marks.

Because timing on motorcycles is normally checked through a small access hole (under a cover or plug) they are often designed to represent a properly timed engine, when the No. 1 cylinder is at or near TDC of the compression stroke and the timing mark is visible through the hole.

Timing procedures vary from manufacturer-to-manufacturer. In the days of points the procedures ranged from using a dial gauge or degree wheel to using a test light or continuity checker to set "static timing." This meant timing was often set WITHOUT the engine running. "Dynamic timing" checks were made on some models, using an automotive style stroboscopic timing light (which makes the timing marks appear to stand still due to the effect of the strobe light).

On most modern motorcycles, timing checks are designed to use a stroboscopic timing light with an inductive pick-up to perform a "dynamic timing" inspection. The timing light's pick-up is clamped to the No. 1 cylinder's spark plug wire and will trigger the timing light each time a pulse is detected in the wire. By pointing the timing light at the timing mark, you can see if it lines up with the appropriate marker or if it centers in the access hole, as required by your specific bike.

➡ **Never pierce a spark plug wire in order to attach a timing light or perform tests. The pierced insulation will eventually lead to an electrical arc and related ignition troubles.**

Carburetor Adjustments

◆ **See Figure 180**

Carburetor tune-up procedures will largely depend upon the type of engine, the type and number of carburetors, what kind of carburetor controls are fitted, and ancillary systems, if fitted, such as oil pumps and the like which operate in conjunction with the carburetor.

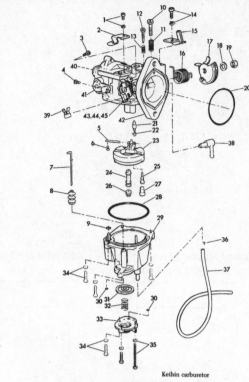

Keihin carburetor

1. Screw & washer	16. Spring	32. Spring
2. Bracket	17. Throttle lever	33. Housing
3. Screw	18. Washer	34. Screw & washer (5)
4. Screw	19. Nut	35. Screw & washer
5. Float pin	20. O-ring	36. Clip
6. Screw	21. Float needle	37. Hose
7. Rod	22. Clip	38. Fitting
8. Boot	23. Float assy.	39. Spacer (not standard)
9. O-ring	24. Main nozzle	40. Choke plate
10. Throttle stop screw	25. Slow jet	(not shown)
11. Spring	26. Main jet	41. Choke lever
12. Low speed	27. Plug	42. Flange
mixture screw	28. O-ring	43. Accel. pump lever
13. Spring	29. Float bowl	44. Rocker arm
14. Screw & washer	30. O-ring (2)	45. Rocker arm spring
15. Bracket	31. Diaphragm	

90994G28

Fig. 180 The typical carburetor is composed of dozens of intricate parts which work together to produce proper air/fuel ratios—they do not respond well to inexperienced and unnecessary tampering

Carburetor adjustments generally fall into 2 major categories:
- **Idle Speed and Mixture**
- **Snychronization**

Periodic carburetor adjustments have become another victim of increasing technology. But this can also be attributed to increasing emissions laws. For years carburetors have been fit with sealed and tamper-resistant screws to prevent adjustment to the air/fuel mixtures. Manufacturers tell us that the mixtures are set at the factory and should NOT be touched in the field. So, if you are riding a bike built from the early-80's on, and it has not been modified, then chances are that you only need to worry about occasionally checking the idle speed and making sure that the carburetors (if it has more than one) are in sync.

Carburetor adjustments must always be made when the engine is at operating temperature.

PRE-ADJUSTMENT CHECKS

◆ **See Figure 181**

Before attempting to make carburetor adjustments, all of the following points should be checked:

1. Carburetor alignment. On flexible mounted units, ensure that the carburetor(s) are vertically oriented, and not tilted to one side or the other. This may effect fuel level and high-speed operation.

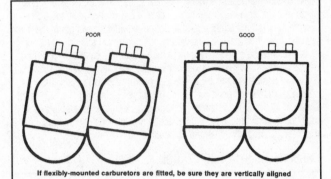

Fig. 181 If the carburetors on your multi-cylinder motorcycle are flexibly-mounted, make sure they are aligned vertically before attempting any adjustments—tilting could adversely affect fuel level and high-speed operation

Fig. 182 Most bikes with multiple carburetors use a single idle speed stop screw—BMW airheads being one of the exceptions since the carburetors are each mounted on opposite sides of the bike

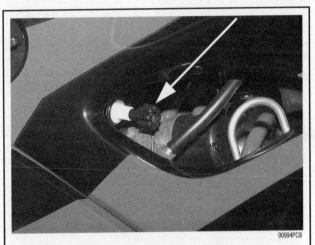

Fig. 183 On many bikes with full fairings the manufacturers are kind enough to supply a remote idle speed adjustment knob attached to the carburetors linkage

2. Cable condition. Check throttle operation, ensuring that the cable(s) are not kinked or binding, and that they and the twist-grip are well-lubricated. If the gas tank has been removed and reinstalled, check that it has not trapped or pinched the throttle cables, or that the cables have not been forced to make sharp bends anywhere along their route.

3. Ancillary systems. Carburetor adjustments should be made last after all other systems have been attended to in order to prevent misleading symptoms. Check that the air cleaner is serviceable, the spark plugs are in good condition, valves are correctly adjusted, and the ignition timing is at least approximately correct. Also ensure that the gasoline is reasonably fresh, of the correct octane, and that foreign material, such as water or dirt, has been purged from the fuel system. Check fuel filters, if applicable.

Cable Adjustment

On most motorcycles, provision is made for adjusting the throttle cable to compensate for stretching. the adjuster is usually found at or near the twist-grip. This device should be adjusted so that the twist-grip has a small amount of noticeable free-play when turned. In general, this free-play should amount to about 10-15° of grip rotation before the slides begin to lift or butterflies begin to turn.

On oil-injection two-strokes, the oil pump cable adjustment must be checked any time the throttle cable is adjusted.

➡**After adjustment, turn the forks slowly from side to side with the engine idling. Idle speed must not change or the cable is too tightly adjusted or too short. Check routing.**

IDLE SPEED & MIXTURE ADJUSTMENTS

◗ See Figures 182 and 183

Idle speeds which are recommended by the manufacturer should be adhered to in most cases. The idle running of a motorcycle engine is usually the most unsatisfactory carburetor range. There are many reasons for this. For one, the quantities of fuel and air which are going into the engine are relatively small, and are controlled by equally smallish passages. These are more likely to become clogged with dirt or varnish than the much larger jets, and the mixture will then be upset. Further, the relative quantities of gas and air are more critical at idle. Finally, since the engine is turning slowly, and is not under load, any irregularities in the mixture flow cause an erratic idle which may be irritating.

On most motorcycles, a satisfactory idle, can be obtained by carefully setting the carburetor(s) idle stop screw to the recommended specifications. As noted, above, idle speed should be set to the recommended specification. An idle speed which is too low may cause trouble by making smooth transition to the slow or mid-range circuit impossible. On some motorcycles, too low an idle may cause damage to bearings and other moving parts due to the great lapse between power pulses or to oil pressures which drop too low below specified idle.

On the other hand, too high an idle speed may cause the rpm to hang up for a moment or so when the throttle is closed. It may also make engaging the gears noisy or difficult, or result in excessive brake lining wear by negating the effects of engine braking. Because of the low engine speeds involved, minor misadjustments or slightly defective components will be much more noticeable at idle.

Because idle speed and mixture adjustments can vary so greatly with model, year and engine design, no attempt can be made to give them all here. If you need to adjust the mixture, either because your bike is that old or it is that modified, you should start with a shop manual. Also, some information regarding proper rejetting of a modified bikes carburetor is provided in the accessorizing section of this manual.

❊❊❊ **CAUTION**

REMEMBER that running internal combustion gasoline engines produce CARBON MONOXIDE which can kill you. NEVER, EVER run an engine (even for a short time) in an enclosed area like a shed or a garage. ALWAYS make sure there is plenty of ventilation (meaning that all garage doors and windows are open and, if at all possible, the exhaust pipes are sticking out through them). Better yet, do it on a nice, sunny day, and perform all adjustments outside.

To check and set idle speed on most bikes:

1. Attach a tachometer to the engine according to the tool manufacturer's instructions. The easiest type to use are the modern tachometers which have an inductive pick-up which you clamp to the No. 1 spark plug wire.

2. Start and run the engine until it reaches normal operating temperature.

3. Locate the idle speed stop screw or idle speed adjusting knob. On models with a single carburetor it is usually found on the carburetor itself. On models with multiple carburetors, there is usually either a single screw attached to a mechanical linkage which actuates the throttle plates of all carburetors or there may be a knurled knob on the end of a cable which is attached to the linkage. The cable type adjuster is usually found on models with extensive body work which would make access to the carburetors very difficult. Unfortunately, this is not true on all models with bodywork. If necessary, remove a side cover or part of the fairing for access to the screw.

➡ **On some models there may be multiple idle screws (one for each carburetor), but at that point setting idle speed becomes part of carburetor synchronization and you should refer to the procedure later in this section.**

4. With the engine running and the hand grip throttle fully closed, turn the idle speed screw until the proper specified idle has been reached.

5. Open and close the throttle a few times, and watch to see that the idle speed returns to specification. Repeat this once or twice to be certain the idle speed remains in spec.

6. With the engine still running at idle speed, slowly turn the handle bars from lock-to-lock. If the idle speed increases, even slightly, the throttle cable should be checked for kinks or binding. If none is found, the throttle cable should be adjusted until normal idle speed can be maintained while the bars are turned through their full range of motion.

Mixture Adjustments

On some older models or on bikes with modified fuel systems, mixture adjustments may be possible. Again, you should follow the bike or the carburetor manufacturer's specific instructions, but here are the basics:

On most carburetors, the idle mixture is determined largely by the pilot air screw which controls the amount of air mixing with the idle circuit jets, or the pilot fuel screw: which controls the amount of gasoline passing into the circuit.

Carburetors may be equipped with one or the other of these screws. While exceptions exist, on most carburetors the location of the screw will indicate whether it is an air screw or a fuel screw. Generally pilot air screws are located on the intake side of the carburetor, while most pilot fuel screws are located between the throttle slide and the engine manifold. Most "CV" carburetors use pilot fuel screws.

It is only important to know whether you have an "air screw" or a "fuel screw" if you intend to make mixture changes based on plug readings or road tests. Turning an air screw in will give a richer mixture, while turning it out will lean the mixture out. For pilot fuel screws, exactly the opposite is true.

Regardless of type pilot screw settings are given by the manufacturer, and should be adhered to, at least to within certain limits. The pilot screw settings are expressed in turns out from the seated position. The pilot screw's tip is tapered and is mated to an air or fuel passage. To make the adjustment, the screw is turned in gently until you can feel that it is lightly seated, then backed out the given number of turns. For example, if your specification for the pilot screw setting is "2½" you will back the screw out this number of times.

When turning these screws in, it is best to be very careful, as it is possible to ruin the tapered portion of the screw if it is turned down too tightly.

When performing a tune-up, always turn the pilot screws out to the given specification, then make any necessary adjustments. It should not be necessary to vary the screw setting more than 1/2 turn from the given setting unless changes have been made to the intake, engine, or exhaust systems. If it is not possible to obtain satisfactory performance with the settings as specified, suspect clogged carburetor passages or air leaks, etc. Due to the large number of differing throttle linkage and carburetor assemblies used today no general procedure will be able to provide all of the information necessary to properly adjust the carburetors on most motorcycles.

CARBURETOR SYNCHRONIZATION

▶ **See Figures 184 thru 191**

If your bike uses more than one carburetor, then at some point you should check the carburetor synchronization to make sure that all cylinders are being fed with the same amount of air/fuel mixture. Essentially, carburetor synchronization makes sure that one cylinder does not try to run faster than the others (which would cause the engine to fight against itself reducing fuel efficiency and power).

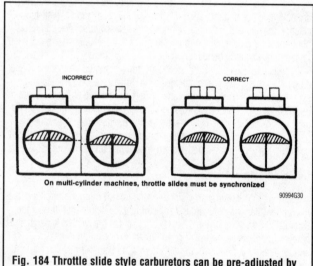

Fig. 184 Throttle slide style carburetors can be pre-adjusted by measuring and evening out the slide heights

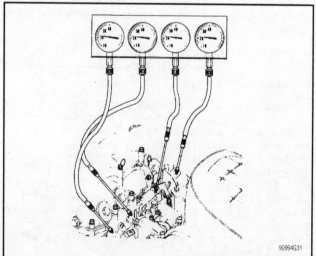

Fig. 185 A vacuum gauge or mercury tube balancer should be connected to vacuum ports for each cylinder being synchronized

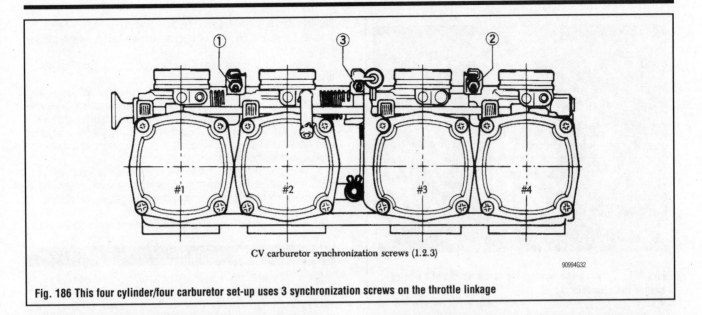

CV carburetor synchronization screws (1.2.3)

90994G32

Fig. 186 This four cylinder/four carburetor set-up uses 3 synchronization screws on the throttle linkage

90994P10

Fig. 187 A close-up view of the throttle linkage from a two cylinder/two carburetor machine . . .

90994PS5

Fig. 189 We attached a vacuum tube to each of the two vacuum ports after reinstalling the carburetors . . .

90994P08

Fig. 188 . . . here is a good view of the throttle linkage synchronization screw

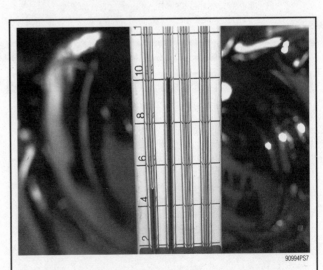

90994PS7

Fig. 190 . . . then we warmed the engine and checked the vacuum—it was out of balance . . .

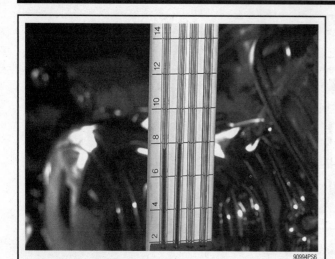

90994PS6

Fig. 191 . . . but a few turns of the screw we showed earlier evened the cylinders out

On bikes equipped with slide type carburetors, you can pre-adjust them by feeling or sighting the height of the slides and adjust them using the cables or linkage until the slides are at the same height.

The best way to synchronize carburetors is by using vacuum gauges on the intake vacuum for each carburetor. Most sync tools are equipped with up to four tubes (if you've got a six cylinder with six carbs, then you might have to buy two tools) each of which can be attached to a vacuum port on the carburetor or the intake manifold, depending on the design.

1. To synchronize the carburetors, start by adjusting the idle speed (and mixture, if appropriate) until the engine is idling at specification.

➡**On some inline four cylinder motorcycles you will have to remove the gas tank in order to install the carb sync tool. If this happens, you will either have to create an auxiliary gas tank so that the engine can be run with the tank off, or you will have to figure out a way to safely hook a fuel line from the regular gas tank (which will have to be supported directly above or above and to the side of the motorcycle) so that it is out of your way, but can still gravity feed the carb float bowls. Smaller fuel tanks from other motorcycles can often be used as an auxiliary tank, check with your local shop or bike boneyard for options, just make sure the tank is clean and free of rust, dirt or debris.**

2. Connect the sync tool to the intake vacuum ports for each cylinder. On most bikes a vacuum port will be provided on the carburetor or intake

manifold and covered with a small plastic cap which can easily be slide from the port nipple. On some carburetors, you will have to remove a plain blanking screw.

3. Start the engine and allow it to idle at normal operating temperature.

4. With the engine warm and running at or near normal idle, adjust the carburetors using the balance screws on the mechanical linkage or the individual screws on each carburetor until all cylinders are showing approximate equal vacuum. A variance of about 0.4–1.6 in. Hg (10–40 mm Hg) is normally allowed between the cylinders, but anything more should be adjusted to bring the cylinder vacuum closer together.

5. When you are finished, remove the sync tool and carefully replug all of the vacuum lines. Remember that a vacuum leak (caused by forgetting to plug the lines or by the plug coming off down the road) will greatly lean your air/fuel mixture and could lead to a burnt valve.

6. Install the gas tank or any bodywork which was removed for access.

Fuel Injection Adjustment

One of the great things about modern electronic fuel injection is that your bike comes with a computer to think about things like air/fuel ratios and ignition timing, so you don't have to. But, fuel injection systems vary, there are some, like the BMW Bosch Motronic systems which do allow for adjustments (but usually they are only necessary right after break-in or some major repair). Suffice it to say that these adjustments require, at the least, a gas analyzer and the BMW computer system interface tools. In fact even seemingly simple adjustments such as the throttle position sensor on Harley's fuel injection system at least require a very expensive break-out box to perform safely.

So what are we getting at here. No periodic adjustments are normally necessary or possible on fuel injected bikes. If you have a rideability problem with your engine, and checks of all maintenance items do not uncover a mechanical culprit, then you should seek advice from your dealer. Also, remember that most fuel injection systems utilize self-diagnostic systems which run checks of the electrical components in the system when the engine is first started (that is why they are equipped with ENGINE lights of some sort). If the computer detects a problem, you will be the second one to know when the light comes on.

Road Test

AWWWW SHUCKS, do I HAVE TO RIDE IT . . .

The last step of a tune-up inspection is to suit up and see how the old bike feels. Only by riding the bike, engine under load, will you know for sure if all of that tweaking paid off. Besides, even if all your bike required was a new set of plugs and some visual checks, do you ever REALLY NEED AN EXCUSE TO RIDE?

CLUTCH & TRANSMISSION MAINTENANCE

Transmission Oil

On bikes without cases that share engine and transmission oil, a separate oil change must be performed in order to keep your transmission in top shape. Remember that most motorcycle transmissions lead a rough life. Most are mounted in close quarters with the engines meaning they get a large amount of the heat from the motor, not to mention the job they normally perform. For example, even though Harley Big-Twin transmissions are bolted to a primary housing and set back slightly from the engine, many of them share oil pans with the engine or are mounted right below the engine oil tank (keeping them close to the source of heat).

➡**Harley-Davidson Sportsters share their transmission fluid, NOT with the engine, but with the primary drive. Please refer to the information on primary drive oils for Sportsters.**

Like engine oil, transmission gear oil will oxidize over time when exposed to moisture and atmospheric contaminants. Luckily, on bikes that don't share their oil with the engine, this process is significantly slower because the oil is not exposed to the acids and other nasty byproducts of combustion. But, that doesn't mean you should ignore it. At least annually, you should drain the transmission fluid, check it for unusual wear or excessive emulsification. If either is found, you should perform more frequent inspections or changes to see if there is a problem developing. If you ride the bike in adverse conditions, such as severe, day long rain, then the fluid level should be checked to make sure too much water didn't find its way in. If the level has gone up (without you adding), you can assume there is too much water in the case and the oil should be changed right away.

SELECTING THE PROPER OIL

Bikes with transmissions that use a separate oil supply, often require special oil for the gears. Most manufacturers of these motorcycles recommend using SAE 80 or SAE 90 EP (extreme pressure) gear oil. Keep in mind that a gear oil viscosity rating does NOT equal an SAE engine oil rating.

➡ **Some two-stroke bikes use a lighter oil in their transmissions. In some cases this may even include SAE engine oils such as 10W-30 or 20W-50.**

Transmission lubrication is an excellent application for synthetic gear oils. Some manufacturer's, like Harley-Davidson for example, even sell synthetic and semi-synthetic gear oils for use in their motorcycles. The extreme operating conditions of a transmission, including the high pressure and shear factors that occur between gears make this an ideal environment for today's premium synthetic gear oils.

Be sure to check your owners manual for your bike manufacturer's particular requirements before selecting a gear oil.

CHECKING YOUR OIL

➡ **Harley-Davidson Sportsters share their transmission fluid, NOT with the engine like many other bikes, but with the primary drive. Please refer to the information on primary drive oils for Sportsters.**

The fluid level of your transmission is usually checked in one of two ways, either using a dipstick OR a fill plug. In both cases the bike should usually be held perfectly upright and level to assure a proper reading.

With A Dipstick

◆ See Figures 192 thru 198

If a dipstick is used, the same rules apply as when checking engine oil. If the dipstick is threaded, DON'T rethread it to check the level, but leave it sitting on top of the threads. Remember to pull it out, wipe it off and reinsert it. Then pull it out and hold it vertically. Oil will not magi-

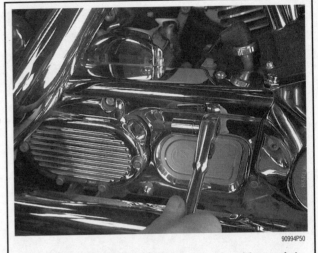
Fig. 193 If it is too tight for an hex key, use a hex driver socket and a ratchet—unless your chrome gets in the way . . .

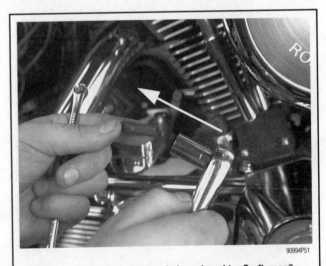
Fig. 194 . . . then you will be glad you bought a Craftsman® socket since the hex can be removed from the socket . . .

Fig. 192 Most transmission dipsticks are retained using hex-head plugs (though some may use thumbwheels)

Fig. 195 . . . and you can use a wrench to turn the hex key

Fig. 196 Like most threaded dispsticks, you check the oil by inserting the dipstick and letting it sit ON TOP OF the threads . .

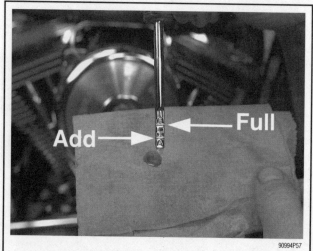

Fig. 197 . . . then withdraw the dipstick and hold it vertically to be assured of a correct reading

Fig. 198 If necessary, add additional fluid through the dipstick opening until the proper level is reached

cally run up the dipstick. If you hold the dipstick vertically, you will never get a false high reading (unless you are thick enough to hold it upside-down, but then you get what you deserve, right?). If oil is necessary, add it through the dipstick opening, SLOWLY. Remember that these transmissions are usually very compact and a few ounces can make quite a difference on the fluid level. Add slowly, let it sit for a minute and then recheck.

With A Filler Plug

♦ **See Figures 199 thru 206**

If a filler plug is used then it is usually just a case of checking it like you would on a 1957 Chevy (or most any other of your favorite cars). Remove the filler plug and see if any runs out. The level should be just to the bottom of the filler plug. If an excessive amount runs out of the case, then the transmission was overfilled OR a lot of moisture has found its way in (and it is time for a fluid change). If you need to add fluid, use a squeeze bottle, a hand held pump or a suction gun (in reverse) to add oil through the filler plug opening. Once the fluid begins to seep back out the opening, install the plug.

Fig. 199 If the transmission uses a filler plug to check fluid level, it is usually found on the side of the transmission housing

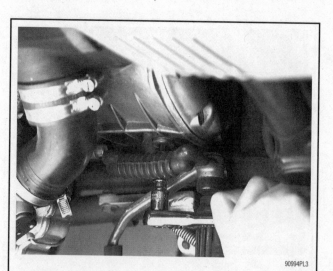

Fig. 200 Remove the plug using a hex key or a driver socket and ratchet

Fig. 201 If fluid runs out, either the transmission was overfilled, or an excessive amount of moisture has mixed with the gear oil

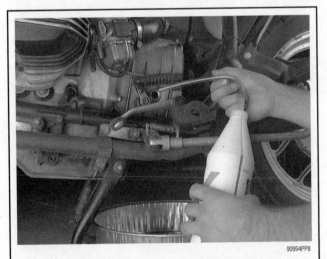

Fig. 202 If the level is low (or if you are refilling it after a change) use a hand pump or a length of rubber hose to add oil

Fig. 203 Attach the hose to the oil bottle, insert the hose in the opening and tilt the bottle to start the oil flowing

Fig. 204 Watch the oil level, it tends to come into sight and over the filler plug opening rather suddenly

Fig. 205 Once the gear oil starts to trickle out, remove the hose and let the level settle

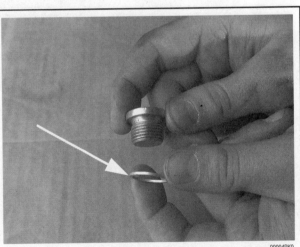

Fig. 206 If the filler plug uses a crush washer, be sure to use a new washer when you install the plug

CHANGING YOUR OIL

◆ **See Figures 207 thru 212**

➥Harley-Davidson Sportsters share their transmission fluid, NOT with the engine like many other bikes, but with the primary drive. Please refer to the information on primary drive oils for Sportsters.

As we said, in order to keep an eye on your transmission's health, be sure to change the fluid AT LEAST once a year, or by your manufacturer's recommended mileage intervals (if they are shorter with your riding style).

Like with all oil changes it is best to drain the oil at normal operating temperature. So once again, suit up and go for a ride. You will eventually learn that if you have a lot of fluids to drain you can buy a couple of drain pans and do them all at once (or you can spend the whole day suiting up, riding, changing an oil, suiting up, riding, changing an oil . . . of course I can think of worse days).

After a decent ride (10–20 minutes depending on how hot it is out already, you'll need less time the hotter the ambient temperature), come back in and remove the transmission drain plug. Allow the transmission to drain fully. On some models the drain plug is not at the lowest point on the

Fig. 209 . . . so be sure to slide the pan in position, then unthread the plug by hand

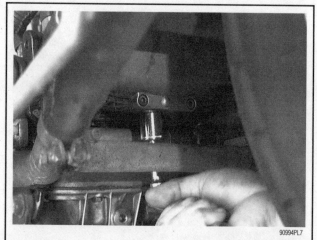

Fig. 207 With the transmission warm from a ride, locate the drain plug, which is usually found directly under the transmission . . .

Fig. 210 With the plug removed, allow the transmission to drain fully

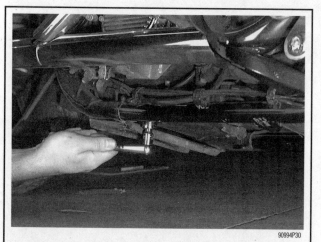

Fig. 208 Loosen the plug using a suitable socket driver and ratchet—Note this model sits so low the drain pan cannot fit under with the ratchet . . .

Fig. 211 Inspect the plug for deposits (since most are magnetic) and check the sealing washers . . .

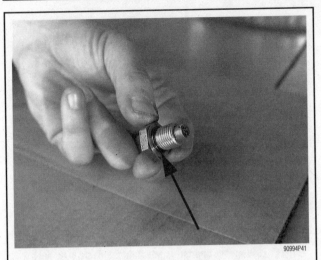

Fig. 212 . . . or in this case, O-rings, to see if they are in good condition or if they must be replaced

transmission if the bike is on its sidestand, if so you should sit on the bike and hold it upright to assure proper draining. Or, since you have to fill the bike with it in the upright position, block it up (using jackstands under the crashbars or wood blocks under the frame) or raise it using a portable bike lift. Of course on models with centerstands, well, let's just say you don't have this problem.

➥**MAKE SURE YOU REMOVE THE CORRECT DRAIN PLUG. You don't want to empty your engine oil, or maybe your primary drive oil instead. If this should happen, you will probably realize it as the oil is draining (since transmission oil is usually not as black as used engine oil, and it tends to smell different), or at worst when you go to add new transmission oil. Be careful because on some bikes it really can be tricky. For example, the transmissions on some late-model Harleys (FLTs and Dynas specifically), share a pan with the oil tank. On these bikes the transmission drain plug is closer to the engine oil fill than the engine drain plug, you can see how it could be confusing.**

Since they do not usually use oil filters, many transmission drain plugs are equipped with a magnet to attract and hold tiny metal deposits which come off gears in use. Be sure to thoroughly clean the metal paste which has collected on the drain plug magnet. Paste is OK, while little teeth could be bad. If chunks are found, be worried (it might be time to have the transmission professionally checked).

When installing the drain plug, check to see if it uses a crush washer or an O-ring. You might have success reusing either of them and you are usually OK reusing an O-ring, as long as it is not cut or dried out and cracked. BUT, if a crush washer was used, then it is best to replace it (don't try to save a few cents on a washer only to lose a few bucks on oil if it starts leaking). Besides, transmissions that leak tend to leak RIGHT IN THE PATH OF THE REAR TIRE and that could be very BAD.

Primary Drive Oil

All motorized vehicles need a method of transmitting power from the engine to the transmission. On cars and trucks this is usually by means of a direct, mechanical connection (through a clutch or a torque converter). But most motorcycle engines have been designed to use a different method (with the exceptions of BMWs and Moto Guzzis). On most bikes a gear set or a drive chain is used to turn the transmission input shaft. On the majority of these, the primary drive is found in the case shared by the engine and transmission (and is usually lubed with engine oil). On these set-ups, no

additional maintenance is required and normal oil changes will serve the primary drive as well.

But, on some motorcycles, such as Harley-Davidsons and Buells, the primary chain is mounted under a cover on the side of the engine case (Sportsters and Buells) or in a completely separate housing (Big-Twins) that is attached to the engine and transmission. On bikes like these, a separate source of oil is often used to lubricate the primary chain and bathe the wet clutch. On Sportster and Buell motors the primary drive fluid is shared with the transmission, which makes transmission/primary oil changes that much more important (because you have all the clutch and chain debris mixing with the gear paste).

Primary drive fluids should be changed at the mileage intervals recommended in your owners manual, OR at least every year. Since they are also the lubricant for your wet clutch, you may want to perform this more often. Besides on most models that use a wet primary, you are going to have to open it up to check and adjust the chain every couple of thousand miles anyway.

SELECTING THE PROPER OIL

Follow the recommendations in your owners manual. A synthetic or semi-synthetic gear oil is usually used for wet primary drives that have their own separate lubricant.

CHECKING YOUR OIL

▶ **See Figures 213, 214, 215, 216 and 217**

➥**The bike must usually be held or supported in the fully upright and level position in order to get the proper fluid level reading.**

The oil level on most wet primary drives is checked through a chain or clutch inspection cover. The exception, of course, would be that most of the Harley Sportsters used a self-leveling filler plug (a filler plug which is removed to allow oil to flow out until the proper level is achieved) until just recently. On most other Harleys (including late-model Sportsters that no longer use the self-leveling plug) the level should be a few millimeters above the bottom of the clutch plates, as seen with the inspection cover removed. As usual, the bike must be upright and completely level before checking.

Harley and Buell inspection covers vary. Many early-models used threaded covers (on the Sportsters they looked almost like little Chevy Bow-Ties). On most late-model bikes, the covers are retained by hex head or Torx® T-27 head screws.

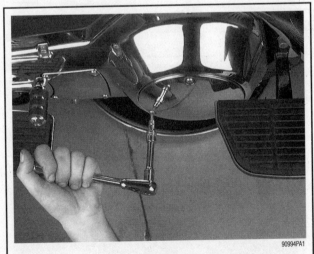

Fig. 213 On most Harleys you have to remove a primary cover in order to check or add fluid

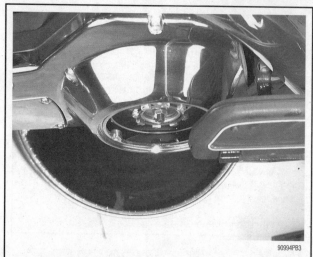

Fig. 214 The fluid should normally be JUST above the bottom of the clutch assembly

Fig. 215 If necessary, add the appropriate fluid . . .

Fig. 216 . . . until the proper level is reached

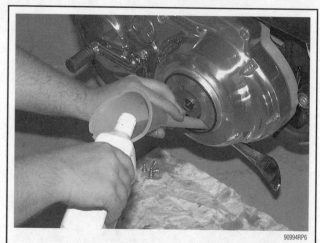

Fig. 217 Late-model Sportsters add fluid the same way, but early-models would add fluid through the chain inspection cover and use a self-leveling plug to equalize the level

✳✳ WARNING

When removing or installing Harley primary covers ALWAYS loosen the bolts gradually in one or two passes of a cross-wise pattern. This is especially important if you are removing a hot cover. Remember that these covers are aluminum and are prone to warping if exposed to uneven clamp loads. For installation, try to wait until the machine is cold, then install and tighten the bolts to specification using a torque wrench. ALSO, always use a light coating of medium strength Blue Loctite® 242 on the bolt threads to keep them from loosening in service. Should one or more of the bolts loosen in service you won't only have an oil leak, you will also have a warped primary inspection cover.

CHANGING YOUR OIL

◆ **See Figures 218 thru 228**

As with all other oil changes it is best to drain the primary case oil while it is at normal operating temperature.

After a short ride (10–20 minutes depending on the ambient temperature), park the bike on its stand and remove the drain plug from the bottom

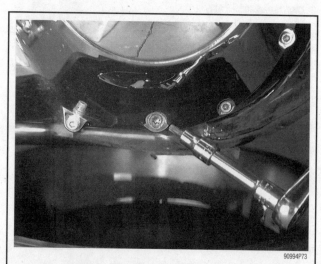

Fig. 218 With the primary drive warm, use a suitable driver (like a Torx bit in this case) to loosen . . .

Fig. 219 . . . and remove the primary drive drain plug

Fig. 220 On Sportsters, the drain plug is usually a hex head bolt that is so close to the rubber kickstand stop that you will need to use a wrench

Fig. 221 Remove the plug and allow the primary fluid to thoroughly drain

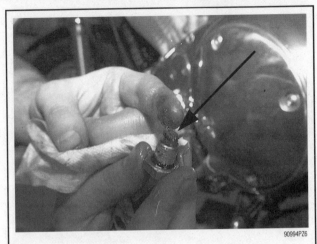

Fig. 222 While the fluid is draining, be sure to clean the deposits from the magnetic drain plug, this one's from a Sportster

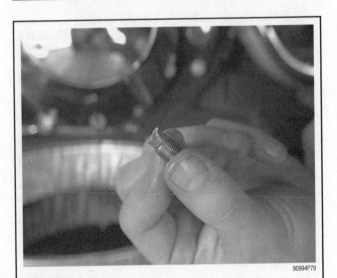

Fig. 223 This drain plug is from a Big-Twin

Fig. 224 Pay close attention when installing the primary cover, the bolts on some models use O-ring washers to prevent leaks

Fig. 225 If the cover O-ring becomes dislodged, be sure to tuck it back into the groove before installing the cover . . .

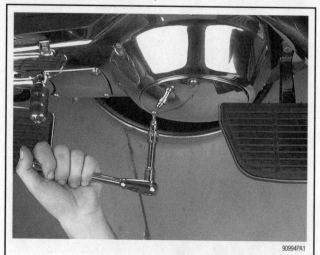

Fig. 228 . . . and carefully install the cover, making sure the O-ring does not get pinched as you gradually tighten the bolts

Fig. 226 . . . though unless you are installing a brand new O-ring, this can be very difficult . . .

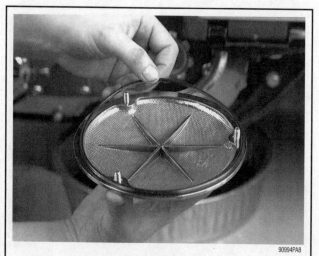

Fig. 227 . . . you may have to use the cover press the O-ring back into position, place the ring around the bolts . . .

of the primary cover. On some models (including most Sportsters) the plug is a hex head threaded straight up into the case (to the rear of the bike from the locknut and threaded primary chain adjuster on Sportster models). On other models the drain plug is a recessed hex or Torx® head bolt in the lower side of the cover. Remove the plug and allow the fluid to drain completely.

Like transmission plugs, most primary case drain plugs are equipped with a magnet to attract and hold tiny metal deposits which come off chains, sprockets and clutch friction discs in use. Be sure to thoroughly clean the metal paste which has collected on the drain plug magnet. Remember that some paste and/or tiny debris is OK, but anything that has a problem fitting through the drain hole is definitely something to worry about. If you find large debris or metal chunks it is time to disassemble your primary case in order to make sure nothing is about to explode.

When installing the drain plug, check to see if it uses a crush washer or an O-ring. Crush washers should be replaced, while O-rings should be checked for wear or damage, and be replaced if any is found. On many late-model Harleys, no gasket is used on the plug, so check the threads for sealant. If the sealant is almost gone, you should thoroughly clean the bolt threads and apply a light coating of thread sealant to make sure there are no leaks.

Harley primary chain and clutch inspection covers use either O-rings or gaskets to keep the oil in the case. O-rings cans be reused if they are not cut or damaged, but gaskets should always be replaced (they won't ever seal again once they are completely soaked with oil, which usually happens when the cover is removed). Also, watch the cover screws, some are equipped with O-ring washers which should be replaced if damaged. All cover screws should be tightened to specification using a torque wrench. DON'T RISK AN UNEVEN CLAMP LOAD which WILL WARP the aluminum cover in service. Although the specifications vary, the inspection cover screws are usually tightened somewhere between 40–110 inch lbs. (5–12 Nm). The most important thing is not whether the spec on your particular bike is 40 inch lbs. or 70 inch lbs. or 110 inch lbs. (this isn't a whole lot of torque), but as long as they are ALL TORQUED EVENLY, your cover will survive.

Primary Drive Chain

CHECKING & ADJUSTMENT

▶ See Figures 229 thru 239

All motorcycles need a method of delivering engine power to the transmission. Most of them do this with a primary drive chain or gear assembly. We say most of them, because there are always exceptions, such as BMW

Fig. 229 To check the primary chain you will have to remove the chain inspection cover—On Sportsters it only takes 2 screws

Fig. 230 Then use a ruler to measure total movement . . .

Fig. 231 . . . of the primary chain while you push up on it using a screwdriver

Fig. 232 The chain can be harder to measure on some Big-Twins, because the top strand is not completely visible . . .

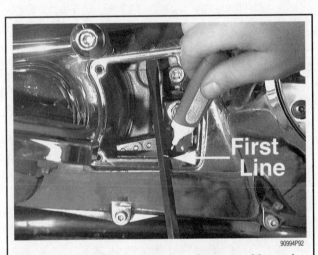

Fig. 233 . . . you can get around this using a screwdriver and some white out, make a line even with the bottom of the inspection hole when the driver JUST touches the chain . . .

Fig. 234 . . . then make another line (also even with the bottom of the cover) after you have pushed upward on the chain, as far as it will go

and Moto Guzzi who use automotive style single plate dry clutches between the transmission input shaft and engine flywheel.

The primary drivetrains on most modern motorcycles are not items to be concerned about during basic maintenance. They are sealed in the engine cases and should only be checked if a new clutch is being installed. But, good old Harley-Davidson likes to do things a little bit different. Since the Big-Twin Harley motors and transmissions are not even bolted to each other, they use a separate, enclosed primary drive chain and wet clutch housing (to which both the motor and transmission attach). On Harley Sportsters it is even more confusing, since the motor and transmission share a case, but NOT an engine oil. The primary chain is enclosed in a housing attached to the side of the case (and shares its fluid with the transmission).

In any case, on all Harley-Davidson motors, the primary drive chain should be checked and adjusted AT LEAST every 5000 miles, but it is a good idea to do that more often if your bike sees hard use. If you are going to change the primary fluid more often (such as with every oil change, then you simply don't have an excuse not to check the chain at the same time).

1. Ok, here's the first irony. It is best to check the primary chain, cold. As in overnight cold. It is best to assure a good measurement, ease of working conditions (since you'll be sticking your hands in an inspection opening in the primary cover) and proper tightening of the inspection cover bolts (to assure the cover does not warp). So what is the problem you might ask? The problem is that fluids are best drained HOT, and you must drain the fluid to perform this check on most Harley motors. Our advice, ride the bike home the night before you plan on checking this and drain all the fluids while it is hot. Then, take the ignition key and place it in the same bag where you have all those bottles of new fluids (just to be sure), and let the bike sit overnight.

To check and adjust the primary chain on Harley-Davidson and Buell motors:

2. Drain the primary chain case of fluid.

3. If possible, raise the rear wheel of the motorcycle off the ground, as it will be easier to check the chain in multiple spots this way.

4. Remove the primary inspection cover. When the cover is bolted on, loosen the cover bolts using two or more passes of a crosswise pattern. These bolts are NOT high torque, but the aluminum covers warp easily so take your time. On most models the clutch inspection cover must also be removed in order to properly refill the primary case (this does not include Sportster models equipped with a self-leveling plug).

➡The inspection covers on late-model Harley and Buell motors usually use a Hex driver or a Torx® T-27 bit. The inspection covers on some earlier bikes where round, threaded plugs.

Fig. 236 If the chain is out of specification you will have to loosen the chain tensioner and reposition it to achieve the proper play

Fig. 237 On Sportsters there is a threaded rod beneath the primary cover that is used to tighten or loosen the chain (but you must loosen the locknut first)

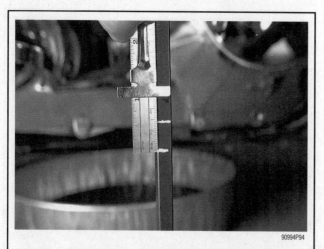
Fig. 235 Remove the screwdriver and measure the distance between the two lines, that is your total chain deflection (free-play)

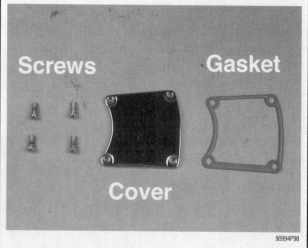
Fig. 238 If the primary chain inspection cover uses a gasket, be sure to replace it each time the cover is removed . . .

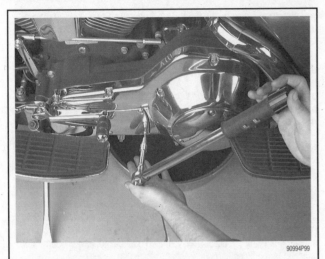

90994P99

Fig. 239 . . . AND ALWAYS use a torque wrench upon installation to prevent the cover from warping in service

5. Remove the cover(s), then remove and discard the gasket. On covers equipped with O-rings, DON'T TOUCH THEM. Once a O-ring is installed in the primary cover groove AND it touches oil, it can be very difficult to reseat. If it unseats, it is a major pain in the but to get it back in the groove. As long as the O-ring is not cut or damaged, leave it alone and you will be fine. If the O-ring comes out, you are better off cleaning the groove thoroughly with some mild solvent and installing a new, dry O-ring.

6. Stick a straight edge into the inspection cover, at as slight an angle as possible, and measure the amount of free-play (the distance the chain will move upward) at multiple points around the chain. This will mean placing the bike in gear and rolling it, bumping it with the starter or turning the rear wheel (with the spark plugs removed unless you're biceps are bigger than your brains) in order move the portion of the chain which is accessible through the cover.

7. Check the specifications for your bike. It is usually ⅝–⅞ in. (16–22mm) COLD or ⅜–⅝ in. (9.5–16mm) HOT on most recent Harley motors. Some older models, including some early 1990's Evos recommended ⅜–½ in. (9.5–13mm) COLD and ¼–⅜ in. (6–9.5mm) HOT. Like most chain adjustments, you would rather it be a little too loose than it be a little too tight, since tight adjustments will cause rapid chain and sprocket wear (as well as possible bearing overloading and failure).

8. If necessary adjust the chain by moving the chain tensioner:

a. On most Big-Twins this involves loosening the locknut on the center of the bracket and then moving the bracket up or down on the serrated teeth at the back of the cover until the adjustment is correct. Once the adjustment is set, tighten the locknut and double check the adjustment.

✽✽ WARNING

DO NOT loosen the adjuster locknut on Big-Twins more than 2 turns or the adjuster bolt may become dislodged in the primary.

b. On Sportsters (here is your turn to make fun of the Big-Twin guys), adjustment is much easier. Loosen the locknut on the lower outside portion of the primary case, then use the hex in the threaded adjuster screw to tighten or loosen the chain adjustment. The adjuster screw is mounted to the tensioner slide which moves upward (tightening the chain) as the screw is threaded inward (clockwise), or moves downward (loosening the chain) as the bolt is threaded outward (counterclockwise).

9. Once the chain adjustment is finished, you probably want to check and adjust the clutch (since you are here anyway and on most models you had to remove the clutch inspection cover anyway).

10. Properly refill the primary chain case with oil. If the rear wheel was raised earlier, make sure it is level now.

11. Install the clutch cover and/or primary chain inspection cover, as applicable. Make sure a new gasket is used on the inspection cover and that the clutch cover O-ring is in its groove.

➥**Remember to check the cover screws for thread lock or sealant. If none is present, use a dab of medium strength Blue Loctite® 242 on the bolt threads to keep them from loosening in service. Should one or more of the bolts loosen in service you won't only have an oil leak, you will have a warped primary inspection cover.**

12. Install the cover screws and lightly seat them using the driver. Then use a torque wrench to tighten the screws to specification. The most important part of this process is to assure that all of the inspection cover fasteners are tightened evenly so that the cover does not warp in service.

Hydraulic Clutch Fluid

Some motorcycles use a clutch master and slave cylinder assembly to actuate the clutch, instead of a mechanical cable. These systems have the advantage of using differences in cylinder bore sizes to give you a mechanical advantage at the hand lever (resulting in reduced lever pressure). Another advantage of these systems is that they are normally self-adjusting.

One of the only down sides to this system is that it gives you another fluid to check and change.

SELECTING THE PROPER FLUID

Most hydraulic clutch systems use DOT 3 or 4 brake fluid. Check the clutch master cylinder cover (as they are usually labeled) or your owners manual to be sure.

CHECKING YOUR FLUID

◆ **See Figures 240 and 241**

Like most brake master cylinders, clutch cylinders tend to use one of 3 methods for fluid checking:

- **Removing the cover**
- **See-through reservoirs**
- **Sight-glass**

The easiest method is the see-through reservoir, which should have one or more fluid level marking on the side of the housing. Covers which have

90994PD9

Fig. 240 On some models, the motorcycle must be upright and the bars centered in order to get a proper reading through the sight glass

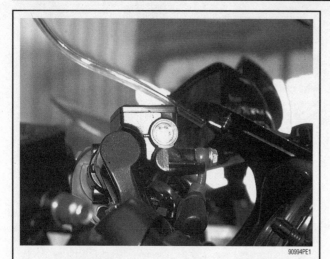

Fig. 241 On other models the bars may have to be turned, full lock, to one side (check your owners manual to be sure)

to be removed are a pain because you will have to take extra care not to spill any fluid AND, they prevent spur of the moment checks (at gas stations and rest stops). Sight-glasses can also be tricky, depending on their design. On some models the sight glass will appear dark whether the reservoir is FULL or EMPTY and will only show a change when the reservoir is somewhere in between (so you can see a little pocket of air or a bubble).

✳✳ WARNING

Remember that Dot 3 and 4 brake fluids EAT PAINT. Take care not to spill any on your motorcycle. If you do, immediately flush the area with plenty of clean water.

Check your owners manual to be sure how your handlebars should be positioned. Especially on models with centerstands (where the bars can be easily turned through their full range of motion while the bike is on the stand), manufacturers will design the reservoirs to be read full only at the proper position. On most bikes, this position is with the clutch reservoir as level as its mounting on the handlebar will allow.

If fluid must be added, clean off and remove the cover, then add fluid and install the cover right away. Don't let contaminants into the fluid by leaving the cover loose or off unnecessarily. Also, ALWAYS use clean, fresh fluid from a sealed container (and preferably from a container that has not been sitting on the shelf too long. If the container is very dusty, you might want to pick another one because even in a seemingly sealed container, brake fluid may absorb some moisture over time.

➡**ALWAYS clean the clutch master cylinder cover of any dirt or debris before removing it. You want to take great care to keep contaminants out of the fluid. And remember that moisture (usually present in the atmosphere) is also a contaminant since DOT 3 or 4 brake fluid is hydroscopic (meaning it tends to absorb water). DO NOT leave the cover off the master cylinder for any length of time, open it up to add fluid and install the cover again, right away.**

It should be normal for the fluid level to decrease slightly with clutch wear. But, if you have to add fluid often, the system should be checked for leaks. Also, if you need to add a large amount of fluid you either have a leak or your clutch may be nearing the end of its useful life. Either situation should be checked and remedied.

CHANGING YOUR FLUID

Since most hydraulic clutch systems use Dot 3 or 4 brake fluid, which is hydroscopic and absorbs moisture from the atmosphere, it is important that

you periodically change the fluid. Over time, moisture in the system can lead to corrosion of the master and slave cylinder internal components (which may in tern lead to scoring of the pistons and bores causing reduced pressure and leaks). Although much less of a danger than with brake systems in which the calipers can be subjected to high heat conditions, the addition of moisture to the fluid will lower the fluid's boiling point. This would make the system more susceptible to a sudden and complete loss of clutching ability should temperatures in the slave cylinder raise high enough to vaporize the water.

Like brake systems, the fluid should be completely drained, refilled and bleed AT LEAST once every two years.

Most systems have a bleed screw located on or near the clutch slave cylinder. To locate it, follow the hydraulic line from the handlebars to the cylinder. Check a shop manual if it is not readily evident. The most common method of changing this fluid is to attach a bleed hose to the screw, open the screw and slowly pump the fluid out using the clutch lever. You can save a little time by first opening the reservoir and draining it with a suction gun or turkey baster. You can also use a hand-held vacuum pump attached to the bleed screw.

Once all of the fluid has been drained, refill the clutch master cylinder reservoir and begin to pump the fresh fluid into the system. Again, a vacuum pump can also be used for this. Once fluid begins to flow from the bleeder screw, tighten the screw and top of the reservoir. Work the hand lever slowly a few times, then bleed it like a brake system. Slowly compress and hold the hand lever, then open the bleed screw allowing trapped air to escape with some fluid. Tighten the bleed screw THEN release the hand lever (if you release the hand level first, you are going to suck air back into the system through the screw). To help prevent this, keep the end of the hose submerged in the fluid you just drained (unless that fluid was REALLY old, in which case you might want to place the hose in a container with a little fresh fluid). Repeat this until NO air bubbles can be seen in the fluid for a couple of tries. Once you are finished, properly top off the fluid level and seal the reservoir.

Clutch Assembly

▶ **See Figure 242**

There are several clutch variations used on motorcycles. Most of them are multi-disc wet or dry clutches known as the countershaft type because they are mounted on the transmission countershaft which runs at somewhere between one half and one third engine speed. In most cases the clutch is chain or gear driven from the crankshaft. The advantage offered by this configuration is that its low operating speed is conducive to smooth high speed shifting. Its greatest disadvantage is its relatively large mass and frictional area which necessitates the use of stiff springs (that often require a lot of lever pressure).

A few machines, notably BMW and Moto Guzzi, use an automotive style single plate clutch known as a flywheel clutch. These clutches are mounted on the crankshaft and spin at engine speed. This, in some cases, makes high rpm shifting a little rougher than on the countershaft type, but the single plate construction makes the lever light to the touch.

A clutch is said to be a "wet-type" if it runs in an oil bath, and a "dry-type" if it does not. The only difference between the two is the type of friction material on the clutch plates. All manual clutches operate in pretty much the same manner, be they wet or dry single or multi-plated. When the clutch lever is actuated the release worm or lever moves in toward the clutch hub and presses the clutch pushrod against the pressure (spring) plate. The force exerted by the pushrod(s) compresses the clutch springs while moving the pressure plate away from the clutch plates, thereby allowing the plates to disengage and spin freely. When the hand lever is released, a return spring moves the release worm or lever back into its original position and the pushrod(s) is pushed back against its seat by the pressure plate which again presses against the clutch plates causing the clutch to engage.

Because clutches wear and cables can stretch with use, the clutch must be checked and adjusted periodically to assure proper operation.

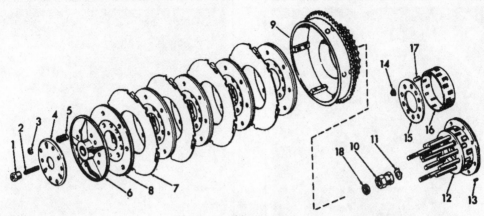

Clutch assembly

1. Pushrod adjusting screw locknut
2. Adjusting screw
3. Spring tension adjusting nut (3)
4. Spring collar
5. Spring (10)
6. Outer disc (pressure plate)
7. Steel disc (4)
8. Friction disc (5)
9. Clutch shell
10. Clutch hub nut
11. Hub nut lockwasher
12. Clutch hub
13. Clutch hub key
14. Bearing plate spring (3)
15. Bearing plate
16. Bearing retainer
17. Bearing roller
18. Bearing nut seal

90994G33

Fig. 242 Exploded view of a typical multi-disc clutch assembly

INSPECTION & ADJUSTMENT

▶ **See Figures 243 thru 249**

Incorrect clutch adjustment can cause problems including early clutch failure, clunky shifting, lack of power and difficulty finding neutral. Too much clutch free-play may not allow the clutch plates to completely separate causing clutch drag (rough shifting and difficulty finding neutral can result). Not enough free-play may cause clutch slippage by keeping the plates from closing fully (which can lead to clutch burning and failure).

Although methods of adjustment vary from machine-to-machine they are usually set with one or more threaded adjusters on the cable (hydraulic systems are usually self-adjusting, taking additional fluid from the reservoir as the clutch wears). Some models have additional clutch adjustments which must be performed at the engine, so be sure to check your owners manual or a good shop manual to be sure you have the proper techniques and specifications.

You will usually know the your clutch on your bike is properly adjusted if there is a small amount of free-play at the lever and you are not experiencing any of the symptoms described earlier. By free-play, we mean the distance the lever moves BEFORE resistance is felt. If there is no detectable free-play at the lever (the clutch begins to release as soon as you begin pulling the lever), then you can't be sure the clutch is fully engaging. If there is an excessive amount of free-play you should check the bike while stopped with the bike in gear on a level surface. Hold the clutch lever fully against the hand grip and, without holding the brake, rev the engine and see if the bike wants to creep forward (if it does, then there

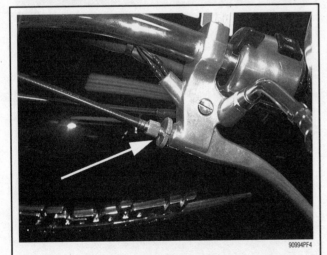

90994PF4

Fig. 243 On most bikes, clutch adjustments are made using a thumbwheel or threaded adjuster at the hand lever . . .

90994PF6

Fig. 244 . . . unless there isn't enough thread, then adjustment should be performed at the other end of the clutch cable

Fig. 245 But, on Harleys Big-Twins, before you adjust the cable, you must open the clutch inspection cover and adjust the lever screw . . .

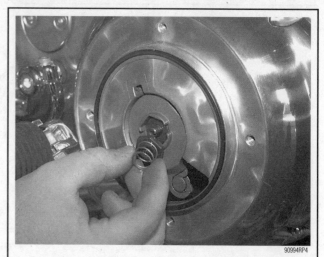

Fig. 247 On Sportsters, the procedure is very similar, but first you must remove the spring loaded lockplate . . .

Fig. 246 . . . then hold it in position and tighten the locknut

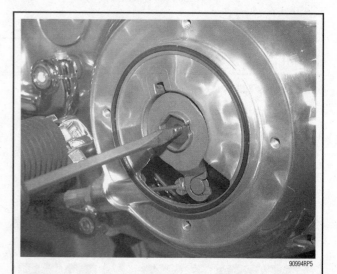

Fig. 248 . . . then you can adjust the lever screw

is probably too much free-play in the cable and the clutch cannot fully disengage).

On most models the clutch free-play adjustment specification is given in inches or mm as the amount of distance the cable can be pulled back from the lever housing by hand or as the distance the lever travels before resistance is felt. Although specifications vary the gap between the cable and lever housing is usually in the neighborhood of 1/16–1/8 in. (2–3mm). Specifications for measuring lever travel as free-play tend to be a little bit higher, usually more like 3/8–3/4 in. (10–20mm) as measured at the end of the lever. Again, check your owners manual for specifications on your bike.

Simple free-play adjustments can usually be made at an adjuster on the cable (sometimes at the handlebar end of the cable, and sometimes a short distance down the cable). On many Japanese and some Euro-pean bikes, there are two cable adjusters, one at each end. On these bikes adjustments should be made at the handlebar end, unless that adjuster reaches the end of its travel, then you would reset it and instead turn to the adjuster on the engine side of the cable. Other bikes may have a cable adjustment one and a lever or pivot adjustment at the engine.

For Harley-Davidson and Buell motors clutch adjustment SHOULD NOT only occur at the cable adjuster. On these models you will have to remove the clutch inspection cover from the primary case and adjust the clutch lever screw. Only after the screw has been set (usually 1/2–1 turn back from lightly seated on Big Twins and late-model Sportsters) is the free-play at the lever adjusted.

Also, pay attention to your manufacturer's recommendations regarding adjustment spec. Some specifications are heat sensitive and must be adjusted either hot or cold. For example, the Harley and Buell clutches are normally set COLD and adjuster screw setting would be incorrect if set on a hot machine.

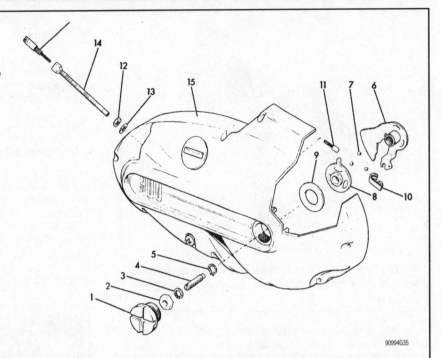

1. Access plug, clutch release adjusting screw
2. Lock nut, adjusting screw
3. Lockwasher, adjusting screw
4. Screw, clutch release adjusting
5. Retaining ring, Truarc
6. Release ramp and lever
7. Ball (3)
8. Release ramp
9. Washer
10. Cable coupling
11. Cable and coil assy.
12. Lock nut, coil adjusting sleeve
13. Washer, coil adjusting sleeve
14. Sleeve, coil adjusting
15. Primary chain case cover

Fig. 249 Although the look of the primary cover has changed a lot over the years, the function of the Sportster's primary and clutch assembly remains essentially the same

Clutch Splines

INSPECTION & LUBRICATION

On motorcycles with dry, single-plate automotive style clutches, the manufacturer may recommend that the splines on the transmission input shaft be periodically lubricated. In use, the clutch disc for these motorcycles slides toward the engine (when the clutch is applied), or away from it slightly (when the clutch is disengaged). It must be able to do so freely in order to release properly and a lack of lubrication can cause excessive wear to the transmission input shaft (which is not a cheap part!).

Recommendations for frequency of this service have varied over the years. At one time BMW recommended annual spline lubrications. On oil-heads, BMW currently recommends 40,000 mile intervals. If you are uncertain what is recommended for your bike, check the owners manual AND check with the dealer. If you have an old enough bike, the dealer might have updated information that your owners manual does not.

The first signs that a bike with this style clutch needs a spline lubrication is if the clutch begins to drag, causing rough transmission shifting. Missed

or difficult downshifts are often an indication that the splines should be lubricated.

On some models (such as the BMW airheads) the transmission does not have to be fully removed from the motorcycle in order to lube the shaft splines. For these bikes, the rear suspension and swingarm can be partially undone to swing the transmission and driveshaft back from the engine. With the transmission slide rearward about an inch, a long handled brush can be used to CAREFULLY apply grease to the splines on the input shaft. This should be done with GREAT CARE to keep any grease OFF the clutch discs. Do not over-apply the grease either, since excess will either be scrubbed of flung off (and will likely wind up contaminating the clutch disc).

On other models the transmission should really be removed in order to get better access (and allow for a thorough cleaning, inspection and lubrication for the splines, clutch disc and flywheel). If the transmission is removed, this is a good time to check for rear main seal seepage and to check the clutch disc for wear. A clutch which has worn below specification (as measured in thickness or amount of material above a rivet head, depending on the clutch) should be replaced. If the transmission is removed completely for this, be sure to remove all clutch dust and lubricant from the input shaft. A spray brake cleaner is usually good for this and it can be used on the clutch disc as well.

FINAL DRIVE MAINTENANCE

There are basically 3 types of final drive systems (used to transmit power from the transmission to the rear wheel) on motorcycles today:
- **Driveshaft**
- **Chain**
- **Belt**

Each system has its advantages (and disadvantages), but they all share one thing, a need for periodic attention to make sure that they keep doing their jobs. Shaft drive is probably the most maintenance free of these, only requiring periodic fluid changes and inspections. Belts are the next closest to maintenance free, requiring periodic inspection and adjustment. Chains, which are the weapons of choice for most high powered motorcycles and sport bikes, require the most attention with cleaning, inspecting, lubricating and adjusting on their list.

Final Drive and Driveshaft Oil

♦ **See Figure 250**

A good number of motorcycles from Japan and many from Europe (including BMW and Moto Guzzi) are equipped with driveshafts Driveshaft-equipped motorcycles are increasing in popularity, especially among riders who find the maintenance of the drive chain irksome, and are willing to pay extra for the reliability of shaft drive.

On most shaft-drive motorcycles, the crankshaft is parallel with the rear wheel, so that power transmission is no problem. On others, however, the engine sits transversely in the frame, so that a special fitting is needed to drive the final driveshaft.

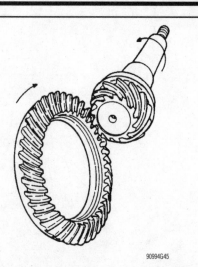

Fig. 250 Shaft final drive is relatively maintenance and trouble free, just check and change the oil on a regular basis and you will be set

The driveshaft must transmit power through a 90° angle. The flow of power moves from the engine in approximately a straight line with constant velocity joints allowing the rear wheel to move up and down, but, at the rear axle, the power must be turned at right angles from the line of the driveshaft and directed to the rear wheel. This is accomplished by a pinion drive gear which turns a circular ring gear.

Drive boxes are built quite strongly for the loads they must carry, so it is unlikely that trouble will ever be encountered provided that routine oil changes are carried out on schedule.

Most designs use one or more bearings to support the pinion shaft. These are lubricated by the oil in the box. The ring gear is supported by a large ball bearing, which is lubricated by the same method.

Driveshafts may be permanently lubricated and sealed, may be run dry or may require their own oil changes, depending on the model.

SELECTING THE PROPER OIL

▶ **See Figure 251**

Most manufacturers recommend using some form of gear oil in their driveshafts or final drives, usually a SAE 80 or SAE 90 EP (extreme pressure)

gear oil. Keep in mind that a gear oil viscosity rating does NOT equal an SAE engine oil rating.

Final drives are also good places to use synthetic gear oils. The same extreme operating conditions which occur in a transmission can be found in the final drive, including the high pressure and shear factors

Be sure to check your owners manual for your bike manufacturer's particular requirements before selecting a gear oil.

CHECKING YOUR OIL

▶ **See Figures 252 thru 259**

Basically, you should treat the final drive and driveshaft in the same manner you would the transmission. The fluid should be checked periodically to make sure that none has leaked out undetected AND to be certain that the level has not increased from moisture that has entered the housing.

Like with most fluid checks, the final drive or driveshaft oils should usually be checked with the bike completely upright and on a level surface. If centerstand is not provided, you may have to secure the bike upright using blocks.

On most bikes, the fluid level of your driveshaft or final drive housing is checked using a filler plug. And on most of these, the level should be up to

Fig. 252 Most driveshaft models use a filler plug to obtain the proper fluid level, oil is added up to the base of the plug threads

Fig. 251 Some manufacturers are kind enough to place a label on the driveshaft or final drive, telling you what type of oil is required

Fig. 253 When used, always replace the crush washer to prevent possible leaks

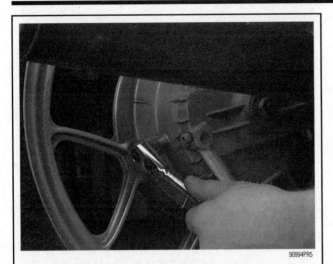

Fig. 254 Other models use a self-leveling plug to determine proper fluid level . . .

Fig. 257 . . . and allowed to seep out of the plug, until it bleeds itself to the proper level

Fig. 255 . . . on this model, the plug is removed . . .

Fig. 258 On BMW airheads, a drift or other small tool can be used as a dipstick . . .

Fig. 256 . . . then fluid is added . . .

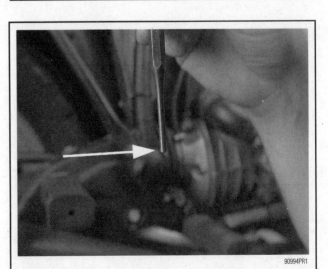

Fig. 259 . . . the fluid level specification is measured in millimeters as read on the makeshift dipstick

the bottom of the threads. We say most, because there are some exceptions. Airhead BMWs, for instance, use a driveshaft housing which is checked by inserting a drift into the filler plug opening and then measuring how high the fluid is on the drift.

Some bikes use a self-leveling plug to properly adjust the level of the final drive fluid. On these, you remove the plug and see if any comes out. If necessary, add fluid through the separate filler plug opening until oil begins to run from the level check opening. Be sure to allow the fluid to set it's own level on this style by letting the flow from the check opening continue until it stops on its own.

✳✳ CAUTION

BE VERY CAREFUL TO KEEP GEAR OIL OFF YOUR TIRES. This is especially true when adding oil to a self-leveling final drive. Position a drain pan so that no oil drips from the housing onto the tire.

When checking the fluid level on any final drive or driveshaft check to see if the fluid has been contaminated from moisture. If an excessive amount runs out of the case, then the transmission was overfilled OR a lot of moisture has found its way in. Emulsified or contaminated oil should be changed right away to prevent unnecessary wear or corrosion to the final drive.

CHANGING YOUR OIL

▸ **See Figures 260 thru 266**

In order to monitor the health of your driveshaft or final drive, be sure to change the fluid AT LEAST once a year, or by your manufacturer's recommended mileage intervals (if they are shorter with your riding style).

Like with all oil changes it is best to drain the oil at normal operating temperature. So suit up and go for a ride. If you have enough drain pans, it is good to drain this fluid at the same time you perform engine and transmission.

After a decent ride (10–20 minutes depending on how hot it is out already, you'll need less time the hotter the ambient temperature), come back in and remove the drain plug. Allow the fluid to drain fully.

Since they do not use oil filters, most driveshaft and final drive housing drain plugs are equipped with a magnet to attract and hold tiny metal deposits which come off splines in use. Be sure to thoroughly clean the metal paste which has collected on the drain plug magnet. Paste is no a problem, don't worry about it. But, if large metal chunks or pieces of the splines are found, be worried (it might be time to have the unit).

When installing the drain plug, check to see if it uses a crush washer or an O-ring. You might have success reusing either of them and you are usually OK reusing an O-ring, as long as it is not cut or dried out and cracked.

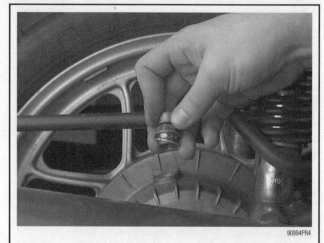

Fig. 261 . . . just in case you have a problem removing it and will be unable to add fluid (at least you will find out before DRAINING this way)

Fig. 262 Position a catch pan below the driveshaft drain plug, then loosen and remove the plug . . .

Fig. 260 No matter what fluids you are changing, ALWAYS remove the filler plug first . . .

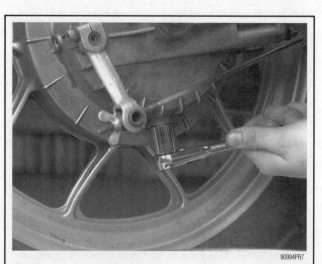

Fig. 263 . . . and/or the rear drive drain plug, as applicable (be careful to keep oil off the rear tire!)

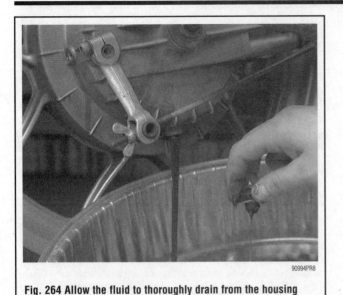

Fig. 264 Allow the fluid to thoroughly drain from the housing

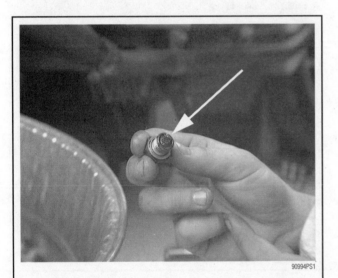

Fig. 265 Examine the drain plug for deposits, then clean it off

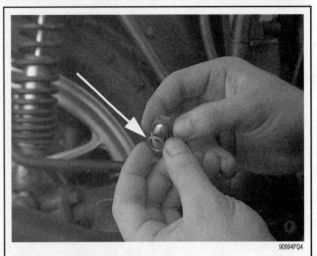

Fig. 266 If a crush washer was used, it should be replaced to assure a proper seal

BUT, if a crush washer was used, then it is best to replace it (don't try to save a few cents on a washer only to lose a few bucks on oil if it starts leaking).

✷✷ CAUTION

Remember that, because of their location, a leaky driveshaft or final drive plug will likely deposit oil on your rear tire. This could lead to a spectacular, but very unnecessary off.

Final Drive Chain & Sprockets

▸ See Figure 267

Final drive by means of a roller chain and sprockets is a very common method of power transmission in motorcycles today. The method is cheap, compact, and quite reliable—provided that certain precautions are taken.

In truth, drive chains are remarkable in the amount of punishment that they absorb in the course of normal operation. They must be able to stand tremendous torque developed by the engine. This torque is not always applied smoothly due to variations in clutch slippage, throttle application, and other factors such as acceleration, deceleration, and gear shifting.

Furthermore, the chain is subjected to varying tension as it rotates since the rear wheel is moving up and down on the swing arm. If the engine sprocket

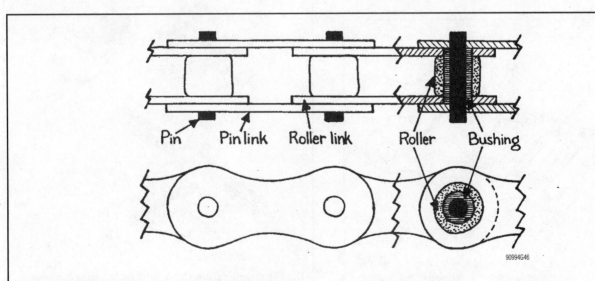

Fig. 267 Cutaway view of a typical motorcycle drive chain

was concentric with the swing arm pivot, this tension variation would be minimized, but this is not often the case. Even the motion of the chain around the sprockets themselves puts pressure on the links. The smaller the sprocket, the more tension the chain must endure. As if this was not enough, the chain is exposed to dirt, moisture, and exposure to the elements.

It is very wise, therefore, to pay some attention to the chain and its sprockets to ensure a long service life.

Chains are designated using a size (based on ⅛ of an inch) and number of links. The first two numbers of a chain's designation will give you its critical measurements. For instance, on a 620 chain, the 6 refers to the pitch between the pins (6⁄8 of an inch), while the 2 refers to the width of the roller (2⁄8 of an inch, or better known as ¼ in.).

CLEANING & LUBRICATION

▶ **See Figures 268, 269, 270, 271 and 272**

Most models now come with permanently lubricated O-ring drive chains, but some still don't. If your bike does not have an O-ring chain, you should seriously consider adding one when it comes up for replacement. Modern O-ring chains last longer and work better with less maintenance than their non-permanently lubricated counterparts.

The term permanently lubricated is somewhat misleading, because you might think that you could ignore a chain like that. The truth is that ALL chains require periodic cleaning and lubrication in order to fight corrosion and wear. Some older bikes were equipped with automatic oiling devices to meter engine oil onto the chain, but this oil is not usually sufficient to keep the chain well lubricated.

The first thing you will need to do is buy some supplies. A good brand of lubricant designed specifically for motorcycle drive chains is recommended. You will also want a stiff bristled brush and a mild solvent or kerosene to clean the chain (but before buying it check with the motorcycle or chain manufacturer to see what they recommend as safe for your O-rings). There are some clever devices out there which can be used for chain cleaning and lubrication. Some of the better ones enclose a few links of the chain with a stiff brush for cleaning and have a tube to which you can attach a spray lubricant. You can rotate the chain through these while cleaning and lubricating the chain. But, for seriously neglected chains, a prior hand cleaning is usually recommended and necessary.

➡**If your model does NOT have a centerstand, then you are going to want to purchase some form of bike lift in order to get the rear wheel of the ground. To properly lubricate and clean a chain you will be constantly turning the rear wheel and pushing the bike back and forth get tiring (besides you are more likely to rush or skip part of the chain if it is a pain in the butt to clean and lube).**

Frequency of cleaning and lubrication is dependent upon the type of lubricant used, riding habits, average speeds, weather conditions, and so on. The rider should check chain condition frequently until he finds the maintenance interval compatible with his/her riding style. As in the case of engine oil, maintenance will be necessary at shorter intervals if the chain is subjected to severe use: high speeds, off-road riding, jack-rabbit acceleration, etc.

Many riders find that an application of chain lube every 300 miles or so allows for excellent chain life.

✳✳ WARNING

Using the wrong solvent for cleaning could cause damage to your O-ring chain. Be sure to only use a cleaner that is recommended by your bike's or chain's manufacturer.

Before attempting to lubricate, inspect or adjust your chain, you should always clean it thoroughly. The BEST way to clean the chain is to remove it from the bike so it can be thoroughly cleaned (this will also make inspection easier). But, there is no need to remove the chain from the bike every 300 miles. You will want to settle on an extended interval, say every 2000 miles or 5000 miles (that corresponds with another major service) and always remove the chain for more thorough cleaning at that time. If nothing else, remove it for cleaning at least once a year.

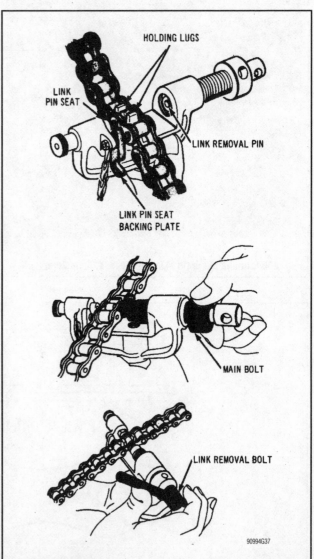

Fig. 269 A chain service tool is VERY helpful when removing or installing a chain . . .

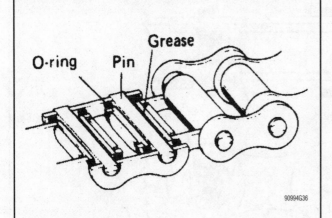

Fig. 268 Cutaway view of an O-ring chain—an O-ring chain has lubricating grease sealed over the pins by O-rings which helps the chain last longer and require less attention

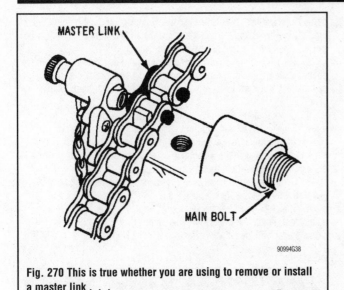

Fig. 270 This is true whether you are using to remove or install a master link . . .

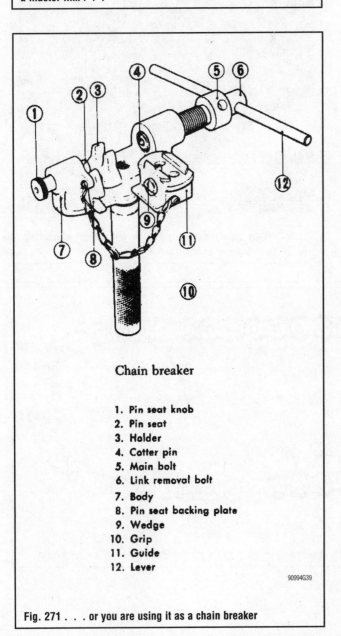

Chain breaker

1. Pin seat knob
2. Pin seat
3. Holder
4. Cotter pin
5. Main bolt
6. Link removal bolt
7. Body
8. Pin seat backing plate
9. Wedge
10. Grip
11. Guide
12. Lever

Fig. 271 . . . or you are using it as a chain breaker

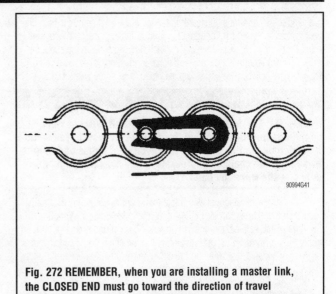

Fig. 272 REMEMBER, when you are installing a master link, the CLOSED END must go toward the direction of travel

➡Models with endless chains will require a special tool to break the chain. On all models, removal and installation of the masterlink spring clip should be done with a pliers or a small prytool—to avoid deforming the spring clip.

Having an old chain on hand makes removal somewhat simpler, since the old chain can be attached to one end of the chain on the bike and pulled through over the engine sprocket, so that it is not necessary to remove the sprocket cover or other components.

To clean the chain, remove heavy deposits of dirt and grease with a stiff brush and suitable solvent (many manufacturer's recommend the use of kerosene). If you have removed the chain, soak it in the solvent for 10 minutes or so, then remove it and clean it again with a brush.

Check that each chain link can pivot freely If there are any kinked or binding links which cannot be freed, or if the chain is rusted or has suffered damage from corrosion (such as might happen if it is touched by acid from an incorrectly routed battery overflow tube), replace it. Methods of measuring chain wear are discussed in a following section. If the chain has been removed for cleaning, take the opportunity to measure chain stretch now, this way you won't risk wasting your time lubricating it only to decide it must be replaced.

After cleaning the chain it is time to oil it. It is your choice whether you would like to oil it now or after it is refitted. There are advantages to both. Oiling the chain while it is removed gives you a good opportunity to hit all of the wear surfaces which can be harder to access when the chain is in place. Of course, it could mean that you have a messy chain to work with when refitting (though if you properly oil and clean the excess off, it should not be a big problem. Of course, if you refit it to the machine first, that will give you an opportunity to warm the bearing surfaces so they better absorb oil (one alternative is to use a hair dryer to warm and oil the chain before installation). The choice is yours.

When installing the chain, note the following points: models which use an endless type chain will require a new masterlink. On other models, the masterlink may be reused if in good condition. Also, check the condition of the masterlink spring clip. Be sure to install the spring clip with the closed end facing the direction of chain rotation. Also, if the clip is "sprung," the concave side must face the chain.

Next it is time to lubricate the chain. For this you are going to have to warm the chain so that the lubricant can better soak into the bearing surfaces. Although this can be done using a hair dryer or a heat gun, it is a LOT more fun to go for a 10–20 minute ride.

Once the chain is warm, you can begin applying the chain lube. Be sure to follow the lubricant manufacturer's instructions for use. Many lubes are dispensed in a very fluid state. This facilitates their penetration into the chain. In a few minutes they become thick and sticky, enabling them to adhere to the chain as it spins around the sprockets while riding.

Many people improperly lube motorcycle chains, wasting too much of their time and lubricant on the outside of the links, where all it can do is help prevent corrosion. It is most important to lubricate in the places that wear occurs most (where there is metal-to-metal contact). Instead of worrying about the rollers (which require little, if any additional lubrication), make sure you get the lubricant between the link side plate where most of the wear occurs.

✳✳ CAUTION

NEVER USE THE MOTOR TO TURN THE REAR WHEEL, should something become caught in the chain or a sprocket you could be seriously injured or killed. Keep you hair, hands and fingers away from the chain and sprockets as much as possible and only turn the wheel by hand.

With rear wheel raised, slowly rotate the wheel as you spray the chain lube onto the inside (sprocket side) of the chain side plates. Work on either the right or left side plates, don't try to cover both at one time. Continue to apply the lubricant for two full revolutions of the chain (to be certain nothing was missed). Then switch to the opposite row of side plates (still spraying from the inside of the chain) and continue to lubricate the links for two revolutions. Give the lubricant a few minutes to soak in and thicken.

Once the lubricant has thickened, apply a small amount of solvent to a shop rag and CAREFULLY turn the rear wheel while you wipe the excess lubricant back off. Too much lubricant is going to hold dirt in suspension which will just accelerate wear.

Once the chain is clean and lubricated, it is time to inspect and adjust it.

INSPECTION & ADJUSTMENT

▶ **See Figures 273 thru 281**

1. First make a visual inspection of the chain and its sprockets. If the chain is rust red in color, it has probably suffered too long without proper lubrication, and should be replaced as the damage done to the pin bushings (which you cannot see) is already beyond repair. The chain must also be replaced if it has any broken or cracked rollers. If the chain is very dirty, covered with grease and dirt, it should be removed and cleaned (refer to the previous section).

2. Check the battery overflow tube, and ensure that it has been so routed as to avoid the chain completely. White deposits on the links is a sign that sulfuric acid from the battery has come in contact with the chain.

If this has happened, the acid has probably damaged one or more of the links. This will weaken them to the point where the chain can no longer be trusted. The chain should be replaced immediately.

3. The drive chain slack is the total up and down movement of the chain measured at a point midway between the sprockets. The specifications may differ for various machines, but is usually about 25mm (1 in.).

4. Conditions under which the chain slack is measured differ from make to make. Some manufacturer's specify that the machine be on the center stand with the rear wheel off the ground, while others state that the slack is measured with the weight of a rider on the bike. Refer to your owners manual for the correct method.

5. On all machines, however, it is imperative that the chain be clean and well lubricated before checking slack.

6. The chain must be checked for tight spots before making this adjustment. Rotate the wheel slowly and note any variances in chain tension. Tension will always vary slightly, but if the tension varies greatly, it is

Fig. 273 Many bikes today are equipped with a label which tells you the specification for chain slack

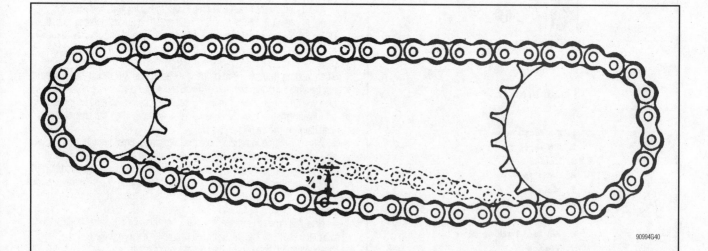

Fig. 274 Chain slack is defined as the total up and down movement of a chain when measured at a point midway between the sprockets

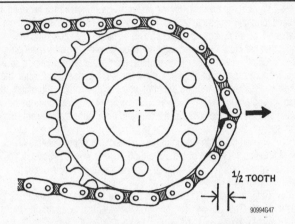

Fig. 275 A quick way to check chain stretch (after the slack is adjusted) is by pulling the chain off the rear sprocket. If you can see more than ½ tooth, then the chain is stretched and should be replaced

probable that the chain or the sprockets are worn to the point of replacement. If a tight spot is found, make a mark on the rear sprocket relative to some fixed point. Continue to rotate the wheel. If the chain becomes tight each time the sprocket mark passes the point you chose, the sprocket is warped and should be replaced. If there is no relation between the periods of chain tightness and the rotation of the sprocket, chances are that the chain itself is the problem.

7. Although a chain with an excessive tight spot must soon be replaced, if it must remain in service for a period of time be sure to adjust the chain tension to the given specification at the tight spot. This will probably mean that the chain will have some very loose spots at which it may slap and hit the chainguard, but the potential of breaking the chain will be somewhat reduced.

8. If your slack measurement shows that the chain must be adjusted, remove the cotter pin and loosen the axle nut, then use the adjuster nuts on each side of the swingarm to tighten or loosen the chain, as necessary.

➡ In order to preserve alignment of the rear wheel, ALWAYS turn the adjusters exactly the same amount on each side of the swingarm. Use a deep socket with a line painted on it for reference, and rotate the socket in ½ turns which are easy to judge.

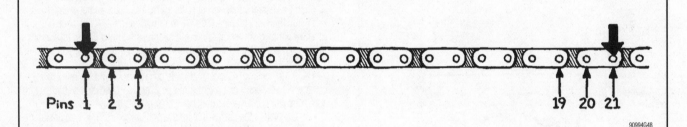

Fig. 276 A more precise method of checking chain stretch is to measure the distance of a set number of links (in this example, 20 links which means the distance between 21 pins) and compare it to specification

Fig. 277 Most bikes also have markings to tell you when the chain has stretched beyond its service limit . . .

Fig. 278 . . . though the markings will vary a bit from model-to-model

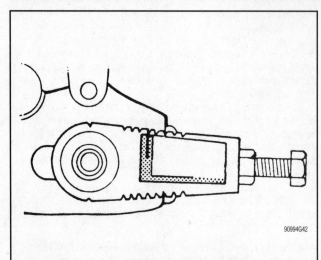

90994G42

Fig. 279 On this model, the chain should be replaced when the shaded zone aligns with the end of the swingarm

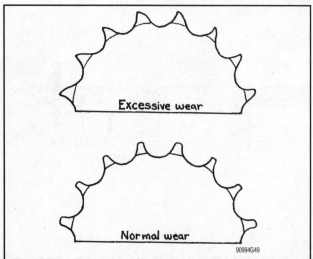

Excessive wear

Normal wear

90994G49

Fig. 280 You should also periodically check the sprockets for wear . . .

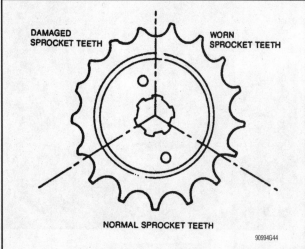

DAMAGED SPROCKET TEETH

WORN SPROCKET TEETH

NORMAL SPROCKET TEETH

90994G44

Fig. 281 . . . any sprockets showing damage, or excessive wear should be replaced

9. Proper alignment of the rear wheel is very important for handling as well as for chain and sprocket life. Most motorcycles have axle alignment marks on the swing arm, and care should be taken when adjusting the chain that the index on the adjuster are lined up with the same mark on both sides of the wheel. BUT, these marks are not always accurate. If such alignment marks are not fitted or are not trusted, it is possible to align the wheel by "eyeballing" it using the front wheel as a reference. Alternately, if there is not too much in the way, you can measure the distance from the swing arm pivot to the center of the axle and make sure it is the same on both sides.

10. After adjusting the chain to the manufacturer's specification, check for wear by attempting to pull the chain off the rear wheel sprocket. If you can see more than ½ of the sprocket tooth at the point this is done, the chain is worn and should be replaced as soon as possible.

11. Other methods of checking the chain for wear involve measuring the chain stretch. This can be done on or off the machine depending on the method you use:

a. If the chain is off the bike, stretch the chain out to its full length and measure it. Then compress the links so that the chain is as short as possible, but not bent. Measure the chain again. If the difference between the two measurements amounts to more than 3% of its total length, the chain should be replaced.

b. If the chain is still installed, you will have to calculate the proper length for a sub-section of the chain (a length that can be measured while it is installed). Do this with the information we provided earlier on chain sizes and their designations. For example, on a 620 chain, the pitch (or distance between pins) is ⅝ in. The distance between 21 pins should equal 20 pitches (20 x ⅝ in.) or 15 in. total. A 3% stretch would allow a maximum length of 15.45 in. across 20 links. If you take a measurement of a longer length across 20 links of a 620 chain, you should replace it.

12. In the event of a worn chain, the sprockets should be inspected closely. A badly worn chain can ruin sprockets, and conversely, badly worn sprockets will quickly wear out a new chain.

13. Check that the sprocket teeth are not hooked. This is the most common sign of a damaged sprocket. Also check for wear on the edges and sides of the teeth. If possible, remove the sprockets, place them on a flat surface and check for warpage. The sprockets must be perfectly flat. If one of the sprockets is worn, it is recommended that both of them be replaced.

14. After lubrication and adjustment, road test the bike to check chain operation. If the motorcycle vibrates at intervals, it could be that the chain is too tight, or that one of the sprockets is warped or worn. If the chain slaps the chainguard or swing arm, it is too loose and must be adjusted. Another symptom of a badly adjusted or worn chain or sprockets is noise while coasting. This can be checked by simply rolling the bike down hill for a short distance.

Final Drive Belt & Sprockets

Over the years, final drive belts have started to come back in popularity. New developments in belt technology have produced very strong and reliable toothed belts. These belts are extremely quiet and low maintenance. Once they are worn in, they tend to hold adjustment for 5,000–10,000 miles under normal usage. They have been known to last anywhere from 30,000–100,000 miles.

Probably their weakest link (no pun intended) is the lack of a master link, which makes removal and installation a little harder than your average chain. Of course, during a normal life, they should not require removal or installation anywhere NEAR the frequency of a chain.

CLEANING & VISUAL INSPECTION

The belt and sprocket should be visually inspected at every oil change. Just take a moment to make sure no rocks have wedged themselves into the sprocket and that no abnormal wear appears on the rear sprocket or the belt. Clean the belt with soap and water, checking to make sure the teeth are intact and that there is no evidence of it rubbing on anything it should not.

CHECKING & ADJUSTING TENSION

◆ See Figures 282 thru 288

Check your owners manual, since models vary on how you check the belt. On some bikes the rider and luggage must be in position, while on others, the bike should be unloaded and resting on its sidestand. The belt should normally be checked overnight cold and at the center of its lower strand. Some models may have gradation lines and a cutaway in the belt guard to make this easier.

➠All Harley-Davidson models should have their belt deflection measured with 10 lbs. of pressure at the measurement point. To do this you will need a belt tension gauge. Harley dealers sell a very inexpensive one which is sized just right to cradle the belt and is easy to use.

Like chains, the belt should turned and checked at various spots, making the adjustment with the tightest spot on the belt turned to its midway. Tolerances for belt slack tend to be smaller than chain slack, more in the neighborhood of ⅜ in. (10mm), but check your owners manual to be sure of the specification for your bike.

Fig. 284 Softails use a slightly different configuration, when you tighten the bolt on them, it pushes the axle rearward (still tightening the belt)

Fig. 282 Whether your bike is a Buell . . .

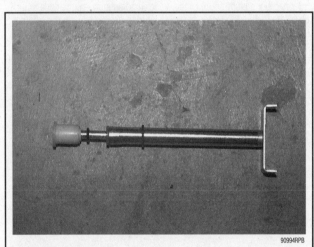

Fig. 285 In order to check the belt, you will need a tension gauge, this one is sold by Harley and is calibrated to their specification of 10 lbs.

Fig. 283 A FLT, Dyna, FXR or Sportster, most swingarm adjusters for final drive belts are similar, as you tighten the nut, it pulls the axle rearward

Push Up

Fig. 286 Measure the amount of deflection (the distance the belt moves) between rest and 10 lbs. of pressure

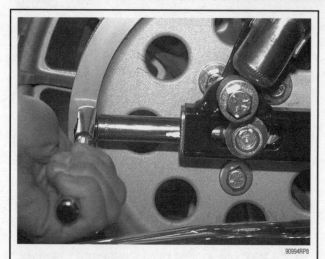

Fig. 287 If necessary, adjust the tension using the adjuster nuts (or bolts) . . .

Fig. 288 . . . mark a socket and turn the adjusters THE EXACT same amount of times on each side of the swingarm in order to keep your axle in alignment

Remember, that too tight or too loose an adjustment can damage your bike. If the belt is too loose it can whip during use, which can damage the belt and will increase wear on the sprocket as the teeth come in and out of the grooves. If the belt is too tight, it can put an additional stress on the transmission bearings causing untimely wear and seal leaks. Of the two, fall on the side of the loose, but stay in spec.

If your belt requires adjustment, take a deep socket (a shallow one will do on Softails) and paint a thin line on one side. The axle adjuster on each side of the swingarm MUST be turned the SAME NUMBER of times in order to preserve axle alignment. To be sure of this, start with the painted line facing DIRECTLY UPWARD and then turn the adjusters using ¼ or ½ turn increments using the line as a guide.

If you get yourself in trouble, use a straight edge (not rope since it can stretch) to measure the distance from the axle adjuster to the swingarm bearing on each side. The distance should be equal if the axle is in proper alignment.

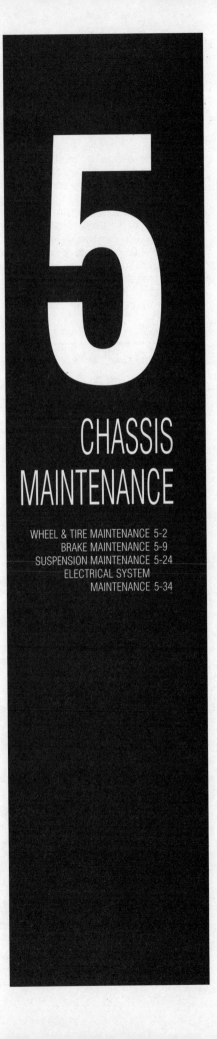

5

CHASSIS MAINTENANCE

WHEEL & TIRE MAINTENANCE

Tires

The old adage "Where the rubber meets the road," takes on special meaning to the motorcyclist. See, bikes fall over if not supported, and unless you are dragging your feet, the only thing holding up your bike is the tires! OK, ok, I won't go into all the physics of spinning wheels and normal forces, but you get the point. You rely on your tires to translate everything the engine is doing, everything the brakes are doing and everything the chassis is doing into controlling forces on the bike.

If you look at only one thing on your motorcycle before heading off, it should be the tires. Unless you ride a trike, you only have two tires keeping your pretty rims from digging into the asphalt. It is very important that your tires be in excellent condition before heading off on a ride. It doesn't take long to properly inspect your wheels and tires, so get down on your knees and start looking!

INSPECTION

▶ See Figures 1, 2, 3 and 4

All righty now! What should you be looking for on my wheels and tires? Not to worry! We will guide you through the mysteries of the wheel and tire combination. The wheel and tire work in combination, and can be inspected as a unit.

The following steps should be done as a minimum before heading out for any ride, no matter how short. They don't take much time and it will help prolong the life of your tires and maybe even you!

1. Do a visual check of the tread depth at the center of the tire. Make sure the tire has a reasonable amount of tread left. There are tread depth indicator bars molded into all modern tires. These bars travel the width of the tire and when they are even with the tread blocks, the tread has reached its minimum useful depth. Keep in mind, sufficient tread depth doesn't mean your tires are good, it just means that there is enough tread! A worn tire can take on a square shape that will effect the handling of the motorcycle.

2. Look for cuts and punctures. Glance over the entire tread area and the sidewalls, too. Look between the tread blocks for embedded items, such as nails, screws, cactus thorns and small furry animals (OK, they would have to be real small, but with the size of sportbike tires nowadays, anything is possible). If there is damage to the sidewall, it is time for a new tire. Sidewall damage is not repairable and isn't to be trifled with. A puncture to the inner two thirds of the tread can be repaired, but it is still recommended that the tire be replaced.

✳✳ CAUTION

Tires that have been repaired should be ridden at lower speeds than normal until they can be replaced with new, undamaged tires. Motorcycle tires do not take to being repaired very well and if the repair should fail, the results can be unappealing!

3. Check the sidewalls for signs of dryrot and cracking. Older tires or those that have been exposed to daylight for extended periods of time (such as bikes stored outdoors) can start to crack down near the tire bead, where it flexes. Ultraviolet light and ozone can start to degrade the rubber that composes the tire. After a while, these cracks will compromise the integrity of the tire and may cause it to fail. Replace dryrotted tires.

4. Check the tire pressure. We will go into more detail below, but suffice it to say that without the proper air pressure in the tires, you are risking damage to your tires, wheels and the performance of the bike. Know what your tire pressures should be and keep them there!

5. Check the integrity of the wheels. Look for dents, cracks, gouges and missing chunks. A slightly scraped wheel may just be unsightly, but a

Fig. 2 Check the tire for wear and damage. Look for squared off tire profiles

Fig. 1 It is a good idea to check the lug bolt torque on bikes with this type of wheel retention scheme

Fig. 3 Look for worn treads and foreign objects embedded in the rubber

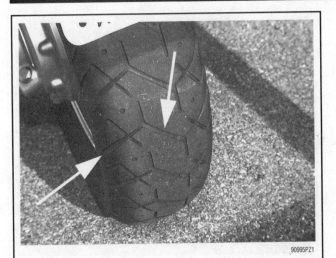

Fig. 4 This tread is squared off. The tread depth at the outside is deeper than the inside

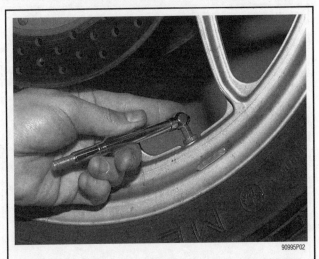

Fig. 6 The pencil type of tire pressure gauge is also very accurate and takes up little room on the bike

wheel with a missing chunk or a bend that exposes the tire bead is dangerous. If you have spoked wheels, check for loose or bent spokes. Look below for more information.

6. Check for out of round wheels. With the wheel off the ground and free to spin, rotate the wheel and look for excessive side-to-side movement. The wheel should be almost perfectly straight with only the tiniest amount of wobble allowed (maybe 0.02 in. (0.5mm), at best). Also check that the wheel doesn't move up and down as if it had an egg shape. Either of these conditions require the wheel to be replaced with a straight unit.

PRESSURE

▶ See Figures 5 thru 12

A tire can support only so much weight by itself. The tire is inflated with air (or nitrogen for you track junkies) and it is the pressurized air that supports the rest of the weight. The air pressure inside the tire lends rigidity in some amount to the tire and limits how much the tire flexes. If the tire has too little air in it, the rubber will flex and eventually heat up. If too much heat is allowed to build up, the rubber can start to degrade, leading to failure of the tire. At the same time, too much air can lead to changes in the way the bike handles and it can become skittish or may bounce over imperfections in the road. Either way, the bike will not main-

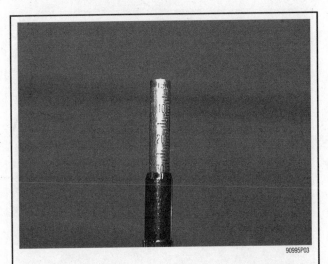

Fig. 7 Make sure you are reading the correct lines on a pencil type gauge as misreading one line can put you a few pounds off!

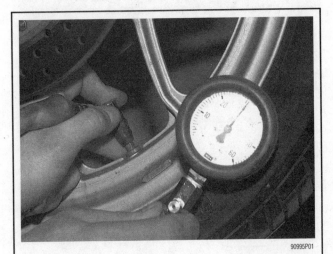

Fig. 5 The dial type of tire pressure gauge is usually very accurate, but a bit large to be carrying aboard

Fig. 8 Right angle adapters such as this are made to help you add or check the air pressure. Remove them when you are done

Fig. 9 My bike actually has a place to mount this tire pump. I have no excuse to be riding on flat tires!

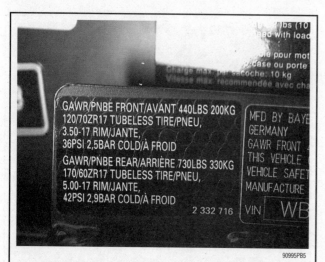

Fig. 10 Somewhere on your bike you should find a sticker like this telling you how much air to put in the tires

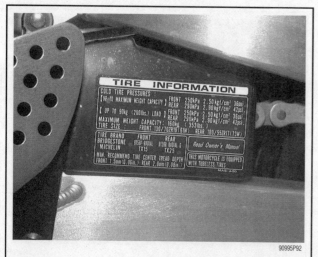

Fig. 11 Some stickers will have a grid to help you figure exactly how much pressure to run

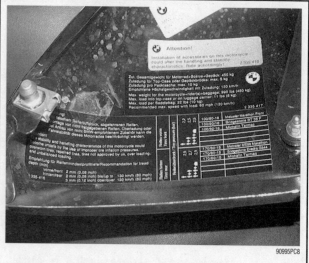

Fig. 12 Some stickers have entire stories to tell!

tain stability. Proper air pressure is more than just important, it is imperative!

Your motorcycle was designed with a certain range of tire pressures in mind. Trust the engineers who designed your bike; They know what is good for you and your bike! Your owners manual will have a listing of what pressures to use in what situations. My old BMW has an actual chart listing the different combinations of driver/passenger, travel speeds and amount of luggage! The range of pressures for my bike can range up to 8 psi difference from one extreme to another; A pound or two in either direction can really be felt. If the chart isn't in your owners manual, you will probably find it on a sticker attached somewhere on your bike, under a seat or sidecover.

Most tire pressures are taken when cold. This means you should check the pressures before you head off. How convenient since you should check them before a ride anyway! As the tire temperature goes up, so will the pressure. If you check your pressures on a hot tire and then adjust the pressure to what the sticker says, you will have actually ended up with a pressure lower than it should be.

Use a tire pressure gauge of good quality and repeatability. Some inexpensive, pencil type gauges may give different results each time it is used. I use a very nice pencil gauge sold by BMW and it has proven to be very accurate and repeatable. It even comes with a cool little valve core tightening tool attached to it! It takes up very little room in my bike and it is convenient to use. I also use a dial type gauge with an attached hose (I stole it from my old track car), but I keep it in the garage as it takes up too much space in my bike. I have compared the reading from both gauges and they agree within a half pound, so I feel safe in using either unit.

WHEEL REMOVAL AND INSTALLATION

You will need to remove your wheels and tires at some point if you need to change a tube on the side of the road or you want to take them to a bike shop to have new tires installed. You may need to replace a bent rim or have the spokes tightened. On certain bikes, you need to remove a wheel to access the brakes. Whatever the reason, there is a good chance that you will find yourself staring at an axle nut or two in the time you own your bike.

Exact instructions for removing and installing a wheel on your bike will be contained in your owners manual (possibly), the factory repair manual (most likely) or an aftermarket repair manual. The following procedure is to give you a general guide to wheel removal and should be enough to get you by in a pinch, but it is no replacement for having the full set of instructions in front of you.

1. Support the bike so the wheel is off the ground. If your bike has a centerstand the job is easy. If your bike doesn't, you will need some way of

holding the wheel in the air. Aftermarket centerstands or bike lifts will do the job. Make sure the bike is stable since you would be bummed if the bike came toppling down on top of you!

2. On bikes with disk brakes, sometimes the caliper(s) need to be removed and hung out of the way to be able to remove the wheel from the frame. Remove the caliper bolts and support them out of the way of the wheel. Do not allow them to hang by their hydraulic lines or they may be damaged.

3. On bikes with drum brakes, you may need to back off the adjustment for the shoes. This may be as simple as unscrewing a wingnut on the brake pushrod, but it will vary by bike.

4. If the wheel to be removed is a rear wheel on a bike with a chain or a belt drive, loosen the axle nut. If you have to move the axle forward for some reason, mark the position of the adjuster before removing the wheel so it can be replaced in its original position. Slide the wheel forward so the chain or belt can be slipped off. You may also have to remove or reposition the muffler canisters to be able to slide the axle out.

5. The wheel axle may be held by a big nut on clamped by pinch bolts. Loosen them and slide out the axle. Some bikes have a hole drilled into one end of the axle so a rod can be placed in it and used to help twist out the axle.

6. Some bikes actually just have lugbolts or lugnuts holding the wheel onto a hub. In these cases, just remove the lugs and slip off the wheel. This type of setup is common on BMW's with single-sided swingarms.

7. Pay attention to any spacers, washers or bearings that may come out with the wheel and axle. These will need to be replaced in the exact locations from which they were removed. If they aren't put back correctly, the wheel my wobble or be off center.

8. Replace the wheel and axle with all the correct hardware. Tighten the bolts or nuts to the specification set by the manufacture. Bolt on the calipers or adjust the drum brake and you are set!

TIRE CHANGING

▶ **See Figures 13 thru 20**

To change a tire you will need two motorcycle tire irons, a lubricant such as soapy water or dishwashing liquid, and a plastic mallet which, while not entirely necessary, is certainly helpful.

You can purchase suitable tire irons at any motorcycle shop, or it is possible that they may have been included in your bike's toolkit. Tire irons are specifically designed for the job. They are angled to provide good leverage and have smooth, rounded spoons to prevent pinching the tube. Although some irons may seem small, if you are using the right method they should provide sufficient leverage to get the tire off the rim. There is no acceptable substitute for good tire irons. Attempting to use screwdrivers or other levers for this job is only asking for trouble.

Fig. 14 A slightly inflated tube will make handling it easier

Fig. 15 Make sure the tube valve is aligned with the hole in the rim so the tube isn't twisted during installation

Fig. 13 Keep the bead well lubricated during tire changing and things will go more smoothly at all steps

Fig. 16 Don't forget the valve stem locknut!

Fig. 17 Gently lever the lower bead into the rim trying not to pinch the tube

Fig. 20 The curved parts of the tire irons allow extra leverage and a good grip on the rim/tire

Fig. 18 Relubricate the bead to keep things sliding

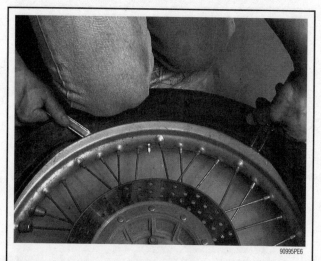

Fig. 19 Use your knee to hold the tire while levering it around the wheel

If you have cast alloy wheels, tire irons should be used with care to avoid damaging the wheel. The same is true to a lesser extent with alloy spoked rims which can be scratched. It may be possible to cover the shaft of the irons with a piece of an old inner tube or the like to reduce the chances of damage. Wheel protection plastic covers are available that fit onto the rim where you are prying to protect the finish.

A large sheet of cardboard can also decrease chances of damage to the wheel or brake disc (if fitted). Changing the tire on a concrete surface can easily chip chrome or scratch the rim or brake disc, while changing it on the lawn will certainly get dirt or grass into the wheel bearings unless a rag is placed under the hub. A large drum with the top removed also makes a handy tire changing stand with some slit rubber hose fitted over the edge of the metal to protect the rim.

1. After removing the wheel from the motorcycle, take out the valve core. Remove the valve stem nut(s). If a rimlock is fitted, remove its nut and push the rimlock down off the fire bead. If the same tire is to be refitted, mark the location of the valve stem and the direction of rotation on the tire sidewall.

2. Place the wheel on the ground and walk around the tire to break the bead off the rim. This may be necessary if the tire has been on the rim for some time. If that doesn't work, you may need to use a bead breaker which looks like a big clamp or use a vise. Cover the jaws of the vise with rubber or cloth to protect the rim from scratching.

3. Smear some soapy water or dishwashing liquid around the beads on both sides of the tire.

4. Beginning at the valve stem, use the tire irons to lever one bead off the rim. The tire bead opposite the valve stem should be pressed well down into the rim well. Kneel on the tire, if necessary to hold the bead down. Start by inserting both tire irons under the bead a few inches apart. Do not insert them too deeply or you may catch the tube (if a tube type tire). Pull back on both irons simultaneously until a portion of the bead is over the rim. Then remove one of the irons and use it again several inches away from its first position. Continue around the tire until one side is completely free of the rim.

5. Pull out the tube, if equipped. If the tire is to be replaced, remove the rimlock (if equipped) and lever the remaining bead off the rim.

6. Check the tube for leaks. Patching the tube is not recommended except in emergency situations. The patch may leak or may upset tire balance. Get a new tube if a puncture is evident.

7. Carefully remove the rim band and, using a wire brush, remove any rust deposits from the rim. Excessive use of tire lubricant can cause rust on steel rims. Check the bead of the tire as well if it is to be reused. Remove any deposits with a wire brush.

8. Check the spokes for looseness and tighten if necessary. If this is done, check that no spoke end protrudes from its nipple. Grind down any protruding spoke ends to obviate the chances of a puncture. Carefully refit the rim band so that it covers all the nipples. A piece of duct tape can be used

under the rim band to help seal the spokes if leakage has been a problem.

9. The tire must be mounted so that the mark on the sidewall aligns with the valve stem. New tires will have this alignment mark painted near the bead. Also note direction of rotation, if applicable. On some tires the direction of rotation will be different depending on whether the tire is mounted on the front or the rear of the motorcycle. If a rimlock is fitted, be sure to install it before the tube, but do not fit its locknut.

10. If you have only replaced the tube, and the tire is still on the rim, care must be exercised when stuffing the tube into the tire since it is possible to twist it If the tire has been completely removed, the easiest method is to mount tire and tube together. Install the valve core into the stem and put just a few pounds of air in the tube. You should inflate the tube just enough so that it holds its shape, but not so much that the tube expands. Place the inflated tube into the tire. Approximately aligning the valve stem and the hole in the rim, lever the tire and tube together over the rim. Be sure to lubricate the tire beads as on removal.

11. If it is very difficult to lever the tire bead on, use a plastic mallet to strike the bead, thus forcing it over the edge of the rim as you move around the tire with the tire irons.

12. After the tire and tube are installed, temporarily overinflate to seat the tire. The tire will have an aligning mark which is a thin line molded into the sidewall and which will appear just above the edge of the rim. This line should be equidistant from the rim edge all the way around the tire. If it is not concentric, the tire is not properly seated. This is sometimes caused by rust on the rim and can often be remedied by thoroughly lubricating the beads and temporarily overinflating.

13. After the tire or tube has been inflated to the correct pressure tighten the valve stem locknut(s) and the nut on the rimlock (if one is fitted).

14. The wheel should be balanced after completing this operation.

✳✳ CAUTION

A new tire needs to be broken in or "scuffed in" as the racers say. The tires are coated with a slippery layer that needs to be worn off before the full width of the tread can be used. Ride some miles, taking it easy, then slowly increase your lean angles.

CHECKING SPOKES

▶ **See Figures 21 and 22**

1. Spokes should be checked periodically for proper tension. Spin the wheel slowly while striking each spoke lightly with a screwdriver. Each one should emit a "ping" of approximately the same pitch.

2. A loose spoke will emit a dull sound. Such spokes should be tight-

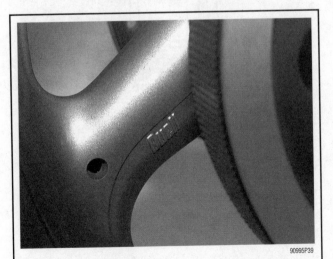

Fig. 21 We don't mean this type of spokes! We mean wire spokes!

Fig. 22 Tap on the spokes and listen to the tone. Loose spokes will sound different than tight ones

ened. The nipple, however, should not be turned more than two revolutions. To exceed this risks puncturing the tube with the end of the spoke. If two turns will not tighten the spoke, remove the tire and tube before continuing. Spoke nipples should be turned only with a genuine spoke nipple wrench which you should be able to purchase from your dealer.

3. If more than two adjacent spokes are found to be loose, the rim should be checked for run-out, and trued if necessary. On-bike tightening of loose spokes is intended only to secure spokes which may have loosened from vibration or settling. It is not intended to true up rims which have been knocked out of kilter. Continuous loosening of spokes should be remedied by removing the wheel and having it properly trued.

WHEEL BALANCING

Wheels should be balanced each time the tire is removed or replaced. A badly balanced tire may make itself evident by vibration (especially if the front tire is out of balance) or by unusual tire wear.

1. Wheels should be balanced on a wheel stand or bubble balancer. This procedure is for a wheel stand, but use of the bubble balancer is about the same , except you just let the wheel tilt to one side or another without spinning it. Balancing on the bike is not recommended due to drag imposed by chains, brake pads, and even wheel bearing grease seals. If a stand is not available, it is permissible to hang the wheel by the axle between two benches or chairs. Only make sure that both surfaces are of equal height. To obtain the most accurate balance it is necessary to remove as much rotational friction as possible. On some designs, wheel bearing grease seals contribute to friction, and really should be removed if possible. It may also be helpful to oil the axle as the wheel is turned. If the wheel will not rotate freely, determine the cause (i.e. bad bearings) before balancing.

2. The tire and tube must be in place and properly installed during balancing. If the wheel has a disc brake, leave the disc in place. Drum brake hubs should be removed.

3. If there are tire balancing weights already on the wheel, leave them there. Remove or reposition these weights once you are into the procedure. Hey, if by some chance the wheel is in balance, why double your work?

4. Balance weights are available in several forms, the most popular for spoke wheels being the type which fits over the spoke nipple and is secured with pliers. Another kind is an almost-flat piece of lead which attaches to steel rims by means of adhesive. Cast alloy wheels may require special kinds of balance weights. On this kind of wheel, always install the balance weight on the outer part of the rim, not on the sides of the spokes or webbing. Balance weights may be available in different weights. Use the lightest ones to start. If you have to add more than three or four weights to correct balance, there is probably something amiss.

5. Spin the wheel slowly several times in succession (or let the bubble balancer tilt to one side), marking the tire with a grease pencil or the like at the lowest part of the wheel each time it stops. If the same mark rotates (or tilts) to the lowest position several times in succession, this is the heaviest part of the assembly. Ideally, the wheel would stop rotating at random locations. If a heavy point is noted, attach a tire balance weight to the wheel directly opposite the heavy point. Repeat procedure, adding or repositioning weights so that the wheel will not stop at any one point in particular when it is spun.

CHECKING RIM RUN-OUT

▶ **See Figures 23 and 24**

The adjustment portion of this procedure is for spoked wheels. Spoked wheels can be adjusted for run-out. Cast wheels can be checked, but not adjusted. If a cast wheel is found to be out of spec, it will need to be replaced.

1. Rim run-out can be checked with a dial gauge or a simple pointer. This check can be made with the wheels on the motorcycle. Before this is done, however, be sure that the wheel bearings are in good condition or misleading results may be obtained. All spokes must be secure.

2. Rims should be checked for lateral (side to side) run-out, and for concentricity (up and down movement). The maximum acceptable variance is typically in the neighborhood of 0.035 in. (0.9mm.) vertically and 0.020 in. (0.5mm) laterally, but check the factory specifications. If either lateral or vertical run-out exceeds this amount, the rim should be trued. To true a rim, the tire and tube must be removed, and a wheel stand should be used.

3. It is not possible to true rims which are bent, even if the damage is slight, since the spokes cannot exert enough force to bend the rim back into shape. Such rims must be replaced.

4. If the rim shows both lateral and vertical run-out, the vertical run-out should be corrected first. This can be done by first loosening those spokes opposite the high spot, and then tightening the spokes at the high-spot. Spokes should be loosened or tightened in small, even increments since lateral run-out will be affected while correcting vertical run-out.

5. If a new rim is being fitted, it is necessary to have the rim at least approximately centered on the hub before attempting to true it. This can be accomplished in most cases by tightening the spoke nipples by approximately the same amount: that is, so that about the same number of spoke threads show at each nipple. File off the ends of any protruding spokes.

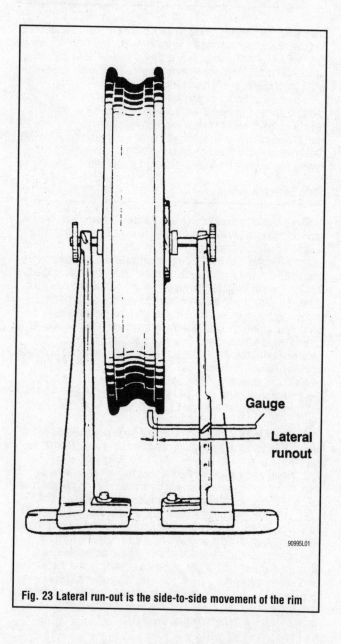

Fig. 23 Lateral run-out is the side-to-side movement of the rim

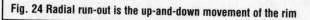

Fig. 24 Radial run-out is the up-and-down movement of the rim

BRAKE MAINTENANCE

Brakes come all sorts of flavors such as these 6 piston, fixed calipers

This brake caliper has three pistons on one side and sliding design

This is a standard set up on today's bikes with twin, multi-piston calipers

This caliper uses a dual piston, sliding design, but notice the pistons are different sizes to help equalize the pressure across the pad during use

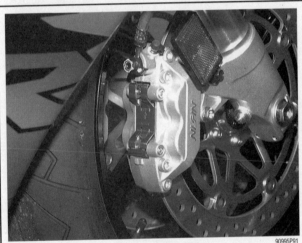

This is an open back, fixed caliper that is bridgeless. The spring on back is used for pad retention and anti-rattle purposes

Brake Fluid

SELECTING THE PROPER FLUID

▶ **See Figures 25, 26 and 27**

Selecting the proper brake fluid is as easy as looking on the cover of your master cylinder and reading the DOT type that the manufacturer calls for. You will find the cover calls for DOT 3, 4 or 5 brake fluid. In general DOT 4 fluid can be used in place of DOT 3, but NEVER mix DOT 5 fluid with DOT 3 or 4. While DOT 3 and 4 fluids have the same general chemical properties, DOT 5 is a whole different ball game.

The difference between DOT 3 and 4 is how well the fluid resists boiling. Temperature ratings for DOT 4 are higher than those of DOT 3. DOT 5 fluids have a temperature rating like the DOT 3 and 4 fluids, but they are silicone based and unless your brake system is designed for DOT 5, do not use it. Harley Davidson brakes typically use silicone DOT 5 fluid.

Silicone based DOT 5 fluids do not absorb water in the way that DOT 3 and 4 fluids do. Water contamination is what kills brake fluid and since DOT 5 fluid won't absorb moisture, it would seem that DOT 5 is the way to go. Unfortunately water can get into a DOT 5 brake system and when it does, it forms

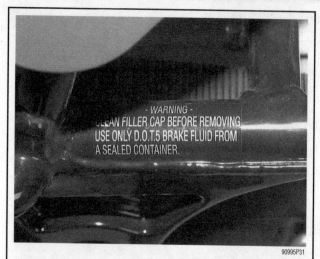

Fig. 25 Before adding brake fluid, check any stickers or warnings on the bike for additional information

droplets. If a droplet gets heated to the point of boiling, it will flash into steam and cause all sorts of nastiness that will result in a loss of braking or possibly locking up the brakes. It isn't very likely this will happen, but it can. Changing the brake fluid is as important on a DOT 5 system as it is on any other.

The DOT 3 and 4 brake fluids are hydroscopic meaning they absorb fluid. As the moisture content goes up, the resistance to boiling goes down. This is the reason why it is so important to change and flush brake fluid on a regular basis. It is a good idea to change the fluid at least once a year, maybe more if you do a lot of wet weather riding and use your brakes more severely than the average rider.

The brand of brake fluid isn't very critical as long as you choose a high quality name brand or the manufacturers offering. There are racing brake fluids out there, but unless they meet a DOT rating, I don't recommend their use on the street. The cost of brake fluid is fairly small compared to the job it performs, so don't skimp on quality here!

CHECKING YOUR FLUID

▶ **See Figures 28 thru 35**

Take a quick glance in your owners manual. You will find exact instructions on how to check your brake fluid. In general, it is as simple as look-

Fig. 26 Always use new fluid from an unopened bottle

Fig. 28 Clean the cap before removing to keep the schmutz from falling in

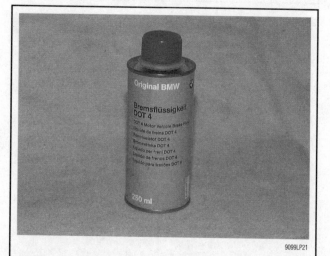

Fig. 27 You won't go wrong using the factory recommended brake fluid

Fig. 29 Most brake fluid reservoirs have some method of checking the level without removing the lid. This one has a sight glass

Fig. 30 This reservoir is translucent allowing you to see the level at a glance

Fig. 33 Some rear reservoirs can be buried like this . . .

Fig. 31 Make sure the reservoir is level when checking the fluid

Fig. 34 . . . or easily seen like this

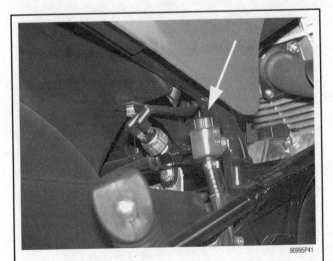

Fig. 32 The rear brake reservoir will typically be a small tank like this

Fig. 35 This rear brake reservoir requires a cut out in the body-work to be seen

ing at a translucent reservoir or into a sight glass. The trick is finding out if the handle bars need to be turned one way or the other to make an accurate check. Most likely you will have to turn the bars so that the master cylinder is level. On rear brake master cylinders, the reservoirs are either integral with the master or separate, but either way, just by holding the bike upright will get the fluid level check that you need.

If your bike doesn't have a translucent reservoir or a sight glass, you may have to take the lid off the reservoir and look down into it to check the level. Be sure to clean off the fill cover before removing it. You don't want any dirt to fall in.

BLEEDING YOUR BRAKES

▶ **See Figures 36 and 37**

A mushy feeling at the brake lever or pedal is most often due to air in the lines. This can happen if the fluid level drops too low, or if a line or hose is disconnected for any reason. This requires brake bleeding to remove the air.

Brake bleeding can be done manually, where the fluid is pumped out using the master cylinder, or vacuum pump, or by gravity. A vacuum pump sucks the old fluid out through the bleeder. Gravity bleeding allows the fluid to flow out over a period of time. Manual bleeding is the most common method and tends to be quick. Vacuum bleeding requires use of a vacuum

Fig. 36 Keep an eye on the fluid being expelled and continue until all the old fluid and bubbles pass

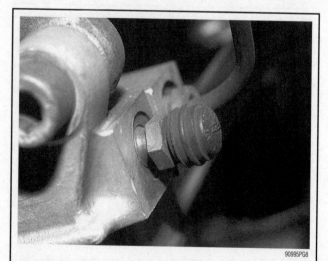

Fig. 37 When you are done, re-install the bleeder cap as it will keep the crud out of the passage

pump and is very quick, but air sucked in through the threads of the bleeder can sometimes obscure the vision of real air bubbles in the fluid. Gravity bleeding is the easiest, but it can take a while and not dislodge stubborn air bubbles.

Certain precautions should be taken when working with brake fluid.
- Brake fluid absorbs moisture very quickly, and then becomes useless. Therefore, never use fluid from an old or unsealed container.
- Do not mix brake fluids of different types.
- DOT 3 or 4 hydraulic disc brake fluid is recommended for almost all motorcycles at this time, with Harley-Davidson being one notable exception. You should check your owners manual to be sure.
- Brake fluid will quickly remove paint Avoid damage to the gas tank by placing a protective cover over it.

Manual Bleeding

1. To bleed the brake system, obtain a length of transparent plastic hose, the inside diameter of which is such that the hose will fit tightly over the bleed nipple of the brake caliper. Also needed is a small cup.
2. Fit the plastic hose to the bleed nipple, and put the other end in the cup which should have an inch or so of new brake fluid in it. Be sure that the end of the hose is below the surface of the fluid in the cup.
3. The hose should not have any sharp bends or kinks in it. It should loop up from the bleed nipple, and then down towards the cup.
4. The motorcycle should be on the centerstand with the handlebars centered. If your bike doesn't have a centerstand, support it in a vertical position.
5. Check that the fluid level is topped up to the indicated line.
6. Apply the brake lever slowly several times, then hold it.
7. While holding the brake lever, loosen the caliper bleed nipple. The brake lever will be pulled towards the handgrip (or if a rear brake, will bottom out), and fluid will be forced through the plastic hose. Try to tighten the bleed nipple before the lever bottoms out.
8. Note the brake fluid being forced out of the plastic hose. If there was air in the lines, air bubbles will be noted coming out of the hose.
9. Pump up the lever again, and loosen the nipple as before, once again checking the fluid being forced out. When air bubbles no longer issue from the plastic hose, the system is bled.
10. Be sure that the master cylinder reservoir is kept topped up during the bleeding procedure. Top off when completed.

Vacuum Bleeding

Vacuum bleeding requires the use of a vacuum pump. The pumps can be handheld or driven from a compressed air source. In simplistic terms, a vacuum is applied to the bleeder screw and then the screw is opened. The fluid is sucked from the system along with any trapped air. The bleeder screw is tightened when done and the fluid reservoir topped off. If you choose to use this method, follow the directions provided with the vacuum pump. Be careful not to suck all the fluid from the system!

Gravity Bleeding

To gravity bleed a system, simply attach a hose to the bleeder nipple and place the open end in a container. Open the bleeder nipple and let the fluid flow out. Keep the reservoir topped off and check the progress from time to time. The longer you let it go, the more bleeding you have done.

FLUSHING THE BRAKE SYSTEM

▶ **See Figure 38**

The procedure for flushing a brake system is identical to that for bleeding, except that the process should be continued until new brake fluid begins to issue from the plastic hose. Remove as much of the old fluid from the reservoir as possible before you start and top off with new. You will begin by pumping out the old fluid with the lever while adding the new fluid in its place. After the new fluid starts coming out, begin checking for air bubbles and continue until you get a solid flow with no bubbles present.

Fig. 38 Keep the fluid topped off while bleeding and flushing

Brake Lines

INSPECTION

Periodically check condition of the hoses and lines. Be sure that all hoses are arranged as the manufacturer intended, and are properly mounted. Check for abrasion damage. Check banjo fittings for signs of seepage.

Over a period of time, brake hoses tend to get hard and lose their flexibility. They can become prone to cracking both internally and externally. Even a hose that looks good on the outside can be breaking down on the inside leading to restricted flow or trapped pressure in the system.

If you have an older bike and you have any doubts to the condition of the brake hoses, replace them. There are many choices available in replacement hose; You can buy original equipment hose, aftermarket hoses or high performance braided steel or kevlar hoses. The choice is yours. If you go with aftermarket hoses of any style, check that they are DOT approved and can be used on the street, if you have a street bike. Non-DOT hoses are made for off-road and racing bikes.

REPLACEMENT

1. Before attacking your motorcycles brake hoses or lines, inspect the hoses and compare the replacements with the originals. Make sure they are identical! Hoses that are too short or too long can cause problems with routing or performance.

2. Make a diagram of the brake line and hose routing before you even get your tools out. Note the location of every clip, tab and bracket that the lines go through. If any of them are damaged, get a replacement for it (maybe two).

3. Protect the paint or bodywork near where you will be working as spilled brake fluid can be harmful to surfaces. As a matter of fact, brake fluid can be a pretty good paint remover, so you get my point! This is true for DOT 3 and 4 fluids as DOT 5 silicone fluids aren't as reactive to paint, but you should still be careful.

4. Remove the brake fluid from the master cylinder using a siphon or suction bulb.

5. Clean the connections of dirt and crud. This will prevent dirt from entering the system. In the case of flare nut fittings, clean the area between the nut and the tube. This will make spinning the nut off easier.

6. If the hose connection is a flare nut, use a backup wrench on the female side of the connection and a flare nut wrench on the nut itself.

7. Install the new hose or line and route it the way the original was.

8. Make the connections at either end and tighten.

9. Check the lines for interference with other things on the bike and check that the fork can move freely if it was a fork mounted line.

10. Fill and bleed the system
11. Apply pressure to the system and check the connections for leaks

Brake Linkage

INSPECTION

▶ **See Figures 39 and 40**

Most brake linkages consist of a push or pull rod that goes from the brake pedal to the brake itself. Inspection consists of looking at the connection points and bushings to check for corrosion and wear. If wear is apparent, the linkage portion affected needs to be replaced. Corrosion should be cleaned off in preparation for relubrication.

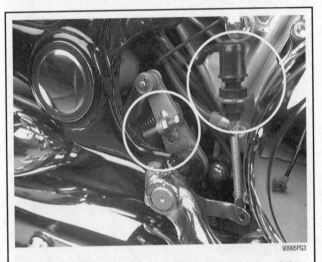

Fig. 39 This rear brake linkage incorporates a stop bolt and the brake light switch

Fig. 40 The linkage works its way back from the pedal to the rear drum to work on the actuating lever

MAINTENANCE

Most linkages are essentially maintenance free, except for periodic lubrication. Some linkages will have greasing points and other will just need some oil spread on the bushings. By keeping the linkage adjusted and lubricated, it should provide a lifetime of use with minimum problems.

Disc Brakes

INSPECTION

♦ **See Figures 41, 42, 43 and 44**

Disc brake systems need little routine maintenance other than an occasional check on pad wear and fluid level.

1. Pads should be replaced when they are worn to the limit lines. These are cut outs or grooves cut into the friction material and indicate the minimum thickness when they are completely gone. Other types will have tab wear indicators. For others still, the manufacturer will specify minimum pad thickness.

2. The master cylinder fluid level is usually inscribed on the master cylinder. The fluid level may drop slightly over a period of time as the pads wear, but this drop will be slight. Do not top up a master cylinder reservoir whose level has dropped slightly due to pad wear, since the level will return to the normal level when new pads are fitted. An exception, of course, will be made if braking effectiveness is reduced due to a low level, but by then, air may have introduced to the system and will need to be bled out.

3. Check the surface of the brake rotor for scoring, grooves, hot spots or any other damage. Check the rotor for warp. This can be done by sighting the

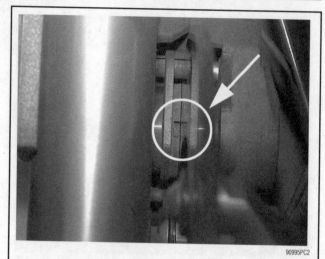

Fig. 43 In this example, when the indentations are worn out of the pads, minimum thickness has been reached.

Fig. 41 Pad thickness can be checked by looking in the back of the caliper if the pads are exposed

Fig. 44 Some pads will have a central groove that will disappear when minimum thickness is reached

Fig. 42 On this BMW pad, when the rotor is seen through the hole on the left, it is time to replace them

edge of the rotor while spinning the wheel assembly. A dial indicator may be used, but why go through the extra effort if a simple visual test can be used.

PAD REPLACEMENT

This procedure will vary according to the make and model of the motorcycle, but all have basic points in common.

• When new pads are fitted, avoid hard braking if possible for at least 50–100 miles (110–220 km) to give the new pads a chance to seat themselves.

• Brake fluid and solvents must be kept off the brake pads.

• A few older design calipers must be adjusted periodically. This procedure should be outlined in your shop manual or owners manual.

There are different styles of brake calipers, each with a different method of removing the pads. In general, disc brakes fall into three categories: fixed, sliding (or floating), and pivoting.

Fixed Calipers

Fixed calipers can be identified by having opposed pistons. A fixed caliper doesn't move during brake application. Fixed calipers are firmly bolted to the fork or swing arm and have no moving portion as does a sliding or pivoting caliper.

Fixed calipers come in two basic flavors: open back and closed back. Open back calipers have an opening from which the brake pads are removed and installed. Closed back calipers require the removal of the caliper to change the brake pads.

OPEN BACK

▶ **See Figures 45 thru 55**

There are many different fixed calipers mounted on motorcycles, but they all change the pads in a similar fashion.

1. Remove the caliper dust cover to expose the tops of the pads and the pad retaining pins.

2. The pad retaining pins will either have to be knocked out with a punch from the back side or just pushed out after a retaining clip is removed. If there is no retaining clip that goes through a hole in the pins, they will have to be driven out.

3. After removing the pins, remove the spring from the caliper. This spring keeps the pads retracted when the brakes aren't applied and also keeps the pads from rattling. Make a note of how the spring fits.

4. Remove some brake fluid from the reservoir if the level is at or near the full mark.

Fig. 47 Don't lose these little clips and they are what keep the pins from sliding out

Fig. 45 A cover may need to be removed to expose the pads and pins

Fig. 48 Press down on the spring and pull out the pins

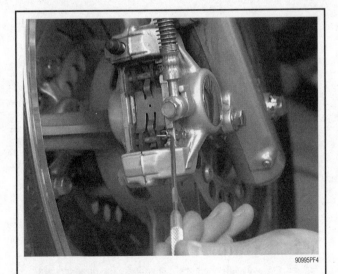

Fig. 46 Use a pick to pull out the clips

Fig. 49 Always replace the spring with the pads as it keeps the pads from rattling and dragging

Fig. 50 This is a performance oriented six piston caliper. It uses an open back with a bolted bridge

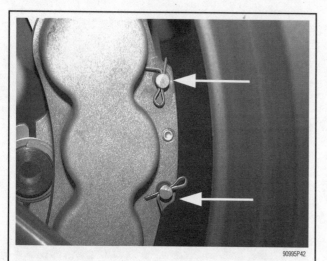

Fig. 51 The pad retention pins are held by these cotters. Use new cotter pins when replacing the pads

Fig. 52 The pins will easily slip out once the cotter pins are removed

Fig. 53 The bolted bridge stiffens the back of the caliper and requires a hex bit to remove.

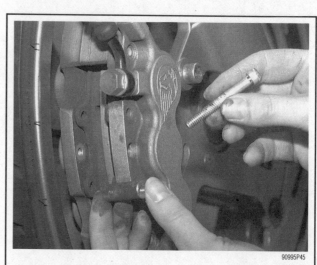

Fig. 54 The spacer isn't retained by anything but the bolt. It will drop out when the bolt is removed

Fig. 55 The pads will slip out of the caliper. The three inboard pistons are visible in this shot

5. Remove the pads and press the pistons back into their bores. If the opposite piston pushes out while you push in the other one, place a pad or piece of wood between it and the rotor to keep it from moving out. Do not pry on the rotor when pushing in the piston as you can bend or crack it.

6. Clean the caliper of brake dust and road grime. Dirt can prevent proper action of the caliper.

7. Drop in the new pads and align the holes for the pad retaining pin.

8. Install the spring and the pad retaining pins. The spring may be held under the pins in some designs.

9. Pump up the brakes until you see the pads compress against the rotor. Check that both sides apply at the same time.

10. Install the dust shield.

11. Check the level of brake fluid and top off. Bleed the brakes as necessary.

CLOSED BACK

▶ **See Figures 56 thru 61**

Closed back design calipers are very common on today's hyperperformance bikes as they allow a stronger bridge area on the caliper. This results in less flex and better braking performance.

Fig. 58 Notice that this pad retention pin has a slot in it to help align the hole for the clip, not to unscrew the pin

Fig. 56 On closed back bixed caliper, you will need to unbolt the caliper from the bike to service the pads

Fig. 59 The pad retention pin may need a light tap to push it out

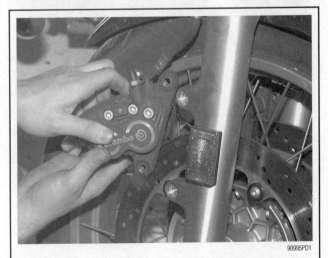

Fig. 57 If the flexible hose is short, don't twist the caliper more than you need

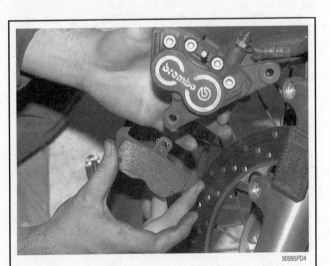

Fig. 60 The pads will slide out of the bottom of the caliper in a closed back design

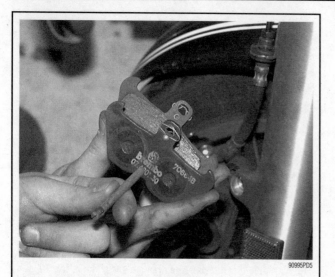

Fig. 61 The pads may have springs that act to suppress rattling

Fig. 62 This rear mounted Brembo caliper is what we consider a floating type. A sliding type is very similar

1. The caliper must be dismounted from the bike to change the pads. Loosen the clamps or brackets holding the brake line to the bike. This will keep the lines from being bent or the hoses from twisting severely.

2. Unbolt the caliper and pull off the bike. Support the caliper so it doesn't hang on the brake line

3. Remove the pad retaining pin(s). A pin may be held by a clip or screwed into the body of the caliper.

4. Remove the pads from the caliper.

5. Clean the body of the caliper and the surfaces on which the pads move.

6. Remove some brake fluid from the reservoir if the level is at or near the full mark.

7. Compress the pistons back into the caliper body .

8. Install the new pads.

9. Install the pad retention pin(s) with its clip or by screwing in.

10. Install the caliper on the bike and tighten the mounting bolts. Use a threadlocking compound to prevent the caliper bolts from loosening.

11. Replace the clips and brackets holding the brake lines or hoses.

12. Apply the brakes to seat the pads. Pump the lever or pedal until it gets firm.

13. Check the level of brake fluid and top off. Bleed the brakes as necessary.

Sliding and Floating Calipers

▶ See Figure 62

Sliding and floating calipers have one or more pistons working on one side of the caliper. When the piston presses the pad against the rotor, the caliper slides over and applies the pad on the opposite side as well. Most of the time these calipers will have two rubber bellows on pins from which the caliper body slides. This is the floating type. The sliding type moves on machined areas of the calipers and doesn't use pins. On either type, there typically will also be a flexible hose going to the caliper versus a rigid pipe.

SLIDING CALIPER

▶ See Figures 63 thru 70

1. On some bikes equipped with this type of caliper, the wheel must be removed. If the wheel is removed, you may not have to dismount the caliper from the bike, otherwise remove the mounting hardware and pull the caliper off the bike.

2. If the pad opposite the piston has a screw on the back, remove the screw and pull off the pad. If there is no screw, the pad will most likely pry out of the caliper.

3. Remove the pad from the piston side of the caliper.

4. Clean the body of the caliper and the surface on which the pads move. Lubricate the sliding surfaces.

Fig. 63 This Harley caliper is a cross between a sliding and floating caliper. The lower bolt acts as a slide

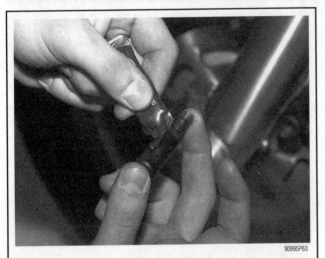

Fig. 64 The slide must be kept lubricated with a brake caliper grease

Fig. 67 There are slots and tabs that align the pad holder with slide boot

Fig. 65 The upper bolt mounts the caliper to the fork leg

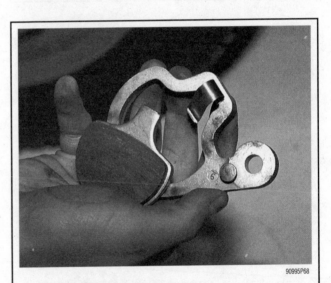

Fig. 68 The piston side pad rides in this holder

Fig. 66 Pull the caliper from the bike to be able to get at the pads

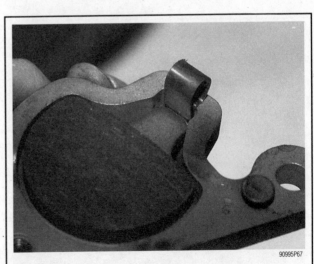

Fig. 69 The spring must be positioned to tension the pad when installed

Fig. 70 The inner pad is held in by this screw

Fig. 72 Use the proper tools when working on today's bikes as they can have unusual bolt materials such as stainless steel or titanium

5. Remove some brake fluid from the reservoir if the level is at or near the full mark..

6. Compress the piston back into the caliper body with either your hands or with a large pair of pliers.

7. Install the new pads and replace the pad retention screw, if equipped. Use non-permanent thread locking compound on the screw.

8. Install the wheel, if removed.

9. Apply the brakes to seat the pads. Pump the lever or pedal until it firms up.

10. Check the level of brake fluid and top off. Bleed the brakes as necessary.

FLOATING CALIPER

▶ **See Figures 71 thru 76**

1. The caliper must be dismounted from the bike to change the pads. Loosen the clamps or brackets holding the brake line to the bike. This will keep the lines from being bent or the hoses from twisting severely.

2. Unbolt the caliper and pull off the bike. Always support the caliper to keep the brake line from being stressed.

Fig. 73 On this caliper, remove the two bolts that attach the caliper to the reaction bracket

Fig. 71 This caliper needs to be dismounted to change the pads

Fig. 74 When pulling the caliper off, move it straight up and don't kink the brake hose

Fig. 75 This inner pad has to slide off the pins to be removed. You might have to push the pad back to achieve this

Fig. 76 This outer pad just pops out of the piston with a prying motion

3. If equipped, remove the pad retaining pin(s). The pin(s) may be held by a clip or screwed into the body of the caliper.

4. Remove the pads from the caliper.

5. Clean the body of the caliper and where the pads move. Lubricate the surfaces on which the pads slide.

6. Remove some brake fluid from the reservoir if the level is at or near the full mark.

7. Compress the piston(s) back into the caliper body with either your hands or a large pair of pliers.

8. Install the anti-rattle spring if equipped.

9. Install the new pads and replace the pad retention pin with its clip. You may have to slide the caliper to get the holes in the pads to line up with the pins on some designs.

10. Install the caliper on the bike and tighten the mounting bolts. Use a threadlocking compound to prevent the caliper bolts from loosening.

11. Replace the clips and brackets holding the brake lines or hoses.

12. Apply the brakes to seat the pads. Pump the lever or pedal until it becomes firm.

13. Check the level of brake fluid and top off. Bleed the brakes as necessary.

Pivoting Caliper

▶ See Figures 77 thru 86

A pivoting caliper uses a solid caliper body that pivots on a single shaft. This necessitates the use of brake pads with a bevel on them. The calipers also need to be adjusted after pad installation. This type of caliper was typically used on older BMW's and some older Hondas.

1. The caliper should be dismounted from the bike to change the pads. The wheel can be removed to do the job, but you won't be able to access the pivot to clean it. Loosen the clamps or brackets holding the brake line to the bike. This will keep the lines from being bent or the hoses from twisting severely.

2. There may be a cover over the pivot on the fork. Remove this cover to access the pivot.

3. The pivot may need to have a bolt threaded into it to allow it to be pulled out of its bore.

4. Remove the pivot and pull the caliper off the bike.

5. Remove the pad retaining spring and remove the pad from the caliper. Remove the other pad from the caliper piston.

6. Clean the entire pivot and caliper. Lubricate the pivot with brake grease. Replace any damaged O-rings

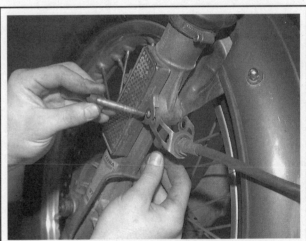
Fig. 77 The caliper will need to be removed and it has a solid line going to it, requiring the removal of the line's bracket

Fig. 78 Unscrewing the lower cover exposes a spring and the bottom of the pivot which is up in the body of the caliper

Fig. 79 Screw the bolt from the brake line bracket into the bottom of the pivot to act a handle

Fig. 80 Use the bolt to pull out the pivot from the fork leg and caliper

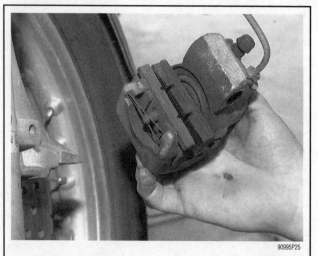

Fig. 81 Once the caliper is removed, access is gained for the pads and retention spring

Fig. 82 This spring does all the pad retention duties on the inboard side

Fig. 83 With the spring removed, the pad can be pried out of the caliper

Fig. 84 The inboard pad is held in the piston by the projection and an O-ring

Fig. 85 The pivot is eccentric to allow adjustment of the pads and their alignment with the rotor. The pivot should be cleaned and lubricated before reinstallation

Fig. 86 The retention spring needs to installed so it does its job. This one wasn't when we took apart the caliper, but it is going back correctly

7. Remove some brake fluid from the reservoir if the level is at or near the full mark.

8. Compress the piston back into the caliper body with your fingers or a large pair of pliers.

9. Press one pad into the caliper piston. Install the other pad into the caliper and clip on the retaining spring.

10. Install the caliper on the fork leg and replace the pivot.

11. Adjust the pivot until the pad is parallel with the rotor. This can be done by marking the rotor with piece of chalk and rotating the wheel with the caliper pressed against the rotor. When the marks are cleanly wiped off across the entire face of the rotor, the caliper is adjusted correctly.

12. If the pivot cover had a spring, apply grease to the spring and replace the cover.

13. Install the clips and brackets holding the brake lines or hoses.

14. Apply the brakes to seat the pads.

15. Check the level of brake fluid and top off. Bleed the brakes as necessary.

Drum Brakes

INSPECTION & ADJUSTMENT

▶ See Figure 87

Drum brakes are becoming a rarity. They used to be used on almost every bike, but discs have taken over most braking duties. You will find some bikes with rear drums, but front drums can usually only be found of some lighter and less expensive models.

1. Drum brakes are operated by either cable or rod. In most cases, front brakes have cable adjusters at the brake plate and at the hand lever. Rear brakes usually have an adjuster at the brake plate. Generally, brake adjustment should be maintained so that the brake hand lever or brake pedal has about 1 in. (24.5mm) of movement before the linings contact the drum. In the case of rod-operated rear brakes, this adjustment should be made with the machine off the stands and with a rider sitting on it. The reason for this is that the movement of the swing arm may vary the distance between the brake cam and the pedal pivot, thereby changing the brake adjustment as the machine is operated.

2. On front brakes, the adjustment is usually made at the brake plate, with fine adjustments made at the hand lever.

3. Twin-leading shoe brakes are fitted with a linkage connecting the two cams, and the linkage may not need routine adjustment unless the brake plate has been disassembled or new shoes have been fitted. One type of the linkage has both brake levers connected with a cable and the levers are pulled together when the brake is applied. This type is self-adjusting. A more common method is to have the brake cable connected to one brake lever, the remaining lever being connected to the first by means of a rod and clevises. The rod is usually threaded as a means of varying the length to make an adjustment.

4. To check the adjustment, disconnect the rod at the main brake lever. There is usually a retaining clip or cotter pin at the clevis pin. Apply the brake hand lever until the shoe contacts the drum. Holding this position, apply the secondary brake lever with your hand until that shoe contacts the drum. The clevis holes should line up at this point. If they do not, lengthen or shorten the brake rod so that the holes align.

5. Some drum brakes have wear indicators fitted to the brake cam. In most cases these consist of arrows. If the arrows align when the brake is applied, the brake linings are worn to the point of replacement.

Fig. 87 Most manufacturers have been nice enough to include these wear gauges right at the actuating lever negating the need to pull everything apart to look at the brake shoes

6. Brakes not fitted with indicators can be checked with the wheel in place. When the brake is applied, the angle formed by the brake rod or cable and the brake lever should not exceed 90 degrees. After this point, braking effectiveness will be reduced.

7. On brakes without wear indicators, an occasional check of lining thickness is recommended. Minimum allowable lining thickness is usually given by the manufacturer, and may be given in your state's motor vehicle code. It is approximately 0.08 in. (2.0 mm) measured at the lining's thinnest point, but this value is only a generalization, and the exact figure must be obtained from your owners manual or shop manual, as it differs from bike-to-bike. On machines with riveted brake shoes, the thickness of the lining must be measured from the top of the rivets. On bonded shoes, it is measured from the surface of the shoe casting.

REPLACEMENT

The following procedure is to be considered a general guide to inspecting and servicing a drum brake assembly. The procedure may vary in detail depending upon the design of the brake assembly in question.

1. Remove the wheel from the motorcycle and separate the hub from the brake plate assembly.

2. Wear of brake linings can be checked with the linings in place. Be sure to measure brake lining thickness at the linings' thinnest points. On riveted brakes, measure the distance from the top of the rivets to the lining surface.

3. Check the linings for grooves, scoring, or other signs of unusual wear. Most damage of this sort is caused by particles of dirt, which have entered the brake drum. If badly scored, the shoes must be replaced. If the shoes are scored, the drum should be checked for the same type of damage. Make sure that there is no oil or grease present of the linings. Oil-impregnated linings must be replaced. If the linings show this condition, determine the source of the lubricant: defective wheel bearing grease seals, excessive chain lube, etc.

4. If the linings are usable, rough up their surface with sandpaper. Then clean them with alcohol or lacquer thinner. Polish the brake drum surface removing any rust or dirt and clean the drum thoroughly.

5. To disassemble the brake plate, remove the shoes. On some models, this is possible simply by grasping both shoes and folding them towards the center of the brake plate. Other models, however, are fitted with retainers or guards. Remove any cotter pins and washers from the brake cam(s), then remove the shoes.

➡**The plurals refer to the twin leading shoe brakes.**

6. To remove the cam(s) from the brake plate, remove the brake lever pinch bolt(s). Most brake levers are fitted on splines and will have to be pried off carefully. After the lever is removed, the brake cam can be tapped or pushed out of the brake plate. Note any dust seals or washers on the brake cam.

7. Check that the brake lever pinch bolts are not bent. This can easily happen if they are overtightened. Replace any bolts in this condition. Inspect the brake lever splines and replace the lever(s) if these are worn or stripped.

8. Inspect the splines on the brake cam(s). These should be in good condition. Check that the brake cam(s) are not bent and that they can rotate freely in the brake plate passage. If it will not, use a fine grade of sandpaper on the camshafts and the surface of the brake plate passage.

9. Clean the cam(s) thoroughly in a solvent to remove any old grease, rust, or corrosion. Use sandpaper or emery cloth to polish the cams. Clean off any residue; before reassembly, smear the cams with chassis grease.

10. Inspect the brake plate for cracks or fractures, and replace it if necessary.

11. On twin-leading shoe brakes, the brake plate linkage should be checked. The connecting rod is secured to each brake lever by a clevis pin and cotter pin or clip. They should be checked for wear, especially on high mileage machines, and replaced if necessary.

12. Check the condition of the brake springs, noting any twisted or fatigued hooks. Replace any broken, rusted, or old springs with new ones. Check spring free length if specified for your bike.

13. Clean all metal parts thoroughly with a suitable solvent, making a special effort to remove the dust and built-up dirt from the backing plate.

14. When reassembling the brake plate, note the following points:
   a. Ensure that the brake cams are lubricated with chassis grease.
   b. The use of new dust seals is recommended.
   c. Lubricate the brake shoe pivot points with a little grease.
   d. Install the shoes as on removal. Hook them together with the springs, and fold them down over the brake cam(s) and pivot(s). Install new cotter pins to the pivot points.
   e. When installing the brake lever on the brake cam, be sure that the punch marks on the lever and cam align, if applicable.

15. The drum should be checked for concentricity. An out-of-round condition is usually noticeable as an on-off-on feeling when the brake is applied while riding. With the wheel assembly mounted on the machine, spin the wheel while applying the brake very lightly. The rubbing noise of the brakes against the drum should be heard for the entire revolution of the wheel.

16. An out-of-round condition and most scoring can be removed by having the drum turned on a lathe. This operation should be entrusted to a qualified specialist with the proper equipment. Usually, the tire and wheel bearings will have to be removed so that the wheel can be checked to the lathe. If a spoke rim needs to be trued, have this done before any work on the drum is performed, as the action of the spokes while truing the rim may further aggravate the drum warpage.

SUSPENSION MAINTENANCE

Air Adjustable Suspensions

INSPECTION

There isn't much to check on an air suspension as most of the working parts of it are buried within the body of a shock or fork. You can check the condition of the system by looking for symptoms and a visual look-see.

1. Apply compressed air to the system at the highest recommended pressure. Ride the bike and allow it to sit over night. Check the pressure again and see if any was lost. If it was, there is a leak somewhere in the system that needs to be fixed.

2. Inspect the air lines and their connections for damage. Check for signs of leakage by applying soapy water to all the joints.

3. Most air suspensions use a standard Schrader type air valve. Use a valve stem core wrench to check the tightness of the core.

ADJUSTMENT

▶ **See Figure 88**

The manufacturer of your bike will recommend a range of pressures to be used in the suspension. Changing the pressure is done to adapt the bike for different types of riding and riding conditions. Typically you will use a higher pressure when the bike is more heavily loaded and a lower

Fig. 88 The air pressure is adjusted by adding or removing air from a valve like this one

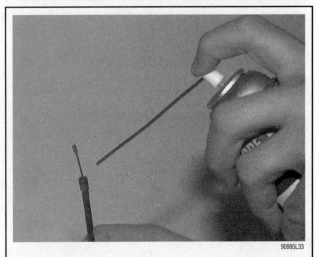

Fig. 90 Use a good cable lubricant at the ends of the cables and allow it to work its way down

pressure for lower weights. Experiment with the suspension pressures to get a feel for the differences in handling and bike behavior.

Control And Chassis Lubrication

CONTROL CABLES

▶ **See Figures 89 and 90**

Cables need routine maintenance to operate smoothly and prevent breakage. A sign of a control cable that needs lubrication is sticky operation or a snatching feeling in the control.

1. Disconnect the cable and drip cable lubricant down the housing. There are special cable lubricating fittings that make this easier and neater. Add lubricant until it runs out of the other end of the cable.

➡**Do not lubricate Teflon lined cables as the cable is designed to be self lubricating. Adding lubricant will only cause problems. Check with the manufacturer of the bike or the cables to see what type you have.**

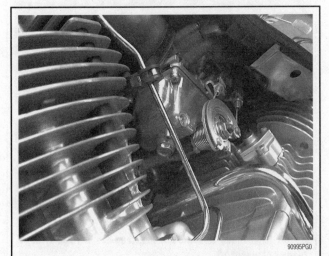

Fig. 89 Without good lubrication or a clean sheath, these throttle cables can't give good smooth performance

2. Lubricate the ends of the cable with grease where they connect to the controls and levers. A dab of grease at the cable openings will help prevent the entry of dirt and moisture into the cable.

3. Disassemble and lubricate the throttle tube and gear. Reassemble and check for proper motion.

SHIFTER & BRAKE LINKAGE

Any linkages on the bike including the shifter need to be lubricated on a regular basis.

1. Apply oil or light grease to all bushings and sliding surfaces. If the bike is equipped with grease fittings, use an appropriate grease gun with the lubricant specified by the manufacturer.

2. Check the condition of the pivots and wear areas. Replace as needed.

3. Clean around the linkage pivots to prevent wear and galling at the bearing surfaces.

HEAD BEARINGS/STEERING STEM

▶ **See Figure 91**

The steering stem assembly consists of the upper and lower triple clamps, their connecting shaft, and the bearings on which the assembly rides in the frame lug.

The bearings in most cases are uncaged balls which ride on bearing races, the inner halves of which are pressed into the frame lug. Some models use tapered roller bearings, or caged ball bearings, or a combination of the two.

Inspection

A problem with the bearings may be indicated by a clunk felt through the handlebars when the brakes are first applied. The condition of the steering stem bearings should be checked periodically in the following manner:

1. Support the front wheel of the motorcycle off the ground.

2. Grasp the fork sliders, and attempt to move them back and forth in line with the motorcycle. No play should be noted here. An alternate method, applicable to machines with a sturdy front fender is to grasp the tip of the fender and pull upwards, placing your other hand at the junction of the triple clamp and frame to feel for play. Ordinarily, play indicated by either of these two methods can be remedied by simply adjusting the bearings. There is, in most cases, a nut or nuts beneath the upper triple clamp which are used to make this adjustment.

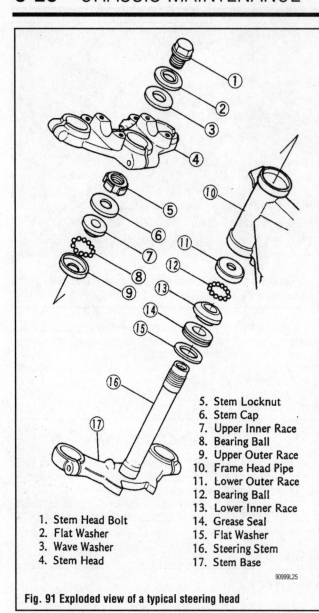

5. Stem Locknut
6. Stem Cap
7. Upper Inner Race
8. Bearing Ball
9. Upper Outer Race
10. Frame Head Pipe
11. Lower Outer Race
12. Bearing Ball
13. Lower Inner Race
14. Grease Seal
15. Flat Washer
16. Steering Stem
17. Stem Base

1. Stem Head Bolt
2. Flat Washer
3. Wave Washer
4. Stem Head

90999L25

Fig. 91 Exploded view of a typical steering head

race of the lower bearing is usually a tight fit on the steering stem and will have to be chiseled off. If you have disassembled the steering stem for routine lubrication, you can check the condition of the balls and races after cleaning them thoroughly in solvent to remove all the old grease.

Any balls which are pitted, rusted, or dented will necessitate replacement of the entire bearing and race assembly. Races themselves should be checked for a rippled surface, indentations, and other imperfections. Frame races should not be removed unless defective, since they will probably be rendered useless by the removal procedure. The same is true of the steering stem lower race. When installing a steering stem assembly, always be sure that the proper number of balls are fitted to each race. Inbed and cover the balls in a high grade bearing grease.

2. Adjust the bearings so that fork action conforms to those standards as outlined above. If new frame races have been installed, make frequent checks of adjustment during the first several hundred miles, since the frame races will probably settle over a period of time.

Lubrication

Lubricating the head bearings can be as simple as applying a grease gun to a zerk fitting or be as tedious as disassembling the whole unit. If your bike doesn't have a grease fitting, follow the replacement procedures for your steering bearings, but simply repack the bearings instead of replacing them.

SIDESTANDS AND CENTERSTANDS

◆ See Figures 92 and 93

It is important to inspect sidestands and centerstands as a failure of the spring(s) or a pivot can allow the stands to drag on the ground. This is a very dangerous situation. The pivots must be kept lubricated to prevent wear of the bushings or pivot itself. Some less-enlightened companies don't use a pivot bushing leading to wear of the frame tab itself and in those cases, you can't fix the damage.

1. Inspect the stand pivots for wear and damage.
2. Lubricate the pivot points.
3. Inspect the springs to make sure the stand is held completely up to the bikes frame.

3. With the front wheel free of the ground, and any steering damper loosened or disconnected, turn the forks slowly from lock to lock. Movement should be smooth, effortless, and without noise. If fork movement is rough, or if there seems to be a detent spot somewhere during the movement of the forks, the bearings or races may be worn.

4. Position the forks off the centered position and release them. The forks should fall to either side of their own weight. If they do not, the bearings may be too tightly adjusted.

5. In general, bearings which cannot be properly adjusted, or will not hold an adjustment for any length of time, can be said to be worn to the point of replacement. For uncaged ball bearings, all of the balls and all races must be replaced at the same time.

Replacement

1. Removal procedures vary for different types of assemblies. In all cases, however, the frame races must be driven out with a drift, and installed with a block of wood until firmly seated in the flame lug. The outer

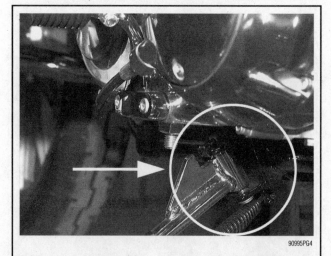

90995PG4

Fig. 92 Inspect and lubricate the sidestand bushing and pivot as regular maintenance

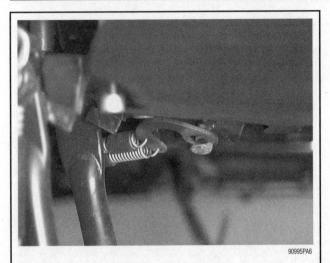

Fig. 93 Inspect the springs that hold the stands as you don't want them to fall at a bad time

Fork Oil

ROUTINE MAINTENANCE

Telescopic fork components are usually long-lived, the most common problem being slider seal leakage. Other components wear much less slowly, and deterioration of fork operation may come on so gradually as to be unnoticeable. Other potential troublespots include permanent spring compression, slider bushing wear, damage to fork tube plating, and damper wear.

Telescopic front forks all require routine oil changes at intervals which will be specified by the manufacturer of the motorcycle. This is necessary to extend seal life, and to drain off dirt or water which may have gotten into the oil supply to cause accelerated wear to the damper components.

Earle's type and leading-link front forks (as opposed to telescopic types) require little or no maintenance, except for those few which may have grease fittings on the link pivots. For the most part, inspection is confined to noting whether operation is satisfactory. If it is not, check the condition of the shock absorbers; leakage would tend to be the most common problem. The shock units are sealed, and replacement is the remedy if problems are in evidence. Link bushings should also be checked for excessive play.

SELECTING THE PROPER OIL

A wide range of fork oils is available including specially-designed motorcycle fork oil, several viscosities of plain motor oil, and Automatic Transmission Fluid (ATF) or hydraulic fluid. The type of oil recommended by the manufacturer should be used, and this will be specified in the owners manual.

The viscosity of the oil used in the forks will to some extent determine the fork's damping characteristics, a heavier oil giving stiffer damping, and vice-versa. This is not always true, however, some forks such as those used on late-model Moto Guzzis having sealed damper units, the fork oil being used only to lubricate the moving parts.

Therefore, oils of varying viscosities may be experimented with, until you find one which suits your needs. It is wise, however, not to vary the recommended oil type or viscosity without due cause.

As important as choosing the correct oil viscosity is choosing an oil which is compatible with the oil already in the forks. Of course, if the forks are disassembled and cleaned, there is no problem here. But routine oil changes always leave some of the old oil in the sliders, and refilling them with an incompatible brand will probably have an adverse effect on damping. Fork capacities are given by the manufacturer and can be found in the owners manual or shop manual. The amount is always given for each fork leg. It is important to realize, however, that some of the old fork oil will remain in the slider as we noted above, and this will naturally affect the amount

you add. Some bike makers will give two fork capacities: one for routine changes, the other for a completely dry fork. In general, the amount added to a dry fork will be about 10% greater than that for routine oil changes. That is, if you are to add 0.4 pints (200cc) of fluid to each leg for a routine change, about 0.44 pints (220cc) should be added if the fork has been disassembled.

CHECKING YOUR OIL

There isn't a sight glass on forks so you have to determine if the fork is behaving correctly to guess what is going on with the fork oil.

If there is visible leaking oil, then you need to get the problem solved.

If the fork travels down and feels fine, but flies up, uncontrolled during extension, there may be a loss of fork oil.

CHANGING YOUR OIL

▶ **See Figures 94 thru 103**

1. Most every bike has drain plugs fitted near the bottom of each fork slider. To remove the old oil, take out the drain plug once you have placed a reasonably sized container beneath it.

Fig. 94 Remove the drain plugs at the bottom of the forks. Do not confuse them with the axle pinch bolts

Fig. 95 The drain plugs will usually have a crush washer under them to seal the joint

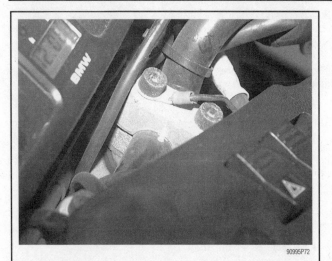

Fig. 96 Dismounting the handlebars and pulling them forward will usually gain you enough room to work on the fork fillers

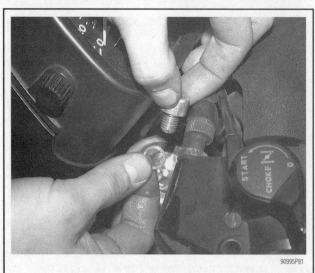

Fig. 99 The fill plug may have a crush washer to seal it

Fig. 97 Some forks will have a cover over the fill plugs. This one just pried up for removal

Fig. 100 To add fluid through this hole, you will need a small diameter tube. Clean the area before filling

Fig. 98 If needed, hold the top still while removing the fill plug

Fig. 101 This fork required a funnel with a tube attached to get the fluid into the fill port

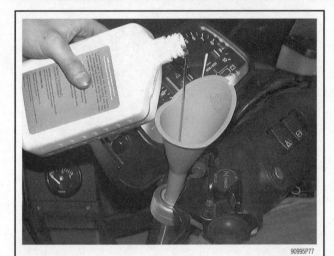

Fig. 102 Some fill holes for the forks will be big enough so you can just use a funnel

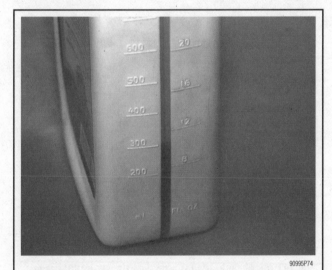

Fig. 103 Before adding the fluid, premeasure it

2. On some models, removal of the drain plug will allow the oil to come out. On others, however, it will be necessary to pump the slider up and down to force out the oil. The easiest way to do this is by applying the front brake and pushing the bike forward (off the stands). Pressure may force the oil stream out several inches, so position the container accordingly. Pump the forks until oil stops coming out. Turn the forks all the way to the right to completely drain the right fork leg, and to the left for the left leg. Check the condition of the drain plug gasket, if applicable, then refit the plug and tighten securely.

3. Check the condition of the drained oil. If oil changes have been carried out reasonably close to the recommended schedule, the oil should be free of dirt, water, etc. If water has been present for some time, the oil may have a foamy consistency and may be tinged green in color for some kinds of oil. Water or dirt in the fork oil may indicate defective fork gaiters or dust covers which have allowed such matter to get to the slider seals and from there into the oil supply. Any gaiters with tears or other damage should be replaced. Dust seals are found on many forks with internal springs. These are attached to the slider just above the oil seals. These dust seals are necessary to keep dirt and water away from the slider oil seals, and they should be replaced if they are cracked, ripped, or dry-rotted. Impurities in the oil can also be due to bad fork slider oil seals.

4. To add oil to the forks, first put the machine on the center stand or otherwise support the front wheel off the ground. This is a safety measure since removing the filler caps on some forks will release the fork spring, causing the forks to collapse and possibly toppling the machine. This is not true of all forks, and on some it may be necessary to compress the forks to free the filler cap from fork body.

✴✴ CAUTION

On models that don't have a separate fill cap and the entire fork cap has to be removed, be aware that the fork spring will try to launch the cap off the bike. Wear eye protection or maybe your full face helmet!

➡️**If you are not sure of the exact procedure, have the front wheel off the ground when the filler cap is removed.**

5. Remove one cap, fill the fork leg with the correct amount of oil, and reinstall the cap before removing the other one. If you have the kind of fork which may collapse in the way explained previously, leaving one filler cap in place at all times will serve to keep the forks extended during the oil change procedure.

6. Fork oil should be measured out carefully, and one way to do this is with a plastic baby bottle which is calibrated in "cc" or ounces. It will be necessary to cut off the end of the nipple to allow the oil to flow freely. On some machines, you can get away with a simple measuring cup, while on others, the close proximity of handlebars, instruments, etc., will make spillage likely.

7. After adding oil, be sure to tighten the filler caps very securely. Check for seepage around the slider oil seals after several miles of operation. Oil leakage indicates that the seals should be replaced.

SEAL REPLACEMENT

▶ **See Figure 104**

1. Fork slider oil seals may simply wear out over a period of time and then begin to leak. Some causes of rapid wear of the seal lips include damage during installation, dirty, contaminated fork oil, damaged dust seals or fork gaiters, rust, corrosion, or scratches on the fork tube, a bent fork tube, or rubber-damaging oil in the forks. Seals may also leak if the forks are over-filled.

2. On most motorcycles, the seals can be replaced simply by removing the fork sliders. It is necessary to remove the front wheel, fender, brake caliper (if applicable), etc. Refer to a shop manual for removal procedures. These will of course vary depending on the make and model of the machine.

Fig. 104 Replacing the fork seals requires disassembly of the forks to get at them

3. The slider seals are pressed into the top of the fork sliders on most bikes, although on a few, the seals may be in the circular nut threaded onto the top of the slider. Seals must be pried out with a suitable lever. Seals should always be replaced once the slider is removed from the fork tube.

4. Condition of the seals cannot be determined from examination of the lips. When prying out the seals, be sure to protect the upper lip of the fork slider. This can be accomplished by placing a soft metal pad beneath your lever. Also take care that the end of the lever does not score the inner wall of the slider.

5. Install new seals by pressing them straight into the slider. Often, one of the old seals can be used, placing it on top of the new seal and tapping around the edges to force the new seal into place. Alternately, a suitably sized socket can be placed over the seal to use as a drift.

6. Always coat the lips of seals with the type of oil you are going to put in the forks.

Wheel Bearings

REPACKING THE BEARINGS

▶ **See Figures 105 thru 112**

The following procedures are for non-sealed bearings. Sealed bearings require no maintenance. Check in your owners or shop manual for the type installed in your bike.

Most motorcycle wheels are fitted with ball bearings, although a few use roller or tapered roller bearings. Each wheel typically has two bearings which in most cases are press-fit into the hub and are separated by a spacer tube. Some wheels use threaded retainers or perhaps circlips to secure one or both bearings. Grease seals are usually fitted to both sides of the hub to keep the bearing grease in and dirt and moisture out.

Some-larger bikes also have a "wheel bearing" in the rear wheel sprocket assembly for added rigidity. Wheel bearings can usually be inspected on the bike simply by grasping either side of the tire and checking for play. There should be none. If play is evident, the bearings may be worn and replacement will be in order. Bearings are always replaced in pairs.

Removal of the bearings is obviously necessary for replacement and also for repacking which should be carried out in accordance with the periodic maintenance schedule for your motorcycle.

➡ **You should note that the removal process may ruin ball bearings because they are press-fit in the hub and must be driven out.. This is especially true on high-mileage machines. In addition, grease seals should always be replaced with new ones if removed. Tapered bearings do not require driving out**

Fig. 106 Support the bike with jack stands or something to help keep the bike stable while lifted

Fig. 107 The wheel bearing is what the axle passes through in the wheel

Fig. 105 If your bike doesn't have a centerstand (this bike doesn't have one due to cost cutting), using a bike lift will be necessary

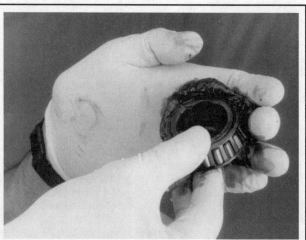
Fig. 108 Packing bearings can be fun and messy all at the same time

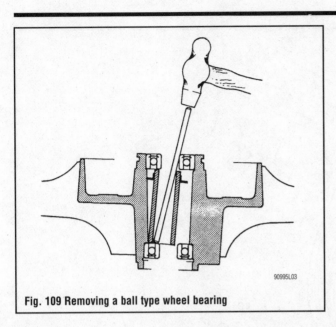

Fig. 109 Removing a ball type wheel bearing

1. Remove the wheel from the motorcycle.
2. Remove any dust covers, spacers, etc. from either side of the hub. Make a note of the location and order of all the removed parts.
3. Pry out the grease seals, if accessible. Machines with tapered-roller bearings use the seals to hold the bearings, and once the seals are removed, the bearings will come out.
4. Remove any retainers or circlips from the hub. Note that some threaded retainers are left-hand thread. Be cognizant of situations such as this, and check your shop manual to be sure.
5. Wheel bearings are driven out with a drift in most cases. It is sometimes helpful to heat the hub very gently to facilitate removal. Heating the hub with a rag soaked in boiling water is one way to due this. Some manufacturers specify that the hub should not be heated to more than 212°F (100°C).
6. The best way to remove wheel bearings is to tap around the outer race with a punch and hammer. This is not possible in most cases, however. If the axle is suitable, it can be inserted into the bearings. A sharp blow on one side of the axle may then be used to dislodge the bearing on the opposite side. It is possible that the bearing will not even look like it moved, but check anyway. In some instances a slight movement is all that is necessary, and the bearings will be free. If this is not possible, the bear-

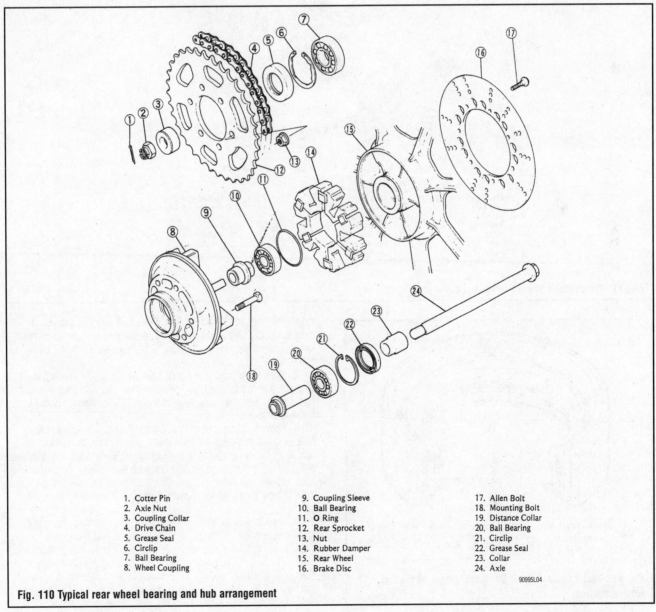

1. Cotter Pin	9. Coupling Sleeve	17. Allen Bolt
2. Axle Nut	10. Ball Bearing	18. Mounting Bolt
3. Coupling Collar	11. O Ring	19. Distance Collar
4. Drive Chain	12. Rear Sprocket	20. Ball Bearing
5. Grease Seal	13. Nut	21. Circlip
6. Circlip	14. Rubber Damper	22. Grease Seal
7. Ball Bearing	15. Rear Wheel	23. Collar
8. Wheel Coupling	16. Brake Disc	24. Axle

Fig. 110 Typical rear wheel bearing and hub arrangement

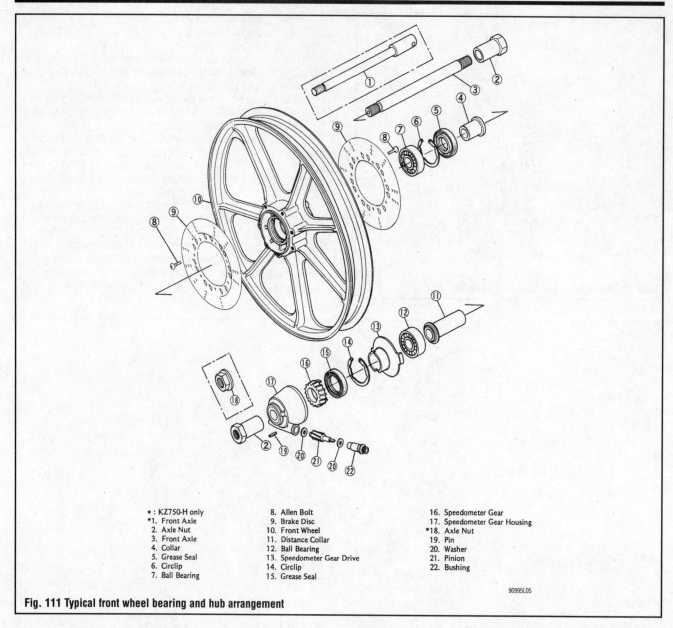

* : KZ750-H only	8. Allen Bolt	16. Speedometer Gear
*1. Front Axle	9. Brake Disc	17. Speedometer Gear Housing
2. Axle Nut	10. Front Wheel	*18. Axle Nut
3. Front Axle	11. Distance Collar	19. Pin
4. Collar	12. Ball Bearing	20. Washer
5. Grease Seal	13. Speedometer Gear Drive	21. Pinion
6. Circlip	14. Circlip	22. Bushing
7. Ball Bearing	15. Grease Seal	

90995L05

Fig. 111 Typical front wheel bearing and hub arrangement

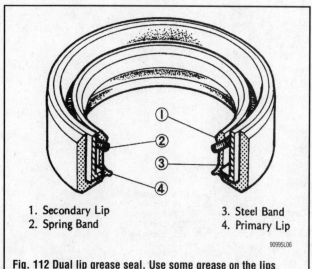

1. Secondary Lip
2. Spring Band
3. Steel Band
4. Primary Lip

90995L06

Fig. 112 Dual lip grease seal. Use some grease on the lips when installing

ing can be removed by reaching through the hub with a long punch. Try to move the spacer tube to one side so that ample purchase can be obtained. Tap the bearing out evenly, alternating your blows around the circumference of the race.

7. Once one bearing is removed, you can take out the spacer tube. If this is only a routine repacking, leave the other bearing in place if possible. As noted, removal risks ruining the bearings, and repacking is possible with one removed.

8. Remove old grease from the hub and the bearings with a solvent. After the bearing is clean, lubricate it with oil and check for smooth rotation. Any roughness, binding or clicking sounds which appear indicate that both bearings should be replaced. Place each bearing on a flat surface and hold the outer race firmly in place. Attempt to move the inner race back and forth. Little or no movement should be noted, or a worn bearing is indicated.

9. Repack bearings with a good grade of wheel bearing grease of the type recommended for your motorcycle. Grease should be pressed into the bearing until it is full. Place a quantity of grease into the hub as well.

10. Bearings should be installed by tapping them into place using a bearing driver tool or properly sized socket. Drive the bearing in squarely and evenly. Do not allow the bearing to become cocked while entering the hub. Tap on the outer bearing race only. Bearings which have one side

sealed are always installed with the sealed side facing out. If a retainer or circlip is fitted to one side of the hub, the bearing on that side should be installed first. After the bearing is installed, fit the retainer or circlip. This will ensure proper location of the bearing to ease fitting the other one.

11. Install new grease seals.
12. Install the dust covers, spacers, etc. in their original locations.
13. Install the wheel and check for play.

Swing Arm

INSPECTION AND MAINTENANCE

◆ **See Figures 113 thru 119**

Except on shaft-drive motorcycle, swing arms are very simple components and usually free of trouble. Swing arms are usually attached to the frame by means of a heavy shaft which may ride in bushings or needle bearings. Wear to these bushings is the prime trouble spot of the swing arm.

To check your swing arm, proceed as follows:

1. Remove the rear wheel, shock absorbers, and belt or chain guard (as applicable).

Fig. 115 Just to be different (and to make a great suspension) BMW hung a swing arm on the front of the bike too. This is their "Telelever" front suspension

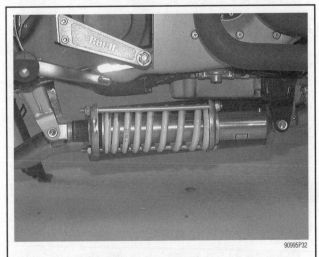
Fig. 113 Some swingarms have the shocks attached via a linkage and aren't connected directly

Fig. 116 This is the lubricating point for the swing arm bushing on my BMW

Fig. 114 Other swingarms have the shock connected directly

Fig. 117 This spiffy greasegun is the BMW factory approved tool to grease the swingarm bushings. It has a tapered point and doesn't use a more standard zerk fitting

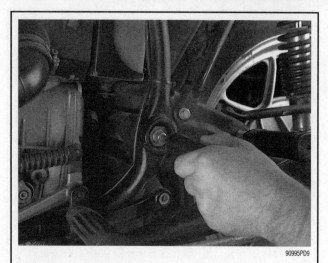

Fig. 118 A few pushes of grease is enough to displace the old, used grease and replenish it with new

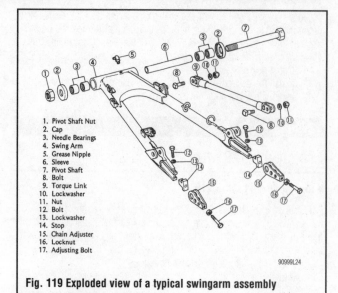

1. Pivot Shaft Nut
2. Cap
3. Needle Bearings
4. Swing Arm
5. Grease Nipple
6. Sleeve
7. Pivot Shaft
8. Bolt
9. Torque Link
10. Lockwasher
11. Nut
12. Bolt
13. Lockwasher
14. Stop
15. Chain Adjuster
16. Locknut
17. Adjusting Bolt

Fig. 119 Exploded view of a typical swingarm assembly

2. On a twin shock bike, measure the distance between the top and bottom shock absorber mounts on both sides. The two measurements must be identical, or the swing arm will have to be replaced.

3. Check that the rear wheel mounting plates are parallel.

4. Grasp the legs of the swing arm and attempt to move it from side-to-side. Any noticeable side-play will indicate that the swing arm bushings need replacement

5. The swing arm is most likely to be damaged if the machine is operated for any length of time with a broken or otherwise defective shock absorber.

6. Bushings are usually press-fit in swing arms, and, if worn, they should be driven out and replaced with new ones. Do not remove pressed-in bushings unless you intend to replace them, since they will be ruined by the removal process

7. When disassembling a swing arm bushing, make careful note of how each component is installed as placement of shims, bushings, sleeves, etc., is critical. Bushings should be lubricated according to manufacturer's instructions. Most have a grease fitting on the swing arm shaft to facilitate the operation, while others must be lubricated by hand. After a rebuilt swing arm is installed, tighten the shaft nut (if fitted) to the properly torque, and check for free movement of the swing arm. Movement should be relatively free (not loose) and noiseless.

8. New bushings should be checked carefully before installation. Be sure they are the correct ones for your machine, and that any lubrication holes or grooves which are supposed to be there are there.

ELECTRICAL SYSTEM MAINTENANCE

Battery

▶ See Figures 120, 121 and 122

The battery is the heart of the motorcycle in many ways. Face it, without a battery we would all be stomping away at kickstarters thinking that there had to be a better way! The battery gets the bike going in the morning, acts a mediator for the electrical system satisfying the demands of all the components on the bike and it does it with very little demands on the operator of the bike!

The battery is like a pet goldfish; It needs little to keep it alive, but it has a limited life. Feed it properly and keep its environment clean and it will live as long as it can. Neglect or abuse it and you will find it belly up at the most inopportune times.

Fig. 120 The Battery Tender® allows you to keep the battery plugged in without fear of overcharging

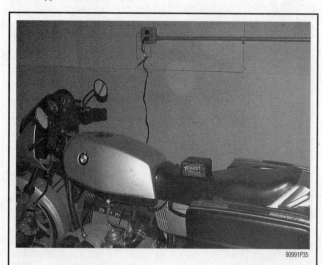

Fig. 121 By keeping the battery charged, even short rides won't discharge it

Fig. 122 A quick connect allows easy set up and no hassles getting to the battery terminals

CHECKING FLUID LEVEL

▶ See Figures 123 thru 128

Most batteries, up until recently have been classified as "wet cells" meaning that the electrolyte in the unit has been in liquid form and the level of fluid had to be topped off at times. All motorcycle type batteries uses two dissimilar materials with some type of electrolyte between them. Wet cell batteries that we need to check are what most of us are used to, but recent advances have brought sealed batteries to the motorcycle world. As motorcycles get more advanced and complicated, the batteries are getting buried deeper and deeper in the depths of the bike. Sealed batteries make routine electrolyte checking unnecessary.

Standard batteries can have some of the electrolytes water portion go away with time. We need to add water back to the battery to bring the level back up to the proper point.

All batteries have some type of electrolyte in them, but sealed batteries recycle the fluid in them and don't lose it to the atmosphere as a standard battery would. As a result, you do not need to check the fluid level in a sealed battery.

Standard batteries will have a level range marked on the case. There will be a high and low level mark. They may have the words "High" and "Low"

Fig. 124 The electrolyte level can be checked by looking at the side of most batteries

Fig. 125 Looky here! A sealed battery that requires no electrolyte maintenance

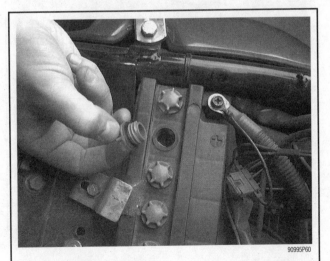

Fig. 123 This battery has standard screw caps that allow access to the electrolyte for filling and level checking

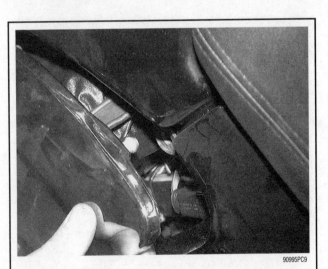

Fig. 126 On this bike, the side cover needs to be removed to access the battery

Fig. 127 Once the side cover is removed, we see the side of the battery to check the electrolyte level, but no visible means to get it out!

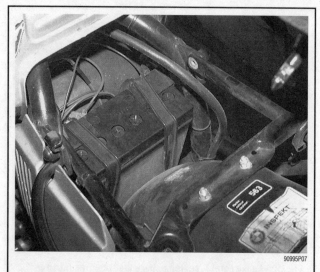

Fig. 128 From this position the battery caps can be reached

marked on them or just be a set of parallel lines. If there are no lines, there will be a level tab in the inside of the filler hole.

1. The level of the electrolyte must be maintained between the lines or up to the level tab. Check in all six cells and not just an end one. Some bikes will require that a side panel be removed or something else be moved to see all six cells.

2. If the fluid needs to be topped off, gain clear access to the top of the battery and clean the top with a clean rag to remove any dirt.

3. Remove the cell cap and use a small funnel to add distilled water to the cell. Bring the level up to the mark. Do not use battery acid or the balance of the electrolyte will be effected. Fill only to the mark; Do not over-fill.

➡Only pure, distilled water should be used as regular water contains minerals and chemicals which can contaminate the battery.

4. Do this to all the cells that need it and replace the caps tightly.

TESTING THE BATTERY

Batteries typically test themselves by failing on us! To prevent this from happening, we can test the electrolyte and voltage to give us an idea about what is happening inside the battery.

1. With the motorcycle not running, the battery voltage should be 12.6 volts minimum (12 volt system) or 6.3 volts (6 volt system). If the voltage is lower than this, charge the battery and let sit off the charger for 3 or 4 hours. Recheck the voltage. If the voltage is still low, the battery is bad. If the battery holds the voltage, look for problems with the bikes charging system

2. If the battery allows for individual cells to be checked (rare nowadays), each cell should read a minimum of 2.1 volts. If nothing else, all the cells should read about the same. If one is lower than the rest, replace the battery. In all honesty, most batteries today don't allow this kind of testing, but I had to add it for the antique crowd!

3. Remove the caps to the battery and test the electrolyte with a hydrometer. The hydrometer will indicate the state of charge in each cell by measuring the specific gravity of the electrolyte. Read the instructions that came with the hydrometer to learn how to interpret the scale on the tool. Some have floating balls and others have pointers. All the cells should have similar readings otherwise you will need to replace the battery due to a dead cell.

CLEANING THE BATTERY

▶ **See Figures 129, 130, 131 and 132**

After a hard ride, I'm sure you like to get cleaned up and brushed off. So does your battery! OK, so you don't have to do it after every ride, but cleaning your battery and connections needs to be on your list of scheduled maintenance items.

1. Remove the battery and clean the outer casing with a solution of baking soda and water. Baking soda will neutralize acid. Make sure the caps are on good and tight!

2. Clean the battery connections and terminals with the same baking soda and water solution. Inspect the cables for frayed ends and corroded wires.

3. Still using the solution, clean the battery tray. Inspect the tray for damage and corrosion. If the tray is rusty, consider cleaning it and

Fig. 129 After pulling off the seat, the battery terminals lay exposed for checking and cleaning

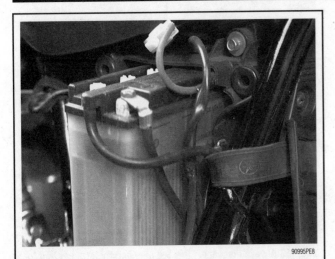

Fig. 130 This bike requires you to pull off a side panel and then slide the battery out to get at it

Fig. 131 Look what may be awaiting you under your battery!

Fig. 132 Clean and rinse the battery tray to get rid of the corrosion

repainting it. If the corrosion isn't fixed, the battery tray will not live a long life.

4. Install the battery and use some terminal protection gel on the connections. You can buy this at any auto parts place and it will help keep the white powder from attacking for a while.

SELECTING A REPLACEMENT

♦ **See Figures 133 thru 141**

Since a dead battery can take all the fun out of riding, you want to use a good quality battery in your bike at all times. Batteries for my bike are expensive, but I have averaged a life span of 4 years on one and that lowers the yearly price to livable levels.

Use a high quality battery. You can't go wrong with the factory supplied battery, but they tend to be expensive. You can go with the aftermarket, but find out from your riding pals what brands they have had good luck with. Check warrantees and where you can get replacements if needed. A cheap battery with a good warrantee doesn't do you any good if you can only get a replacement at one store in the entire country.

Find the proper sized battery both physically and powerwise. The battery needs to fit well in the stock battery tray and to be held by the battery hold

Fig. 133 Sealed batteries first appeared as original equipment on some bikes but are now available as replacement units for other bikes

Fig. 134 To gain access to the battery on this bike, you need to remove the under seat storage . . .

Fig. 135 . . . and the side covers

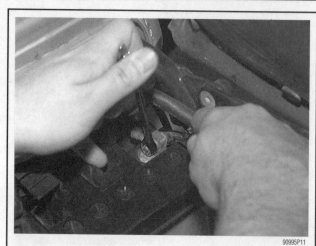

Fig. 138 Always disconnect the negative battery terminal first to avoid doing unintended arc-welding of the positive terminal to the frame

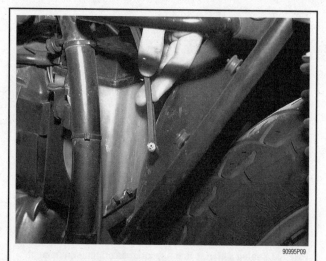

Fig. 136 These rubber straps hold the battery down and must be installed when reassembling

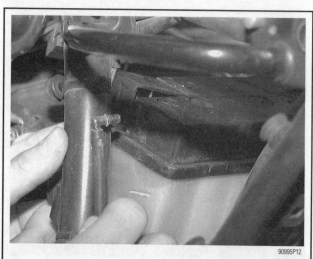

Fig. 139 Remove the vent tube before pulling the battery out if it will interfere

Fig. 137 Inspect the hold downs when removed. These are heading towards the end of their lives

Fig. 140 The battery on this bikes pulls out from the top, but others may slide out the side

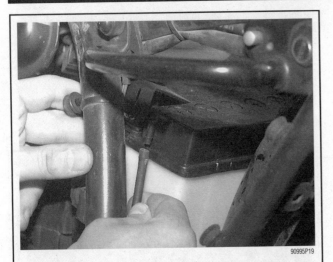

Fig. 141 After installing the new battery, make sure you connect the vent tube or corroded frame tubes will result

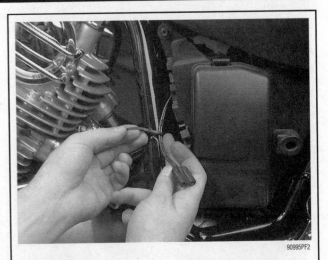

Fig. 143 To make charging easier, a permanent plug can be attached to the battery for the charger to be plugged into

downs, plus have the terminals match. The battery needs to have at least the electrical capacity of the original. Most motorcycle batteries are rated in amp hours. This number will be printed on the case of the battery or in the literature that came with the battery.

With good choices made you will have a battery that will help get you and your bike on the road every time. Choose poorly and it will be a push start for you!

CHARGERS

▶ See Figures 142 and 143

There will be a time in your bike's life that it will need to have some extra help in the form of a battery charger. When looking for a charger for your car, almost any will do, but a motorcycle is a different animal. A motorcycle battery is quite a bit smaller than a car battery and its needs are different.

If you use a car battery charger on a motorcycle battery, you can boil out all the electrolyte and kill it. The charging requirements for the motorcycle battery are much lower and are in the range of 2 amps or less. If you have no choice and have to use a car battery, choose the lowest power range (typically 2 amps) and check the battery often during the charge. If it is getting hot or bubbling excessively, remove it from the charger.

The best bet for charging a motorcycle battery is using a motorcycle battery charger (like, duh). Probably the most convenient is a smart charger such as the Deltran Battery Tender®. This type of charger will provide a low charging rate (say 1.25 amps) until the battery is completely charged and then switch to a safe storage rate. This storage rate will keep the battery at peak condition indefinitely and not harm the battery. I keep my bike on one when it isn't being ridden and I know it will be ready for me even if I have ridden in a few days or weeks.

Be careful of low priced battery chargers with questionable monitoring circuits. They may not have the smarts to keep your battery from overcharging and boiling off. If you chose a low priced unit, keep an eye on the battery to make sure it is doing OK and not getting hot or off gassing too much.

Some motorcycle battery chargers come with a harness that you can connect directly to you battery and plug in the charger instead of having to use big clips on the terminals. Some chargers will have a plug that will match the accessory power port on the bike. BMW motorcycles have this type of port and so do many touring bikes. If your bike doesn't have a power port, it is easy to attach one.

JUMP STARTING

Let us say right from the beginning that jump starting your bike is something we think that you will want to stay away from. Your bikes battery and charging system can be damaged during a jump. It is safer to charge the battery and go from there.

If you get stuck somewhere and you have to jump your bike, try to connect the batteries of the two vehicles and just let the good battery charge the bad one, disconnect them and then try starting the bike. If that doesn't work, connect the batteries again, but don't run the engine of the vehicle with the good battery. Try starting the bike.

The problem with using a car to jump a bike is that a car battery can provide enough electrical energy to weld the entire wiring harness of the bike to itself in a flash if there is a short somewhere. Use thin gauge wire (12 or 14 gauge) to make the jumper cables to limit the amount of current that can be passed during the starting. This will help protect your bike.

Fig. 142 Getting to this terminal to charge the battery can be a problem since it is in close quarters with a frame tube and the protective cover right there

Light Bulb Replacement

Visibility is of paramount importance to the motorcyclist. If they can't see you, then you are in deep trouble. It is bad enough that most drivers don't really look where they are going, but we don't need to compound the problem with burned out lights and turn signals. Working lights aren't just a good idea, they're the law! (Sorry, I couldn't resist!)

TURN SIGNALS, RUNNING LIGHTS AND BRAKE LIGHTS

Bulb Replacement

▶ **See Figures 144, 145 and 146**

Most turn signal bulbs are held in the reflectors under the lens and simply removing the lens gains you access to the bulb. The lens may be held on by a screw or two or possibly the lens just pries off. Sometimes the entire housing will have to be removed from the bike and disassembled to get at the bulb. I have seen housings held by screws, bolts or thumbscrews.

1. Remove the lens or housing. The mounting screws can be hidden behind a piece of bodywork or buried in a tailhousing. Look for screws, bolts or thumbscrews that will need to be removed.

2. Remove the bulb from the socket.

3. Check the socket for corrosion or damage. Light corrosion can be removed by cleaning with a contact cleaner available at auto parts stores

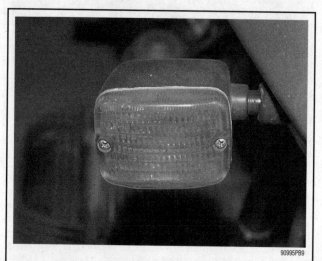

Fig. 144 The lens of this light is held by two screws and exposes the bulb once removed

90995PB9

Fig. 145 The entire light housing lens removes with two screws on this bike

90995PC0

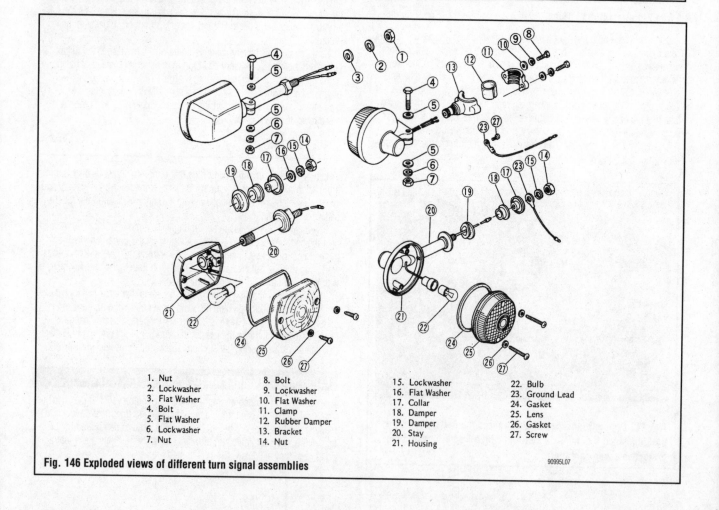

1. Nut	8. Bolt	15. Lockwasher	22. Bulb
2. Lockwasher	9. Lockwasher	16. Flat Washer	23. Ground Lead
3. Flat Washer	10. Flat Washer	17. Collar	24. Gasket
4. Bolt	11. Clamp	18. Damper	25. Lens
5. Flat Washer	12. Rubber Damper	19. Damper	26. Gasket
6. Lockwasher	13. Bracket	20. Stay	27. Screw
7. Nut	14. Nut	21. Housing	

Fig. 146 Exploded views of different turn signal assemblies

90995L07

or electronics stores. Heavy corrosion may require replacement of the socket or maybe the entire housing if the socket isn't available separately.

4. Clean the interior of the reflector, removing the dust and dirt that accumulates there.

5. Clean the lens with soapy water and dry before installation.

6. Replace the bulb with a proper part. Be careful that you install the proper wattage and size bulb, otherwise the light may not work correctly or could damage the socket and lens. You may want to use a dab of dielectric grease to protect the socket from corrosion.

7. Replace the lens and housing. Check the bulb for proper operation.

Stalk Replacement

▶ **See Figure 147**

Whoosh! Bamm! Crack! DAMN!!!! There goes another turn signal stalk!

If it hasn't happened to you, it probably will at some point. Turn signal stalks are often the first thing to hit the ground when a bike falls over or something brushes too close to it. Most stalks are designed to crack off fairly easily. This is so the fairing and body work isn't hurt too badly, but it really seems like the parts manufactures do it to make even more money with the ease that they snap.

Thankfully most stalks are easy to replace and the job doesn't take too long. For the more popular bikes aftermarket stalks are available at a price much lower than the manufacturers part. There are even generic, yet stylish, stalks that the price for a pair may be less than a single factory part. This may be a good choice if the factory part is too expensive or no longer available.

1. Most stalks are held on the backside of the mounting base with a screw or bolt that the wire goes through. Gain access to the back of the mounting point.

2. If the electrical connection is made by a plug, disconnect the plug and set aside. If there isn't a plug, check the new stalk and see where the supplied wire ends. Cut the current wire at this point so you can splice the wire together.

3. Dismount the old stalk and put the new one in place.

4. Connect the wires if a plug is used. If the wires need to be spliced, use a good quality butt splice and a chunk of heat shrink tubing or solder the wires and protect with heat shrink tubing.

5. Put a bulb into the stalk and check for proper operation of the lights.

Fig. 147 This stalk is rubber mounted and is easily replaced if need be

HEADLIGHTS

▶ **See Figures 148, 149 and 150**

Headlights come in two general camps: florescent and acetylene gas. Just kidding. They are either a sealed beam unit such as came on your grandfather '63 Chevy or a reflector/bulb combination. The latter is the more popular technology as it provides better lighting.

Sealed beam bulbs get replaced as a unit, reflector and all. Reflector/bulb type lamps just need the bulb to be replaced. Most sealed beams can be replaced by an H4 type reflector/bulb lamp unit from the aftermarket. These units will provide superior lighting and replaceable bulbs with a choice of wattage's.

The headlight can be held by a retaining ring or in a nacelle or maybe it will be built into the fairing. There are about as many different mounting schemes as there are motorcycles.

1. If the headlight is held by a retaining ring, remove the ring and pull the lamp forward.

2. If the lamp is built into the fairing, gain access to the back of the lamp by whatever means is needed. This may include removing body work or an access panel built just for that purpose.

Fig. 148 A single screw holds the trim ring on this headlight

Fig. 149 To access this headlight, the upper portion of the fairing needs to be removed

3. If the lamp is held in a nacelle, you may have to remove the nacelle to access the wiring and plug for the lamp.

4. Disconnect the plug from the back of the bulb.

5. If the lamp is a sealed beam unit, remove the lamp. If the lamp is a separate bulb, pull of the rubber cover and unclip the retainer. Pull the bulb out of the housing.

6. Replace the sealed beam with a new bulb and plug in the connector.

Install the retaining ring. If you are replacing just a bulb, be sure not to touch the new bulb with your skin or the life will be severely reduced. If the bulb was touched, clean with alcohol and a lint-free wipe. Install the retainer and rubber cover.

7. Install any removed parts and check the aim of the light. Adjust if needed.

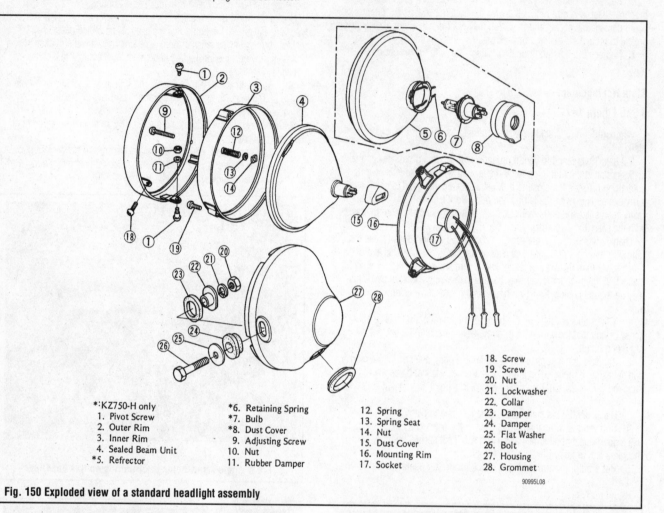

*:KZ750-H only
1. Pivot Screw
2. Outer Rim
3. Inner Rim
4. Sealed Beam Unit
*5. Refrector

*6. Retaining Spring
*7. Bulb
*8. Dust Cover
9. Adjusting Screw
10. Nut
11. Rubber Damper

12. Spring
13. Spring Seat
14. Nut
15. Dust Cover
16. Mounting Rim
17. Socket

18. Screw
19. Screw
20. Nut
21. Lockwasher
22. Collar
23. Damper
24. Damper
25. Flat Washer
26. Bolt
27. Housing
28. Grommet

90995L08

Fig. 150 Exploded view of a standard headlight assembly

90995PG5

Maintaining a shop full of bikes isn't as daunting as a task as it may seem. Just take your time and you will be all set to ride

90995P18

Building the shop, on the other hand can, be a daunting task!

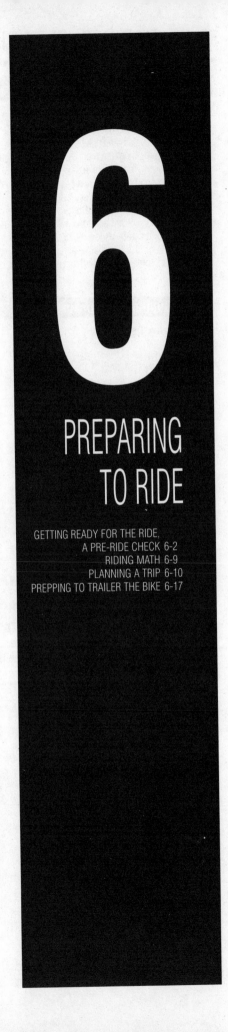

6

PREPARING
TO RIDE

GETTING READY FOR THE RIDE, A PRE-RIDE CHECK

It would be great if we could just jump on our bikes, hit the button and ride off into the sunset, but unfortunately, it just doesn't (or shouldn't) work that way. Motorcycles aren't like cars where if something goes wrong, you just coast to the side of the road and get on with your life. The results can be a bit more extreme on a bike. If a tire goes down, you don't just slap on the spare and head to the nearest gas station. If the bike stops running in the middle of a thunderstorm, you can't just turn up the radio and wait for a dry spell (unless you are on a Goldwing, of course!)

With a little bit of care and time, we can make our riding experience as pleasurable as it can be. A few moments before each ride is all that is necessary to help reduce the chance of running into a bad situation. It isn't hard and with some practice and discipline, it becomes an integral part of the riding experience.

What Should I Be Looking For?

▶ See Figures 1 and 2

If you keep up on your everyday maintenance, the pre-ride check should be short and sweet. In general, the check includes items which effect safety and driveability. You will look at items like your tires, oil level, coolant

level, brake pads, lights and controls. Depending on the bike, the actual items may change as appropriate (check your owners manual), but use the following list as a guide:

TIRES

▶ See Figures 3 thru 13

Check the tire pressure and the condition of the wheel/tire combination. If the tire pressure is not correct, adjust it to specification. Without the proper tire pressure, the bike can become unstable or the tire may be damaged. By checking the pressure every time you ride, you can see trends; If the pressure stays mostly even every time you check it and then one day it is way down, you will be alerted that another problem may exist, like a puncture or bad tube. While down on your knees checking the pressure, give the wheels a spin and look for damage to the tire and rim. You might spot a nail the has just stuck into the tread and be able to remove it before the tire goes down in the middle of no where. Tap on the spokes if your wheels have them. They should make a nice ringing sound. If you find one that doesn't, it means that the spoke is loose and needs to be tightened.

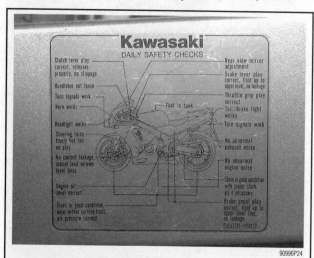

Fig. 1 This bike makes it very clear what needs to be checked every day

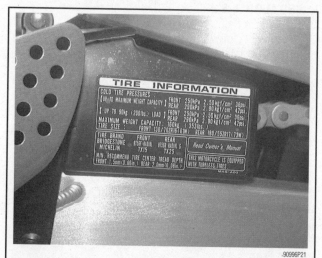

Fig. 3 Almost every bike will have a sticker on it with the proper tire pressures listed

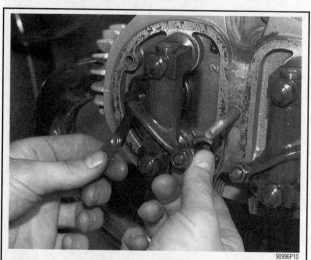

Fig. 2 If you keep up on your maintenance, your needs on the road will be reduced

Fig. 4 Keep on top of your tire pressures or bad things can happen like . . .

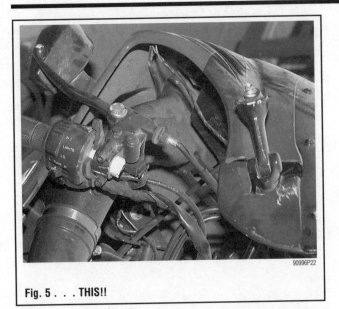

Fig. 5 . . . THIS!!

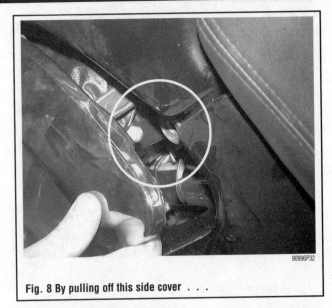

Fig. 8 By pulling off this side cover . . .

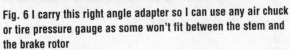

Fig. 6 I carry this right angle adapter so I can use any air chuck or tire pressure gauge as some won't fit between the stem and the brake rotor

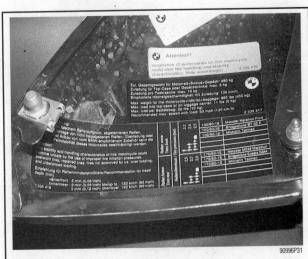

Fig. 9 . . . you can expose the sticker which tells you almost anything you need to know about this bike

Fig. 7 Know what your tire pressures should be

Fig. 10 Playing xylophone on the spokes can tell you if any are loose

Fig. 11 Look at the treads of the rear and . . .

Fig. 12 . . . front tires

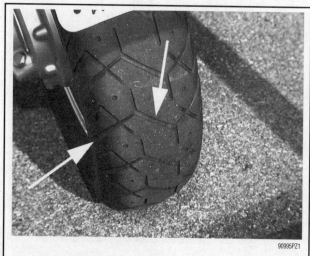

Fig. 13 This tire is squared off. The tread on the outside is deeper than in the center

OIL LEVEL

♦ **See Figures 14 thru 19**

An engine of any type uses oil to lubricate and cool itself. Most bikes provide some type of quick check of the oil level, such as a dipstick or sight glass. Read your owners manual to help decide how the level is to be read. Some bikes need to be held straight up and down for the level to be correct and others should be on the side stand. If the bike has a dipstick, typically the level is read when it isn't pushed or screwed all the way it. For example: On my BMW, you unscrew the dipstick, wipe it down and then put it back into the engine with out rethreading it. If you thread it back in before reading it, the level will be incorrect. The notable exception to this rule is Harley-Davidson. They require the dipstick to be pushed in all the way (they always have to be different). Some bikes have a sightglass on the side of the motor. Most of these have to be read while the bike is straight up and down. That is easy if you have a centerstand, but if you don't you will need a helper or some way of holding up the bike while you look into the sight glass.

Fig. 14 Checking the oil can be as simple as a glance at a sight glass

Fig. 15 The oil dipstick is located under the seat on this Buell, but it is easy to remove with this thumbscrew

Fig. 16 This dipstick is just a push fit in the tank

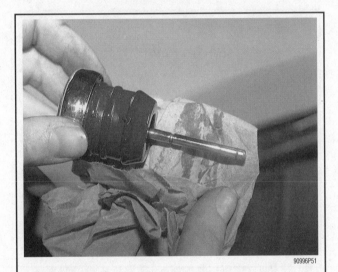

Fig. 17 Make sure the level is in between the lines

Fig. 18 My BMW has the oil dipstick right on the side of the engine

Fig. 19 Most bikes with dipsticks are filled with oil through the dipstick hole

LIGHTS

Check that all your lights work. This includes the running lamps, the headlamp (high and low beams), the turn signals and the brake lights. Make sure the brake lights come on with both the front lever and the foot pedal. I know from experience that you need to check this every time you get on the bike. I had a front brake switch go bad on me in the middle of a ride! That was a bummer since people had no idea I was braking unless I used my rear brake. Good thing I wasn't run over. Turn signals and running lights are the way the other vehicle spot you on the road, so give a glance at them too. It is also worth the time to make sure all your warning lights on the instrument pad light up when you turn on the key because you don't want to find out the hard way that your oil pressure light is burned out!

HORN

Go ahead! Toot your own horn! It's fun and educational! And you don't have to wait until you are in a tunnel to do it!

COOLANT

▶ **See Figure 20**

If your bike is water cooled, take a peek at the coolant level in the reservoir. Coolant has a mysterious way of slowly disappearing over a period of time, so even if you don't have any visible leaks, you may be low. You may also spot a slow leak by having to add coolant on a regular basis even if it doesn't leave any drips on the floor.

BATTERY ELECTROLYTE

Check the battery for the proper level of electrolyte. Some bikes have the battery in plain sight, yet others are buried. If you can check it easily, make it a habit to do so. If it isn't easy to see, make it part of your regular maintenance routine.

BRAKE PADS AND SHOES

▶ **See Figures 21 and 22**

Some bikes have brake pads that are easily seen and can be checked with a glance. Look for enough material left on the pad for your ride. Drum brakes aren't as easy if they don't have wear indicators on the linkage, but if

Fig. 20 This coolant reservoir is filled from under the seat, but can be checked from outside the bike

Fig. 21 The rear drum on this bike has a quick check for brake shoe wear on the lever. The pointer will tell you at a glance if the shoes are in good shape

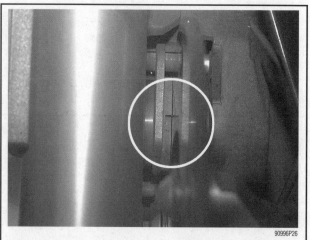

Fig. 22 These pads have wear indicators. They are the indentations in the friction material and the pads need replacement when the indentations are gone

there is an inspection opening, use it! Front brakes are more critical on most bikes due to the weight transfer during braking, but on heavily loaded bikes and touring machines, the rear brakes become more or as important.

CONTROLS, CABLES AND GRIPS

▶ See Figures 23, 24, 25, 26 and 27

It is real bummer to have a throttle or clutch cable snap during a ride. Look at the cable ends for fraying and damage. Look for worn grips and controls in need of lubrication. Check the level of brake fluid in the reservoir and also in the clutch reservoir (if your bike has a hydraulic clutch). Look for worn out foot pegs and foot peg covers. Worn-out covers may allow your foot to slip during braking or shifting. This is mostly an inconvenience, but in the wrong circumstance, it can be come dangerous.

LEAKS

Look over the engine and driveline for obvious leaks. A small leak now may turn into a gusher just as you are entering a turn. It is also a good way to keep a tab on the mechanical condition of the bike. If it has always

Fig. 23 This reservoir cap removes via three screws and pops right off

Fig. 24 Keep the fluid topped off in the reservoir

Fig. 25 The brake fluid level stares back at you from the reservoir. You don't have any choice but to check it!

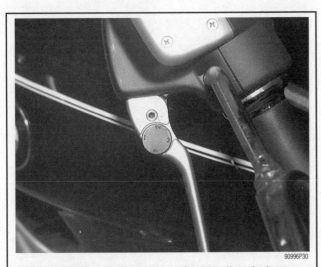

Fig. 26 On some bikes you use this wheel to adjust the lever pull to suit you

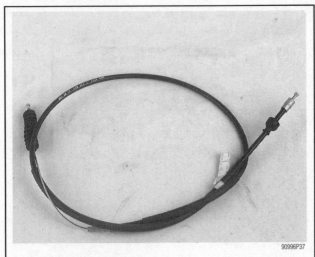

Fig. 27 This spare clutch cable has ridden many miles and has never seen action. I hope to keep it that way

stayed dry and now it has a sheen of oil on the belly of the bike, you have a problem that you need to look into.

SIDE AND CENTERSTANDS

Check that the side and centerstand springs are tight. If the spring is weak or fails, it will allow the stand to drag on the ground, possibly resulting in a fall. Not a good thing! The OTHER author of this book had a 1200 Sportster that refused to keep its side stand in the upright and locked position; This resulted in many long trails of sparks off his bike during left turns. It looked impressive, but didn't do much good for either the bike or the side stand! Even a replacement spring didn't help matters and at that point we discovered a worn pivot pin and frame tab. The pivot pin was an easy replacement job, but the worn tab was something Kev just had to live with (so he bought a new fuel injected Road King as a repair).

EXHAUST SYSTEM

▶ **See Figures 28 and 29**

Inspect the exhaust system for holes and damage. Check that it is securely mounted and that all of its hardware is in place. You don't want that cool carbon fiber canister falling off, do ya?

Fig. 28 This is the rear exhaust hanger of a bike we had as a demo. It wasn't doing its job very well!

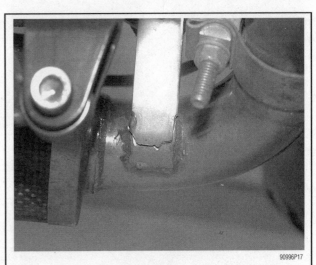

Fig. 29 This is the rear hanger of the same demo bike. Gee, I wonder what was holding this muffler on?

CHAIN AND BELT

▶ See Figure 30

Your bike will have either a chain or belt if it isn't a shaft drive. Take a look at the slack in the chain or belt and make sure that it isn't excessive. Look for kinked portions of the chain and signs of reddish rust on the side links. Look for missing teeth and frayed areas on the drive belt. Check the sprockets for damage while you have your nose down that far.

Fig. 30 This bike will tell you when the chain is too worn, the adjustment will reach a certain point

SETTING THE SUSPENSION TO FIT YOUR RIDE

▶ See Figures 31, 32, 33 and 34

Before heading out, you should set the suspension to fit the riding you are planning to do. You should adjust the spring preload and the damping. In general you will want to crank up the preload for heavier loads like passengers or luggage. In conjunction with that you will most likely want to up the damping rates. If your bike has air suspension, set the pressure in the forks and/or shocks.

Fig. 31 The fork damping is adjustable right at the top of the fork on this bike

Fig. 32 The preload on the rear shock of this bike is adjusted with this spanner wrench provided in the bikes tool kit

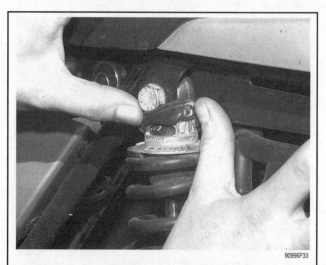

Fig. 33 I owned this bike for a year before I realized that there was a damping adjustment on my rear shocks

Fig. 34 Most air suspensions have a fill valve like this one. Look in your owners manual for locations

AND THE LAST CHECK!

And by the way: Did you check to see if there was fuel in the tank?

90996P12

This guy is all set for an easy ride home. I hope he has enough fuel!

What Do You Really Need To Look For (Lawyers Vs Convenience)?

The short answer is: all of the above, but we all know that sometimes it just isn't possible to do all the items in the list. In this (hopefully rare) case, pick the most important items such as tire pressure, oil level and brake lights. If you have been looking at all the items in the above list on a continuing basis, you should have a good feel for the condition of the bike and skipping an item or two shouldn't hurt once in a while. It still is very much a good idea to always check these items when you get on the bike each day and some of the more basic items (tires, oil, lights, etc.) a few more times during the day during a long ride. Just remember that the check is there for your safety and convenience, not to make life tougher on you. If you miss one item on that list and it causes you a problem, it is all on you. Motorcycling should be fun, but the responsibility of riding is great and you should respect that, just not for you, but for your rider if you have one.

RIDING MATH

When we were deciding who would write this section of the book, it was decided that I was the best person for the job since my degree says "engineering" somewhere on it. Nevermind the fact I took Calculus 1 four times, but it is better than an English major trying to do arithmetic! (Um, Kev wanted me to tell you that he only took Engineering Calculus 1 two times, but then again, we wouldn't expect an English major to know how to count.) You don't have to be a rocket scientist to figure out riding math, and everyone should know the basics. If you ride, you will need to know how far a tank of fuel will get you or how far the ride will be that day. If you are a riding with a group of people all with different bikes and tank capacities, you will need to know how to plan out the days ride without anyone running their tank out.

Mileage Math (Fuel Vs Distance Vs Your Reserve Capacity)

Ok everyone grab your calculator, your owners manual and some gas station receipts. Warm up those button pushing fingers because we have some work to do! We need to figure out how far that tank of fuel is going to take you and in the process, figure out how far each one of those gallons (liters) of fuel is going to keep propelling you forward.

You may be of the camp that just rides until you hit reserve then head for the nearest gas station. It doesn't work that way all the time anymore. Fuel injection is a wonderful thing to have on motorcycles nowadays, but along with the advantages, some disadvantages popped up. One of those is the loss of the petcock reserve switch. Why is this a big deal? Simple, unless you pay attention to your fuel gauge/low level light (and they can be pretty inaccurate), you will run out of fuel and there won't be any reserve to switch to! Also keep in mind that in some parts of the country, the distances between fuel stops is pretty far and you have to plan your riding to correspond to gas availability.

Even if your bike still has a reserve, you should know what type of mileage you can expect from the bike. This comes in handy when planning a ride for the day or when riding with friends with differing ranges of fuel capacity. It can also help point out engine problems if you notice your fuel economy takes a sudden change.

FUEL ECONOMY

Everyone should know how to do this from driving cars or at least 6th grade math, but lets go over figuring fuel economy.

1. Fill up your fuel tank until completely filled and zero the trip odometer or note the mileage of the regular odometer.
2. Ride until you hit reserve or whenever is convenient.
3. If possible completely fill up again at the same pump you filled up at originally since every pump nozzle has a slightly different shut-off point. If not, no big deal.
4. Note the distance traveled on your trip odometer or subtract the original mileage on your regular odometer from the current reading.
5. Divide that distance by the units of fuel you put into the bike. If you use the English measurement system, you will divide miles by gallons of fuel. If you use metric measurements, you will divide kilometers by liters.
6. The resulting number reflects the units of mileage you can travel per a unit of fuel, either miles per gallon or kilometers per liter.
7. Keep track of your results and note what type of riding you did for each tank full. You will see that the days you did some canyon carving tend to have a lower number than the days you just went for a cruise. After a while you will get a feel for the type of fuel economy to expect during a days ride.

RANGE

Figuring out the range of your bike becomes more important as your trip size increases. If you just run out for a 5 mile ride to the local diner, your bikes range won't make much a difference to you, but if you ride all day long, range is very important.

1. Find out the capacity of the fuel tank on your bike. If the bike has reserve capacity in the tank, take note of this number.
2. Multiply the capacity of the tank by the average mileage you figured out in the above section.
3. If your bike has a reserve, do the same calculation for the amount of fuel before hitting reserve. For example: A bike with a 5 gallon tank and a reserve capacity of 1 gallon has a capacity to reserve of 4 gallons (5 minus 1 equals 4).

PLANNING A TRIP

▶ **See Figure 35**

One of the greatest joys I get out of riding is taking medium to long trips with a group of friends. Planning a trip requires more than just a destination. With some preliminary thought and smart planning, an average trip can be turned into a truly great ride to remember with a minimum of hassles.

I don't advocate over-planning a trip. When on a bike, "things" just happen to and your plans, if they were to inflexible, can be ruined. Those "things" can include mechanical problems (Damn! That coil is acting up again!), health problems (Damn! I knew I shouldn't have eaten that onion last night or maybe, it was the tequilla!), lodging problems (Damn! What do you mean you have no more campsites open?) or even detours that you might want to take (Damn! You mean we are only 100 miles from Deals Gap? Let's go!). Leave some slack in your schedule.

Let me tell you a true story about a trip I took with a bunch of guys from work and how good planning and a little luck kept us on the road. It started out before the actual trip began. I was washing my bike and had problems getting it started afterwards. I figured that the old ignition wires were beat and bought a new set for the ride. After installation, I tested them with a fine spray of water only to find out that the wires weren't at fault, but a cracked ignition coil was! It was too late in the day to get a new one, so I told the guys in the group that I couldn't go due to mechanical problems. They convinced me to go along and that we'd all deal with the problem if it came up. Three days into the trip we hit the first rain and sure enough, my bike quit soon after the first few drops came down.

I pulled in the clutch and rolled under the first overpass we had seen on the Blue Ridge Parkway in hundreds of miles. What luck! With a plastic soft drink bottle and a can of WD-40, we were on our way. (We also met a very nice couple on a touring rig who stopped under the same overpass. We talked bikes and met their dog who rode with them on the tank!) When we stopped for the night at a hotel somewhere in Tennessee, I tried to make a more permanent fix and only managed to completely break the coil! I was now stuck. I had no luck locating a new part in the local area and I told the guys that I would have to stay an extra night or two and catch up with them at our final destination. They said "No way!" and we all hit the phones. My local dealer had missed the last next-day air pick up and couldn't get the part out to me on time. With the realization that the West Coast is three hours behind the East Coast, a call to California netted me a brand new coil being next-day aired out to me for delivery in the morning! The time zone difference saved me!

The next day my package was waiting for me at the hotel counter at 9 am and by 10 am the entire group was on the road! We had only wasted an hour total and my bike was running great with the new coil. If I had planned that trip too tightly, the trip would have been thrown way off schedule. Enough time was placed into our daily plans to accommodate such occurrences.

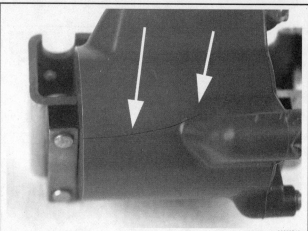

This is the culprit ignition coil that caused my bike to stop running. Had I seen this before the trip, the problem may have been prevented

This is the replacement ignition coil that was installed less than an hour after receiving it next-day air

Planning Your Route

▶ **See Figure 36**

Once you decide where you want to go, now you have to figure out how to get there. Do you want to take back roads? Do you want to hit the highways and make some time? Do you want the most scenic route? Ask yourself these questions and then hit the books.

Find out what travel conditions are like in the areas you will be traveling through. Most states have a travel bureau that will send you all sorts of info just for the asking. They should also be able to fill you in with any major traffic considerations such as highway construction or at least tell you who can help you out.

Travel services such as the American Automobile Association with their trip routing service can be a great way to plan your trip. Even if you don't follow their suggestion down to the last detail, they can be a great way to base your travel plans. Check with motorcycle groups, such as the AMA, for similar services.

A favorite of the computer crowd is the new mapping software available for personal computers and on the Internet. These programs allow you to

Fig. 35 All packed up and ready to go!

Fig. 36 Maps are your friends in times of need and for finding your way around unfamiliar areas

Fig. 37 Bring both a clear and a tinted shield with you whenever you ride

plug in your starting point, your ending point and any additional waypoints you choose. The program will ask you if you want scenery or speed and then chug out a series of maps to guide you on your way. Do be careful as some of the programs can be based on old information and be misleading at times.

Bring an atlas with you! This can be a great way to see what else is around where you are riding and get you to areas that may not be on your pre-planned route. It will also help if after a days riding you find yourself not where you expected to be! A good map is worth its weight in 20W-50 if it gets you out of a jam.

You may want to invest in a tank bag with a map pocket on the top of it. This makes it easy to keep your map handy when you are riding. I don't suggest you read it while on the road, but come to a stop and investigate as much as you want. Some riding clothing manufacturers, such as Aerostitch® make arm and thigh mounted map pockets for people who might find them more handy.

What to Wear—"What you wear when you leave might be a lot different from what you need when you return."

▶ See Figures 37 thru 43

A short story: Wow! What a bright and shiny, beautiful day! I think I will jump on the old scoot and go for a ride. (An hour later and 50 miles away from home) Gee, the sky is getting pretty dark out there and my, it is getting cold. Hey! Is that rain hitting my face? (The sky lets loose with torrents of rain) Dang it! I knew I should have brought my full faced helmet and rain suit! Blah!

What the hero of the previous paragraph didn't take into account is that weather changes! Conditions change! If they didn't, we wouldn't need painfully dull weather forecasters on the local TV stations! Now imagine that you are about to leave on a multiday trip and you can expect that conditions will change. You will have to plan for all contingencies.

THE DAY TRIP

If you are just heading out for the day, you can pretty much know what is going to happen during the day. You will know basically what the weather will be like and you can bring what is appropriate. But even so, I recommend that you always bring a rain suit with you. The rain suit is handy just not for those times of wet stuff falling from the sky, but if you get into an area that is colder that what you were prepared for, it makes a great wind break and extra layer to help keep you warm.

Fig. 38 From heated gloves or waterproof to summer weight, there are gloves to fit all riding needs and you may need more than one set on a ride

Fig. 39 This is my current favorite riding outfit, an Aerostitch® Roadcrafter, with a water resistant finish and pockets galore

Fig. 40 It is hard to beat a good leather jacket to ride in

Fig. 42 Three different choices for riding in the rain: Gore-Tex, one piece rain suit and big rubber bag (no, not the editor on the right, his rain suit)

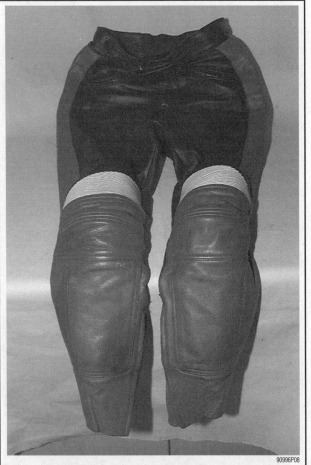

Fig. 41 Leather pants should be worn instead of a pair of jeans. Leather is more skid resistant than cotton and these leathers have been tested!

I also recommend bringing both clear and tinted face shields for your helmet. If you get stuck out later than you expected, there isn't anything more scary than trying to ride in the dark with a dark tinted visor on!

THE WEEKENDER

The weekend trip is about the same as the day trip except you should look at the distance you are traveling. If the distance takes you out the immediate area you are starting in, you may run the risk of not really now what kind of weather is being predicted.

Take the extra visors and the rain suit. You may also want to bring extra gloves and riding apparel. Keep in mind that you have a few days of riding and you need to be comfortable for the entire trip. You can withstand almost anything for one day, but it gets old quickly if you have to ride in unpleasant conditions for two or three days.

Fig. 43 Rainsuits don't take up much room when packed correctly

THE WEEKLONG TRIP AND BEYOND

This is were all the stops get pulled out. Bring the spare visors for the helmet, bring the rainsuit, bring the heated vest. If you have to give up some space in your luggage for that extra tuxedo you wanted to bring so you can have that extra pair of socks and gloves, so be it. It is more important that you be comfortable on the road than where it is you end up.

You will be riding day in and day out, so comfort is the key. I have found that absorbent underclothing designed for athletes is great stuff to wear under leathers as it absorbs and wicks away any sweat that may build up as you ride. I have even found that gel-type bicycling shorts help when I ride motorcycles with stiff seat cushions. If you wear Cordura type riding gear (such as Aerostitch®) with street clothing underneath, make sure the street clothing doesn't bunch up and cause you problems down the road (pardon the pun). A minor irritation today may become unbearably painful two days from now.

Because space is a concern on a long trip, try to find clothing that will be useful in more than one situation. Cordura type clothing, such as Aerostitch®, is mostly waterproof and may negate the need for a rainsuit. I wear a pair of waterproof leather boots that won't soak through in a rain and are comfortable enough to wear walking around in all day so I don't need an extra pair of shoes (I have to admit they look sorta silly when wearing them with shorts, but you get the idea). If you wear a leather jacket, get one that won't look too out of place when you stop for the night and you head to the local diner; the "Boy Racer" type jacket may look cool, but you may find yourself having to pack a "normal" jacket for the night life!

What to Bring—"Expect the unexpected"

What you should bring along will vary according to what you plan the trip to be. Sounds obvious, but it requires some forethought if you haven't done any motorcycle trips before. Since space on the bike is limited as compared to a car, you want to maximize the utility of everything you bring. You have to put some thought into what not to bring also. Just because you have always taken that 40 quart cooler with you on all your camping trips, doesn't mean you can bring it now!

BIKE GEAR

You should prepare the bike gear before the trip starts. Get your riding clothing all set up and the protective gear. This is the same as any other trip. You have your helmet, spare visors, gloves and boots already to go, right? Now, look at what you have and decide if any of it can work double duty. Does the fleece liner work as a warm jacket for the nights around the campfire? Can you live in your riding pants once you get to your destination?? Will you be comfortable in your riding boots as you walk around the rally site? If the gear you bring works for you in more than one way, it will leave extra room for other stuff you my want to bring on the trip.

You will need to bring some bike spares too. Unless your bike is brand new, you may want to bring some things like extra spark plugs or a spare throttle cable. Check with other people who have the same type of bike that you have; they can tell you what you might want to bring along.

Remember, if you will be out in the middle of the forest or a remote campground; a motorcycle store probably won't be right next door! A portable tire pump is a good idea since most campgrounds or hotels won't have an air compressor. Bring a piece of wood or a flat metal plate to put the bikes side or center stand on in case the ground or asphalt is soft where you park the bike. Bring a towel that you can use to wipe off the dew in the morning (and the bird dropping from the tree you parked it under!).

Most campgrounds and hotels are safe, friendly places, but you may want to be able to lock up your stuff at night or if you go away from your bike. Look into cable locks that can be used to lock the bike and some of your gear too. Also look for waterproof storage containers if you have to store your gear outside your tent.

CLOTHING AND PERSONAL ITEMS

After you have looked at all your riding gear and have decided what can do double duty as "street" cloths, you have to decide what to pack for the rest of the time you aren't on the bike. I will leave the decision up to you as to how many pairs of underwear you want to stuff in your tank bag or how many extra socks you need to get you through the trip. You do have to consider things like an extra pair of shoes for times you aren't riding or maybe a pair of sandals to wear into communal showers at a rally site (athletes foot in riding boots isn't fun). Will you need spare towels for the showers you may find? Do you want one "nice" outfit for a night on the town when you don't want to look like an extra from "A Rebel Without A Clue."

If you are planning a long trip, you may be able to pack a minimum of clothing and stop at a coin laundry to freshen up your gear. One trick I use is packing a minimum of shirts and buying a few new ones as the trip progresses. This keeps you in fresh shirts as you ride!

Do leave some extra room on your bike to pack all the new stuff you will pick up along the way. You may buy a few extra T-shirts for the gang at home, or pick up a bottle or two of that great wine you tasted at the vineyard you stopped at. How could you pass up that great deal on a pair of vintage mirrors for your project bike in the garage.

I pack all of my gear in waterproof bags when I leave for a trip. I even use a form of bag liner in my hard bags attached to the bike. This helps protect my gear from water and even road dust. It is also convenient to be able to grab my stuff, already packed neatly, and load up the bike for the days riding.

MOTORCYCLE CAMPING TRIPS

▶ **See Figures 44 thru 49**

This is my favorite type of motorcycle trip. For some reason, motorcycles and camping just plain seem to go together. Spending the day bombing the backroads followed by a night under the stars is a great feeling.

Packing for the trip should start with the necessities: Camping gear, motorcycle gear and your clothing. You should consider your motorcycle gear first since that is what is going to get you to the camping site in the first place! Then the camping gear since a good nights sleep is paramount to a good day riding. Lastly, your clothing (not riding clothing) needs to be looked at, but since the needs of the riding and the camping are so important, they may dictate what your bring or don't to put on your back.

90996P93

Fig. 44 This is a synthetic insulation sleeping bag. When packed, it compresses to 9 x 17 inches (220 x 416mm)

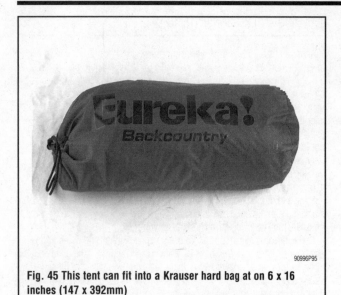

90996P95

Fig. 45 This tent can fit into a Krauser hard bag at on 6 x 16 inches (147 x 392mm)

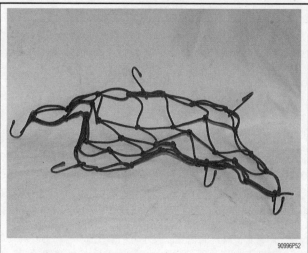

90996P52

Fig. 48 Carry two of these bungee nets with you at all times. You will be glad you did

90996P94

Fig. 46 I recommend a self-inflating sleeping pad to help cushion you from the hard ground

90996PZ1

Fig. 49 Packed for a camping trip

90996P46

Fig. 47 Don't forget a flashlight and other handy gear

An important consideration when going motorcycle camping is whether you are going to need gear for just you or you and a passenger. This impacts the size of what gear you get. For example: Most tent rated for two people really only hold one person and their clothing. A two person tent is great if it is only you on the bike. If you will be sleeping two people in your tent, consider a 3 or 4 person tent. This will leave room for you and your gear. On the negative side, a 3 or 4 person tent is quite a bit bigger when broken down, but you may not have a choice. I use a nice little tent that folds down to 6 x 16 inches (147 x 392mm). It can actually fit into one of my saddle bags along with a ground cloth, tent pegs and some camping extras. It took me a while to find one that collapsed this small, but it was worth the effort. They manufacturer of the gear made the same tent in two versions: one with fiberglass poles that folded down to 5 x 22 inches (122 x 540mm) and then my version with aluminum poles with the smaller folded dimensions. It cost some extra dough, but the space savings was worth it.

Sleeping bags are one area where you can either save some space or take up almost all you have. Sleeping bags are listed by "comfort ratings." This is typically a minimum temperature at which an average person will be comfortable at. The lower the temperature rating, the more insulation a sleeping bag will need to keep the occupant from getting cold. If you choose a bag with too low a rating, say 0°F (-16°C), the bag will be too warm to use during a warm spring night or any time during the summer. There are some modular system bags that come as two parts and you mix or match the pieces as temperature dictates. Some manufactures even make models designed for women with different arrangements of size and insulation distribution.

Sleeping bags come with a few different types of insulating materials loosely broken up into synthetics and natural. The natural insulating material is almost always down. Down is hard to beat for its insulating properties. You need relatively little down to keep you warm at night. It also compresses into the smallest package making storage easier on a tightly packed bike. The negative of down is that it loses its insulating properties when it gets wet, plus it takes a long time to dry out. Some people are also allergic to feathers. If you can find a way to keep a down sleeping bag dry during a ride in a rainstorm, it may be the best choice for its size versus performance ratio.

Synthetic insulating materials don't pack quite as well as down, but some of the premium materials come close. The big advantage of the synthetics is the ability to maintain the ability to insulate even when wet. They also dry out quicker after they get wet. Since I ride in the relatively wet eastern part of the country, I chose a synthetic bag and keep it in a waterproof outer bag, just in case. I don't like sliding into a cold, wet bag when it comes time to snooze off for the night!

You can fill a book with the different types of camping gear, but a tent and sleeping bag are the most basic. The choice to carry cooking utensils, portable showers, rock climbing gear or folding chairs is up to you. Just remember that every pound extra you pack on board, is one more pound weighing the bike down and one more item to pack up after each night! And you did pack the extra toilet paper, didn't you?

Trouble on the Road—"Cell Phone, Tire Kit, Tools . . ."

▶ **See Figure 50**

I just knew I should have changed that part! Well, it just happened to you. You are stuck on the side of the road with a dead or broken bike. What to do? Hopefully this won't happen to you since you have prepped your bike so well, but it can occur to anyone at anytime. A few minutes of preparation can help you out of a jam.

Anything can happen out on the road. A tire can go down. An ignition coil can go bad. You may get sick and need some medical attention. Think ahead and any misfortune you may encounter can be minimized.

RESOURCES ON THE ROAD

▶ **See Figure 51**

Motorcycle organizations can be your best friend when on the road. Many of the groups publish books with lists of people who are willing to help out when the need arises. These people have volunteered to provide a place to work on your bike, or make spare parts available or even just provide a resting place where a nice cup of coffee is waiting along with some good conversation.

These books will typically have a listing of dealers around the country and good contacts for other needs you may have. Join a motorcycle club if you haven't already and get a copy of the book if they publish one.

Fig. 51 This is the BMW MOA Anonymous book. It has telephone numbers for people, shops and dealers who can help in times of need

MEDICAL PROBLEMS

▶ **See Figure 52**

If you have an existing medical problem or if you are healthy but are going into unknown areas during your trip, take some time and try to find out where medical help will be located along the way. Make a list of the

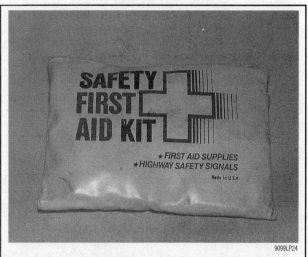

Fig. 52 Carry a small medical kit with you to take care of any minor problems you may come across

Fig. 50 Some of the spare parts that live in the tail section of my bike

medical centers and hospitals in the areas you are going to and keep it in an easily accessed location.

If you have medical needs that an emergency medical technician may need to know, wear a Med-Alert bracelet or pendant. This may save your life. If you are traveling with others, let everyone else know your medical problem so they can alert medical personnel of the concern if the need arises.

If you take medicine on a regular basis, make sure you have enough to last the trip and bring some extra jut in case you get stuck somewhere for a while. Bring your prescription in case you need to get a refill on the road.

EMERGENCY KIT

Cellular Telephones

▶ See Figure 53

In the past, this section in the book may have been filled with emergency procedures that explained how to survive in the wilderness using nothing more than a can of beans and a shoelace, but it is different nowadays: We have cellular phones!

Fig. 54 This is my solution to tube patching; I carry a spare
90996P42

Fig. 53 Cell phones have become cheap and the areas that they can be used are increasing every day
90996P47

The cell phone is a boon to the motorcyclist. You can travel all over knowing that help is only a phone call away. If you have a cell phone, remember to keep the batteries charged and have the instructions handy. Make sure you remember all of your passcodes and to activate the roaming feature so you can call from outside your home area.

If you are traveling with a cell phone, keep in mind that it may not work in all areas or in geographical features that block signals. Your cell phone company will be able to help you identify what areas aren't covered by cells or what types of terrain may cause the phone not to work.

Tire and Tube Repair Kits

▶ See Figures 54, 55 and 56

Some new motorcycles are coming with tubeless tire repair kits as standard. These kits consist of a tire plug and plug tool, plus a means to inflate the tire after the repair. If your bike doesn't come with a kit like this, they are available from almost any motorcycle dealer or mail order house. The punctured tire is rasped out with the tire plug tool and then a plug is pressed into the opening. When the tool is removed, the plug is left behind to fill the void. The tire is then reinflated using a carbon dioxide canister or a small pump. The entire process can take place with the wheel and tire still mounted to the bike.

Fig. 55 A tube patch kit will get you back on the road as long as the tube is repairable
90996P34

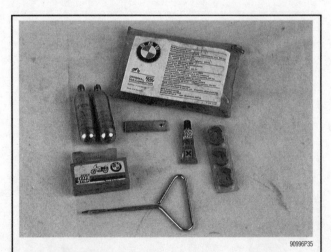
Fig. 56 A tubeless tire plug kit is quick and easy to use. You may want to practice on a used tire just so you know how to do it
90996P35

Tube repair kits have been around for as long as there have been tubes (maybe even longer, but it is tough to prove). These kits require the tire to be dismounted and the tube removed for patching. It is just like what you remember when you were a kid working on your bicycle. You scuff the tube where the puncture is and then spread the glue on the area. A small patch of rubber is pressed into place and allowed to set.

The kits can be used to get the bike back on the road until a permanent repair is made (like replacing the tire!) A repaired tire should only be used as a temporary fix and the speed you travel on it reduced. Don't take risks with a patched tire or tube. It isn't worth it.

Tool Kit

▶ **See Figures 57, 58 and 59**

Some of your nicer motorcycle manufacturers include a fairly comprehensive tool kit with the bike. Some manufactures don't see the need for a tool kit, while yet others give you tools that are useless, they can be jettisoned from the bike right after you get it.

If your bike doesn't come with a tool kit, you can buy one all ready made from the aftermarket or you can gather your own set of tools.

If you decide to put together your own kit, only bring what would be needed for a standard tune-up and anything else that has an obvious need. Unless you expect to be rebuilding the head on the side of the road, leave the heavy stuff at home.

When the other author of this book was planning a cross country trip, he did a standard service on his bike and made a pile of all the tools he used.

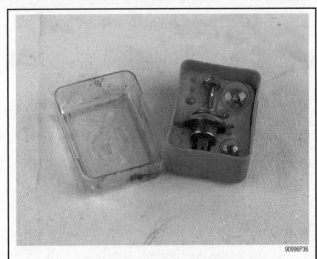

Fig. 58 This set of spare bulbs contains one of almost every bulb used on the bike

From this group of tools, he made up a kit that accompanied him from coast-to-coast and it didn't take up too much room on the bike.

There are manufacturers of tool kits made specifically with the needs of bikes in mind. These kits are compact and well thought out. Most have quality tools, but you will want to check that closely.

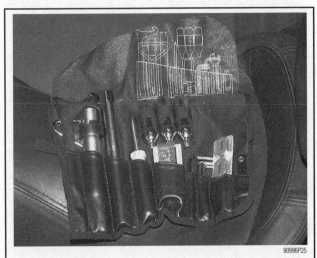

Fig. 57 Just doesn't this manufacture give you a tool kit, but the tool kit has a diagram to help keep it organized!

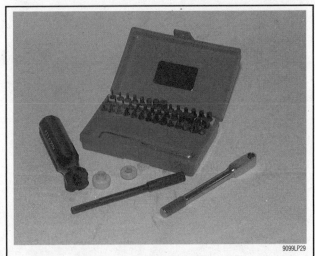

Fig. 59 This tool kit isn't much larger than a deck of cards yet contains various handy bits and drivers

PREPPING TO TRAILER THE BIKE

Either by choice or need, at some point we will need to put our bikes on a trailer. Maybe the bike broke and can't be ridden (hopefully not). Maybe you are taking your track prepped bike out to the track or ORV (Off Road Vehicle) park (hopefully!).

Tiedowns

There are specific motorcycle tiedown straps that are designed to go over the bars and pull down on the forks. This is nice to have, but the same effect can be had with a set of one inch wide ratcheting tiedowns. The trick is to pull down evenly without damaging any parts of the bike. Do not use rope as it doesn't allow for easy tensioning.

➡**Tieing a bike down to a trailer or truck requires two people to do it safely. You may want to have an experienced person show you how to do it properly before you try it yourself.**

1. Place the bike upright and not on its sidestand or centerstand.
2. Place the straps on the bike and position them so they won't pull down on anything that can be damaged. Place soft cloths in between the straps and bike to prevent scuffing. The straps should be positioned so there is one on each side of the bike pulling down at an angle to the tiedown point on the trailer or truck bed.
3. Alternately tighten the straps on each side to compress the front suspension; the bike will hold itself upright. Use additional straps to act as backups in case one of the main straps loosens or breaks.

4. Tie down the rear of the bike in the same manner so it doesn't hop from side-to-side.

Trailers and Trucks

You can use a trailer to haul a bike around or the back of a truck if it is big enough. Using the bed of a pickup is fine, but it has some disadvantages. The bed sits high in the air and pushing the bike up the ramp can be a problem. The wheels of a bike should be held in a channel or by using blocks on the sides of the tires to keep it from slipping sideways; Most trucks won't have channels unless you bolt them in. The good part about using a truck is that it is convenient. No worries about trailering or additional tolls on the turnpike for multiple axles.

Trailers are probably the best to use if you are serious about hauling some bikes around. A dedicated motorcycle trailer is your best choice, but a good flatbed trailer with tiedown point and a tire rail is also serviceable. Trailers have a lower load height and have properly spaced tiedown points for the straps. On the negative side you have to have a vehicle to tow the trailer with a hitch, lighting harness and some experience driving a vehicle with trailer attached. There is additional maintenance to be done to the trailer and inspections/registration for states that require it.

A good basic motorcycle trailer can be relatively inexpensive for a small unit, but the price can jump up quickly as you pile on the options. If you went really nuts, you can get an enclosed trailer that will protect your bike from the elements. That is perfect for show bikes or restored bikes.

If you use a trailer, make sure the vehicle you use to tow it with has the capacity to handle the load safely. A big tour bike, trailer and some accessories can start to push the limits of many light trucks and most cars if they aren't equipped for towing.

Protecting The Bike

When the bike is loaded on a trailer, it is subjected to a constant spray of road crud from the rear tires of the tow vehicle. Some trailers have kickups at the front edge to help keep objects from hitting the cargo. A good set of mud flaps on the toe vehicle can help reduce the amount of stuff thrown into the air.

You can use a bike cover to help keep the crud off the bike, but this has its problems. The wind from moving down the road can cause the cover to flap and wear at the finish on the bike. It will also cause a "sail" effect and make the trailer more sensitive to cross winds. The best bet is to simply clean the bike after you arrive at your destination!

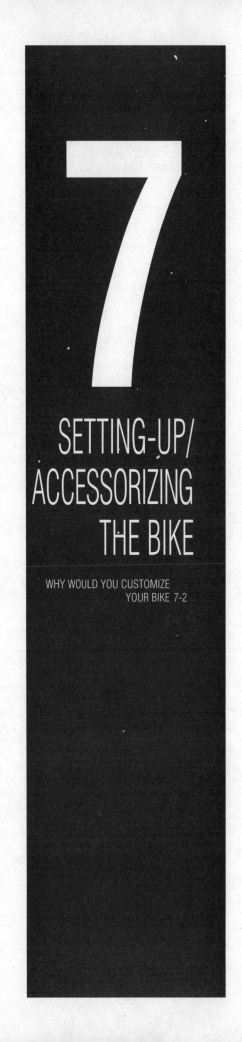

7
SETTING-UP/ ACCESSORIZING THE BIKE

WHY WOULD YOU CUSTOMIZE YOUR BIKE

Motocyclists live for customizing their bikes. Sometimes we do it to make our rides more individual. Sometimes we do it to make our bike work better for our needs. Sometimes we do it just because we can! There is no right or wrong when it comes to customizing your bike. If you like what you did, then it was the right thing to do. Just ignore the crowds of people gathering around your bike to see the chrome plated tires and flamed chain links! It is your ride and you can do what you want!

This section is designed to help you choose the proper accessories to help your bike better fit you and work for you. The goal here is familiarize you with what options are available when it comes to buying accessories and with what features you should look for in them. We have chosen examples of accessories from some of the industries known leaders (and in some cases from lesser known but just as high quality manufacturers), and we would like to thank the manufacturers again for their help with the production of this section. That is not to say the brands pictured here are your only options. However it is to say that they are VERY GOOD examples of the high quality accessories that are available, and as such are excellent standards for comparison with the accessories you look at when deciding on a purchase.

Selecting the Accessories to Fit Your Needs

When looking at modifying your bike with accessories, you have to determine what your goals are; Are you looking to make the bike more comfortable on a long ride? Do you want your bike to stand out in a crowd of rumbling v-twins? Do you want a bit more growl when the throttle twists to its stops? A rider who is into cruising the main strip is bound to have vastly different needs from a member of the sport touring crowd.

Pick up a copy of a motorcycle catalog or magazine and you will find it full of neato toys and tricks just waiting to be bolted to your bike. You will find seats, mirrors, chrome, camshafts, shocks, mufflers, sprockets, lights, luggage, tires, fork springs, neon colored doodads and a few hundred more items I didn't list.

Down to business: Make a list of what you want the bike to do. OK, now that you have that, make a list of possible accessories that will help you achieve your goals. Decide if any of the accessories may degrade other aspects of your riding that you don't want to and cross them off the list.

The nice thing about motorcycles and the aftermarket is that you can get almost anything you want (and in almost any color, too!) Take your list to your dealer, the local motorcycle shop or the catalog houses. They will help you with obtaining the stuff you want. Keep in mind that the manufactures often have accessories for your bike that fit and work as the factory intended. You don't have to hit the aftermarket for everything!

What types of accessories may I want on my bike? Let's look at some of the different types of riders and what they may outfit their bikes with: The cruiser may want a set of slash cut pipes and chrome galore. He/she may want more flash out of their ride as long term comfort isn't real high on their needs list. They want to be seen and noticed. A cool look and "don't mess with me" attitude is the recipe for the day. Or they may go in the other direction and outfit their bike with saddlebags, a comfy seat and a decent windshield so they can put on the miles aboard a slick looking machine.

The sport bike dude may be into as much neon as possible (sorta passé at this point, but it is still around) or they may want their rocket to look, sound and feel like a GP bike. A pair of carbon canisters, rear sets and carbon fiber fenders may be needed to fill their want list. I was going to avoid the term "squid," but I had to mention that squidlyness is more a riding style than a fashion style. Not all sport bike folks are squids, so don't let the sight of carbon fiber fool ya!

The luxo-touring folks have some needs that can't be met on anything other than a full boat tour machine. The Gold Wingers and Voyagerians want things like cup holders and communications systems. They may need back rests or a trailer hitch. They want comfort all day long and can put as many miles on their bike in a week as some riders put on in a year! They know what works and what doesn't; Check with an experienced tour rider and they can help you with your choices.

I consider myself to be a sport tourer. I like some nice twisties on my way to someplace. As a result, I like some performance mods along with a place to but my gear for the night. I need luggage and comfort to match my riding goals for the day. I will be out in the weather all day long so I will need some protection, but I don't want to hinder my fun when Deals Gap opens up in front of my fender.

There are many different needs and even more answers. Ask the guys at the local bike shop what they think will meet your needs. Call the catalog houses as they answer those questions all day long and can help point out your choices. Talk to the dealer that sold you your bike; They may show you that the manufacturer already makes something that you want. Chat it up! You will find most bikers will help you out with your questions.

Helping to Make Your Bike Fit You

An often overlooked aspect of motorcycle ownership is how well the bike fits you. This means its purpose as well as the physical fit. We have already gone over the different types of bikes in another section now that you have made your choice of style of bike, we can try to tweak the bike to make you most comfortable with it.

You can pick and choose accessories to make it fit your needs better. The most basic change in terms of comfort is the seating position. Where your butt ends up determines how everything else on your body fits the bike. It will effect the distance between your upper body and the handlebars. It will effect how bent your legs get when resting on the pegs. It will also effect how your body gets positioned on the bike: crouched, upright, laid back, etc.

Once you have decided on your seating position, you can look at things like handlebars and how your upper body reacts to them. You can choose a set of grips to make your hands comfortable. The pegs that your feet rest on can change the way you read the motions of the bike. If you aren't comfortable on the bike, you won't be happy with the bike. If you aren't happy with the bike, you won't do the things you want to do.

You can add items like a fairing or windshield to protect you from the wind and elements. This will extend the range of weather you are willing to ride in. It will help keep you comfortable and keep you from being to badly beat up by Mother Nature.

If you are comfortable on the bike, you will find it enjoyable to ride all day. If you do that, you might find you need some additional storage spaces to stash things like toll tickets and toll money. Your trips may take you through some nice twisties and the stock suspension that is great on the highway may need some help in the form of stiffer springs and better shocks. You may also find yourself riding at night wishing for some extra light to brighten the roadway.

If you enjoy riding with a friend on the passenger pillion, you will want a method of communicating without resorting to the helmet tapping Morse code. A two way communicator may be just the trick. You may also want to add some road tunes in the form of a radio or CD player.

Even if you are just out for quickie back road burn, you may find that your stock pipes just don't give you that growl that you so enjoy. A new set of exhaust pipes or slip-ons may be what the doctor ordered.

The possibilities are endless. You can tune your bike to fit your mind and body. All it takes is some time, research and desire to do it (money can help also). Don't be afraid to try things out or ask around for opinions. Even if you make a modification that doesn't work out, you are now one step closer to knowing what you need or want. In fact, you may be able to buy something that someone else decided didn't work for them allowing you to pick up their mistake for a song! If you make a mistake, there will almost always be someone there to buy your goofs too.

Seats

HOW TO SELECT

▶ **See Figures 1 thru 7**

Unfortunately seats are one of the most subjective topics in motorcycling. Due to the extremely wide range of shapes of the human behind, it is impossible to get empirical data on which to compare the comfort of seats. You need to look at the design of the seat and what its purpose is.

There are touring seats with wider bases and more supportive padding so the 700 mile (1150 km) a day rider can do so in comfort. The road racer needs a saddle that allows them to slide around on the seat to better position their bodies in turns. A sport tourer needs something in the middle; It can't be too restrictive or you won't be able to move about, yet you need the support and comfort of a touring type seat.

The cruiser crowds go for more style in their saddles. Materials like leather find their way into high quality seats and that makes the seat look like a million bucks. Conchos, fringe and other ornamentation can help make a box standard bike stand out from the crowd.

If you take a passenger, you may want to consider a saddle with improved accommodations for the passenger. Some aftermarket seats, such as Corbin®, can be had with removable back rests for both rider and passenger. These seats come with a more comfortable passenger area and sometimes the riders backrest comes equipped with a pouch to help store little things like toll tickets and money. These are items best handled by the passenger and now they have a place to put them.

You need to talk to a retailer of aftermarket seats or to the maker of the seat itself to try to figure out what is best for you. Most of these people are more than happy to help guide you. Talk to the dealer as some of the bike manufactures have other seats available for your bike. If you go that route, you get to keep your machine all original and the parts tend to fit the way they were intended.

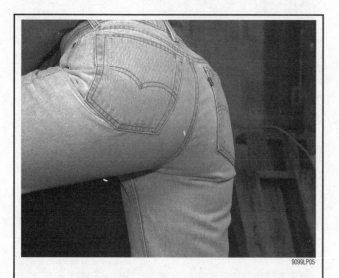

Fig. 1 The trick is to get your bike to fit this

Fig. 3 The new seat provides better support for the rider and passenger

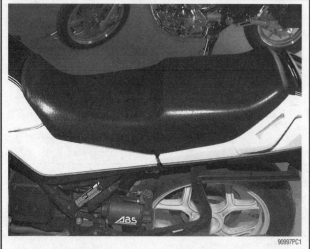

Fig. 2 This stock seat has seen many miles down the road and is ready to be changed

Fig. 4 A common desire for a seat is an adjustable back rest. This one can be used in both rider and passenger positions

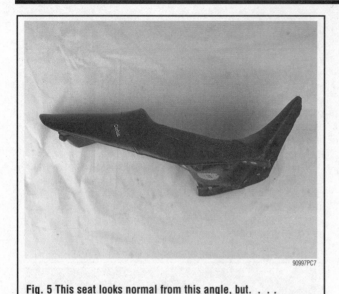

Fig. 5 This seat looks normal from this angle, but. . . .

Fig. 6 . . . . this cutaway shows how a seat is constructed

Fig. 7 This Corbin® seat is made of fiber reinforced plastic, with a cushion of special closed cell foam and custom upholstery

You should also talk to a few owners of bikes similar to yours and find out what they have experienced with seats. Some seats need a break-in period and can feel downright awful when first installed. Some one with experience with that brand seat can fill you in and keep you from judging too quickly.

A seat can help lower the effective height of a bike to help people with shorter inseams. At the same time, the seat can be rebuilt to increase its height as so to leave some extra leg room between the butt of the rider and the pegs. Either of these modifications will help make the bike fit you and not the other way around!

Quality seats are manufactured with multiple layers of materials; Each layer serves a function. The seat pan forms the shape of the seat and provides the mounting points. There may be one or more layers of foam in differing densities that form the cushioning part of the seat. The foam is the heart of the seat and can make or break its comfort. The foam is what makes up the shape of the scoop of the seating area. This is the pocket where your rump goes.

On top of the foam may be a gel pad that helps absorb vibration and keeps pressure points from forming. This gel is also used in gloves, bicycle riding shorts and some medical applications. Many custom seat manufacturers will modify your seat or one of theirs to accommodate a gel pad.

The final layer of a seat is the upholstery. This is the outer layer of the seat and is the contact point between you and the bike. The covering may be made of vinyl or leather, but the synthetic material is the most common as it withstands weather with little maintenance. The material can be smooth or textured and it can come in various colors to match the bike. You can pick what you want and make your bike meet your needs.

A big name in the aftermarket seat game is Corbin®. A quick glance at the Chilton riders bikes shows that over half of our bikes are equipped with a Corbin® seat. This probably has to do with Kevin's comfortable experience with a custom Corbin® leather saddle that he put 6 days in a row at 650 miles (1050 km) per day on. That was enough for the rest of us to be convinved of the value of a Corbin® seat. (Then again, Kevin has never been quite the same since that trip. Maybe it was from sitting on his central nervous system for so long?)

HOW TO INSTALL

▸ See Figures 8 thru 21

Most motorcycle seats are easy to replace. Many just unclip from the frame and reinstall just as easy. Some require a bit more doing. Check your owners manual for specific instructions.

If your seat hinges from the side, such as on a BMW and many other manufactures, most of the time you just have to open up the seat, remove a clip or two from the hinges and unhook it from the bike. To install the new seat, you may have to swap over some hardware from the old set to the new, adjust the latches and hinges, then go riding!

Some bikes, like Harleys, have the seat bolted down with one or more screws at the back or along the perimeter. It can be as simple as removing a screw and pulling back on the seat to disengage it from a tab at the front. Slide the new seat in and install the screw.

Some seats are bolted to the bodywork and require you to remove the body work to the point where you can access the mounting hardware. This will be more common on the hard-core sport bikes.

Your bike may have a seat that pops out with out any hardware. The seat may be adjustable from the factory and fit into various slots. It may come off to allow access to the engine or storage compartments. Installing an aftermarket or replacement seat is as simple as popping the new one in (as long as it fits properly).

When installing a new seat, you should check that the seat doesn't rub the paint anywhere or foul anything else of importance. You can use clear tape to protect the paintwork from scuffing. You should also check that the new seat mounts at least as firmly as the original seat did.

New seats may require a breaking in period that can last as long as 2000 miles (3250 km)! Find this out in advance so you can allow an appropriate time period before judging the comfort of the seat. Until the seat is broken in, take it easy on yourself as a new seat can cause pressure points and be very uncomfortable to the point of soreness. Maybe that pair of gel-pad biking shorts can get double duty!

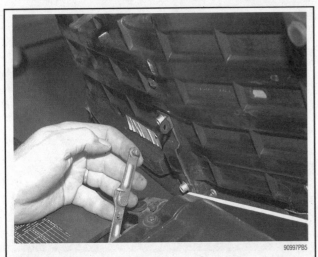

Fig. 8 This type of seat is hinged and requires the limit strap to be disconnected

Fig. 9 Only a few bolts and pins hold this seat on

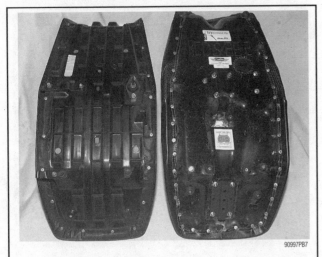

Fig. 10 The stock seat and the replacement may look different at the seat pan, but all the mounting points are the same

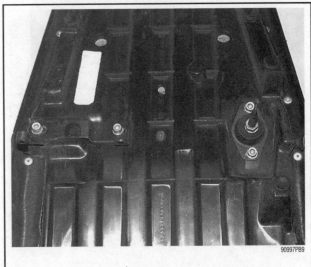

Fig. 11 The stock hardware may need to be swapped . . .

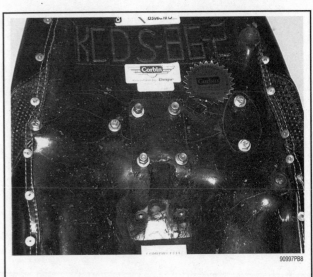

Fig. 12 . . . onto the new seat

Fig. 13 This seat is held by a screw at the front . . .

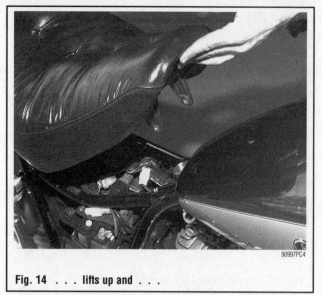

Fig. 14 . . . lifts up and . . .

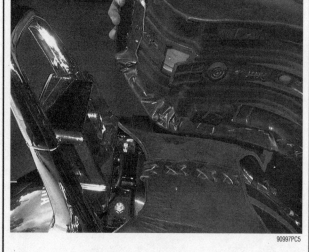

Fig. 15 . . . pulls out from the rear

Fig. 16 This is a mighty small stock seat for a mighty big rider

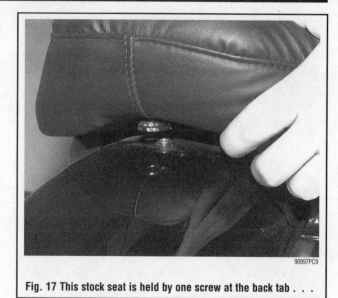

Fig. 17 This stock seat is held by one screw at the back tab . . .

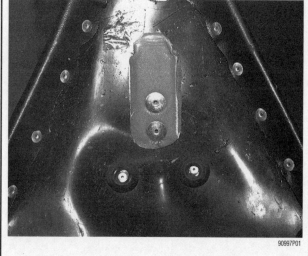

Fig. 18 . . . while the front is held by a slot and tab

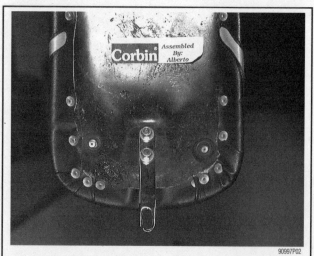

Fig. 19 The rear of the new seat is held in the same fashion as the stock seat

Fig. 20 The new seat requires that the threaded insert be moved to a position that already exists in the Sportsters rear fender

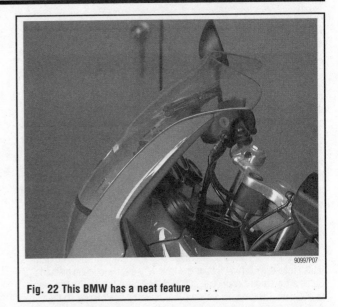

Fig. 22 This BMW has a neat feature . . .

Fig. 21 This is more like it for an easy ride on the weekend

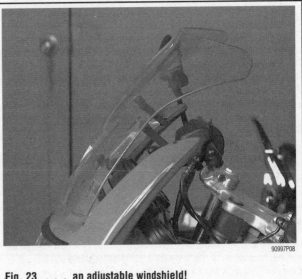

Fig. 23 . . . an adjustable windshield!

Windshields

♦ See Figures 22 and 23

Many bikes come with a windshield with the job of protecting the rider. Some bikes come with no windshield, but have optional ones from the manufacturer. Other bikes are just plain bare with no OEM windshield available. The aftermarket has provided solutions for people who want a windshield for their naked bike, or to change the one that came with the bike.

HOW TO SELECT

Windshields come in many shapes, sizes and configurations. Some are separate pieces that bolt onto the bike via brackets; Others are integrated into the fairing and bodywork. Some are fixed in place, while others are adjustable either by moving the brackets or by hitting a button (power windows for bikes!).

If your bike already has a windshield, but it doesn't meet your needs, you have to determine what changes will help make the situation better. A typical problem with windshields is an improper height for the rider. If the windshield has a low top to it, the air swirling off the upper lip may cause the riders helmet to get caught in the turbulence. The solution is to get a windshield that is either higher to force the air over the riders helmet, or lower to keep the turbulence off the head and keeping the helmet in clean air. If winter riding is your thing, the first choice is probably the correct one, but if you like having the air going through the vents on your helmet in the middle of the summer, the latter is the way to go. You may want to buy a taller windshield for the winter and a shorter one (or cut down a standard one) for summer use. Switch off between the two for all year riding!

If the windshield is too narrow, you hands can be sitting out in the elements getting cold, wet or otherwise unhappy. Increasing the width of the windshield can help better enclose the rider in a still air pocket and keep the rider isolated from the elements.

If you don't have a windshield for your bike, you will have to determine if one was available from the manufacturer or not. If there was one available, decide if you like it or not and if you do, does the price fit your pocketbook? If not, what is available from the aftermarket. Are there units made specifically for your bike or will you have to go with a universal unit?

Some of the best places to see windshields is at motorcycle rallies. You get to talk to people actually using them and they can give you firsthand accounts of what they will do. You can see how they are fitted and what they look like on the bike. Motorcycle shops and dealerships are also great places to check out windshields. The staff at the shops can fill you in with cost and what it takes to mount them. Lastly catalogs and advertisements in motorcycle magazines are good places to see the many different styles of windshields, except you won't be able to see what they look like in real person or how they mount. If you buy one mail order, make sure there is a return policy and take care of the unit until you decide to keep it.

The needs of a touring bike are much different from those of a sportbike. On a touring bike, you will probably want a fairly upright windshield that makes a pocket of still air behind it. The windshield will force you to look through it, so good optical properties are very important. You don't want a wavy distorted view of the road.

A sportbike's fairing and windshield is only designed to move the air up a little so the windblast hits the riders chest. This helps the rider hold themselves up at speed. It also forms a pocket of still air down closer to the tank and instrument panel so the rider can get into a full racer-boy tuck at rocket warp speeds and not be blown off the bike. Some stock windshields can be too radical and provide no real world protection for the rider. The aftermarket has come up with slightly taller units that bolt in place of the stock ones and lift the air up higher.

When looking for a windshield, check the manufactures catalogs for other similar bikes as yours that may come with a windshield. The OEM units are usually very well built and have very clean mounting methods. Some are even quick removal units such as Harley-Davidson's "Convertible" series. These accessories mount a quick release bracket on the bike and allows use of different windshields. Some models may be expensive, but they are very convenient!

If you tend to just want a good basic windshield and have no preferences to style or brand, there are some very good generic units on the market. They have universal mounting arms with almost infinite adjustment and allow mounting on most any bike. There is a windshield that I know of that has passed through many owners hands and each time it was mounted on a different type of bike, yet the windshield looked natural on each one of them. Talk about getting your moneys worth!

Something to keep in mind about windshield is that they change the way a bike handles. If you mount a windshield on a bike that didn't have one before, be very careful the first time you ride it. You may be in for a surprise! You now have a big sail effecting the aerodynamics of the bike. If you change an existing windshield, you still need to be careful as things are different from what you are used to.

HOW TO INSTALL

◆ **See Figures 24, 25, 26, 27 and 28**

It is almost impossible to describe every method of windshield mounting, but here are a few general guidelines. The windshield you buy will come with instructions or the seller should be able to give you some tips on how to do it.

Regardless of what type of windshield you get, you have to be careful during the installation not to trap any control cables or block the lighting. You may have to route the cables differently or remount the turn signals in a different location.

If you are replacing a windshield with a new one and it mounts in the same fashion, you are good to go. Simply unbolting or unscrewing the old unit and swapping it out is straight forward. Sportbike windshields often are just screwed to the fairing and a few minutes of effort will get you where you need to be.

If the windshield you are putting on doesn't mount in the same fashion as the original or your bike didn't have a windshield to begin with, follow the instruction of the mounting kit. It may direct you to remove certain items or relocate them. You may have to dismount the handlebars or remove parts of the fairing. If you have to do this, make sure that you remount everything in its proper location and tighten the fasteners to spec. You wouldn't want your handlebars to fold down on you at speed, now would you?

Universal windshields often use band clamps to attach to the handlebars and fork legs. It is very important to check that the mounting hardware doesn't get in the way of the mirrors, controls or lights. You will also want to check that nothing can hit the windshield when the fork goes to full compression. Check that the windshield doesn't block the turn signals or head

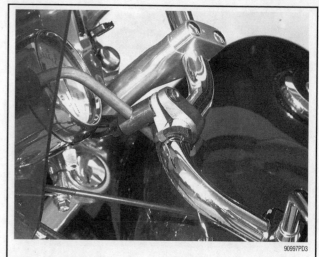

Fig. 24 This universal mount windshield clamps to the handlebars

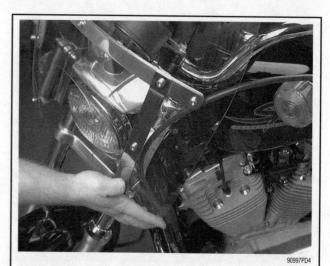

Fig. 25 Test fit the windshield before making any permanent changes as you might have to make some adjustments

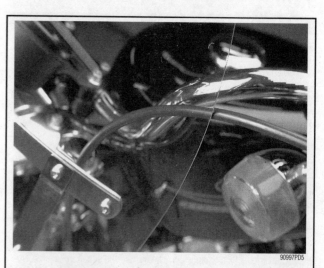

Fig. 26 When fitting a windshield, check for interference with controls and cables

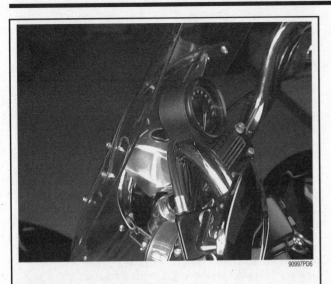

Fig. 27 This control cable required . . .

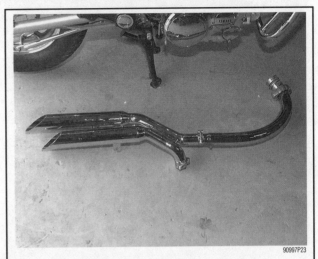

Fig. 29 A good reason to swap an exhaust system is to go to a lightweight aftermarket system like this . . .

Fig. 28 . . . some rerouting

Fig. 30 . . . from a heavyweight stock system, like this

light. Move the bars from full lock to the opposite side to make sure the windshield doesn't lessen the amount of steering you have at full turn.

On your first ride, be very careful as the bike will behave differently than you may be used to. Its reaction in side winds will also be different. One thing that always gets me is body mounted fairings and windshields since my bike has a fork mounted fairing. On my bike the instruments move with the forks, but on others the instruments don't. Freaks me out every time! If you aren't used to the mounting style you just put on, be super careful until you are used to it.

Exhaust Systems

HOW TO SELECT

▶ **See Figures 29, 30, 31 and 32**

There is probably no other modification that can so completely change the personality of a motorcycle than the exhaust system. From super quiet touring systems to barking drag pipes, there is an exhaust system to make your bike into what you want it to be heard as. Granted, a set of drag pipes on a 250 Rebel isn't going to turn it into a bad-boy ride, but a set of tuned

pipes on a Road King may make your time on a tour bike more visceral and liven things up a bit.

We all have been subjected to exhaust systems that are too loud. There is a camp that feels that the louder the pipes are, the better. This goes for the cruiser crowd as well as the sportbike crowd (I haven't run into too many Gold Wingers without baffles, so I feel safe to leave them out of the story). The plain truth is, loud pipes annoy the outside world. I admit that one of the sweetest sounds I have heard coming from a bike was a Ducati 916 being fired up for its new owner with a set of carbon canisters, but if you were trying to sleep or have a quiet picnic, those pipes wouldn't sound so hot. Leave the drag pipes for the drag strip and keep those baffles in the canisters if you aren't on a track.

There are many reasons to replace the stock exhaust system on you bike. Maybe yours is rotted out and you wanted something different. Possibly you want a little more rumble to make you grin. Most aftermarket pipes can help you reduce the weight of your bike, sometimes as much as 20 pounds (44 kilos) or more! Maybe you just wanted a new look for the old steed. All are good reasons. For myself, I opted for a set of stock replacement mufflers as they were the only units that matched the style of the bike (I ride a fairly rare BMW that didn't have too much aftermarket support, but I'm sure that if I had dug enough I would have found some different pipes).

Fig. 31 Another good reason to change the exhaust is to get a new look or sound for your bike

Fig. 32 Exhaust systems can help define the style of the bike

There are many different styles of replacement exhaust systems. Some systems are simply replacement mufflers that "slip on" to the existing factory pipes. These are the simplest systems. Other systems replace the entire set of pipes from the cylinder head back. Some of these systems resemble the stock systems, but use bigger pipes or have some other sort of difference. Other systems may be completely different from the stock system. You have to be careful with systems like these as you may lose use of centerstands or block easy access to maintenance items such as oil filters.

HOW TO INSTALL

♦ **See Figures 33 thru 57**

One of the biggest concerns when replacing an exhaust system is how much effect it is going to have on the tuning of the engine. Simply bolting a set of mufflers to your bike is not all you have to concern yourself with. Replacement exhaust systems from the aftermarket or performance arm of the manufacturer will typically have higher rates of flow than the stock systems. This helps engine performance if tuned to take advantage of it. If you don't tune the engine and adjust the mixture, chances are that you will cause the engine to run lean. A lean running engine will run hot and even-

tually damage itself. Low restriction pipes equal higher flow of gases through the engine. Higher flow of gases mean more air coming into the engine. More air means more fuel that the engine can burn. The end result is that you have to rejet your carbs or diddle with the fuel injection (if the fuel injection doesn't self adjust).

Talk to the manufacturer of the system you intend to use. They will be able to give you an idea about what modifications to the carburetion will have to be done. Sometimes they can give you specific changes and might be able to supply a jetting kit matched to the exhaust system. If they don't have that, they can give you some guidance as to typical setting to use as a baseline. If you have done extensive modifications to your engine, the manufacturer may not be able to help you as they can't possibly know every combination of parts that can be bolted to a bike. In this case, a shop familiar with your type of bike may have already done a similar modification and can help you get your bike dialed in.

1. Once you have figured out what to do with your fuel mixture, now you can start thinking about actually installing the exhaust system. Look through the manufacturers instructions. They should give you a list of parts you will need during the job. If they say to reuse any parts, like gaskets, you may want to pick up new ones just in case the old ones are damaged during the removal process.

2. Before removing any bolts, hold up the new exhaust system to the bike and try to look for all the places the new system will mount. Look for the way the pipes attach to each other. Check that the pipes and mount will match up. Most quality manufacturers test fit their products so you don't have to do any modifications to the system. Sometimes you will find that the lower priced systems out there require a fair bit of modification to get them to fit. You usually get what you pay for.

3. If you are sure everything will fit fine and you have all the parts you need, it is time to remove the old system. This can be lotsa fun as old exhaust system hardware tends to fuse itself together over a period of time. Liberal doses of rust penetrating lubricant can help break free some of the more stubborn fasteners. Sometimes nothing short of a torch will help free things up, just be careful not to damage anything in the process. Loosen all the connections and mounting bolts.

4. Some bikes require that other parts be removed for access to the exhaust system. Bodywork, fairings, engine guards, centerstands, sidestands, brake levers, foot boards, etc, etc. All may need to be removed or moved out of the way. If the bike is equipped with a fuel injection system with an oxygen sensor, remove it and its wire. If the bike has an exhaust power valve, remove its linkage and actuating assembly, as appropriate.

5. When you have removed the mounting fasteners and disconnected the pipes, be ready to drop the old system. Be careful as the old system may be quite a bit heavier than it may seem, but hey, isn't that one of the reasons you are changing it?

6. With the old system out, this is a great time to inspect the mounting tabs on the bike and any areas that are normally covered by the exhaust system. Check for rust and corrosion. Clean and paint any areas that may need it. Check the threads on the cylinder head where the pipe attaches to; Often these threads get buggered up due to the high heat encountered at an exhaust port. Check the inside of the exhaust port for excessive carbon or for signs of burning valves. You might catch a problem before an engine teardown is needed. If you are only installing a set of slip on mufflers, check that the end of the pipe is still round and not squashed out of shape. A small pipe expander can help round out a damaged pipe.

7. Test fit the new exhaust system. Put everything into place, but don't tighten anything yet. Check for clearances at items such as the rear swing arm, rear shocks, luggage mounts, brake lines and levers, chassis tubes, sidestands, centerstands, bodywork and other accessories. If there are clearance problems, you might have to bend some mounting tabs or make up spacers. Some race oriented exhaust systems don't make any provision for side or centerstands. This is the time to find out if the system won't fit correctly or if you have all of the parts needed for the job. The Cobra(REG)kit we installed in the Chilton shop was complete and required no modifications to make it fit.

8. Once you are convinced that everything is as it should be, you can install the new gaskets, put anti-seize paste on fittings and get set to bolt

everything down. Check your instructions to see if there are any sequences that you have to follow when tightening the various part of the system. Chance are that you need to start closest to the engine and work your way back. While doing this, keep checking the system alignment as it can change as things snug up.

9. With the system completely bolted down, reinstall anything that had to come off in the process. Tighten the fasteners properly and use thread locking compounds where appropriate.

10. Install any luggage that may hang close to the exhaust system and check for clearance. You wouldn't want to get to the campsite to find your underwear turned into toasty critters.

11. If your carbs will need readjustment or be rejetted, do this now, before firing up the bike. Once it is complete, check for any fuel leakage before starting the bike.

12. Ok, now that you have everything done, fire it up! Check for leaking connections and tighten them up. Run the bike for a while and recheck the connections once they have cooled back down. They may need retorquing. After riding the bike for a few hundred miles, go back over everything and check that nothing has started to leak or rattle off. If everything is good at this point, you should be set for many years of trouble free service from your new exhaust.

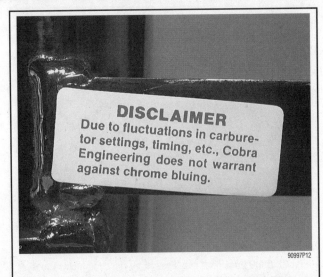

Fig. 35 Take heed of any warnings the manufacturer gives you

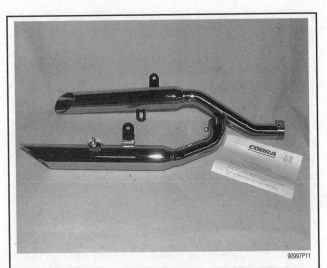

Fig. 33 Check that you have everything you need for your exhaust system. This kit from Cobra® is very complete

Fig. 36 You may have to disassemble more of the exhaust system than just the mufflers when swapping canisters

Fig. 34 You may need to install a carb jet kit to adjust for the change in mixture caused by a higher flow exhaust system

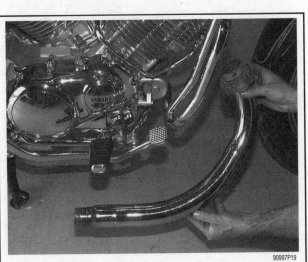

Fig. 37 On this bike, dropping the headpipe was the first step in the process (after removing the engine guards)

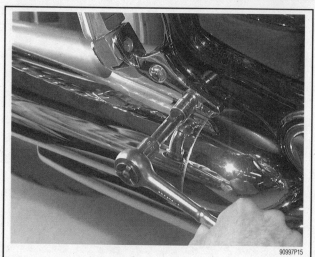

Fig. 38 Other items that may need to be removed include foot pegs

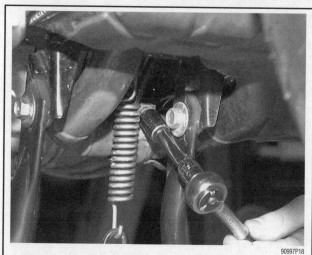

Fig. 41 Band clamps made this job go much easier since the pipes don't get crushed

Fig. 39 This foot peg bracket had a bolt that also supported a muffler mount

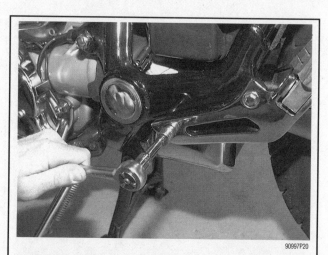

Fig. 42 This seemingly uninvolved bolt actually supported the stock exhaust resonator and needed to be removed before the exhaust would drop

Fig. 40 Hidden until we got into the job was this crossover pipe that resides under the centerstand

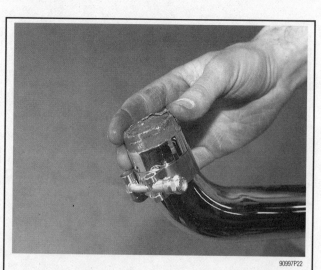

Fig. 43 The exhaust manufacturer said that this gasket could be reused, but a new one is always a good idea

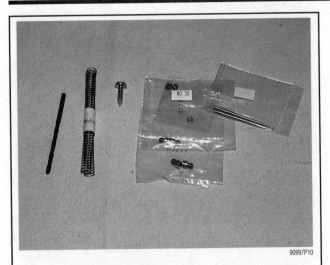

Fig. 44 The rejetting kit came with new jets, springs, needles and clips

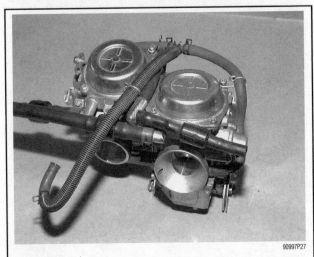

Fig. 47 With the carbs removed, access to everything was easy. Do not separate the carbs

Fig. 45 The jet kit maker said that the job could be done on the bike. We don't think so!

Fig. 48 Removing the carb tops exposed the slides and springs

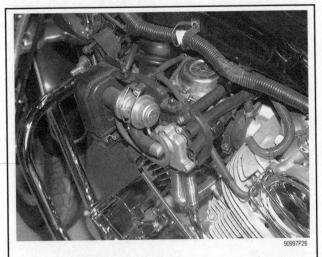

Fig. 46 Removing the carbs wasn't so bad as all the hoses just slipped right off and stayed in place

Fig. 49 This is the needle that is replaced by the one in the kit

Fig. 50 The main jet sits at the bottom of the float bowl (removed)

Fig. 53 The jet sits right above the bowl drain plug. Don't forget the crush washer

Fig. 51 Be careful when removing the main jets as they are made of brass and can be damaged by harder tools

Fig. 54 This screw starter made it easy to replace the main jet

Fig. 52 Another way of getting at the main jet is through the bowl drain plug

Fig. 55 You may need to sync the carbs when finished if the any of the balance screws were disturbed

Fig. 56 The idle screws may need to be tweaked after the jet kit is installed

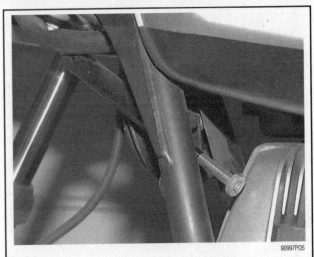

One suspension accessory you can add is a steering damper . . .

Fig. 57 Check for leaks once everything is buttoned up

. . . that allows adjustment for different riding conditions

Shocks & Springs

Most people who drive cars never think twice about the suspension holding their car up. Motorcyclists on the other hand, are constantly adjusting preload, playing with the rebound dampening and otherwise twisting the dials of their suspensions. The reason for this is that the rider and payload of a motorcycle is a much larger percentage of the total weight of the vehicle as compared to a car or truck.

If we have only ourselves on the bike, it will handle in one fashion, but add another rider or a stack of camping gear, the bike can turn into something completely different. We need to adjust the suspension of the bike to fit our needs and preferences. A sporting rider may want something different from a bike than a touring type person who owns the same type of bike. Motorcycles were meant for personal involvement and suspensions are just one more area we can get involved in.

HOW TO SELECT

♦ See Figures 58, 59 and 60

There are many reasons to change the suspension on a motorcycle. Sometimes the reason is handling and performance; The rider wants more control from the bike. They may want to stiffen up the chassis so it becomes more reactive and predictable.

Other riders want a ride that is tailored to their laid back cruising or touring style. Maybe they carry a ton of gear with them and need the load carrying capability increased over stock. They don't need a super hard suspension as they will be touring the country's highways at a sedate pace.

Possibly the rider is a bit lacking in the amount of inseam they have and need to lower the set height of their motorcycle. They just need an extra inch from the saddle height so they can flat foot the bike at stop signs.

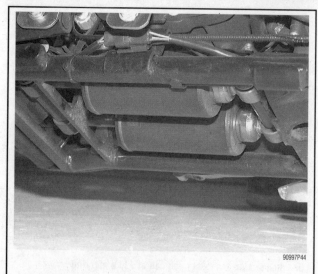

Fig. 58 The rear shocks on a Harley Fat Boy

Fig. 59 A typical threaded adjuster on a sportbike rear shock

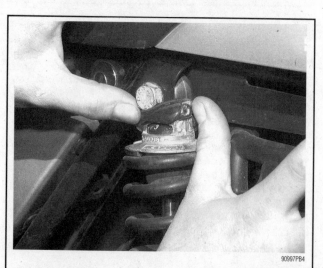

Fig. 60 Many aftermarket shocks will have adjustments that the stock shocks will not

Bikes like early BMW's are known for their nice supple ride, but nose-dive heavily under braking due to soft fork springs. Many people put heavy duty springs in the front forks of their bikes to help alleviate the problem.

The motorcycle manufacturers have to build machines that will meet the needs of most, but can't really make a bike that will meet the desires of all. Certain compromises have to be made so the greatest amount of people will be able to ride the bike. It is great if the stock suspension happens to work for you, but a lot of the time, the bike can be made better with a few tweaks. Sometimes simply replacing worn out stock components with new can make a bike return to its original form, but why not take the chance to replace the equipment with some high class suspension componentry?

In general, you can replace either the dampers or the springs in either the front suspension or rear. The rear suspension is typically made up of a shock and a spring assembly, or pair of them on older design bikes. The front is usually a fork that contains springs and the damper valves, except on the new BMW's that use the Telelever front suspension with a control arm and coilover shock similar to the rear unit on most bikes. Also slightly different is the Harley-Davidson Springer front suspension with its exposed springs. There have been a few other forkless designs, but they aren't very common.

It is recommended that the front and rear suspensions be modified at the same time with matched components. If you only modify one end of the bike, the suspension can be adversely effected and the bike will not handle in a proper manner. Ask the retailer or manufacturer of the suspension for their recommendations as to what would be appropriate for the bike to do the modification correctly.

You have to decide what your goals are in the suspension modification game. If you are looking for better handling or better control of the bike under extreme loads, you will be aiming for a different set up than the person who wants to lower their bike. If you are trying to solve a particular suspension problem, check with the suspension manufacturers. They probably have already figured out the solution and have it ready to install.

We called Progessive Suspension® when we wanted to upgrade our presidents bike. Well over 6 feet tall and we won't even discuss his weight, he needed some real expertise for setting up his BMW K-bike correctly. The folks at Progressive gave us the equipment and information we needed to set up his bike to suit his needs.

Most stock suspensions have a minimum of adjustments. They usually come with a preload adjustment and sometimes a damping adjustment. Aftermarket suspensions come with a full range of possibilities. Some aftermarket suspensions resemble the stock pieces, but may have a few little tweaks or maybe finer performance.

Other aftermarket suspensions come with enough dials, wheels, adjustments and doodads to keep the most techno oriented rider sated. I have seen rear shocks for bikes that have hydraulic (not the typical ramp and peg) preload adjustment, compression damping adjustments, rebound damping adjustment (both with what seemed to be millions of adjustment positions), a remote gas filled reservoir and a very pretty aluminum housing. It was almost a shame to mount this unit on a bike. It should have been put on the wall with a frame around it. Joking aside, this shock helped turn a fine handling bike into an awesome handling bike with the capability to be adjusted to almost any riding situation.

Check with your dealer to find out what they recommend for suspensions. They have a lot of experience with your type of bike. Also check with other people who ride your type of bike and do your type of riding. They can offer some personal insights. Call the manufacturers and find out what they have to offer. They may already offer the suspension you need, already to go packed up in a box.

When you buy a suspension for your bike, you will typically buy a set of fork springs and a rear shock with spring (or a pair as needed). Either can be installed by the do it yourselfer in most cases. All it takes is some patience and effort.

HOW TO INSTALL

Fork Springs

▶ See Figures 61 thru 78

A glance in a repair manual will draw gasps of horror from anyone who has never been inside a fork leg before. The exploded view of most forks show very complicated and seemingly incomprehensible collections of parts. I know the first time I did fork springs I was a bit nervous about popping off those fork caps! Once I got myself calmed down, I realized that the job was very straight forward and almost (almost!) easy.

1. The first step in changing fork springs on most bikes is getting rid of the old fork oil. Occasionally you might find a freak bike without drain plugs. On these bikes you will have to remove the forks to get the oil out. Refer to your shop manual for that information. On most other bike there will be a drain plug at the bottom of the fork leg. You need to remove the old fork oil by draining it. I recommend catching the old oil and measuring how much came out. It can help guide you to the amount you will need to put back in.

2. Support the front of the bike so the forks hang at full extension. This will lesson or remove the spring preload. If your bike has a centerstand,

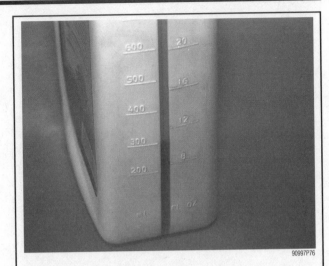

Fig. 63 Measure the amount of fork oil that was drained from each fork leg

Fig. 61 Most fork drain plugs are at the bottom of the fork leg and are easy to get at

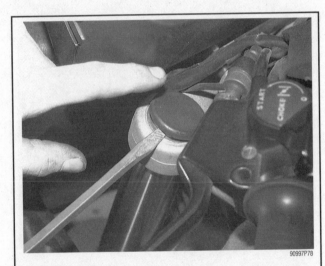

Fig. 64 With the handlebars out of the way, the tops of the fork legs are exposed

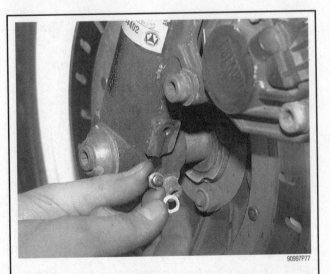

Fig. 62 Make sure to replace the crush ring under the drain bolt

Fig. 65 This fork uses a retaining ring in a groove to hold the cap in place

Fig. 66 Pressing down on this cap will allow removal of its retaining ring

Fig. 69 A hooked wire will reach down into the fork to get at the fork spring

Fig. 67 Pull the cap out of the fork leg (if it didn't already pop out and bounce across the shop floor)

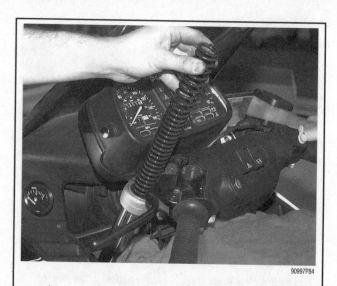

Fig. 70 This bike had two spacers and two springs per fork leg

Fig. 68 Pull out any spacers that may be installed

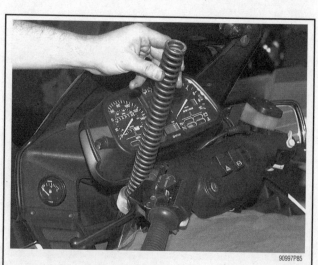

Fig. 71 The new spring from Progressive Suspension® just drops in along with . . .

you are good to go. If you don't have a centerstand on your bike you will have to use a jack or bike lift. Just make sure the bike doesn't tip in the other direction!

3. You will need to access the tops of the fork tubes. Some bikes have the tube tops exposed, others will require you to reposition the handlebars to get at the tube tops. If you have to dismount the handlebars, matchmark them and try to move them without disconnecting any of the controls; See if you can just undo the bolts holding the handlebar and move it to a better location. This is simply a way of reducing work for you. You will have to disconnect controls if you find that they might get damaged if you move them too far or you will have to readjust everything.

4. With the fork tube tops exposed, you will have to remove the plugs. Some just unscrew, other have a retaining ring holding them in. In either case, it is very important to be careful when removing them as there is a spring beneath them ready to pop the cap off and toss it across the room! If the cap is the screw type, use a correct size wrench to turn the plug out (or go running all over the town looking for a wrench big enough when you discover you don't have one! Been there!). If the plug doesn't thread out and is held by a retaining ring, press down on the plug to expose the retaining ring and remove it. Gently ease the pressure on the plug and allow the spring to push the plug up and out of the bore.

5. With the plugs removed, take note of where the end of the springs are. Do they protrude from the top of the fork legs or are they even with the tops? Maybe they are recessed down a bit from the edge. This is important information as it may be needed to set the preload of the new springs.

6. Pullout the old springs and spacers noting the location of each. Check the instructions that came with the fork springs as to the proper pre-loading of them. Sometimes the new springs have to be spaced so they are even with the top of the fork leg, othertimes not. Only the instructions will know for sure.

7. If you need to make spacers, use PVC pipe or metal pipe. If you use the plastic, make sure to use a metal washer between the two so the plastic doesn't get chewed up.

8. Place the new springs and spacers into position.

9. This is a good time to add the proper amount of fork oil as this is the easiest time to do this. In the case of some bikes, this is the only time to do this as they don't have seperate oil fill plugs on the fork leg plugs.

10. Check the condition of any seals and install the fork leg plugs.

11. Install the handlebars, using the matchmarks as a guide, and get the bike back on the ground to pump up the forks. This will distribute the fork oil throughout the inner workings of the damper assembly.

12. Take an easy test ride on the bike to get used to the new suspension.

Fig. 73 . . . makes it flush with the top of the fork leg

Fig. 74 Use a pre-measured amount of new fork oil in each leg as required

Fig. 72 . . . a spacer cut to the proper length that . . .

Fig. 75 Install the fork cap, button up the rest of the bike and you are done

Fig. 76 This fork cap has a place to add fork oil without having to remove the whole cap

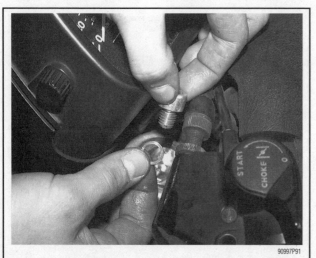

Fig. 77 The fork oil fill uses a crush washer that needs to be replaced each time it is removed

Fig. 78 Small hole! A small tube and patience will get that fork leg filled during future fluid changes

Rear Shocks

◆ **See Figures 79 thru 93**

Most rear shocks are relatively easy to get at and that is what this procedure describes. Some shocks are buried in the bowels of the bike and require some major disassembly to get at them, but once you are there, removal or installation should basically be the same. Refer to a repair manual for shock replacement if you have this type of bike.

1. Raise the bike so all the weight is off of the rear wheel and it is hanging at full travel. Use the centerstand or jack up the bike to get the rear tire off the ground.

2. Remove any components that may be in the way of removing the shock. Items that may need to be removed include: luggage, luggage racks, exhaust systems, side panels and other side mounted items.

3. If the shocks are air filled, bleed off the air from the units. Disconnect the air lines if fitted with a single air filling port.

4. Remove the upper and lower mounting hardware. Keep track of the washers and spacers that may come off with the shock.

5. Install the new shock and use the supplied mounting hardware. New performance shocks may be equipped with spherical bearings in place of the original rubber bushings. There may be spacers used that aren't used in

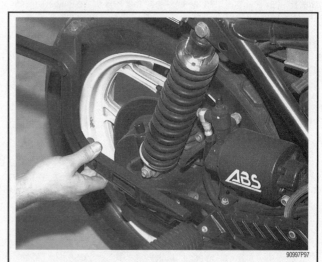

Fig. 79 This bike needed to have the luggage mount removed to get the shock off the stud

Fig. 80 To get at the mounting hardware on some bikes, you may have to take off more than what you would think!

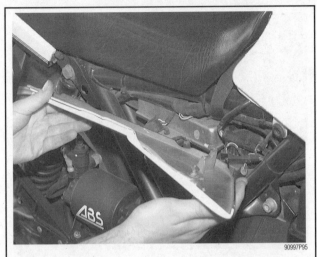

Fig. 81 The side panel popped off on this bike to expose the upper shock mount

Fig. 82 We used this crowbar to raise the suspension enough to take the weight off the mounting hardware

Fig. 83 Look on the rear of the fastening hardware. You might need to use a backup wrench

Fig. 84 If the weight is off the hardware, the bolts should just slip out

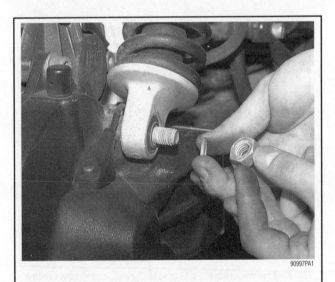

Fig. 85 The lower mount on this bike is just a stud

Fig. 86 Once all the hardware is off, the shock just slips out

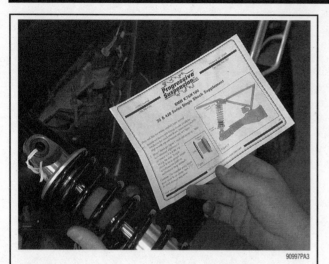

Fig. 87 Always read the instructions for specific information for your bike

Fig. 88 This performance shock used O-rings and spacers in the heim joint mount

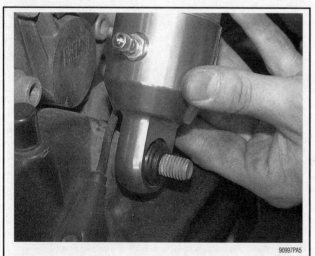

Fig. 89 Make sure any and all spacers are in place before tightening down anything

Fig. 90 Make sure the shock is in the correct orientation or adjustment dials may not be able to be reached

Fig. 91 Always tighten the mounting hardware, lower . . .

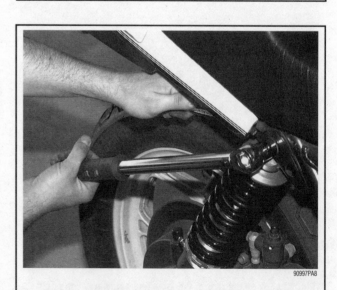

Fig. 92 . . . and upper to specifications

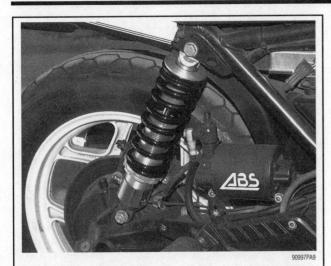

Fig. 93 With the shock installed, it is time to make the initial adjustments

the original mounting scheme. The installation instructions will show the proper mounting. Tighten the mounting hardware.

6. Install any parts that may have had to come off to gain access to the shocks.

7. Do the basic adjustment to the shocks to get baseline. Adjust the spring preload so the sag (the difference in length of the shock when loaded and unloaded) is approximately 20 to 30 percent of the total travel. Turn all the damper adjustments to the default setting as determined by the manufacturer.

8. Test ride the bike and make any adjustments as needed.

If the bikes suspension feels harsh over bumps then loosen up on the compression damping. If the suspension feels bouncy, increase the rebound damping. If the suspension bottoms out, increase the spring preload. You will find additional suspension set-up information in Section 9 of this book.

Luggage

Just a quick note here: Milk crates strapped to the back of the bike are very passé! Not to mention it is a crime to steal them. With out milk crates to attach to our bikes, we need to find a good substitute. Fortunately the aftermarket and OEMs have come to the rescue with a huge selection of add-on luggage.

HOW TO SELECT

The variety of luggage for bike is pretty darn impressive. There is a piece of luggage that will fit your needs; You just have to find it! There are different styles available and some are more appropriate for your type of riding than others. Some will fit well on your bike, while others won't. You need to sift through the collection of luggage and find what best suit your needs.

Some things to consider are how much space do you really want or need? Will you be carrying a passenger and won't be able to use the seat as additional luggage space. Do you want something that is waterproof? Can you mount it on your bike?

Saddlebags/Panniers
◆ See Figures 94, 95, 96, 97 and 98

The traditional motorcycle luggage is the saddlebag, also known as panniers. The saddlebag mounts so each of the two compartments hangs on a side of the bike, typically behind the rider. The bags can be thrown over the rear seat, or some mount the connecting piece under the rear seat. Some are pieces of hard luggage that mount to racks on either side of the bike.

They come in all sorts of styles. Some are basic rectangular bags, while others are more triangular shaped to match the lines of a sport bike's tail section. Some are just big black boxes that resemble suitcases mounted to the sides of your ride.

For the most part, saddlebags and panniers will give you the most amount of storage space on the bike. They also keep the loads weight lower than any other storage system, which is good for handling.

Some bags can even hold a helmet and can lock it away for the time you must leave your bike. Some bags can be removed from their racks and be carried around like a suitcase, which is great for long tours and when you want a quick way to move your stuff into your tent or hotel room.

Most hard luggage requires that you attach a luggage mount to the bike. Some of the mounts blend into the bike easily, while others stand out and are very noticeable. If that is a concern for you, you may not want to consider hard luggage.

If you pick soft luggage, be careful when mounting it. On some bikes, the luggage will hang down very closely to the rear wheel. If your bike has this problem, you will have to come up with some type of guard to keep the bags from flapping into the spokes. I once saw a Ducati 916 with custom made luggage guards for just that purpose. It just goes to show that you can put luggage on darn near anything!

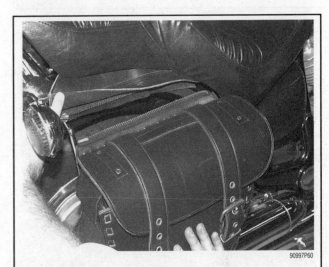

Fig. 94 These leather saddlebags unzip so you can take them away with you

Fig. 95 This is a more generic type of fabric saddlebag that can work with almost any bike (and is waterproof to boot)

Fig. 96 Some saddlebags are custom made to fit the look of the bike

Fig. 97 These hard bags release from the bike after pulling a few levers

Fig. 98 This style of saddlebag has its mount under the seat

Tank Bags

▶ **See Figure 99**

Some people love tank bags while others hate them. Tank bags mount in front of the rider on top of the tank portion of the bike. They are very handy since they have many little pockets to stash toll tickets, money, maps and sunglasses. Tank bags are the best place to keep everyday items on a bike since it is the most easily accessed.

Tank bags mount with either a strap system or magnets. The strap system is the most secure, but not as convenient as a magnetic mount. A magnetic mount has a series of magnets built into the base and sticks itself to the bike. Keep in mind that not all bikes have steel tanks and those with plastic covers or aluminum tanks won't be able to use them. You will also want to keep away anything that may be effected by the magnetic field like credit cards or audio tapes.

Tank bags come in all sizes from thin units that are basically map pouches to mongo bags that expand so much you have to look around them! Some tank bags have adjustable sections or removable parts so you can customize the size as you need. Look for a bag with good water resistance and the ability to cover it with a rain cover if it gets drippy out.

Fig. 99 This tank bag has a map pouch and is expandable to hold a days worth of riding gear

Some tankbags have separate bases that attach to the bike and allow you to merely unzip or unclip the bag from the base. This makes it easy to take your stuff off the bike without having to redo all the straps. Some manufactures make bases specific to a bike. This custom fit makes for a very secure bag.

Trunks/Tail Bags

▶ **See Figures 100 and 101**

Storage that is mounted on the tail section of the bike is often referred to as tail bags when they are soft luggage or trunks when it is a hard case. Most trunks mount to a rack or get bolted directly to the bike. The mounts are usually permanent parts of the bike and the trunks have a quick release on them so you can easily take them off when needed. Tail bags are often just strapped to the passenger seating area with bungees or straps.

There are versions of the tail bags that mount to a passenger backrest and resemble a back pack. These units are bigger than a traditional tail bag and stand in a vertical position. It allows you to pack a lot of stuff on a bike that may not have a large amount of other storage possibilities

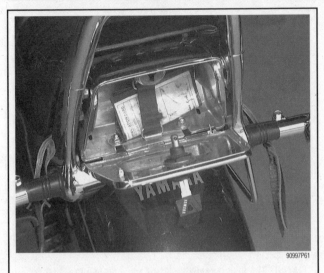

Fig. 100 This bike even has a built in trunk

Fig. 102 The owner of this bike keeps a few spare tools in this windshield bag

Fig. 101 You can even mount bags on things like crash bars

Windshield Bags

▶ See Figure 102

Windshield bags are often just small bags that mount to the base of the windshield at the forks. They are used to store some small tools and they are popular with the cruiser crowd. Most of the time they are black leather and sometimes come decorated with conchos and fringe; Not something you are likely to find to a CBR900RR! Keep in mind when adding anything to the front forks, you will effect the handling of the bike. As a result, keep the bag small and lightweight if you decide to use one. Check that they don't contact the front fender under suspension compression.

HOW TO INSTALL

The mounting method will vary according to the type of bag or luggage you get. Any of them will come with instruction that you should follow exactly.

Soft luggage

▶ See Figures 103, 104, 105, 106 and 107

Soft luggage has the advantage of adapting to many styles of bikes. Because of this, it is impossible to explain exactly how to mount it to every bike! In general, soft luggage has a set of straps that reach down to the frame of the bike or other strong mounting points. The trick is to locate the straps so the bag has even tension on all the straps and the bag can't slide around. Nothing is worse than a bag getting loose at 60 mph (100 kph)!

Saddle bags hang on each side of the bike and are held together by a central strap or web. Sometimes this center part mounts under the seat or through the frame at the rear. The bags can also be slung over the seat. Most bags will have stabilizing straps to keep them from flapping or dislocating.

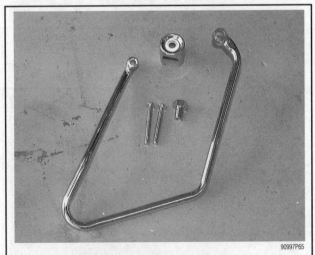

Fig. 103 Some bikes require that you install a bag guard to keep soft luggage out of the rear tire and swingarm

Fig. 104 The kit was made by the bike manufacturer and used existing holes

Fig. 107 The bike is ready to accept soft luggage now that the guards are in place

Fig. 105 This kit provided matching hardware so the new bolts didn't clash with the chrome

Tank bags, whether magnetic or not, will usually have a strap the goes around the steering head to act as an anchor. On magnetic bags, this strap is a tether in the unlikely case that the bag breaks its magnetic bonds with the tank. Be careful with any tank bag where it contacts the bodywork. Make some type of provision to protect the paint from scuffing by the bag or its straps. I have a nice hole in the clearcoat of my tank from where a tank bag strap buckle dug in during one trip.

Tail packs have the dubious honor of occasionally turning into back rests and as a result, need to be very secure. They aren't designed to be back rests, but riders tend to slide back and put a lot of pressure on the mounting straps. Make sure the straps will hold up to the double job!

Hard luggage

♦ **See Figures 108, 109 and 110**

Hard luggage requires the bike to have some type of permanent mount that the bags attach to. Whether or not the bags are removable from the bike, the mounts themselves are permanent. Some bikes such as BMW'S, have factory hard luggage available and thus can be bought (or equipped) with the luggage mounts. Some other bikes need the support of the aftermarket for hard bags and yet others come stock with them.

Fig. 106 Take care when replacing hardware that might affect the bikes handling, like this shock mounting nut

Fig. 108 This is a Krauser made hard bag. It is the standard bearer of bike luggage

Fig. 109 Not exactly the most beautiful bag, but it has proven to be functional

Fig. 111 Luggage racks are convenient mounting spots for bulky items

Fig. 110 This is a modern hard bag mounted on a BMW K100

If factory luggage is available, it is usually a simple matter of acquiring the factory mounts and bolting them up to the factory made holes. If the bags came from the aftermarket, you will be at the whim of the bag maker. There are a number of excellent and reputable hard luggage manufacturers that provide instructions along with a full mounting kit. You may or may not have to drill parts of your bike to mount the new hardware. Talk to the supplier of the kit to determine what it will take to get your luggage attached.

Luggage Racks

▶ See Figure 111

Luggage racks are usually mounted behind the seat and are used as a mounting platform for strapping down things (but not milk crates!).

HOW TO SELECT

Check the manufacture of your bike for factory luggage racks. Many bikes have accessory racks available for them. If not, the aftermarket has a selection of racks out there. Some racks will be small and are used for small payloads. This is common for bikes with limited space behind the seat. Larger racks are available for bikes with solo seats or on larger tour

machines. These racks can mount all sorts of stuff, but keep the load rating of your bike and luggage rack in mind when packing!

Some luggage racks act as mounting points for tail trunks. This makes for a convenient set up that is usually quick dismounting.

HOW TO INSTALL

Luggage racks are like hard bags mounts. They bolt to the bike using holes already provided or by sharing mounting points with other items such as fenders or brackets. The rack will come with a diagram and/or instructions on proper mounting. If the rack shares a mounting point with another item, be sure to tighten the fastener so proper clamping forces are applied to the joint.

Check that the rack doesn't interfere with turn signals or the visibility of the tail light as some racks can extend over the stock light.

Grips/Pegs

HOW TO SELECT

▶ See Figures 112, 113 and 114

If you really want to be amused, pick up a cruiser accessory catalog and try to list all the available styles of grips and pegs. There are seemingly as many different styles as there are motorcycles on the road.

I classify grips and pegs in two categories: fashion and function. The fashionable units are made with prettiness in mind and are not necessarily the hot ticket for usability. On some bikes this won't matter. If the bike isn't ridden very far or is used as a show bike, who cares if you have chrome steel grips with o-rings as the sole friction surface? They look cool!

On the other hand, functional units can include factory replacement grips and pegs or aftermarket units that hope to improve on what was originally there.

Grip styles include solid rubber, gel cushioned, foam rubber and heated. Heated grips are usually available as an option on a new bike, but they can be retrofitted to unequipped models. There are also some aftermarket heaters that are thin membranes that fit under the regular grip and get wired to the bikes electrical system.

People tend to gravitate to either rubber or foam grips. If you like thicker grips, foam is probably the way to go. They also tend to damp some vibration that comes through the handlebars. The downside is that they wear quickly and require frequent replacement. I happen to like them and they aren't too expensive, even for BMW factory replacement units.

Regular rubber grips are good, long lasting choices for a standard bike. The thinner design fits many peoples hands better than the thicker foam grips. Their life can also be rated in seasons and not mere months!

Fig. 112 Stock pegs tend to be big, heavy and vibration dampening

Fig. 113 Highway pegs allow the rider to stretch out a bit

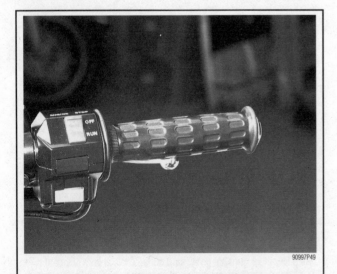

Fig. 114 Grips come in all sorts of sizes, materials and shapes

Pegs can come in a few different functional styles based on how they mount and their stated purpose. Some pegs are simple metal bars made of light alloy for the racer crowd. They provide a smidgen more cornering clearance. Some are designed as "highway pegs." These mount out in front of the rider and allow the rider to stretch out in the saddle. They may be paired with forward controls that move the shifter and brakes up to the position of the pegs. Conversely "rear sets" move the controls further back so the rider can get into more of a crouch for boy racer duty.

In addition to the solid metal ones, pegs can be solid rubber or hollow to help reduce vibration.

Keeping your grips and pegs in good shape will help you maintain control of your bike by keeping your hands and feet where they are supposed to be!

HOW TO INSTALL

Grips

▶ **See Figures 115, 116, 117 and 118**

1. The old grips can be removed by either sliding them off (unlikely) or making a slit down its length and peeling it off (most likely).

Fig. 115 This foam grip lead a hard life and needs to be replaced

Fig. 116 Rubber grips tend to live forever, but should be renewed to regain some tackiness

Fig. 117 Some rubber grips are cushioned to help absorb some vibration

Fig. 118 The shiny areas on this grip indicate smooth and slippery places. It needs to be replaced

2. Clean the handle bar where the grip mounts on the left or the throttle sleeve on the right. Make sure that the surface is perfectly clean or the new grips may have difficulty sliding on.

3. Some grips will just slide right on while others will be very stubborn. In those cases, lubricate the insides of the grips with contact cleaner and slide the grip on quickly before it evaporates. If you are using gel type or foam rubber, coat the inside of the grips with contact cement and allow to dry. After the cement is dry, use the contact cleaner trick to get them on. The cement will help prevent the grips from rotating.

4. If there were end caps supplied with the grips, use some contact cement and install them to the bar ends.

Pegs

▶ **See Figure 119**

Most pegs simply bolt on and off. Make sure that the clamps are tight enough to prevent the pegs from rotating. Some designs will use spring washers to preload the pegs. If equipped with them, make sure they are in place. Forward controls and rear sets are more involved and will come with exact instructions to deal with the relocation of the rods and linkages.

Fig. 119 This chrome and rubber peg kit comes with everything needed to bolt it on

Handlebars

HOW TO SELECT

▶ **See Figures 120 and 121**

Handlebars will effect the way you the rider interact with the dynamics of the bike and will make a real change to its aesthetics. You can chose to change bars to better suit your desire of the style of the bike or to make a change to the way you fit on the bike. Keep in mind that changing one will effect the other.

There are many styles of handlebars. The old cruisers of yore had what were known as "ape hangers." These bars brought the riders hands almost above their heads in a show of something, but what exactly, I don't know. A more reasonable version of this is the buckhorn bars. These bars have a moderate pullback and angled grips. This bar is typically used on cruisers with laid back riding positions. Some touring rigs use a modified version of this as it promotes a relaxed riding style, good for many hours on the road.

As the ride moves towards the sporting, the bars tend to get flatter and less angled back. There are different amounts of rise which is the distance

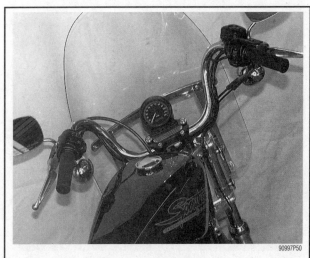

Fig. 120 These buckhorn bars are popular on cruisers due to the pull back and therefore, sit back design

Fig. 121 A sport touring bike has a flatter, less pulled back design than a cruisers bar

between the mounting clamps and the level of the controls. The flatter the bar, the more direct the steering becomes. Also, the wider the bars, the easier it is to lever the bike into turns, but at the expense of spreading the rider into the wind more.

At the far sporting extreme, there are bars known as "clip ons." These are short stubs of bars that get attached directly to the fork legs with the grip actually below the level of the triple clamp! There are modified versions that have the grip above the triple clamp for a slightly better street riding position. Pure clip ons are usually reserved for the race track.

If you like your handlebars but feel you need them a bit closer to you, there are adapters that bolt in place of the stock bars and then the bars mount to them. They raise and move back the handlebars. You don't need to change anything on some bikes, but others will require new cables and hoses, plus lengthening any wires that are too short.

HOW TO INSTALL

◆ See Figure 122

Installing handlebars requires the removal of the controls and subsequent reinstallation with proper adjustments. Brake lines have to be disconnected and later bled. Bodywork and instrument panels may have to be

Fig. 122 Most, but not all, bars are held by clamps on the triple tree

removed. New cables and brake lines may have to be installed to accommodate the change of position of the controls.

If you plan on replacing your handle bars, use a shop manual to walk you through the procedure so you don't miss any steps. Making a mistake can result in loss of control of the bike. Not a happy thing to happen! It can be done by the DIY'er, but it isn't a first time wrencher project; You should have some experience with the various systems that will be effected.

Engine Guards

HOW TO SELECT

◆ See Figures 123 and 124

Engine guards are typically hoops of metal the mount to the front frame of the bike and prevent the engine cases from contacting the ground in case of a fall. They are also known as "crash bars" but that has such a negative connotation!

Engine guards can also help prevent a bike from going completely on its side in case of a fall. This is good because some of the heavier tour rigs are

Fig. 123 Engine guards are designed to take the force of a fall and keep it away from the engine (and if you are lucky, keep the engine off your legs!)

Fig. 124 The engine guard spreads the force of a fall over multiple points along the bike's frame

almost impossible to get upright by yourself when they are laying on their sides. The downside is that they may limit your lean angles, but only in extreme situations.

Engine guards aren't just for the engine any more! Some bikes have additional hoops located further back on the bike to help prevent damage to the rear portion of the bike. This is useful on tour rigs that have luggage affixed to the bike.

On BMW oilheads there is a design of engine guard that bolts over the cylinder head cover. This is to protect the engine from knocks and scrapes in case the bike goes over, as the first thing to hit the ground is the cylinders of an opposed twin. Don't ask me how I know.

While they aren't accessories, there are bikes out there that have fall over protection in the form of hard points built into the bike that prevent damage to the softer bodywork. These hard points will typically take the form of little "wings" or bumps mounted low in the bodywork. They connect to the frame or engine and take the place of metal hoops.

HOW TO INSTALL

▶ See Figures 125 and 126

Engine guards can either bolt to the frame of the bike or clamp to the frame. Most original engine guards will bolt up to points on the frame, but

90997P40

Fig. 125 Upper mounting of a typical stock engine guard

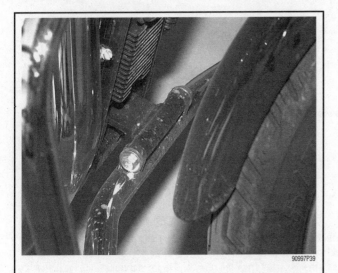

90997P39

Fig. 126 Lower mounting point of a typical stock engine guard

the aftermarket units may use the clamps to make it more universal. As the guard will be taking the full weight of the bike in a fall, I think the bolted systems will stand up better.

The engine guards will install in a fairly straight forward manner. A typical unit will bolt to the frame under the steering head at the top of the hoop and then down at the bottom on either side of the engine. There may be a brace going back along the bikes frame to help secure the guard.

Check that the engine guard doesn't interfere with any controls, cables, linkages, pedals or anything else.

Accessory Lighting

Good lighting is a must on a motorcycle. It is a good idea on any vehicle, but even more so on a bike. Just not does lighting help you see, but it will also help others see you. With some changes to the stock lighting on a bike, you can help out both sides.

HOW TO SELECT

When considering the stock lighting on your motorcycle, please contact the local authorities and find out the regulations for vehicle lighting. You may find that the modification you wanted to make will be illegal in your area and it is better to find this out before you do the work.

Running Lights

One of the most amazing sights I have seen was a full boat tour bike decked out for a light parade. This bike had lights everywhere on it! I'm not sure if they qualified as running lights, but they certainly got the job done!

Accessory running lights are used in conjunction with the stock lamps to make the bike noticeable to other traffic on the road. Some accessory running lights are adaptations of the stock turn signals to include another filament that is lit all the time. The stock single filament turn signal bulb is replaced by a dual filament bulb with one filament wired as the turn signal and the other as the running lamp.

There are LED panels coming onto the market that mount in the reflector housings and perform the same job as the above described dual filament bulb.

Complete housings can be added to the bike to act as running lamps and are often mounted on the perimeter of the bike as to make the outline of the bike show up at night time.

Passing/Driving Lamps

You can never have too much light! Some motorcycle lighting is excellent with modern designs and well thought out lighting patterns. Others are nothing short of pathetic. Most are in between the two and can stand a little help at times. Additional light can be put on almost any bike, with only two real concerns: Can the bike provide enough juice to run them and can you find some that you won't mind hanging on your bike?

One choice you have, if your bike is equipped with sealed beams, is to replace them with a reflector/bulb combination. Most new bikes are already equipped with this type of lighting, but a few bikes come without.

There are many designs available today. Some lamps resemble the old searchlights of yore and come standard on certain "nostalgia" oriented machines. These are the big chrome housing units that bolt on either side of the main headlamp. Other more modern units use fancy optics that allow the units to come in small housings that are easy to tuck away under fairings or in the bodywork.

There are even units that bolt to the fork legs providing lighting wherever the forks are turned (never mind that during turning the countersteer will point the lamps away from where you are going!).

When buying an accessory driving lamp, be sure to buy a quality unit. Low quality lights will have bad light distribution, reflectors that will fog quickly and sockets that burn out. Their mounting hardware will not be very good and may cause the lamps to vibrate. Spend your money wisely.

Good lights can come in different lighting patterns, but share similar housings. This will allow you to mount "fog," "cornering," or "driving" lights. Fog lights have a broad pattern, but allow practically no light to be sent upwards to reflect off the fog and blinding the rider. Cornering lights have short patterns that extend out illuminating the sides of the road. Driving lights have beams that project out far down the road. This allows for excellent illumination and forewarning of what is coming your way.

Any additional lamp will need to be aimed carefully, otherwise oncoming traffic may be blinded by your lights. Also check the local laws concerning additional lighting.

Additional Brake Lamps

STOP!!!!!

That is what you want to announce to all the people behind you when you hit the binders. Motorcycles are small compared to cars or trucks and drivers of other vehicles just don't see us well. They tend to look around us or not see us at all. This is a bad thing when everyone is rolling along, but even worse when we are slowing down. We want to prevent being rear ended because that is a very nasty thing on a bike.

One way to help the situation is to make it more obvious that we are slowing down. By adding more or brighter brake lights, we make ourselves more noticeable. Once again, check the local laws dealing with this type of thing, but I doubt you will find anyone who could complain about added safety.

You can simply add some lights that come on with the brake light to help matters out, but there are other choices. Relatively new are high output LED units that mount in the tail light housing and come on with either a steady light or a pulsing light. They can really make the back of the bike stand out. Similar units are made to stick to the rear bodywork. These units are small enough that they aren't noticeable until they light up. A quick glance will not show them to the looker.

There are brake light modulators that flash your standard brake light when actuated. They work well, but I would pick one of the LED devices that flash to put on my bike.

HOW TO INSTALL

▶ **See Figure 127**

When adding any kind of lighting to your bike, you have a few items to consider: location, load and legality. Any additional lighting may be subject to the whims (laws) in your area. Check out the laws and how they effect your plans for the bike. The laws may place restrictions on the size, placement, color and brightness of the lamps. Don't approach the laws as being restrictive, consider them as guidelines. You may find that they will give you ideas on how to implement a lighting scheme for your bike.

Check the output of your charging system. The specifications sheet in your owners manual should list this. The rating will probably be listed in watts. If it lists voltage and amperage, multiply the two together to get watts. There should also be a list of what bulbs the bike uses and if it doesn't, the repair manual will. Add up all the wattage's of the bulbs and take a guess at how much the rest of the electrical system draws; A call to a dealer should net you that information. Total all of it together and subtract from the alternator output. This result will give you a guideline as to how much additional lighting you can use. Some bikes have low output generators like my old BMW boxer; I have to be careful how much power I draw from the bike before I overload the alternator and cause the battery to discharge.

Any additional lighting whether driving lights, brake lamps or running lights will draw electrical current beyond what the bike's engineers planned for in the lighting circuits. Simply replacing the fuse with a higher rated one is not a good idea. The wires may not be sized to take the additional load. This is usually not a problem with brake light circuits since they are only used for short periods of time, but running light and head light circuits can be a problem. Driving lights should be wired as their own circuits anyway so they shouldn't pose a problem.

To get around the wiring limitations, use relays to drive the additional lighting. Use the stock lighting circuit to drive the relay and have the relays switch power the new lights. On any general purpose relay there will be four terminals; Two go to the coil and two go to the switch. The relay will be

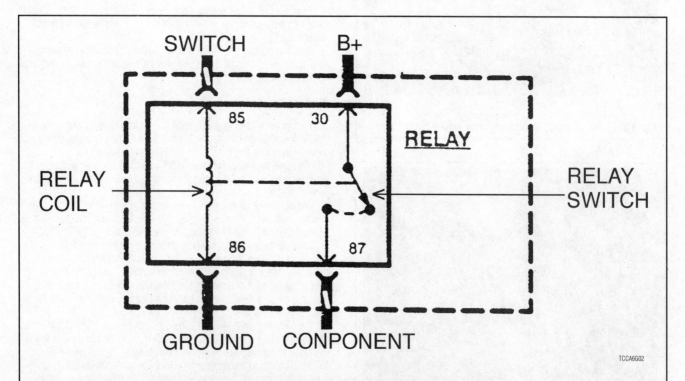

TCCA6G02

Fig. 127 Relays are composed of a coil and a switch. These two components are linked together so that when one operates, the other operates at the same time. The large wires in the circuit are connected from the battery to one side of the relay switch (B+) and from the opposite side of the relay switch to the load (component). Smaller wires are connected from the relay coil to the control switch for the circuit and from the opposite side of the relay coil to ground

marked with which terminal is which. Connect one of the coil wires to ground and connect the other to the stock lighting circuit. Connect one of the switch terminals to a fused lead from the battery and run the other to your additional lights. It is that easy!

Use wire that is of appropriate size for the circuit. For most lighting circuits except head lights and driving lights, use 16 gauge wire. For head lights and running lights, use 14 gauge. These are just guidelines, but they will get you in the ballpark.

I recommend against using wire taps. These are the little plastic (usually blue) pieces that you lay a piece of wire in and it pierces the insulation to make contact with the copper inside. They have a tendency to nick the wires and cause them to break over a period of time. They can also allow moisture to make its way into the wire and corrode it. If you need to tap into a circuit, trace the wire back to the connector and find the end. You should be able to make a connection there by extracting the terminal and soldering an additional wire to it.

If you buy driving lights from a good manufacturer, they will provide excellent instructions and often provide a pre-built wiring harness. Connect the ends and you are ready to go once you have mounted the lights. Always route the wires away from anything that may damage them.

Horns

HOW TO SELECT

Go out and hit the horn on your bike. Kinda wimpy isn't it? Now imagine cruising along at 60mph (100 kph) and have a truck start to move over on you. That horn you have seems inadequate doesn't it? There is a solution!

There are extra load horns available on the market. They take the form of either special electrical units or air power units. The Air horns have the most distinctive and loudest sound. The problem is that they need a lot of mounting room for the compressor, hoses and two trumpets.

The other choice is super loud electrical horns. They do a great job and mount in place of the original horn. These are the easiest to deal with overall.

HOW TO INSTALL

▶ **See Figure 128**

The electrical type horns simply mount in place of the original units and require nothing more than unbolting the old ones and replacing with the new. Sometimes a new bracket may be needed, but a piece of strap metal and a drill bit will fix your problem.

An air horn requires you to find a place to mount the compressor and

two trumpets. On larger bikes with plenty of bodywork this may not be a problem, but most every other bike will be. You also need to use a relay from the stock horn system to drive the new compressor as it will draw more current than the stock unit and may burn out the wiring or horn button if left stock. This may be a lot of work, but if you have the time, energy and space for it, air horns are a great addition to the bike.

Communications Systems

HOW TO SELECT

There comes a time where tapping Morse code on each others helmet isn't the best way of communicating between rider and passenger. Also, this is no way to communicate between bikes! The aftermarket has answered the problem with a slew of products aimed at making communication between riders easy and effective.

The earliest communications systems we have seen are nothing more than tubes that run between the helmets of rider and passenger. There were no batteries or connections to go bad. On the otherhand, there were no volume controls and it sounded like you were talking through a pipe (which you were!). We found one in the saddlebag of a bike one of us picked up at an auction. At first we thought it was just a jumble of tubes that got stuck in there, but once untangled, we saw what they were!

Lucky for us, the electronics manufacturers came out with simple communicators connecting speakers and microphones mounted in your helmet to a control unit allowing individual control of volume. Some have noise control features or the ability to attach an external audio source like a radio or CD player so the riders can jam to some music while cruising down the turnpike.

Another feature is the two way communicators that allow riders on different bikes to talk. This is very convenient when riding in pairs or larger groups. You can just talk instead of making crazy hand signals to get your point across. Just what is the international hand signal for "I need to make a rest room stop?"

HOW TO INSTALL

▶ **See Figures 129, 130 and 131**

Most helmet-to-helmet communicators mount the control box to the helmet of the rider. This way the volume controls are accessible to bother rider and passenger. The microphones and speakers mount inside the helmet with doublesided tape or hook and loop fasteners. Sometimes the helmets have ear pockets that the speakers can just slip in to.

Be careful when routing the wires; You don't want to get the wires caught

Fig. 128 The openings of the horns should face down so any collected water can drain out

Fig. 129 This communicator can be used as a wired system between rider and passenger or wireless between bikes

Fig. 130 The ear speakers mount in the helmet as close as possible to the users ears

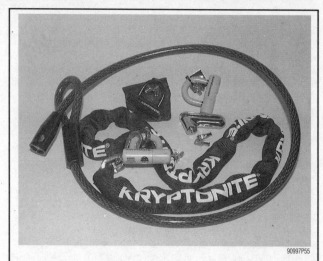

Fig. 132 With a selection like this from manufacturers like Kryptonite®, there is sure to be a lock to fit your needs

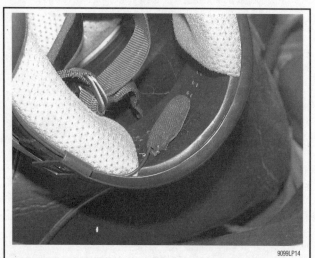

Fig. 131 The microphone mounts in the chin bar of a full face helmet

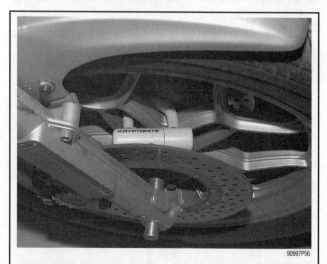

Fig. 133 Just putting a lock around the spokes of a wheel makes the bike hard to move

on any moving parts. You also don't want the wires to wrap around you in case you have to get off the bike in a hurry. Do remember when dismounting the bike that you are connected to each other and pull the plug before walking away.

When using communicators, keep the volume low enough that you don't block out all the external sounds. You still want to hear what is going on around you.

Alarm/Theft Deterrent Systems

HOW TO SELECT

Locks

▶ See Figures 132 thru 138

There are probably dozens, if not hundreds, of different ways of locking your bike up. Locks fall in the category of theft deterrent, not prevention, as a thief who really wants your bike will get it. A lock isn't going to prevent them from taking what they really want, only slow them down. The trick is to make your bike look like it will take too much time to steal and the thief will move on to another target.

Fig. 134 Nothing short of a blow torch is going to cut through this chain

Fig. 135 Some Harleys use this type of tab style fork lock

Fig. 136 A disk lock is a convenient and obvious way of showing your bike is protected

Fig. 137 Cable locks aren't as secure as some of the other types, but are very handy to use

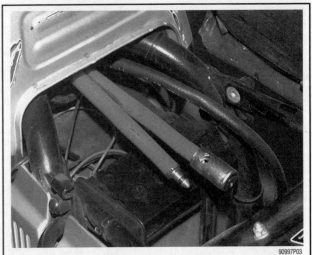

Fig. 138 BMW has gone as far as providing a place to store a cable lock

Some bikes have locks built in to them. My bike has a locking fork, a locking seat and a place to store a cable lock. This is nice, but none of the built in locks are very visible. Only by using my cable lock do I give passerbys any notion that my bike is protected.

The aftermarket has realized that security is as much conspicuity as it is strong locks. One of the more popular motorcycle locks is the disk lock. This style lock fastens through the front brake rotor or on the wheel spokes. The manufactures have gone ahead and made them in bright colors so they are noticeable to potential thieves. They are also noticeable to the rider who starts to ride off without removing the lock, hopefully preventing a very sudden stop!

Other types of locks include cable locks which thread through the frame or fork of the bike and then can be attached to a post or just left entangling the bike. Once again, they tend to be brightly colored as to be highly visible.

A new twist to the old fashioned chain and padlock is a specialty chain made up of flat links encased in a protective sleeve. The chain is bigger and stronger than almost anything else out there. The one down side is that it weighs as much as a boat anchor! The good part is that no one is likely to defeat it.

Some bikes, namely some Harleys, use a fork lock which is nothing more than a tab on the fork that aligns with a tab on the frame. A pair of holes line up to allow a padlock to be placed in them. This locks the fork solidly to the frame. A standard padlock can be used, but the aftermarket has responded with a higher security barrel lock type with a plastic coating to prevent scratches to the bikes finish.

A popular style is the "U" lock. This lock has a long locking bar shaped like a "U" naturally and the end is closed off by the lock itself. This style allows the bar to pass through the bike and around something else or just catch a few different parts of the bike. This is also a handy lock to use to secure helmets to the bike.

Keep in mind that locks only work when they are used and they won't do you a bit of good hidden in the bikes storage area. Get them out and noticed. They may not stop a thief who absolutely has to have your ride, but it will make their job a bit tougher.

Alarms

Motorcycles can now be equipped with alarms in a similar style as automobiles. They have some of the same features and functions except for automatic window roll up! Alarms are a great addition when using a lock since the combination will resist even the most persistent thief.

Alarms are hard wired into the bike and use sensors to detect when someone is messing with your baby. The alarm may use a vibration sensor or a tilt detector. A vibration sensor detects tiny movements on the bike such as someone starting to touch it. A tilt detector will be set off when the angle that the bike is sitting at is changed. The alarm may also use a current sensor, in case the thief manages to bypass the other sensors. The current sensor detects when an electrical circuit is turned on like an ignition switch.

Another sensor technology is the mass sensor. This sensor projects an ultrasonic field around the bike and senses when the field is entered by some mass (read: person). Usually the alarm will chirp to notify the intruder that the bike is protected and if the person doesn't move, the alarm will sound.

The alarm can be equipped with a siren to warn anyone in the area that your bike alarm has been triggered. Most alarms will turn off after a set period of time if the input that triggered the alarm doesn't exist anymore.

Another method of alerting that the alarm has been triggered is a pager. You can wear a pager and it will tell you if your alarm has been tripped. This is good if you live in an area where car alarms are commonly set off and no one pays attention to them anymore.

A good alarm will arm itself once the bike is turned off or allow you to arm it via a remote control. Some units come with anti-carjacking features which will allow the bike to be ridden away, but with a click of the remote, the alarm will shut the bike down on the thief. This allows the bike-jacker to get away from you, but not to get to far and be caught by the police.

Another handy feature of some alarms is the starter interrupt. This feature cuts the power to the starter, so even if the thief gets through all the other protection layers, they won't be able to get the bike started.

HOW TO INSTALL

Most alarms come with detailed instructions on how to install the unit. Some are very easy to install as they are self contained units requiring only a power lead to go to it. As the options go up, such as light flashers and starter cut-outs, the number of wires involved increase.

The big trick when installing an alarm is hiding it enough that a thief can't disable it. Unlike a lock that needs to be obvious, you want to bury the alarm controller as deep as possible to keep it safe. Putting where it can't be seen is the trick and that goes for the siren too. It may be tough but spend some time figuring a good place to put the unit and the results will be worth it.

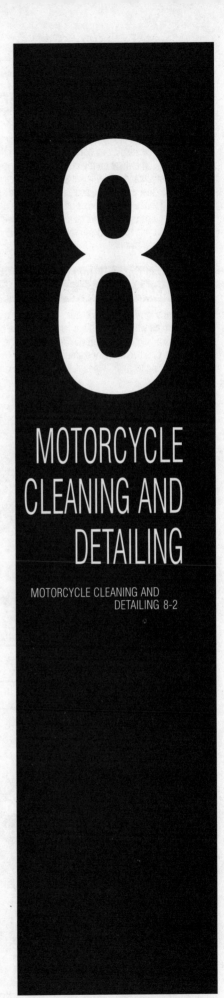

8

MOTORCYCLE CLEANING AND DETAILING

MOTORCYCLE CLEANING AND DETAILING

This is the section for those of us who like looking at our bikes and seeing a bright, shiny motorcycle. Now I have to admit that if you looked at my car you would be suspicious of me putting this section together (I think there is paint somewhere on my car, but don't ask me what color it is). My bike on the otherhand is a different story; I enjoy cleaning and polishing my Bimmer. With just a little time and effort, the grime and muck that coats a bike after a good hard ride comes off and leaves a motorcycle to be proud of. I think motorcyclists in general take pride in their rides. I can prove this: Go to a motorcycle rally and you will see a field full of bikes that are cleaner than their owners!

The Differences Between Cleaning a Motorcycle and Cleaning a Car

There are a few differences between a motorcycle and a car that we need to keep in mind when washing our bikes. All of the controls and instruments are exposed on a motorcycle and you need to be careful when spraying cleaners or solvents on and around the bike.

Since the engine and all the related controls are exposed to the ele-

Yuck!

90998P17

Getting ready to polish it up!

90998P15

ments, we need to keep an eye out for potential problem points. For example: You don't want to spray some heavy duty solvent on the engine to find out later you just doused the electronic control unit for the ignition with water and cleaner! Avoid electronic parts and switches when spraying direct streams of water.

Don't use a high pressure cleaning wand to spray down a motorcycle; Water and cleaner can be forced past seals and gaskets into lubricants or other areas not tolerant of water. Use only a low pressure garden hose or equivalent.

Don't wash a road salt covered bike with warm water! This will only speed up the effect of the salt on the bikes finish. Wash it down with cold water first.

Paint Detailing

UNDERSTANDING YOUR MOTORCYCLE'S FINISH

If all you want is a shine, you can have it. Wash the motorcycle. Apply wax or one of the cleaner/wax combination products. Buff with a clean cloth. The finish will shine—but it won't be "detailed."

For some bike owners, a shine is enough, because, as the miles and months and years go by, they forget the mirror-like brilliance and vibrant color perfection of their motorcycle's finish when it was fresh from the factory. However, that "wet look," as though the finish had been applied only moments before, was probably a key reason they bought the bike!

Detailing aims to do nothing less than recapture, insofar as possible, a motorcycle's original showroom look. And to restore the factory-fresh "wet look" to its finish. A mere wash and wax won't do it.

To understand why not is to understand how to refresh and restore its showroom look: how to detail its finish.

Two progressive afflictions, oxidation and scratches, first dim, then dull, and finally degrade a motorcycle's finish, as described below.

Oxidation

Oxidation is a chemical reaction between atmospheric pollutants and the paint's pigments. The oxidation of conventional motorcycle paint (and, to a lesser extent, the newer clearcoat finishes) creates an ever-growing layer of scum on the paint's surface. In conventional finishes, the scum is "dead paint": the oxidized top color layer of paint. In clearcoat finishes, what's oxidized is the see-through protective top layer of the clearcoat. Unless the finish is regularly detailed and the scum removed, the oxidation layer thickens and builds and dulls the paint.

Waxing does not remove the oxidation. It merely covers it up. No amount of waxing alone can recapture oxidized paint's original color or vibrancy. Only detailing can.

Scratches

Look closely at your bike's finish. Better, examine it with a magnifying glass. The finish—whether conventional or clearcoat—is cross-hatched by a myriad tiny scratches. Wear and tear from many sources—from washing brushes to wind friction— cause motorcycle paint scratches. Whether in conventional paint or in the top layer of clearcoat, scratches have the same effect: they opaque the paint, bending (refracting) light rays from their normal straight paths. The result is ever-diminishing clarity. (Pro-detailers call clarity DOI—Distinction of Image.)

Waxing does not remove or correct a finish's light refracting hairline scratches; however, detailing can. Detailing removes the oxidation, the finish's "dead paint." Doing so, it uncovers and exposes a fresh, original color layer once covered and obscured by oxidation; or, in the case of clearcoat, removes what amounts to a film that blurs its see-through clarity. Detailing also removes or fills in the light-bending scratches and, with oxidation removed and scratches filled in, protects the revitalized finish from further oxidation or scratching.

DETAILING PRODUCTS

▶ **See Figure 1**

You can pick and choose from dozens of motorcycle products formulated to remove the oxidized paint layer, fill in the scratches, and protect the revitalized paint or clearcoat from further degradation. Here is how finish detailing products are generally classified:

- Oxidation removers (in order, from the most abrasive to the least abrasive): rubbing compounds, polishing compounds, cleaners, and polishes.
- Scratch removers: polish and glaze.
- Scratch fillers: glaze and sealer.
- Finish protectors: wax.

If, reading various product labels, you're confused as to what is a "cleaner" and what is a "polish," to say nothing of "compounds," you aren't alone. Even their makers only hazily differentiate between "cleaners" and `polishes."

There is, however, a critical difference between the four types of oxidation-removers. The critical difference is their degree of abrasives. Whatever their type, most oxidation removers contain grit, a sandlike abrasive that acts much like sandpaper to remove surface imperfections. Oxidation is a surface imperfection.

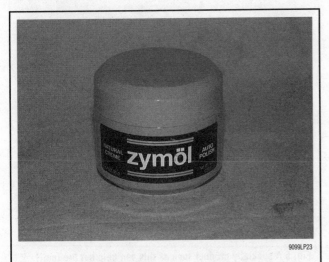

Fig. 1 Using high quality products can make the process of detailing your bike easier

Polishes, Cleaners and Compounds

▶ **See Figure 2**

In detailing your motorcycle's finish, start with the least abrasive, a polish. (So fine are some grits used in the polishes and cleaners especially formulated for clearcoat finishes, which cannot tolerate abrasion, that they produce a paste that is not abrasive in the usual sense.) If polish doesn't remove the oxidation, progress to a slightly more abrasive oxidation remover, a cleaner. If you are absolutely convinced that something even more abrasive is needed to remove badly oxidized finish, usually found on long neglected paint jobs, use the even more abrasive product, a polishing compound— but use it with great care and with minimum application pressure SO as not to cut right through the finish and down to base metal. Rubbing compounds are SO abrasive ("aggressive," in detailing lingo) that they should probably only be used by pro-detailers and paint shop experts. Improper use of such products puts your paint job at risk.

Fig. 2 Polishing and rubbing compounds need to be respected when using as they can mess up a finish faster than they can help them!

Glazes

Often a watery, sometimes transparent liquid, glaze has two primary jobs: to fill in tiny scratches and, buffed, to produce a brilliant shine. Glaze is applied with a clean, non abrasive 100% cotton cloth and allowed to dry. The glaze dries as a haze, which is buffed to a lustrous shine. Buffed semi-wet, glaze often produces an ultimate shine—a shine which, almost immediately, must be protected by wax. If left unwaxed, glaze and its benefits are quickly dissipated by sunlight.

Sealers

Sealers perform and are applied much like glaze. The chief difference between a sealer and a glaze is the visible effect on the finish. Glaze gives the finish a higher luster than does sealer. However, sealers generally do a better job of enhancing a finish's depth of color and reflective clarity (DOI). Like glaze, most sealers lose their effect unless protected by wax.

Wax

▶ **See Figure 3**

Wax, in motorcycle detailing, has four important functions:
1. It protects the newly exposed fresh paint or clear-coat layer.
2. It protects the scratch-filling glaze or sealer.
3. It produces a brilliant, mirror-like shine.
4. It weatherproofs and waterproofs the finish.

What about combination products which claim to do two, even three, things in one step? Among combination products are cleaner/waxes, sealer/waxes, polish/waxes, and wash/waxes. Most combinations are easy and quick to apply, but the combinations seldom if ever do either job as well as do single-purpose products. Exceptions may he some sealer/glazes and some cleaner/polishes. Both partners in these combinations do essentially the same job.

If it's simply a shine you want, the combinations may deliver it, and in considerably less time than the sequential application of two to four single-purpose detailing products. However, if you want your motorcycle s finish to be the best it can be, detailing's ultimate promise, stick with single-purpose products.

Before you begin detailing the finish, you need to know whether your motorcycle has a conventional finish (the kind of paints all motorcycles were painted with, until recently) or the newer clear-coated finish. Abrasive polishes and cleaners, as previously noted, must never be used on

Fig. 3 There are many waxes on the market. Check the applications on the label before using them

Fig. 4 The old standby bucket and sponge may not be enough to make your bike sparkle

clearcoat finish. Abrasives can permanently scratch the clearcoat, destroying its see-through clarity.

If you are unsure whether your motorcycle's finish is conventional or clearcoat, check your owners manual or ask the dealer from whom you bought the motorcycle. A quick test of the finish may also help you to decide: With a non abrasive cloth, apply wax or a mild polish to a few inches of finish in some out-of-sight place. Rub firmly but gently. If finish color comes off on the cloth, the motorcycle probably has a conventional finish. If no paint shows on the cloth, the finish is probably clearcoat.

One last decision remains before you set to work. Should you randomly select various finish-detailing products, such as cleaner, polish, glaze, and wax? Or should you use a step-by-step, product-by-product detailing "system" as formulated and tested by the various product makers? While finish restorative systems invariably use only a particular maker's products, these maker-recommended products—and their step-by-step application—all but guarantee superlative results. The systems take the guesswork out of product selection and help you avoid finish-damaging mistakes.

❋❋ WARNING

If you are in doubt about whether your paint job is conventional or clearcoat, treat it and detail it as though it were clearcoat finish. Use only products whose labels specify that they may be used on clearcoat finish.

DETAILING THE BODYWORK

Washing

▶ See Figures 4, 5 and 6

Three basic rules about washing:
1. Do not wash and detail your motorcycle in the sun.
2. In extremely cold weather, do your washing and detailing indoors (preferably in a heated place).
3. Work only on a cool motorcycle (hand-test the motorcycle's surface temperature before you begin).

While wash products will remove most oil and grease stains, road tar—which may smudge a motorcycle's lower parts—may need special effort and special products. Stubborn, dried tar and grease can be removed with special tar removers, but they also remove wax. Specially formulated tar cleaners are available from most local automotive supply retailers.

Steps:
4. With your hose's nozzle adjusted to medium spray, thoroughly wet the motorcycle's finish, washing off loose grit, dirt, and pollutants.

Fig. 5 A specialty product such as this can help get the really tough crud off the finish

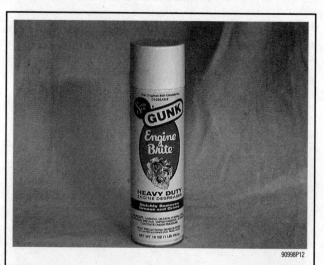

Fig. 6 A product like this may attack aluminum engine components, so be careful when using them

5. Soak towels thoroughly in sudsy wash solution. Use minimum application pressure. The sudsy solution acts as a lubricant between your wash cloth and the motorcycle's finish. The aim is to loosen surface dirt and pollutants, float them off the finish, and hold them in suspension within the solution. Floating them off prevents them from scratching the finish. Dunk the cloth frequently in your bucket of wash water to get rid of suspended, potentially abrasive particles. Work with a clean, sopping wet cloth, heavy with solution. While application in a circular motion is easier, and for most detailers more natural, a forward-backward motion is better because it does not leave circular swirl marks in the finish.

6. Some pro-detailers wash the dirtiest parts—wheels, fenders, and lower body area—first. Others start at the top and work their way down. Either way, replace dirty water with fresh as you finish each area and switch to clean towels to prevent trapped dirt from contaminating the areas you just cleaned.

7. Pay particular attention to hard-to-reach places: areas behind the fairing, inside fenders, wheel spokes, front and taillight assemblies.

8. Rinse well with a medium spray from the hose, flooding areas to float particles off.

9. Dry with clean, non abrasive cotton cloths, preferably terry towels, or with a soft chamois or sponge.

Quick-dry tip: Ride around the block. Air and wind will get rid of excess rinse water, especially in hard to dry places as the grills, vents, and emblems. But don't drive so far as to dry the finish. Some moisture must remain to prevent spotting during final towel-drying.

As you dry, be sure not to let any water droplets remain, because they'll leave spots in the finish. Don't neglect to dry wheels and chrome. If any dirt comes off on your drying cloth, you didn't wash the finish well enough.

Removing Oxidation

If the finish is heavily oxidized, use a good cleaner; use a polish if the finish is only moderately or marginally oxidized. Whatever the product, make sure its label specifies it's to be used for your motorcycle's type of finish (conventional or clearcoat, or both).

There are many cleaners available for either conventional or clearcoat finishes. Read labels carefully to determine what is appropriate for your motorcycle's finish.

Polishes, cleaners, sealers, and glazes, when manually applied, are allowed to dry only up to the point of being "nearly dry"—then they are wiped and buffed. Allowing any of these products to dry completely before rubbing them off and buffing the finish risks the possibility of abrasive "chalking"; that is, the tiny particles of hard, dried product can, themselves, become abrasives.

Steps:

1. Apply cleaner or polish to a 1-foot-square area with a clean, non abrasive, 100% cotton cloth.

2. Use the preferred back-and-forth motion if you can; use a circular motion if you must. Apply only enough cleaner or polish, and buff with only enough pressure, to remove oxidation. Stop frequently to observe results. When oxidation is removed from a conventional finish, the newly exposed color layer shows deep, original color; a clearcoat finish relieved of oxidation has renewed, see-through clarity. Guidelines for buffing conventional finishes and clearcoat finishes appear below:

a. **CONVENTIONAL FINISH** Since you're working directly on pigmented paint, expect some color to come off on your rag. You are working to remove only the oxidized, dead paint, and to expose a fresh layer; when deep-toned, fresh paint shows, stop. You want to remove as little paint as possible. Removing more than necessary will only thin the pigment layer, not improve its color.

b. **CLEARCOAT FINISH** To remove the oxidized top layer of clearcoat, follow the procedure given for conventional paint—but be aware that clearcoat can be tricky. Because you aren't working on color pigment, but rather on the finish's transparent protective paint, no color shows on your cloth. You must therefore stop more frequently to observe results. When the clarity of the clearcoat has been restored and the deep-toned color underlying the clearcoat shows through, stop. Further application of cleaner or polish will needlessly remove good clearcoat, reducing the clearcoat's protective thickness.

3. When a small area has been cleaned and buffed, move to an adjacent small area. Doing one small area at a time reduces the chances of the product thoroughly drying and abrasively "chalking."

4. Work carefully around insignias, headlights, taillights, moldings, crevice areas, and the "opening" edges of fairings and luggage—places where cleaner or polish, if allowed to dry thoroughly, will be tedious to remove.

5. Hand-buff to a high gloss.

Glazing/Sealing

Closely inspect the cleaned, oxidation-free finish and note where hairline scratches are most severe. Glaze and/or sealer fills in minute scratches and is buffed to a high shine. The finish's ultimate shine depends on the shine you buff into the glaze or sealer, not on the shine of its final wax protective coating. Glazes buff to a high luster; sealers generally do not buff to as high a luster, but they produce deeper-toned color.

If you use glaze, use a single-purpose product; if you choose to use a sealer, use a combination product, such as a glaze/sealer. Single-purpose sealers have other finish corrective uses not discussed in this book.

Steps:

1. Apply successively to small finish areas with a clean, non abrasive 100% cotton cloth. (Some detailers prefer cheesecloth available at your local automotive parts retailer.)

2. Allow it to semi-dry to a haze. Buff to a high gloss.

3. If you can't achieve a high gloss, reapply glaze or sealer/glaze and buff again.

Waxing

▶ See Figures 7, 8 and 9

Waxing after application of glaze or sealer is essential to protect the glaze from dissipation by sunlight and to achieve ultimate depth of color in conventional finishes and ultimate clarity in clearcoat finishes.

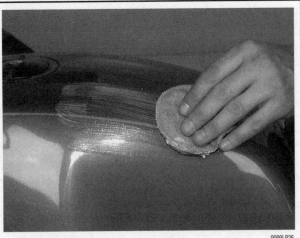

9099LP26

Fig. 7 Apply a thin layer of wax using a soft terry cloth applicator like this one

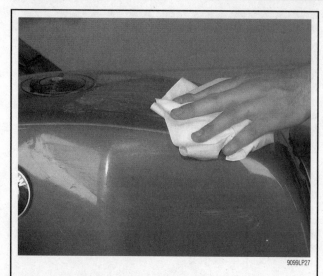

Fig. 8 Use a lint-free cloth to remove the wax

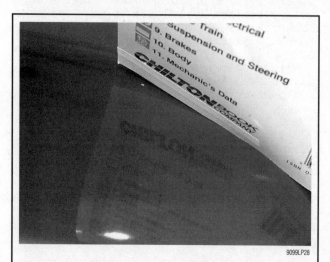

Fig. 9 A well waxed surface allows you to see well-defined reflections in the paint

There are a few exceptions to this wax-after-glazing rule. Some glazes do not require wax protection; however, these glazes must be reapplied frequently—too frequently to suit most driveway detailers. Most glazes of this type are used to super-shine show bikes being entered in a competition (in which motorcycles are judged on their excellence of appearance).

For a long-lasting wax job the best choice is Carnauba. The wax, derived from the Brazilian Carnauba palm, is nature's hardest wax, providing hard, long-lasting finish protection. Carnauba also has the highest melting point of any natural wax. It remains protective even at temperatures of 200°F (94°C). During summer's hottest days, in the hottest regions (as the Southwest), a black motorcycle left in the sun can reach such elevated temperatures.

➡**Waxing is seldom a one-step operation. Far better to apply a thin coat of wax initially, then buff it, then apply a second thin coat. The first merely gets into the "pores" of the finish; the second fully overcoats the finish.**

Choose a Carnauba paste wax over a Carnauba liquid wax. The paste contains a slightly greater percentage of Carnauba. Spray-on waxes contain considerably less Carnauba because the formula must be thinned to spray. With the paste, it is also easier to apply the wax in a very thin layer, which gives best results and which buffs easiest to a super shine. Two thin wax

applications with buffing in between is usually the best approach for long-lasting results. Properly applied, Carnauba wax may continue to protect your finish, depending on climate and other conditions, for as long as 3–6 months—and sometimes longer. The areas that receive lots of sun may need waxing more frequently.

Steps:

1. Apply successively to small areas of the finish with a damp 100% cotton cloth. A terry cloth towel that has been laundered in fabric softener is the best applicator.

2. With back-forth motion (or circular motion, if you must), apply a thin, even layer of wax.

3. Buff with a clean non abrasive cloth. Repeat until the finish is completely waxed and buffed to a brilliant shine.

Cleanup

Wherever cleaner or wax has hardened in crevices (on edges and the like), remove it with a cotton swab or a used, soft-bristled toothbrush. Also recommended: a soft paintbrush, its bristles trimmed to about a 2-inch (50mm) length, which can get into the smallest places.

BASIC TOUCH-UP TECHNIQUE

▶ **See Figure 10**

Apply enough thin layers (coats) of color-matching paint so that the surface of the touch-up is level with, or slightly higher than, the surface of the surrounding finish. If higher, level the touch-up, when absolutely dry. to finish height using extremely fine wet-sanding paper (at least 600 grit), followed by a polishing compound (only experienced nick-fixers should use rubbing compound, which is more abrasive). Then detail the repaired nick place and a small finish area surrounding it as you would ordinarily detail the finish: apply glaze or polish; then wax and buff

Fig. 10 Touch up paint is available in small tubes like these with brush applicators

Quick Fix For Very Small, Nonrusted Nicks

Time required: 5-20 minutes (per nick)
Materials needed:

1. All-purpose cleaner or carwash solution color-match paint
2. Artist's brush
3. Extremely fine wet-sanding paper (at least 600 grit)
4. Masking tape (optional, depending on scratch size and location)
5. Cotton swab
6. Glaze
7. Wax

Steps:

8. Thoroughly clean the nick area, using a cotton swab wetted with all-purpose cleaner or carwash solution.

9. When dry, apply a dab of color-match paint to the nick using a modeler's or artist's brush. (Some detailers use the tear-off end of a match from a matchbook.)

10. Let dry. If the surface of the touch-up is not even with, or slightly above the surface of the surrounding finish, repeat the dab-and-dry cycle until it is.

11. Wait a day or more, even a week, to let the touch-up thoroughly dry. Paint takes far longer to dry completely than most bike owners believe.

12. When you are sure the touch-up is dry, very carefully level it (if it is not already level) with the surface of the surrounding finish. Rub the spot gently and only enough to bring it level, using a very small piece of 600 grit (or finer) wet-sanding paper.

13. Apply glaze to fill in any scratches left by the sandpaper. Then wax and buff the touch-up and a small area surrounding it.

Touching Up Larger Nicks And Scratches

Time required: 30-60 minutes (per touch-up)
Materials needed:
1. All-purpose cleaner or carwash solution
2. Masking tape
3. Cotton swab
4. Artist's brush
5. Fine steel wool (000 or 0000)
6. Color-match paint; primer, if needed extremely fine wet-sanding paper (600 grit or higher) polishing compound
7. Glaze
8. Wax

This procedure is similar to that given above for the quick fix, but there are some important differences:

Steps:

9. Mask closely and completely around the nick to protect the surrounding finish. The width of the masking should be at least 1 inches (25mm); 2 inches (50mm) wide is better.

10. If the nick is rusted, very gently remove visible rust with fine steel wool (000 or 0000) or with extremely fine wet-sanding paper (600 grit or finer).

11. If the nick or chip has penetrated to bare metal, apply a base coat (primer) as the first few coats in the paint buildup. When primer coats are thoroughly dry, begin applying thin coats of the color-matching finish paint. If the finish is clearcoat the final coats must he a clearcoat finish compatible with the original.

POLISHING CHROME (RACKS, MOLDING, TRIM)

A good chrome polish renews and shines most chrome. Once chrome has been cleaned and shined, apply the same Carnauba wax used on the finish. Waxing a motorcycle's chrome is as important as waxing its finish. Wax preserves chrome's brilliance and prevents rusting. Most chrome is cleaned and polished with a dual-purpose chrome cleaner/polish. Where chrome is pitted or rusting, a two-step chemical cleaning treatment often works best. Chrome-plated plastics are best cleaned and protected by products specially designed for chromed plastics.

➡ **Do not wax chrome exhaust pipes as the heat will burn off the wax and possibly discolor them.**

Clean and polish body chrome before glazing the finish (just after you apply cleaner or polish) to prevent chrome cleaner from streaking the glaze. When you wax the finish, wax body chrome, too. Non-body chromed parts, like luggage racks, can be cleaned, polished, and waxed later.

Steps:

1. With a soft cloth, apply chrome cleaner/polish to a small area of chrome. Let it dry, then rub and buff with a clean cloth.

2. Inspect the cleaned area. Remove any road tar with tar remover. If there are pits or scratches in the chrome, soak a toothbrush in cleaner and scour them clean. Rusty places may require two or three applications of cleaner and gentle use of steel wool (00 or 000).

3. Be careful not to get chrome cleaner on the finish, or in the crevices of chromed fittings (for example, headlight and taillight assemblies). Most chrome polish, once dry, is hard to remove from crevices, rubber, and plastic components (such as taillight lenses). Removing the cleaner from unwanted places is time-consuming and tedious, even using a clean toothbrush or cotton swab. Shorten the cleanup time by not getting the cleaner where you don't want it.

4. When the chrome is clean and shined, wax it.

Making Chrome Rust Disappear

Some suggested rust removal detailing aids:
1. Grease remover
2. Steel wool (grades 00, very fine; 0000, super fine, and 000, mid range fine)
3. Steel.wool soap pads
4. Wet sandpaper, 600-1200 grit
5. Chrome cleaner/polish (one-step cleaner/rust remover and polish; two-step acid-neutralizer chrome cleaner; or both)
6. Artist's knife
7. Artist's paint brush
8. Aluminum paint
9. Automotive quick-dry spray-on clear lacquer or urethane (gloss or flat finish)

Chrome rust on small areas, such as luggage racks, mirror fixtures, wire wheel spokes, handles, or molding, calls for a decision: (1) Have it rechromed; or (2) detail it back to good looks and renewed life by removing the rust, repairing (if possible) the rusted area, then preserving its restored good looks with a coat, or several, of clear, spray-on lacquer or urethane, a liquid plastic.

The easy way is to have it rechromed. You merely remove the rusted parts and have a chrome shop rechrome them. However, rechroming can be expensive as well as vexing. And unless the chrome shop is reputable, you stand an odds-even chance of having to rechrome again 5 years or so down the road.

Also, just as with repainting, it is probably true that not even the best rechrome job can match the quality or life expectancy of original factory chrome.

Even if you find a reputable chrome shop (look under "Plating" in the Yellow Pages), it may not handle small jobs, whatever the price. Many plating companies replate only jewelry, silverware . . and, yes, plumbing fixtures! Even those which make it their business to rechrome antique automotive parts like bumpers often don't handle automotive or motorcycle bric-a-brac, such as luggage racks.

The logical, inexpensive choice is to detail it yourself. Detailing can often restore rusted chrome to a reasonable-and-usable-semblance of its original, gleaming self. Whether or not a rust-corroded small part can be returned to its former glitter depends, obviously, on the extent of the rust. First, do as pro-detailers do: carefully inspect the rust-affected chrome surface, including weld areas, if any. If whole areas of chrome are missing, literally peeled away, no amount of detailing will restore what's no longer there. You have no choice: either have it rechromed or buy new.

If your careful inspection seems to indicate surface rust—rust which coats, rather than digs deep into, the chrome—try a simple experiment. Find a small area where rust seems heaviest, and work over the area very lightly with fine steel wool. You may get an unexpected surprise: just a few light strokes with steel wool may clear the surface of rust. Beneath lies gleaming chrome. You've discovered a rusted part that can be restored to near-new, usable condition.

Pro-detailers prefer three extremely fine grades of steel wool when working with chrome rust. None, with proper use, will scratch, mar, or remove chrome. Proper use almost always means light use. You exert the absolute minimum pressure necessary to clean and polish the chrome surface, no more. All three of these pro-detailer preferred grades of steel wool polish chrome as they clean and remove rust. And all have myriad other uses in detailing; for example, cleaning and restoring the sidewall areas of tires.

The finest, least abrasive steel wool is "quadruple-0," so called because its numerical grade designation is 0000. It is also often called super fine or 4-0 steel wool.

Only slightly more abrasive but widely used by pro-detailers because it gets the job done faster without risk of chrome-surface damage is "double-0" steel wool, whose grade designation is 00 (or 2-0). It is often called veryfine steel wool.

Mid-range between these two is "triple-0" (3-0) steel wool, whose grade designation is 000. Many pro detailers prefer the "triple-0" because it "works" faster than the super fine 0000 but is less abrasive than the 00.

The more zeros in a steel wool's grade designation, the less abrasive it is. All three grades are inexpensive, usually come in ready-to-use pads, and are available in hardware, home center, and auto supply stores.

You can test the detailability of most surface-rusted parts and accessories—that luggage rack, for one—without rushing out to buy steel wool. You probably already have steel wool soap pads in the kitchen. One of these will do an effective job of surface-testing rusted automotive chrome. But the steel wool is coarser (typically 01), so you have to use a super-light touch.

Some pro-detailers rid chrome of rust using 600 to 1200 grit wet "sandpaper." These useful papers actually contain no sand, but rather waterproof silicon carbide. This is the same type of "sandpaper" that gives fine furniture and fine cars their final, super-smooth, mirror-like finish.

True to its name, wet sandpaper is used wet. Soak the sandpaper in water. Keep it and the corroded surface wet as you sand away the rust; 600 to 1200 papers are only mildly abrasive (the higher the grade number, the less abrasive). Still, they must be used judiciously, with only light application of pressure. You want to rid the chrome of rust, not remove or thin the chrome itself.

Among the least abrasive wet "sandpapers" available are 1200 to 2000 grit wet sandpaper, often used by pro-detailers to achieve a mirror finish on newly repainted cars, including those with a clearcoat finish. Judiciously worked with water-wetted 1200 to 2000 grit paper, then waxed, a finish coat achieves a depth of luster and sheen that often looks fresh from the factory.

All abrasive rust-removers are used by pro-detailers with a single purpose: to quickly remove the worst surface rust. Rust that is below the chrome surface must be removed by other, nonabrasive means.

Restoring Chrome

Time required: 45-60 minutes for usual exterior chrome; 3-4 hours for large chrome accessories (such as luggage racks)

Materials needed:
1. Dropcloths
2. Newspaper
3. Masking tape
4. Spray-on lacquer or urethane
5. Household steel wool soap pad
6. 00 steel wool; 000 or 0000 steel wool
7. Household scouring cleanser and soft-bristled tooth-brush or spray-on acid-neutralizer chrome cleaner (for removing weld-seam rust)
8. Aluminum paint and an artist's brush (to cover weld-seam rust that resists removal)
9. Chrome cleaner
10. Wax

Let's detail a typical chromed accessory luggage rack:

First, remove the rack from the bike. All readily detachable chrome bric-a-brac should be removed for detailing, since you risk damaging the bike's finish with rust-removal agents.

Once you have removed the rack (or other part), if the rust is heavy, you might begin as do some pro-detailers—with a very light going over with a household steel wool soap pad soaked in water to release suds. The pad's relatively coarse steel wool should only be used in the initial rust removal step. Switch to slightly abrasive 00 steel wool. Use dry. Then as most of the rust is removed—and you begin working on the original chrome surface—switch to less abrasive 000 or least abrasive 0000 steel wool. Remove as much of the rust as possible including tiny pinhole deposits, without marring or removing any of the chrome.

Chrome is often thin. It doesn't take much rubbing to rub right through it. The first indication that you have done so is often a dulling of the now-clean chrome surface. That, or the chrome seems off-color because you have reached, or at least are approaching, the underlying plating layers, the top one often being copper.

Happily, on such bric-a-brac as luggage carriers, which are bolted to a bikes frame, the heaviest rust is often virtually out of sight—on the underside of the rack's crossmembers. This is because underside areas collect more moisture (rain, dew, snow), are in the shade (not in direct, drying sunlight), and are areas most often neglected in routine cleaning and waxing.

Welds present a special problem. Weld seams (where two frame members are joined by welding) collect rust, too. But with one difference: rust in weld joints is almost impossible to reach or remove with steel wool alone.

How do you get at, and remove, weld seam rust? Sometimes you can work a household scouring cleanser into the weld seam with a toothbrush. Simply moisten a soft-bristled toothbrush with water, dip the wetted bristles into the scouring powder. and go to work on the rusted weld seams.

Or you might try any of several spray-on acid-neutralizer chrome cleaners. These products were developed primarily for cleaning chromed wire wheels (and their spokes) and for chromed bumpers. but may work on weld seam rust as well.

If you use one of the chrome cleaners, follow the directions carefully. If weld seam rust is still visible, there's an effective last resort. To obliterate the last visible rust from a chromed weld, carefully paint the seams with aluminum paint. The painted joint will not exactly match the tone or color of the chrome. but if you do the job right, the aluminum-painted seam will scarcely be noticeable.

To conceal tiny rusted weld seams with aluminum paint, you need: (1) quick-drying aluminum paint: (2) an artist's brush—a #2 fine-bristled brush works best; and (3) a steady eye and equally steady hand. The object is to paint just the rusted seams and not the surrounding chrome.

Some detailers paint seams before polishing, before a final spray-on coat of clear lacquer or urethane. Other detailers polish the chrome first because some chrome cleaner-polishes remove the paint, even when it's thoroughly dry.

With seams painted and rust removed, give the chrome parts a final cleaning and polish before lacquer spraying. Be careful to avoid leaving finger or hand prints on the polished chrome. Grasp the workpiece with a clean rag or paper towel.

Any number of good chrome cleaner/polishes are available at auto supply stores. There are roughly two types of readily available chrome cleaners: those applied and then almost immediately rubbed off with a soft, clean rag; and those which are allowed to dry before polishing. The best products of both types will brighten even once-rusted chrome to almost-new appearance. The let-it-dry/rub-it-off chrome polishes may do a slightly better job than the wipe-off-wet type, but dried residue, while easy to rub off, has a habit of lingering in cracks, seams and crevices. Cleaning every last vestige of dried cleaner/polish from such hard-to-reach places adds considerable time and work to the detailing job.

No polishing product, whatever its claim, seals in the shine of refurbished chrome with the permanence of a spray coat of clear lacquer or urethane, available in handy spray cans at most auto and paint stores.

For chrome, especially if you've used aluminum paint, choose gloss, not flat, lacquer or urethane. Both are clear final coats, meaning they are see-through, no-color finishes. But the gloss adds luster to the painted seam areas, making them blend in with the rest of the chrome.

You don't have to be a spray-paint artist to do a credible job. But you need patience. Rush the spraying, and you'll botch this final, critical step in chrome refurbishing.

On complex parts, such as a luggage carrier, with its crossmembers and front/back/side surfaces, the spraying can be spread over several hours, even several days. Why? Because you spray on a very thin coat of clear finish, then let it dry. Next, apply a second coat. Then turn the rack over and repeat the process until every surface and crevice is overcoated with a clear final finish.

For each of the several critical steps in spray-coating refurbished chrome, there's a right and wrong way to do it.

Steps:

11. Start right. Provide protection against overspraying, even when the detailed part has been removed from your bike. Low-cost dropcloths are extremely thin sheets of plastic, some less than 1/10th of a mil thick. Position the dropcloth behind, under, and all around the part you're spray painting. If the part you're spraying is attached to the bike, mask all around it with newspaper. Then cover a wide area, 6 to 10 feet all around, with a dropcloth, held in place with masking tape. If there's even a whisper of a breeze (don't spray-paint in anything heftier), extend your masking even more. Breeze-carried overspray can reach distant areas you never dreamed it could reach.

12. Thoroughly mix (shake) the spray can contents. Most directions tell you to shake at least one full minute before using, and shorter periods while you're spraying. Many users don't. The result is something less than a satisfactory job. Most spray cans contain a little ball that mixes the paint; when the ball begins to do its mixing job, you can hear it rattling. Keep shaking the can a full minute (better, two minutes) after the ball begins to rattle.

13. Spray it right. For professional results, spray in quick, thin coats. It's easy to spray too much clear lacquer or urethane because it is colorless and all but invisible. Hold the can 12 inches—or better, 16 to 18 inches—from what you're painting. Make quick, smooth passes, applying a very thin coating. Then stop. Let the thin layer thoroughly dry before you apply another thin layer. Let that dry thoroughly and repeat the process until the entire bric-a-brac is sealed in a crystal clear, glossy cocoon of lacquer or urethane.

14. Wax it. When the protective see-through coating is absolutely dry, wax it with a high-grade wax, such as 100% carnauba. Waxing is essential protection for the lacquer or urethane, just as wax is the essential protector of your bike's body finish.

Rushing to apply successive coats almost always gives poor results. Sure, the chrome may look and feel dry, but insufficient time between coats results in a rough, splotched finish, not the desired glossy smoothness. A rough lacquer finish can't be repainted unless you want to wet sand and start all over again at square one.

Another helpful tip: Spray cans, for all their convenience, have the nasty habit of clogging. Once the nozzle is clogged, it's next to impossible to unclog. But it won't clog if you follow the simple directions on the label (something a lot of users don't heed). When finished with a spray pass, hold the can upside down, nozzle down, and depress the plunger for about 3 seconds so that the propellant cleans and clears the nozzle.

DETAILING VINYL AND RUBBER PARTS

Vinyl or plastic parts, such as seats, after washing, are cleaned with a vinyl cleaner/polish. Clean black vinyl or rubber parts with any good vinyl cleaner, followed by waxing. There are products available that are specially designed for cleaning and restoring black vinyl and rubber parts. Do not use these types of products on the tires as they can be slippery. Why would you want to make your tires slippery if you had the choice?

There are common products on the market that are touted as "protectants". Be careful with these products. If they contain petroleum products, they may actually remove the plasticizers from the materials you put them on and over a period of time, damage the material. These products leave a nice shiny surface and are quick to use, but in light of the future damage they may cause, you may choose to stay away from them.

DETAILING WHEELS AND TIRES

▶ **See Figure 11**

Wheels and tires are "show parts." In detailing wheels, especially, consult your owners manual for any special manufacturer's instructions. Clear-coated or painted wheels can be scratched or permanently damaged by abrasive cleaners or polishes. Wheels made of magnesium ("Mag") or aluminum clean and shine best and safest with special products. Not too many motorcycle wheels are made of magnesium, but some old racing bikes being restored for show just might have them. It works best to detail one wheel at a time and to detail the tire/sidewall areas first.

90998P16

Fig. 11 This wheel is in need of some help!

Detailing Tires

Only if you have to, put any kind of product on your tires. If you do, only put it on the sidewall, not the tread. Use only products designed for use on tires; Some protectants are very slippery and you don't want them anywhere near your treads! Some petroleum based products can degrade the rubber over a period of time, so take the effort to read the label on the product to make sure it is safe for use on tires.

Steps:

1. Use a tire brush and an all-purpose cleaner to clean the tire to the tread line.
2. Let the tire dry.
3. Apply a protectant to all visible black tire sidewall areas. Do not put on the tread area. Protectant brings out and renews the tire's deep black color. Most protectants work best when you leave them on for several hours (or, even better, overnight) before wiping off any residue.

✳✳ CAUTION

Putting anything on the tires of your bike risks reducing available traction. We do not recommend using anything on your tires.

Detailing Wheels

▶ **See Figures 12 and 13**

Steps:

1. Rewash wheels. Then apply an all-purpose cleaner, as for tires, above. Wheels and their wheel wells are often the dirtiest parts of your motorcycle (other than a non-detailed engine!). Wheels pick up road tar, grease, and black brake dust.
2. With a soft cloth apply a good wheel cleaner. You can use one of the specialty wheel cleaners designed for the type of wheels you have (Mag, aluminum, or painted), or you can use one of the cleaners that work safely and efficiently on most kinds of wheels.
3. Whatever cleaner you use, use it gently. Wheels are surprisingly scratchable, especially if clear-coated. If your wheels are clear-coated, use only wheel cleaners specified for clearcoat. Work the cleaner into wheel recesses using a toothbrush or cotton swab.
4. Spoked wheels and wheels with intricate designs take some extra doing—generally with a toothbrush, swabs, and a non abrasive cloth soaked in cleaner or soap suds. And, yes, your fingers, too, which can reach into places many cleaning aids can't (many motorcycle enthusiasts even detail in the hub!). It's a labor-intensive job, but the good news is that once done right, spoked, finned, and other wheels are easier to clean the next time around.

Fig. 12 A variety of brushes will be needed to get at all the nooks and crannies of a bike's wheel

Fig. 14 Spray bottles are a good way of applying cleaners and other products

Fig. 13 Make sure the wheel cleaner you will be using is compatible with the type of wheels you have

Fig. 15 Don't forget cleaning products for the other parts of your bike

5. Rinse with a hose or bucket(s) of water and let dry.
6. Wax with the same wax you used on the finish.

DETAILING'S DETAILS

▶ **See Figures 14 and 15**

Here's a quick checklist of detailing's details:
• Antennas. Use a good chrome cleaner. Polish, then wax. If the antenna is clear-coated, treat as clearcoat finish.
• Gas fill port and cap. They were spotless when you bought the motorcycle; detail them to showroom condition.
• Chromed tailpipes. Use 00 or 000 steel wool to rid them of rust; then use chrome polish. Tailpipe heat makes waxing a waste of time.
• Plastic taillight and headlight lenses. An all-purpose cleaner and soft-bristled toothbrush (an old toothbrush, not a new one) routes grime and road film from crevices without scratching scratch-prone lenses. After cleaning, apply a plastic polish.
• Radiator grille. If your motorcycle has an exposed one, go over it grille piece by grille piece, topside as well as bottom, with an all-purpose cleaner. If chromed, follow with chrome polish. Finally, apply wax. Leave no recess undetailed.

Your motorcycle's initial fender-to-fender detailing, described here step-by-step, admittedly takes time, effort, and energy. But the upkeep—keeping it detailed—is relatively easy. And, if detailing is done regularly— perhaps three to four times a year—requires relatively little time. Some things get easier once done right; detailing is one of them.

A MASTER DETAILER DISCUSSES CLEARCOAT FINISHES

The new painting systems rely on clearcoats to help preserve the beauty of new paint finishes. The following section discusses clearcoats in general terms. Pay attention and you will learn something about motorcycle finishes that apply to your motorcycle and maybe even to your car or truck.

Clearcoat: New High-Tech Finish

Today, on many makes and models of motorcycles, there is a whole new system of finishes, high-tech motorcycle paints which differ fundamentally from their predecessors in construction and in the way they must be cared for and detailed.

In simplest terms, the final, top layer of finish on all motorcycles of the past, and still on some today (mostly repaints), is a pigmented paint. Detailing these conventional finishes, you work directly on the motorcycle's color—the paint layer that gives a motorcycle its color. Using polish or cleaner, color actually comes off on your polishing cloth or buffing pad if the paint, aging, is oxidized. But this does not happen if your motorcycle is clear-coated.

On motorcycles with a clearcoat finish, the paint's color layer lies protected by a clear, colorless, usually urethane or polyurethane final finish. The urethanes are part of a new family of high-tech motorcycle finishes.

The urethanes and polyurethanes—often called the clearcoat because they comprise the clear, see-through final top finish overlying the pigmented paint layers—are more forgiving than conventional finishes, yet, oddly, they need more care.

Faults in the clearcoat finish can be more easily corrected than in such pigmented finishes as enamel, acrylic, lacquer, or other conventional motorcycle paints. Scuffs or scratches in these pigmented paint layers are difficult to correct. For one reason, a scratch or deep scuff actually penetrates, and likely mars or even discolors, the finish's pigmented color layers, since the paint's color layers are the finish's top layers.

In the clearcoat, many scuffs—minor scratches, for example—never reach the paint layers. And while in the clearcoat they may be visible, they are usually not nearly as obvious as would he damage to the finish's color layers.

Still, the clearcoat is vulnerable not only to casual damage, but to environmental damage and degradation. The clearcoat, to maintain its luster and impregnability, demands more frequent washing: once a week, certainly.

An example of casual damage is the scuffing and scratching that happens when somebody uses his or her motorcycle as a shelf for a bag. Slide the bag off the clearcoat, and you leave a scuff mark. With clear-coating, a scuff mark like that is relatively easier to repair than when the damage is in the top, color layer of conventional paint.

Protecting Clearcoat From Environmental Damage

Environmental damage is a clear and present danger to the clearcoat. And even more so than for conventional finishes. If you live in an area where there's a lot of traffic or you commute long distances, carbon black from other vehicle exhausts builds up on the clear-coat. Live or drive near an airport and there's fallout from jet fuel. In industrial zones of the Eastern and Northeastern states, and moving farther south every year, is industrial pollution, including acid rain. Acid fog is common in Southern California. So, in the industrial north, is acid snow (only a concern if you store your bike outside in the winter). Include, too, early morning's acid mist. Every form of precipitation carries the threat of acid fallout and clearcoat damage.

What happens is this: If your motorcycle isn't frequently washed, it becomes coated with acid fallout. A light rain, a morning mist, fog, or dew mixes with the acid particles, putting them into solution. Now your motorcycle's finish is wetted with an acid solution. All that's needed for catalytic activity—an increase in finish-destroying chemical action—is heat. It doesn't take much sunlight to supply it. And you have all the ingredients for acid-burning the finish. It probably won't happen in one day, or two. Or even a week. But the damaging process, unless you frequently wash your motorcycle, goes on day after day: more acid fallout, an ever stronger acid solution, more catalytic action spurred, day after day, by the sun's heat and light.

Only washing the motorcycle to rid it of acid fallout breaks this potentially damaging cycle. That's why it's so important, especially with the clearcoats, to wash your motorcycle frequently.

Washing Your Motorcycle's Clearcoat

The key to washing a motorcycle to rid it of acid build up is to use the right techniques, the right products, and the right tools.

Two things are basic: (1) you don't ever want to wash your motorcycle in sunlight, and (2) you don't ever want to wash a hot motorcycle.

Before you use a wash product on a sun-warmed hot motorcycle, rinse it with cool, clear water. Rinsing washes away the heaviest concentrations of atmospheric pollutants. And, just as important, pre-rinsing cools the finish.

Neglect the pre-rinse, and you aid and abet chemical activity. The reason is basic: the chemical activity of many wash solutions, among them the

detergents, is accelerated by a motorcycle's body heat. A chemical reaction is produced which can either streak or burn the finish, especially if it's a clearcoat. Before you use a wash product, rinse the motorcycle with a flood of cool water. Rinsing quick-cools a hot motorcycle. Also, a clean water pre-rinse also gets rid of possibly abrasive materials.

Basic Clearcoat Systems

Understanding your motorcycle's clearcoat is a first step toward properly caring for—and detailing—it.

Currently, there are several basic clearcoat systems, although the technology is changing rapidly. There are urethane, polyurethane, polyester, and fluorine high-tech clearcoat systems. All are pretty much built up, layer by layer, in the same way: you've got a primer coat (the first coat on the motorcycle's bare metal skin), then one color coat or several (this is the `base coat,' which is often surprisingly thin), and lastly, the far thicker final clearcoat.

The actual color coat can be quite thin in clearcoat finishes because all it does is introduce the color. When, in conventional finishes, the color is contained in the final paint layer, the color layer is quite thick because it serves both as the color-carrying layer and as the final, protective top coat. Today's clearcoat is probably twice as thick (total) as the combined thickness of the primer and colored base coats. It's not unusual for the clearcoat layer to have three times the thickness of the color (pigment) coat layer—and sometimes more.

Clearcoat: A See-Through Solar Window

Consider the clearcoat as a kind of window. As viewed through the clearcoat window, the base coat is dull. What illuminates and lusterizes it are properties in the clearcoat—among them screening agents which screen out ultraviolet rays, which, in conventional motorcycle finishes, bleach and fade the color layer. The clear-coat's ultraviolet screening agents also protect the color coat from fading. Conventional finishes have no such protection. So, what you have in the clearcoat is not just a window, but a solar window.

You've got to keep that solar window clean to maintain, in the color finish, what the industry calls DOI—Distinction of Image. In essence, DOI is the deep gloss you are trying to maintain in your motorcycle's finish.

To test for this reflective depth of image, hold a newspaper over the finish. If you can read it from its reflection in the finish, you have depth and clarity in the finish. The same thing happens when, polishing or waxing the clearcoat, you look into the finish for a reflection of yourself. Detailing or clearcoat flaws show up when your reflected image is wavy or imperfect.

In detailing, you aim to achieve a slippery wet look in the finish. One example is the wet look of those faddish motorcycles painted with neon colors. The dazzle colors you see are the result of looking through the finish's clearcoat window. For most motorcycles, however, the wet look achieved by the clearcoat is harder to describe precisely—even though it's one of the beauties you get with a clearcoat finish.

Abrasives: Clearcoat's Kiss Of Death

But you can destroy that look if you use the wrong products in detailing the clearcoat. The clearcoat is not designed to have anything—let us repeat and emphasize, anything—used on it which is abrasive. Anything abrasive used on the clearcoat can scuff and scar its surface. Abrasives are the kiss of death to a clearcoat finish.

Now, when we emphasize no abrasives, we're talking about products used by the do-it-yourself detailer. Paint shops, in repairing clearcoats and when finishing a newly repainted/clear-coated motorcycle or repair, do use abrasive products and techniques. Commonly used by pro-detailers is ultra-fine wet sanding paper, with an almost non abrasive 1500–2000 grit rating. Wet-sanding enhances the clearcoat finish by removing sags, dust, and other flaws. Flaws removed, the new clearcoat finish is allowed to dry anywhere from 72 hours to 30 days, and then, when cured and dry, is cleaned with a non abrasive cleaner and then polished. Finally, the clearcoat is waxed.

Certainly the skilled weekend detailer can wet sand a clearcoat when virtually everything else has failed to restore its original, new motorcycle look. But you need skill and a feel for the clearcoat to do it without further surface damage.

Choosing The Right Wash Product

♦ **See Figure 16**

Now, in washing the clearcoat—and, in fact any motorcycle paint finish—you should use a wash product specifically formulated for motorcycle finishes.

We know, dishwashing detergents have been recommended for motorcycle washing. On the basis of overwhelming evidence, we totally disagree. Dishwashing detergent is formulated to wash dishes—specifically, to remove grease. That same formulation is going to remove the wax from the motorcycle's finish and also any protective silicones. Silicones are contained in many motorcycle polishes and in some car waxes. Use dishwashing detergent and you remove them—which means, at the very least, that every time the motorcycle is washed with detergent you have to reapply polish and wax.

Saying this, I have to again concede that some professional detailers use all-purpose cleaners and dishwashing detergents. They do so for the very reason the do-it-yourself detailer should seldom, if ever, use them. The professional detailer wants to strip all the wax from the finish. This enables him, starting from scratch, to better polish and wax the motorcycle. Eliminated by using those products is one of the chores he'd normally have to do—remove the wax.

Unless, after washing the motorcycle, you intend to polish (glaze) and wax it, you don't want to remove the wax. You don't because the wax's purpose isn't simply to shine a motorcycle's finish. Wax forms a protective barrier and also a slipperiness which tends to deflect street debris, such as stones, which might otherwise chip the finish. It also resists scuffing, caused, for example, by somebody rubbing against the motorcycle in a parking lot. The wax, being slippery, reduces possible abrasive damage. The analogy is the difference between a waxed kitchen floor and one that's unwaxed. Drag something across an unwaxed floor and you leave scratches. Drag something across your motorcycle's unwaxed finish and it scratches.

If you've waxed the motorcycle, you certainly don't want to undo what you've done by washing it with an aggressive, all-purpose cleaner. If a wash solution degreases the finish or body parts, you can be sure it will also de-wax the finish.

To wash clearcoats, use any of a number of products specially formulated for clearcoat washing. Almost all are liquids, not powders. Powders may not completely dissolve in your wash water. The tiny, undissolved granules have the potential to become abrasives.

Defining The Just-Right Clearcoat Wash Product

The proper and ideal slippery, soapy solution for frictionless dirt removal from an automotive finish, including clearcoat, can be defined by a number of characteristics:

- High-foaming—inherent cleaning action
- High lubricity—slipperiness, like a lubricant
- Free-rinsing—a solution which, in itself, leaves no residue
- pH balance—a product with an acid-alkaline balance which is slightly alkaline to counter the acidic nature of a finish's collected fallout pollutants

What commonly available wash products fit these criteria? There are several available (check labels carefully). The choice comes down to personal preference.

Clearcoats must also be critically washed in a specific way. The tools you use should be just as critically designed for clearcoat washing. Among these tools are natural fiber body brushes, synthetic-wool washing mitts, sponges, and terry cloth towels.

Washing Clearcoat Finish

♦ **See Figure 17**

Whatever washing tools you use, the basic washing techniques for clearcoat are the same. First, you hose and clean-water flush the finish to remove any loose dirt or pollutants. Then you wash the finish with a free-rinsing wash solution.

The first step—flushing with water—purges the surface of anything loose that can be quickly and easily removed.

If any dirt remains, it's got to be removed with a minimum of friction. What is likely holding dirt on the clearcoat finish is surface tension. To remove stubborn dirt or other stick-to-surface materials—bird and tree droppings being the most common—you've got to disturb the surface tension without creating friction enough to scratch the clearcoat.

Ideally, what you want your wash solution—your wash water—to do is free-rinse, that is, to dislodge and rinse all pollutants, including abrasives, from the clearcoat and hold them in frictionless, non abrasive suspension within the wash water. What does it is a soapy, slippery wash solution that meets the criteria for an ideal clearcoat wash product.

Keep these same criteria in mind when choosing your washing tool. A sponge is not a free-rinsing tool, because grit and dirt can get caught in the sponge's pores. Even less free-rinsing is a towel, or a diaper, because of the weave of the cloth. You're going to trap dirt and grit in the weave of the towel or the diaper, even if you wash with a soapy solution that has high lubricity and is high-foaming, two of the more important criteria of a clearcoat wash solution.

90998P06

Fig. 16 Hmmm, it says "car wash" on it; Will it work for a motorcycle too? Probably, but there are bike specific products

90998P02

Fig. 17 The body brush is a great tool for washing bodywork

The ideal tool for washing clearcoat finishes is a natural fiber body brush. This usually imported, bleached pig's hair brush is super soft. Commonly, the hair is set into a mahogany block with epoxy cement. These aren't usually available in everyday auto supply houses, but can be sourced from detailing specialty suppliers.

Natural fiber body brushes (they're designed for motorcycle washing) are user-friendly tools for washing clear-coats. Using them, you need exert only minimal pressure. That means less friction on the clearcoat—and less washing effort, too.

The brush has a nap that's about 3 inches (76mm) deep. You use only the tips of the brush's super-fine hairs—just the first ½–¾ inch of the nap. You use very little pressure. All you want to do is loosen the dirt's surface tension and get the dirt into the carrier solution—your soapy wash water or finish shampoo. If you can't find a body brush, then use the second-choice ideal clearcoat washing tool: a synthetic wool mitt.

One caution: Not all wash brushes are the hog hair—China bristle natural fiber kind I'm describing. Some, with coarser hair, may be too aggressive—too abrasive—for clearcoat finishes.

You may have to settle for something less than the ideal clearcoat washing tool. A terry cloth towel, perhaps, or even a sponge. If you keep them forever lubricated in your wash water to make sure they are clean, and if you use them carefully and with minimum pressure, they'll generally do a satisfactory job on clearcoat finishes.

Clearcoat Polishes and Cleaners

✵ WARNING

The use of abrasive compounds on clearcoat can be fatal to the finish.

Polish. A lot of detailing pros use the words polish and glaze interchangeably. As if they are the same things. Generally, they are not. A polish is a polish. A glaze is a glaze. And a cleaner is a cleaner. Whatever the product, use the least aggressive—the least abrasive. A more abrasive product generally gets the polishing job done faster. But an overly aggressive polishing/cleaning product also risks scratching, and in fact removing, some of the finish—such as the clearcoat.

A polish is a minimally abrasive cleaner and lusterizer. A cleaner, more aggressive than a polish, contains chemical cleaning agents. Even more abrasive—often very abrasive—are compounding products. Compounds are sometimes the preferred products for treating heavily oxidized conventional finishes. Using a compound—called compounding—you are apt to remove paint as well as oxidation. Today, the cleaners—far less abrasive than compounds—are usually all you need to work with on even the most oxidized conventional finishes.

While compounds can be used—and still often are—on conventional paints, their use on clearcoat finishes risks major damage. The minute particles of pumice, which give the compounds their cutting action, cut little holes in the clearcoat. The result: swirl marks which are difficult, and sometimes impossible, to remove from the clearcoat.

Swirls are residual evidences of abrasive polishing. There should, of course, be no evidences in a finish that it has been polished—just an even, unbroken, reflective shine. Hand-polish swirls are irregular, non-reflective blotches in the finish's polished surface. Machine-polish swirls—evidence of machine buffing— tend to be circular blotches. Swirl marks are the nemesis of detailers, whether pros or weekenders.

If you get swirl marks when you buff a finish by hand, it means there are abrasive particles in the prod uct you're using. Or, perhaps, some abrasives in whatever you're using to apply the product—a rough towel, for example. Or a foam sponge applicator that's not clean and has some grit or hardened cleaner in its pores. In short, there are only two ways that swirls develop when cleaning, polishing or buffing a clearcoat. finish: (1) the product you're using, whether hand- or machine-applied, is too abrasive; (2) the polishing tool is abrasive.

In machine polishing, the problem is often a wool buffing pad. Wool buffing pads are, by their very nature, abrasive. Wool buffing pads are an anachronism in today's era of high-tech clearcoat motorcycle finishes. They are plainly out of date, although wool buffing pads are still being used on conventional non-clearcoat finishes. But not on clearcoats. There's no question about it: in machine buffing, wool buffer pads are the number one swirl-maker.

Today's preferred and widely used machine polishing pads for clearcoat are made of synthetic foam. They all but eliminate swirl marks, and they can be used on both conventional and clearcoat finishes.

How Do You Know If It's Clear-Coated?

One vexing question: How do you know, in this era of fast-changing technology, whether your motorcycle has a conventional or clearcoat finish?

It isn't always easy to tell. One test is to gently rub an out-of-sight place on the finish with a mild cleaner. If color comes off on your cloth, you can be fairly sure it's conventional finish. If no color comes off, you can be almost as sure it's clear-coated.

Still, there's only one sure-sale rule-of-thumb: When in doubt, treat it as a clearcoat finish. Obviously, if your motorcycle is clear-coated, it needs special handling and special care.

Cleaning Leather

♦ **See Figures 18 and 19**

Leather shows up on many bikes in the form of accesories, baggage and seats. It is a wonderful material, still not matched by anything man made, but it does require some special care:

1. Remove all dirt and grit from the leather after a ride. Use a good quality leather cleaner like Lexol®. If you can't clean the grit, at least wipe down the surface with a clean cloth. The grit can work its way into the pores of the leather and act as an abrasive, wearing out the leather prematurely.

2. Test any product you buy on a hidden area of the leather first. This will tell you if the leather will tolerate the product. If the leather isn't very high quality, the color may come off or streak.

3. Clean with a good leather cleaner, but do not use anything containing silicones or solvents. Use a good leather care product and impregnating spray when cleaning. This will help preserve the leather surfaces.

4. After washing, allow the leather to dry completely before riding.

5. If the leather is spotted with dirt that isn't soluable in water, use pure petroleum spirits to dab at the stain. Do not rub. After cleaning the spot, use a leather care product to help preserve the treated area.

6. Leather will change over time; This is natural. Be careful not to get non-colorfast materials in contact with the leather as color transfer can

Fig. 18 Use a good quality leather cleaner to help bring the dirt out of the pores

Fig. 19 Leather conditioner should be used after each cleaning

occur (Just remember what your hands looked like when those cheap gloves you bought stained your skin!)

7. Treat the leather on a regular schedule and it will last for a long time. (This is also good advice for you riding leathers too!)

Cleaning Carbon Fiber

Carbon fiber as it is used on bikes falls into two general catagories, purposeful and decorative. Purposeful carbon fiber may include fenders, exhaust canister and bodywork. Decorative carbon fiber may actually be a decal that looks like carbon fiber, or simply a layer of carbon fiber over a cheaper substrate, such as fiberglass or plastic.

Most of the spiffy new carbon fiber used on motorcycles has been painted with a clearcoat. This is to protect the resin used in the fiber matrix from the ultraviolet rays in sunlight. Treat the carbon fiber as you would a painted surface.

If the carbon fiber is actually a decal, well, just wash it with some soap and water. You should be fine.

Cleaning Plastic, Lexan, and Plastic Windshields

If the plastic part has been painted, refer to the paint care portions of this chapter. If the plastic has the color molded into it, simply cleaning with a soapy water solution and a non abrasive cloth will keep it looking good. The trick is not to scratch the surface during cleaning. If the surface does get scratched, a good commercial plastic polish will help get the scratches out and restore the looks of the piece.

Windshields should be cleaned with plenty of soapy water and a clean towel. You want to avoid getting any grit trapped in the towel leading to scratches in the plastic. Never use a dry towel or scratches will be formed instantly. You want to use enough water to float away any dirt that is on the windshield.

Plastic windshields can be restored using plastic polishes and scratch removers. Any good auto parts place or your motorcycle dealer will carry such products. There are differenct grades of products to match the severity of the damage to the windsheild.

Some products are designed for maintenance type use, helping to keep the tiny scratches polished out of the plastic. Others are for heavier damage and to reclaim deeper scratched windshields. Follow the instructions on the bottle exactly. Some manufactures are very specific in the use of their products and recommend that their system be used since each product is matched to the next.

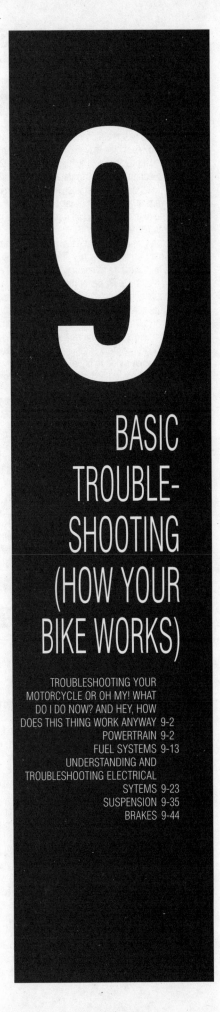

9

BASIC TROUBLE-SHOOTING (HOW YOUR BIKE WORKS)

TROUBLESHOOTING YOUR MOTORCYCLE OR OH MY! WHAT DO I DO NOW? AND HEY, HOW DOES THIS THING WORK ANYWAY?

Even with the best maintenance, a motorcycle can sometimes fail to perform as hoped. Your bike may refuse to start or it may stop running right. You may have a problem with its handling or maybe one of your accessories stops working. A motorcycle is a mechanical device subject to wear and failure. With good maintenance most problems can be avoided, but once in a while a gremlin can sneak up and bite you. In this section we will look at some of the ways you can troubleshoot your motorcycle and get it back in tip-top shape.

The Motorcycle Safety Foundation (MSF) teaches its students the word "SIPDE." That stands for "Scan," " "Identify," "Predict," "Decide, " and "Execute." This is the mantra a motorcyclist should be repeating every second they are on their bike. By performing "SIPDE" the motorcyclist keeps a clear view of what is going on around them and they can keep one step ahead of the traffic. The concept can be applied to troubleshooting your motorcycle.

Fixing a problem should not be a hit or miss proposition. By charting a plan of action using all the information available to you, the process of troubleshooting should be straightforward, if not easy. The biggest mistake people make when trying to figure out a problem is not taking an organized approach to it, choosing instead to guess at the solution.

The Basic Steps Of Troubleshooting:

Many hours and dollars were spent designing your motorcycle. Some of the worlds best engineers make their livings designing our source of enjoyment. They used standard engineering practices to design them and by keeping this in mind, we can use the same type of thought patterns to fix them.

1. **Scan:** Look the bike over. Are there any obvious problems? Are there any parts out of place or hanging off? Are all the connectors fitted tightly? Is there fuel in the tank? Are any wires disconnected? Are there fluids leaking from anyplace they shouldn't (or in any amounts more than usual!)? Is the battery charged? These are all items that can be done at a glance. The

"Scan" portion of troubleshooting should be part of your pre-ride check and by keeping a close eye on your bike, you might catch something that may become a problem later. You would be amazed at how many problems present themselves with just a good looking over. Never skip this step!

2. **Identify:** What may cause this type of problem? For example: If the bike won't start, there is no need to check the transmission. Try to narrow down your search. Was the bike making a noise? Ask yourself what might possibly make that kind of noise and start looking in that area. Did you smell something like burning oil or spilled gasoline? Look for areas that contain those fluids. The idea is to eliminate as many potential areas as possible so your search becomes smaller. Remember that the engineer who designed your bike took it one part at a time; You should also.

3. **Predict**: Now that you have identified the most likely area to explore, it is time to dig a bit deeper. Now it is time to pull out the tools and testers to see if you were right. Pick an area or item that seems to be the most likely culprit. You have been using logic as your detective and now the suspect is in sight. Start testing your assumptions and see if you choose wisely.

4. **Decide:** Did your tests conclude that the item you just tested was the guilty party? Is the problem identified? Can you go onto repairing the problem or is further narrowing required? Will this fix the problem or just cure the symptom? These are things you need to think about. Many times people just fix some symptoms without actually curing the underlying cause. Replacing a tire may fix a wobble caused by uneven wear, but what caused the uneven wear? Make sure you have reached the root of the problem.

5. **Execute:** Go ahead! Fix that problem! You may be able to fix the problem right in your own driveway or on the side of the road, but maybe you can't and will need professional help. Either way, you have figured out what the problem is and you can decide what direction you want to go.

In the rest of this section we will explain how the various systems of the bike work in order to help you troubleshoot your problems.

POWERTRAIN

Piston Port Two-Stroke Engines

▶ **See Figures 1, 2, 3 and 4**

Before you try to determine what's wrong with your engine you should know how it works when everything is right. The simplest type is the piston port two stroke single which only has three main moving parts. The ports are located in the cylinder wall and are opened and closed by the piston's movement. Their functions are:

1. Intake port—admits fresh fuel mixture from the carburetor into the crankcase. Transfer ports—provide passages for the mixture between the crankcase and combustion chamber. These are also known as scavenging ports.

2. Exhaust port—releases burned gases from the combustion chamber into the exhaust pipe.

Basically, this is what happens during a 360 degree rotation of the crankshaft, beginning with the piston at top dead center (TDC):

3. Downstroke—the piston descends from the previous cycle and exposes the exhaust port, jetting out the expanding burned gases. Simultaneously, the piston's downward movement compresses the fuel mixture from the previous cycle in the airtight crankcase.

As the piston continues to descend, it also exposes the transfer ports. The compressed mixture waiting in the crankcase now rushes through the ports and fills the combustion chamber, while at the same time sweeping any remaining burned gases out the exhaust port.

4. Upstroke—after reaching its lowest point of travel, the piston begins to ascend and closes off the transfer ports. At the same time, the piston's upward movement creates a partial vacuum in the crankcase. As the piston

continues to ascend, it closes off the exhaust port and begins to compress the mixture in the combustion chamber.

Meanwhile, the bottom of the piston exposes the intake port and a fresh fuel mixture is sucked into the crankcase. When the piston approaches top dead center, ignition occurs and the piston once again descends to begin another cycle. As described, ignition occurs once every 360 degrees or, more appropriately, once every two strokes of the piston (one down and one up). Hence, the term two-stroke engine.

A recent improvement in piston port design is the five-port cylinder, and the main difference between it and the conventional type lies in the five-port cylinder's more efficient exhaust sweep.

The earlier Schnuerle loop scavenging system has two transfer ports that aim streams of fresh mixture toward the back of the cylinder; this sweeps out most of the remaining exhaust gases, but leaves one area untouched in the middle of the combustion chamber. The five-port system, on the other hand, has two additional auxiliary transfer ports. These extra ports direct a small charge of fresh mixture right at the dead spot and force it out the exhaust port. This complete exhaust sweep creates more space for the incoming mixture, and, as a result, the engine has more low and mid-range power, runs cooler, and consumes less fuel.

The newest development in two-stroke engineering is the seven-port cylinder used in conjunction with a reed valve. The die-cast aluminum valve consists of a block with flexible stainless steel reeds that open and close the intake port. The reeds are actuated by crankcase vacuum and, therefore, admit only the necessary amount of fuel. When combined with the improved scavenging ability of the seven-port cylinder, the valve helps reduce fuel consumption, increase low-end pulling power, and flatten out the horsepower and torque curves.

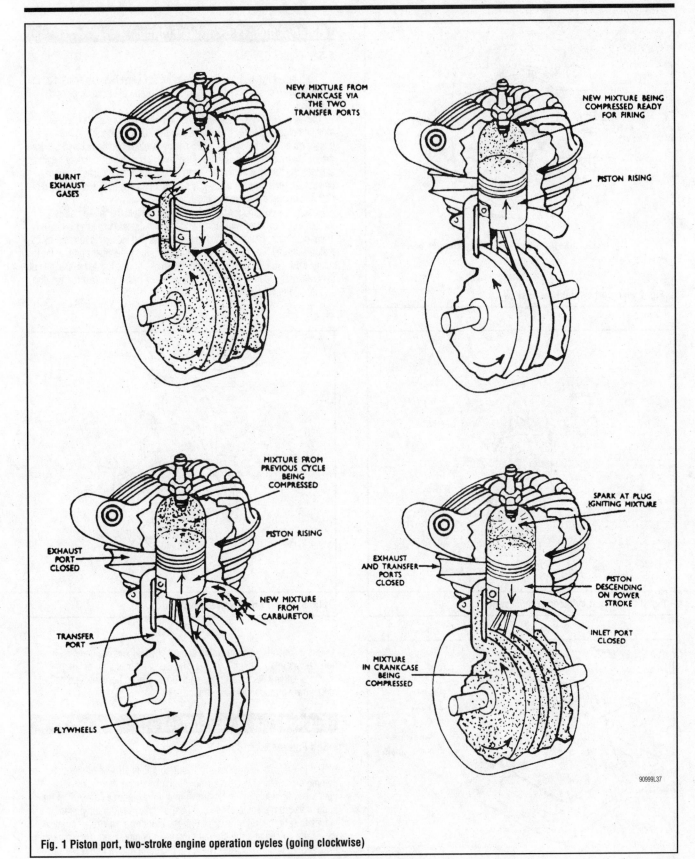

Fig. 1 Piston port, two-stroke engine operation cycles (going clockwise)

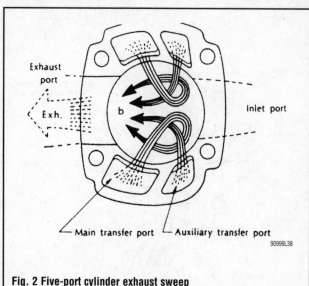

Fig. 2 Five-port cylinder exhaust sweep

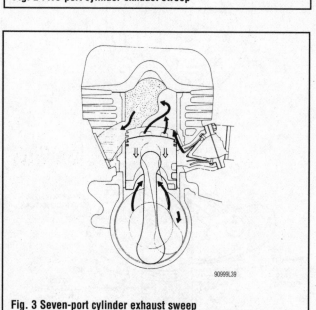

Fig. 3 Seven-port cylinder exhaust sweep

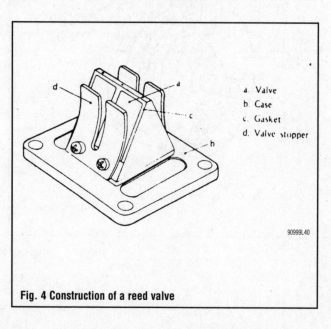

a. Valve
b. Case
c. Gasket
d. Valve stopper

Fig. 4 Construction of a reed valve

Rotary-Valve Two-Stroke Engines

▶ **See Figure 5**

The rotary-valve two-stroke operates on the same basic principles as the piston-port type, but is constructed differently and offers some distinct advantages.

The valve itself is a resin hardened fiber disc with a cutaway section along its circumference. The disc is mounted directly to the end of the crankshaft and is enclosed within a narrow sealed chamber located between the crankcase and the carburetor. As the valve rotates, the cutaway section exposes the port and allows the fresh fuel mixture to be sucked into the crankcase. Then, when the cutaway section ends, the port is sealed by the disc and no more mixture can enter.

What is the advantage? In the piston port system the intake port is located in the cylinder wall along with the transfer and exhaust ports. Therefore, intake timing (when the port opens and closes) is dictated by the piston skirt and limited by the size and position of the other ports. In the rotary-valve type, on the other hand, the intake port is located in the side of the crankcase, and intake timing is determined by the position (on the disc) and duration of the valve cutaway.

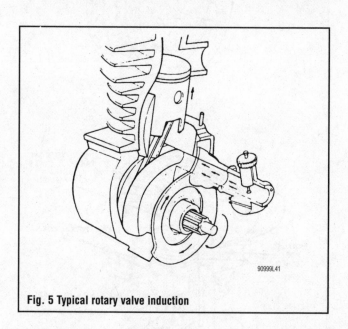

Fig. 5 Typical rotary valve induction

This independence from piston control and cylinder design complications allows intake timing to be set, and easily adjusted, for optimum engine breathing. As a result, the engine has greater flexibility and delivers more power throughout a wider range.

Pushrod Four-Stroke Engines

▶ **See Figures 6, 7, 8 and 9**

The four-stroke engine requires four complete strokes of the piston to complete one power cycle. During the intake stroke the intake valve opens and the fuel mixture is drawn into the cylinder as a result of the sudden vacuum created in the combustion chamber. As the piston moves toward the top of its travel on the compression stroke, both valves are closed and the fuel/air mixture is compressed. The spark plug fires and ignites the charge. The resulting combustion forces the piston down in the power stroke. As the piston moves down toward its lowest point of travel, the exhaust valve opens, and as the action of the flywheel sends the piston back up on the exhaust stroke, the remains of the previous charge are forced out past the exhaust valve. Just before the piston reaches the top of its travel, the intake valve opens and the exhaust

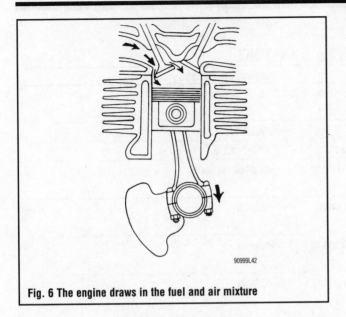

Fig. 6 The engine draws in the fuel and air mixture

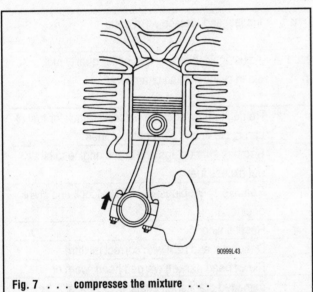

Fig. 7 . . . compresses the mixture . . .

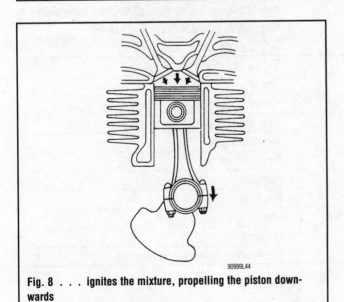

Fig. 8 . . . ignites the mixture, propelling the piston downwards

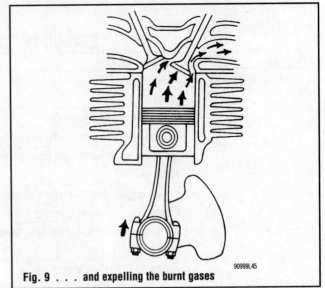

Fig. 9 . . . and expelling the burnt gases

flow induces the intake flow which continues while the exhaust valve closes. The process then repeats itself since each of the four cycles has been completed.

The basic valve train of four-stroke engines consists of camshaft driven pushrods which actuate rocker arms, which in turn, operate the valves. The camshaft can be driven directly by the crankshaft through gears which reduce the rate of rotation to 1/2 the engine speed. Cams can also be chain driven off the crank.

Overhead Camshaft Four-Stroke Engines

Overhead cam engines are those which have the cam mounted above the valves.

The cam or cams ride in the cylinder head supported by plain bearings, usually with inserts, but sometimes directly on the alloy head casting itself, or on ball or roller bearings.

The cam(s) may be driven by chain which necessitates the fitting of a chain tensioner somewhere. Both single and duplex chains are used. Other types of cam drives include spur gears (MV Agusta), shaft and bevel gear (Ducati), and reciprocating rods (NSU). Chain-driven overhead cams predominate since this method is cheaper, quieter, and more compact than other methods, but, as noted, a tensioner is necessary to compensate for stretching of the chain. Tensioners are sometimes fully automatic, relying on oil pressure to function, but more often they are simply mechanical devices which must be set by hand. Usually the tensioner will have a spring-loaded arm which, when released, will push against the chain, and a bolt is then tightened to secure it in this position.

Single overhead cam engines use rocker arms to actuate the valves, while more sophisticated dual overhead cam engines may have the cams located directly above the valve stems, obviating the need for any intermediate device. The chief drawback of this letter method is the difficulty of valve adjustment, which must be done with precisely measured shims, but the advantage is in the higher rpm obtainable, and the longer interval between valve adjustments. There are dual overhead cam engines that use threaded adjusters, but they are not the norm.

The advantage of an overhead cam design is that the reduced weight of the valve train allows the engine to turn higher rpm. In addition to this, overhead cam engines have much less valve floating problems than pushrod engines where the engine can begin to turn faster than the valves can operate. The only disadvantage of an overhead cam design is that it necessitates a tall engine which raises the center of balance and makes designing a handling frame more difficult.

ENGINE TROUBLESHOOTING

Problem	Possible Cause	Inspection/Remedy
Abnormal engine noise	Piston slap; piston-to-cylinder wall clearance too great	Check clearance
	Excessive valve clearance	Adjust
	Excessive carbon in combustion chamber	Decarbonize
	Maladjusted or worn cam chain; worn cam sprocket	Adjust or replace
	Knock (especially noticeable at idle): worn connecting rod big end bearing	Replace
	Worn connecting rod small end bearings or wrist pin	Replace
	Rumble at idle developing into whine at high rpm: crankshaft main bearings worn or damaged	Replace
	Defective or worn transmission gears or shaft bearings	Inspect and replace worn parts
	Pinging or spark knock: timing too advanced; low quality fuel; excessive carbon buildup in combustion chambers	Adjust ignition timing; use better quality fuel; clean cylinder head chambers
Engine fails to start, but has spark at the plug	No fuel in the tank; fuel petcock closed or clogged; fuel line clogged	Refuel; turn on or clean petcock; check for fuel at carbs; clean and blow out fuel lines
	Engine flooded	Remove spark plugs and crank engine to blow out excess fuel
	Crankcase flooded (2-stroke)	Remove spark plugs, shut off petcock and crank engine
	Ignition timing incorrect	Reset timing
	Improper fuel/oil ratio (2-stroke)	Drain tank and refill with correct mixture
	Low or no compression	Blown head gasket; warped head; worn or damaged crankshaft seals; poor seal at crankcase mating surface (2-stroke); worn piston rings; worn cylinder bore; bad valves
	Carb adjustments wrong	Adjust carb; check float height
Engine fails to start (no spark at plug)	Ignition switched off	Turn on ignition
	Kill switch off	Reset
	Spark plug worn or fouled	Clean or replace
	Spark plug heat range too cold	Replace with proper spark plug
	Spark plug gap too wide	Reset the gap
	Spark plug resistor cap defective	Replace cap
	Plug lead defective or damaged	Replace
	Ignition coil defective	Replace
	Condenser defective (points type ignition)	Replace
	Points worn, dirty or damaged	Replace
	Points wire disconnected	Reattach and check connections

ENGINE TROUBLESHOOTING

Problem	Possible Cause	Inspection/Remedy
Engine fails to start (cont.)	Dead battery	Recharge or replace battery
	Blown fuse, circuit breaker or fusible link	Replace or reset
	Loose or corroded battery terminals	Clean and secure the connections
Engine is hard to start	Worn, dirty or improperly gapped plug; improper heat range (too cold)	Clean or replace plugs with proper heat range
	Points dirty, pitted or out of adjustment	Replace and adjust
	Carburetor idle settings wrong; pilot air or fuel passages clogged	Adjust idle settings or clean carburetors
	Battery low	Recharge or replace battery
	Ignition timing out of specification	Adjust
	Spark plug lead cracked or dirty	Replace
	Loose or intermittently grounded wires at coil, points or connectors	Check connections and condition of wiring
	Defective coils or condensers	Replace
	Worn internal engine component	Rebuild engine
Engine starts but refuses to run	Fuel feed problem	Check fuel supply; check petcock, lines, carburetor for blocked passages; fuel tank vent
	Valve clearance incorrect	Adjust
	Ignition timing incorrect	Adjust
	Spark plugs too cold or worn	Replace with proper heat range plugs
Engine idles poorly and misfires under acceleration	Incorrect carburetor adjustment	Adjust
	Spark plugs dirty, worn or incorrect gap	Clean or replace spark plugs
	Poor wiring connections in ignition circuit	Check connections at each ignition component
	Defective ignition coils or condensers	Replace
	Ignition timing incorrect	Adjust
	Air leaks at carburetor manifolds	Fix leaks
	Water in carburetors or tank	Drain carburetor float bowls or drain fuel tank
	Carburetor main jet clogged	Remove and clean
	Fuel tank vent clogged	Clean
	Petcock clogged	Clean
	Float bowl level too low	Adjust float height
Spark plugs foul repeatedly	Plug gap too narrow	Adjust to proper gap
	Plug heat range too low for conditions	Fit a higher heat range plug
	Fuel mixture set too rich	Adjust fuel mixture
	Too much oil in fuel (2-stroke)	Check ratio or mixing pump
	Piston rings worn	Replace
Engine surges or runs unevenly at standard throttle opening	Air leaks at carburetor manifolds	Check for leaks and fix
	Partial seizure of engine due to overheating	Determine reason for overheating and fix

ENGINE TROUBLESHOOTING

Problem	Possible Cause	Inspection/Remedy
Engine breaks up or misfires while running	Dead battery	Recharge or replace battery
	Loose or intermittent connections in ignition circuit	Check connections
	Carburetor float level incorrect	Check float height and that the needle valve is seating
Loss of compression or power	Holed or damaged piston	Replace
	Piston partially seizing	Determine cause and fix
	Worn piston rings	Replace
	Blown or leaking head gasket	Replace
	Muffler or exhaust port clogged with carbon (2-stroke)	Decarbonize
	Clogged air filter	Clean or replace
Poor low speed operation	Incorrect ignition timing	Adjust timing
	Bad points	Replace
	Defective coil or condenser	Replace
	Carburetor float level incorrect	Adjust
	Pilot screw not adjusted properly	Adjust carburetor
	Spark plug gap too big	Adjust
Poor high speed operation	Ignition timing incorrect	Adjust
	Spark plug gap too small	Adjust
	Defective ignition coil	Replace
	Carburetor float level incorrect	Adjust float level
	Low compression	Check engine mechanical condition and repair
	Engine carbon fouled	Decarbonize
	Exhaust pipe loose at engine	Tighten connection
	Weak breaker points spring	Replace points
	Air cleaner dirty or clogged	Clean or replace
Engine partially seizes or slows after high speed operation	Spark plug too hot	Use colder range plugs
	Piston seizure	Determine cause and repair
	Fuel mixture too lean	Adjust carburetor
	Insufficient lubricant in fuel mixture (2-stroke)	Check mixture ratio or oil mixing pump
	Air leaks at carburetor manifolds	Repair leaks
Engine overheats	Engine is carbon fouled	Decarbonize
	Water pump not working	Repair
	Radiator clogged internally	Replace
Engine overheats (cont.)	Loss of coolant	Repair leak and fill with proper coolant
	Ignition timing too retarded or too advanced	Adjust
	Cooling fins clogged with dirt	Clean
	Air/fuel mixture too lean	Adjust
Engine detonates or preignites	Spark plugs too hot for application	Replace with cooler spark plugs
	Ignition timing too advanced	Adjust
	Insufficient oil in fuel (2-stroke)	Check mixture ratio or oil mixture pump

90999C07

ENGINE TROUBLESHOOTING

Problem	Possible Cause	Inspection/Remedy
Engine detonates or preignites (cont.)	Air/fuel mixture too lean	Adjust
	Air leaks at carburetor manifolds	Fix
	Engine carbon fouled	Decarbonize
	Fuel octane too low	Use higher octane fuel
Engine backfires	Ignition timing too advanced	Adjust
Rapid piston and cylinder wear	Ineffective air cleaner	Replace
	Excess fuel washing cylinder walls	Adjust mixture leaner
Popping at muffler after shutting off throttle	Mixture too lean	Adjust idle circuit and float level. Check for air leaks.
Exhaust smoke accompanied by oil consumption	Too much oil in engine	Set to correct level
	Worn rings or bore	Rebuild
	Worn valve guides or seals	Replace
	Scored cylinder	Bore to oversize
Black smoke from exhaust pipes	Excessive carbon buildup in engine	Decarbonize
	Overly rich mixture	Adjust carb
	Obstructed air cleaner element	Install new element
	Malfunctioning choke mechanism	Repair the mechanism
Piston seizure	Low oil level	Maintain oil at proper level
	Engine overheating due to too advanced ignition timing, insufficient valve clearance, stuck valves	Check settings
	Insufficient oil	Check oil pump
Burned valves	Clearances adjusted too tightly	Replace valves; check guides; maintain adjustment
	Overly lean mixture	Adjust carb; inspect fuel delivery system for malfunctioning or obstructions
	Timing too retarded	Adjust
Bent valves or broken valve guides	Valve hitting piston because of over-revving the engine, or weak valve springs	Check top end components; inspect for incorrect valve timing
Bad connecting rod bearings	Insufficient or contaminated oil	Check oil, filter, and oil pump
	Over-revving engine	Abide by tachometer red line
	Extended use of the engine with ignition timing too advanced, high-speed misfire etc.	Adjust ignition timing; fix misfire problem
Bad crankshaft bearings	Insufficient or contaminated oil	Change oil and filter when directed
	Over-revving engine	Abide by tachometer red line
	Extended use of the motorcycle with one weak or misfiring cylinder	Fix misfire problem
Worn cam lobes or bearings	Insufficient or contaminated oil	Maintain oil at proper level; change filter when directed
	Failure to allow engine sufficient warm-up	Allow additional warm-up when starting cold engine
	Defective oil pump or clogged oil passages in engine	Replace

ENGINE TROUBLESHOOTING

Problem	Possible Cause	Inspection/Remedy
Worn cylinder and rings	Damaged or leaking air cleaner	Replace element; secure connections
	Low oil level or contaminated oil	Maintain oil at proper level; change oil and filter at proper intervals
	Defective oil pump	Replace
	Failure to allow engine sufficient warm-up	Allow at least one minute for warm-up when starting cold engine

90999C09

TRANSMISSION TROUBLESHOOTING

Problem	Possible Cause	Inspection/Remedy
Clutch slips	Release mechanism improperly adjusted	Readjust
	Release worm and lever sticking	Check cable for binding, and lever spring for damage
	Clutch spring tension too loose	Readjust progressively, and evenly, until proper operation is achieved
	Worn or damaged clutch spring(s)	Replace as necessary
	Friction discs or steel plates worn, warped, or oil impregnated	Replace as necessary
	Distorted pressure plate	Replace as necessary
Clutch drags	Release mechanism incorrectly adjusted	Readjust
	Release worm and lever, or throwout bearing, excessively worn or damaged	Replace as necessary
	Clutch spring tension too tight	Readjust
	Friction discs gummy and sticking	Replace as necessary
	Steel plates or pressure plate warped or damaged	Replace as necessary
	Clutch sprocket keys excessively worn or damaged	Replace as necessary
Clutch chatters	Clutch disc rivets loose	Replace as necessary
	Pressure plate excessively flattened	Replace as necessary
	Excessive play in the clutch drive chain	None.
	Bad clutch hub bearing	Replace as necessary
Grinding when shifting	Clutch drags	Consult the Clutch Drags section
	Worn gear dogs	Replace as necessary
	Worn shifter mechanism (ie. distorted selector forks or worn shift drum or cam)	Replace as necessary
	Bad transmission shaft bearings	Replace as necessary
	Worn transmission shafts	Replace as necessary
	Foreign objects in the gearbox	Flush out gearbox
	Idle speed too high	Adjust
	Excessive oil level in the primary case	Drain and refill according to specifications
	Transmission oil too heavy for conditions	Drain and refill with lighter oil
	Insufficient or diluted gearbox oil	Drain and refill
Transmission pops out of gear	Shifter rods improperly adjusted or damaged	Readjust or replace as necessary
	Shifter forks improperly adjusted or damaged	Readjust or replace as necessary
	Insufficient shifter spring tension	Replace as necessary
	Worn or damaged gear dogs	Replace as necessary
	Worn transmission shaft splines	Replace the shafts as necessary
	Worn, damaged, or improperly adjusted shifter mechanism	Replace or adjust as necessary
	Improperly adjusted or damaged shift linkage	Readjust or replace as necessary

90999C10

TRANSMISSION TROUBLESHOOTING

Problem	Possible Cause	Inspection/Remedy
Transmission shifts hard	Clutch drags	Consult the Clutch Drags section
	Worn, damaged, or maladjusted shifter	Readjust or replace as necessary
	Worn or damaged gear dogs	Replace as necessary
	Worn return spring	Replace as necessary
	Improper mainshaft and countershaft alignment	Replace as necessary
	Transmission oil too heavy for conditions	Drain and refill with a lighter oil
Excessive gear noise	Excessive gear backlash	Replace the worn components as necessary
	Worn or damaged transmission shaft bearings	Replace as necessary
	Worn or damaged gears	Replace as necessary
Foot shifter operates poorly	Worn, damaged, or maladjusted shifter mechanism	Replace or readjust as necessary
	Worn or damaged shift lever return spring	Replace as necessary
	Galled, gritty, or damaged shifter bearing surface	Repair or replace as necessary
	Gritty shifter mechanism	Thoroughly clean out mechanism
	Bent or distorted shifter shaft	Replace as necessary
	Bent shifter lever which contacts engine case	Repair or replace as necessary
Kickstarter jams	First tooth on kick gear badly worn	Replace as necessary
	Damaged ratchet pinion teeth	Replace as necessary
	Broken, worn, or improperly meshed gear teeth	Replace as necessary
	Broken return spring	Replace as necessary
	Grit on kick gear worm or in ratchet mechanism	Thoroughly clean out mechanism
	Kick lever hung up	Repair or replace as necessary
Kickstarter slips	Worn or damaged kick gear or ratchet mechanism	Replace as necessary
	Clutch slips	Consult Clutch Slips section
	Stripped splines between gear pedal and kickstarter shaft	Replace the shafts as necessary
	Bent starter shaft	Replace as necessary
	Lack of engine compression	Determine cause
Chain whine	Chain too tight	Adjust chain correctly
	Chain rusted or kinking	Lubricate or replace chain
Chain slap	Chain too loose	Adjust chain correctly
	Bent chain guard	Repair chain guard so chain rotates freely
Accelerated chain and sprocket wear	Sprockets improperly aligned	Align sprockets
	Rear wheel out of alignment	Align wheels
	One or both sprockets slightly damaged	Replace sprockets and chain
	Chain worn or damaged	Replace chain and sprockets
	Chain insufficiently lubricated	Keep chain lubricated thoroughly

90999C11

FUEL SYSTEMS

Carbureted

▶ See Figures 10, 11, 12, 13 and 14

The fuel system on most bikes is made up of the carburetor(s), fuel filter and occasionally a fuel pump. The following information encompasses the great majority of components currently in use.

Most basically stated, a carburetor mixes air and fuel to form a combustable mixture. Air passes over an opening, drawing gasoline up and into the air stream. The gasoline is atomized as it is sucked from the opening. A throttle plate blocks the airflow to adjust the speed of the engine.

A carb works due to the "venturi effect." A venturi is a passage with a constricted section through which a fluid moves (in this case the fluid is the air). As the air flows through the constriction, the velocity increases and the pressure goes down. It is this lower pressure that draws the gasoline through the opening.

In real life, there must be multiple ways of adjusting the rate of fuel delivery to match the needs of the engine. As a result, the carb can have many different circuits and components. If you wish to know more about this subject, brace yourself and read on. Otherwise, skip to the section on cleaning your chrome and be happy. Carbs aren't for the faint-at-heart!

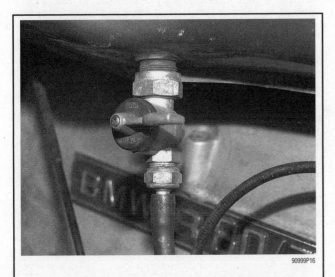

Fig. 10 A standard petcock that is completely manually operated

Fig. 12 Small inline fuel filters will help catch any particles that make their way through the petcock screen

Fig. 11 This petcock is vacuum operated which means it opens up automatically when the engine runs, requiring no input from the rider

Fig. 13 The air filter is the first line of defense and the first part of the air/fuel system

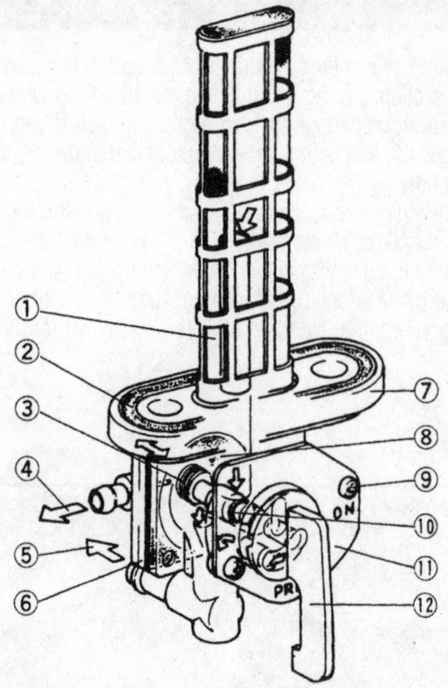

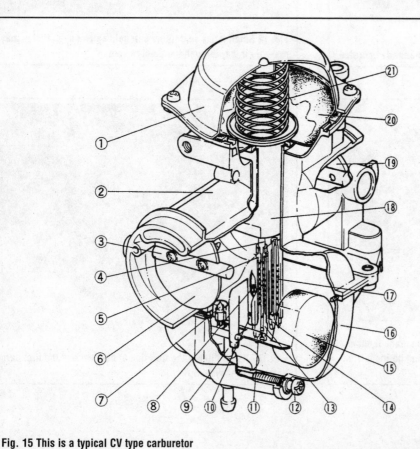

1. Filter
2. O Ring
3. Spring
4. Vacuum
5. Fuel
6. Diaphragm Cover
7. Body
8. Diaphragm
9. Screw
10. O Ring
11. Holding Plate
12. Tap Lever

90999L01

Fig. 14 Cutaway of a vacuum operated petcock

CONSTRUCTION

♦ See Figures 15, 16 and 17

Most carburetors consist of a one-piece body cast from cheap pot metal, although some "racing" units are made from more expensive materials such as magnesium. The body incorporates a bore for the movement of the throttle slide, the venturi, and provides a mounting point for various fuel and air jets.

The body is drilled with a number of fuel and air passages. Among these are the primary air passage, pilot air passage, and pilot outlet or by-pass.

The primary air passage can usually be found just beneath the carburetor intake, and is drilled through to the needle jet. The air taken in through this passage helps to atomize, or mix, the gasoline passing through the needle jet before it enters the venturi. Unless the gasoline is atomized, raw fuel will reach the combustion chamber, resulting in wet-fouled spark plugs, inefficient combustion, and generally poor operation.

The pilot air passage is located alongside the primary air passage on most carburetors. The air taken in through this drilling is used for idle and low-speed operation.

The pilot outlet is a very small drilling which can be seen on the engine side of the throttle slide bore. The fuel/air mixture for idling pass through here and then to the engine.

The carburetor body also has a place for the attachment of the float bowl. The float bowl houses the float assembly and carries the carburetor's gasoline supply. A part of the float assembly is the float valve which usually consists of a small needle and a needle seat.

The float rises and falls according to the amount of gasoline in the float bowl, alternately pressing the needle against its seat and releasing it, thus controlling the fuel flow. The float bulbs may be made of various materials. Most early carburetors used brass bulbs, but plastic has been used more frequently in recent years. Float needles can be plastic, brass, or neoprene-tipped brass, the last proving most effective. Needle seats are almost always brass, and on most carburetors can be unscrewed for cleaning or replacement.

1. Upper Chamber Cover
2. Carburetor Body
3. Choke Shaft
4. Jet Needle
5. Needle Jet
6. Choke Valve
7. Float Valve Needle
8. Pilot Jet
9. Overflow Pipe
10. Plastic Plug
11. Secondary Main Jet
12. Drain Screw
13. Needle Jet Holder
14. Primary Main Jet
15. Float
16. Float Chamber
17. Bleed Pipe
18. Vacuum Piston
19. Throttle Shaft
20. Diaphragm
21. Spring

90999L02

Fig. 15 This is a typical CV type carburetor

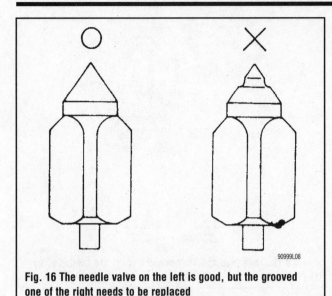

Fig. 16 The needle valve on the left is good, but the grooved one of the right needs to be replaced

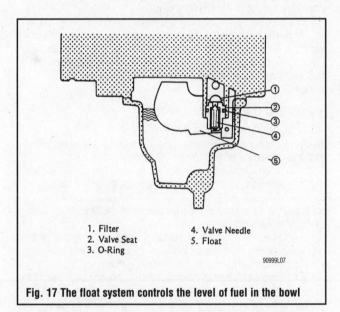

1. Filter
2. Valve Seat
3. O-Ring
4. Valve Needle
5. Float

90999L07

Fig. 17 The float system controls the level of fuel in the bowl

The great majority of modern carburetors mount the float bowl directly beneath the carburetor body. In this position the fuel supply surrounds the main jet ensuring an accurately metered supply of fuel during acceleration, braking, or banking to either side. This type of carburetor is usually known as "concentric." Not all carburetors were constructed in this manner, and separate float bowl carburetors were the rule for many years.

The throttle slide is the chief metering component of the carburetor. It is controlled directly by the throttle cable which runs to the twist grip on direct-control type carburetors. On "CV" units, the throttle cable opens and closes a throttle plate, and the slide itself opens and closes by venturi vacuum (this is explained later).

The throttle slide determines the size of the carburetor venturi and therefore meters the amount of air in the fuel/air mixture at most of the operating range. Additionally, the needle or jet needle is attached to the slide. This needle works in conjunction with the needle jet and determines the amount of gasoline allowed to pass into the engine primarily in the mid-range.

The throttle slide is cylindrical in most carburetors, although there are examples of "square slides" such as used by some Dell `Orto carburetors. The slide has a cutaway at the intake side of the carburetor to allow the entry of air in sufficient quantities to mix with the gasoline when the throttle is closed. The higher the cutaway, the leaner the mixture will be when the

slide is just opened. If the size of the cutaway is not matched to the other metering components and the particular needs of the engine, the transition from idle to the main metering system will be greatly impaired. This is a particularly critical period, since the load on the engine is changing as the clutch is engaged, and smooth starts from a dead stop must be considered a matter of safety in many cases.

Formerly, throttle slides were cast from the same material as the carburetor body, but this was found to cause greatly accelerated wear on both slide and body. Today, the slide is commonly steel, often chromed, bringing wear into more acceptable limits. In CV carburetors, where the slide must be moved by venturi vacuum, the slides must be light in weight, so light alloys are used.

OPERATION

The operation of a practical carburetor can best be described by dividing it into five circuits, and the components which control each one.

Direct-Control Carburetor

STARTING CIRCUIT (0% THROTTLE OPENING)

▶ **See Figure 18**

The engine needs a rich mixture for starting when cold. Since this need is only temporary and the mixture must be balanced when the engine warms up, a manually operated "choke" is incorporated into most carburetors and is controlled by the operator.

There are various ways of creating this rich mixture. The most simple is to reduce the amount of air available to the carb by closing off the mouth with a plate. This method is most often found on Honda motorcycles and on some others as well.

On some units, notably the old Amal Monoblocs and Concentrics, a temporary rich mixture is obtained by flooding or overfilling the float bowl. "Ticklers" are provided on the carburetor. When pushed, they depress the float, allowing the float needle to rise from its seat. The fuel level in the float bowl then exceeds its normal level and rises through the jets into the venturi where it provides a rich starting mixture.

Other carburetors, such as Mikuni and Dell `Orto use a refined version of the tickler. A starter jet is fitted which is activated by a cable or lever. When activated, the jet is opened (in most cases a spring-loaded plunger does the opening and closing), and fuel from the float bowl can bypass the normal fuel jets and pass into the carburetor bore.This is also true for some CV type carbs.

Once the engine is started and warmed up, the choke is switched off, and the fuel/air metering is turned over to the idle circuit components.

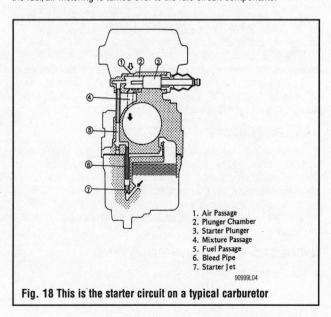

1. Air Passage
2. Plunger Chamber
3. Starter Plunger
4. Mixture Passage
5. Fuel Passage
6. Bleed Pipe
7. Starter Jet

90999L04

Fig. 18 This is the starter circuit on a typical carburetor

IDLE CIRCUIT (0–⅛ THROTTLE OPENING)

▶ **See Figure 19**

At idle, under normal operating conditions, the engine requires very little fuel and air. It does, however, require more accurate metering than pure venturi action can provide while the engine is turning relatively slowly and intake air velocity is low.

The idle circuit on most popular carburetors consists of a pilot jet, pilot air passage, and the throttle slide.

Fuel is provided by the float bowl. The amount of fuel is metered by the pilot jet, while air is taken in through the carburetor venturi and passes under the throttle slide (which is almost, but not quite closed at this point).

Because the idle mixture is so crucial, it is possible to adjust the mixture to compensate for changing conditions so that a good idle is always maintained. For this reason a pilot screw is fitted to most carburetors. The pilot screw is really a tapered needle and is fitted to an air or fuel passage. Turning the screw in or out will change the amount of fuel or air allowed to pass, and hence the mixture. On some carburetors the pilot screw is fitted directly to the pilot air passage and is sometimes called the "pilot air screw." On carburetors of this type, the amount of fuel entering the idling engine is determined by the size of the pilot jet alone, and the amount of air is varied to meet changing conditions.

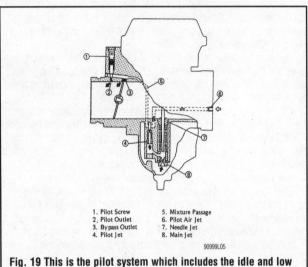

1. Pilot Screw
2. Pilot Outlet
3. Bypass Outlet
4. Pilot Jet
5. Mixture Passage
6. Pilot Air Jet
7. Needle Jet
8. Main Jet

90999L05

Fig. 19 This is the pilot system which includes the idle and low speed circuits

On other types of carburetors, it is the amount of air which is fixed by the size of the pilot air passage. On these carburetors, the pilot screw changes the amount of fuel passing into the engine.

In operation, piston suction creates a low-pressure area behind the throttle slide. To equalize this low pressure, air rushes through the pilot air passage, mixes with fuel from the pilot jet. This mixture is bled into the carburetor's intake tract through the pilot outlet. The air coming in under the throttle slide is added to this mixture and delivers it to the combustion chamber.

LOW-SPEED CIRCUIT (⅛–¼ THROTTLE OPENING)

This circuit uses the same components as the idle circuit. There is, however, an increase in the airflow as the throttle slide rises, and in fuel flow as the needle begins to come out of the needle jet. This effects a transition to the mid-range circuit, since the increased amounts of fuel and air delivered by the needle jet and the venturi overshadow the smaller amounts coming from the pilot outlet, eventually eliminating the idle circuit from the metering system.

MIDRANGE CIRCUIT (¼–¾ THROTTLE OPENING)

▶ **See Figure 20**

In this circuit, air is supplied by two sources: the venturi and the primary air passage. The more important reason for the air going through the primary air passage, however, is that it mixes with the gasoline in the needle

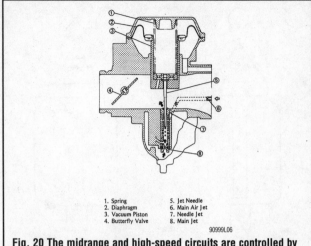

1. Spring
2. Diaphragm
3. Vacuum Piston
4. Butterfly Valve
5. Jet Needle
6. Main Air Jet
7. Needle Jet
8. Main Jet

90999L06

Fig. 20 The midrange and high-speed circuits are controlled by the main jet

jet (the needle jet has a number of holes drilled in it), and this helps to atomize the fuel before it enters the venturi.

Fuel is supplied by the float bowl and metered by the needle jet and needle. The needle jet on most carburetors is located just above the main jet and works in conjunction with the needle suspended from the throttle slide.

As the slide rises, the air flow through the carburetor is increased, and at the same time the tapered needle allows more and more fuel to pass through the needle jet.

HIGH-SPEED CIRCUIT (FULL THROTTLE)

The throttle slide has been lifted clear of the venturi, and no longer controls the amount of air. By the same token, the needle has lifted out of the needle jet, and no longer controls the fuel supply.

Venturi action takes over completely. The amount of air sucked into the engine is determined by the size of the venturi, and the amount of fuel delivered by the size of the main jet. The only other part of the system which still has a significant effect is the primary air passage which continues to aid fuel atomization.

It should be understood that the operating ranges of the various metering circuits overlap somewhat, so there is a gradual, rather than an abrupt, transition from one to another as the throttle is operated.

The relative independence of the various circuits, however, should explain why it is fruitless to make random changes in carburetor settings without first determining the nature of the problem, and the range in which it occurs.

ACCELERATOR PUMPS

Some direct-control carburetors used on four-stroke motors incorporate accelerator pumps which squirt a stream of raw gasoline into the venturi whenever the throttle is opened. The pumps usually consist of a throttle slide-activated plunger which takes fuel directly from the float bowl, bypassing the normal metering components.

Accelerator pumps are incorporated to aid the transition from the idle system to the main metering system. Throttle response is therefore much improved. One disadvantage of the system, however, is that it may have an adverse effect on fuel economy.

Constant-Velocity Carburetors

▶ **See Figure 21**

The constant-velocity carburetor is basically the same as the direct-control type carburetor, except that the throttle twist-grip is not connected directly to the throttle slide, Instead, in the CV carburetor, the throttle grip and cable are connected to a throttle plate located between the intake manifold and throttle slide. As the throttle plate is opened, the manifold vacuum evacuates air from the top of the slide chamber through a passage in the slide. Consequently, on demand from the engine, the slide is raised and more air is admitted, and the tapered needle is proportionally lifted out of the jet tube to admit more fuel,

The term "constant-velocity" (or constant vacuum) refers to the speed of the air passing over the main jet tube and the vacuum in the carburetor throat which remains constant due to the movement of the piston in relation to the vacuum.

As the engine demands more air and the manifold vacuum increases, the slide responds by lifting in proportion to the vacuum. Thus the carburetor air speed and vacuum remain constant, because an increase in vacuum means an increase in slide lift, which in turn increases the amount of air passing through the carburetor by altering the size of the air passage (venturi), and compensating for the increased engine demands with a larger flow of air. A constant vacuum indicates a constant-velocity, and vice versa.

Throttle-Plate Carburetors

The "throttle-plate" carburetor is little different in theory from the throttle-slide types considered above except, of course, that there is no moving slide, In its place is a flat plate which pivots as the twist-grip is rotated to increase the size of the carburetor throat and allow progressively more of the fuel/air mixture to enter the combustion chamber.

Unlike the throttle-slide carburetors described above, the throttle-plate units do not usually have well defined mid-range circuits, and are best described by breaking the operation down into "low-speed" and "high-speed" circuits.

The Bendix 16P12 carburetor is typical of this type and is used in the following explanation. This carburetor was used on most Harley-Davidson V-Twins after 1970, with the exception of late models fitted with a very similar Keihin unit or Evo engines fitted with a Keihin CV type.

STARTING CIRCUIT

A choke plate on the intake side of the carburetor closes off the mouth to yield a rich mixture needed for starting. A hole in the choke plate allows some air to enter to prevent flooding the engine. In addition, an accelerator pump is fitted which injects a stream of gasoline into the venturi when the throttle is opened.

LOW-SPEED CIRCUIT

There are three or four idle discharge holes located at the top engine side of the venturi. The main idle discharge hole is variable in size as it works in conjunction with a tapered idle adjusting needle. At idle, the throttle plate stop screw holds the throttle plate open just enough so that this passage is able to discharge its fuel into the engine.

Drawn by piston suction, gasoline rises from the float bowl through the idle tube. As the fuel passes the idle discharge holes, air is drawn in and mixed with it,

The mixture is then bled into the intake port through the idle hole.The mixture is determined by the idle adjusting needle. If the needle is turned IN, the mixture will be leaned out, and it will be richened if the needle is turned out.

As the throttle is opened slightly, the other idle discharge holes are exposed in turn, each allowing progressively more fuel and air into the intake port.

Eventually, the throttle plate is opened enough so that engine suction is powerful enough to draw gasoline from the main discharge tube and the transition to the high-speed circuit begins.

HIGH-SPEED CIRCUIT

The high-speed circuit begins when all idle discharge holes are exposed, and can no longer supply sufficient gasoline and air for the engine's needs.

As the throttle plate is opened the velocity of the incoming air passing through the venturi is increased, and, as this happens, this air exerts an increasingly powerful suction on the gasoline in the discharge tube just below the venturi. This gasoline is already partially atomized by the air drawn through the well vent.

When the throttle is fully opened, the amount of air in the mixture is determined by the size of the carburetor venturi and the amount of fuel by the size of the main jet.

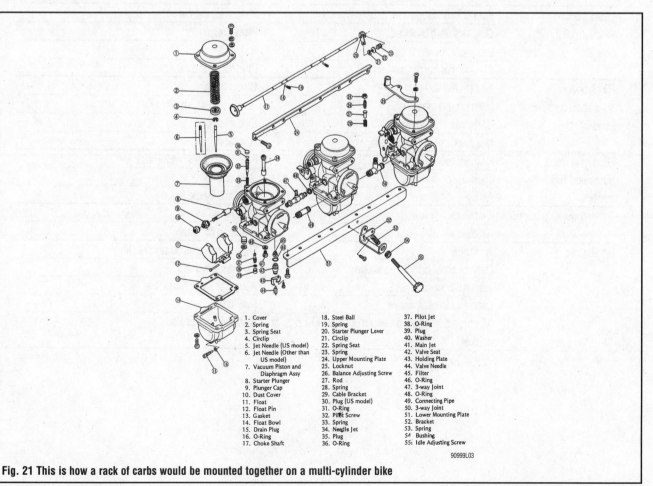

1. Cover	18. Steel Ball	37. Pilot Jet
2. Spring	19. Spring	38. O-Ring
3. Spring Seat	20. Starter Plunger Lever	39. Plug
4. Circlip	21. Circlip	40. Washer
5. Jet Needle (US model)	22. Spring Seat	41. Main Jet
6. Jet Needle (Other than US model)	23. Spring	42. Valve Seat
	24. Upper Mounting Plate	43. Holding Plate
7. Vacuum Piston and Diaphragm Assy	25. Locknut	44. Valve Needle
	26. Balance Adjusting Screw	45. Filter
8. Starter Plunger	27. Rod	46. O-Ring
9. Plunger Cap	28. Spring	47. 3-way Joint
10. Dust Cover	29. Cable Bracket	48. O-Ring
11. Float	30. Plug (US model)	49. Connecting Pipe
12. Float Pin	31. O-Ring	50. 3-way Joint
13. Gasket	32. Pilot Screw	51. Lower Mounting Plate
14. Float Bowl	33. Spring	52. Bracket
15. Drain Plug	34. Needle Jet	53. Spring
16. O-Ring	35. Plug	54. Bushing
17. Choke Shaft	36. O-Ring	55. Idle Adjusting Screw

90999L03

Fig. 21 This is how a rack of carbs would be mounted together on a multi-cylinder bike

CARBURETOR TROUBLESHOOTING

Problem	Possible Cause	Inspection/Remedy
Carburetor floods repeatedly	Float set too high	Adjust
	Float needle sticking	Remove float bowl and clean needle and seat
	Float needle or seat worn or damaged	Replace as necessary
	Float sticking due to misalignment	Correct
	Fuel petcock left open with engine shut off	Shut off the fuel after you stop the engine
	Float punctured	Replace
Idle mixture too lean	Pilot jet too small	Replace with larger jet
	Worn throttle slide	Replace
	Pilot screw out of adjustment	Adjust
Idle mixture too rich	Pilot jet too large	Replace with smaller jet
	Dirt or foreign matter in idle passage	Dismantle and clean carburetor
	Pilot screw out of adjustment	Adjust
Lean mixture at sustained mid-range speeds	jet needle set too lean	Reset needle clip at lower notch
	Needle or main jet clogged	Remove and clean jets
	Intake manifold air leak	Find leak and rectify
Lean mixture at sustained high-speeds	Main jet too small	Replace with larger jet
	Main jet clogged	Remove and clean.
	Float level too low	Remove float and adjust level
Lean mixture during acceleration	Jets clogged	Remove and clean
	Damaged or worn throttle slide	Replace
	Float level too low	Adjust float height
Lean mixture throughout throttle range	Fuel filters clogged or dirty	Remove and clean
	Gas cap vent blocked	Blow clear
	Damaged or worn throttle slide	Replace
	Air leaks at carb manifold	Find leak and rectify
Rich mixture at sustained mid-range speeds	Air cleaner dirty	Clean or replace
	Main jet too large	Replace with smaller jet
	Carburetor flooding	See above
	Needle or needle jet worn	Replace
Rich mixture at sustained high-speeds	Main jet too large	Replace with smaller size jet.
	Carburetor flooding	See above.
	Air cleaner dirty	Replace or clean
Rich mixture throughout	Carburetor flooding	See above
	Air cleaner dirty	Replace or clean
Erratic idle	Air leaks	Determine source and rectify
	Dirty or blocked idle passages	Clean carburetor
	Idle settings incorrect	Adjust to specifications
	Damage to pilot screw	Replace
	Worn or damaged air seals such as O-rings or gaskets	Rebuild carburetor

90999C01

CARBURETOR TROUBLESHOOTING

Problem	Possible Cause	Inspection/Remedy
Erratic idle (cont.)	Unsynchronized carburetors on carburetors. multi-carb machines	Adjust and synchronize
	Defective auto timing advancer	Repair or replace.
	Mixture too lean	Adjust carburetor

90999C02

Fuel Injection

▶ **See Figure 22**

Ok, now that you have digested all that stuff about carburetors, you have to be thinking, "There has got to be a better way!" In fact, there is, and it is called fuel injection. In its most basic form, fuel injection is defined as injecting fuel into the engine via a pressurized fuel source. Carbs on the other hand rely on vacuum to draw the air and fuel into the engine.

If fuel injection is so great, why don't all motorcycles use it? This answer comes down to economics: Carbs are cheaper than fuel injection. Not to mention the fact that the motorcycle manufacturers have done great things with carbs, so why mess with a good thing? But, there are still good reasons for the use of fuel injection.

Fuel injection allows for very precise metering of fuel into the engine. It also allows the mixture to be controlled by a computer that can decide the best course of action for the fuel system in only a few milliseconds. Carbs rely on the shape of needles, the size of orifices and the whims of the person who built or tuned it! Fuel injection is programmed with the purpose of the bike in mind and an attempt is made to optimize the fuel delivery.

COMPONENTS AND THEIR OPERATION

▶ **See Figures 23, 24, 25 and 26**

Depending on the manufacturer, the fuel injection system on any one model of bike may be different from another model. This is because every bike has a different need and goal in life. Your standard Harley-Davidson with fuel injection has a very basic system since the engine runs in a very short rpm range

and doesn't ask much from its owner in terms of performance. That engine is very happy to chug along all day long at 2000 rpm cruising down Route 66.

A BMW K or R bike has a bigger job to do and in its latest versions (as of the time of the writing of this book) is equipped with emissions controls that rival any car. BMW was an early adopter of fuel injection and has learned how to make it work on a motorcycle. Typically a BMW is ridden in

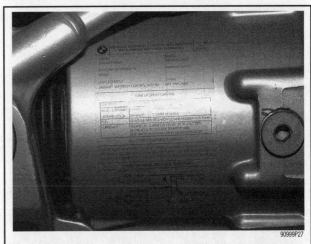

Fig. 23 This is an emissions control sticker on a BMW motorcycle listing all of the specs that need to be adhered to in order to keep the exhaust levels in check

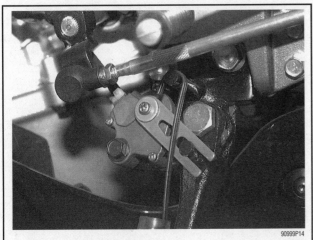

Fig. 22 Even with all the high tech fuel injection on some bikes, something as simple as a bad sidestand switch will keep a bike from starting or running

Fig. 24 This is a fuel injector positioned at the intake port of the cylinder head

Fig. 25 This oxygen sensor measures the exhaust oxygen level and with this information the computer can adjust the fuel mixture on the fly

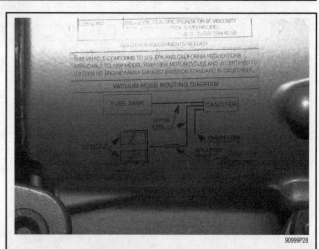

Fig. 27 With emissions controls as important today as they are, a vacuum line diagram is provided by the manufactures so the correct routing can be checked and maintained

Fig. 26 This is an air temperature sensor that the fuel injection computer will consult with while making its decisions

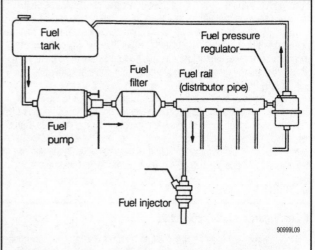

Fig. 28 This is a sample of a fuel supply system for fuel injection

a wider range of conditions to meet its sport touring duty and as a result, a more complicated fuel injection system is needed.

Some other bikes, such as Ducatis and Moto Guzzi (it is as much fun to type Moto Guzzi as it is to say it) has yet another agenda: They are sport bikes and need good solid performance out at the track or in the back roads. It also happens that fuel injection is quite the handy thing to have out at the race track when you want to reprogram the fuel delivery curve to help you beat the competition!

Other manufacturers use fuel injection to meet the needs they set for themselves.

Regardless of the manufacturer, a few rules are held to all fuel injection systems. There must be a fuel supply, a fuel injector (or two or three, etc), a method of determining how much air is going into the engine and a central processor that orchestrates the entire system.

Fuel Supply

▶ See Figures 27 thru 32

Like any other bike, a fuel injected one will have a fuel tank. The only difference is that the fuel tank may contain a high pressure fuel pump and a return line for unused fuel. If the fuel pump is not inside the tank,

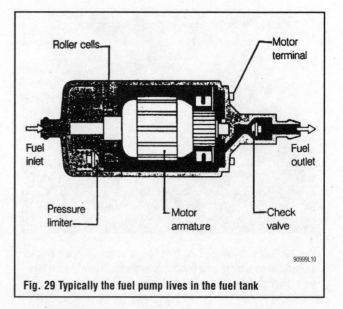

Fig. 29 Typically the fuel pump lives in the fuel tank

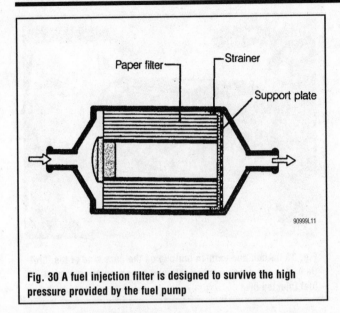

Fig. 30 A fuel injection filter is designed to survive the high pressure provided by the fuel pump

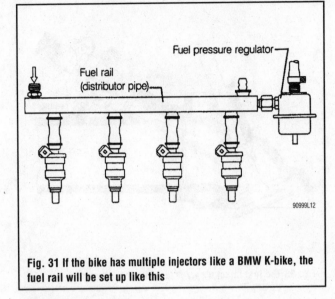

Fig. 31 If the bike has multiple injectors like a BMW K-bike, the fuel rail will be set up like this

it will be mounted somewhere near. A fuel pump on a fuel injected bike will provide fuel at a high pressure so it can be atomized at the fuel injector nozzle. The entire fuel supply will be routed through a fuel filter that will remove any of the nasties that may try to hurt your injectors. A fuel pressure regulator keeps the injectors fed with a fuel at defined pressures.

Fuel Injectors

▶ See Figures 33 and 34

Fuel injectors are typically electromechanical devices which act as valves controlling the flow of fuel into the intake tract of the engine. Fuel is deliv-

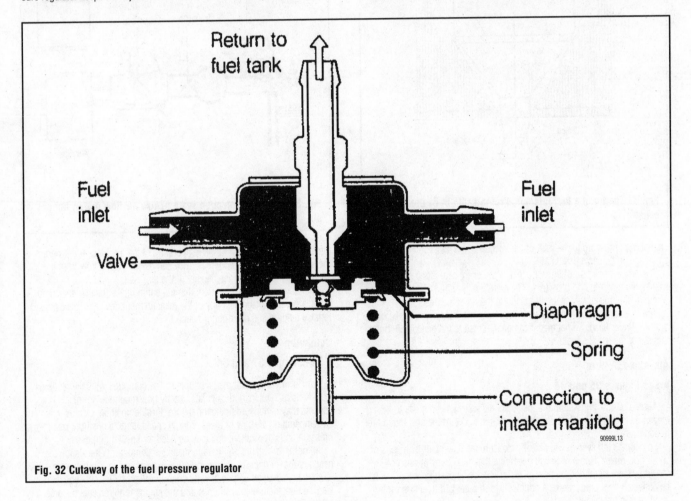

Fig. 32 Cutaway of the fuel pressure regulator

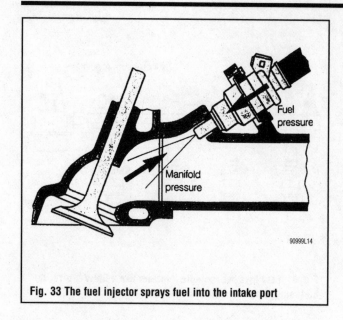

Fig. 33 The fuel injector sprays fuel into the intake port

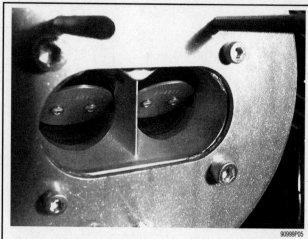

Fig. 35 Carbon and varnish buildup on the back side of the throttle plates can cause a rough idle and poor running even on a fuel injected bike

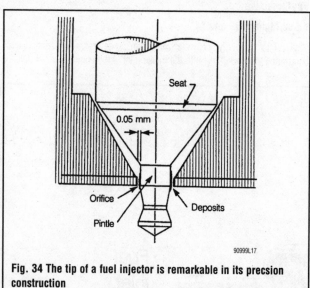

Fig. 34 The tip of a fuel injector is remarkable in its precsion construction

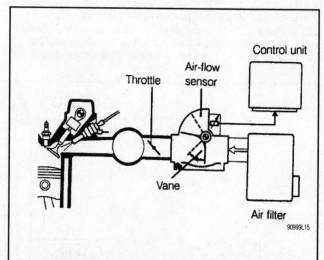

Fig. 36 Some fuel injection systems use air flow meter, but not all

ered at high pressure to the inlet of the injector and it passes through a small screen that acts as a final filter.

There is a small coil of fine wire that, when energized, lifts a pintle off its seat allowing the fuel to pass by it. The fuel then flows out of a nozzle where it is atomized by the small hole(s) in the tip of the injector.

The injector is usually mounted in the intake manifold at the intake port of the cylinder head. Sometimes it can be mounted to the head itself, but this is not the usual situation.

Air Intake System

♦ See Figures 35 and 36

Air is a critical ingredient in a fuel injection system since it has to be measured precisely for the computer to be able to determine how much fuel to add to it.

Sometimes the system will actually measure the flow of air by means of an air flow meter. This device will determine that air flow by means of a moving vane. Depending on how much air is moving past the vane, it will be deflected by a proportional amount. The computer will read this value and use it in the calculations.

In more basic systems, the amount of air will be determined through calculations. The computer will be fed signals from the engine in regards to

the speed of the engine and the temperature of the air. Since the programmers know how big the engine is, they can determine the flow from the speed of the engine and the density of the air.

In either system it is important that the entire intake tract be sealed so there is no air leakage past any of the measurement devices. This can lead to false reading and poor performance.

Computer

♦ See Figures 37 and 38

This is where the real magic happens! The computer will take readings from various sensors and calculate exactly how much fuel to inject. The sensors may include engine temperature, throttle position, exhaust oxygen, air temperature, air flow or mass, engine speed, engine position, barometric pressure and a few others that may be need for special purposes.

All of these sensors are there to make the computer better define the needs of the engine. An engine loping along just above idle has much different needs than an engine at wide open throttle. Mix into the equation varying temperature and altitudes and the engine requirements become very tricky. Due to the ability of the computer to take all of these situations into account and calculate the changes in mere milliseconds, fuel injection can make for a very driveable vehicle. There is nothing more pleasurable than

Fig. 37 Ignition is one of the functions that the fuel injection computer will also control

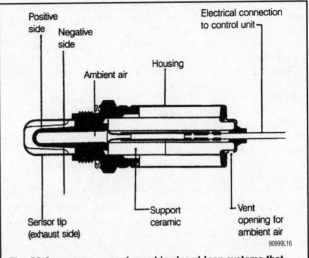

Fig. 38 An oxygen sensor is used in closed loop systems that adjust themselves to varying conditions

going out to your bike on a cold day, hitting the button and having it fire up on the first try!

Some fuel injection systems have built in diagnostics. This means that the computer can actually determine what may be wrong with itself. If a problem is sensed, a light will flash or illuminate on the instrument cluster to warn you. Most fuel injection systems undergo a self-diagnostic routine when the bike is started. Check your owners manual to see if your bike has this capability.

The latest offerings from some of the manufactures are bikes equipped with catalytic converters to help reduce the exhaust gas emissions. On bikes so equipped, there will be an oxygen sensor mounted in the exhaust system to provide feedback to the computer on the amount of oxygen in the exhaust stream. This information allows the computer to keep the fuel mixture in the narrow range in which the catalyst best operates. There are a few bikes, notably Harley-Davidson, that use catalytic converters without a feedback system and the oxygen sensor.

UNDERSTANDING AND TROUBLESHOOTING ELECTRICAL SYSTEMS

Basic Electrical Theory

♦ See Figure 39

For any 12 volt, negative ground, electrical system to operate, the electricity must travel in a complete circuit. This simply means that current (power) from the positive terminal (+) of the battery must eventually return to the negative terminal (-) of the battery. Along the way, this current will travel through wires, fuses, switches and components. If, for any reason, the flow of current through the circuit is interrupted, the component fed by that circuit will cease to function properly.

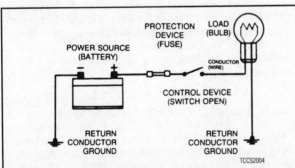

Fig. 39 This example illustrates a simple circuit. When the switch is closed, power from the positive (+) battery terminal flows through the fuse and the switch, and then to the light bulb. The light illuminates and the circuit is completed through the ground wire back to the negative (-) battery terminal. In reality, the two ground points shown in the illustration are attached to the metal frame of the vehicle, which completes the circuit back to the battery

Perhaps the easiest way to visualize a circuit is to think of connecting a light bulb (with two wires attached to it) to the battery—one wire attached to the negative (-) terminal of the battery and the other wire to the positive (+) terminal. With the two wires touching the battery terminals, the circuit would be complete and the light bulb would illuminate. Electricity would follow a path from the battery to the bulb and back to the battery. It's easy to see that with longer wires on our light bulb, it could be mounted anywhere. Further, one wire could be fitted with a switch so that the light could be turned on and off.

The normal motorcycle circuit differs from this simple example in two ways. First, instead of having a return wire from the bulb to the battery, the current travels through the frame of the motorcycle. Since the negative (-) battery cable is attached to the frame (made of electrically conductive metal), the frame of the vehicle can serve as a ground wire to complete the circuit. Secondly, most motorcycle circuits contain multiple components which receive power from a single circuit. This lessens the amount of wire needed to power components on the bike.

HOW DOES ELECTRICITY WORK: THE WATER ANALOGY

Electricity is the flow of electrons—the subatomic particles that constitute the outer shell of an atom. Electrons spin in an orbit around the center core of an atom. The center core is comprised of protons (positive charge) and neutrons (neutral charge). Electrons have a negative charge and balance out the positive charge of the protons. When an outside force causes the number of electrons to unbalance the charge of the protons, the electrons will split off the atom and look for another atom to balance out. If this imbalance is kept up, electrons will continue to move and an electrical flow will exist.

Many people have been taught electrical theory using an analogy with water. In a comparison with water flowing through a pipe, the electrons would be the water and the wire is the pipe.

The flow of electricity can be measured much like the flow of water through a pipe. The unit of measurement used is amperes, frequently abbreviated as amps (**a**). You can compare amperage to the volume of water flowing through a pipe. When connected to a circuit, an ammeter will measure the actual amount of current flowing through the circuit. When relatively few electrons flow through a circuit, the amperage is low. When many electrons flow, the amperage is high.

Water pressure is measured in units such as pounds per square inch (psi); The electrical pressure is measured in units called volts (**v**). When a voltmeter is connected to a circuit, it is measuring the electrical pressure.

The actual flow of electricity depends not only on voltage and amperage, but also on the resistance of the circuit. The higher the resistance, the higher the force necessary to push the current through the circuit. The standard unit for measuring resistance is an ohm (omega). Resistance in a circuit varies depending on the amount and type of components used in the circuit. The main factors which determine resistance are:

• Material—some materials have more resistance than others. Those with high resistance are said to be insulators. Rubber materials (or rubber-like plastics) are some of the most common insulators used in vehicles as they have a very high resistance to electricity. Very low resistance materials are said to be conductors. Copper wire is among the best conductors. Silver is actually a superior conductor to copper and is used in some relay contacts, but its high cost prohibits its use as common wiring. Most motorcycle wiring is made of copper.

• Size—the larger the wire size being used, the less resistance the wire will have. This is why components which use large amounts of electricity usually have large wires supplying current to them.

• Length—for a given thickness of wire, the longer the wire, the greater the resistance. The shorter the wire, the less the resistance. When determining the proper wire for a circuit, both size and length must be considered to design a circuit that can handle the current needs of the component.

• Temperature—with many materials, the higher the temperature, the greater the resistance (positive temperature coefficient). Some materials exhibit the opposite trait of lower resistance with higher temperatures (negative temperature coefficient). These principles are used in many of the sensors on the engine.

OHM'S LAW

There is a direct relationship between current, voltage and resistance. The relationship between current, voltage and resistance can be summed up by a statement known as Ohm's law.

Voltage (E) is equal to amperage (I) times resistance (R): $E = I \times R$

Other forms of the formula are $R = E/I$ and $I = E/R$

In each of these formulas, E is the voltage in volts, I is the current in amps and R is the resistance in ohms. The basic point to remember is that as the resistance of a circuit goes up, the amount of current that flows in the circuit will go down, if voltage remains the same.

The amount of work that the electricity can perform is expressed as power. The unit of power is the watt (w). The relationship between power, voltage and current is expressed as:

Power (w) is equal to amperage (I) times voltage (E): $W = I \times E$

This is only true for direct current (DC) circuits; The alternating current formula is a tad different, but since the electrical circuits in most motorcycles (and cars, for that matter) are DC type, we need not get into AC circuit theory.

Electrical Components

POWER SOURCE

Power is supplied to the motorcycle by two devices: The battery and the alternator. The battery supplies electrical power during starting or during periods when the current demand of the motorcycle's electrical system exceeds the alternator output capacity . The alternator supplies electrical current when the engine is running. Just not does the alternator supply the current needs of the motorcycle, but it recharges the battery.

The Battery

In most modern vehicles, the battery is a lead/acid electrochemical device consisting of three or six 2 volt subsections (cells) connected in series, so that the unit is capable of producing approximately 6 or 12 volts (respectively) of electrical pressure. Each subsection consists of a series of positive and negative plates held a short distance apart in a solution of sulfuric acid and water.

The two types of plates are of dissimilar metals. This sets up a chemical reaction, and it is this reaction which produces current flow from the battery when its positive and negative terminals are connected to an electrical load. The power removed from the battery is replaced by the alternator, restoring the battery to its original chemical state.

The Alternator

On some motorcycles there isn't an alternator, but a generator. The difference is that an alternator supplies alternating current which is then changed to direct current for use on the bike, while a generator produces direct current. Alternators tend to be more efficient and that is why they are used.

Alternators and generators are devices that consist of coils of wires wound together making big electromagnets. One group of coils spins within another set and the interaction of the magnetic fields causes a current to flow. This current is then drawn off the coils and fed into the motorcycle's electrical system.

GROUND

Two types of grounds are used in motorcycle electric circuits. Direct ground components are grounded to the frame through their mounting points. All other components use some sort of ground wire which is attached to the frame or chassis of the vehicle. The electrical current runs through the chassis of the vehicle and returns to the battery through the ground (-) cable. If you look, you'll see that the battery ground cable connects between the battery and the frame or chassis of the vehicle.

➡ **It should be noted that a good percentage of electrical problems can be traced to bad grounds.**

PROTECTIVE DEVICES

♦ **See Figures 40, 41, 42 and 43**

It is possible for large surges of current to pass through the electrical system of your vehicle. If this surge of current were to reach the load in the circuit, it could burn it out or severely damage it. It can also overload the wiring, causing the harness to get hot and melt the insulation. To prevent this, fuses, circuit breakers and/or fusible links are connected into the supply wires of the electrical system. These items are nothing more than a built-in weak spot in the system. When an abnormal amount of current flows through the system, these protective devices work as follows to protect the circuit:

• Fuse—when an excessive electrical current passes through a fuse, it "blows" (the conductor melts) and opens the circuit, preventing the passage of current.

• Circuit Breaker—a circuit breaker is basically a self-repairing fuse. It will open the circuit in the same fashion as a fuse, but when the surge subsides, the circuit breaker can be reset and does not need replacement.

• Fusible Link—a fusible link (fuse link or main link) is a short length of special, high temperature insulated wire that acts as a fuse. When an excessive electrical current passes through a fusible link, the thin gauge wire inside the link melts, creating an intentional open to protect the circuit. To repair the circuit, the link must be replaced. Some newer type fusible links are housed in plug-in modules, which are simply replaced like a fuse, while older type fusible links must be cut and spliced if they melt. Since this link is very early in the electrical path, it's the first place to look if nothing on the vehicle works, but the battery seems to be charged and is properly connected.

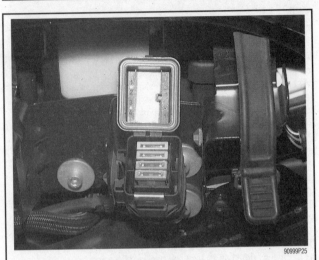

Fig. 40 This is a fuse center on a German bike—with a water-proof cover

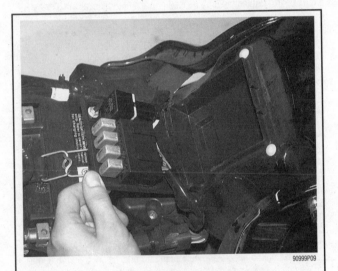

Fig. 41 This bike uses circuit breakers instead of fuses

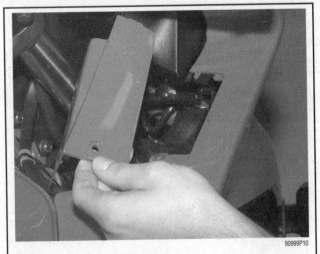

Fig. 42 Feeling quite clever, the manufacturer of this bike hid the fuse panel in the bodywork

Fig. 43 Once the cover is removed, the fuse panel is handy to get at

✻✻ CAUTION

Always replace fuses, circuit breakers and fusible links with identically rated components. Under no circumstances should a component of higher or lower amperage rating be substituted.

SWITCHES & RELAYS

▶ **See Figures 44, 45 and 46**

Switches are used in electrical circuits to control the passage of current. The most common use is to open and close circuits between the battery and the various electric devices in the system. Switches are rated according to the amount of amperage they can handle. If a sufficient amperage rated switch is not used in a circuit, the switch could overload and cause damage.

Some electrical components which require a large amount of current to operate use a special switch called a relay. Since these circuits carry a large amount of current, the thickness of the wire in the circuit is also greater. If this large wire were connected from the load to the control switch, the switch would have to carry the high amperage load and there would be an increased size of the wiring harness. To prevent these problems, a relay is used.

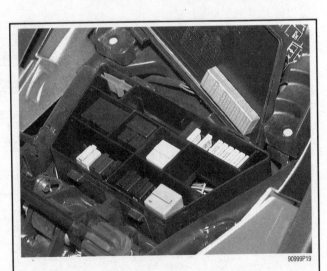

Fig. 44 Todays bikes have fuse and relay centers that can rival a car

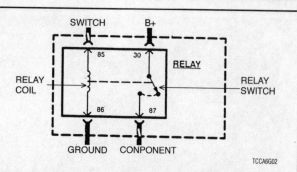

Fig. 45 Relays are composed of a coil and a switch. These two components are linked together so that when one operates, the other operates at the same time. The large wires in the circuit are connected from the battery to one side of the relay switch (B+) and from the opposite side of the relay switch to the load (component). Smaller wires are connected from the relay coil to the control switch for the circuit and from the opposite side of the relay coil to ground

Relays are composed of a coil and a set of contacts. When the coil has a current passed though it, a magnetic field is formed and this field causes the contacts to move together, completing the circuit. Most relays are normally open, preventing current from passing through the circuit, but they can take any electrical form depending on the job they are intended to do. Relays can be considered "remote control switches." They allow a smaller current to operate devices that require higher amperages. When a small current operates the coil, a larger current is allowed to pass by the contacts. Some common circuits which may use relays are the horn, headlights, starter, electric fuel pump and other high draw circuits.

LOAD

Every electrical circuit must include a "load" (something to use the electricity coming from the source). Without this load, the battery would attempt to deliver its entire power supply from one pole to another instantly. This is called a "short circuit." All this electricity would take a short cut to ground and cause a great amount of damage to other components in the circuit by developing a tremendous amount of heat. This condition could develop sufficient heat to melt the insulation on all the surrounding wires and reduce a multiple wire cable to a lump of plastic and copper.

WIRING & HARNESSES

The average motorcycle contains meters and meters of wiring, with hundreds of individual connections. To protect the many wires from damage and to keep them from becoming a confusing tangle, they are organized into bundles, enclosed in plastic or taped together and called wiring harnesses. Different harnesses serve different parts of the vehicle. Individual wires are color coded to help trace them through a harness where sections are hidden from view.

Motorcycle wiring or circuit conductors can be either single strand wire, multi-strand wire or printed circuitry. Single strand wire has a solid metal core and is usually used inside such components as alternators, motors, relays and other devices. Multi-strand wire has a core made of many small strands of wire twisted together into a single conductor. Most of the wiring in a motorcycle electrical system is made up of multi-strand wire, either as a single conductor or grouped together in a harness. All wiring is color coded on the insulator, either as a solid color or as a colored wire with an identification stripe. A printed circuit is a thin film of copper or other conductor that is printed on an insulator backing. Occasionally, a printed circuit is sandwiched between two sheets of plastic for more protection and flexibility. A complete printed circuit, consisting of conductors, insulating material and connectors for lamps or other components is called a printed circuit board. Printed circuitry is used in place of individual wires or harnesses in places where space is limited, such as in instruments.

Since motorcycle electrical systems are very sensitive to changes in resistance, the selection of properly sized wires is critical when systems are repaired. A loose or corroded connection or a replacement wire that is too small for the circuit will add extra resistance and an additional voltage drop to the circuit.

The wire gauge number is an expression of the cross-section area of the conductor. Motorcycles from countries that use the metric system will typically describe the wire size as its cross-sectional area in square millimeters. In this method, the larger the wire, the greater the number. Another common system for expressing wire size is the American Wire Gauge (AWG) system. As gauge number increases, area decreases and the wire becomes smaller. An 18 gauge wire is smaller than a 4 gauge wire. A wire with a higher gauge number will carry less current than a wire with a lower gauge number. Gauge wire size refers to the size of the strands of the conductor, not the size of the complete wire with insulator. It is possible, therefore, to have two wires of the same gauge with different diameters because one may have thicker insulation than the other.

It is essential to understand how a circuit works before trying to figure out why it doesn't. An electrical schematic shows the electrical current paths when a circuit is operating properly. Schematics break the entire electrical system down into individual circuits. In a schematic, usually no

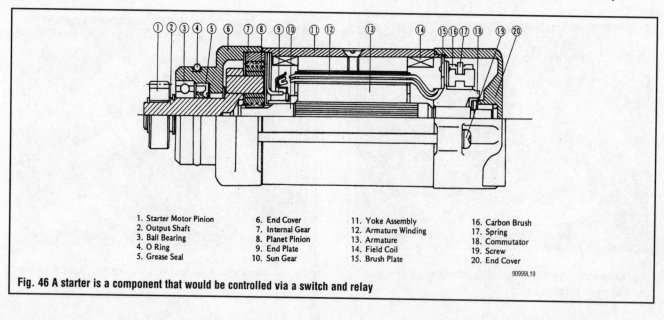

1. Starter Motor Pinion	6. End Cover	11. Yoke Assembly	16. Carbon Brush
2. Output Shaft	7. Internal Gear	12. Armature Winding	17. Spring
3. Ball Bearing	8. Planet Pinion	13. Armature	18. Commutator
4. O Ring	9. End Plate	14. Field Coil	19. Screw
5. Grease Seal	10. Sun Gear	15. Brush Plate	20. End Cover

Fig. 46 A starter is a component that would be controlled via a switch and relay

attempt is made to represent wiring and components as they physically appear on the vehicle; switches and other components are shown as simply as possible. Face views of harness connectors show the cavity or terminal locations in all multi-pin connectors to help locate test points.

CONNECTORS

▶ **See Figure 47**

Three types of connectors are commonly used in motorcycle applications—weatherproof, molded and hard shell.

• Weatherproof—these connectors are most commonly used where the connector is exposed to the elements. Terminals are protected against moisture and dirt by sealing rings which provide a weathertight seal. All repairs require the use of a special terminal and the tool required to service it. Unlike standard blade type terminals, these weatherproof terminals cannot be straightened once they are bent. Make certain that the connectors are properly seated and all of the sealing rings are in place when connecting leads.

• Molded—these connectors require complete replacement of the connector if found to be defective. This means splicing a new connector assembly into the harness. All splices should be soldered to insure proper contact. Use care when probing the connections or replacing terminals in them, as it is possible to create a short circuit between opposite terminals. If this happens to the wrong terminal pair, it is possible to damage certain components. Always use jumper wires between connectors for circuit checking and NEVER probe through weatherproof seals.

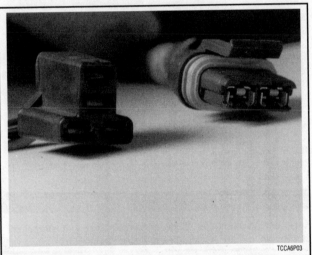

Fig. 47 Hard shell (left) and weatherproof (right) connectors have replaceable terminals

• Hard Shell—unlike molded connectors, the terminal contacts in hard-shell connectors can be replaced. Replacement usually involves the use of a special terminal removal tool that depresses the locking tangs (barbs) on the connector terminal and allows the connector to be removed from the rear of the shell. The connector shell should be replaced if it shows any evidence of burning, melting, cracks, or breaks. Replace individual terminals that are burnt, corroded, distorted or loose.

Test Equipment

▶ **See Figure 48**

Pinpointing the exact cause of trouble in an electrical circuit is most times accomplished by the use of special test equipment. The following describes different types of commonly used test equipment and briefly explains how to use them in diagnosis. In addition to the information covered below, the tool

Fig. 48 All the electronic test equipment in the shop won't help you find a mechanical problem like this cracked coil

manufacturer's instructions booklet (provided with the tester) should be read and clearly understood before attempting any test procedures.

JUMPER WIRES

✵✵ CAUTION

Never use jumper wires made from a thinner gauge wire than the circuit being tested. If the jumper wire is of too small a gauge, it may overheat and possibly melt. Never use jumpers to bypass high resistance loads in a circuit. Bypassing resistance, in effect, creates a short circuit. This may, in turn, cause damage and fire. Jumper wires should only be used to bypass lengths of wire or to simulate switches.

Jumper wires are simple, yet extremely valuable, pieces of test equipment. They are basically test wires which are used to bypass sections of a circuit. Although jumper wires can be purchased, they are usually fabricated from lengths of standard automotive wire and whatever type of connector (alligator clip, spade connector or pin connector) that is required for the particular application being tested. In cramped, hard-to-reach areas, it is advisable to have insulated boots over the jumper wire terminals in order to prevent accidental grounding. It is also advisable to include a standard automotive fuse in any jumper wire. This is commonly referred to as a "fused jumper." By inserting an in-line fuse holder between a set of test leads, a fused jumper wire can be used for bypassing open circuits while still protecting the circuit. Use a 5 amp fuse to provide protection against voltage spikes.

Jumper wires are used primarily to locate open electrical circuits, on either the ground (-) side of the circuit or on the power (+) side. If an electrical component fails to operate, connect the jumper wire between the component and a good ground. If the component operates only with the jumper installed, the ground circuit is open. If the ground circuit is good, but the component does not operate, the circuit between the power feed and component may be open. By moving the jumper wire successively back from the component toward the power source, you can isolate the area of the circuit where the open is located. When the component stops functioning, or the power is cut off, the open is in the segment of wire between the jumper and the point previously tested.

You can sometimes connect the jumper wire directly from the battery to the "hot" terminal of the component, but first make sure the component uses 12 volts in operation. Some electrical components, such as fuel injectors or sensors, may be designed to operate on about 4 to 5 volts, and running 12 volts directly to these components will cause damage.

TEST LIGHTS

♦ **See Figure 49**

The test light is used to check circuits and components while electrical current is flowing through them. It is used for voltage and ground tests. To use a 12 volt test light, connect the ground clip to a good ground and probe wherever necessary with the pick. The test light will illuminate when voltage is detected. This does not necessarily mean that 12 volts (or any particular amount of voltage) is present; it only means that some voltage is present. It is advisable before using the test light to touch its ground clip and probe across the battery posts or terminals to make sure the light is operating properly.

✳✳ WARNING

Do not use a test light to probe electronic ignition, spark plug or coil wires. Never use a pick-type test light to probe wiring on computer controlled systems unless specifically instructed to do so. Any wire insulation that is pierced by the test light probe should be taped and sealed with silicone after testing.

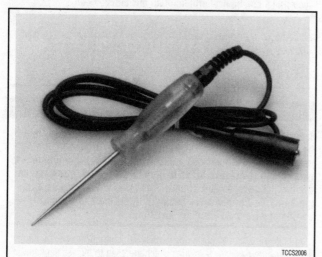

TCCS2006

Fig. 49 A 12 volt test light is used to detect the presence of voltage in a circuit

Like the jumper wire, the 12 volt test light is used to isolate opens in circuits. But, whereas the jumper wire is used to bypass the open to operate the load, the 12 volt test light is used to locate the presence of voltage in a circuit. If the test light illuminates, there is power up to that point in the circuit; if the test light does not illuminate, there is an open circuit (no power). Move the test light in successive steps back toward the power source until the light in the handle illuminates. The open is between the probe and a point which was previously probed.

The self-powered test light is similar in design to the 12 volt test light, but contains a 1.5 volt penlight battery in the handle. It is most often used in place of a multimeter to check for open or short circuits when power is isolated from the circuit (continuity test).

The battery in a self-powered test light does not provide much current. A weak battery may not provide enough power to illuminate the test light even when a complete circuit is made (especially if there is high resistance in the circuit). Always make sure that the test battery is strong. To check the battery, briefly touch the ground clip to the probe; if the light glows brightly, the battery is strong enough for testing.

➡**A self-powered test light should not be used on any computer controlled system or component. The small amount of electricity transmitted by the test light is enough to damage many electronic automotive components.**

MULTIMETERS

Multimeters are an extremely useful tool for troubleshooting electrical problems. They can be purchased in either analog or digital form and have a price range to suit any budget. A multimeter is a voltmeter, ammeter and ohmmeter (along with other features) combined into one instrument. It is often used when testing solid state circuits because of its high input impedance (usually 10 megaohms or more). A brief description of the multimeter main test functions follows:

• Voltmeter—the voltmeter is used to measure voltage at any point in a circuit, or to measure the voltage drop across any part of a circuit. Voltmeters usually have various scales and a selector switch to allow the reading of different voltage ranges. The voltmeter has a positive and a negative lead. To avoid damage to the meter, always connect the negative lead to the negative (-) side of the circuit (to ground or nearest the ground side of the circuit) and connect the positive lead to the positive (+) side of the circuit (to the power source or the nearest power source). Note that the negative voltmeter lead will always be black and that the positive voltmeter will always be some color other than black (usually red).

• Ohmmeter—the ohmmeter is designed to read resistance (measured in ohms) in a circuit or component. Most ohmmeters will have a selector switch which permits the measurement of different ranges of resistance (usually the selector switch allows the multiplication of the meter reading by 10, 100, 1,000 and 10,000). Some ohmmeters are "auto-ranging" which means the meter itself will determine which scale to use. Since the meters are powered by an internal battery, the ohmmeter can be used like a self-powered test light. When the ohmmeter is connected, current from the ohmmeter flows through the circuit or component being tested. Since the ohmmeter's internal resistance and voltage are known values, the amount of current flow through the meter depends on the resistance of the circuit or component being tested. The ohmmeter can also be used to perform a continuity test for suspected open circuits. In using the meter for making continuity checks, do not be concerned with the actual resistance readings. Zero resistance, or any ohm reading, indicates continuity in the circuit. Infinite resistance indicates an opening in the circuit. A high resistance reading where there should be none indicates a problem in the circuit. Checks for short circuits are made in the same manner as checks for open circuits, except that the circuit must be isolated from both power and normal ground. Infinite resistance indicates no continuity, while zero resistance indicates a dead short.

✳✳ WARNING

Never use an ohmmeter to check the resistance of a component or wire while there is voltage applied to the circuit.

• Ammeter—an ammeter measures the amount of current flowing through a circuit in units called amperes or amps. At normal operating voltage, most circuits have a characteristic amount of amperes, called "current draw" which can be measured using an ammeter. By referring to a specified current draw rating, then measuring the amperes and comparing the two values, one can determine what is happening within the circuit to aid in diagnosis. An open circuit, for example, will not allow any current to flow, so the ammeter reading will be zero. A damaged component or circuit will have an increased current draw, so the reading will be high. The ammeter is always connected in series with the circuit being tested. All of the current that normally flows through the circuit must also flow through the ammeter; if there is any other path for the current to follow, the ammeter reading will not be accurate. The ammeter itself has very little resistance to current flow and, therefore, will not affect the circuit, but it will measure current draw only when the circuit is closed and electricity is flowing. Excessive current draw can blow fuses and drain the battery, while a reduced current draw can cause motors to run slowly, lights to dim and other components to not operate properly.

Troubleshooting Electrical Systems

▶ See Figure 50

When diagnosing a specific problem, organized troubleshooting is a must. The complexity of a modern motorcycle demands that you approach any problem in a logical, organized manner. There are certain troubleshooting techniques which are standard:

• Establish when the problem occurs. Does the problem appear only under certain conditions? Were there any noises, odors or other unusual symptoms?

• Isolate the problem area. To do this, make some simple tests and observations, then eliminate the systems that are working properly. Check for obvious problems, such as broken wires and loose or dirty connections. Always check the obvious before assuming something complicated is the cause.

• Test for problems systematically to determine the cause once the problem area is isolated. Are all the components functioning properly? Is there power going to electrical switches and motors. Performing careful, systematic checks will often turn up most causes on the first inspection, without wasting time checking components that have little or no relationship to the problem.

• Test all repairs after the work is done to make sure that the problem is fixed. Some causes can be traced to more than one component, so a careful verification of repair work is important in order to pick up additional mal-

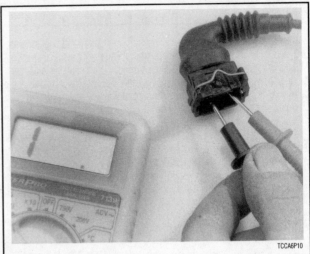

Fig. 51 The infinite reading on this multimeter (1 .) indicates that the circuit is open

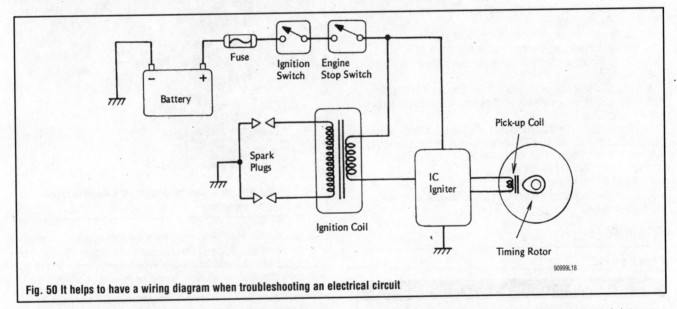

Fig. 50 It helps to have a wiring diagram when troubleshooting an electrical circuit

functions that may cause a problem to reappear or a different problem to arise. A blown fuse, for example, is a simple problem that may require more than another fuse to repair. If you don't look for a problem that caused a fuse to blow, a shorted wire (for example) may go undetected.

Experience has shown that most problems tend to be the result of a fairly simple and obvious cause, such as loose or corroded connectors, bad grounds or damaged wire insulation which causes a short. This makes careful visual inspection of components during testing essential to quick and accurate troubleshooting.

Testing

OPEN CIRCUITS

▶ See Figure 51

This test already assumes the existence of an open in the circuit and it is used to help locate the open portion.

1. Isolate the circuit from power and ground.
2. Connect the self-powered test light or ohmmeter ground clip to the ground side of the circuit and probe sections of the circuit sequentially.

3. If the light is out or there is infinite resistance, the open is between the probe and the circuit ground.
4. If the light is on or the meter shows continuity, the open is between the probe and the end of the circuit toward the power source.

SHORT CIRCUITS

➡ Never use a self-powered test light to perform checks for opens or shorts when power is applied to the circuit under test. The test light can be damaged by outside power.

1. Isolate the circuit from power and ground.
2. Connect the self-powered test light or ohmmeter ground clip to a good ground and probe any easy-to-reach point in the circuit.
3. If the light comes on or there is continuity, there is a short somewhere in the circuit.
4. To isolate the short, probe a test point at either end of the isolated circuit (the light should be on or the meter should indicate continuity).
5. Leave the test light probe engaged and sequentially open connectors or switches, remove parts, etc. until the light goes out or continuity is broken.
6. When the light goes out, the short is between the last two circuit components which were opened.

VOLTAGE

This test determines voltage available from the battery and should be the first step in any electrical troubleshooting procedure after visual inspection. Many electrical problems, especially on computer controlled systems, can be caused by a low state of charge in the battery. Excessive corrosion at the battery cable terminals can cause poor contact that will prevent proper charging and full battery current flow.

1. Set the voltmeter selector switch to the 20V position.
2. Connect the multimeter negative lead to the battery's negative (-) post or terminal and the positive lead to the battery's positive (+) post or terminal.
3. Turn the ignition switch **ON** to provide a load.
4. A well charged battery should register over 12 volts. If the meter reads below 11.5 volts, the battery power may be insufficient to operate the electrical system properly.

VOLTAGE DROP

When current flows through a load, the voltage beyond the load drops. This voltage drop is due to the resistance created by the load and also by small resistance's created by corrosion at the connectors and damaged insulation on the wires. The maximum allowable voltage drop under load is critical, especially if there is more than one load in the circuit, since all voltage drops are cumulative.

1. Set the voltmeter selector switch to the 20 volt position.
2. Connect the multimeter negative lead to a good ground.
3. Operate the circuit and check the voltage prior to the first component (load).
4. There should be little or no voltage drop in the circuit prior to the first component. If a voltage drop exists, the wire or connectors in the circuit are suspect.
5. While operating the first component in the circuit, probe the ground side of the component with the positive meter lead and observe the voltage readings. A small voltage drop should be noticed. This voltage drop is caused by the resistance of the component.
6. Repeat the test for each component (load) down the circuit.
7. If a large voltage drop is noticed, the preceding component, wire or connector is suspect.

RESISTANCE

▶ See Figure 52

✳✳ WARNING

Never use an ohmmeter with power applied to the circuit. The ohmmeter is designed to operate on its own power supply. The normal 12 volt electrical system voltage could damage the meter!

1. Isolate the circuit from the vehicle's power source.
2. Ensure that the ignition key is **OFF** when disconnecting any components or the battery.
3. Where necessary, also isolate at least one side of the circuit to be checked, in order to avoid reading parallel resistances. Parallel circuit resistances will always give a lower reading than the actual resistance of either of the branches.
4. Connect the meter leads to both sides of the circuit (wire or component) and read the actual measured ohms on the meter scale. Make sure the selector switch is set to the proper ohm scale for the circuit being tested, to avoid misreading the ohmmeter test value.

Wire and Connector Repair

Almost anyone can replace damaged wires, as long as the proper tools and parts are available. Wire and terminals are available to fit almost any need. Even the specialized weatherproof, molded and hard shell connectors are now available from aftermarket suppliers.

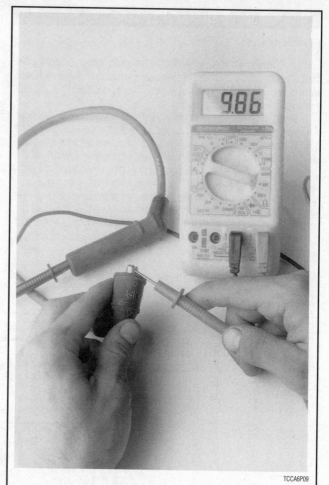

TCCA6P09

Fig. 52 Spark plug wires can be checked for excessive resistance using an ohmmeter

Be sure the ends of all the wires are fitted with the proper terminal hardware and connectors. Wrapping a wire around a stud is never a permanent solution and will only cause trouble later. Replace wires one at a time to avoid confusion. Always route wires exactly the same as the factory.

➡**If connector repair is necessary, only attempt it if you have the proper tools. Weatherproof and hard shell connectors require special tools to release the pins inside the connector. Attempting to repair these connectors with conventional hand tools will damage them.**

Reading Wiring Diagrams

▶ See Figures 53 thru 58

For many people, reading wiring diagrams, or schematics, is a black art. It isn't as bad as it seems, since wiring diagrams are really nothing more than connect-the-dots with wires!

If you look at the sample diagrams, you will see that they contain information such as wire colors, terminal connections and components. The boxes may contain information such as internal configurations as would be handy to figure out what is going on inside a relay or switch.

There is a standard set of symbols used in wiring diagrams to denote various components. If the wiring diagram doesn't provide a reference for the symbols, you should be able to pick out their meanings from other information given.

The wiring diagram will use abbreviations for wire colors. There will be a chart somewhere in the wiring diagram or in the manual you are using to decode them.

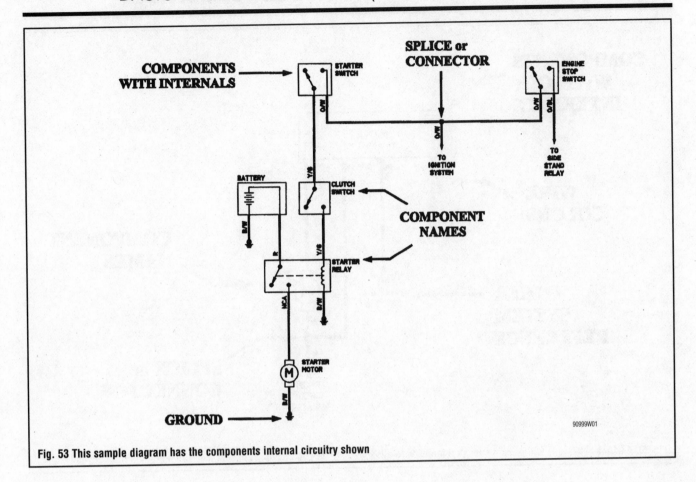

Fig. 53 This sample diagram has the components internal circuitry shown

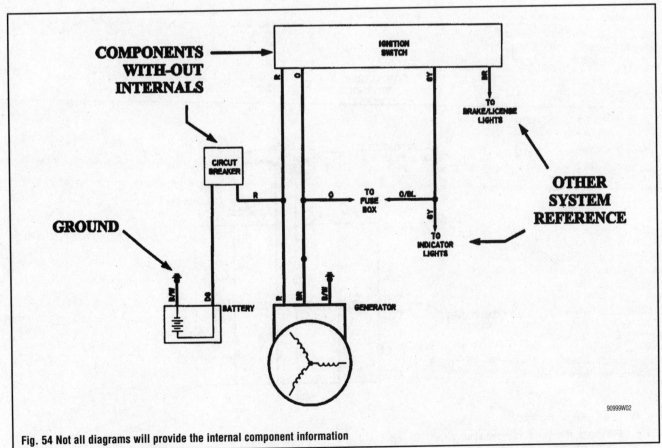

Fig. 54 Not all diagrams will provide the internal component information

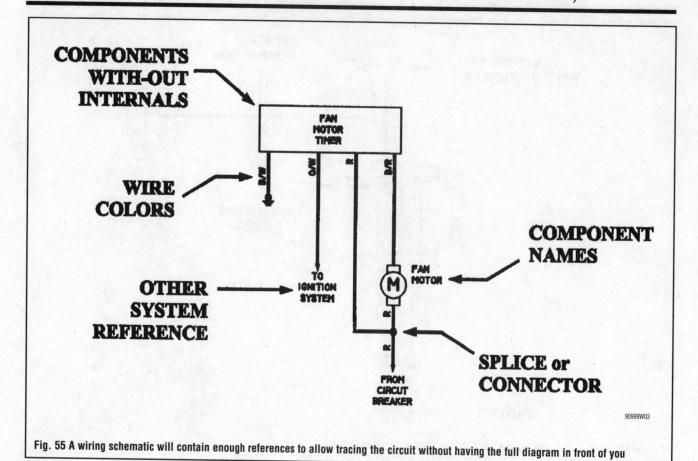

Fig. 55 A wiring schematic will contain enough references to allow tracing the circuit without having the full diagram in front of you

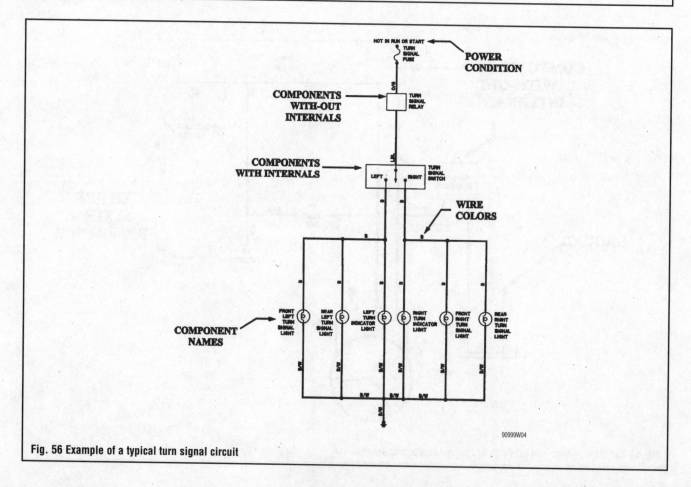

Fig. 56 Example of a typical turn signal circuit

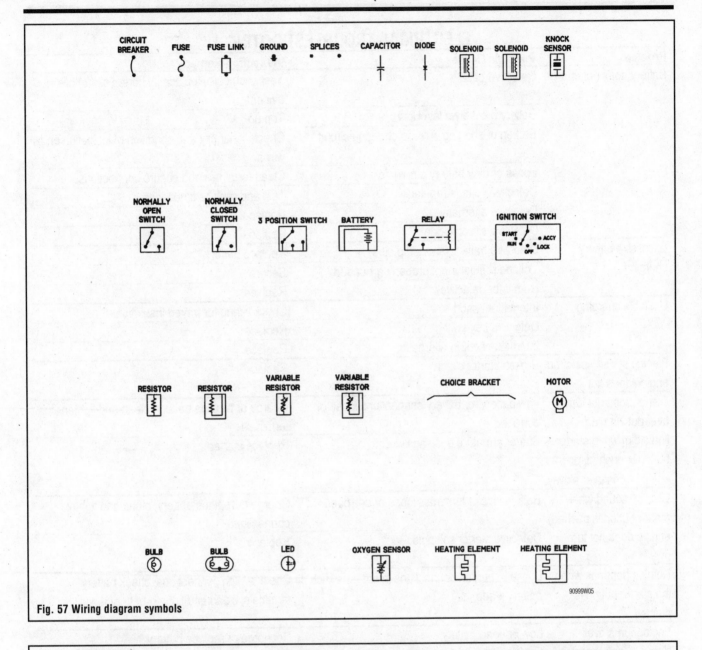

Fig. 57 Wiring diagram symbols

BLACK	B	PINK	PK
BROWN	BR	PURPLE	P
RED	R	GREEN	G
ORANGE	O	WHITE	W
YELLOW	Y	LIGHT BLUE	LBL
GRAY	GY	LIGHT GREEN	LG
BLUE	BL	DARK GREEN	DG
VIOLET	V	DARK BLUE	DBL
TAN	T	NO COLOR AVAILABLE	NCA

Fig. 58 Examples of some wire color abbreviations

ELECTRICAL TROUBLESHOOTING

Problem	Possible Cause	Inspection/Remedy
Battery does not charge	Defective battery	Test each cell. Replace if shorted cell(s) are evident
	Battery electrolyte level low	Top up
	Broken or shorting wires in charging circuit	Check continuity and condition of insulation on all wires
	Loose or dirty battery terminals	Clean terminals and secure connections
	Defective voltage regulator	Test and replace if necessary
	Defective alternator	Replace
	Defective silicon diode	Replace
Excessive battery charging	Defective battery (shorted plates)	Replace battery
	Voltage regulator not properly grounded	Secure
	Regulator defective	Replace
Unstable charging	Intermittent short	Check wiring for frayed insulation
	Defective key switch	Replace
	Intermittent coil in alternator	Replace
Electric starter spins, but engine does not	Broken starter clutch	Replace
Starter does not turn over but warning lights dim when starter button is pushed, or engine turns over slowly	Low battery, or battery connections loose or corroded	Charge or replace battery; clean and tighten terminals
	Starter armature bushings worn	Replace starter
Clicking sound when starter button is pushed; engine does not turn over	Battery low, or terminals loose or corroded	Charge or replace battery; clean and tighten connections.
	Defective starter solenoid	Replace
Nothing happens when the starter button is pushed	Loose or broken connections in starter switch or battery leads	Check switch connections; check battery terminals; clean and tighten battery leads
Engine turns over slowly when starter button is pushed (cold weather)	Low or dead battery	Recharge or replace battery
	Engine oil too thick	Use correct viscosity oil
Turn signal will not light	Burned out bulb	Replace
Turn signal will not flash	One bulb burned out	Replace
	Low battery	Charge or replace battery

90999C03

ELECTRICAL TROUBLESHOOTING

Problem	Possible Cause	Inspection/Remedy
Speed of flasher varies with engine rpm	Low battery	Charge or replace battery
	Defective flasher unit	Replace
No spark or weak spark	Defective ignition coil(s)	Replace
	Defective spark plug(s)	Replace
	Plug lead(s) or wires damaged or disconnected	Check condition of leads and wires; check all connections
Breaker points pitted or burned	Defective condenser	Replace points and condenser
Carbon-fouled spark plugs	Mixture too rich	Adjust carburetors; check air cleaner
	Plugs too cold for conditions	Use hotter plugs
	Idle speed set too high	Adjust carburetors
Oil-fouled spark plugs	Worn rings, cylinders, or valve guides (four-stroke)	Rebuild
	Badly adjusted oil pump cable (two-stroke)	Adjust
Spark plug electrodes burned or overheated	Spark plugs too hot for conditions	Use colder plugs
	Engine overheating	See above
	Ignition timing incorrect	Adjust
	Mixture too lean	See above

90999C04

SUSPENSION

Front Suspension

OPERATIONAL DESCRIPTION

Front forks may be of several different types, but the overwhelming majority of motorcycles in production today use the "telescopic" type. Other kinds of forks include the "Earle's type" which was used on BMWs many, many years ago (and some current sidecar rigs), and the "leading-link" suspension which was found on NSU machines and others such as the Honda "Dream" and a large number of stepthrough "50s" of years gone by. A recent addition to the front suspension fray is the BMW Telelever.

Telescopic Forks

▶ See Figures 59 thru 67

Telescopic forks consist of two fork tubes or stanchions which are attached to the frame by a pair of triple clamps. At the lower end of the tubes are fork sliders which, as the name implies, move up and down on the tubes in response to road irregularities. Cushioning is provided by fork springs, which may be internal or external, that is, either inside the fork tube or outside it. Of the two types, the former is now more popular, although Harley-Davidson uses external springs as a fashion statement on a few of its models. Rebound damping is accomplished by means of a damper unit in the fork tube. On some forks, this damper unit provides both compression and rebound damping, while on others the fork springs themselves are responsible for all compression damping (not very common).

Damper units vary infinitely in design, but basically they carry out the function of slowing the fork slider's movement when the fork spring attempts to force it to the fully extended position.

90999P12

Fig. 59 This fork has adjustable damping that can be changed right at the fork cap

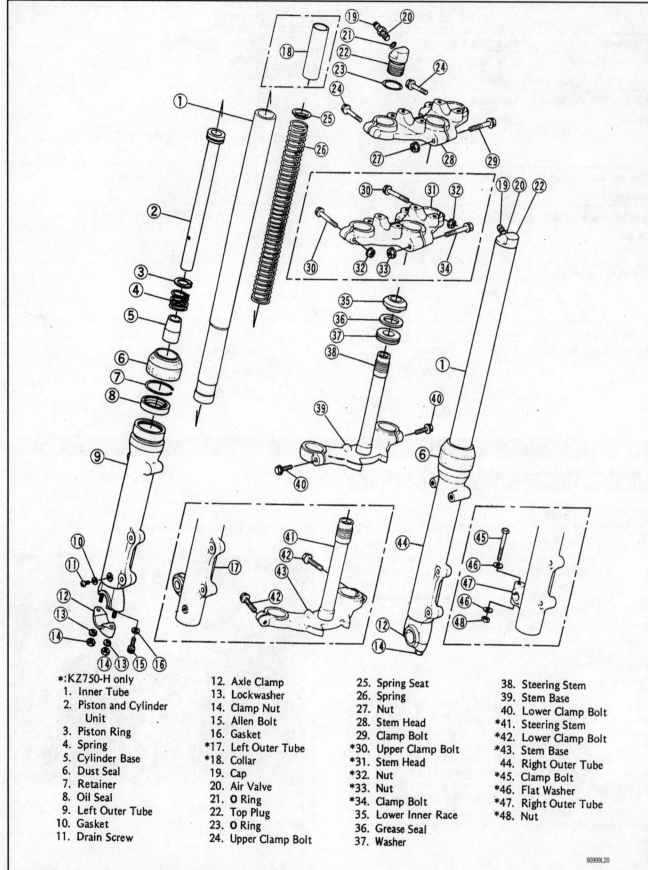

*:KZ750-H only
1. Inner Tube
2. Piston and Cylinder Unit
3. Piston Ring
4. Spring
5. Cylinder Base
6. Dust Seal
7. Retainer
8. Oil Seal
9. Left Outer Tube
10. Gasket
11. Drain Screw
12. Axle Clamp
13. Lockwasher
14. Clamp Nut
15. Allen Bolt
16. Gasket
*17. Left Outer Tube
*18. Collar
19. Cap
20. Air Valve
21. O Ring
22. Top Plug
23. O Ring
24. Upper Clamp Bolt
25. Spring Seat
26. Spring
27. Nut
28. Stem Head
29. Clamp Bolt
*30. Upper Clamp Bolt
*31. Stem Head
*32. Nut
*33. Nut
*34. Clamp Bolt
35. Lower Inner Race
36. Grease Seal
37. Washer
38. Steering Stem
39. Stem Base
40. Lower Clamp Bolt
*41. Steering Stem
*42. Lower Clamp Bolt
*43. Stem Base
44. Right Outer Tube
*45. Clamp Bolt
*46. Flat Washer
*47. Right Outer Tube
*48. Nut

Fig. 60 Exploded view of a standard telescopic fork assembly

90999L20

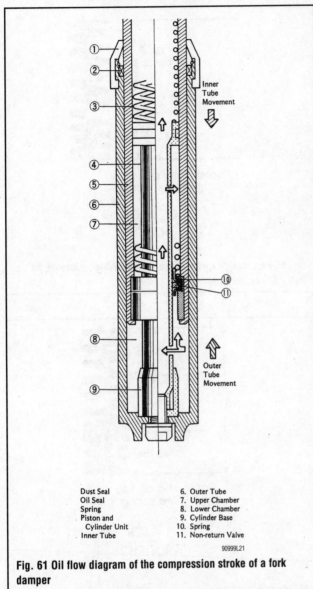

Dust Seal
Oil Seal
Spring
Piston and
  Cylinder Unit
Inner Tube

6. Outer Tube
7. Upper Chamber
8. Lower Chamber
9. Cylinder Base
10. Spring
11. Non-return Valve

90999L21

Fig. 61 Oil flow diagram of the compression stroke of a fork damper

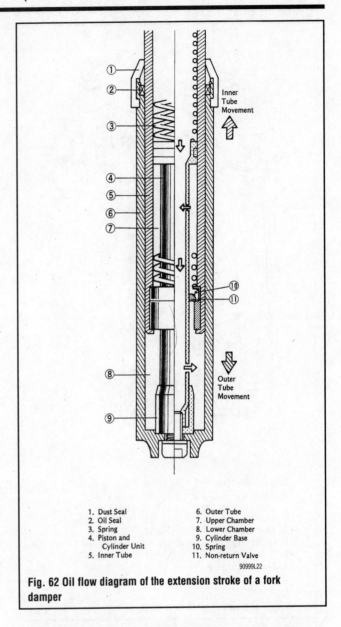

1. Dust Seal
2. Oil Seal
3. Spring
4. Piston and
    Cylinder Unit
5. Inner Tube

6. Outer Tube
7. Upper Chamber
8. Lower Chamber
9. Cylinder Base
10. Spring
11. Non-return Valve

90999L22

Fig. 62 Oil flow diagram of the extension stroke of a fork damper

When the front forks strike a bump in the road, the fork sliders are forced up along the fork tubes, compressing the springs, and, at the same time, forcing oil through a number of orifices in the damper mechanism.

When this force on the sliders is released, the compressed springs attempt to return to their normal length. Rather than allow the sliders to be bounced back to the extended position all at once, the damper mechanism resists sudden movement of the slider, the resistance being provided by the oil which the slider must suck through the orifices as it moves back down the fork tube.

Fork sliders are ususlly alloy castings which are a close fit on the fork tubes. On some forks, this fit is obtained through the use of a replaceable bushing, while on others the slider itself is machined to fit the fork tube. One or two oil seals are incorporated into the top of the slider to hold the damping oil and to prevent the contamination of the damper with dirt and oil.

The fork slider may be secured to the fork by means of a bolt at the bottom of the slider which threads into the damper or the fork tube itself or a large circular nut may be fitted to the top of the slider. Sometimes, both are found.

Fork springs may be one of two types: straight or progressively wound. The difference between the two types is evident upon inspection. A straight-wound spring will compress a given distance by the application of a certain force. Doubling the force will double the compressed distance, and so on. The relationship between the applied force and the compressed distance is therefore linear. Progressively wound springs, however, have no such linear relationship. After the initial force is applied, multiples of that force will provide increasingly less compression. This allows a spring to be softer at lesser compressions and stiffer as the compression increases.

Fork tubes are commonly hard-chromed. Fork tubes are secured by pinchbolts at the triple clamps.

Leading-Link and Earle's Forks

Earle's forks function in exactly the same way as the rear swing arm and shock absorber assembly, consisting of a pivoted arm and two sealed damper units which incorporate the springs.

Leading-link forks are similar in principle but use two pivoted links, which are mounted independently, each of which has its own spring and damper assembly.

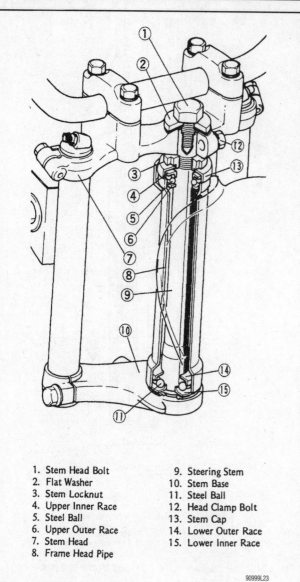

1. Stem Head Bolt
2. Flat Washer
3. Stem Locknut
4. Upper Inner Race
5. Steel Ball
6. Upper Outer Race
7. Stem Head
8. Frame Head Pipe
9. Steering Stem
10. Stem Base
11. Steel Ball
12. Head Clamp Bolt
13. Stem Cap
14. Lower Outer Race
15. Lower Inner Race

90999L23

Fig. 63 Typical steering head for a telescopic fork

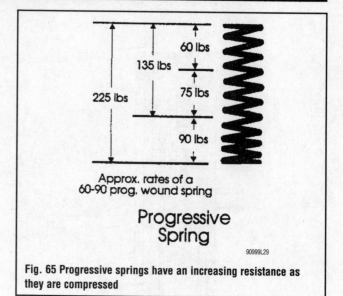

Approx. rates of a
60-90 prog. wound spring

Progressive Spring

90999L29

Fig. 65 Progressive springs have an increasing resistance as they are compressed

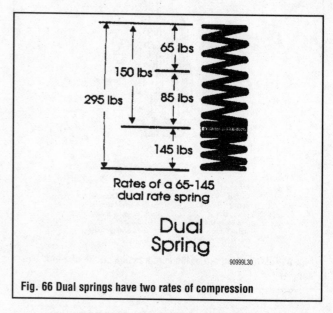

Rates of a 65-145
dual rate spring

Dual Spring

90999L30

Fig. 66 Dual springs have two rates of compression

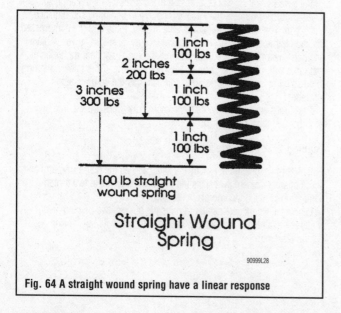

100 lb straight
wound spring

Straight Wound Spring

90999L28

Fig. 64 A straight wound spring have a linear response

90999L31

Fig. 67 Kevin trying to fill his rear air shocks on his Road King

Telelever and Other Forkless Designs

▶ **See Figure 68**

BMW developed the Telelever suspension to get past the limitations of the standard fork designs. The strength of the Telelever is its ability to reduce braking dive while maintaining suspension flexibility. The only way of reducing dive in a standard fork design is to increase the spring rate. The Telelever uses suspension geometry to achieve the same results.

A quick glance at the Telelever makes it look like a standard fork as it has two stanchions that look to be fork legs. These legs are only used as guides and do not fullfill any suspension function. The real job is done by a control arm that guides the front wheel via a ball joint. It looks to be very similar to half of a double wishbone suspension that is found on a race car.

There have been other forkless designs, but they haven't met with much commercial success. Yamaha produced one with a single sided swing arm and that looked like an Earles fork that was missing one side.

Steering Damper

▶ **See Figures 69 and 70**

A steering damper is a device whose purpose is to provide some resistance to the lateral (side-to-side) movement of the forks. This is especially useful for travel over rough terrain or corrugated road surfaces as the damper will resist rapid deflection of the front wheel and will protect to some extent against lock-to-lock oscillations of the fork (a.k.a. tankslapper).

Dampers are of two types: friction type and hydraulic. Friction type dampers rely upon spring loaded "friction plates" to provide resistance to fork turning. These plates are found on the steering stem (or immediately beneath the stem) and are activated by tightening the damper knob which forces them against the steering stem. The knob can be tightened until the desired degree of damping is reached.

A second type of damper is the hydraulic type. This damper is usually fitted between the fork triple clamp and the frame. It functions in much the same manner as the damper unit found on household storm doors, but is, of course, much smaller. Unlike the friction damper, which provides a uniform resistance, the hydraulic unit automatically varies the degree of damping in proportion to the speed at which the forks are turned. For example, if the forks are moved slowly from side-to-side, little damping will be noticed. But if an attempt is made to yank the forks over quickly, a strong damping action will slow the movement.

Steering dampers can be sealed units or have a user adjustment via a knob on the end of the shaft. Typically you will need more damping at high speeds than at low speed. Too high of damping at low speeds can make the forks hard to turn, so be careful not to crank it up too high.

Fig. 69 Typically steering dampers are mounted between the triple tree and the frame of the bike

Fig. 70 Adjustable steering dampers will have a knob like this that can be turned to change its resistance

Rear Suspension

OPERATION

▶ **See Figures 71 thru 80**

Rear shocks are similar in operation to telescopic forks but with external springs. The spring provides controlled restriction for the downward pressure of the bike or the upward pressure of the wheel, and the shock unit itself controls the rebound rate of the spring, most of which are progressively wound, and serve to keep the wheel on the ground while the rest of the bike is bouncing around.

The operation of a typical shock absorber can be described as follows: The compression stroke of the rear shock absorber begins when it receives a load compressing both the outer spring and the shock hydraulic unit itself. The cylinder, which contains fluid, rises along the piston rod, causing pressure on the oil beneath the piston. This slows or "damps" the rate of compression. The oil flows through the piston orifice and enters the space above the piston after pushing up the non-return valve held down by a valve spring. At the same time, a small amount of the oil is forced through

Fig. 68 The BMW Telelever suspension takes some getting used to visually, but one ride and you will see its advantages

Fig. 71 This single sided swingarm has a single coil over shock to do the suspension work

Fig. 73 . . . or is hydraulicly adjusted on shocks that are buried in the bike. . . .

a base valve, and then another base valve, and enters the chamber between the cylinder and the shock outer shell. When the cylinder, rising along the piston rod, meets the rubber bumper at the top of the rod, the compression ends.

The spring tension caused by compression eventually forces the shock absorber to extend to its normal or static length. The cylinder moves down along the piston rod; the oil which had been forced above the piston returns through the piston orifice and through the piston valve to the space beneath the piston. The oil which had been forced between the cylinder and the outer shell also returns to the reservoir beneath the piston after passing through a base valve. The oil resists the attempt of the outer spring to return suddenly to its normal length. This is known as rebound damping.

Some motorcycles use a combination gas/oil shock instead of the oil type just described. They function similarly, except pressurized nitrogen helps prevent the oil from foaming during periods high shock movements

Almost all production motorcycle rear shock absorbers are sealed, and cannot be disassembled. In fact, on some models, it is dangerous to attempt to do so.

If the shock leaks oil, looses its damping ability, is damaged through collision or extreme use, both units should be replaced. The springs, however, should have an unlimited life unless they sag or collapse. Springs can be replaced as a tuning method for the suspension.

Fig. 74 . . . or by a racy looking threaded collar

Fig. 72 Suspension preload is handled by a ramped collar. . .

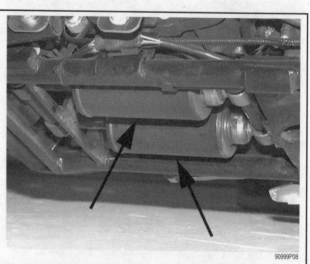

Fig. 75 This bike has hidden the twin shocks and springs under the chassis to simulate a "hardtail" design from the past

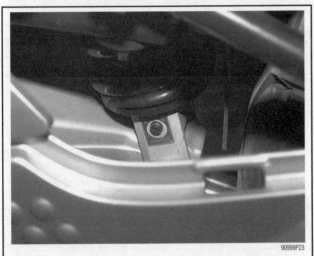

90999P23

Fig. 76 Adjustable damping controls can be exposed like on this shock . . .

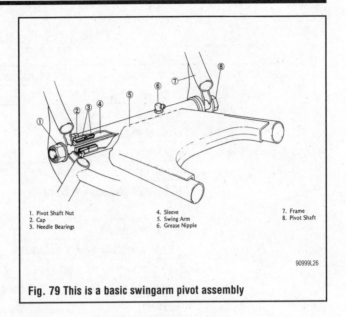

1. Pivot Shaft Nut
2. Cap
3. Needle Bearings
4. Sleeve
5. Swing Arm
6. Grease Nipple
7. Frame
8. Pivot Shaft

90999L26

Fig. 79 This is a basic swingarm pivot assembly

90999P13

Fig. 77 . . . or be accessed through a cut out in the bodywork . . .

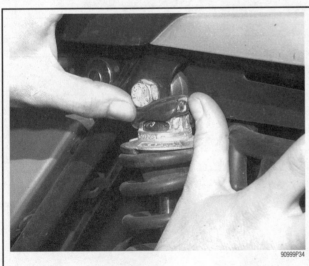

90999P34

Fig. 78 . . . or by a thumbwheel at the top of the shock

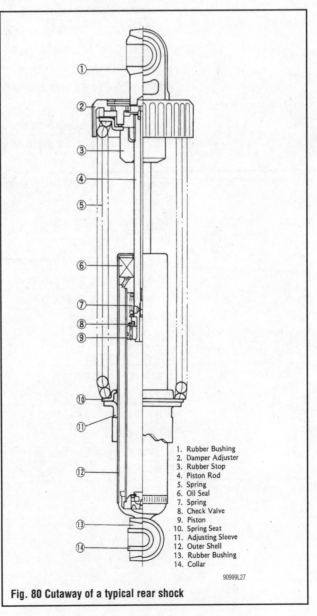

1. Rubber Bushing
2. Damper Adjuster
3. Rubber Stop
4. Piston Rod
5. Spring
6. Oil Seal
7. Spring
8. Check Valve
9. Piston
10. Spring Seat
11. Adjusting Sleeve
12. Outer Shell
13. Rubber Bushing
14. Collar

90999L27

Fig. 80 Cutaway of a typical rear shock

CHASSIS TROUBLESHOOTING

Problem	Possible Cause	Inspection/Remedy
Excessive vibration	Loose, broken, or worn motor mounts	Secure, replace, or repair motor mounts
	Loose axle nuts	Secure axle nuts
	Excessive hub bearing play	Adjust or replace hub bearings
	Loose spokes	Secure spokes and true wheel if necessary
	Rear wheel out of alignment	Align wheels
	Wheel rims out of true or damaged	True or repair wheel rims
	Irregular or peaked tire wear	Replace tire and check wheel alignment and trueness
	Tires overinflated	Check air pressure with tires cold
	Tire and wheel unevenly balanced	Balance wheels
	Worn steering head bearings	Adjust or replace bearings as necessary
	Worn rear shock bushings or shocks	Replace shocks or bushings as necessary
	Swing arm bushings too tight or too loose	Adjust bushings as directed by manufacturer
	Excessive front end loading	Remove excessive weight from front end
	Cylinder head bracket loose or broken (models on which head and frame are attached)	Secure or repair cylinder head bracket
	Broken or bent frame, forks, or swing arm	Repair or replace damaged components
	Primary chain badly worn, insufficiently lubricated, or too tight	Replace, lubricate, and/or adjust chain
	Incorrectly adjusted ignition timing	Adjust timing to specifications
	Incorrectly assembled clutch mechanism	Inspect and repair clutch as necessary
	Excessively worn crankshaft	Repair or replace crankshaft assembly
Uncertain or wobbly	Worn or bad steering head bearings	Adjust or replace bearings
	Worn or bad hub bearings	Adjust or replace bearings
	Bent forks or swing arm	Repair or replace damaged components
	Worn swing arm bushings	Adjust or replace bushings
	Bent steering stem or frame neck	Repair or replace damaged components
	Wheels improperly aligned	Check chassis for alignment of wheels
	Tires improperly seated on rim	Seat tire so bead is even all around
	Tires unevenly worn	Replace tires as necessary
	Defective steering damper	Replace as necessary
	Loose front wheel	Secure wheel
Pulls to one side	Faulty right or left shock	Replace shocks as a set
	Incorrectly adjusted drive chain	Adjust as necessary
	Wheels improperly aligned	Align wheels as necessary
	Wheels out of true	True wheels as necessary
	Incorrectly balanced tires and wheels	Balance wheels as necessary
	Defective steering head bearings	Adjust or replace bearings as necessary

90999C12

CHASSIS TROUBLESHOOTING

Problem	Possible Cause	Inspection/Remedy
Pulls to one side (cont.)	Faulty steering head damper	Replace as necessary
	Bent or damaged forks, frame, or swing arm	Repair or replace damaged components
Heavy or stiff steering	Low front tire pressure	Check tire pressure with tires cold
	Bent or damaged steering stem or frame neck	Repair or replace damaged components
	Bad steering head bearings and/or races	Replace or adjust bearings as necessary
	Defective steering damper	Replace as necessary
	Incorrect damper adjustment	Adjust as necessary
Poor fork operation	Contaminated fork oil	Drain and replace fork oil
	Worn or leaky seals evidenced by dirt or water in the fork oil or by oil on tubes	Replace seals
	Weak or damaged fork springs	Replace springs as necessary, preferably as a set
	Worn shock absorber assembly (leading link type forks)	Replace as a set as necessary
	Worn breather valves	Replace as necessary
	Excessive clearance in slider bushings as evidenced by excessive play between the slider and the tube	Replace worn components as necessary
	Bent tubes, brackets, dampers, or sliders	Replace damaged components as necessary
	Too little fork oil, oil is diluted, or oil is of wrong viscosity	Drain and replace fork oil
	Wrong fork springs in use	Replace springs as necessary
Stiff fork action	Excessive amount of fork oil	Drain and replace fork oil according to specifications
	Wrong fork oil viscosity	Drain and replace oil with a lighter grade
	Wrong fork springs in use	Replace springs as necessary
Worn rear shock	Weak or collapsed springs	Replace springs as a set
	Faulty damper unit	Replace shocks as a set
	Wrong spring in use	Replace springs as necessary
	Shocks adjusted incorrectly	Adjust shocks as necessary
Stiff rear shock	Faulty damper valve	Replace shock absorbers as a set
	Wrong spring in use	Replace springs as necessary
	Shocks incorrectly adjusted	Adjust shocks as necessary
Wheel rotates out of true	Wheel and tire out of balance	Balance wheel as necessary
	Excessive hub bearing play	Adjust or replace bearings
	Deformed wheel rims	Repair or replace rim as necessary

90999C13

CHASSIS TROUBLESHOOTING

Problem	Possible Cause	Inspection/Remedy
Wheel rotates out of true (cont.)	Loose spokes	Adjust spokes for even tension
	Loose swing arm bushings	Adjust as necessary
	Drive chain too tight	Adjust chain as necessary
	Bent frame or swing arm	Repair or replace damaged components

90999C14

BRAKES

Operation

DISC BRAKES

▶ **See Figures 81, 82, 83 and 84**

Disc brakes are all quite similar in operation. The main components of a disc brake system are the master cylinder, the caliper; and the disc or rotor.

The master cylinder is mounted on the handlebar for front disc brakes (most of the time; Some early BMW bikes had cable activated master cylinders mounted on the chassis) or on the chassis for rear wheel discs. The master cylinder contains a fluid reservoir, a piston assembly for applying hydraulic pressure to the system, and a lever for moving the piston assembly.

The caliper(s) is mounted on the forks for front discs, or the swing arm for rear disc brakes. The caliper houses the brake pads which bear against the disc when pressure is applied.

There are several types of calipers. One kind consists of a rigidly mounted caliper with two (or multiples of 2) moveable pistons, one on each side of the disc. Fluid pressure is applied to both pistons, they, in turn, pushing their respective pads against the disc.

Another type of caliper is the "sliding caliper" type. As opposed to the fixed caliper described above, this assembly mounts the caliper to a bracket by means of sliding shafts. There is typically only one piston, and when pressure is applied to this piston, it presses its pad against the disc, and the caliper shifts slightly in the opposite direction bringing the opposing pad into contact as well. The "floating caliper type" is very similar to the "sliding" and can use the same description.

Along the same lines as the "sliding caliper" is the "swinging caliper." This is also a single-piston unit, and the caliper is mounted on a bracket which is pivoted at the fork slider. When the brake is applied, the one piston moves its pad into contact with the disc, and the caliper moves slightly to bring the other pad against the disc.

DRUM BRAKES

In recent history, drum brakes have been mostly banished to service the rear of the motorcycle due to the superior braking ability of disc brakes. Drum brakes are still used as rear brakes on some bikes, but are becoming rarer every model year. Some very small bikes (less than 250cc) may still use a drum up front, but that is even rarer.

Drum brakes can be actuated either by mechanical means, such as a pushrod or cable, or by hydraulic circuits.

Drum brakes are either single leading shoe or double leading shoe types. Four leading shoe brakes as found on machines such as early Moto Guzzi Sports or early Suzuki GT750s are actually two twin leading shoe brake assemblies one mounted on each side of the wheel.

A single leading shoe brake consists of two brake shoes mounted on a plate. On one side, the shoe rests on a stud or pivot, while the other end of the shoes hear against a cam. The shoes are held in place by coil springs. When the brake lever or pedal is activated, the cam is turned, pressing the brake lining against the drum. Since there is only one cam, only one end of the brake shoe is pressed against the drum. The other end is a fixed pivot. No matter how the brake plate is arranged on the motorcycle, the leading side of one shoe and the trailing side of the other will be resting on the cam.

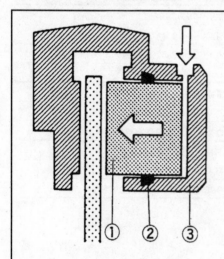
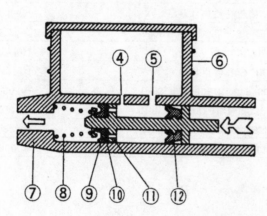

1. Piston
2. Fluid Seal
3. Caliper
4. Relief Port
5. Supply Port
6. Reservoir
7. Master Cylinder
8. Spring
9. Primary Cup
10. Non-return Valve
11. Piston
12. Secondary Cup

90999L32

Fig. 81 When brakes are applied, fluid is forced from the master cylinder to the caliper

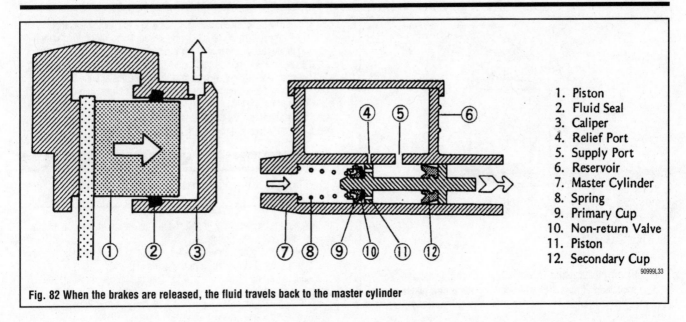

1. Piston
2. Fluid Seal
3. Caliper
4. Relief Port
5. Supply Port
6. Reservoir
7. Master Cylinder
8. Spring
9. Primary Cup
10. Non-return Valve
11. Piston
12. Secondary Cup

90999L33

Fig. 82 When the brakes are released, the fluid travels back to the master cylinder

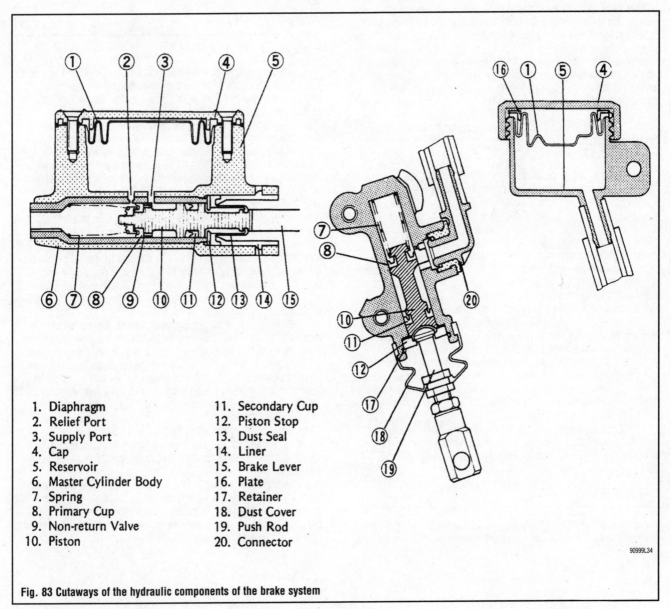

1. Diaphragm
2. Relief Port
3. Supply Port
4. Cap
5. Reservoir
6. Master Cylinder Body
7. Spring
8. Primary Cup
9. Non-return Valve
10. Piston
11. Secondary Cup
12. Piston Stop
13. Dust Seal
14. Liner
15. Brake Lever
16. Plate
17. Retainer
18. Dust Cover
19. Push Rod
20. Connector

90999L34

Fig. 83 Cutaways of the hydraulic components of the brake system

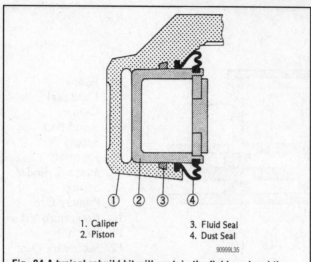

1. Caliper
2. Piston
3. Fluid Seal
4. Dust Seal

90999L35

Fig. 84 A typical rebuild kit will contain the fluid seal and the dust seal. Sometimes they will even include a new piston

Drum brakes are self-energizing. That is, once the leading shoe has been brought into contact with the drum, the drum's rotational movement tends to draw it against it. The trailing shoe, on the other hand, tends to be forced away from the drum.

Twin-leading shoe brakes are different in the following way. Instead of a single fixed pivot and single cam, each shoe is mounted on its own pivot and has its own cam. The shoes are mounted so that the leading end of both shoes are those activated by the cam.

ANTI-LOCK BRAKING SYSTEMS

▶ See Figure 85

For all intents and purposes, the two wheels of a motorcycle must remain in motion for the rider to maintain control. Under braking there is the possibility of going past the capability of the tire to provide traction and the wheel may lock up. This may result in nothing but a rear wheel skid or it may spit you off the high side of the bike in an amazing display of flailing limbs. Technology has helped provide a solution to this problem.

Due to slick portions of the road or overzealous application of the brakes, the wheel may lock up leaving the rider to worry about the outcome. A number of manufactures have developed anti-lock braking systems to help prevent wheel locking under braking situations. Anti-lock brakes will monitor the rotation of the wheels and actually reduce braking at the wheel that is starting to lock up. This will cause the wheel to continue to rotate and help the rider maintain control of the bike.

A computer will monitor a pair of sensors mounted one per wheel. The computer will check the relative speeds of the wheels and if it determine that one or the other wheel is starting to slowdown, pending wheel lockup, it will tell a braking solenoid valve to reduce the brake line pressure on the wheel that is effected. This will reduce the amount of braking at that wheel and allow you to continue to ride.

If the computer fails or sees a fault in the system, it will typically take itself out of operation and illuminate a warning lamp. You still have full use of the hydraulic brake system, but without the benefit of the anti-lock action.

LINKED BRAKING SYSTEMS

Most motorcycle braking systems use a hand actuated lever to operate the front brakes. A foot lever takes care of the rear brakes. The two systems are completely independent of each other. There are some bikes that have a linked braking system where actuating the front lever will provide some braking in the rear. Some systems will actuate a front brake when the rears are actuated. Check your owners manual for specific operation description.

The advantage of a linked system is that you can share the braking chores with both ends of the bike without having to think about it too much. This is good for heavily loaded tour bikes and others that have similar weight distributions. The bad side is that for riders who are used to standard braking systems, it can feel quite bizarre.

Brake Troubleshooting

DISC BRAKES

Refer to the brake system troubleshooting chart for information on how to diagnose disc brake problems.

Common problems with disc brakes include bad fluid seals, damaged or corroded caliper pistons and seized caliper slides.

Using the wrong friction material can lead to improper braking. The brakes may react too strongly or require too much pressure to activate them. If the fluid seal on the caliper is leaking, the friction material can get soaked and lose effectiveness.

INEFFECTIVE DRUM BRAKES

▶ See Figure 86

1. If the brakes become ineffective even if adjustment is correct, check lining thickness first. If thickness is within acceptable limits, the loss of braking power may he caused by an excessive angle between the brake rod or cable and the brake lever.

2. A common cause of poor operation of cable operated drum brakes is caused by the build-up of dirt or corrosion between the inner brake cable and the cable sheath. Ensure proper cable lubrication by periodically disconnecting the brake cable from the hand lever and pouring motor oil or one of the molybdenum disulphide or graphite-based lubricants between the inner and outer cables. Apply sufficient amounts. The lubricant should appear at the lower end of the cable to show that the entire length is lubricated. An alternate method involves removing the cable from the motorcycle completely and immersing it in a pan of light oil. Leave one end of the cable above the oil in the pan so the lubricant can seep through. Try to get some light grease into either end of the cable after lubrication to keep out dirt and moisture. You should note that cables which have gone without periodic lubrication for an extended length of time can usually not be repaired by lubrication. If the sticking or binding persists, the cable must be replaced.

3. Glazed linings can also cause poor braking. This can be fixed by removing the wheel and inspecting the surfaces of the brake linings and the brake drum. Use sandpaper to rough up the linings. Sandpaper can also be used to clean up rust or corrosion on the brake drum. The drum should be shiny. Also, check the drum for wear. On some motorcycles, brake drum maximum allowable diameter is stamped somewhere on the hub. If not, it is contained in the shop manual. Worn drums must be replaced.

4. Although not common, ineffective brakes can be the result of oil or grease on the linings. It is almost impossible to remove lubricant from the porous linings, surfaces and brakes in this condition should be replaced.

5. On some motorcycles, it is necessary to "center the brakes" in the drum any time the wheel has been removed. Failure to do so will cause a decrease in braking power. To perform this operation, and assuming that the axle nut is loose, simply apply the brakes hard, and, holding them on, tighten the axle nut to its proper torque.

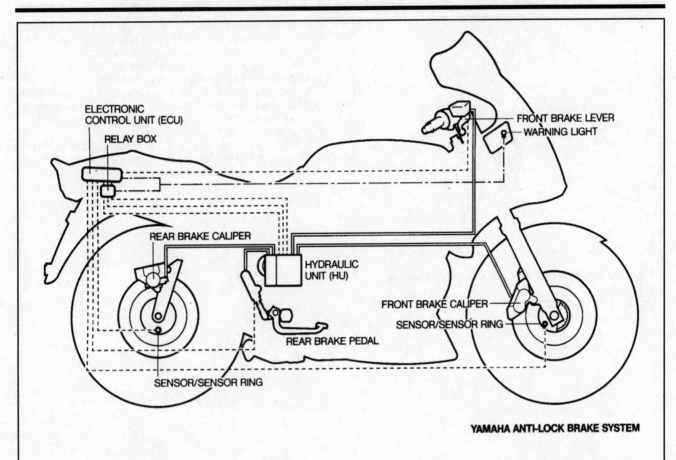

ELECTRONIC
CONTROL UNIT (ECU)

RELAY BOX

FRONT BRAKE LEVER
WARNING LIGHT

REAR BRAKE CALIPER

HYDRAULIC
UNIT (HU)

FRONT BRAKE CALIPER
SENSOR/SENSOR RING

REAR BRAKE PEDAL

SENSOR/SENSOR RING

YAMAHA ANTI-LOCK BRAKE SYSTEM

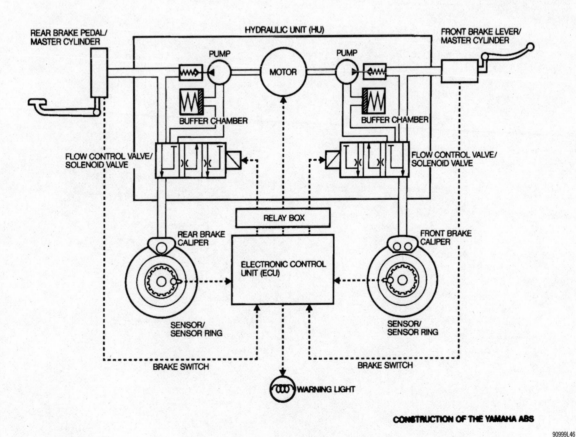

REAR BRAKE PEDAL/
MASTER CYLINDER

HYDRAULIC UNIT (HU)

FRONT BRAKE LEVER/
MASTER CYLINDER

PUMP

MOTOR

PUMP

BUFFER CHAMBER

BUFFER CHAMBER

FLOW CONTROL VALVE/
SOLENOID VALVE

FLOW CONTROL VALVE/
SOLENOID VALVE

REAR BRAKE
CALIPER

RELAY BOX

FRONT BRAKE
CALIPER

ELECTRONIC CONTROL
UNIT (ECU)

SENSOR/
SENSOR RING

SENSOR/
SENSOR RING

BRAKE SWITCH

BRAKE SWITCH

WARNING LIGHT

CONSTRUCTION OF THE YAMAHA ABS

90999L46

Fig. 85 This is a working diagram of a Yamaha ABS system and its components

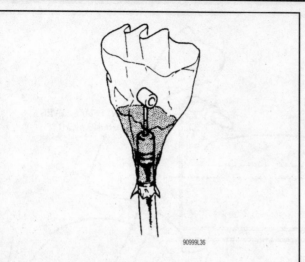

90999L36

Fig. 86 An easy method of applying lubricant to a control or brake cable

6. On twin leading shoe brakes, improper adjustment of the brake connecting rod will cause a lack of performance. Adjust this according to the manufacturers instructions. Another cause, often overlooked, is worn or damaged clevis pins. Once these pins wear a good deal of slop may develop in the brake linkage. The remedy is replacement of the pins.

7. Dragging brakes may be caused by an improperly lubricated cable as discussed above. Other causes include worn or damaged return springs. Most manufacturers give a maximum allowable length for brake springs, and those which exceed this limit should be replaced.

8. Binding of the brake cam(s) in the brake plate is another cause of dragging brakes. This may happen either because the cams have not been properly lubricated or because they are bent.

9. Squealling is most often caused by dirt on the brake linings. Clean linings and drum thoroughly.

BRAKE TROUBLESHOOTING

Problem	Possible Cause	Inspection/Remedy
Brakes do not hold (Drum)	Brake shoes glazed or worn	Repair or replace shoes
	Brake shoes oil or grease impregnated	Replace shoes
	Brake linings worn away	Replace linings
	Brake drum worn or damaged	Replace or have drum turned down
	Air in brake lines or insufficient hydraulic fluid	Drain system and refill with fresh fluid, then bleed system
	Brake linkage incorrectly adjusted	Adjust linkage as necessary
	Brake control cables insufficiently lubricated or binding	Lubricate or replace cable as necessary
Brakes drag (Drum)	Lack of play in the linkage	Adjust linkage as necessary
	Weak or damaged return springs	Replace springs as a set
	Rusted cam and lever shaft	Replace as necessary
Unadjustable Brakes (Drum)	Worn brake shoe linings	Replace shoes or rotate the actuating lever a few degrees on its splined shaft (if applicable)
	Worn brake shoe cam	Replace the cam as necessary
	Worn or damaged brake drum	Replace the drum or have it turned down
Scraping noise (Drum)	Linings worn down to the rivets	Replace the linings and have the drum turned or replaced as necessary
	Broken brake shoe	Replace the shoes and repair or replace the drum as necessary
	Dirt in the drum	Clean out the assembly and replace or repair the drum as necessary
	Scored or out of round brake drum	Repair or replace the drum as necessary
	Broken pivot	Replace the pivot
Brakes shudder (Drum)	Unevenly worn shoes	Replace shoes
	Out of round brake drum	Repair or replace drum
Excessive lever travel with loss of braking power (Disc)	Air in hydraulic system	Drain and replace fluid, then bleed system
	Master cylinder low on fluid	Refill the cylinder and bleed system
	Loose lever adjuster bolt	Secure and adjust lever and bolt
	Leak in hydraulic system as evidenced by fluid loss	Rebuild system as necessary
	Worn disc pads	Replace pads as necessary
Brake squeal (Disc)	Glazed pads	Clean up or replace pads
	Improperly adjusted caliper	Adjust caliper
	Extremely dusty brake assembly	Thoroughly clean out assembly
Brake shudder (Disc)	Distorted pads	Replace pads
	Oil or brake fluid impregnated pads	Replace pads
	Loose mounting bolts	Secure assembly
	Warped disc	Replace disc

90999C15

BRAKE TROUBLESHOOTING

Problem	Possible Cause	Inspection/Remedy
Pads dragging on rotor (Disc)	Loose adjusting ring	Secure adjusting ring
	Piston binding in bore	Rebuild caliper assembly
	Relief port blocked by piston in master cylinder	Rebuild caliper assembly
	Caliper out of adjustment	Adjust
	Caliper pivot frozen	Clean and lubricate pivot

90999C16

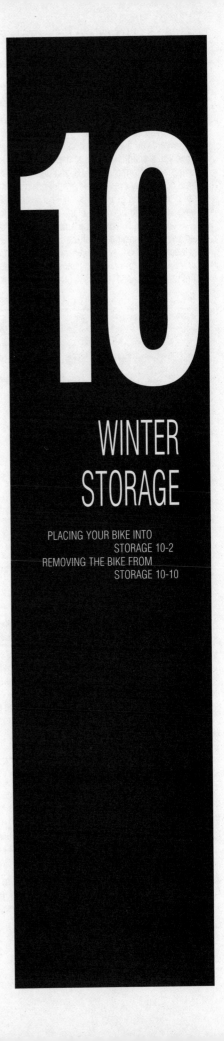

10

WINTER

STORAGE

PLACING YOUR BIKE INTO STORAGE

Not all of us are lucky enough to live in an area where you can ride your motorcycle 12 months out of the year. Depending on the severity of the winters where you live and depending upon your own desire to ride in cold weather, you should take steps to preserve your precious machine(s).

Living in the Northeastern U.S. and being particularly stalwart riders, the authors don't really ever completely put our motorcycles into storage. Our use of proper riding gear (including electric apparel) and well selected winter days allow us to ride most of the year (barring long winter blizzards). But, we take special steps in the winter to assure that our bikes will be protected should an unexpected blizzard keep us off the mounts for more than a few weeks. If you know (or even suspect) that you will be off your motorcycle for a month or longer, you should follow these storage procedures to assure proper care and readiness of your bike.

bike may be exposed to corrosive road salts or damaging cinders and has an even greater need for protection. But even without severe cold weather, your bike's finish should be cleaned and protected year `round.

While detailing the bike you have a perfect opportunity to look out for potential problems. Keep your eyes open for loose or missing fasteners, cracked or damaged components and weeping or leaking seals. A loose or missing fastener may be a wake-up call to pay closer attention to basic maintenance and your pre-ride checks or it could be a warning sign that some other problem is developing with your ride. A good cleaning, followed by observation after operation of the bike will help determine if a seal is leaking badly (and should be replaced) or if a slight amount of weepage is responsible for accumulated fluids, dirt or grime on a part of the bike.

If you live where this sort of scene is even remotely possible, then you should take steps to protect your bike in the winter

Fig. 1 Take some time before winter hits to give your bike a thorough wash . . .

Clean And Protect The Bike

Most people already understand the benefits of detailing your motorcycle. Besides giving you an opportunity to inspect all the various components of your bike (while you clean them), it allows you to protect these parts from moisture and corrosive agents in the atmosphere. Everything from painted parts to powdercoat to chrome should be cleaned and given a coating of some protectant to reduce the possibility of damage or corrosion during storage.

WASH & WAX

◗ See Figures 1, 2, 3 and 4

Refer to the detailing section of this book for recommendations regarding the care and treatment of the different materials on your motorcycle. Obviously leather is not protected in the same fashion as paint or plastic. The key is to completely clean the bike (with a proper wash) and then protect the various surfaces of the bike with quality wax and finish preservers before placing it in storage.

➡The good old wash and wax should be part of your routine whether or not you are planning on putting your bike in storage. If you are going to ride during cold and nasty winter months then your

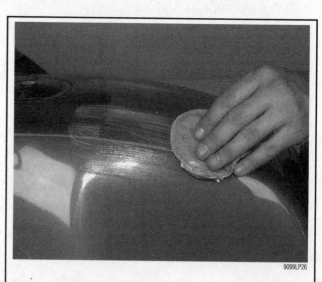

Fig. 2 . . . and a detailed waxing . . .

Fig. 3 . . . using a high quality wax

Fig. 4 The time you take to clean your bike before storage will be well spent to protect your baby over the harsh winter months

The longer that the bike is going to remain in storage, the more important your cleaning and protecting ritual will become. If a bike is only going to be in storage for a few months, chances are that few components are going to wear out just because of time and exposure (unless of course they were just about gone to begin with, but your inspection should have revealed that). If however the bike may be stored for a longer period of time (measured in years instead of months) then your chance of items like seals drying, cracking or melting their way onto shafts becomes greater. One of the biggest advantages of detailing your bike before placing it into storage is, that should a seal give up the ghost during storage, you will more quickly identify it when removing the bike from storage later.

➥Cleaning and protecting the bike before storage is definitely a case of an ounce of prevention being worth a pound of cure. But if your bike requires a pound of cure when it is removed from storage, it will simply require that much LESS than it would if it hadn't been properly detailed.

TREATING RUBBER PARTS

There are a lot of products available to beautify rubber and plastic. Keep in mind, the truth is that rubber will eventually dry out and crack. Exposure to

ultraviolet radiation, the evaporation of component oils and oxidation will take their toll on everything from tires to boots. Most products on the market cannot prevent the natural aging of these components, but you should be able to at least lengthen their usable life while making them better looking in the process.

✳✳ CAUTION

NEVER put any sort of rubber protectant or treatment on the treads of your tires. UNLIKE CARS AND TRUCKS, motorcycles need tire grip to keep from falling over and treating the tires could make them dangerously slippery leading to an embarrassing fall at best or a deadly accident at worst.

Prepare The Drivetrain For Storage

FUEL SYSTEM

▶ **See Figures 5, 6 and 7**

Over time the most volatile compounds found in a sample of gasoline will evaporate, leaving the remaining fluid less combustible. This will lead

Fig. 5 One easy way to empty the carburetor(s) is to run them dry by turning the petcock to OFF while the engine is running . . .

Fig. 6 . . . but the best way is to remove the float bowl drain plug . . .

Fig. 7 . . . of course, how easy it is to access the drain plug(s) will depend on the bike

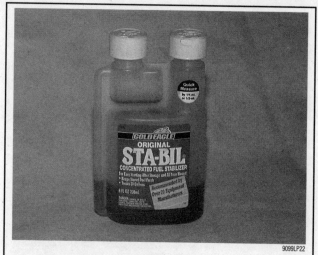

Fig. 8 This bottle of fuel stabilizer comes with a handy feature, a built-in measuring and dispensing cup

to difficult starting and rough running for your engine. BUT, this is the least of your worries when it comes to gasoline and any form of long term storage.

As gasoline evaporates it can leave behind a varnish which will coat and possibly clog critical fuel delivery systems. Needle jets, floats and valves in carburetors can be rendered useless by enough of this varnish. The tiny nozzles on fuel injectors can become clogged (sticking partially open or closed), completely disrupting fuel mixture and atomization. All of this adds up to a poor running motorcycle (if it runs at all) and lengthy or costly repairs as parts must be removed and cleaned or replaced.

You basically have two options when it comes to preventing fuel system damage during months when the bike is idle. Either you can completely drain the fuel system or you can add a fuel stabilizer to the system and make sure it is completely mixed with your bikes gasoline.

Add Stabilizer Or Drain?

Your decision on whether to add fuel stabilizer or to completely drain the system should really depend on how long the bike is going to be stored and how willing you are to go through the trouble. Frankly, adding stabilizer is the easier of the 2 solutions, but for long term storage (again, speaking more in terms of years than months) draining is the better solution.

ADDING FUEL STABILIZER

♦ See Figure 8

This is the solution most people (including the authors prefer) because it is a lot easier than draining the system. But, remember that, using fuel stabilizer is more suited to a storage time that is measured in months and NOT years. This makes it sufficient for most rider's winter storage needs. If you decide to use this method, be sure to follow the stabilizer manufacturer's instructions, but keep the following points in mind:

• It is best to add most stabilizers right before filling the tank, as this gives the stabilizer the best chance to fully mix with the gasoline as the tank is filled.

• After adding stabilizer, be sure to operate the engine for a few minutes to give the fuel/stabilizer mixture an opportunity to reach all parts of the system (fuel lines and carburetors or fuel injectors, as applicable).

• Gas from your last fuel fill-up will be in the system for a long time, so if possible, avoid oxygenated fuels which use alcohol, since alcohol absorbs water and may promote corrosion in the fuel system. If you can't avoid fuel with alcohol in it, then pay extra-close attention to the next point.

• Be sure to TOP-OFF the fuel tank to minimize the amount of air (and therefore moisture) that is present in the tank. If you store a fuel tank with air in it, the moisture will cause rusting on the inside of an uncoated tank and that rust can play havoc with your fuel system come spring.

DRAINING THE SYSTEM

If you are really serious about storing your bike (and you should be if it is going to be stored for time periods measured in years instead of just months), then you should completely drain the fuel system. But remember that if you do remove all of the fuel (and therefore remove the danger of varnish build-up), you have another concern, in the form of corrosion. Remember that air contains a certain amount of moisture, so if you drain the fuel system completely, leaving only air behind, then there will be moisture to help rust metal surfaces in the system.

If you drain the system and don't want to come back and find the fuel tank completely rusted (and in serious need of repair), then you must coat the inner surface with a rust preventative. Carburetor float bowl(s) should removed, coated with a light oil and then reinstalled.

OIL & OTHER FLUIDS

It doesn't matter what the fluid's job is normally, when it comes to storage ALL FLUIDS have one major job. During winter months when the bike is idle, all of your fluids are there simply to fight corrosion. Once the bike is removed from storage, those fluids will be called upon to lubricate, cool and/or transmit power, but for now, you want them to inhibit corrosion and nothing more.

There is a lot of debate between "experts" who will advise you to change all fluids before storage or only after storage. Some people advise that you only change some fluids. Many will draw upon years of experience, saying that they never changed this or that fluid and have never had a problem (and they may be right). But it is hard to make generalizations. What works for one make or model (or in one part of the country) may not work for another.

With that said, we are going to make a generalization here. You never LOSE by changing all of your fluids before storage (except in some cases, you might spend a few dollars more on fluids that you didn't absolutely need). Well guess what, add up all the fluids your bike needs and look at that dollar amount compared to the value of the motorcycle. If the value of the motorcycle is greater (and it should be significantly so in most cases, unless you are fond of riding a rat bike), then your motivation is simple, changing all fluids is CHEAP INSURANCE.

Engine Oil

♦ See Figures 9 and 10

During engine operation all sorts of nasty acids are formed and some work their way into your engine oil. Acids and moisture are enemies of the bearings and metal surfaces found in your engine and should be minimized to assure long life. Luckily, periodic engine oil changes remove most of the

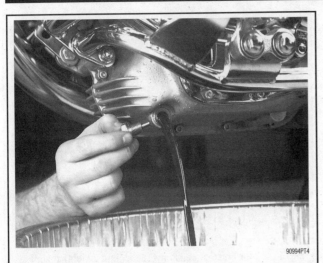

Fig. 9 It is always a good idea to drain all of your old fluids and lubricants, especially the engine oil . . .

Fig. 11 If the coolant in your water cooled engine is due to be changed, DO IT NOW, don't risk the engine block freezing and cracking in storage

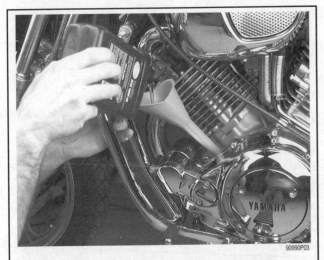

Fig. 10 . . . and refill the bike with fresh fluids immediately before placing it into winter storage

corrosives and the normal operating temperatures of the engine should be sufficient to purge the crankcase of moisture. But, what about when you park the bike for the winter?

The last time the engine is run before storage make sure it comes completely up to operating temperature. This will help to make sure that moisture is boiled-off from inside the mufflers. Then, you should ride straight home from the gas station (where you just added your fuel stabilizer) and drain your engine oil. Change the oil and filter to make sure that you have removed the most corrosive agents and moisture from the engine prior to letting it sleep for the next few months. Your bearings and con-rods will thank you.

Engine Coolant

▶ See Figure 11

Engine coolant has 2 purposes. The primary purpose is temperature control of the engine (to cool it during operation). But it also contains rust inhibitors to prevent corrosion as well as lubricants for the water pump and seals. If your coolant is close to the replacement interval in your bike's owners manual, then you should replace it now, before putting it in storage. Like engine oil, it is best to put nothing but fresh fluids in the system to sit all winter.

✳✳ WARNING

Replacing the coolant before storage is especially important if the bike is to be stored outside or in an unheated garage/shed where it may be subjected to sub-freezing temperatures. As coolant ages it not only loses its ability to inhibit corrosion and cool the motor, it also will lose its ability to resist freezing. As the freezing point of your coolant is raised by age, the possibility of severe engine damage caused by the coolant freezing and expanding increases. It would be a shame to loose an engine all because you wouldn't spring for a gallon of coolant.

Transmission, Primary Drive or Gear Oil

▶ See Figures 12, 13 and 14

Many transmissions, primary cases, and driveshafts or final drives are vented to the atmosphere. They will acquire moisture through condensation as the bike is used. Hopefully during use, the oil heats up sufficiently that moisture will evaporate, but this becomes less likely as winter approaches and ambient temperatures drop. To be sure you have removed as much moisture as possible from your driveline, take this opportunity to change all

Fig. 12 Immediately prior to winter storage is also a good time to change any separate transmission . . .

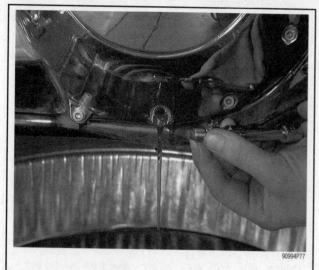

Fig. 13 . . . primary drive . . .

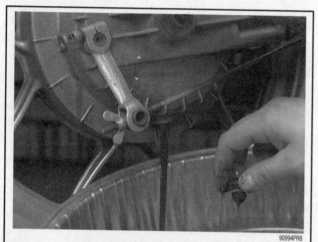

Fig. 14 . . . or gear oils that your bike may use, to make sure fresh, non-emulsified fluids are present to protect it through winter

drive fluids (if you have enough drain pans, do it as the engine oil drains. Remember, do it immediately after you get back from the gas station).

Once again, by changing these fluids you will help to reduce the amount of corrosion which will take place during the time the bike is left in storage.

Brake/Hydraulic Clutch Fluid

◆ See Figure 15

One of the most ignored parts of maintenance tends to be the replacement of hydraulic brake fluids. Remember that DOT 3 & 4 fluids are highly hydroscopic, meaning that they will readily absorb moisture from the atmosphere. Even if you never remove the master cylinder cover, it is likely that some moisture will get into the system over time and this can cause corrosion.

Fig. 15 Is your brake or clutch hydraulic fluid too old? If so it should be replaced before storage . . . but if not, you should still check the level

➡Just because your bike may use DOT 5 fluid (Harleys for instance use silicone brake fluid), doesn't mean that you should ignore brake fluid changes. Silicone fluid may not absorb moisture as readily, but moisture may still find its way into the system and cause corrosion.

Drive Chain

◆ See Figures 16 and 17

If your bike is equipped with a final drive chain, take the opportunity to clean, lube and adjust the chain now. A fresh coating of lubrication will help to assure that the chain and sprockets remain as corrosion free as possible during the long winter months. By adjusting it now, you will be sure the chain is ready when it is time to remove the bike from storage.

Fig. 16 The chain should be checked, cleaned and lubricated before storage. . .

Fig. 17 . . . and, if you adjust it now, it will be ready when the time comes to ride again

SPARK PLUGS & CYLINDERS

♦ See Figure 18

If the engine was run (in order to change the oil) then the cylinders should not require any special attention for normal winter storage (consisting of a few months). But, if the storage is going to be any longer OR if you want the extra level of protection, you can coat the cylinders with some additional engine oil.

Remove and inspect the spark plugs (if they need to be replaced, you might as well do it since you're going through the trouble to remove them anyway). Pour 1–2 tablespoons of fresh, clean engine oil through the spark plug hole. Rotate the engine to spread the oil around the cylinders, then install the spark plugs.

➡Rotating the engine can be done by hand to prevent the addition of gasoline to the cylinders (which is just going to wash the oil back of the cylinder walls).

To rotate the engine, you've got a few options. Keep the spark plugs out to relieve engine compression (so you will be able to accomplish this by hand without hurting yourself). You can put the bike in gear and push it a few yards up and down the driveway. You can lift the rear wheel (using a bike lift or a centerstand), place the bike in gear and turn the rear wheel. Of

Fig. 18 If you want to add extra oil to protect the cylinder walls, you are going to have to remove the spark plugs

course on some older models and on some dirt bikes, you can just use the kick starter to rotate the engine.

➡If you disable the ignition system and drain the carburetor(s) or if you unplug the fuel injectors (depending on your fuel system) you can turn the engine once or twice using the electric starter. Just be sure that you won't be introducing any gasoline into the cylinders or your effort will all be for naught.

Prepare The Battery For Storage

CHECKING THE FLUID

♦ See Figure 19

One of the most important parts of battery care is to maintain the fluid level. If the electrolyte level is allowed to drop beyond a certain point the plates will corrode and the battery will not be able to receive or hold a charge. Before placing the bike into storage be sure to remove the cell cap(s) and check the fluid level. If necessary, top-off any cells using DISTILLED water. Only fill the battery to the fill lines on the case or to the bottom of the cell opening in the top of the battery case if no fill line is present (or as directed by the battery manufacturer).

Fig. 19 Unless you have a sealed, maintenance-free battery, you should remove the caps and check the battery fluid level before storage

➡After adding any water to the battery, be sure that it gets a chance to mix with the electrolyte. The best way to do this is to operate the motorcycle (but since you just went through a lot of trouble to NOT OPERATE IT, we recommend attaching a TRICKle charger for a few hours, this should do the trick. Uhhhhh, no pun intended.)

If you are using a sealed dry cell or gel cell battery, you obviously won't be opening any cell caps to add distilled water, but there still may be a way to check the electrolyte. Automotive batteries use sight glasses in the top of the battery case, so check with the battery manufacturer to see if they have provided a similar method of checking your battery.

REMOVE IT OR TEND IT?

♦ See Figures 20, 21, 22 and 23

The second most important part of battery maintenance is making sure that it is properly charged. If you have just checked the fluid level, then you are in the perfect position to check the charge using a hydrometer designed just for that purpose. Because the specific gravity of electrolyte will change with the amount of charge present, you will be able to check the exact condition of each battery cell by using a hydrometer (that is, unless it is a sealed battery).

But even if the charge is fine now, there is no telling how it is going to be in a few months. Actually, we just lied, we can tell you one thing for certain, it is NOT going to be fully charged anymore and it could be dead. Batteries will self discharge over time (which will allow for changes to the chemical composition of the plates inside the battery). If allowed to discharge often enough or long enough, the battery will become permanently discharged and useless.

For this reason you are going to want to make sure that the battery is fully charged when you put the bike into storage and then either hook it up to an automatic charger (such as the Battery Tender®) which will maintain a proper charge without overcharging it. Or, if you do not have an automatic battery charger, use a trickle charger for a few hours at least once every month.

If you are lucky enough to be storing the motorcycle in a heated or attached garage, then you will be fine leaving the battery in place. You will be fine, that is, as long as an extension cord or outlet is handy to make sure the battery can be kept fully charged. But, if the bike is to be stored outside or in a detached garage or shed, you really should remove the battery from the bike and store it somewhere warmer. Remember that as a bat-

Fig. 22 An automatic charger, like the Battery Tender® can be left attached to your bike all winter long . . .

Fig. 20 If the bike is not going to be stored in a heated or attached garage, then you are best off removing the battery and storing it where it can't freeze

Fig. 23 . . . it will monitor your battery's voltage and keep it properly charged (without overcharging)

tery discharges more of the electrolyte is converted to water, which could freeze. Should the electrolyte freeze, come spring, you will likely find a dead battery, with a cracked case that has spilled a weakened acid (but an acid nonetheless) all over your bike.

Prepare The Chassis For Storage

You are just about ready to put your baby to sleep for a while, with only the chassis remaining to be given some attention.

LUBING THE CHASSIS

Now is a good time to lube and grease any pivot points from cables and levers to steering head bearings. The depth to which you pursue lubing will have something to do with your normal maintenance routine.

If you have a tire that is close to replacement, then you probably won't bother removing the wheel just to repack the bearings (especially if your bike uses sealed bearings that don't require periodic repacking) since you will likely be removing the wheel sometime in early spring. If lubing your steering head bearing only involves a grease gun and a zerk fitting you will be much more likely to do that now (regardless of when it is next due), then you would be if it involved removing the steering head to repack the bearing by hand.

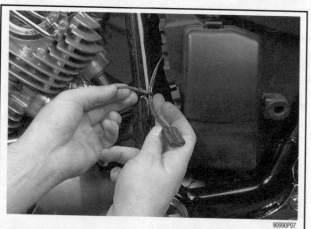

Fig. 21 If the battery is going to be left on the bike, then some type of wiring harness should be installed so you can easily attach a battery charger—in this case, the electric glove harness can be used

CHECKING THE TIRES

▶ **See Figures 24 and 25**

If your tires are approaching replacement time, NOW IS NOT THE TIME TO DO IT, wait for spring.

If you are really lucky, or if you time it just right, your tires will be worn, close to the end of their usable lives right before storage. This will allow you to pay little attention to them and not worry about what affect storage and time will have on them.

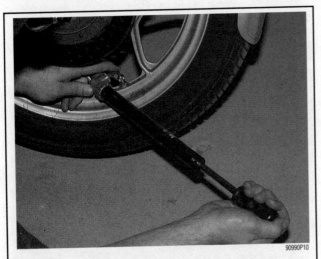

Fig. 24 Before placing the bike in storage, make sure the tires are properly inflated

Fig. 25 If possible, raise the bike so that the tires are off the ground, but MAKE CERTAIN it is SECURE and can't fall

But since it is rare that we are that lucky or that methodical let's tell you how to best get your tires through the winter. There are 3 things you can do to help assure your tire's survival:

• **Make sure they are properly inflated**—The first and most important thing to do is to inflate your tires to the manufacturer's specification.

• **Cover the bike or keep it out of direct sunlight**—Since ultraviolet radiation is probably the most significant cause of dry rotting and cracking, the next most important thing to do for your tires is to keep them out of direct sunlight.

• **Raise the tires off the ground**—The last thing you can do to preserve your tires is relatively easy if you have a center stand and much less so if you don't. Support the motorcycle securely, under the frame, to keep the wheels off the ground.

➡**Remember that time is a tire's enemy just as much as is usage. If the bike is going to be stored for a LONG time (measured in years and not months) then there may be nothing you can do to assure that the tires will be good when the time period ends. But, following our recommendations will give you the best shot.**

COVERING & PROTECTING THE BIKE

Ideally, you will want to place a high quality bike cover over the machine to keep it away from prying eyes, ultraviolet radiation, and whatever else might come its way. BUT, there are a few things to be careful of with covers. If you are going to buy one, make sure it has a soft inner lining to prevent scratching of painted surfaces. Also, make sure it is not made of a plastic material, but instead choose one that breathes. A non-breathable, plastic material will trap condensation and promote corrosion and mold, while a breathing cover will allow moisture to evaporate, further protecting your baby.

Unfortunately motorcycles have lots of neat, tight, little nooks and crannies (like Thomas' English Muffins®). This is not only a problem when it comes to detailing, but when it comes to RODENTS. Unfortunately, many small, furry animals are attracted to these nooks and may think it is nest building time. They also have the unfortunate habit of shredding things like saddles, wiring harnesses and air filters. If possible, set a rodent trap or two in order to protect your baby. Or if you are THAT humane about it, check the bike every week or so to discourage nesting. Hey, you can always get a cat and allow them access to the storage area (as long as they don't like to stretch their claws on your saddle).

Leaving It In Storage

Once you have put it in storage, LEAVE IT ALONE. You can drool on it (as long as you dry it afterwards). You can rub body parts against it (as long as you don't scratch it or remove too much wax). You can get in your leathers, sit on it and go "Vroom . . .Vroom." while spitting on yourself. But don't start it just to listen or to "warm the motor." Idling it won't warm the motor very much, probably will not charge the battery, definitely won't do anything for the drivetrain and will most likely leave some condensation in the exhaust to rust your precious pipes and mufflers. LEAVE IT ALONE UNTIL IT IS PROPERLY REMOVED FROM STORAGE.

REMOVING THE BIKE FROM STORAGE

If you followed our instructions last fall, then you should be in GREAT SHAPE and we will have you riding by the afternoon (barring any unexpected problems).

BUT if you were an idiot (and we both must confess to having been idiots before), then it is going to take a little more time.

Also, if you come across an abandoned baby (the proverbial bike that has been forgotten about in the shed or barn for the past decade or so) then you should follow these steps towards reawakening a bike. Of course, the longer the bike has been in storage, the more items you are going to need to check. If the bike was stored for more than one winter you should start to suspect ANY RUBBER item (tires, hoses, seals) and any wear items (cables, fluids, lights). Don't assume that anything is in good shape until you have checked and proven it to be serviceable.

Check The Chassis After Storage

PERFORMING A MICKEY MOUSE CHECK

▶ **See Figure 26**

Before attempting to wake your sleeping baby, check for evidence of visiting or nesting rodents. Look for signs that your bike has not wintered alone such as small turds, gnawed wiring, shredded hide of the naugha (that strange, elusive animal with a fake leather skin), etc.

Make sure there are no rodents sleeping in the machine (and that no nesting rodents have left anything behind). The only way to be sure of this is to disassemble the air intake track (air cleaner and any ducting) as well as any bodywork (fairing, tail section and/or side covers) which could hide a sleeping rodent. This is an excellent time to check the condition of the air filter and clean or replace it, as necessary and as applicable to your model. Use a flashlight to inspect the opening in the muffler(s) to make sure no one is residing in there either. You WON'T BELIEVE the smell if you miss a nest in the muffler and start the bike.

✳✳ WARNING

If any evidence of extra-rodential activity is found, be sure to check the bikes electrical, air intake and exhaust systems VERY CAREFULLY to avoid causing unexpected damage when attempting to start the motor.

Fig. 26 Air cleaners and intake ducts are popular places for rodents to winter (I guess they can't afford the south of France), so always check before starting the bike after winter storage

CHECKING THE TIRES

▶ **See Figure 27**

Start by grabbing your trusty tire gauge and check that the tires are properly inflated. The longer the bike has been in storage, the less likely this is to be true. Use a hand pump, portable air tank or an air compressor to pump the tires back up to specification. Listen for any audible air leaks.

With the tires properly inflated, check for cracks or dry rotting. Look between the tread blocks and check the sidewalls for any evidence of weathering or cracking. Remember that you only get 2 tires on a motorcycle. ANY TIRE which shows ANY EVIDENCE of dry rotting should be replaced. Don't risk a possible tire failure.

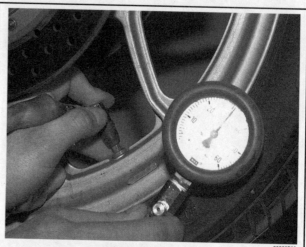

Fig. 27 Even the best valve stems will loose some air over time, so ALWAYS check your tire pressure after storage

CHECKING LUBE POINTS

▶ **See Figures 28 and 29**

Make sure that all levers, pivot points and cables move freely without binding or excessive resistance. Check the swingarm, forks and steering

Fig. 28 Make sure all levers and controls move freely, without binding, and lubricate or replace them as necessary

Fig. 29 If your model does not use sealed wheel bearings, you should clean, inspect and repack the bearings when replacing tires

head for proper travel. If you are replacing any tires it is also a good idea to check the wheel bearings. If the bearings are not sealed on your brand, it is time to clean, inspect and repack the bearings too.

It is never a bad idea to lube all chassis points when you are removing the bike from storage. If it has been more than one winter of storage for this machine, then you MUST lube all points to prevent sudden and troubling binding.

❊❊ CAUTION

Any source of binding or excessive resistance on levers or pivot points MUST be found and repaired before any attempt is made to ride the motorcycle. Chassis or control instability could easily lead to a very serious accident. Improperly operating components may be signs of an impending equipment failure.

Check The Battery After Storage

Once again, if you have had the battery on a Battery Tender® or other automatic charger, then you are probably in good shape, but just to be sure make an electrolyte level and charge check. Remove the vent caps (unless it is a sealed battery) and make sure the fluid is at the proper level. Use a hydrometer to check for proper charge.

➡ **While you are checking the fluid level, use a flashlight to take a look at the tops of the battery plates. If there is a significant amount of white corrosion, then your battery is either toast or almost toast and you really should replace it, even if it does seem to take a charge. You don't want it to strand you next week, do you?**

If the battery is not fully charged, place it on a charger to make sure it is ready to go when you are finished prepping the bike.

If the battery is completely discharged, you are going to want to consider replacing it. Even though you may be able to get it to hold a charge, a battery which has sat discharged for any length of time will never hold a full charge again. And the longer it sat discharged, the worse off it will be. It may very well give up the ghost at an inconvenient time (like in the middle of a trip, or early one morning when you are trying to start the bike and ride to work).

Check The Drivetrain After Storage

CHECKING ALL FLUIDS

♦ See Figure 30

Engine Oil

DO NOT CRANK OR ATTEMPT TO START THE MOTOR YET!

Whether or not you properly prepped the bike you should change the engine oil at this time. If the oil filter was replaced when the bike was put into storage you can reuse it, but be sure to drain as much oil as possible from the filter or from the cartridge housing (as applicable).

OK, it is obvious why you would change the oil if the bike was found in a barn a decade after it was placed there by someone else, right? But, you are probably asking, "If I followed the proper storage preparations last fall, why should I trash that perfectly good oil now?" Well, the answer is simple. If the oil is worth more than the bike, don't sweat it and don't bother changing it either. But if the bike is worth more than the oil (and I really hope it is for your sake) then it is cheap insurance. Even if you kept the bike in a heated garage, there is no guarantee that no condensation formed and that all of the nasty corrosives were removed by the last change, so we recommend that you don't risk it.

If the bike was stored outdoors or in a non-temperature controlled area, then the chances are good that you have got nasties in the crankcase or in the oil bag (as applicable) so why give those nasties a shot at your engine?

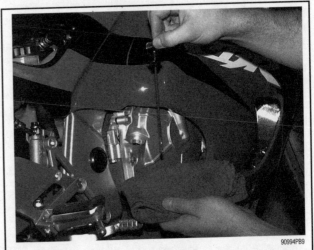

Fig. 30 Before removing a bike from storage, ALL fluids should be checked, and some should be replaced

Engine Coolant

If the bike was properly prepped and the coolant was changed before storage, just make a quick level check.

If the bike is being resurrected or if you didn't change the coolant before storage, you should at least check the level and check the specific gravity. Specialized hydrometers are available to give you an indication of the coolants ability to resist freezing and boiling. If the level is OK and the coolant is still giving adequate protection, then you are free to leave it in the system.

Of course, if you don't know how long the coolant has been in the system, you should change it. Remember that the other job coolant performs is to prevent corrosion while lubricating the water pump seal(s). Coolant usually looses its ability to do these jobs properly LONG BEFORE a hydrometer will tell you that it is bad. If the coolant is more than a year old, then you probably want to save yourself the hassle down the road and replace it now.

Transmission, Primary Chain or Gear Oil

I'm starting to sound like a broken record but I'll say it again: If you followed the storage routine and replaced these fluids last fall, then you are probably in good shape. BUT, you will still want to check the fluid level. If the level has gone down (look for a leak). If the level has gone up, then you have a significant amount of condensation mixed in with the oil and it should be replaced to prevent damage to the bike's components.

➡**Keep in mind that although these fluids will not contain the corrosive byproducts of combustion, they are JUST as likely to contain condensation. If you want to be certain that your gears and shafts are protected from moisture, then you should replace the oil before running the bike.**

As usual, if you are resurrecting a beast which has been in storage for some years, then do yourself a favor, just drain and replace all gear oils now.

Brake/Hydraulic Clutch Fluid

Check the fluid level in the clutch and/or brake master cylinders, as applicable. If the bike has a mechanical brake, double check that the linkage moves freely.

More and more manufacturer's are recommending annual or bi-annual brake or clutch hydraulic fluid changing. Obviously this is an area that a lot of people ignore with seemingly little trouble (until their machines start to age and a caliper piston freezes or seals are torn by corrosion and begin to leak. If your fluid is due for a change, there is really no better time than the present. But, even if it is not due for one, consider performing one now anyway. We aren't talking about a lot of fluid in most cases. The smartest course of action is to flush and refill these systems EVERY YEAR. It is the best way you can assure yourself that the system components will continue to operate properly and remain corrosion free for many years.

Of course, if you don't know when any of the hydraulic fluids were changed last, DO IT NOW!!!

CHECKING ADJUSTMENTS

♦ See Figure 31

Drive Chain or Belt

Refer to the drivetrain maintenance section of this manual and to your bike's owners manual. Check the final drive belt or chain adjustment before you trust your life to this thing. If necessary, the chain and sprockets can be cleaned and pre-lubed, but since chains should usually be lubed hot, you will have to redo this after your first ride.

Levers, Pedals or Linkage

You should have checked the levers and pedals for freedom of movement while you were checking the chassis out, but now it is time to make sure they are all properly adjusted. Refer to the maintenance sections of this book and check your bike's owners manual to make sure that all controls and linkage are properly adjusted within specification. Improperly adjusted controls can lead to VERY SHORT and VERY DANGEROUS rides.

REMOVE & INSPECT THE SPARK PLUGS

If you checked the spark plugs and coated the cylinders with fresh oil before storing the bike, then the plugs are almost certain to be in good shape, but you will still want to pull them so you can recoat the cylinder walls with oil before attempting to start the bike.

Fig. 31 If you didn't do this before storage, you better check and adjust the final drive belt or chain before riding the bike. Hey, it's your life

But if you didn't properly prep the bike or if you are resurrecting a beast after a lengthy storage, you are definitely going to want to check the plugs and prime the cylinders with oil. This can be done easily enough:

1. Remove the spark plugs and check their gaps. Replace the plugs and/or adjust the gap, as necessary.

➡**Remember that a sleeping bike may be difficult enough to awaken without adding poor spark to the equation.**

2. Pour 1–2 tablespoons of fresh, clean engine oil through the spark plug hole.
3. Rotate the engine to spread the oil around the cylinders. You have a few choices on how to rotate the engine. You can rotate it by hand, which is slower and more gentle (lowering the chance of gouging a cylinder wall if a ring is reluctant at first) or you can use the electric starter (if you are more sure that the rings won't be reluctant):

   a. To rotate the engine by hand, keep the spark plugs out to relieve engine compression.

   b. Place the bike in gear and turn the rear wheel using the drivetrain to rotate the engine crank. This can be done with the rear wheel raised (grasping the wheel by hand) or by pushing the bike along using the handlebars).

   c. Of course on some older models and on some dirt bikes, you can use the kick starter to rotate the engine by hand (or foot as the case may be).
4. Install the spark plugs.

FILL THE FUEL TANK

If you drained the fuel system before storage then it is time to refill the gas tank and prime the system using fresh gasoline. As usual, be very careful when working around gasoline.

☀☀ CAUTION

Gasoline is VERY DANGEROUS STUFF. It is HIGHLY flammable and it is very easy to get yourself dead doing really dumb things. Don't work around open flames or things that might cause a spark.

If you used fuel stabilizer, than you've got another choice to make here. The longer the bike has been in storage, the less volatile the fuel will be, even if you used stabilizer. If you just stored it for one winter, then you are likely to be in good shape. If you are in doubt, then drain the fuel tank and pour that fuel into your car or truck's tank (where it will mix with a greater amount of fuel and likely cause no problem . . . besides even if it does cause a problem, better your car than your bike RIGHT?).

If you didn't add stabilizer or if you are resurrecting a long forgotten beast, then chances are that your fuel system is clogged with varnish and that the inside of your fuel tank is covered with rust. Both of these potential nightmares must be remedied before the bike can come to life.

Rust in the fuel tank can get by the fuel filter and clog carburetor passages or destroy fuel injectors. If you are unsure, use the petcock (if equipped) to dispense a little fuel into a clear container and check for dirt, rust or debris. You can also use a mechanic's mirror and a flashlight to inspect the inside of the tank.

As for the fuel tank, if it contains rust you will have to clean and seal the tank before it can be safely used.

If your carburetors contain varnish, then they may require a rebuild before they will perform properly. To help determine if this is going to be a problem, remove the float bowls (we are assuming that you have drained any fuel that was left, or that it was in storage so long that no fuel is present). Once the float bowl(s) have been removed from the carburetor(s), examine each float and chamber for varnish. If varnish is evident, you are probably going to have to disassemble and clean or completely rebuild the carburetors.

Priming The System

▶ See Figure 32

Once you are ready to go you will want to prime the fuel system before attempting to start the engine (this helps to prevent unwanted excessive drain on your new or freshly charged battery). If you have a carbureted bike then chances are that priming is as easy as turning on the petcock. BUT, you may have a vacuum actuated petcock which prevent fuel from flowing to the carburetor(s) unless engine vacuum is applied to one side of a pressure valve. Most vacuum actuated petcocks have a prime setting which allows fuel to flow without vacuum, but if yours does not then you will either need a hand held vacuum pump, or you are simply going to have to crank for a little while.

If you have a fuel injected bike, then chances are that the fuel pump will prime itself when the ignition switch is turned on. Most fuel injection systems run the pump for a few seconds whenever the key is turned. A good way to determine this is to simply listen for the pump (since it is usually in your gas tank, it is not hard to hear on a motorcycle). If you have problems starting a fuel injected bike, after storage, check the bike's owners manual to make sure there is no other special way to prime the system.

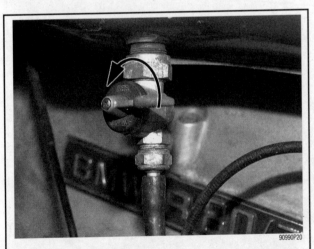

Fig. 32 If the fuel system was drained you should prime the carburetors by turning the petcock to PRIME or RESERVE, as applicable

Performing The Pre-Ride Check

▶ See Figure 33

Before attempting to start and ride the bike, you should now take an opportunity to perform a COMPLETE pre-ride check as detailed elsewhere in this manual. Obviously you have already addressed some of the items (like checking fluids and tires), but you don't want to leave anything out. Make sure the lights, turn signals and horn all work. Make sure the bike is completely ready before you take it for a spin.

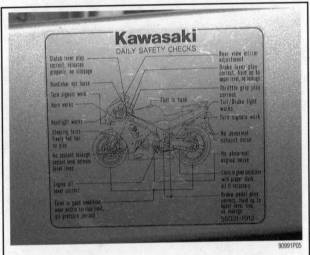

Fig. 33 Before starting and riding the bike, perform a COMPLETE pre-ride safety check

Starting And Riding The Bike

Once you are certain everything is working, hop on and give the starter a whirl. If the engine is tough to start, remember that a starter needs time to cool down between tries. DON'T hold the starter button for more than a few seconds and try to wait a minute between tries. I know it can be frustrating, but there is no reason to burn out a perfectly good starter motor with excessive cranking, especially when your bike is just waking up for the first time this season.

If the bike does not seem to catch after a few tries, double check the basics. "FINE-C" as the Motorcycle Safety Foundation preaches:

- Is the FUEL on?
- Is the IGNITION on?
- Is the bike in NEUTRAL (with the kickstand up on some models)?
- Is the ENGINE kill switch in the run position?
- Is the CLUTCH lever pulled in?

If the bike will still not start, refer to the troubleshooting section to see what you've forgotten.

When the bike fires. Give the engine a few seconds to begin warming and for the oil to circulate before revving the motor. Follow your usual warm-up routine, which probably means riding slowly and moderately until the engine has fully warmed. During that first ride of the season, take special care to listen and feel for potential problems you may have missed. You probably want to avoid busy highways until you and the bike are sure of each other again.

THEN, RIDE SAFE(ly) . . . the copy editor forced me to add the LY, Bastard.

90990P16

After a long, hard winter, you can always tell the Chilton parking lot, by the amount of bikes lined-up

90990P11

By following the care and maintenance instructions in this book, your bike can look this good after 20 years too

GLOSSARY

Understanding your mechanic (should you decide to use the services of one) is as important as understanding your bike. Many riders have difficulty understanding mechanical terminology. Talking the language of motorcycles and machines makes it easier to effectively communicate with professional technicians. It isn't necessary (or recommended) that you diagnose the problem for him/her, but it will save time, and you money, if you can accurately describe what is happening. It will also help you to know why your bike does what it is doing, and what repairs were made.

ABS: Anti-lock braking system. An electro-mechanical braking system which is designed to minimize or prevent wheel lock-up during braking.

ACCELERATOR PUMP: A small pump located in the carburetor that feeds fuel into the air/fuel mixture during acceleration.

ADVANCE: Setting the ignition timing so that spark occurs earlier before the piston reaches top dead center (TDC).

AFTER TOP DEAD CENTER (ATDC): Some point after the piston reaches the top of its travel on the compression stroke.

AIR CLEANER: An assembly consisting of a housing, filter and any connecting ductwork. The filter element is made up of a porous paper, sometimes with a wire mesh screening, and is designed to prevent airborne particles from entering the engine through the carburetor or throttle body.

AIR/FUEL RATIO: The ratio of air-to-gasoline by weight in the fuel mixture drawn into the engine.

ALTERNATING CURRENT (AC): Electric current that flows first in one direction, then in the opposite direction, continually reversing flow.

ALTERNATOR: A device which produces AC (alternating current) which is converted to DC (direct current) to charge the bike's battery and run the bike's current consuming devices.

AMMETER: An instrument, calibrated in amperes, used to measure the flow of an electrical current in a circuit. Ammeters are always connected in series with the circuit being tested.

AMP/HR. RATING (BATTERY): Measurement of the ability of a battery to deliver a stated amount of current for a stated period of time. The higher the amp/hr. rating, the better the battery.

AMPERE: The rate of flow of electrical current present when one volt of electrical pressure is applied against one ohm of electrical resistance.

ANALOG COMPUTER: Any microprocessor that uses similar (analogous) electrical signals to make its calculations.

ANTIFREEZE: A substance (ethylene or propylene glycol) added to the coolant to prevent freezing in cold weather.

ANTI-LOCK BRAKING SYSTEM: A supplementary system to the base hydraulic system that prevents sustained lock-up of the wheels during braking as well as automatically controlling wheel slip.

ARMATURE: A laminated, soft iron core wrapped by a wire that converts electrical energy to mechanical energy as in a motor or relay. When rotated in a magnetic field, it changes mechanical energy into electrical energy as in a generator.

ATDC: After Top Dead Center.

ATMOSPHERIC PRESSURE: The pressure on the Earth's surface caused by the weight of the air in the atmosphere. At sea level, this pressure is 14.7 psi at 32°F (101 kPa at 0°C).

ATOMIZATION: The breaking down of a liquid into a fine mist that can be suspended in air.

AXIAL PLAY: Movement parallel to a shaft or bearing bore.

AXLE: A shaft that is used to provide support across portions of the forks, frame or swingarm.

AXLE CAPACITY: The maximum load-carrying capacity of the axle itself, as specified by the manufacturer. This is usually a higher number than the GAWR.

BACKFIRE: The sudden combustion of gases in the intake or exhaust system that results in a loud explosion.

BACKLASH: The clearance or play between two parts, such as meshed gears.

BACKPRESSURE: Restrictions in the exhaust system that slow the exit of exhaust gases from the combustion chamber.

BAKELITE®: A heat resistant, plastic insulator material commonly used in printed circuit boards and transistorized components.

BALL BEARING: A bearing made up of hardened inner and outer races between which hardened steel balls roll.

BALL JOINT: A ball and matching socket connecting suspension components (steering head to control arm on the BMW Telelever fork). It permits rotating movement in any direction between the components that are joined.

BALLAST RESISTOR: A resistor in the primary ignition circuit that lowers voltage after the engine is started to reduce wear on ignition components.

BATTERY: A direct current electrical storage unit, consisting of the basic active materials of lead and sulfuric acid, which converts chemical energy into electrical energy. Used to provide current for the operation of the starter as well as other equipment, such as the radio, lighting, etc.

BEAD: The portion of a tire that holds it on the rim.

BEARING: A friction reducing, supportive device usually located between a stationary part and a moving part.

BEFORE TOP DEAD CENTER (BTDC): The point just before the piston reaches the top of its travel on the compression stroke.

BEZEL: Piece of metal surrounding radio, headlights, gauges or similar fairing mounted components; sometimes used to hold the glass face of a gauge in the dash.

BI-METAL TEMPERATURE SENSOR: Any sensor or switch made of two dissimilar types of metal that bend when heated or cooled due to the different expansion rates of the alloys. These types of sensors usually function as an on/off switch.

BLOW-BY: Combustion gases, composed of water vapor and unburned fuel, that leak past the piston rings into the crankcase during normal engine operation. These gases are removed by the breather system to prevent the buildup of harmful acids in the crankcase.

BOOK TIME: See Labor Time.

BOOK VALUE: The average value of a bike, widely used to determine trade-in and resale value.

BORE: Diameter of a cylinder.

BRAKE CALIPER: The housing that fits over the brake disc. The caliper holds the brake pads, which are pressed against the discs by the caliper pistons when the lever or brake pedal is depressed.

BRAKE FADE: Loss of braking power, usually caused by excessive heat after repeated brake applications.

BRAKE HORSEPOWER: Usable horsepower of an engine measured at the crankshaft.

BRAKE PAD: A brake backing plate and lining assembly used with disc brakes.

BRAKE SHOE: The backing for the brake lining. The term is, however, usually applied to the assembly of the brake backing and lining.

BREAKER POINTS: A set of points inside the distributor, operated by a cam, which make and break the ignition circuit.

BTDC: Before Top Dead Center.

BUSHING: A liner, usually removable, for a bearing; an anti-friction liner used in place of a bearing.

CALIFORNIA ENGINE: An engine certified by the EPA for use in California only; conforms to more stringent emission regulations than Federal engine.

CALIPER: A hydraulically activated device in a disc brake system, which is mounted straddling the brake rotor (disc). The caliper contains at least one piston and two brake pads. Hydraulic pressure on the piston(s) forces the pads against the rotor.

CAMSHAFT: A shaft in the engine on which are the lobes (cams) which operate the valves. The camshaft is driven by the crankshaft, via a belt, chain or gears, at one half the crankshaft speed.

CANCER: Rust on a body part.

CAPACITOR: A device which stores an electrical charge.

CARBON MONOXIDE (CO): A colorless, odorless gas given off as a normal byproduct of combustion. It is poisonous and extremely dangerous in confined areas, building up slowly to toxic levels without warning if adequate ventilation is not available.

CARBURETOR: A device, usually mounted to the intake manifold of an engine, which mixes the air and fuel in the proper proportion to allow even combustion.

CATALYTIC CONVERTER: A device installed in the exhaust system of some modern bikes, like a muffler, that converts harmful byproducts of combustion into carbon dioxide and water vapor by means of a heat-producing chemical reaction.

CENTRIFUGAL ADVANCE: A mechanical method of advancing the spark timing by using flyweights in the distributor that react to centrifugal force generated by the distributor shaft rotation.

CHECK VALVE: Any one-way valve installed to permit the flow of air, fuel or vacuum in one direction only.

CHOKE: The valve/plate that restricts the amount of air entering an engine on the induction stroke, thereby enriching the air to fuel ratio.

CIRCLIP: A split steel snapring that fits into a groove to hold various parts in place.

CIRCUIT BREAKER: A switch which protects an electrical circuit from overload by opening the circuit when the current flow exceeds a pre-determined level. Some circuit breakers must be reset manually, while most reset automatically.

CIRCUIT: Any unbroken path through which an electrical current can flow. Also used to describe fuel flow in some instances.

CLEARCOAT: A transparent layer which, when sprayed over a vehicle's paint job, adds gloss and depth as well as an additional protective coating to the finish.

CLUTCH: Part of the power train used to connect/disconnect power to the rear wheel.

COIL: Part of the ignition system that boosts the relatively low voltage supplied by the electrical system to the high voltage required to fire the spark plugs.

COMBUSTION CHAMBER: The part of the engine in the cylinder head where combustion takes place.

COMPRESSION CHECK: A test involving removing each spark plug and inserting a gauge. When the engine is cranked, the gauge will record a pressure reading in the individual cylinder. General operating condition can be determined from a compression check.

COMPRESSION RATIO: The ratio of the volume between the piston and cylinder head when the piston is at the bottom of its stroke (bottom dead center) and when the piston is at the top of its stroke (top dead center).

CONDENSER: An electrical device which acts to store an electrical charge, preventing voltage surges..

CONDUCTOR: Any material through which an electrical current can be transmitted easily.

CONNECTING ROD: The connecting link between the crankshaft and piston.

CONTINUITY: Continuous or complete circuit. Can be checked with an ohmmeter.

CONTROL ARM: A suspension component found on a few motorcycles (such as modern BMWs with a Telelever Suspension) which is mounted on the frame and supports the ball joint.

CONVENTIONAL IGNITION: Ignition system which uses breaker points.

COOLANT: Mixture of water and anti-freeze circulated through the engine to carry off heat produced by the engine.

COUNTERSHAFT: An intermediate shaft which is rotated by a mainshaft and transmits, in turn, that rotation to a working part.

CRANKCASE: The lower part of an engine in which the crankshaft and related parts operate.

CRANKSHAFT: Engine component (connected to pistons by connecting rods) which converts the reciprocating (up and down) motion of pistons to rotary motion used to turn the driveshaft.

CURB WEIGHT: The weight of a vehicle without passengers or payload, but including all fluids (oil, gas, coolant, etc.) and other equipment specified as standard.

CYLINDER HEAD: The detachable portion of the engine, usually fastened to the top of the cylinder block or jugs and containing all or most of the combustion chambers. On overhead valve engines, it contains the valves and their operating parts. On overhead cam engines, it contains the camshaft as well.

CYLINDER: In an engine, the round holes in the engine block or the jugs which attach to the engine case in which the piston(s) ride.

DEAD CENTER: The extreme top or bottom of the piston stroke.

DETERGENT: An additive in engine oil to improve its operating characteristics.

DETONATION: An unwanted explosion of the air/fuel mixture in the combustion chamber caused by excess heat and compression, advanced timing, or an overly lean mixture. Also referred to as "ping".

DIAPHRAGM: A thin, flexible wall separating two cavities, such as in a CV carburetor.

DIESELING: The engine continues to run after the key is shut off; caused by fuel continuing to be burned in the combustion chamber.

DIGITAL VOLT OHMMETER: An electronic diagnostic tool used to measure voltage, ohms and amps as well as several other functions, with the readings displayed on a digital screen in tenths, hundredths and thousandths.

DIODE: An electrical device that will allow current to flow in one direction only.

DIRECT CURRENT (DC): Electrical current that flows in one direction only.

DISC BRAKE: A hydraulic braking assembly consisting of a brake disc, or rotor, usually mounted on a wheel, and a caliper assembly usually containing two brake pads which are activated by hydraulic pressure. The pads are forced against the sides of the disc, creating friction which slows the bike.

DISPLACEMENT: The total volume of air that is displaced by all pistons as the engine turns through one complete revolution.

DOHC: Double overhead camshaft.

DOUBLE OVERHEAD CAMSHAFT: An engine type that utilizes two camshafts mounted in one cylinder head. One camshaft normally operates the exhaust valves, while the other operates the intake valves.

DOWEL PIN: A pin, inserted in mating holes in two different parts allowing those parts to maintain a fixed relationship.

DRIVE TRAIN: The components that transmit the flow of power from the engine to the rear wheel. The components can include the primary drive, clutch, transmission, driveshaft, chain or belt

DRUM BRAKE: A braking system which consists of two brake shoes mounted on a fixed backing plate, and a brake drum, mounted on an axle or wheel, which revolves around the assembly.

DRY CHARGED BATTERY: Battery to which electrolyte is added when the battery is placed in service.

DVOM: Digital volt ohmmeter

DWELL: The rate, measured in degrees of shaft rotation, at which an electrical circuit cycles on and off.

ECU: Electronic control unit.

ELECTRODE: Conductor (positive or negative) of electric current.

ELECTROLYTE: A solution of water and sulfuric acid used to activate the battery. Electrolyte is extremely corrosive.

ELECTRONIC CONTROL UNIT: A digital computer that controls engine (and sometimes the Anti-Lock Brake system) functions based on data received from various sensors.

ELECTRONIC IGNITION: A system in which the timing and firing of the spark plugs is controlled by an electronic control unit, usually called a module. These systems have no points or condenser.

ENAMEL: Type of paint that dries to a smooth, glossy finish.

END-PLAY: The measured amount of axial movement in a shaft.

ENGINE: The primary motor or power apparatus of a vehicle, which converts liquid or gas fuel into mechanical energy.

ENGINE CASE: The basic engine casting containing the crankshaft main bearings, as well as machined surfaces for the mounting of other components such as the jugs or cylinder head, oil pan. On many bikes it may also hose the transmission shafts and gears.

EP LUBRICANT: EP (extreme pressure) lubricants are specially formulated for use with gears involving heavy loads (transmissions, rears, etc.).

ETHYL: A substance added to gasoline to improve its resistance to knock, by slowing down the rate of combustion.

ETHYLENE GLYCOL: The base substance of most antifreeze.

EXHAUST MANIFOLD: A set of pipes which conduct exhaust gases from the engine.

FAST IDLE: The speed of the engine when the choke is on. Fast idle speeds engine warm-up.

FEDERAL ENGINE: An engine certified by the EPA for use in states other than those which adopt California standards.

FEELER GAUGE: A blade, usually metal, of precisely predetermined thickness, used to measure the clearance between two parts.

FILAMENT: The part of a bulb that glows; the filament creates high resistance to current flow and actually glows from the resulting heat.

FINAL DRIVE: The system used to transmit power from the engine to the transmission. Usually a chain or gear, but can be a belt or driveshaft as well.

FIRING ORDER: The order in which combustion occurs in the cylinders of an engine.

FLAME FRONT: The term used to describe certain aspects of the fuel explosion in the cylinders. The flame front should move in a controlled pattern across the cylinder, rather than simply exploding immediately.

FLAT ENGINE: Engine design in which the pistons are horizontally opposed. BMW Boxer motors are examples of flat engines.

FLAT RATE: A shop term referring to the amount of money paid to a technician for a repair or diagnostic service based on that particular service versus dealership's labor time (NOT based on the actual time the technician spent on the job).

FLAT SPOT: A point during acceleration when the engine seems to lose power for an instant.

FLOODING: The presence of too much fuel in the intake manifold and combustion chamber which prevents the air/fuel mixture from firing, thereby causing a no-start situation.

FLYWHEEL: A heavy disc of metal attached to the rear of the crankshaft. It smoothes the firing impulses of the engine and keeps the crankshaft turning during periods when no firing takes place. The starter also engages the flywheel to start the engine.

FOOT POUND (ft. lbs. or sometimes, ft. lb.): The amount of energy or work needed to raise an item weighing one pound, a distance of one foot.

FUEL FILTER: A component of the fuel system containing a porous paper element used to prevent any impurities from entering the engine through the fuel system.

FUEL INJECTION: A system replacing the carburetor that sprays fuel into the cylinder or intake through nozzles. The amount of fuel can be more precisely controlled with fuel injection.

FUSE: A protective device in a circuit which prevents circuit overload by breaking the circuit when a specific amperage is present. The device is constructed around a strip or wire of a lower amperage rating than the circuit it is designed to protect.

When an amperage higher than that stamped on the fuse is present in the circuit, the strip or wire melts, opening the circuit.

FUSIBLE LINK: A piece of wire in a wiring harness that performs the same job as a fuse. If overloaded, the fusible link will melt and interrupt the circuit.

GAWR: (Gross axle weight rating) the total maximum weight an axle is designed to carry.

GCW: (Gross combined weight) total combined weight of a tow vehicle and trailer.

GEAR RATIO: A ratio expressing the number of turns a smaller gear will make to turn a larger gear through one revolution. The ratio is found by dividing the number of teeth on the smaller gear into the number of teeth on the larger gear.

GEARBOX: Transmission

GEL COAT: A thin coat of plastic resin covering fiberglass body panels.

GENERATOR: A device which produces Direct Current (DC) necessary to charge the battery.

GVWR: (Gross vehicle weight rating) total maximum weight a vehicle is designed to carry including the weight of the bike, passenger, equipment, gas, oil, etc.

HALOGEN: A special type of lamp known for its quality of brilliant white light. Originally used for fog lights and driving lights.

HEAT RANGE: A term used to describe the ability of a spark plug to carry away heat. Plugs with longer nosed insulators take longer to carry heat off effectively.

HEMI: A name given an engine using hemispherical combustion chambers.

HORSEPOWER: A measurement of the amount of work; one horsepower is the amount of work necessary to lift 33,000 lbs. one foot in one minute. Brake horsepower (bhp) is the horsepower delivered by an engine on a dynamometer. Net horsepower is the power remaining (measured at the flywheel of the engine) that can be used to turn the rear wheel after power is consumed through friction and running the engine accessories (water pump, alternator, etc.)

HUB: The center part of a wheel or gear.

HYDROCARBON (HC): Any chemical compound made up of hydrogen and carbon. A major pollutant formed by the engine as a by-product of combustion.

HYDROMETER: An instrument used to measure the specific gravity of a solution.

HYDROPLANING: A phenomenon of driving when water builds up under the tire tread, causing it to lose contact with the road. Slowing down will usually restore normal tire contact with the road. Deadly on a motorcycle!

IDLE MIXTURE: The mixture of air and fuel being fed to the cylinders when the engine is running at base speed (no throttle applied). The idle mixture screw(s) are sometimes adjusted as part of a tune-up.

INCH POUND (inch lbs.; sometimes in. lb. or in. lbs.): One twelfth of a foot pound.

INDUCTION: A means of transferring electrical energy in the form of a magnetic field. Principle used in the ignition coil to increase voltage.

INJECTOR: A device which receives metered fuel under pressure and is activated to inject the fuel into the engine at a predetermined time.

INPUT SHAFT: The shaft in a transmission to which torque is applied, usually carrying the driving gear or gears.

INTAKE MANIFOLD: A casting or passage used to conduct air or a fuel/air mixture to the cylinders.

JOURNAL: The bearing surface within which a shaft operates.

JUMPER CABLES: Two heavy duty wires with large clamps used to provide power from a charged battery to a discharged battery mounted in a vehicle.

JUMPSTART: Utilizing the sufficiently charged battery of one bike to start the engine of another bike with a discharged battery by the use of jumper cables.

KEY: A small block, usually fitted in a notch between a shaft and a hub to prevent slippage of the two parts.

KNOCK: Noise which results from the spontaneous ignition of a portion of the air-fuel mixture in the engine cylinder caused by overly advanced ignition timing or use of incorrectly low octane fuel for that engine.

LABOR TIME: A specific amount of time required to perform a certain repair or diagnostic service as defined by a vehicle or after-market manufacturer .

LACQUER: A quick-drying paint.

LITHIUM-BASE GREASE: Chassis and wheel bearing grease using lithium as a base. Not compatible with sodium-base grease.

LOCK RING: See Circlip or Snapring

MANIFOLD VACUUM: Low pressure in an engine intake manifold formed just below the throttle plates. Manifold vacuum is highest at idle and drops under acceleration.

MANIFOLD: A casting of passages or set of pipes which connect the cylinders to an inlet or outlet source.

MASTER CYLINDER: The primary fluid pressurizing device in a hydraulic system. On bikes, it is found in brake and hydraulic clutch systems and is lever or pedal activated.

MISFIRE: Condition occurring when the fuel mixture in a cylinder fails to ignite, causing the engine to run roughly.

MODULE: Electronic control unit, amplifier or igniter of solid state or integrated design which controls the current flow in the ignition primary circuit based on input from the pick-up coil. When the module opens the primary circuit, high secondary voltage is induced in the coil.

MULTI-WEIGHT: Type of oil that provides adequate lubrication at both high and low temperatures.

NEEDLE BEARING: A bearing which consists of a number (usually a large number) of long, thin rollers.

NITROGEN OXIDE (NOx): One of the three basic pollutants found in the exhaust emission of an internal combustion engine. The amount of NOx usually varies in an inverse proportion to the amount of HC and CO.

OCTANE RATING: A number, indicating the quality of gasoline based on its ability to resist knock. The higher the number, the better the quality. Higher compression engines require higher octane gas.

OEM: Original Equipment Manufactured. OEM equipment is that furnished standard by the manufacturer.

OHM: The unit used to measure the resistance of conductor-to-electrical flow. One ohm is the amount of resistance that limits current flow to one ampere in a circuit with one volt of pressure.

OHMMETER: An instrument used for measuring the resistance, in ohms, in an electrical circuit.

OSCILLOSCOPE: A piece of test equipment that shows electric impulses as a pattern on a screen. Engine performance can be analyzed by interpreting these patterns.

O2 SENSOR: See oxygen sensor.

OUTPUT SHAFT: The shaft which transmits torque from a device, such as a transmission.

OVERHEAD CAMSHAFT (OHC): An engine configuration in which the camshaft is mounted on top of the cylinder head and operates the valve either directly or by means of rocker arms.

OVERHEAD VALVE (OHV): An engine configuration in which all of the valves are located in the cylinder head and the camshaft is located in the engine case. The camshaft operates the valves via lifters and pushrods.

OXIDES OF NITROGEN: See nitrogen oxide (NOx).

OXYGEN SENSOR: Used with a feedback system to sense the presence of oxygen in the exhaust gas and signal the computer which can use the voltage signal to determine engine operating efficiency and adjust the air/fuel ratio.

PARTS WASHER: A basin or tub, usually with a built-in pump mechanism and hose used for circulating chemical solvent for the purpose of cleaning greasy, oily and dirty components.

PAYLOAD: The weight the vehicle is capable of carrying in addition to its own weight. Payload includes weight of the driver, passenger and cargo, but not coolant, fuel, lubricant, spare tire, etc.

PERCOLATION: A condition in which the fuel actually "boils," due to excessive heat. Percolation prevents proper atomization of the fuel causing rough running.

PICK-UP COIL: The coil in which voltage is induced in an electronic ignition.

PING: A metallic rattling sound produced by the engine during acceleration. It is usually due to incorrect ignition timing or a poor grade of gasoline.

PINION: The smaller of two gears. The rear axle pinion drives the ring gear which transmits motion to the axle shaft.

PISTON RING: An open-ended ring which fits into a groove on the outer diameter of the piston. Its chief function is to form a seal between the piston and cylinder wall. Most bike pistons have three rings: two for compression sealing; one for oil sealing.

POLARITY: Indication (positive or negative) of the two poles of a battery.

POWER-TO-WEIGHT RATIO: Ratio of horsepower to weight of a bike.

POWERTRAIN: See Drive train.

PCM: See Electronic Control Unit (ECU).

Ppm: Parts per million; unit used to measure exhaust emissions.

PREIGNITION: Early ignition of fuel in the cylinder, sometimes due to glowing carbon deposits in the combustion chamber. Preignition can be damaging since combustion takes place prematurely.

PRELOAD: A predetermined load placed on a bearing during assembly or by adjustment. Also used to describe the amount of weight a shock is adjusted for by pre-compressing its spring.

PRESS FIT: The mating of two parts under pressure, due to the inner diameter of one being smaller than the outer diameter of the other, or vice versa; an interference fit.

PRIMARY CIRCUIT: The low voltage side of the ignition system which consists of the ignition switch, ballast resistor or resistance wire, bypass, coil, electronic control unit and pick-up coil as well as the connecting wires and harnesses.

PRIMARY DRIVE: The system used to transmit power from the transmission to the rear wheel. Usually a chain, belt or driveshaft.

PROFILE: Term used for tire measurement (tire series), which is the ratio of tire height to tread width.

Psi: Pounds per square inch; a measurement of pressure.

PUSHROD: A steel rod between the valve lifter and the valve rocker arm in OverHead Valve (OHV) engines.

RACE: The surface on the inner or outer ring of a bearing on which the balls, needles or rollers move.

RADIATOR: Part of the cooling system for a water-cooled engine, usually mounted in the front of the engine and connected to the engine with rubber hoses. Through the radiator, excess combustion heat is dissipated into the atmosphere through forced convection using a water and glycol based mixture that circulates through, and cools, the engine.

RAKE: The angle of the steering head, as measured in degrees.

RECTIFIER: A device (used primarily in alternators) that permits electrical current to flow in one direction only.

REGULATOR: A device which maintains the amperage and/or voltage levels of a circuit at predetermined values.

RELAY: A switch which automatically opens and/or closes a circuit.

RELUCTOR: A wheel that rotates inside a housing and triggers the release of voltage in an electronic ignition.

RESIN: A liquid plastic used in body work.

RESISTANCE: The opposition to the flow of current through a circuit or electrical device, and is measured in ohms. Resistance is equal to the voltage divided by the amperage.

RESISTOR SPARK PLUG: A spark plug using a resistor to shorten the spark duration. This suppresses radio interference and lengthens plug life.

RESISTOR: A device, sometimes made of wire, which offers a preset amount of resistance in an electrical circuit.

RETARD: Set the ignition timing so that spark occurs later (fewer degrees before TDC).

ROCKER ARM: A lever which rotates around a shaft pushing down (opening) the valve when the other end is pushed up by the pushrod. Spring pressure will later close the valve.

ROLLER BEARING: A bearing made up of hardened inner and outer races between which hardened steel rollers move.

ROTOR: The disc-shaped part of a disc brake assembly, upon which the brake pads bear; also called, brake disc.

RPM: Revolutions per minute (usually indicates engine speed).

RUN-ON: Condition when the engine continues to run, even when the key is turned off. See dieseling.

SEALED BEAM: A headlight or running light in which the lens, reflector and filament form a single unit.

SECONDARY CIRCUIT: The high voltage side of the ignition system, usually above 20,000 volts. The secondary includes the ignition coil, coil wire, distributor cap and rotor, spark plug wires and spark plugs.

SENDING UNIT: A mechanical, electrical, hydraulic or electromagnetic device which transmits information to a gauge.

SENSOR: Any device designed to measure engine operating conditions or ambient pressures and temperatures. Usually electronic in nature and designed to send a voltage signal to an on-board computer, some sensors may operate as a simple on/off switch or they may provide a variable voltage signal (like a potentiometer) as conditions or measured parameters change.

SHIM: Spacers of precise, predetermined thickness used between parts to establish a proper working relationship.

SHIMMY: Vibration (sometimes violent) in the bike, sometimes caused by misaligned components, out of balance tires or worn suspension components.

SHORT CIRCUIT: An electrical malfunction where current takes the path of least resistance to ground (usually through damaged insulation). Current flow is excessive from low resistance resulting in a blown fuse.

SINGLE OVERHEAD CAMSHAFT: See overhead camshaft.

SKIDPLATE: A metal plate attached to the underside of the body to protect the fuel tank, transfer case or other vulnerable parts from damage.

SLAVE CYLINDER: A device in the hydraulic clutch system which is activated by hydraulic force, disengaging the clutch.

SLUDGE: Thick, black deposits in engine formed from dirt, oil, water, etc. It is usually formed in engines when oil changes are neglected.

SNAPRING: A circular retaining clip used inside or outside a shaft or part to secure a shaft, such as a floating wrist pin.

SOHC: Single overhead camshaft.

SOLENOID: An electrically operated, magnetic switching device.

SPARK PLUG: A device screwed into the combustion chamber of a spark ignition engine. The basic construction is a conductive core inside of a ceramic insulator, mounted in an outer conductive base. An electrical charge from the spark plug wire travels along the conductive core and jumps a preset air gap to a grounding point or points at the end of the conductive base. The resultant spark ignites the fuel/air mixture in the combustion chamber.

SPECIFIC GRAVITY (BATTERY): The relative weight of liquid (battery electrolyte) as compared to the weight of an equal volume of water.

SPLINES: Ridges machined or cast onto the outer diameter of a shaft or inner diameter of a bore to enable parts to mate without rotation.

SPONGY LEVER (OR PEDAL): A soft or spongy feeling when the brake is applied. It is usually due to air in the brake lines.

SPRUNG WEIGHT: The weight of a bike supported by the springs.

STARTER: A high-torque electric motor used for the purpose of starting the engine, typically through a high ratio geared drive connected to the flywheel ring gear.

STRAIGHT WEIGHT: Term designating motor oil as suitable for use within a narrow range of temperatures. Outside the narrow temperature range its flow characteristics will not adequately lubricate.

STROKE: The distance the piston travels from bottom dead center to top dead center.

SUPERCHARGER: An air pump driven mechanically by the engine through belts, chains, shafts or gears from the crankshaft. Two general types of supercharger are the positive displacement and centrifugal type, which pump air in direct relationship to the speed of the engine.

SWING ARM: Typically a single or double sided assembly that attaches the rear wheel to the frame, while allowing the wheel to move up and down for suspension travel.

SYNTHETIC OIL: Non-petroleum based oil.

TACHOMETER: A device used to measure the rotary speed of an engine, shaft, gear, etc., usually in rotations per minute.

TDC: Top dead center. The exact top of the piston's stroke.

THERMOSTAT: A valve, located in the cooling system of an engine, which is closed when cold and opens gradually in response to engine heating, controlling the temperature of the coolant and rate of coolant flow.

TIMING BELT: A square-toothed, reinforced rubber belt that is driven by the crankshaft and operates the camshaft.

TIMING CHAIN: A roller chain that is driven by the crankshaft and operates the camshaft.

TOP DEAD CENTER (TDC): The point at which the piston reaches the top of its travel on the compression stroke.

TORQUE: Measurement of turning or twisting force, expressed as foot-pounds or inch-pounds.

TRAIL: The distance between the imaginary point where the steering head axis strikes the ground and the center of the tire contact patch.

TRANSDUCER: A device used to change a force into an electrical signal.

TRANSISTOR: A semi-conductor component which can be actuated by a small voltage to perform an electrical switching function.

TREAD WEAR INDICATOR: Bars molded into the tire at right angles to the tread that appear as horizontal bars when only a small amount of tread remains.

TIPLE CLAMP (TREE): An assembly used to position the front fork tubes of a motorcycle. It normally consists of the steering stem and two brackets (an upper and lower).

TUNE-UP: A regular maintenance function, usually associated with the replacement and adjustment of parts and components in the electrical and fuel systems of a vehicle for the purpose of attaining optimum performance.

TURBOCHARGER: An exhaust driven pump which compresses intake air and forces it into the combustion chambers at higher than atmospheric pressures. The increased air pressure allows more fuel to be burned and results in increased horsepower being produced.

UNLEADED FUEL: Fuel which contains no lead (a once common gasoline additive). The presence of lead in fuel will destroy the functioning elements of a catalytic converter, making it useless.

UNSPRUNG WEIGHT: The weight of components not supported by the springs (wheels, tires, brakes, rear axle, control arms, etc.).

VACUUM GAUGE: An instrument used to measure the presence of vacuum in a chamber.

VALVE CLEARANCE: The measured gap between the end of the valve stem and the rocker arm, cam lobe or follower that activates the valve.

VALVE GUIDES: The guide through which the stem of the valve passes. The guide is designed to keep the valve in proper alignment.

VALVE LASH (clearance): The operating clearance in the valve train.

VALVE TRAIN: The system that operates intake and exhaust valves, consisting of components like camshaft(s), valves, springs (except on Ducatis), lifters or shims, pushrods (sometimes) and rocker arms.

VALVE: A device which control the pressure, direction of flow or rate of flow of a liquid or gas.

VAPOR LOCK: Boiling of the fuel in the fuel lines due to excess heat. This will interfere with the flow of fuel in the lines and can completely stop the flow. Vapor lock normally only occurs in hot weather.

VARNISH: Term applied to the residue formed when gasoline gets old and stale.

VISCOSITY: The ability of a fluid to flow. The lower the viscosity rating, the easier the fluid will flow. For example, a 10 weight motor oil will flow much easier than 40 weight motor oil.

VOLT: Unit used to measure the force or pressure of electricity. It is defined as the pressure

VOLTAGE REGULATOR: A device that controls the current output of the alternator or generator.

VOLTMETER: An instrument used for measuring electrical force in units called volts. Voltmeters are always connected parallel with the circuit being tested.

WANKEL ENGINE: An engine which uses rotary pistons. In place of standard pistons, triangular-shaped rotors revolve in specially shaped housings.

WATER PUMP: A belt, chain or gear driven component of the cooling system that mounts on the engine, circulating the coolant under pressure.

WHEEL WEIGHT: Small weights attached to the wheel to balance the wheel and tire assembly. Out-of-balance tires quickly wear out and also give erratic handling when installed on the front.

WHEELBASE: Distance between the center of front wheel and the center of rear wheel.

MASTER
INDEX